Children's Writers' & Artists' YEARBOOK 2023

NINETEENTH EDITION

The essential guide for children's writers and artists
on how to get published and who to contact

BLOOMSBURY

LONDON · OXFORD · NEW YORK · NEW DELHI · SYDNEY

BLOOMSBURY YEARBOOKS
Bloomsbury Publishing Plc
50 Bedford Square, London, WC1B 3DP, UK
29 Earlsfort Terrace, Dublin 2, Ireland

BLOOMSBURY YEARBOOKS, WRITERS' & ARTISTS' and the Diana logo are
trademarks of Bloomsbury Publishing Plc

This edition published 2022

A catalogue record for this book is available from the British Library

ISBN: PB: 978-1-4729-9132-4; eBook: 978-1-4729-9131-7

2 4 6 8 10 9 7 5 3 1

Typeset by DLxml, a division of RefineCatch Limited, Bungay, Suffolk
Printed and bound in Great Britain by CPI Group (UK) Ltd, Croydon, CRO 4YY

To find out more about our authors and books visit www.bloomsbury.com and sign up for our
newsletters.

Writers' & Artists' team
Editor Alysoun Owen
Assistant editor Eden Phillips Harrington
Articles copy-editor Virginia Klein
Listings editors Lisa Carden, Rebecca Collins, Lauren MacGowan
Editorial assistance Emily Camera; Sophia Blackwell (poetry)
Production controller Jonathon Leech

About the *Yearbook*

The Editor welcomes readers to this edition of the *Children's Writers' & Artists' Yearbook.*

In her *Foreword* on page xi, Smriti Halls emphasises how: 'Words are my happy place'. This is a sentiment most authors, publishers, editors, agents (and readers too we hope) share. Smriti describes the challenge of balancing everyday life with finding time to write and acknowledges that the perfect circumstances for writing do not exist. Regardless of someone's background or circumstance, what unites us together is our collective love of words and the influence that they can have. This *Yearbook* can be your stepping-stone as you take the plunge into the worlds of writing and publishing. The insightful and inspirational articles, along with the up-to-date contact details of thousands of individuals across media organisations and companies, will help guide you through the process from start to finish.

New articles this year provide support for new and established writers, from *Connecting with your readers* by Clare Povey (page 119) to *Creating your cast of characters* by Aisling Fowler (page 151). Former teacher turned literary agent Kate Scarborough suggests *Why teachers make great children's writers* on page 225 and Beth Cox gives her expert insight into the importance of *Authentic inclusion in children's books* on page 9. Lauren James tells us how to approach *Writing hopeful climate fiction* (page 165) and commissioning editor for *Teen Breathe* magazine, Chloe Rhodes, offers tips on *Writing for teens* (page 277). In her article *Finding an agent for your picture book* (page 221), literary agent Jodie Hodges highlights what all aspiring picture book artists seeking representation should know. A trilogy of articles will take you through the acquisition process from a range of perspectives. Take a look at what happened for one debut author with her YA novel, in *Getting published - the author's story* by Nicola Garrard (page 15), *Getting published - the agent's story* by Abi Fellows (page 17) and *Getting published - the publisher's story* by Rosemarie Hudson (page 20).

Whether you are just starting out as a writer or illustrator, or if you wish to develop your work or consolidate your knowledge further, or you are keen to locate the most appropriate agent or publisher, there will be much in this *Yearbook* to help you on your way.

Alysoun Owen, Editor

Contents

Praise for the *Yearbook*

'Take the great advice that's in this *Yearbook*.'
David Almond

'[An] impressive raft of advice and notes on every aspect of the business.'
Quentin Blake

'Riffle these pages and turn your dream into an ambition.'
Frank Cottrell Boyce

'To find your way as a children's author, *CWAYB* should be your first port of call.'
Sarah Crossan

'Between the covers of this book is everything you need to know to get published.'
Julia Donaldson

'Contains a wealth of essays, articles and advice.'
Frances Hardinge

'Stuffed full of useful facts to help you get writing (and drawing).'
Liz Pichon

'Whenever people ask me about how to get their work for children
published ... the first words to come out of my mouth are always:
Children's Writers' & Artists' Yearbook.'
Michael Rosen

'A goldmine of invaluable information.'
Francesca Simon

'Filled with practical and creative advice.'
William Sutcliffe

'I wish you all the luck in the world. Don't be a ninny
like me, practically giving up at the first rejection.
Consult the excellent *Children's Writers' & Artists' Yearbook*.'
Jacqueline Wilson

More than a book

The Writers & Artists **website** (www.writersandartists.co.uk) relaunched in 2021 and offers more free content and resources than ever before.

Here you will find hundreds of **articles** on the writing and publishing process, regular **writing competitions**, and a **community** space to share your work or ask questions about the entire creative process. Brand new features, such as being able to annotate and bookmark pages, can be accessed by creating your **free user account**. As a registered member of the *Writers' & Artists'* community, you will receive – straight to your dashboard – exclusive discounts on books, events and editing services and regular content to match your particular interests.

You can find details of our range of **editing services** as well as our **writing courses** and **masterclass evenings**. A selection of bursaries are available as well as payment instalment plans.

Our **Listings subscription** provides access to the entire database of contacts in the latest edition of the renowned *Writers' & Artists' Yearbook*, as well as hundreds of additional online-only entries.

Whatever your needs, we hope that *Writers' & Artists'* resources, whether delivered in an ebook, print, online or at our events, will provide you with the information, advice and inspiration you are looking for.

Short story competition

The annual *Writers' & Artists' Yearbook* Short Story Competition offers published and aspiring writers the chance to win a place on an Arvon Residential Writing Week (worth £850). In addition, the winner's story will be published on the Writers & Artists website.

To enter the competition, submit a short story (for adults) of no more than 2,000 words, on the theme of 'love' by 14 February 2023 to waybcompetitions@bloomsbury.com. For full details, terms and conditions, and to find out more about how to submit your entry, visit www.writersandartists.co.uk/competitions.

You can find details of competitions for children's writing under *Children's book and illustration prizes and awards* on page 359.

ARVON hosts residential creative writing courses in three rural writing houses in the UK. With the opportunity to live and work with professional writers, participants transform their writing through workshops, one-to-one tutorials, time and space to write. Five-day courses and shorter courses are available in a wide range of genres and have provided inspiration to thousands of people at all stages of their writing lives. An online programme of writing courses, masterclasses and live readings also runs year-round. Find out more and book a course online at www.arvon.org.

Foreword

Smriti Halls

Words are my happy place. Playing with them, nudging them, giving them a little squeeze. From as far back as I can remember they've been my companions, filling me to the brim with joy. It wasn't much of a surprise, then, that they became the tools of my trade – as teacher, copywriter, staff writer and editor. Any excuse to keep tinkering. The surprising bit was that those same words started prodding at *ME* – playing with me, nudging me, giving *me* a little squeeze … Soon they were filling me to the brim with stories of my own that I felt compelled to write – books that reflected my own passions, preoccupations and perspectives; stories I wanted the world to hear, written in my own voice.

Pursuing this path seemed neither sensible nor sane and, at first, I tried to ignore it, knowing full well that I didn't have the luxury of an office or even a desk at home – much less the idyllic writer's shed, den or hut to retreat to. But those mischievous words wouldn't let me go. I quickly realised that writing in my spare time, around a full-time job, daily commute and three gorgeous children, was not sustainable. And so, gathering all my courage, I plunged into the life of a full-time, freelance writer.

How I longed for a room of my own (frankly I'd have made do with a small cupboard) – just somewhere to shut the door and concentrate for five minutes together – but that simply wasn't an option. Instead, I focused on grabbing the moments I could, in the space that was available. I negotiated with my husband for some clear working days and accepted every offer of help. I paid for a childminder (and tried not to be put off by the sound of pound coins clinking into an invisible jar, for every word not written). And little by little, one by one, with comedic haphazardness, my books began to be written – at the library, in my sister's spare bedroom, on the train, in waiting rooms and coffee shops. I wrote at the kitchen table, kneeling up to the sofa, with babies asleep in the back of the car, whilst on holiday, and once (only once) I got out of bed and wrote the first draft of a picture book at three in the morning. On one memorable camping trip, I charged across several fields in the rain, was pursued by a bull and lost a shoe in a ditch – all in pursuit of a pub where I could use the WiFi to send off a manuscript. Naturally, the minute I got there, out of puff, dishevelled and smelling fragrantly of manure, the laptop ran out of charge.

It's now exactly ten years since my first picture book was published and, in that time, my books have grown from one to 50 titles – brought to life by a host of incredible illustrators. Some have seen success, others none at all, but I'm proud of every single one. Each is fingerprinted with love and is a snapshot of my life at a particular moment. Together, they are a photo album of the joys, the tears, the laughter – and the tantrums too! The books I write are created right at the centre of my topsy-turvy, everyday life. That obviously brings significant challenges (*No, you may not build a den out of my proofs!*), but whenever I bemoan the lack of space to escape to, I remember that I wrote a Number One bestseller standing up in my living room with a child on one hip and another toddling on the floor – which helps lend a bit of perspective.

I'm humbled to know that some of the words I've written have walked alongside people in their deepest, most profound moments. They've been used in beauty and brokenness, used as marriage vows and as last rites; I sometimes wonder whether their creation, amidst the idiosyncrasies and imperfections of my own life, imbues them with something that speaks into the real-life moments of other people's lives. I don't know. What I *do* know is that not a word would have been written if I'd waited for what I foolishly believed were the ideal circumstances.

So, my advice?

- Don't waste time trying to get everything in order – embrace the chaos and roll with it.
- Enjoy your work and the pleasure it brings you.
- The path may not look as you expected, it might be leading somewhere spectacular ... You won't find out unless you get started, so get going and enjoy the journey!

And if you need just one trusty friend for the road, you won't find better than the *Children's Writers' & Artists' Yearbook*. It was placed into my hands when I first started out and I recommend it to everyone who asks me for advice. It's a one-stop welcome to the world of publishing – an invaluable guide to who's who and what's what. For anyone new to the business, it's worth its weight in gold.

As for me, I'll still daydream about my writing room (and you have an open invitation to come and visit me there one day), but for now I'll be content living in and out of words. *They're* my happy place.

Smriti Halls is an award-winning, internationally bestselling children's author, published in 40 languages worldwide. Her books include modern picture book classics *Rain Before Rainbows* (Walker Books 2020), the *I'm Sticking With You* series (Simon & Schuster 2020), *Elephant in My Kitchen* (Farshore 2020), *The Little Island* (Andersen Press 2019), *The Ways of the Wolf* (Wren & Rook 2017) and US Number One bestselling *I Love you Night and Day* (Bloomsbury 2014). She is an ambassador for children's books, a contributor to the Bedtime Stories Prison Project and a guest speaker for the HarperCollins Author Academy, supporting under-represented voices. She was BookTrust's Writer in Residence September 2020–March 2021 and is a patron for the School Library Association. Smriti has been a judge for several prizes, including the Costa Book Awards, the BookTrust Lifetime Achievement Award and Faber & Faber's FAB Award. She works widely with schools, libraries, festivals and bookshops to bring a love of reading to the widest possible audience. Smriti lives in London and is also published as Smriti Prasadam-Halls. See www.smriti.co.uk for more information.

Books
Spotting talent

Publishers and literary agents are not looking for what *they* like but for what children will like. Chicken House publisher Barry Cunningham famously accepted the manuscript of the first *Harry Potter* book which – as everyone knows – turned out to be the first of an international bestselling series. He explains here what he is looking for when he reads a new manuscript.

I'm a fan: I love reading and I love great stories. For many years I travelled with Penguin the length and breadth of the country – on tours with authors like Roald Dahl, to schools with the Puffin Book Club or to lonely writers' festivals. It was during this time that I learnt the most important part of my trade – how children react to the books they love, the authors that they adore, and how they put up with the material that they are coerced into reading. Reluctant readers indeed! Entertaining, inspiring and challenging young readers should always be at the heart of our industry.

At Chicken House, we love to celebrate new authors – and discover new voices for young readers – through our *Times*/Chicken House Children's Fiction Competition for unpublished writers. We're on the lookout for original ideas, a fresh voice, a diverse range of entries and stories that children will love. More on this later.

First steps

All publishers get streams of brown envelopes – especially, like divorces, after Christmas or the summer holidays – when writers finally feel something must be done with that story they've been working on.

So, how do you get your manuscript read by a publisher? Firstly, find out what the publisher wants: A sample? The complete manuscript? Perhaps, like us, they only accept submissions through specific avenues – for us, it's *The Times*/Chicken House Children's Fiction Competition. For most editors, first on the reading list are the submissions from agents, manuscripts recommended by other authors or by someone whose judgement they trust. So, if you know someone who knows someone, use the contact.

Next, know a little about the list you are submitting to: look at their catalogue or read some of their books. Let publishers know how much you like their publications (we all like those sorts of comments!) and how you think your novel might sit with the rest of their titles.

Then, write a short snappy synopsis – a page will do (I've had some that are as long as half the novel itself!). It should tell the publisher what the book is about, its characters and why they should read it. Also include a little bit about you, the author. Don't forget that. It can be almost as important as anything else in these days of marketing and personality promotion (no, you don't *have* to have had an exciting job, but it does give an impetus to read on …).

I worked with a very famous editor in my first job who was talking one day about her regular advice to first-time writers. Her advice began with a simple question: 'Have you thought of starting at Chapter 2?' Strangely, I find myself repeating this regularly. Often I find the first chapter is tortured and difficult, before the writer relaxes into the flow of the story in Chapter 2. And often things improve if we start straight into the action, and come back and explain later. But more importantly, first novels often fail because the editor doesn't get past a poor opening section. Beginnings are crucial, because I know children won't persevere if the story has a poor start, either.

So what am I looking for?

Back to the heart of things ... There are writers who know a lot about children – they might be teachers or parents – so does this mean they can write more relevantly for young people? There are authors who know nothing about modern children, don't even really like children – does this mean they will never understand what a child wants? There are 'crossover' books that don't appear to be for real children at all. There are books with children in them that aren't children's books. Confused?

To me it's simple. Books that really work for children are written from a child's perspective through an age-appropriate memory of how the author felt and dreamed and wondered. The best children's writers carry that childhood wonder, its worry and concern, or even its fear and disappointment, around with them. They have kept the child within alive – so writing is not a professional task of storytelling for tiny tots but a simple glorious act of recreating the excitement of childhood.

That's part one of what you need. Part two, in my view, is a concentration on your audience. I've worked with adult writers too and there is a difference here. Children's authors are creating for a distinctly different readership – they need to think in a more *humble* way than if their work was for their contemporaries. What I mean is that they have to be mindful of how their work will impact on children. Characters must have convincing voices, descriptions must be good enough for children to visualise, and authors must be aware of things like children's attention span when it comes to detailed explanations.

But perhaps even more important is an awareness of the emotional effect of a story on a child. We must always remember their hunger for hope and a bright tomorrow, the closeness and importance of relationships – how easily a world can be upset by parents, or loss of an animal or a friend – and the way in which action really does speak to children, for fantasy and adventure is part of the process of literally growing an imagination.

(If all this means nothing to you, and writing for children is just another category, then I don't think you should bother. That's not to say all this should operate consciously in the mind of the new writer – but that's what a publisher seeks, and that's what I'm looking for).

Categories and concepts

Everyone has read about the older children's market, and its lucrative crossover into the kind of children's book that adults buy for themselves. I think this will continue to be a growing phenomenon – but the best books in the field will still be clear in their intent: not looking 'over their shoulder' at adults, but true to themselves and their subjects.

I'm sure fantasy will continue to hold a firm following – but with the best books based around character and not simply wild lands and strange people. Historical fiction is poised for a comeback for older children – showing the rich material and heritage we have in our shared everyday culture, as well as the 'big battles' of yore.

At last all kinds of young adult fiction has found a firm market and any number of clear voices: hard-edged, romantic, comic, or a wild mixture of all three! Both here and in the

USA, the 13–18 age group is firmly established as a permanent adjunct to the children's market, buying for themselves thrillers, dystopian adventures and books that speak to crises and concerns.

But my favourite category is the most neglected – real stories and novels for 7–9 year-olds. This was once the classic area of children's books, with the biggest names and the greatest longevity of appeal. Sadly, it has become the haunt of derivative series and boring chapter books. But there are clear signs of revival, with bestselling stories for this age group and the slightly older 9–12 category coming thick and fast. It's a great area for new talent; Chicken House has enjoyed many runaway bestsellers in this category, including *The Girl of Ink & Stars* by Kiran Millwood Hargrave (winner of the Waterstones Children's Book Prize) and *Asha & the Spirit Bird* by Jasbinder Bilan (winner of the Costa Book Award).

Picture books have had a great revival – seeing off the apparent challenges of apps and new technology to reassert the love of a beautifully-produced picture story, so I expect more innovations coming here. The success of cartoon novels and graphic story treatments for older readers has shown how story and illustration can work together in amusing and stimulating ways, enticing those who are looking for something a little bit different.

Language and setting

It's often said that, like exams, children's books are getting easier, that the language is getting 'younger' while the plots are getting more sophisticated. I don't think this is true. Certainly, for all markets, dialogue is more important than ever – and less time is taken in description. Children are used to characters who say what they mean, and whose motivations and subtleties emerge in speech. But largely I think this makes for more interpretation and imagination. Descriptions now concentrate on setting and atmosphere, rather than telling us authoritatively what the hero or heroine feels. All to the good in my view, and something new writers for children should absorb.

Also welcome in contemporary children's books is the freeing up of the adult! These characters are no longer confined to small walk-on parts and 'parental' or 'villainous' roles. Nowadays, adults in children's novels are as well drawn as the children, sometimes as touchingly vulnerable people themselves. But as in life, the most potent and frightening image in any children's book remains the bad or exploitative parent.

International scope

Children's literature is truly one of our most glorious 'hidden exports'. British writers continue to be very successful around the world, particularly in the USA and Europe. It is worth remembering this – while setting is not so important as inspiration, obviously UK-centred plots, regional dialogue and purely domestic issues, if not absolutely necessary, are best avoided. But there is no need either – like a creaky old British film – to introduce 'an American boy' or mid-Atlantic slang to your work to appeal to another audience. This seldom works and is often excruciating!

The marketplace

The market still remains delightfully unpredictable. It is hopeless to look at last year's trends and try to speculate. The sound and timelessly good advice is to find your own voice and, above all, to write from the heart. If you can touch what moved you as a child or still moves the child within you, then there's your 'market appeal'. Whether it's aboard the frigate of your imagination or in the quieter but equally dangerous seas of the lonely soul, skill and inspiration will win you your readership.

So, if you're up to the challenge, we'd love to read your story. *The Times*/Chicken House Children's Fiction Competition is an annual competition – so if you've missed the deadline this year, never fear. The prize is a £10,000 publishing contract with Chicken House, and every short- and longlisted writer will receive an editorial report on how to make their story the best it can possibly be.

Oh, and finally, don't give up - as I once said to a certain young woman about a boy called Harry ...

Barry Cunningham OBE was the editor who originally signed J.K. Rowling to Bloomsbury Children's Books. He now runs his own publishing company, Chicken House (see page 25), specialising in introducing new children's writers to the UK and USA. Notable recent successes include James Dashner, Cornelia Funke, M. G. Leonard, Kiran Millwood Hargrave, Jasbinder Bilan, Maz Evans and Lucy Christopher. Chicken House and *The Times* jointly run an annual competition to find new writers which awards a £10,000 publishing contract as the first prize; visit www.chickenhousebooks.com or see page 367. Barry was awarded an OBE in 2010 for services to publishing.

Breaking down the market: where does your book sit?

Author, editor and book packager Jasmine Richards provides a breakdown of the established market categories used by publishers and booksellers to help budding authors know where their own work might fit in.

Writing for children is big business. Around 10,000 children's books are published every year in the UK. Publishers and agents are saying that children's books are having a renaissance. That's despite the fact that, ten years ago, some in the industry were pronouncing the death of the printed book for young readers. We now know that parents are worried about screen time and its effects. Parents want their children to turn pages rather than swipe left. To tell the truth, adults still seem to prefer reading printed text also. There is something comforting and nourishing about the physical book and that realisation is why sales of that format will continue to increase.

So, if the children's market is so buoyant, why is it so hard to get published? The fact is, the children's market is a very established and mature business, and competition is ferocious. It also has some very big players who have a lot of the market share, from Julia Donaldson to Jacqueline Wilson.

Thrown into the mix, you also have celebrity fiction from musicians, TV personalities, YouTubers and sports stars. Then you have the perennial children's classics that book buyers return to again and again because they are excellent stories that stand the test of time. Established adult writers have also entered the marketplace, creating books for young adults and increasing their range of readers downwards. Finally, you have several well-established series each written by a team of writers on a rapid publishing cycle (such as the *Rainbow Magic* and *Beast Quest* series). There are an awful lot of books on the shelves and, for a new book to go on, another will have to come off. Obviously, there is infinite space online – but that doesn't help with discoverability.

In this fiercely competitive market, publishers are looking for exceptional books – novels that will stand out in this crowded arena and grab, not just the readers' attention, but also the attention of all the gatekeepers who will encounter the book before it even reaches the bookshop. A new book needs to convince sales directors selling in and also the head buyers at the main book chains, planning their offering. The book will need to be able to hold its own; it needs to be 'sticky' or, in other words, memorable and really easy to pitch. People in the industry love books, but the bottom line is that publishing is a business. Each book needs to have the potential to perform, if it is going to be published and if it is going to stay in print.

So, what can an author do to give themselves the best chance? Well – write a great story! A story with characters that readers will care about. A plot that turns the pages for the reader. A world that feels real and rich. A children's author must produce all those things, but it would be wise for them also to master an understanding of the market so they can appreciate the universe their book will operate in. There are a few ways to do this:

• Attend writing conferences or children's book events put on by people like SCBWI (see page 330) where you'll see people in the industry talking about what they are buying and why.

• Spend lots of time in bookshops and see what kind of books are on the table tops or in promotion.

• Keep an eye on what novels are winning key children's book awards or getting a lot of reviews in the print media.

• Read publications like *The Bookseller* to see what is happening in the world of publishing.

• Follow authors, book publicists, agents, booksellers and editors on social media to see what they are saying about the industry.

• It's also worth visiting libraries or talking to teachers about what books kids are reading.

• Most importantly, chat to children and ask what they are enjoying about the books they're reading. Their answers might surprise and inspire you.

Authors also need to get an understanding of the age ranges of children's books, a sense of word lengths for each of those age brackets, and some of the other features that are unique to certain parts of the market. Editors, including this one, can be a bit reticent when it comes to defining word counts. There is a good reason for this caginess. Books are works of art. They are an author's creative endeavour and thus not something that will always sit neatly in predefined categories. Still, if a book is going to sit outside some of the established norms when it comes to word count, then that needs to be for a good reason.

There are also some practical considerations to do with word counts; the bigger the book, the more it costs to print, after all, but there are set price points at the different age ranges. For instance, a middle-grade book will normally have a higher price point than a book for a 5–7 year-old and the middle-grade book can take a heftier page count because the publisher can charge more for that book.

You also need to consider the reading stamina of the children at the different age ranges. If an author writes a 70,000-word book for a 7–9 year-old, when the average is 10,000–15,000 words, then they are asking an awful lot of that reader. That's not to say that some readers won't be up to the task, but is that extended word count really serving the story well? Is it giving the book its best chance of being published? Is it giving the child reader the best reading experience? The guidelines provided below are just that: a guide – the average word count for the different age ranges of books – but there will always be exceptions. Ultimately, a story should be as long or as short as it *needs* to be.

Picture books

Golden rule: keep picture book text short! Remember, the pictures will do a lot of the telling in the story. The best picture books really take advantage of that fact. Picture books are often split out into two categories:

Books for age 0–2. These will not have many words at all (300 words or fewer) but they will have very strong images that tend to relate to the everyday and familiar rather than more fantastical settings or themes.

Books for 2–5 year-olds (although older children will still get a lot out of picture books and will be reading these alongside first chapter books). These books are on average between 300 and 1,500 words, but some books might just be one word! Although short, these books need to have definite story beats, and twists and turns that will delight both the adult reader and child listener. They should explore the experiences and possible feelings that young children may be dealing with for the first time. The best picture books are those where a kind of magic happens in that space between the images and the text, and in which that interplay brings new meaning. The picture book should be a pleasure to read out loud, with rhythm but not necessarily rhyme – as this could have an impact on how well the book sells internationally. Rhyme can be pretty tricky to make work in translation, although not impossible!

Printing a book in full colour is not cheap; the publishing house that commissions the title needs to be sure that they will achieve co-editions with overseas publishers to keep printing costs down and make the book profitable. When writing a picture book, it is worth keeping the 32-page format front and centre – this roughly works out at 24 pages or 12 spreads in which to tell the story. The narrative needs to offer ample opportunity for illustration, but that does not mean the author should dictate what these illustrations might be. It is a collaboration. Part of the publisher's role in the process of publishing a picture book is to find the perfect pairing of author and illustrator.

Younger readers
Books for readers aged 5–7. These tend to have shorter sentences and simpler diction. Some may feature chapters, and illustration can either be in colour or in black-and-white. They average between 500 and 4,000 words.

Books for readers 7–9. These are on average between 10,000 and 15,000 words but can be longer. Readers at this age will have a bit more confidence and may be devouring a lot of series fiction and enjoying the fact that they are reading whole novels. The age of the protagonists in these books will tend to be at the top end of the actual readership or perhaps even older.

Middle-grade fiction or core readers
Novels for 9–12 year-olds will be significantly longer than the previous category and average at about 30,000-40,000 words. A novel can be much longer for this age range, especially if it is a fantasy title. Whatever the number, the words should serve the story and ensure that it is being delivered in the optimal way. If the novel is going to be 80,000 words that can work, but there should be a very good reason for it.

Generally, readers in this age range have a lot more stamina. They will identify strongly with the hero, so a close third-person perspective or first-person narrative can work very well here. The protagonist tends to be aspirational and so often they are aged around 13. Readers in this age range can deal with more complex stories and themes, but a more challenging style choice might be off-putting.

Books for teenagers and YA
Books for readers aged 12+ can be anything from 30,000 words upwards. There is series fiction for teenagers, but the idea of author as the main brand is perhaps something teenagers identify with more commonly, rather than a series title. Teenagers are interested in exploring big ideas, regardless of the genre, and an author can take a few more risks with the style choice or perspective in order to help get those big ideas across.

The protagonists in these books tend to be teenagers rather than 20+ year-olds. There is also a burgeoning category – called NA or New Adult – of books which feature protagonists in their early 20s. In the UK this age range has not become firmly fixed as yet, but may well do in the future.

Jasmine Richards is an author who has written over a dozen books for children and teenagers. Her most recent novel, *Keeper of Myths*, is published by HarperCollins Children's Books in the US. She is also the co-creative on the *Aziza's Secret Fairy Door* series published by Macmillan and *Future Hero* published by Scholastic. She has over 15 years' worth of publishing experience having worked at Puffin, Working Partners and Oxford University Press as an editor and story developer. In 2019 Jasmine founded Storymix: The Inclusive Fiction Development Studio (www.storymix.co.uk), which creates series with protagonists of colour for publishers. Storymix also supports and incubates writers from minority ethnic backgrounds and offers a pathway into being published. She's always looking for talented writers and illustrators to work with, especially if they are keen to develop their writer's craft with Storymix's team of editors. Her author website is www.jasminerichards.com and you can follow her on Facebook and Twitter @JRichardsAuthor and @storymixstudio.

See also...

● *What are children's publishers looking for?*, page 13

Authentic inclusion in children's books

Beth Cox, inclusion and equality consultant, shares advice on how to make books authentically inclusive, based on her 17 years' experience of doing just that, and explores why inclusion is vital for the wellbeing of all children.

There is no doubt that inclusion and diversity are on everyone's mind in publishing right now. But what do we mean by inclusion and diversity and are the terms interchangeable? There are two core approaches when it comes to the content of books: books that focus on or teach about 'diversity' or a particular facet of it, and books that just happen to include a diverse range of characters. The former certainly have a place – they help us understand things that we don't have lived experience of, they open up conversations, and they show the challenges that many marginalised people face. However – and it's a big however – if books 'about' diversity are all that children are exposed to, they are still 'othering'; they still say, 'This is different', 'This is unusual', 'People with this experience only have challenges and face suffering, never joy'. I refer to these types of books as 'diverse books'.

What we need most, what I'm passionate about, and what my work focuses on are 'inclusive books'. These are great stories (or high-quality content if non-fiction) that include a diverse range of characters incidentally. In such books, the reason that characters are traditionally marginalised is irrelevant or only a minor part of the plot, the characters are fully rounded and more than the aspect(s) that make them 'different'. Because all humans are different. All humans are diverse. Talking about 'diverse books' suggests there is a 'norm' – a white, heterosexual, male, cisgender, nuclear family norm. But there is no such thing. Normal is subjective.

At this point I want to emphasise that, when I talk about inclusion and diversity, I'm referring to all facets of diversity and the many ways in which all humans are 'different'. A lot of the time the focus is solely on ethnic diversity, but no one facet exists in isolation, and they often intersect, which impacts experiences of marginalisation.

Why is inclusion so important?

The most common answer to this question is the 'windows and mirrors' explanation, first introduced by Emily Style in 1988 and expanded on by Rudine Sims Bishop in 1990 to include the further analogy of sliding doors. The phrase explains that books should be windows onto that which is outside a reader's experience and mirrors for them to see themselves. The sliding door is a metaphor for how books allow a reader to step into and experience a world created by an author. Now, there is absolutely nothing wrong with this analogy, but it's only part of the reason inclusive books are important. They do so much more than this.

The limitation with the windows and mirrors analogy is that, even if such a book exists, a reader might not come across a book that reflects their personal experience. Books that present a stereotypical 'norm' again and again and again suggest there is just one way of being. However, if books represent a multitude of ways of being, if books represent that there are a multitude of ways to be happy, readers will see, regardless of whether their own precise experience is reflected, that it's okay and safe for everyone to be exactly who they are. That whoever they are – that's okay. They are of value. They are enough. They belong. Inclusion in books isn't just important as a way of challenging marginalisation and discrimination, it is important for the mental wellbeing of every child (and adult).

I've been working in publishing for nearly 20 years and since 2005, when I joined the steering group for Scope's 'In The Picture' project, I've been committed more than ever to making books inclusive. Thankfully, the way inclusion is thought about and approached in the industry has changed a lot in that time. When Alexandra Strick and I founded Inclusive Minds in 2013, our focus was very much on convincing publishers of the need for incidentally inclusive books and exploring the barriers they faced in creating these, as well as seeking solutions. More recently, Inclusive Minds has been able to focus on supporting authors and publishers to ensure authenticity, mainly through its network of Inclusion Ambassadors – young people with lived experience of marginalisation who are willing to be connected with publishers, authors and illustrators to help them build authentic characters and plots.

It's important to be clear that Inclusion Ambassadors are NOT sensitivity readers. Sensitivity readers are too often brought in at a very late stage in the publishing process to 'check' that there is nothing in a book that could 'cause offence', but this isn't an effective approach. Not only is it too late in the publishing process to make large changes, should core problems be identified, but it can lead to authors feeling as though they are being censored because they had already pretty much finalised their text. Working with people with lived experience should be part of the research and development process. When authors are building characters and working out plots, they should be having conversations with people who have experienced marginalisation, to enable them to sense-check the authenticity of their ideas and build in nuance that only someone with lived experience would know about. This will result in a much more authentic representation than using a sensitivity check at the end of the book.

So, where do you start?

The first piece of advice I always give is to **focus on similarities first**, not differences. Often when a traditionally marginalised character appears in a book there is an emphasis on what makes them different. But this approach 'others' them further. The way readers initially engage with characters is by identifying things they have in common. This is what builds empathy – a reader's sense that 'Oh, I do/feel/think that' (or that someone they know does). Once a connection with a character has been made, it's easier to explore or understand what might make that character different, if that's even necessary, without danger of them being othered. After all, this is how we make friends. We initially connect with people because of something we have in common, and then, as a friendship develops, we find out how we are different; we have conversations that might challenge our thinking; we understand how their 'normal' is different from ours.

Very closely linked to this is **ensuring that your characters are fully rounded** – that they are more than the aspect for which they are marginalised. Humans are multifaceted and should be treated as such. Everyone has a multitude of hopes, interests, passions, concerns, fears. Know who your character is, inside and out. Even if that isn't all explored in the text, it will ensure that they come across as a real person rather than a caricature.

Books

Be aware of your world-view and any privilege you may hold. Regardless of how much research you do and how many people you speak to, you will still write or approach a project from your own personal world-view and experience. It's important therefore to try to look at your work, dispassionately if you can, and consider how your writing might come across to someone with a different lived experience from yours. This isn't an easy thing to do, but the more you understand about inclusion and the various facets of diversity, and the more you try, the easier it becomes. Overthinking is a positive skill here. You need to think about all the possible ways that something could be perceived, and whether one of these interpretations will perpetuate a stereotype. Of course, there will be a point where you have to accept that one book can't do everything, and times when you might decide that, although a character could perpetuate one stereotype, they challenge many others. And that's fine. The important thing is for that to be a conscious decision.

Consider what you have done to ensure authenticity. Basing a character on what you've been exposed to in other media isn't enough, as the media is often based on stereotypes. What research has gone into the plot and character to ensure that these will ring true?

Further resources

• **The Danger of a Single Story**
Chimamanda Ngozi Adichie's TED Talk
www.ted.com/talks/chimamanda_ngozi_adichie_the_danger_of_a_single_story

• **Inclusive Minds**
Organisation with a large network of Inclusion Ambassadors, who can be connected to book creators to help them.
www.inclusiveminds.com

• **Inclusion and equality training**
The Inclusion Incubator (for publishers) and Foundations for Inclusion (for freelancers, authors and illustrators) combine training, implementation tasks and consultancy.
www.bethcox.co.uk

• **What is intersectionality?**
A simple explanation from Kimberlé Crenshaw who coined the word.
www.youtube.com/watch?v=ViDtnfQ9FHc

• **Inclusive and accessible to all? An evaluation of children's picture books and their representation of physical disability**
Dissertation by Caroline Linnea Oestergaard
https://whatcarolineread.co.uk/inclusive-and-accessible-to-all

• **#BAMEOver – Statement for the UK**
Inc Arts guide to terminology, based on a survey of and discussion by and of people with lived experience of racism.
https://incarts.uk/%23bameover-the-statement

• **Reflecting Realities**
The 2019 report has a useful section on exemplifications of good practice and reiterates in detail the various 'degrees of erasure' by which ethnically marginalized characters are kept in the background. The section on ensuring children's literature reflect realities provides useful questions to ask when producing or working on inclusive books.
https://clpe.org.uk/research/reflecting-realities

Finally, remember that **this is a constant learning journey**. After so many years I'm still learning all the time. I also look back at some of the things I've done in the past with the awareness that I would do them differently now. You might still get something wrong; in that case the most important thing is to apologise and ask, or see, how you can learn from it.

Where can you get support?

The good news is that you don't have to go on this journey alone. I realised, after working on numerous books over the years, that if authors, illustrators, editors, designers and publishers understood the basic principles of inclusion, the children's book landscape could be transformed much more quickly. So I designed a programme based on everything I've learned, not just about inclusion, diversity and equality, but also about creating books and, most importantly, about combining the two.

Foundations for Inclusion offers a unique combination of training, implementation tasks, mindset work and live group sessions with me to help anyone who is self-employed in the children's book world, including authors and illustrators, understand and explore those basic principles. I also deliver a version of this programme, the Inclusion Incubator, to publishers.

And if you want to explore the best inclusive books, I'd highly recommend becoming a member of and purchasing books from **Letterbox Library**, who curate the most authentic inclusive books and sell them individually or in collections. But please do support by buying from them, as their sales fund their valuable curation work.

Beth Cox is an inclusion and equality consultant (and editor) who has been working in the publishing industry since 2003. She worked at Child's Play International Ltd for almost eight years before becoming self-employed. From 2005-08 she was on the steering group for the lottery-funded Scope 'In the Picture' project. She is the co-founder of Inclusive Minds alongside Alexandra Strick and speaks on inclusion at conferences across the UK and overseas. Beth is the author of four books in the *Level Headers* series published by B small publishing. For more information visit www.bethcox.co.uk and follow her on LinkedIn and Instagram @BethCInclusion.

See also...
• *A message for under-represented writers: We Want You,* page 229

What are children's publishers looking for?

Editorial director Rebecca Hill highlights the key ingredients that combine to produce a children's book that will inspire the passion of an editor, publishing team and readers. She urges writers to focus on their craft, knowing that a great book relies on a great story, one with its own fully developed world that captures the reader from start to finish.

Stories! Each year publishers send thousands of books out into the world, into the hands of eager children, so how can you make sure your story gets to the top of a publisher's pile? Every editor is a fan of reading, but the truth is we get sent more material than we can hope to acquire. What we are all looking for when we open up a new manuscript is a story that allows us to do what we love best ... *read*.

It really is that simple. What I'm looking for when I start a story is to be that writer's biggest fan. The books we publish at Usborne have all given me that feeling of wanting to shout about them from the rooftops: 'Listen to this sentence, everybody! Turn the page and gasp, dear reader ... Hide under the covers and tremble, if you dare dive into this one.' Stepping into a world that is thoroughly developed, and has characters that live and breathe, is a feeling unlike any other. So, if a book can hook me in and make me laugh, make me cry, affect me more than anything else I've read that week, I know that's the one to be passionate about. And passion is what every editor needs – first at an editorial meeting, then at an acquisition meeting and at every available opportunity after that, until that book ends up on a bookseller's table.

As an editorial director, when I'm building Usborne's list I'm always aware of providing a book for every reader. After all, there are lots of tastes that need catering for. But it is essential to see a company's passion for each and every book – from the very first editorial meeting when a submission is discussed. That is exactly what is needed to make a book a success because, beyond the editor's door, a whole team of people will need to love and champion a book: the cover designer, the sales teams, the publicist, the rights team and the marketing department. Without company-wide passion a book could disappear, but with it a book will fly, because we come together to become its superfans.

But before editors even start reading a story and becoming superfans, we make judgements based on your **title**. The title is the crucial 'first sell' of your book to the reader; I can't emphasise enough that a title needs to work hard, and you need to work hard on making it right. As publishers, we are not looking for a set of clumsily arranged buzz words – *The Secrets of the Forbidden Girl in the Magical Dragon Kingdom with Unicorns* – but we are looking for a title that tells us what kind of book you are writing. Strong titles should shine a light on something about your novel, be that the character, the tone or the central interest. Great titles should make us want to know what your book is about. Great titles should make us want to read on.

After the title, the **start** of your story is essential. I so often find myself getting distracted from the story in front of me by a plot that doesn't quite know where it is heading, or a character that doesn't leap out from the pages to ensure I don't return to the demands of office life. Make sure your opening is as strong and grabby as you can make it, without throwing the whole of the kitchen sink in there. Openings are the reason we carry on but, more importantly, they are the reason *children* carry on reading, and that is who we, as editors, are always thinking of when we read. Child readers are harsher than any editor, so make sure you work on making your opening as perfect as you can get it. That prologue – do you actually need it? Where should the first chapter start? Often the story gets going just before your inciting incident, so make *that* the kicking off point!

And carry that **guiding light**; ask yourself, what was it that made you want to write this book? What idea? What theme? What was it you wanted to say? What is it you want children to feel? Make sure you keep those things with you when writing and editing, and keep coming back to them, because what editors want to see, when looking for books to acquire, is authors who are in control of their material; authors who understand how their world is built and understand who their characters are; authors who will tell me at some stage of the editing process: *No, no! My character would never do that, but they would do this instead.*

Always, always think about your **audience**. The children's book market is split into age groups, and you need to be aware of what works for those categories – what content is appropriate, what subjects appeal and what word counts are expected.

Then there's the **ending**: this is another area that I often work hard on with authors. Plan where you want your story to go, and what message and emotion you want to leave the reader with. Make sure that when we finish your book we want to thrust it straight into someone else's hands to read!

But how do publishers *really* decide what to publish?

There are many important things for a publisher to consider when acquiring a book. Will children love it? Will international publishing partners want to buy the rights? Does the author have many more stories to tell? If it is a series, how quickly can the author write the next book? Does this book fit the type of publishing house that we are? Is this something that is missing on our list, or is it something that the competition is doing well with? I always hope the answer to all of these questions is 'Yes', but the truth is, my mind is set when I'm about a third of the way through a book – because by then I have fallen in love with the story.

After that comes the editing, the positioning, the building up of the campaign, the writing of sales material, the development of a cover... These things all combine to help make a great story into a great book. Great stories will always find readers, because stories make us who we are, and help us to become what we want to be.

So, how *do* you make sure your book gets to the top of the editor's pile? Focus on your craft! When the market is ever-changing, do publishers really know what trend is coming next? Can we look into a crystal ball and see what will become a bestseller? I'll let you into a secret here: the answer is no and ...erm... no. But I do know a good story, as soon as it arrives on my desk. I open it up, settle down, and then I read, and read and read – doing what every editor loves best. All I want is a story that won't let me stop reading.

Rebecca Hill is fiction editorial director at Usborne Books. She was named Editor of the Year at the British Book Awards 2019, the first children's editor ever to win this coveted prize. Rebecca has acquired and published bestselling authors Holly Bourne, Peter Bunzl, Sophie Anderson and P.G. Bell alongside award-winning titles such as *After the Fire* by Will Hill, winner of the 2018 YA Book Prize, and *Kick* by Mitch Johnson, winner of the Branford Boase Award 2018.

Getting published: the author's story

In this, the first of three articles tracking the course of her debut novel, *29 Locks*, from concept through to publication and beyond, author Nicola Garrard describes what motivated her to write it, the steps, decisions and people involved in each stage of the process, and the highs and lows encountered along the way.

My journey to publication was unplanned. I'd been a secondary English teacher since 1998, but I never thought to write a novel until 2017, when one of my loveliest students was stabbed to death in London. I started writing with a clear intention: to show how poverty, knife crime and child criminal exploitation rot childhoods but also how young people resist and succeed. Having taught boys groomed by gangs for many years, I was able to illustrate the pressures to which they are exposed and celebrate their many special qualities which are often unappreciated by wider society.

These early attempts at writing developed into the story of an inner-city teenager, Donny, who was raised in poverty and exploited by gangs, but who gets the opportunity to leave London, learn about boats and make friends with rural teenagers. He then returns, via the eponymous 29 canal lock gates, to take his revenge on the drugs importers who have hurt his family, friends and community. I wrote the first draft rapidly when my young children were asleep and hit 'send' to literary agents as soon as it seemed 'finished'. I wouldn't advise you to do this but, perhaps because of its emotive subject and the passion with which I wrote, a number of agents quickly replied with variations of 'This is important but needs work … Try this …' and I was thrilled to be telephoned by a top agent. Encouraged by 'revise and resubmit' requests, I returned to the manuscript and worked with Islington teenagers and former students who had been groomed by gangs to make sure my representations of their lived experience and London dialect were respectful and accurate.

A few months later, I submitted a draft to the Lucy Cavendish Fiction Prize and the Mslexia Children's Novel Award; both competitions shortlisted *29 Locks*. At this point I was made four offers of representation. I met the agents and chose The Good Literary Agency, which was founded by Nikesh Shukla and Julia Kingsford to promote under-represented voices, such as BAME, working class, disabled and LGBTQ+ writers. I was star-struck when Nikesh Shukla appeared with the TGLA team for coffee and signed my copies of his YA novels. I had never met a novelist before! The other agencies were equally impressive, but I wanted my writing to generate income that would one day be reinvested into under-represented writers. As a teacher committed to social justice, I needed my writing career to align with those values.

After signing with TGLA I completed a new draft, taking on board the editorial suggestions of the agency team which works collegiately on their titles. Next, my agent Abi Fellows pitched in person to publishers. There was immediate interest. Abi took me to meetings with a publishing director, head of PR and commissioning editor at a 'Big 5' publishing house in central London. Sadly, *29 Locks* did not clear the acquisitions stage. This is an aspect of publishing that is seldom acknowledged: that a writer can find literary representation yet still not find a publisher. Having sailed through all the milestones – prize shortlistings, signing with an agent, submission to publishers – my young adult novel stumbled at the last post.

But my agent didn't give up. I was delighted when, many months after I had accepted the idea that *29 Locks* might never be published, Abi phoned with an offer from Rosemarie Hudson at HopeRoad. It was a perfect fit. When I looked up HopeRoad, I discovered that their remit is to further Asian, Caribbean and African diaspora stories, and to fight negative cultural representations. As a Black publisher, with decades of experience, Rosemarie was uniquely placed to champion *29 Locks* and its multicultural cast of characters. She was also keen to build opportunities in publishing, such as commissioning a young illustrator whose degree portfolio was inspired by the Bristol Black Lives Matter movement. HopeRoad's editor, Joan Deitch, brought decades of publishing experience to bear on the final stages of structural revision, copy-editing and preparation of the manuscript for publication. My overwhelming sense was that the entire team of this small, award-winning independent publisher wanted to make my novel the best it could be and to bring Donny's story to readers.

Since publication, throughout the publicity and promotion phase, Rosemarie and her friendly team give ongoing support. Rosemarie sends encouraging texts before I do an event or interview, and recently called to give me a much-needed pep talk about writing my next novel. I'm told that this level of attention would be unlikely with a large publisher, and I am very grateful for her kind and supportive introduction to the industry. As a result, my experience of publishing has been enormously fulfilling and *29 Locks* (HopeRoad 2012) was soon recognised in literary prizes, such as the Branford Boase Award (see page 361), and reviews, making the *Financial Times* 'Best Books of 2021' list.

Abi, an enthusiastic but pragmatic agent who manages my expectations, is always available to answer questions about publishing, contracts and marketing, and to guide my next steps following a successful debut. We were both very excited to be consulted in the choice of actor for the upcoming audiobook of *29 Locks* and, as a rule, I follow her advice whenever opportunities arise. I would advise aspiring authors to be open to independent publishers, and to manage their expectations because – even with an outstanding manuscript – there remains a huge element of luck. Say yes to all promotional opportunities sent your way, be energetic in generating your own, and remember that the right agent and publisher for you are the ones who care deeply about your story's intentions and the readers for whom it was written.

As a small indie, HopeRoad doesn't have the budget of large publishers to place their titles in trade publication listings, supermarkets and on bookseller's shop tables, but their high-quality production values, personal touch and passionate belief in *29 Locks* has already inspired support from award-winning authors, reading organisations, librarians, teachers, reviewers, grass-roots youth organisations and the readers who matter: teenagers seeking to make sense of the world, develop empathy with others, and most importantly, find hope. I am deeply grateful to Abi and Rosemarie who have brought my story to their hands.

Nicola Garrard is a teacher and author. Her debut novel, *29 Locks* (HopeRoad 2021), was shortlisted for the Lucy Cavendish Fiction Prize and the Mslexia Children's Novel Competition, longlisted for the 2022 Branford Boase Award, and included in the *Financial Times* Best Books 2021. Nicola has taught in secondary schools for 23 years, including 15 in an Islington comprehensive. She studied English Literature, with a focus on representations of race in Early Modern theatre. For more information see https://nicola-garrard.co.uk. Follow her on Twitter @nmgarrard.

See also...

- *Choosing the right agent*, page 218
- *Getting published: the agent's story*, page 17
- *Getting published: the publisher's story*, page 20

Getting published: the agent's story

Abi Fellows, in this second of three articles tracking the course of Nicola Garrard's debut novel *29 Locks* from concept to publication, recounts how she came to sign Nicola as one of her first authors at The Good Literary Agency (TGLA) and to support her along that journey. She describes the qualities she looks for in books to add to her list, and in their authors, and what her multifaceted role as literary agent entails.

Often, when I do workshops and panels, writers ask that golden question: what are agents looking for? For me personally, as an agent, what is most important is the potential for impact. Because I work across fiction and non-fiction, for adults and for children, this potential can manifest in a number of ways. My list is very diverse, but what unites my authors is their commitment to, and passion for, creating narratives that spark conversation, raise awareness, advocate for positive change and engender hope – narratives for readers who haven't seen themselves, their histories and their stories in books before, or enough.

The importance of representation is at the forefront of my mind when I'm considering children's publishing specifically. When I first read the manuscript of *29 Locks*, I had been volunteering as a school governor in southeast London schools for several years and was acutely aware of the issues that Nicola's writing shone a spotlight on: grooming, gang violence and knife crime. I also knew that teachers were always looking for ways to open up conversations with their students about the realities of young people's lives, realities which are – sadly – often challenging and bleak, in a way that British-originated young adult fiction doesn't always acknowledge. The thing that struck me most on my first reading of *29 Locks* was the impact it could have in terms of raising awareness about issues which have been neglected by politicians but which impact a huge number of teenagers, and younger children too. To jump forward for a moment, this was hammered home to me when Nicola told me about the number of safeguarding referrals made at one of the schools she visited, after *29 Locks* was published, for a session with the students. It is devastating that the novel's themes and plot resonate with so many young people, but also heartening to know that, because of seeing themselves in the novel, some youngsters felt better equipped to ask for help.

Authors often wonder whether agents are more moved by polish than by potential. Potential is the thing that excites me, personally, coupled with talking to the writer and believing they have the tenacity and persistence writers need to progress from manuscript to published book. Most agents these days will do some editorial work (some more than others), and, to be sure that your vision is aligned with theirs, I would always advise writers to ask any prospective agents about this. I'm lucky enough to be able to invest both my own time and energy and the support of colleagues when giving editorial feedback, and I was able to use this collegiate approach when working with Nicola ahead of submission.

Working on an edit – or more often several edits – before submitting a book to publishers is one of my favourite parts of the job. While my client is hard at work re-drafting, based on the feedback that I have given them, I am busy perfecting my pitch and drumming up some buzz with editors. Cultivating relationships with editors is a vital part of an agent's job, as we need to keep up to date with what editors are looking for and how their lists are evolving. Alas, this is not all 'Call my Agent'-style long lunches and parties (although we're grateful to see some of these events returning); it also involves phone calls, Zooms, office meetings, reading published books to keep an eye on the market, and a little bit of stalking editors on Twitter. But even with the most enthusiastic pitch and a superb manuscript, submissions don't always go quite as we agents hope. In Nicola's case, wider conversations about the market at that time were a tricky road bump that we had to navigate. The least fun part of an agent's job is having to make the call to say that an anticipated offer has not come through after all – but it's where we go together, as agent and author, from that point that is important.

Rejection is a part of an agent's life, just as it is an author's, and we don't talk about this enough as an industry. In fact, I think we are overly keen to give the impression that all debuts sell overnight in massive pre-empts. Would it were so! There are many routes to publication, not all of them quick or direct, and resilience is a huge necessity of life for most authors. It's important to be aware that the journey to publication can have unexpected hiccups along the way. But we agents are a tenacious species, and the key thing is to find an ally and champion of your work who will hold tight during these challenging times. As agents we are here to give moral support to our authors whilst they are waiting for news of an offer. This can be a time in a writer's career when working on something else is a great distraction. In Nicola's case, she was buzzing with new ideas so it made sense to start exploring those, talking together about her wider goals and what the strategy for her career should look like moving forward.

Choosing an agent is generally a decision that is made in a moment of excitement, and it marks a great stage of achievement in a writer's life. It's important to consider what kind of advisor that person is going to be in the tougher moments and how you will communicate when things are tricky. It's worth remembering that it is not always an author's first book to go on submission that lands a deal. This can be down to shifting trends and tastes more than the quality of the work itself. I'm a great believer in never giving up on a project and will always keep my ear to the ground for unexplored opportunities, new imprints and editors. And that is how I ended up having a very fortuitous conversation with Rosemarie at HopeRoad about *29 Locks*. Key for both Nicola and I was to hold on to our belief in what made *29 Locks* special and the impact it could have, a belief which – happily – Rosemarie and her team at HopeRoad shared. We knew we needed a publisher who would put this book out into the world sensitively and in a way that would enable both the book and Nicola to have the impact that had motivated her to write it.

Agents are often thought of as the 15-percenters who do the deal, keep their commission, and move on. But our work encompasses so much, both before and after the deal is done. Once the contract is signed, the agent's role shifts into one of overseeing, occasional troubleshooting, and a lot of cheerleading. In the case of *29 Locks*, the publishers made my job very easy. One of the things that I love about working with independent publishers is the personal touch and the shared vision that runs through the team, along with the vast amount of energy that goes into every single launch. Particularly important was that the team fully supported Nicola's wish to use the book to create opportunities for up-and-coming creatives, such as the artist who designed the cover and the young actor who voiced the audio edition.

I am thrilled that, in HopeRoad, we found powerful advocates and collaborators who shared our vision of the impact *29 Locks* could have. Its publication is a wonderful example of how author, agent and editor can work together as a team.

Abi Fellows is a literary agent who has worked at The Good Literary Agency since 2019. She has previously worked as a literary agent at Georgina Capel Associates, a literary scout at Rosalind Ramsay Ltd, and also as a bookseller at Blackwell's and on the sales team at Faber & Faber. Abi has a BA in English Literature from Bristol University and an MA in English Literature from UCL. See www.thegoodliteraryagency.org/about/abi for more information, and follow her on Twitter @AbiRFellows.

See also...
- *A message for under-represented writers: We Want You*, page 229
- *Choosing the right agent*, page 218
- *Getting published: the author's story*, page 15
- *Getting published: the publisher's story*, page 20
- *What do agents do for their commission?*, page 211

Getting published: the publisher's story

Following on from the author's story and that of the agent, Rosemarie Hudson, publisher at HopeRoad Publishing, describes her role and experience as commissioning editor of *29 Locks* by Nicola Garrard, and gives advice for other new authors on how to tackle the publishing process.

On my first reading of the manuscript for *29 Locks*, I was immediately struck by the relevance of the content and also deeply moved by the loving relationship between the main protagonist, Donny, and his addicted mother. The story was written with so much passion – passion, and sometimes anger, at the suffering of the young hero and his contemporaries in their real-life settings of inner-city deprivation. By publishing *29 Locks* (HopeRoad 2021), I hoped the story would inspire young readers *not* to take up the knife or a life of drugs. I vowed to do my very best for this book, because it was a story that was worth telling and sharing. I knew it would hit the mark with young adult readers. There was no need to give the manuscript out to any of our readers, nor to spend much time deliberating about my decision – you see, I fell in love with Nicola's story immediately and by the end of Chapter One I knew it was perfect for HopeRoad's young adult list. (A 'reader' will assess a manuscript and report on its merits, advising the commissioning editor if it is well written, if the language is age appropriate, etc.) The story reminded me so much of award-winning and now well-established author Alex Wheatle's debut novel *Brixton Rock* (Arcadia Books 2004) in its rawness and in its depiction of the protagonist's struggles. Alex, in fact, later read the proofs of *29 Locks* and gave us a lovely quote for the front cover of the book, saying that the text 'crackles off the page'.

From the very start, I could see that *29 Locks* had a distinct selling point – it was written by a teacher with first-hand experience of the subject. It's a contemporary tale of love and redemption, a London coming-of-age novel, filled with cultural references to Africa and the Caribbean. The text supports discussions with teachers and students about poverty, knife crime, drugs and child grooming. I knew I could promote it well to the public and get it into schools, libraries and bookshops. Teachers and librarians, as well as booksellers, are real experts when it comes to knowing what readers want and what sells well, so asking them for their views and tapping into their knowledge is an important part of being a publisher. Publishers have an eye on book prizes, as being longlisted, shortlisted or winning one can propel a title up the sales charts. I sensed that *29 Locks* would shine in the young adult fiction category of some of our most prestigious prizes. Suzi Feay, writing for the *Financial Times*, loved it and it became one of her Best Books for YA readers for 2021. At the time of writing, *29 Locks* is on the longlists for the Branford-Boase Award 2022 (see page 361) and the Berkshire Book Award. At HopeRoad we feel that *29 Locks* is a classic book that will continue to sell.

It is worth noting that we did not use many professional reviewers pre-publication; these can be especially valuable for quotations and endorsements to use in marketing. Instead, we sent the proofs out to real 'beta' teenage readers, and to reading groups in young offenders' institutions, from whom we received original and enthusiastic feedback. The book resonated with these readers in a way that is truly authentic; many could see their own lives, and choices they had made, reflected in the text. As publishers, we are really grateful for their input as it helped confirm my own views about Nicola's manuscript and to hint at a receptive market for her story.

To sign Nicola up as one of our authors, I swiftly contacted her literary agent Abi Fellows at The Good Literary Agency. We negotiated and arrived at an agreement that worked well for all of us. The cover design for the book was hugely important – it is what readers see first, so needs to have impact and compel them to pick it up. We needed a cover that properly reflected the content and was fresh as well as enticing. Our brilliant designer, James Nunn, working alongside his gifted mentee Olivia Anthony, came up with our fabulous design, which sums up exactly the mood of the novel.

Nicola is a dream author to work with; this was her first book, so she was a little anxious at first but adapted speedily to the publishing process. An extremely hard worker, Nicola's own ideas come thick and fast, and she's a great communicator. It's important for publisher and author to work well together, and especially key is finding the right copy-editor to work with an author – someone who is on their wavelength. When Nicola learned that Joan Deitch had worked on *Brixton Rock* back in the day, she was reassured; they loved working together. One of the high points of the whole process for me was the launch event, which took place on 'Word on the Water', the London Bookbarge on the Regent's Canal towpath. I also enjoyed reading the reviews that confirmed our own high regard for the book. It was a joy to watch Nicola talking about her book during interviews. With her talent at communication, she takes great pleasure in visiting schools and discussing the book and its themes.

Were there any downsides to the whole process? Yes! Thanks to Covid, the book had to be put back from a summer publication to an autumn one. Getting everything done on time, when staff illness (which had an impact throughout the industry) was delaying deadlines and causing breaks in the chain of production, caused quite a bit of panic. Schedules were turned upside down. And, of course, during Covid we couldn't take advantage of public events, as they were cancelled (and Zoom will never replace face-to-face!). Events, such as readings and book signings, allow authors to meet their audiences, discover new communities and sell books.

Here is my top advice for all new authors:

• **Know the market**. Know who you are writing for – who is your book aimed at? Who is your reader? Make sure you have a good story to tell, one that is believable, and write it well. Persevere. Rejection and dejection are part of the learning curve; they are not the end of the world. And success does not always come with the first book.

• **Research and read**. Know where to look for information about publishers who produce books like your own. This book, *Children's Writers' & Artists' Yearbook*, is a key resource. Also, do plenty of research in the bookshops and online. Find out who is publishing what. Read lots.

• **Get your work edited**. You need to have it edited by a professional before you send it out to an agent or publisher. A good copy-editor will help with presentation and polish. Always check the Acknowledgement pages at the end of books in the same genre as your own, as they can give valuable clues about the copy-editors and agents that the author worked with.

• **Work hard**. Be prepared to work hard both at the editing stage and at publication. Once your book has been acquired, the work does not stop there. Social media helps to sell books, so be on top of your game. Post publication, be prepared to do interviews, to be in the public eye and travel to events to promote your book. Don't be shy. Your publisher and their team will support you at all times. And finally ...

• **Keep writing**.

Rosemarie Hudson is a publisher and commissioning editor, and the founder and managing director of HopeRoad Publishing Ltd, www.hoperoadpublishing.com.

See also...
● *Getting published: the agent's story*, page 17
● *Getting published: the author's story*, page 15

Children's book publishers UK and Ireland

There are changes to listings in this section every year. We aim to provide a comprehensive list of publishing imprints, the name or brand under which a specific set of titles are sold by a publisher. Any one publisher might have several imprints. The imprint usually appears on the spine of a book. Imprints are included either under a publisher's main entry or in some cases as entries themselves. Information is provided in a way that is of most use to a reader. The listings that follow are updated by the Writers' & Artists' editors based on information supplied by those listed.

*Member of the Publishers Association or Publishing Scotland
†Member of Publishing Ireland, the Irish Book Publishers' Association
‡Member of the Independent Publishers Guild

Alanna Max

38 Oakfield Road, London N4 4NL
email info@alannamax.com
website www.alannamax.com
Publisher Ken Wilson Max, *Editor-At-Large* Anna McQuinn

Children's picture books. See website for submissions guidelines. Founded 2012.

Amgueddfa Cymru – National Museum Wales‡

Cathays Park, Cardiff CF10 3NP
tel 029-2057 3235
email post@museumwales.ac.uk
website www.museumwales.ac.uk
Twitter @AmgueddfaBooks
Head of Publishing Mari Gordon

Books based on the collections and research of Amgueddfa Cymru for adults, schools and children, in both Welsh and English. Founded 1907.

Andersen Press Ltd*

20 Vauxhall Bridge Road, London SW1V 2SA
tel 020-7840 8703 (editorial) / 020-7840 8701 (general)
email anderseneditorial@penguinrandomhouse.co.uk
website www.andersenpress.co.uk
Managing Director Mark Hendle, *Publisher* Klaus Flugge, *Director* Philip Durrance, *Publishing Director* Charlie Sheppard, *Editorial Director* Sue Buswell (picture books).

Children's publisher of picture books, fiction for 5–8 and 9–12 years and young adult fiction. Publisher of the *Elmer* series by David McKee, the *Little Princess* series by Tony Ross, *The Proudest Blue* by Ibtihaj Muhammad, S.K. Ali and Hatem Aly, *The Bolds* series by Julian Clary and David Roberts, as well as award-winning fiction by Phil Earle and Kwame Alexander. Founded 1976.

Arachne Press

email cherry@arachnepress.com
website https://arachnepress.com/
Director Cherry Potts

Small, independent publisher of award-winning short fiction, poetry and select non-fiction, for adults and children. Founded 2012.

Arcturus Publishing Ltd

26–27 Bickels Yard, 151–153 Bermondsey Street, London SE1 3HA
tel 020-7407 9400
email info@arcturuspublishing.com
website www.arcturuspublishing.com
Editorial Manager Joe Harris (children's)

Children's non-fiction, including activity books, reference, education, practical art, geography, history and science. No unsolicited MSS. Founded 1993.

Aurora Metro‡

67 Grove Avenue, Twickenham TW1 4HX
tel 020-3261 0000
email submissions@aurorametro.com
website www.aurorametro.com
Facebook www.facebook.com/AuroraMetroBooks
Twitter @aurorametro
Managing Director Cheryl Robson

Adult fiction, young adult fiction, biography, drama (including plays for young people), non-fiction, theatre, cookery and translation. Submissions: send synopsis and three chapters. Runs a biennial competition for women novelists (odd years): Virginia Prize For Fiction. Entry fee for submission of either adult or young adult novel. See website: www.aurorametro.com/VirginiaPrize. Imprints include Aurora Metro Books and Supernova Books. Founded 1996.

Award Publications Ltd

The Old Riding School, The Welbeck Estate, Worksop, Notts. S80 3LR

tel (01909) 478170
email info@awardpublications.co.uk
Facebook www.facebook.com/awardpublications
Twitter @award_books
Instagram @award.books

Picture story books, fiction, early learning, information and activity books for 0–12 years. No unsolicited material. Refer to social media sites for details of submission windows. Founded 1972.

b small publishing limited
website www.bsmall.co.uk
Managing Director Catherine Bruzzone, *Publisher* Sam Hutchinson

Activity books and foreign language learning books for 2–12 years. Written in-house. No unsolicited MSS. Founded 1990.

Badger Learning*
Oldmedow Road, King's Lynn, Norfolk PE30 4JJ
tel (01553) 816083
email info@badgerlearning.co.uk
website www.badgerlearning.co.uk
Publisher Sarah Rudd

Educational publishing for pupils and teachers across the curriculum, from KS3–KS5. Specialists in publishing teen fiction and books for children 7+ years who are struggling or reluctant readers. Range covers high interest age/low reading age titles. Series include *Teen Reads*, *YA Reads*, *Papercuts*, *Between the Lines*, *Strange Town*, *Snow-Man*, *The League of Enchanted Heroes*, *Full Flight*, *First Flight* and *Graphic Novels*. Email for submission guidelines. Founded 2001.

Barrington Stoke*
18 Walker Street, Edinburgh EH3 7LP
tel 0131 225 4113
email info@barringtonstoke.co.uk
website www.barringtonstoke.co.uk

Fiction for reluctant, dyslexic or under-confident readers: fiction for children 8–12 years with a reading age of 8+, fiction for teenagers with a reading age of 8+, fiction for 8–12 years with a reading age of below 8, fiction for teenagers with a reading age of below 8, non-fiction for children 8–14 years with a reading age of 8+, graphic novels. Resources for readers and their teachers. No unsolicited MSS. All work is commissioned from well-known authors and adapted for reluctant readers. Founded 1998.

Big Picture Press
Victoria House, Bloomsbury Square,
London WC1B 4DA
tel 020-3770 8888
email hello@templarco.co.uk
website www.templarco.co.uk,
www.bonnierbooks.co.uk
Twitter @BigPicturePress
Publisher Sophie Hallam

Non-fiction and illustrated gift books. First publications include Mizielinski's *Maps* and Katie Scott's *Animalium*. Focusing on visual presentation, collaborates with artists such as Chris Wormell (*Planetarium*) and Ximo Abadia (*The Speed of Starlight*). An imprint of Bonnier Books UK (below).

Bloomsbury Publishing Plc*‡
50 Bedford Square, London WC1B 3DP
tel 020-7631 5600
website www.bloomsbury.com
Founder & Chief Executive Nigel Newton, CBE

A leading independent publishing house with authors who have won the Nobel, Pulitzer and Booker prizes. Bloomsbury has offices in London, New York (page 51), New Delhi, Oxford and Sydney (page 41). MSS must normally be channelled through literary agents, with the exception of academic and professional titles. Founded 1986.

BLOOMSBURY CONSUMER DIVISION
Managing Director Ian Hudson

Imprints include: Absolute Press, Bloomsbury Activity Books, Bloomsbury Children's Books, Bloomsbury Circus, Bloomsbury India, Bloomsbury Press, Bloomsbury Publishing, Bloomsbury USA, Bloomsbury USA Children's Books, Raven Books.

Bloomsbury Children's Books
Publishing Director & International Editor-in-Chief Rebecca McNally, *Publishing Director* Sharon Hutton (non-fiction), *Head of Fiction* Ellen Holgate, *Editorial Directors* Zoe Griffiths (fiction), Saskia Gwinn (non-fiction)

Shortlisted for Children's Publisher of the Year 2021 in the British Book Awards. Bestselling authors include J.K. Rowling, Louis Sachar, Neil Gaiman, Sarah J. Maas, Sarah Crossan, Brian Conaghan. No unsolicited MSS.

Bloomsbury Education
Head of Education Helen Diamond, *Editorial Director* Hannah Rolls (educational fiction, poetry & digital resources), *Senior Commissioning Editor* Hannah Marston (education – CPD)

Publishes around 75 print titles per year: educational fiction, children's poetry, teacher's books, apps and digital platforms. Imprints include AB-CLIO, Bloomsbury Education, Andrew Brodie, Featherstone Education, Red Globe Press. No submissions by email. Look at recently published titles and catalogues to gauge current publishing interests. Much of the list is educationally focused and publishes in series. Allow 8–10 weeks for a response.

Bonnier Books UK*
Victoria House, Bloomsbury Square,
London WC1B 4DA
tel 020-377 0888

email hello@bonnierbooks.co.uk
website www.bonnierbooks.co.uk
Ceo Perminder Mann, *Managing Directors* Kate
Parkin (adult trade), Jane Harris (children trade)

Publishes across a wide variety of genres for different
ages. From crime to reading group fiction; memoir to
self-help; activity to reference. Publishers of twelve
imprints: adult trade (Zaffre, Manilla Press, Blink
Publishing, John Blake); Children's trade (Piccadilly
Press (page 35), Hot Key Books (page 30), Templar
(page 39), Big Picture Press (page 23), Studio Press
(page 38)). Founded 2015.

The Book Guild Ltd

Unit E2 Airfield Busines Park, Harrison Road,
Market Harborough, Leics. LE16 7UL
tel 0800 999 2982
email info@bookguild.co.uk
website www.bookguild.co.uk
Facebook www.facebook.com/thebookguild
Twitter @BookGuild
Directors Jeremy Thompson (managing), Jane
Rowland (operations)

Offers traditional and partnership publishing
arrangements, with all titles published being funded
or co-funded by The Book Guild Ltd (does not offer
self-publishing). MSS accepted in fiction, children's
and non-fiction genres, please see the website for
details. The Book Guild is part of parent company
Troubador Publishing Ltd. Founded 1996.

Boxer Books Ltd

email info@boxerbooks.com
website www.boxerbooks.com
Publisher David Bennett

Publishes innovative baby board books, picture
books, young fiction and stunning story collections.
No unsolicited MSS in any form unless via a
recognised agency. Acquired by Sterling Publishing in
2022. Founded 2005.

Bright Red Publishing*

Mitchelston Drive Business Centre,
Mitchelston Drive, Kirkcaldy KY1 3NB
tel 0131 220 5804
email info@brightredpublishing.co.uk
website www.brightredpublishing.co.uk
Facebook www.facebook.com/BrightRedBooks
Twitter @_BrightRed
Instagram @bright_red_publishing
Directors John MacPherson, Alan Grierson

Educational publishing for Scotland's students and
teachers. Founded 2008.

Brilliant Publications Ltd*‡

Unit 10, Sparrow Hall Farm, Edlesborough,
Dunstable LU6 2ES
tel (01525) 222292

email info@brilliantpublications.co.uk
website www.brilliantpublications.co.uk
Facebook www.facebook.com/Brilliant.Publications
Twitter @Brilliantpub, @BrillCreative
Managing Director Priscilla Hannaford

Publishes easy-to-use educational resources, featuring
engaging approaches to learning, across a wide range
of curriculum areas, including English, foreign
languages, maths, art and design, thinking skills and
PSHE. No children's picture books, non-fiction
books or one-off fiction books. See Guidelines for
Authors on website before sending proposal.
Founded 1993.

The British Museum Press

Great Russell Street, London WC1B 3DG
tel 020-7323 8000
email publicity@britishmuseum.org
website www.britishmuseum.org/publishing
Head of Publishing Claudia Bloch

Award-winning illustrated books for children, young
readers and families, inspired by the famous
collections of the British Museum. Titles range across
picture books, activity books and illustrated non-
fiction. Founded 1973.

Buster Books

16 Lion Yard, Tremadoc Road, London SW4 7NQ
tel 020-7720 8643
email enquiries@mombooks.com
website www.mombooks.com/buster
Facebook www.facebook.com/BusterBooks
Twitter @BusterBooks
Instagram @buster_books

Reference, activity, board and picture books for 0+
years. Publishes approx. 60 titles a year. Buster's
publications include puzzle books, including the
Clever Kids series, and a wide selection of children's
illustrated non-fiction, colouring, drawing, sticker,
activity and picture books. Titles range from
enlightening books such as *This Book is Full of Brains*,
A Day in the Life of a Caveman, *A Queen and
Everything In Between* and *Dr Maggie's Grand Tour of
the Solar System* to quirky books such as *Does a Bear
Poo in the Woods?*, *The Dinosaur Department Store*
and *Feeling Good About Me*. Bestselling colouring
books include the *I Heart Colouring* series and *The
Amazing Book of Beasts*. No unsolicited MSS.
Founded 1985.

Cambridge University Press*‡

University Printing House, Shaftesbury Road,
Cambridge CB2 8BS
tel (01223) 358331
email information@cambridge.org
website www.cambridge.org
Facebook www.facebook.com/
CambridgeUniversityPress
Twitter @CambridgeUP

Chief Executive Peter Phillips; *Managing Directors* Mandy Hill (academic), Christine Özden (International Assessment Education), Rod Smith (Cambridge Education)

For children: curriculum-based education books and software for schools and colleges (primary, secondary and international). For adult and younger learners: ELT. Founded 1534.

Campbell – see Pan Macmillan

Candy Jar Books
Mackintosh House, 136 Newport Road, Cardiff CF24 1DJ
tel 029-2115 7202
email submissions@candyjarbooks.co.uk
website www.candy-jar.co.uk/books
Facebook www.facebook.com/CandyJarLimited
Twitter @Candy_Jar
Head of Publishing Shaun Russell

Non-fiction and fiction for children aged 7+. Will consider unsolicited MSS. Check website for submission details. Founded 2010.

Cassava Republic Press‡
9 Eri Studio C11, Mainyard Studios, 94 Wallis Road, London E9 5LN
email info@cassavarepublic.biz
website https://cassavarepublic.biz/
Facebook www.facebook.com/CassavaRepublic
Twitter @cassavarepublic
Instagram @cassavarepublicpress
Founders Bibi Bakare-Yusuf, Jeremy Weate

Publishes contemporary Black and African writing. Aims to bring high-quality fiction and non-fiction for adults and children to a global audience. Has offices in Abuja and London. Founded 2006.

Caterpillar Books – see Little Tiger Group

Catnip Publishing Ltd
320 City Road, London EC1V 2NZ
tel 020-7138 3650
email editorial@catnippublishing.co.uk
website www.bouncemarketing.co.uk/publisher/catnip-publishing
Twitter @catnipbooks
Managing Director Robert Snuggs

New and previously published titles from picture books to teen fiction. Acquires new titles from overseas publishers, reissues out-of-print titles by top authors and commissions original fiction for 7–9 years, 9–12 years and young adult readers. Publishes 15–20 books a year. Recently published books by Pippa Goodhart, Jason Beresford, Berlie Doherty, Sarah Baker, Sophie Plowden, Joan Lingard, Keris Stainton and Anne Booth. Will only consider agented submissions. Founded 2005.

CGP
Coordination Group Publications, Broughton House, Broughton-in-Furness, Cumbria LA20 6HH
tel (01229) 715753
email ewt@cgpbooks.co.uk
website www.cgpbooks.co.uk

Educational books centred around the National Curriculum, including revision guides and study books for Reception, KS1, KS2, KS3, GCSE, iGCSE and A level. Subjects include maths, English, science, history, geography, computing, ICT, computer science, psychology, business studies, economics, religious studies, design and technology, PE, music, French, German, Spanish, sociology, 11+, 13+ and functional skills. On the lookout for top teachers at all levels, in all subjects. Potential authors and proofreaders should email the external writing team with their name, subject area, level and experience, plus contact address, ready for when a project comes up in their subject area. Founded 1996.

Chicken House
2 Palmer Street, Frome, Somerset BA11 1DS
tel (01373) 454488
email hello@chickenhousebooks.com
website www.chickenhousebooks.com
Twitter @chickenhsebooks
Managing Director & Publisher Barry Cunningham, *Deputy Managing Director* Rachel Hickman

Fiction for 7+ years and young adult. No unsolicited MSS. Successes include James Dashner (the *Maze Runner* series), Cornelia Funke (*Inkheart* and *Dragon Rider* series) and Kiran Millwood Hargrave (*The Girl of Ink & Stars*). See website for details of *The Times/* Chicken House Children's Fiction Competition for unpublished writers. Founded 2000.

Child's Play (International) Ltd
Ashworth Road, Bridgemead, Swindon, Wilts. SN5 7YD
tel (01793) 616286
email office@childs-play.com
website www.childs-play.com
Facebook www.facebook.com/ChildsPlayBooks
Twitter @ChildsPlayBooks
Chairman Adriana Twinn, *Publisher* Neil Burden

Children's educational books: board, picture, activity and play books; fiction and non-fiction. Founded 1972.

Christian Education
5/6 Imperial Court, 12 Sovereign Road, Birmingham B30 3FH
tel 0121 472 4242
email sales@christianeducation.org.uk
website https://shop.christianeducation.org.uk/, www.retoday.org.uk
Facebook www.facebook.com/RETodayServices
Twitter @IBRAbibleread

Incorporating RE Today Services and International Bible Reading Association. Publications and services for teachers and other professionals in religious education including *REtoday* magazine, curriculum booklets and classroom resources. Also publishes bible reading materials. Founded 2001.

Cicada Books*

Unit 9, 6 Cliff Road, Cliff Road Studios, London NW1 9AN
email info@cicadabooks.co.uk
website www.cicadabooks.co.uk
Twitter @cicadabooks
Instagram @cicadabooks

Award-winning independent publisher specialising in highly illustrated books for children. Publishes between 10 and 12 titles a year. Founded 2009.

Colourpoint Creative Ltd†

Colourpoint House, Jubilee Business Park, 21 Jubilee Road, Newtownards, Co. Down BT23 4YH
tel 028-9182 6339 (within UK) / +353 (0)48 91846339 (Republic of Ireland)
email sales@colourpoint.co.uk
website www.colourpoint.co.uk
Twitter @colourpointedu
Commissioning Editor Wesley Johnston

Textbooks for Northern Ireland CCEA board. Educational textbooks for KS3 (11–14 years), KS3 Special Educational Needs (10–14 years), GCSE (14–16 years) and A-Level/undergraduates (age 17+). Not primary. Subjects include, but not limited to, biology, business studies, chemistry, design and technology, English, French, geography, history, HE, ICT, Irish, life and health sciences, LLW, MVRUS, PE, physics, politics, science and RE. Short queries by email. Full submission in writing including details of proposal, sample chapter/section to show ability to connect with target age group, qualification/experience in the subject, full contact details and sae. Textbooks, workbooks and electronic resources all considered. Founded 1993.

Cranachan Publishing*

Blacksheep Croft, 52 North Galson, Isle of Lewis HS2 0SJ
tel (01851) 850700
email hello@cranachanpublishing.co.uk
website www.cranachanpublishing.co.uk
Twitter @cranachanbooks
Instagram @cranachanbooks
Publisher & Founder Anne Glennie

A small, independent publisher based on the Isle of Lewis, focusing exclusively on high-quality children's fiction for 9–12 years (Pokey Hat imprint) and young adult fiction for teens and 12+ years (Gob Stopper imprint) with a Scottish flavour. Also publishes educational resources for teachers. Founded 2015.

Cranthorpe Millner Publishers

9 Hills Road, Cambridge CB2 1GE
tel 020-3441 9212
email kirsty.jackson@cranthorpemillner.com
website www.cranthorpemillner.com
Facebook facebook.com/CranthorpeMillner
Twitter @CranthorpeBooks
Instagram @CranthorpeMillner
Directors Kirsty Jackson (managing), David Hahn (chairman)

Titles include fiction and non-fiction: memoir, celeb autobiographies, history, science fiction, young adult, historical fiction, crime/thriller, literary fiction. Founded 2018.

Critical Publishing Ltd‡

3 Connaught Road, St Albans AL3 5RX
tel (01727) 851462
email admin@criticalpublishing.com
website www.criticalpublishing.com
Facebook www.facebook.com/CriticalPublishing
Twitter @criticalpub
Directors Di Page (sales & marketing) Julia Morris (editorial)

Award winning publisher of books for teachers – from trainee, through CPD and on to leadership. Titles are practical but research-based and are suited for those teaching across all age ranges. Founded 2012.

Crown House Publishing Ltd‡

Crown Buildings, Bancyfelin, Carmarthen SA33 5ND
tel (01267) 211345
email books@crownhouse.co.uk
website www.crownhouse.co.uk
Facebook www.facebook.com/CrownHousePub
Twitter @CrownHousePub
Instagram @crownhousepub
Directors David Bowman (managing), Karen Bowman

Award-winning independent publisher specialising in the areas of education, coaching, business training and development, leadership, NLP, hypnotherapy, psychotherapy, self-help and personal growth. Founded 1998.

Independent Thinking Press

email books@independentthinkingpress.com
website www.independentthinkingpress.com
Publishes CPD books and resources for teachers and school leaders, including business, training and development, coaching, health and wellbeing, NLP, hypnosis, counselling and psychotherapy. Publishes a range of children's books.

Dinosaur Books Ltd

tel 020-7737 6737
email info@dinosaurbooks.co.uk
website www.dinosaurbooks.co.uk
Twitter @dinosaurbooksco
Director Sonya McGilchrist

Chapter books for children 5–14 years. Submissions by email only: submissions@dinosaurbooks.co.uk. Founded 2014.

DK*
One Embassy Gardens, 8 Viaduct Gardens, London SW11 7BW
tel 020-7139 2000
website www.dk.com
Ceo Carston Coefeld

A member of the Penguin Random House (page 35) division of Bertelsmann, publishing illustrated books for adults and children: travel, licensing, reference, education, gardening, food and drink. Founded 1974.

Dogberry Ltd
13 The Rafters, Nottingham NG7 7FG
email contact@memoirist.org
website www.dogberrybooks.com
Publisher Auriel Roe

English language publisher of humorous literary fiction, young adult fiction and memoir. Founded 2020.

Dorling Kindersley – see DK

Dref Wen
28 Church Road, Whitchurch, Cardiff CF14 2EA
tel 029-2061 7860
website www.drefwen.com
Directors Roger Boore, Anne Boore, Gwilym Boore, Alun Boore, Rhys Boore

Welsh language publisher. Original, adaptations and translations of foreign and English language full-colour picture story books for children. Also activity books, novelty books, Welsh language fiction for children 7–14 years, teenage fiction, reference, religion, audiobooks and poetry. Educational material for primary and secondary school children in Wales and England, including dictionaries, revision guides and Welsh as a Second Language. Publishes approx. 50 titles a year and has 450 in print. No unsolicited MSS. Phone first. Founded 1970.

The Educational Company of Ireland
Ballymount Road, Walkinstown, Dublin D12 R25C, Republic of Ireland
tel +353 (0)14 500611
email info@edco.ie
website www.edco.ie
Ceo Martina Harford

Educational (primary and post-primary) books in the Irish language. Publishes approx. 60–70 titles each year and has 600–700 in print. Ancillary materials include digital resources, concrete resources and CDs. A member of the Smurfit Kappa Group plc. Submissions to: amolumby@edco.ie. Please include: a brief description of the project's scope and content; table of contents; sample chapter and biographical

details. Allow three months for response. Founded 1910.

Electric Monkey – see HarperCollins Publishers

Everything With Words Ltd
16 Limekiln Place, London SE19 2RE
tel 020-8771 2974
email info@everythingwithwords.com
website www.everythingwithwords.com
Managing Director & Publisher Mikka Bott

Children's fiction for 5 years to young adult. Accepts unsolicited MSS. Founded 2016.

Faber & Faber Ltd*‡
Bloomsbury House, 74–77 Great Russell Street, London WC1B 3DA
tel 020-7927 3800
website www.faber.co.uk
Twitter @FaberChildrens
Publisher Leah Thaxton (children's)

High-quality picture books, general fiction and non-fiction, drama, film, music, poetry. For children: fiction for 5–8 and 9–12 years, teenage fiction, poetry and some non-fiction. Authors include T.S. Eliot, Ted Hughes, Philip Ardagh, Justin Fletcher, Harry Hill, Betty G. Birney, Francesca Simon, Karen McCombie, Jennifer Gray, Mackenzie Crook, Natasha Farrant. Founded 1929.

Fairlight Books Ltd‡
Summertown Pavilion, 18–24 Middle Way, Oxford OX2 7LG
email submissions@fairlightbooks.com
website www.fairlightbooks.co.uk
Facebook www.facebook.com/FairlightBooks
Twitter @fairlightbooks
Instagram @fairlightbooks

Specialises in literary fiction, particularly novellas (the Fairlight Moderns) and online short stories. Founded in 2017.

CJ Fallon
Ground Floor, Block B, Liffey Valley Office Campus, Dublin D22 X0Y3, Republic of Ireland
tel +353 (0)16 166400
email editorial@cjfallon.ie
website www.cjfallon.ie
Executive Director Brian Gilsenan

Educational textbooks. Founded 1927.

Farshore Books – see HarperCollins Publishers

David Fickling Books
31 Beaumont Street, Oxford OX1 2NP
tel (01865) 339000
website www.davidficklingbooks.com
Publisher David Fickling, *Publishing Director* Liz Cross

Books

Independent publisher of picture books, novels and non-fiction for all ages, as well as graphic novels. Currently not accepting unsolicited MSS submissions. Founded 1999.

Fine Feather Press

The Coach House, Elstead Road, Farnham, Surrey GU10 1JE
tel 07968 607981
email enquries@finefeatherpreess.com
website www.finefeatherpress.com
Facebook www.facebook.com/finefeatherpress
Twitter @NatureActivity
Contact Andrea Pinnington

Photographic non-fiction children's books focusing on the natural world. Not accepting submissions. Founded 2011.

Firefly Press Ltd*

25 Gabalfa Road, Llandaff North, Cardiff CF14 2JJ
email hello@fireflypress.co.uk
website www.fireflypress.co.uk
Facebook www.facebook.com/FireflyPress
Twitter @fireflypress
Publisher Penny Thomas, *Editors* Janet Thomas, Leonie Lock

Award-winning publisher of fiction for 5–19 years. Founded 2013.

Fisherton Press

email general@fishertonpress.co.uk
website www.fishertonpress.co.uk
Facebook www.facebook.com/FishertonPress
Twitter @fishertonpress
Director Ellie Levenson

A small, independent publisher producing picture books for children under 7 years. Not currently accepting proposals but illustrators are welcome to send links to a portfolio. Founded 2013.

Floris Books*

Canal Court, 40 Craiglockhart Avenue, Edinburgh EH14 1LT
email floris@florisbooks.co.uk
website www.florisbooks.co.uk
Facebook www.facebook.com/FlorisBooks
Twitter @FlorisBooks
Commissioning Editors Sally Polson, Eleanor Collins

Children's board books, picture books, story anthologies. Approx. 50 titles each year. Founded 1978.

Kelpies

website www.discoverkelpies.co.uk
Contemporary Scottish fiction – picture books (3–6 years), young readers series (6–8 years) and novels (8–15 years). Successes include *The Nowhere Emporium* by Ross MacKenzie and *There Was a Wee Lassie Who Swallowed a Midgie* by Rebecca Colby. See website for submission details.

Galore Park Publishing Ltd*

Carmelite House, 50 Victoria Embankment, London EC4Y 0DZ
tel 020-7873 6412
website www.galorepark.co.uk

Educational textbooks and revision guides for students studying at independent schools. *So You Really Want To Learn* range of textbooks for children 11+ years and *Junior* range for children 8–10 years. Courses include Latin, French, English, Spanish, maths and science. Founded 1999.

W.F. Graham

2 Pondwood Close, Moulton Park, Northampton NN3 6RT
tel (01604) 645537
email books@wfgraham.co.uk
website www.wfgraham.co.uk

Activity books including colouring, dot-to-dot, magic painting, puzzle, word search and sticker books.

Neil Griffiths Consultancy

Willow Cottage, 26 Purton Stoke, Swindon SN5 4JF
tel 07976 574627
email neil@cornertolearn.co.uk
website www.cornertolearn.co.uk
Publisher Neil Griffiths

Training books and learning materials aimed at teachers and parents with young children. Imprint: Red Robin Books. Founded 2008.

Guppy Publishing Ltd‡

Bracken Hill, Cotswold Road, Oxford OX2 9JG
tel 07884 068983
email bella@guppybooks.co.uk
website www.guppybooks.co.uk
Facebook www.facebook.com/guppybooks
Twitter @guppybooks
Instagram @guppypublishing
Director Bella Pearson

Publishing children's and young adult fiction for 5–18 years. Illustrated books for newly emerging readers, fiction for middle-grade readers and novels for young adults. Poetry, prose, graphic novels. Founded 2019.

Hachette Children's Group*

Carmelite House, 50 Victoria Embankment, London EC4Y 0DZ
email editorial@hachettechildrens.co.uk
website www.hachettechildrens.co.uk
Twitter @HachetteKids
Ceo Hilary Murray Hill, *Senior Trade Publisher* Ruth Alltimes, *Trade Publisher* Emma Blackburn, *Education Publisher* Paul Rockett

One of the largest children's publishers in the UK. Publishes baby and pre-school books, picture books, gift, fiction, non-fiction, series fiction, books for the school and library market and licensed publishing. Comprises the imprints Hodder Children's Books; Orchard Books; Orion Children's Books; Little, Brown Books for Young Readers; Quercus Children's Books; Pat-a-Cake; Wren & Rook; Franklin Watts; Wayland Books. Owner of Enid Blyton Entertainment. Generally only accepts submissions sent via an agent. Occasionally holds periods of open submissions for a limited time period or a specific genre. See social media channels for details. Founded 1986.

Hachette UK*

Carmelite House, 50 Victoria Embankment, London EC4Y 0DZ
tel 020-3122 6000
website www.hachette.co.uk
Ceo David Shelley

Part of Hachette Livre SA since 2004. Hachette UK group companies: Hachette Children's Group (see above); Hachette Ireland; Hachette Australia (page 41); Hachette New Zealand; Headline Book Publishing; Hodder Education Group; Hodder & Stoughton; Hodder Faith; Illuminate Publishing (page 30); Little, Brown Book Group; John Murray; Orion Group; Octopus Group. Founded 1986.

Happy Yak

The Old Brewery, 6 Blundell Street, London N7 9BH
tel 020-7000 8084
website www.quartoknows.com/happy-yak

A children's imprint of the Quarto Group, Inc. (page 36). Publishes pre-school, picture books and illustrated non-fiction for children 0–7 years, with a focus on fun, accessible content and contemporary illustration. Founded 2021.

HarperCollins Publishers*

The News Building, 1 London Bridge Street, London SE1 9GF
tel 020-8741 7070
Alternative address Westerhill Road, Bishopbriggs, Glasgow G64 2QT
tel 0141 772 3200
website www.harpercollins.co.uk
Ceo Charlie Redmayne

For adults: fiction (commercial and literary) and non-fiction. Subjects include history; celebrity memoirs; biographies; popular science; mind, body & spirit; dictionaries; maps and reference. All fiction and trade non-fiction must be submitted through an agent. Owned by News Corporation. Founded 1817.

Farshore Books
website www.farshore.com
Executive Publisher Cally Poplak

Children's fiction, young adult (Electric Monkey), picture books, non-fiction (Red Shed), novelty and gift, and licensed books. Fiction authors include: Michael Morpurgo, Laura Ellen Anderson, Andy Stanton, Lemony Snicket, Holly Jackson, Michael Grant and David Levithan. Picture Book authors include: Matt Lucas, Julia Donaldson and Chris Packham. Books published under licence include Winnie-the-Pooh, Thomas the Tank Engine, Mr. Men and Minecraft. Visit website to see current policy on manuscript submissions. Previously known as Egmont UK, acquired by HarperCollins Publishers 2021.

HarperCollins
Managing Director Kate Elton, *Executive Publishers* Oliver Malcolm, Kimberly Young
Imprints include: HarperFiction, NonFiction, Avon, One More Chapter, HarperNorth and HarperCollins Ireland.

HarperCollins Audio
Group Digital Director Joanna Surman, *Publishing Director* Fionnuala Barrett
Publishes various audio formats. Leading publisher of trade fiction and non-fiction audiobooks for children and adults, as well as standalone audio projects. Publishes in excess of 700 audiobooks each year.

HarperCollins Children's Books
Executive Publisher Ann-Janine Murtagh
Activity books, novelty books, pre-school brands, picture books, pop-up books and book and CD sets. Fiction for 5–8 and 9–12 years, young adult fiction and series fiction; film/TV tie-ins. Publishes approx. 265 titles each year. Picture book authors include Oliver Jeffers, Judith Kerr and Emma Chichester Clark, and fiction by David Walliams, Michael Morpurgo, David Baddiel and Lauren Child. Books published under licence include Dr Seuss, Bing, Twirlywoos and Paddington Bear. No unsolicited MSS: only accepts submissions via agents.

Hawthorn Press*‡

1 Lansdown Lane, Stroud, Glos. GL5 1BJ
tel (01453) 757040
email info@hawthornpress.com
website www.hawthornpress.com
Director Martin Large

Publishes books and ebooks. Series include *Early Years, Steiner/Waldorf Education, Crafts, Personal Development, Art and Science, Storytelling*. Founded 1981.

Head of Zeus - Zephyr

Clerkenwell House, 5–8 Hardwick Street, London EC1R 4RG
tel 020-7253 5557
email hello@headofzeus.com
website www.headofzeus.com
Facebook www.facebook.com/headofzeus
Twitter @_ZephyrBooks
Chairman Anthony Cheetham, *Publishing Director* Fiona Kennedy

Children's imprint. Founded 2002.

Books

Hogs Back Books Ltd

34 Long Street, Devizes, Wilts. SN10 1NT
tel (01483) 506030
email enquiries@hogsbackbooks.com
website www.hogsbackbooks.com

Children's picture books and teenage fiction.
Welcomes texts and submissions from illustrators but
cannot return material without prior arrangement.
Founded 2009.

Hopscotch

St Jude's Church, Dulwich Road, London SE24 0PB
tel 020-7501 6736
email orders@hopscotchbooks.com
website www.hopscotchbooks.com
Associate Publisher Angela Morano Shaw

A division of MA Education. Teaching resources for
primary school teachers. Founded 1997.

Practical Pre-School Books

Early years teaching resources.

Hot Key Books

Victoria House, Bloomsbury Square,
London WC1B 4DA
tel 020-3770 8888
email hello@hotkeybooks.com
website www.hotkeybooks.com,
www.bonnierbooks.co.uk
Twitter @HotKeyBooksYA
Executive Publisher Emma Matthewson

Publishes books for teen and older readers, some of
which appeal to an adult audience. An imprint of
Bonnier Books UK (page 23). Founded 2012.

Igloo Books Ltd

Cottage Farm, Mears Ashby Road, Sywell,
Northants. NN6 0BJ
tel (01604) 741116
email customerservices@igloobooks.com
website www.igloobooks.com
Twitter @igloo_books

Children's: fiction (adult), licensed books, novelty,
board, picture, activity books and education. Not
currently accepting submissions. Founded 2005.

Illuminate Publishing

Carmelite House, 50 Victoria Embankment,
London EC4Y 0DZ
tel 01235 827720
email sales@illuminatepublishing.com
website www.illuminatepublishing.com

An award-winning independent publisher of teaching
and learning resources. Publishes across a wide range
of secondary subjects: academic and vocational. Part
of Hachette UK (page 29). Founded 2010.

Imagine That Publishing Ltd

Marine House, Tide Mill Way, Woodbridge,
Suffolk IP12 1AP
tel (01394) 386651
email customerservice@imaginethat.com
website www.imaginethat.com
Facebook www.facebook.com/ImagineThatPublishing
Twitter @imaginethatbook
Instagram @imaginethatbook
Chairman Barrie Henderson, *Managing Director*
David Henderson

Children's activity books, novelty books, picture
books, reference, character, gift books and early
learning books. Founded 1999.

Top That

Books plus kits.

IWM (Imperial War Museums) Publishing

Lambeth Road, London SE1 6HZ
tel 020-7416 5000
email publishing@iwm.org.uk
website www.iwm.org.uk
Facebook www.facebook.com/iwm.london
Twitter @I_W_M

IWM tells the stories of people who have lived,
fought and died in conflicts involving Britain and the
Commonwealth since 1914. Produces a range of
books, drawing on the expertise and archives of the
museum. Books are produced both in-house and in
partnership with other publishers. Founded 1917.

Jolly Learning Ltd*‡

77 Hornbeam Road, Buckhurst Hill, Essex IG9 6JX
tel 020-8501 0405
email info@jollylearning.co.uk
website www.jollylearning.co.uk
Director Christopher Jolly

Educational: primary and English as a Bilingual
Language. Publishes approx. 25 titles each year and
has 300 in print. Successes include *Jolly Phonics Extra*,
My Jolly Phonics and *Jolly Dictionary*. Imprint: Jolly
Phonics. Unsolicited MSS are only considered for
add-ons to existing products. Founded 1987.

Miles Kelly Publishing

Harding's Barn, Bardfield End Green, Thaxted,
Essex CM6 3PX
tel (01371) 832440
email hello@mileskelly.net
website www.mileskelly.net
Director Gerard Kelly

High-quality illustrated non-fiction and fiction titles
for children and family: activity books, board books,
story books, picture books, poetry, reference, posters
and wallcharts. Age groups: preschool, 5–10, 10–15,
15+. Founded 1996.

Kelpies – see Floris Books

The King's England Press
111 Meltham Road, Lockwood, Huddersfield,
West Yorks. HD4 7BG
tel (01484) 663790
email sales@kingsengland.com
website www.kingsengland.com

Poetry collections for both adults and children plus
history books. Successes include *The Spot on My
Bum: Horrible Poems for Horrible Children* by Gez
Walsh, *Revudeville* and *Turned Out Nice Again* by
Deborah Tyler-Bennett and *Jordan's Guide to British
Steam Locomotives* by Owen Jordan. Also publishes
reprints of Arthur Mee's *The King's England* series of
1930s guidebooks and books on folklore, and local
and ecclesiastical history, plus children's and adult
fiction. See website for guidelines. However, currently
not accepting new unsolicited proposals.
Founded 1989.

Knights Of*
97 Granville Avenue, Brixton Village,
London SW9 8PS
website https://knightsof.media
Twitter @_KnightsOf
Managing Director Aimée Felone, *Editorial Director*
Eishar Brar, *Creative Director* Marssaié Jordan

Children's commercial fiction publisher,
championing authors and illustrators from diverse
backgrounds. Founded 2016.

Kube Publishing Ltd
Markfield Conference Centre, Ratby Lane,
Markfield, Leics. LE67 9SY
tel (01530) 249230
email info@kubepublishing.com
website www.kubepublishing.com
Managing Director Haris Ahmad

Publishes books of a Muslim interest. Founded 2006.

Ladybird Books
One Embassy Gardens, 8 Viaduct Gardens,
London SW11 7BW
tel 020-7139 3000
email ladybird@penguinrandomhouse.co.uk
website www.ladybird.co.uk

Ladybird publishes books across a wide range of
formats for children aged from 0–7 years. They
include tactile books for babies, nursery rhymes,
classic fairy tales and reading schemes, alongside
licensed character publishing. Part of Penguin
Random House UK (page 35). Founded 1867.

Lantana Publishing
The Oxford Foundry, 3–5 Hythe Bridge Street,
Oxford OX1 2EW
email info@lantanapublishing.com
website https://lantanapublishing.com/
Facebook www.facebook.com/lantanapublishing

Twitter @lantanapub
Instagram @lantana_publishing
Ceo Alice Curry, *Commissioning Editors* Holly Tonks,
Katrina Gutierrez

An award-winning children's book publisher and
social enterprise publishing inclusive books by
authors from under-represented groups. Looking for
inclusive fiction for babies and toddlers, 5–8 years
and 9–12 years. Authors should send full MS,
illustrators their portfolio and link to their website
and author-illustrators a complete book dummy. See
submissions page on website for how to submit.
Founded 2014.

Leckie*
Dipford House, Queens Square Business Park,
Huddersfield Road, Honley, Holmfirth HD9 6QZ
email leckiescotland@harpercollins.co.uk
website www.leckiescotland.co.uk

Publishes educational books and resources for over
20 subjects in secondary education, specifically for
Scotland. It has recently expanded into primary,
publishing maths and health and wellbeing for the
primary Curriculum for Excellence. Founded 1989.

Frances Lincoln
The Old Brewery, 6 Blundell Street, London N7 9BH
tel 020-7700 6700
email reception@frances-lincoln.com
website www.quartoknows.com/Frances-Lincoln
Publisher Philip Cooper

Imprint of The Quarto Group (page 36). Children's
books. Founded 1977.

Frances Lincoln Children's Books
The Old Brewery, 6 Blundell Street, London N7 9BH
tel 020-7700 6700
email katie.cotton@quarto.com
website www.quartoknows.com/Frances-Lincoln-
Childrens-Books
Facebook www.facebook.com/Quartokids
Twitter @QuartoKids
Publisher Katie Cotton

Imprint of The Quarto Group (page 36). Illustrated
children's books: arts and the great outdoors, visual
storytelling and cultural diversity. Founded 1983.

Lion Hudson Ltd‡
Prama House, 267 Banbury Road, Summertown,
Oxford OX2 7HT
tel (01865) 302750
email info@lionhudson.com
website www.lionhudson.com
Managing Director Suzanne Wilson-Higgins

Bible story retellings, prayer books, picture
storybooks, illustrated non-fiction and information
books on the Christian faith and world religions. Also
specialises in gift books, occasion books, seasonal
books for Christmas and Easter and bible activity

books. Children's submissions: hardcopy with sae if return required. Part of the SPCK Group. Founded 1971.

Lion Fiction

Historical fiction, mystery, fantasy and heart-warming tales from authors with a Christian world-view.

Lion Scholar

Bible-related reference works for the serious reader or first year undergraduate.

Little Door Books

email submissions@littledoorbooks.co.uk
website www.littledoorbooks.co.uk
Twitter @littledoorbooks

Award-winning independent publisher specialising in children's books. Publishes four or five books a year. Not currently accepting unsolicited MSS. Founded 2016.

Little Tiger Group

1 Coda Studios, 189 Munster Road, London SW6 6AW
tel 020-7385 6333
email contact@littletiger.co.uk
website www.littletiger.co.uk
Group Publishing Director Thomas Truong, Publisher Jude Evans

Acquired by Penguin Random House UK (page 35) in 2019. Founded 1987.

Caterpillar Books
website www.littletiger.co.uk/imprint/caterpillar-books
Editorial Director Pat Hegarty
Books for children, including novelty board and picture books.

Little Tiger Press
website www.littletiger.co.uk
Editorial Director Eleanor Farmer
Children's picture books, board books and novelty books for preschool–7 years. See website for submissions guidelines. Founded 1987.

Stripes
website www.littletiger.co.uk/imprint/stripes-publishing
Editorial Director Lauren Ace
Fiction for children 6–12 years and young adult. Quality standalone titles and series publishing in all age groups. Will consider new material from authors and illustrators; see website for guidelines. Founded 2005.

360 Degrees
website www.littletiger.co.uk/special/360degrees
Editorial Director Pat Hegarty
Non-fiction novelty for children aged 5–12 years. Founded 2015.

LOM ART

16 Lion Yard, Tremadoc Road, London SW4 7NQ
tel 020-7720 8643
email enquiries@mombooks.com
website www.mombooks.com/lom
Facebook www.facebook.com/MichaelOMaraBooks
Twitter @OMaraBooks
Managing Director Lesley O'Mara, Publisher Philippa Wingate

Illustrated non-fiction for children. Publishes approx. 10 titles a year. Titles include Fantomorphia, Maybe the Moon, The Van Gogh Activity Book and Life Lessons From My Cat, plus a range of artist-led drawing, colouring and picture book titles. Unable to guarantee a reply to every submission received, include a sae if submission to be returned. Imprint of Michael O'Mara Books Ltd. Founded 2015.

Longman – see Pearson UK

Mabecron Books Ltd

3 Briston Orchard, St Mellion, Saltash, Cornwall PL12 6RQ
tel (01579) 350885
email ronjohns@mabecronbooks.co.uk
website www.mabecronbooks.co.uk
Twitter @mabecronbooks

Award-winning publisher. Produces children's picture books and books with a Cornish or west country subject. Linked to bookshops in Falmouth, St Ives and Padstow. Founded 1998.

McGraw-Hill School Education*

8th Floor, 338 Euston Road, London NW1 3BH
tel (01628) 502730
email helpme@mheducation.com
website www.mheducation.co.uk
Facebook www.facebook.com/UKSchoolsMHE
Twitter @UKSchoolsMHE

Educational publisher for primary and secondary education in English, maths, science, humanities and other subject areas, including intervention and learning support. Founded 1888.

Magic Cat Publishing‡

Unit 2, Empress Works, 24 Grove Passage, London E2 9FQ
email marketing@magiccatpublishing.co.uk
website www.magiccatpublishing.co.uk
Instagram @magiccatpublishing
Directors Jenny Broom, Rachel Williams

A small, independent children's publisher. Publishes family-focused non-fiction and gift books. Founded 2019.

Mama Makes Books Ltd‡

49 Newlands Road, Tunbridge Wells, Kent TN4 9AS
tel 07790 468405

email info@mamamakesbooks.com
website www.mamamakesbooks.com
Facebook www.facebook.com/mamamakesbooks.com
Twitter @mamamakesbooks
Instagram @mamamakesbooks
Director Penny Worms

A small, independent children's publisher of illustrated books for children 0–8 years: baby books, novelty, early learning and non-fiction. Founded 2020.

Mantra Lingua Ltd

Global House, 303 Ballards Lane, London N12 8NP
tel 020-8445 5123
email info@mantralingua.com
website https://uk.mantralingua.com/
Facebook www.facebook.com/Mantralingua
Twitter @mantralingua
Managing Director R. Dutta

Publishes bilingual picture books and educational resources for UK, US, Swedish and German audiences. Looking for illustrators with ability to draw diverse racial faces and authors and storytellers with ability to interpret or imagine modern city lives. Commission and royalty based relationships with print runs covering between 10 and 15 language editions. Translators and audio narrators, tel: 0845 600 1361. Founded 2002.

Maverick Books

Studio 11, City Business Centre, 6 Brighton Road, Horsham, West Sussex RH13 5BB
tel (01403) 256941
email submissions@maverickbooks.co.uk
website www.maverickbooks.co.uk
Facebook www.facebook.com/Maverick-Childrens-Books
Twitter @maverickbooks
Managing Director Steve Bicknell, *Managing Editor* Kimara Nye

Publishes titles across the formats of picture books, early readers, graphic reluctant readers, junior fiction and middle grade. Maverick has a strong ethos of championing new authors and emerging illustrators. For submissions, please see submission guidelines page on website. Submissions by email only. Founded 2009.

Kevin Mayhew Ltd

Fengate Farm, Rattlesden, Suffolk IP30 0SZ
tel (01449) 737978
email info@kevinmayhew.com
website www.kevinmayhew.com
Director Barbara Mayhew

Christianity: prayer and spirituality, pastoral care, preaching, liturgy worship, children's, youth work, drama, instant art, educational. Music: hymns, organ and choral, contemporary worship, piano and instrumental, tutors. Read submissions section on website before sending MSS/synopses. Founded 1976.

The Mercier Press[†]

email info@mercierpress.ie
website www.mercierpress.ie
General Manager Mary Feehan

Books for adults and children. Subjects include Irish literature; folklore; history; politics; humour; current affairs; health; mind, body & spirit; general non-fiction. Founded 1944.

Moonlight Publishing

Garden House at Vine House, Chapel Square, East Hendred, Oxon OX12 8JN
email info@moonlightpublishing.co.uk
website https://moonlightpublishing.co.uk/

An independent, family-run company specialising in illustrated information books for children 4–10 years. Founded 1980.

Nobrow Books*

27 Westgate Street, London E8 3RL
tel 020-7033 4430
email info@nobrow.net
website https://nobrow.net/
Twitter @NobrowPress

Publishes picture books, illustrated fiction and non-fiction and graphic novels. Founded 2008.

Flying Eye Books

email info@nobrow.net
website www.flyingeyebooks.com
Twitter @FlyingEyeBooks
Children's imprint. Fiction and non-fiction. Founded 2013.

Nosy Crow*[‡]

14 Baden Place, Crosby Row, London SE1 1YW
tel 020-7089 7575
email hello@nosycrow.com
website www.nosycrow.com
Managing Director Kate Wilson, *Head of Fiction* Kirsty Stansfield, *Head of Picture Books* Louise Bolongaro, *Head of Non-Fiction & Novelty* Rachel Kellehar

Independent children's publisher. Publishes child-focused, parent-friendly children's books. Also children's publisher for The National Trust and The British Museum. Founded 2010.

The O'Brien Press Ltd[†]

12 Terenure Road East, Rathgar, Dublin D06 HD27, Republic of Ireland
tel +353 (0)1 4923333
email books@obrien.ie
website obrien.ie
Directors Michael O'Brien, Ivan O'Brien, Kunak McGann

Children: picture books; fiction for all ages; illustrated fiction for ages 3+, 5+, 6+, 8+ years, novels (10+ and young adult): contemporary, historical, fantasy. Non-

Books

fiction. No poetry or academic. Unsolicited MSS (sample chapters only), synopses and ideas for books welcome – submissions will not be returned. Founded 1974.

Old Barn Books‡

Warren Barn, Bedham Lane, Fittleworth, West Sussex RH20 1JW
tel (01798) 865010
email ruth@oldbarnbooks.com
website www.oldbarnbooks.com
Facebook www.facebook.com/oldbarnbooks
Twitter @oldbarnbooks
Instagram @oldbarnbooks

Independent publisher of picture books and fiction for children up to 14 years and the occasional gift book for adults. Interested in the natural world and promoting empathy. Not currently accepting unsolicited submissions. Founded 2015.

Otter-Barry Books Ltd‡

Little Orchard, Burley Gate, Herts. HR1 3QS
tel (01432) 820915
email info@otterbarrybooks.com
website www.otterbarrybooks.com
Twitter @otterbarrybooks
Publisher Janetta Otter-Barry

Publishes illustrated books for children 0–11+ years. Authors and illustrators include Jackie Morris, Joseph Coelho, Chitra Soundar, Petr Horáček and Ken Wilson-Max. Founded 2015.

Owlet Press

tel 07920 446328
email sam@owletpress.com
website https://www.owletpress.com/
Facebook www.facebook.com/owletpress
Twitter @oweletpress

Independent publisher of children's books. Works with established and new, under-represented authors and illustrators. Founded 2017.

Oxford University Press*

Great Clarendon Street, Oxford OX2 6DP
tel (01865) 556767
email enquiry@oup.com
website www.oup.com
Ceo Nigel Portwood

Archaeology, architecture, art, belles lettres, bibles, bibliography, children's books (fiction, non-fiction, picture), commerce, current affairs, dictionaries, drama, economics, educational (foundation, primary, secondary, technical, university), encyclopedias, ELT, electronic publishing, essays, foreign language learning, general history, hymn and service books, journals, law, medical, music, oriental, philosophy, political economy, prayer books, reference, science, sociology, theology and religion; educational software; *Grove Dictionaries of Music & Art*. Trade

paperbacks published under the imprint of Oxford Paperbacks. Founded 1478.

Children's and Educational Division

Picture books, fiction, poetry and dictionaries. Authors include Tim Bowler, Gillian Cross, Julie Hearne and Geraldine McCaughrean.

Pan Macmillan

6 Briset St, Farringdon, London EC1M 5NR
tel 020-7014 6000
email publicity@macmillan.com
website www.panmacmillan.com
Ceo Joanna Prior

For children: fiction and non-fiction including popular reference. Founded 1843.

Campbell

Early learning, pop-up, novelty, board books for the preschool market.

Kingfisher

Illustrated non-fiction books for children.

Macmillan Children's Books

Imprint for Macmillan Children's Books.

Two Hoots

Illustrated children's books.

Tor

Science fiction and fantasy published in hardback and paperback.

Patrician Press

12 Lushington Road, Manningtree CO11 1EF
tel 07968 288651
email patricia@patricianpress.com
website www.patricianpress.com
Facebook www.facebook.com/patricianpress, www.facebook.com/puddingpress
Twitter @PatricianCom
Publisher Patricia Borlenghi

Publishes fiction and poetry. Imprint: Pudding Press. Founded 2012.

Pearson UK*

Edinburgh Gate, Harlow, Essex CM20 2JE
tel 0845 313 6666
email schools@longman.co.uk
website www.pearsoned.co.uk
Ceo Andy Bird

Consists of five divisions: Virtual Learning, Higher Education, English Language Learning, Workforce Skills and Assessment and Qualifications. Imprints include: Addison-Wesley Professional, Adobe Press, Allyn & Bacon, BBC Active, Benjamin Cummings, Causeway Press, Cisco Press, Edexcel, Exam Cram, FT Press (formerly FT Prentice Hall), Ginn & Company, Edwin Ginn, Harvester Wheatsheaf, IBM

Press, InformIT, LifeBound, Macromedia Press, Maths Champs, MySQL Press, New Riders, Novell Press, Oliver & Boyd, Payne Galway, Peachpit, Pearson Custom Publishing, Pearson Longman (formerly Longman), Penguin Books, Pi Press, Pitman, Prentice Hall, Propero, Puffin, Que Publishing, Rigby, SAMS Publishing, VangoBooks, Wharton School Publishing and York Notes. Founded 1998.

Penguin Random House Children's UK*
One Embassy Gardens, 8 Viaduct Gardens, London SW11 7AY
tel 020-7139 3000
website www.penguin.co.uk
Managing Director Francesca Dow, *Publishing Director* Amanda Punter (Puffin fiction, non-fiction, licensing, preschool brands & picture books), *Publishers* Ruth Knowles (Puffin fiction, non-fiction & licensing for 6+ readers), Anna Barnes-Robinson (Puffin preschool brands & picture books), Leanne Gill (Ladybird licensing), Lou Grosart (Ladybird Trade), *Publishing Director* Kate Heald (Education), *Art Director* Anna Billson, *Commercial Director* David Sprei (Penguin Ventures), *Licensing & Consumer Products Director* Susan Bolsover (Penguin Ventures)

Part of Penguin Random House UK (see below). Children's paperback and hardback books: wide range of picture books, board books, gift books and novelties; fiction; non-fiction, popular culture, digital and audio. Preschool illustrated developmental books for 0–6 years; licensed brands; children's classic publishing and merchandising properties. No unsolicited MSS or original artwork or text. Imprints: Ladybird, Puffin, Penguin. Founded 2013.

Penguin Random House UK*
One Embassy Gardens, 8 Viaduct Gardens, London SW11 7AY
tel 020-7840 8400
website www.penguin.co.uk
Directors Markus Dohle (Ceo Penguin Random House), Tom Weldon (Ceo Penguin Random House UK)

Penguin Random House UK group companies which publish books for children: Penguin Random House Children's UK (see above). Founded 2013.

Phaidon Press Ltd
2 Cooperage Yard, London E15 2GR
tel 020-7843 1000
email enquiries@phaidon.com
website www.phaidon.com
Editorial Director Tracey Smith, *Vice President & Publisher* Deborah Aaronson, *Associate Publisher, Children's Books* Maya Gartner.

Visual arts, lifestyle, culture and food. Founded 1923.

Piccadilly Press
Victoria House, Bloomsbury Square, London WC1B 4DA
tel 020-3770 8888
email hello@piccadillypress.co.uk
website www.piccadillypress.co.uk, www.bonnierbooks.co.uk
Twitter @PiccadillyPress
Executive Publisher Emma Matthewson *Senior Commissioning Editor* Felicity Alexander

Publishes fun, family-orientated stories in any genre. Titles can be standalone stories or part of a series and use design and illustration that is integral to the content when appropriate. Publishes books primarily for 5–12 years. Imprint of Bonnier Books UK (page 23). Founded 1983.

Pikku Publishing‡
7 High Stree, Barkway, Royston, Herts. SG8 8EE
tel (01763) 849656
email info@pikkupublishing.com
website https://pikkupublishing.com/
Twitter @pikkupublishing

Publishes original, illustrated books for 3–13 years. Founded 2020.

Poolbeg Press Ltd
123 Grange Hill, Baldoyle, Dublin D13 N529, Republic of Ireland
tel +353 (0)18 063825
email info@poolbeg.com
website www.poolbeg.com
Directors Kieran Devlin, Barbara Devlin

Children's and teenage fiction. Imprints: Poolbeg, In a Nut Shell. Founded 1976.

Priddy Books
The Stables, 4 Crinan Stree, London N1 9XW
tel 020-7418 5515
website www.priddybooks.com
Publisher Roger Priddy

Specialises in baby/toddler and preschool books: activity books, board books, novelty books, picture books. Founded 2000.

Prim-Ed Publishing
Marshmeadows, New Ross, Co. Wexford Y34 TA46, Republic of Ireland
tel 0851 440075
email marketing@prim-ed.com
website www.prim-ed.com
Managing Director Seamus McGuinness

Educational publisher specialising in copymasters (photocopiable teaching resources) for primary school and special educational needs lower second level pupils. Books written by practising classroom teachers. Founded 1993.

Puffin – see Penguin Random House Children's UK

Pure Indigo Ltd

Publishing Department, 17 The Herons, Cottenham, Cambridge CB24 8XX
tel 07981 395258
email ashley.martin@pureindigo.co.uk
website www.pureindigo.co.uk/publishing
Commissioning Editor Ashley Martin

Develops innovative junior series fiction and software products that complement the product range. The junior series fiction titles are developed in-house and on occasion authors and illustrators are commissioned to complete project-based work. For consideration for commissions, visit the website. Founded 2005.

Pushkin Press*

71–75 Shelton Street, London WC2H 9JQ
email books@pushkinpress.com
website www.pushkinpress.com
Facebook www.facebook.com/PushkinPress
Twitter @pushkinpress
Publisher Adam Freudenheim, *Deputy Publisher* Laura Macaulay, *Commissioning Editor* Daniel Setón

Publishes European classics of the 20th century and novels, essays, memoirs, children's books (Pushkin's Children's Books). Imprints: Pushkin Press, Pushkin Children's Books, Pushkin Vertigo, ONE. Founded 1997.

The Quarto Group, Inc.

The Old Brewery, 6 Blundell Street, London N7 9BH
tel 020-7700 9000 / 020-7700 8066
email dan.rosenberg@quarto.com
website www.quarto.com
Chairman Peter Read

Composed of three publishing divisions: Quarto International Co-editions Group, Quarto Publishing Group US and Quarto Publishing Group UK. Quarto has nine children's imprints and these are: Quarto International Co-editions Group (Quarto Children's Books, QED Publishing, Ivy Kids, small world creations, Happy Yak (page 29)), Quarto Publishing Group UK (Wide Eyed Editions (page 40), Frances Lincoln Children's Books (page 31) and Quarto Publishing Group US (Walter Foster Jr.). Founded 1976.

Ransom Publishing Ltd*

Unit 7, Brocklands Farm, West Meon GU32 1JN
tel (01730) 829091
email ransom@ransom.co.uk
website www.ransom.co.uk
Directors Jenny Ertle (managing), Steve Rickard (creative)

Children's fiction and non-fiction, phonics and school reading programmes, and books for children and adults who are reluctant or struggling readers. Range covers high interest age/low reading age titles, quick reads and reading schemes. Currently not accepting any unsolicited submissions. Founded 1995.

Raven Books

Publishes fiction for children 8–14 years.

Really Decent Books

156 Newbridge Road, Bath BA1 3LE
tel (01225) 334747
email info@reallydecentbooks.co.uk
website www.reallydecentbooks.co.uk
Facebook www.facebook.com/reallydecentbooks
Twitter @ReallyDecent
Publisher Phil Dauncey

Independent publisher of books for babies, toddlers and children. Founded 2012.

Red Bird Publishing

Kiln Farm, East End Green, Brightlingsea, Colchester, Essex CO7 0SX
tel (01206) 303525
email info@red-bird.co.uk
website www.red-bird.co.uk

Innovative children's activity packs and books produced with a mix of techniques and materials. Activity books, novelty books, picture books, painting and colouring books, teaching books, posters, hobbies, nature and the environment, science. Age groups: preschool, 5–10, 10–15. Authors are specialists in their fields. No unsolicited MSS. Founded 1998.

Rockpool Children's Books Ltd

6 Kitchener Terrace, Ferryhill,
Co. Durham DL17 8AX
tel 07711 351691
email stuarttrotter3@gmail.com
website www.rockpoolchildrensbooks.co.uk
Facebook www.facebook.com/RockpoolChildrensBooks
Twitter @rockpooltweets
Instagram @rockpool_childrens_books
Publisher & Creative Director Stuart Trotter

Independent publisher of quality children's picture books. Founded 2006.

Ruby Tuesday Books Ltd‡

6 Newlands Road, Tunbridge Wells, Kent TN4 9AT
tel (01892) 557767
email shan@rubytuesdaybooks.com
website www.rubytuesdaybooks.com
Twitter @RubyTuesdaybk
Publisher & Author Ruth Owen

Publishes children's books. Founded 2008.

SAGE Publishing*‡

1 Oliver's Yard, 55 City Road, London EC1Y 1SP
tel 020-7324 8500

email info@sagepub.co.uk
website www.sagepublishing.com
Facebook www.facebook.com/SAGEPublishing
Twitter @SAGE_Publishing
Instagram @sage_publishing

Journals, books and library products for the educational, scholarly and professional markets. Founded 1965.

Salariya Book Company Ltd*‡

Book House, 25 Marlborough Place, Brighton BN1 1UB
tel (01273) 603306
email salariya@salariya.com
website www.salariya.com,
www.youwouldntwantto.be
Facebook www.facebook.com/theSalariya
Twitter @theSalariya
Instagram @salariyabooks
Managing Director David Salariya

Children's art, picture books, fiction and non-fiction. Imprints: Book House, Scribblers, Scribo. No unsolicited MSS. Founded 1989.

Scallywag Press Ltd*

10 Sutherland Row, London SW1V 4JT
tel 07910 278462
email publisher@scallywagpress.com
website www.scallywagpress.com
Twitter @scallywagpress
Instagram @scallywagpress
Contact Sarah Pakenham

Publishes works by newcomers as well as established authors and illustrators. Currently not accepting unsolicited MSS. Founded 2018.

Schofield & Sims Ltd*

Unit 11, The Piano Works,
113–117 Farringdon Road, London EC1R 3BX
tel (01484) 607080
email editorial@schofieldandsims.co.uk
website www.schofieldandsims.co.uk

Educational: nursery, infants, primary; posters. Founded 1901.

Scholastic Ltd*

Euston House, 24 Eversholt Street,
London NW1 1DB
tel 020-7756 7756
website www.scholastic.co.uk
President & Ceo Peter Warwick

Children's fiction, non-fiction and picture books, education resources for primary schools. Owned by Scholastic Inc. Founded 1964.

Chicken House

See page 25.

Scholastic Children's Books

tel 020-7756 7761
email submissions@scholastic.co.uk
website www.scholastic.co.uk
Twitter @scholasticuk
Fiction Publisher Lauren Fortune, *Non-Fiction Publisher & Licensing* Elizabeth Scoggins, *Editorial Director, Illustrated Books* Felicity Osborne

Activity books, novelty books, picture books, fiction for 5–12 years, teenage fiction, series fiction and film/TV tie-ins. Successes include *Tom Gates* series by Liz Pichon, *Horrible Histories* by Terry Deary and Martin Brown, *His Dark Materials* by Philip Pullman, *The Hunger Games* by Suzanne Collins, and picture books by Julia Donaldson and Axel Scheffler including *Stick Man*, *Zog*, *Tiddler* and *The Highway Rat* and the *Wonkey Donkey* by Craig Smith and Katz Cowley. Imprints: Scholastic, Alison Green Books. No unsolicited MSS. Unsolicited illustrations are accepted, but do not send any original artwork as it will not be returned.

Scholastic Educational Resources

Book End, Range Road, Witney, Oxon OX29 0YD
tel (01993) 893456
Publishing Director Robin Hunt

Professional books, classroom materials, home learning books and online resources for primary teachers, and GCSE support material.

Scripture Union

Trinity House, Opal Court, Fox Milne,
Milton Keynes MK15 0DF
tel (01908) 856000
email hello@scriptureunion.org.uk
website www.scriptureunion.org.uk
Director of Ministry Development (Publishing) Terry Clutterham

Christian books and bible reading materials for people of all ages; educational and worship resources for churches; adult fiction and non-fiction; children's fiction and non-fiction (age groups: under 5, 5–8 years, 8–10 years and youth). Publishes approx. 40 titles each year for children/young people and has 200–250 in print. Successes include the *Bible Storybook* series and *Essential 100* by Whitney Kuniholm. Will not consider unsolicited MSS. Founded 1867.

SEN Press Ltd

1 Necton Road, Wheathampstead AL4 8AT
tel (01582) 833205
email info@senpress.org
website www.senpress.org
Publisher Janie Nicholas

Literacy and life skills resources for 14–19 years with special educational needs. Founded 2003.

Shepheard-Walwyn (Publishers) Ltd‡

107 Parkway House, Sheen Lane, London SW14 8LS
tel 020-8241 5927

email books@shepheard-walwyn.com
website www.shepheard-walwyn.com,
www.ethicaleconomics.org.uk
Facebook www.facebook.com/
ShepheardWalwynPublishers
Twitter @SWPublishing
Instagram @shepheard.walwyn
Director M. Lombardo, *Marketing Manager* T.
Kerrigan, *Production Manager* K. Tot

Publishes books for children with a focus on the
environment. Publishing partner of The School of
Philosophy and Economic Science, London. IPG
member. Hosts a podcast:
www.shepheardwalwyn.podbean.com. Founded 1971.

Simon & Schuster UK Ltd*

222 Gray's Inn Road, London WC1X 8HB
tel 020-7316 1900
email enquiries@simonandschuster.co.uk
website www.simonandschuster.co.uk
Facebook www.facebook.com/simonschusterUK
Twitter @simonschusteruk
Directors Ian Chapman (Ceo), Alex Maramenides
(managing director, children's), Jane Griffiths
(editorial director, children's)

Children's and young adult fiction, picture books,
novelty, pop-up and licensed character.
Founded 1986.

Smart Learning

Unit 2, Aston Way, Middlewich, Cheshire CW10 0HS
tel (01423) 206 200
email admin@smart-learning.co.uk
website www.smart-learning.co.uk

High-quality teaching and learning resources for both
teachers and children – from Foundation Stage
through to KS3. Publishes software and books to
enhance the teaching and learning of ICT, phonics,
literacy, PSHE and citizenship and English.
Founded 2012.

SRL Publishing Ltd*

email admin@srlpublishing.co.uk
website www.srlpublishing.co.uk
Facebook www.facebook.com/srlpublishing
Twitter @srlpublishing
Instagram @srlpublishing

A climate-positive publisher. Titles range from young
adult, new adult, contemporary fiction and crime/
thriller to non-fiction. Founded 2014.

Strident Publishing Ltd

22 Strathwhillan Drive, Hairmyres, Glasgow G75 8GT
tel (01355) 220588
email info@stridentpublishing.co.uk
website www.stridentpublishing.co.uk

Fiction for children 7–18 years. Publishes approx. 15
books a year. Works closely with authors who present
in schools/at festivals. Email proposed blurb together
with the first three chapters and covering letter
stating why book is likely to appeal to readers.
Founded 2005.

Stripes – see Little Tiger Group

Studio Press

Victoria House, Bloomsbury Square,
London WC1B 4DA
tel 020-3770 8888
email hello@studiopressbooks.co.uk
website www.studiopressbooks.co.uk,
www.bonnierbooks.co.uk
Twitter @StudioPress
Executive Director Helen Wicks

Presents trend, brand and celebrity-led publishing to
both the children's and adult market in the UK and
seeks to capture current trends in social media,
gaming, film, art and design. Publishes a diverse
range of formats, including fiction, non-fiction,
picture books, gift, humour and activity, An imprint
of Bonnier Books UK (page 23). Founded 2015.

Sweet Cherry Publishing*‡

Unit 4U18, The Book Brothers Business Park,
Tolwell Road, Leicester LE4 1BR
tel 0116 253 6796
email info@sweetcherrypublishing.com
website www.sweetcherrypublishing.com
Facebook www.facebook.com/sweetcherrypublishing
Twitter @sweetcherrypub
Director A. Thadha

Award-winning specialist in children's fiction series.
Children's picture books, novelty books, gift books,
board books, educational books and fiction series for
all ages. Also welcomes young adult novels and series.
See website for submission guidelines. Imprints
include Clock Tower and Cherry Stone. Clock Tower
aims to champion marginalised voices and values
diversity, inclusivity and representation.
Founded 2011.

Tarquin Publications

Suite 74, 17 Holywell Hill, St Albans AL1 1DT
tel (01727) 833866
email info@tarquinbooks.com
website www.tarquinbooks.com

Mathematical models, puzzles, codes and logic and
paper engineering books for children. Publishes 7–8
titles each year and has over 100 in print. Successes
include *Magic Moving Images* and *Mini Mathematical
Murder Mysteries*. Do not send unsolicited MSS. Send
a one-page proposal of idea. Founded 1970.

Taylor & Francis Group*

2 and 4 Park Square, Milton Park, Abingdon,
Oxon OX14 4RN
tel 020-7017 6000
email enquiries@taylorandfrancis.com
website https://taylorandfrancis.com/

Ceo Annie Callanan, *Managing Director* Jeremy North (Taylor & Francis, Academic Learning)

Academic and reference books, including education. Imprints include CRC Press, Europa, Garland Science, Psychology Press, Routledge, Spon and Taylor & Francis. Founded 1988.

Templar Books

Victoria House, Bloomsbury Square,
London WC1B 4DA
tel 020-3770 8888
email hello@templarco.co.uk
website www.templarco.co.uk,
www.bonnierbooks.co.uk
Twitter @templarbooks
Editorial Director Katie Haworth, *Publisher* Sophie Hallam

Publishes illustrated children's non-fiction, picture books, fiction, gift and novelty books for all ages. Templar is an imprint of Bonnier Books UK (page 23). Founded 1978.

Tiny Owl Publishing Ltd

6 Hatfield road, London W4 1AF
email info@tinyowl.co.uk
website www.tinyowl.co.uk
Facebook www.facebook.com/tinyowlpublishing
Twitter @TinyOwl_Books
Publisher Delaram Ghanimifard

An independent publisher of global children's literature. Publishes high-quality picture books for children 3–11 years. Aims to promote diversity and human rights values. Founded 2015.

Tiptoe Books

United House, North Road, London N7 9DP
tel 020-7520 7600
email enquiries@amberbooks.co.uk
website www.tiptoebooks.co.uk

Illustrated non-fiction, multi-volume sets, calendars and sticker books for children of all ages. Subjects include history, ancient civilisations, the natural world, fantasy and general reference. Opportunities for freelancers. Children's books imprint of Amber Books Ltd.

Troika*

Troika Books Ltd, Well House, Green Lane,
Ardleigh, Colchester, Essex CO7 7PD
email info@troikabooks.com
website www.troikabooks.com
Publisher Martin West, *Publicity, Marketing & Editorial* Roy Johnson

Publishes picture books, poetry and fiction for all ages, with an emphasis on quality, accessibility and diversity. Founded 2012.

Usborne Publishing Ltd‡

Usborne House, 83–85 Saffron Hill,
London EC1N 8RT

tel 020-7430 2800
email mail@usborne.co.uk
website www.usborne.com
Directors Peter Usborne, Jenny Tyler (editorial), Andrea Parsons, Nicola Usborne

An independent, family publisher of books for children of all ages, including baby, preschool, novelty, activity, non-fiction and fiction. Looking for high-quality imaginative children's fiction. No unsolicited MSS. Founded 1973.

Wacky Bee Books*

Shakespeare House, 168 Lavender Hill,
London SW11 5TG
tel 020-7801 6300
email hello@wackybeebooks.com
website www.wackybeebooks.com
Facebook www.facebook.com/wackybeebooks
Twitter @wackybeebooks
Director Louise Jordan

Publishing books with a buzz for children 3–12 years. Picture books for 3+ years, early readers for 5–7 years, general fiction for 8–12 years. Submission enquiries by email to submissions@wackybeebooks.com. Founded 2014.

Walker Books Ltd*‡

87 Vauxhall Walk, London SE11 5HJ
tel 020-7793 0909
website www.walker.co.uk
Facebook www.facebook.com/walkerbooks
Twitter @walkerbooksuk
Instagram @walkerbooksuk
Editors Karen Lotz, Jane Winterbotham, Denise Johnstone-Burt, Annalie Grainger

An independent company with a global reach, publishing activity books, novelty books, picture books, fiction for 5–8 years and 9–12 years, young adult fiction, series fiction, film/TV tie-ins, plays, poetry, digital and audio. Publishes approx. 300 titles each year and has 2,000 in print. Continuing successes include the *Alex Rider* series by Anthony Horowitz, *Chaos Walking* by Patrick Ness, *Maisy* by Lucy Cousins, *Where's Wally?* by Martin Handford, the *Mortal Instruments* series by Cassandra Clare and a wide range of award-winning novels and picture books by other authors and illustrators. Imprint: Walker Books, Walker Studio, MIT Kids Press, MITeen Press and Walker Entertainment. Write to the editor, enclosing sae, and allow six months for response. Founded 1980.

Welbeck Publishing Group

20 Mortimer Street, London W1T 3JW
tel 020-7612 0400
email enquiries@welbeckpublishing.com
website www.welbeckpublishing.com

No unsolicited MSS; synopses and ideas welcome, but no fiction or poetry. Founded 2019.

Mortimer
Children's entertainment, licensing and gaming.

Welbeck Flame
Associate Publisher *Felicity Alexander*
Children's fiction.

Wide Eyed Editions
The Old Brewery, 6 Blundell Street, London N7 9BH
tel 020-7700 6700
website www.quartoknows.com/Wide-Eyed-Editions

Imprint of the Quarto Group, Inc. (page 36). Creates original non-fiction for children. Founded 2014.

Y Lolfa Cyf
Talybont, Ceredigion SY24 5HE
tel (01970) 832304
email ylolfa@ylolfa.com
website www.ylolfa.com
Director Garmon Gruffudd, *Editor* Lefi Gruffudd

Welsh language books and English books of Welsh and Celtic interest, popular biographies and sports books. Founded 1967.

ZigZag Education
Unit 3, Greenway Business Centre, Doncaster Road, Bristol BS10 5PY
tel 0117 950 3199
email submissions@publishmenow.co.uk
website www.zigzageducation.co.uk,
www.publishmenow.co.uk

Development Director John-Lloyd Hagger, *Strategy Director* Mike Stephens

Secondary school teaching resources: English, maths, ICT, geography, history, science, business, politics, P.E., media studies. Founded 1998.

ZooBooKoo International Ltd
4 Gurdon Road, Grundisburgh, Woodbridge, Suffolk IP13 6XA
tel (01473) 735346
email karen@zoobookoo.com
website www.zoobookoo.com

Multi-level educational folding cube books. Successes include *World Football, Human Body, Kings and Queens, French Phrases* and *United Kingdom*. Founded 1996.

ZunTold
email elainebous@gmail.com
website https://zuntold.com/
Facebook www.facebook.com/zuntoldbooks
Twitter @zuntold
Instagram @zuntold_books
Director Elaine Bousfield

Publishes new fiction for children and young people and young adults. Also supports young people in their own writing. Interested in middle grade fiction (9–12), teens, young adults and crossover fiction. Agent submissions send a copy of synopsis and the first three chapters. Submissions opened for authors without an agent in June (for young adult, new adult, cross over fiction) and in December (for middle grade). Does not work with picture books. Founded 2016.

Children's book publishers overseas

Listings are given for children's book publishers in Australia (below), Canada (page 43), France (page 45), Germany (page 46), Italy (page 46), the Netherlands (page 47), New Zealand (page 47), South Africa (page 48), Spain (page 49) and the USA (page 50).

AUSTRALIA

*Member of the Australian Publishers Association

ACER Press*
19 Prospect Hill Road, Private Bag 55, Camberwell, VIC 3124
tel +61 (0)3 9277 5555
email proposals@acer.org
website www.acer.org/au

Publisher of the Australian Council for Educational Research. Produces a range of books and assessments including professional resources for teachers, psychologists and special educational needs professionals. Founded 1930.

Affirm Press
28 Thistlethwaite Street, South Melbourne, VIC 3205
tel +61 (0)3 8695 9623
email info@affirmpress.com.au
website https://affirmpress.com.au/
Facebook www.facebook.com/affirmpress
Twitter @affirmpress
Ceo & Publishing Director Martin Hughes

Non-fiction, fiction and young fiction. Founded 2010.

Allen & Unwin Pty Ltd*
83 Alexander Street, Crows Nest, NSW 2065
Postal address PO Box 8500, St Leonards, NSW 1590
tel +61 (0)2 8425 0100
website www.allenandunwin.com
Chairman Patrick Gallagher, Ceo Robert Gorman, Publishing Director Tom Gilliatt, Publishing Director Jane Morrow (Murdoch Books), Publishing Director Eva Mills (children and young adult)

Fiction for children 5–9 and 10–13 years, teenage fiction, series fiction and narrative non-fiction. Also adult/general trade books, including fiction and broad-ranging non-fiction. Imprints include: Allen & Unwin, Albert Street Books, Inspired Living, Crows Nest, House of Books, Murdoch Books, Peir 9. Submission guidelines: will consider unsolicited MSS (but not picture book texts). Will only accept MSS through the electronic Friday Pitch system. Founded 1990.

Bloomsbury Publishing Pty Ltd*
Level 6, 387 George Street, Sydney, NSW 2000
tel +61 (0)2 8820 4900
email au@bloomsbury.com
website www.bloomsbury.com/au
Facebook www.facebook.com/bloomsburypublishingaustralia
Twitter @BloomsburySyd
Managing Director Cristina Cappelluto

Supports the worldwide publishing activities of Bloomsbury Publishing: caters for the Australia and New Zealand territories. Bloomsbury Publishing Plc founded 1986.

Brolly Books*
Suite 330, 45 Glenferrie Road, Malvern, VIC 3181
tel + 61 3 95338863
email andrew@brollybooks.com
website https://brollybooks.com/

An independent Australian publishing house specialising in Australian children's books, boxed picture jigsaws, and general non-fiction. Founded 1997.

Cengage Learning Australia*
Level 7, 80 Dorcas Street, South Melbourne, VIC 3205
tel +61 (0)3 9685 4111
website www.cengage.com.au
Vice President Higher Education Paul Petrulis, Vice President School Division Nicole McCarten

Educational books. Founded 2007.

Exisle Publishing
Unit 11, 201 Main Street, Gosford, NSW 2250
website https://exislepublishing.com/
Facebook www.facebook.com/exislepublishing
Twitter @exislebooks
Ceo Gareth St John Thomas

Publishes non-fiction for both adults and children. Children's imprint: Ex Books. Founded 1991.

Hachette Australia Pty Ltd*
Level 17, 207 Kent Street, Sydney, NSW 2000
tel +61 (0)2 8248 0800
email auspub@hachette.com.au
website www.hachette.com.au
Ceo Louise Stark

General, children's: picture books, fiction for children 5–8 and 9–12 years, teenage fiction and series fiction. Accepts MSS via website. Founded 1971.

HarperCollins Publishers (Australia) Pty Ltd Group*

Postal address PO Box A565, Sydney South, NSW 1235
tel +61 (0)2 9952 5000
website www.harpercollins.com.au

Literary fiction and non-fiction, popular fiction, children's, reference, biography, autobiography, current affairs, sport, lifestyle, health/self-help, humour, true crime, travel, Australiana, history, business, gift, religion. Founded 1989.

Little Hare Books*

Ground Floor, Building 1, 658 Church Street, Richmond, VIC 3121
tel +61 (0)3 8520 6444
email info@hardiegrantchildrenspublishing.com.au
website www.hardiegrant.com/au/hardie-grant-childrens-publishing

Imprint of Hardie Grant Egmont Children's Publishing. Publishes high-quality children's books in Australia and New Zealand. Check website for details of when submissions are accepted. Founded 2010.

McGraw-Hill Australia Pty Ltd*

Level 2, 82 Waterloo Road, North Ryde, NSW 2113
Postal address Private Bag 2233, Business Centre, North Ryde, NSW 1670
tel +61 (0)2 9900 1800
website www.mcgraw-hill.com.au

Educational publisher: higher education, primary education and professional (including medical, general and reference). Division of the McGraw-Hill Companies. Founded 1964.

New Frontier Publishing*

48 Ross Street, Glebe, NSW 2037
tel +61 (0)2 9660 4614
email info@newfrontier.com.au
website www.newfrontier.com.au
Director Sophia Whitfield

Aims to uplift, educate and inspire through its range of children's books. Activity books, board books, picture books, middle-grade fiction, dictionaries, textbooks. Caters for children 2–12 years. Unsolicited MSS accepted. Understanding of existing list crucial. Downloadable submissions pack available via website. Founded 2002.

Pan Macmillan Australia Pty Ltd*

Level 25, 1 Market Street, Sydney, NSW 2000
tel +61 (0)2 9285 9100
email pan.reception@macmillan.com.au
website www.panmacmillan.com.au
Directors Ingrid Ohlsson (publishing)

Commercial and literary fiction; children's and young adult fiction; non-fiction and character products; general non-fiction; sport; cooking and lifestyle. Founded 1843.

Penguin Random House Australia Pty Ltd*

Sydney office Level 3, 100 Pacific Highway, North Sydney, NSW 2060
tel +61 (0)2 9954 9966
email information@penguinrandomhouse.com.au
Melbourne office 707 Collins Street, Melbourne, VIC 3008
website www.penguinrandomhouse.com.au
Ceo Julie Burland, *Publishing Director* Justin Ratcliffe, *Group Publishing Director* Nikki Christer, *Publishing Director, Penguin Young Readers* Laura Harris, *Publicity Director* Karen Reid

General fiction and non-fiction; children's, illustrated. MS submissions for non-fiction accepted, unbound in hard copy addressed to Submissions Editor. Fiction submissions are only accepted from previously published authors, or authors represented by an agent or accompanied by a report from an accredited assessment service. Imprints: Arrow, Bantam, Ebury, Hamish Hamilton, Knopf, Michael Joseph, Penguin, Viking, Vintage and William Heinemann. Subsidiary of Bertelsmann AG. Founded 2013.

University of Queensland Press*

PO Box 6042, St Lucia, QLD 4067
tel +61 (0)7 3365 7244
email reception@uqp.com.au
website www.uqp.com.au

Publishes children's and young adult as well as fiction, non-fiction and poetry for all ages. Founded 1948.

R.I.C. Publications Pty Ltd

5 Bendsten Place, Balcatta, WA 6021
tel +61 (0)8 9240 9888
website www.ricpublications.com.au

Educational publisher specialising in blackline master or copymasters and student workbooks for schools and homeschoolers. Founded 1986.

Rhiza Edge

PO Box 302, Chinchilla, QLD 4413
tel +61 (0)7 3245 1938
email editor@rhizaedge.com.au
website www.rhizaedge.com.au
Facebook www.facebook.com/rhizaedge
Commissioning Editor Emily Lighezzolo

Publishes issue-based stories for young adult readers. Imprint of Wombat Books (page 43). Founded 2018.

Scholastic Australia Pty Ltd*

76–80 Railway Crescent, Lisarow, Gosford, NSW 2250
tel +61 (0)2 4328 3555
website www.scholastic.com.au
Chairman David Peagram

Children's fiction and non-fiction. Founded 1968.

Wombat Books*

PO Box 302, Chinchilla, QLD 4413
tel +61 (0)7 3245 1938
email website@wombatrhiza.com.au
website www.wombatrhiza.com.au
Facebook www.facebook.com/wombatbooks
Publisher Rochelle Manners

An independent publisher of children's picture books
and books for early readers. Young adult and adult
imprint: Rhiza Edge (page 42). Founded 2009.

CANADA

*Member of the Canadian Publishers' Council
†Member of the Association of Canadian Publishers

Annick Press Ltd†

388 Carlaw Avenue, Suite 200 Toronto,
ON M4M 2T4
tel +1 416-221-4802
email annickpress@annickpress.com
website www.annickpress.com
Owner & Director Rick Wilks

Preschool to young adult fiction and non-fiction.
Approximately 25% of books are by first-time
authors. Founded 1975.

Breakwater Books†

Suite 213, 321 Carlaw Avenue, Toronto,
ON M4M 2S1
tel +1 709-722-6680
email orders@breakwaterbooks.com
website https://breakwaterbooks.com/
Facebook www.facebook.com/breakwaterbooksltd
Twitter @breakwaterbooks
President & Publisher Rebecca Rose

Publishes award-winning writing in all literary genres:
fiction, non-fiction, poetry, drama, art, young adult
and children's books, as well as cookbooks,
guidebooks and educational resources.
Founded 1973.

Dundurn Press†

1382 Queen St E, Toronto, ON M4L 1C9
tel +1 416-214-5544
email submissions@dundurn.com
Publisher Kirk Howard

Young adult fiction. Founded 1972.

Fitzhenry & Whiteside Ltd

195 Allstate Parkway, Markham, ON L3R 4T8
tel +1 800-387-9776
email bookinfo@fitzhenry.ca
website www.fitzhenry.ca
Facebook www.facebook.com/FitzWhits
Twitter @FitzWhits
Ceo Sharon Fitzhenry

Fiction and non-fiction (social studies, visual arts,
biography, environment). Publishes ten picture

books, five early readers/chapter books, six middle
novels and seven young adult books each year.
Approximately 10% of books are by first-time
authors. Emphasis is on Canadian authors and
illustrators, subject or perspective. Will review MS/
illustration packages from artists. Submit outline and
copy of sample illustration. For illustrations only,
send samples and promotional sheet. Responds in
three months. Samples returned with sase.
Founded 1966.

HarperCollins Publishers Ltd*

22 Adelaide Street West, 41st Floor, Toronto,
ON M5H 4E3
tel +1 416-975-9334
email hcOrder@harpercollins.com
website www.harpercollins.ca

Literary fiction and non-fiction, history, politics,
biography, spiritual and children's books.
Founded 1989.

House of Anansi Press and Groundwood Books

128 Sterling Road, Lower Level, Toronto,
ON M6R 2B7
tel +1 416-363-4343
email publicity@houseofanansi.com
website https://houseofanansi.com/
Facebook www.facebook.com/groundwoodbooks
Twitter @GroundwoodBooks
Publisher Scott Griffin

Groundwood Books publishes boosks for all ages,
including fiction, picture books, graphic novels and
non-fiction. Founded 1974.

Kids Can Press Ltd†

25 Dockside Drive, Toronto, ON M5A 0B5
tel +1 416-479-7000
email customerservice@kidscan.com
website www.kidscanpress.com
Editorial Director Yvette Ghione

Middle grade/young adult fiction and non-fiction.
Publishes picture books, young readers, middle
readers and young adult titles. Approximately
10–15% of books are by first-time authors. Submit
outline/synopsis and between two and three sample
chapters. See website for submission guidelines.
Founded 1973.

McGraw-Hill Ryerson Ltd*

145 Kings Street West, Suite 1501,
Toronto ON M5H 1J8
tel +1 800-565-5758
website www.mheducation.ca

Educational and trade books. Founded 1972.

Nelson Education*

1120 Birchmount Road, Toronto, ON M1K 5G4
tel +1 416-752-9448

website www.nelson.com
President & Ceo Steve Brown

Educational publishing: school (K–12), college and university, career education, measurement and guidance, professional and reference, ESL titles. Division of Thomson Canada Ltd. Founded 1914.

Nimbus Publishing†

PO Box 9166, Halifax, NS B3K 5M8
tel +1 800-646-2879
website https://nimbus.ca/
Facebook www.facebook.com/nimbuspub
Twitter @nimbuspub

Publishes children's picture books and fiction, literary non-fiction, social and cultural history, nature photography, current events, biography, sports and cultural issues. Founded 1978.

Oberon Press

145 Spruce Street, Ottawa, ON K1R 6P1
tel +1 613-238-3275
email oberon@sympatico.ca
website www.oberonpress.ca

General fiction, short stories, poetry, some biographies, art and children's. Only publishes Canadian writers. Currently not accepting unsolicited MS. Founded 1985.

Orca Book Publishers†

1016 Balmoral Road Victoria, BC V8T 1A8
tel +1 800-210-5277
email orca@orcabook.com
website www.orcabook.com

Books for children and young adults. Will consider MSS from Canadian writers only. No submissions by fax or email. See website for submission guidelines. No poetry. Founded 1984.

Pajama Press†

11 Davies Avenue, Suite 103, Toronto, ON M4M 2A9
website https://pajamapress.ca/
Facebook www.facebook.com/pajamapress
Twitter @pajamapress
Publisher Gail Winskill

Children's: picture books, our new sturdy books for the very young, early chapter books for new readers, middle grade novels, young adult novels for pre-high school audiences, and literary non-fiction. Founded 2011.

Pearson Canada*

26 Prince Andrew Place, North York, ON M3C 2T8
tel +1 800-361-6128
website www.pearson.com/ca/en.html
Ceo Dan Lee

Academic, technical, educational, children's and adult, trade. Founded 1998.

Penguin Random House Canada Ltd*

320 Front Street West, Suite 1400, Toronto, ON M5V 3B6
tel +1 416-364-4449
website www.penguinrandomhouse.ca
Ceo Kristin Cochrane

Literary fiction, commercial fiction, memoir, non-fiction (history, business, current events, sports), adult, teen and young readers. No unsolicited MSS; submissions via an agent only. Imprints: Allen Lane Canada, Anchor Canada, Appetite by Random House, Bond Street Books, Doubleday Canada, Emblem, Hamish Hamilton Canada, Knopf Canada, McClelland & Stewart, Penguin Canada, Penguin Teen, Portfolio Canada, Puffin Canada, Random House Canada, Seal Books, Signal, Strange Light, Tundra Books, Viking Canada, Vintage Canada. Subsidiary of Penguin Random House. Founded 2013.

Rebel Mountain Press†

email rebelmountainpress@gmail.com
Facebook www.facebook.com/rebelmountainpress
Twitter @rebelmountain1
Publisher Lori Shwydky

Publishes children's and young adult literature, anthologies and poetry that feature characters and authors who are BIPOC, LGBTQ2IA+ and/or have disabilities. Founded 2015.

Red Deer Press

195 Allstate Parkway, Markham, ON L3R 4T8
tel +1 800-387-9776
email rdp@reddeerpress.com
website www.reddeerpress.com

Literary fiction, science fiction, non-fiction, children's illustrated books, young adult fiction, teen fiction. Publishes books that are written or illustrated by Canadians and that are about or of interest to Canadians. Imprint: RJS (Robert J. Sawyer) Books (science fiction). Publishes 14–18 new books a year. Children's picture books MSS from established authors with a demonstrable record of publishing success are preferred. Currently accepting new MSS. Founded 1975.

Ronsdale Press†

3350 West 21st Avenue, Vancouver, BC V6S 1G7
tel +1 604-738-4688
email ronsdale@shaw.ca
website www.ronsdalepress.com
Facebook www.facebook.com/ronsdalepress
Twitter @ronsdalepress
Director Veronica Hatch

A Canadian publisher based in Vancouver with some 300 books in print. Not currently accepting picture books. Founded 1988.

Scholastic Canada Ltd*

175 Hillmount Road, Markham, ON L6C 1Z7
tel +1 800-268-3860
email custserv@scholastic.ca
website www.scholastic.ca
Facebook www.facebook.com/ScholasticCanada
Twitter @scholasticCDA
Instagram @scholasticcda
Art Director Andrea Casault

Serves children, parents and teachers through a variety of businesses including Scholastic Reading Club and Book Fairs, Scholastic Education, Classroom Magazines, Trade and Éditions Scholastic. Publishes recreational reading for children and young people from preschoolers to teens and educational materials for kindergarten to Grade 8 in both official languages. Its publishing focus is on books by Canadians. Wholly owned subsidiary of Scholastic Inc. Scholastic Canada is currently interested in reviewing unpublished material by writers from underrepresented communities, including Black writers, Indigenous writers, writers of colour, writers with disabilities, LGBTQIA2S+ writers and writers who identify with other marginalized groups. Canadian artists may submit electronic samples of their work along with their website/contact information to the art director. Never send originals. Please see website for submission guidelines. Founded 1920.

Second Story Press†

20 Maud Street, Suite 401, Toronto, ON M5V 2M5
tel +1 416-537-7850
email info@secondstorypress.ca
website https://secondstorypress.ca/
Facebook www.facebook.com/secondstorypress
Twitter @secondstory

Publishes feminist-inspired fiction and non-fiction for adults, children and young adults. Founded 2015.

University of Toronto Press

800 Bay Street, Mezzanine, Toronto, ON M5S 3A9
tel +1 416-978-2239
email publishing@utpress.utoronto.ca
website www.utorontopress.com

Imprints include: Aevo UTP; New Jewish Press; Rotman-UTP Publishing. Publishers of non-fiction, monographs, textbooks and academic books, ESL/EFL, teacher reference, adult basic education and school texts. Founded 1901.

Tundra Books

320 Front Street West, Suite 1400, Toronto, ON M5V 3B6
tel +1 416-364-4449
email submissions@tundrabooks.com
email art@tundrabooks.com
website www.penguinrandomhouse.ca/imprints/TU/tundra-books

Facebook www.facebook.com/tundrabooks
Twitter @TundraBooks

Publisher of high-quality children's picture books and novels, renowned for its innovations. Publishes books for children to teens. Imprints: Penguin Teen Canada, Puffin Canada, Tundra Books. A division of Penguin Random House Canada Ltd. Founded 1967.

FRANCE

l'école des loisirs

11 rue de Sevres, 75006 Paris
tel +33 (0)1 4222 9410
email edl@ecoledesloisirs.com
website www.ecoledesloisirs.fr
Managing Director Louis Delas

Specialises in children's literature from picture books to young adult fiction. Founded 1965.

Flammarion

1 place de l'Odéon, 75006 Paris
tel +33 (0)1 4051 3346
website https://editions.flammarion.com
Ceo Gilles Haéri

Leading French publisher. Children's imprints include: Albums du Père Castor, Castor Poche, Tribal, Etonnants Classiques, GF – Flammarion, Chan – OK. Founded 1875.

Père Castor

Children's Publisher Céline Dehaine

Children's picture books, junior fiction, activity books, board books, how-to books, comics, gift books, fairy tales, dictionaries and records and tapes. Covers 0–16 years.

Gallimard Jeunesse

5 rue Gaston Gallimard, 75328 Paris
tel +33 (0)1 4954 4200
website www.gallimard-jeunesse.fr
Children's Publisher Hedwige Pasquet

Publisher of high-quality children's fiction and non-fiction including board books, novelty books, picture books, pop-up books. Founded 1911.

Hachette Livre/Gautier-Languereau

53 rue Jean Bleuzen, 92170 Vanves
tel +33 (0)1 4392 3030
website www.gautier-languereau.fr
Director Sarah Koegler, *Editor Director* Brigitte Leblanc

One shot picture books for children. Imaginative stories for children aged from 2–10 years. Illustrated books, pop ups, laser dye-cut books, books with CD. Major illustrators: Antoine Guilloppé, Hélène Druvert, Rébecca Dautremer, Philippe Jalbert, Amanda Minazio, Aurelia Fronty. Publishes approximately 55 titles each year. Will consider

Books

unsolicited MSS. Allow four months for response. Contacts on website. Founded 1885.

Kaléidoscope

11 rue de Sèvres, 75006 Paris
tel +33 (0)1 4544 0708
website www.editions-kaleidoscope.com
Children's Publisher Isabel Finkenstaedt

Specialises in up-market picture books for children 0–6 years. Founded 1989.

Editions Sarbacane

35 rue d'Hauteville, 75010 Paris
tel +33 (0)1 4246 3727
email e.beulque@sarbacane.net
website www.editions-sarbacane.com

High-quality activity books, board books, picture books and young adult fiction, fiction for children from preschool age to adult.

Le Sorbier

25 boulevard Romain Rolland, 75014 Paris
tel +33 (0)1 4148 8000
website www.editionsdelamartiniere.fr

High-quality picture books for children up to 10 years and illustrated reference books for 9–12 years. Imprint: De La Martinière Jeunesse.

GERMANY

Carlsen Verlag

Postfach 50 03 80, 22703 Hamburg
tel +49 (0)40 398040
email info@carlsen.de
website www.carlsen.de
Directors Renate Herre, Joachim Kaufmann

Children's picture books, board books and novelty books. Illustrated fiction and non-fiction. Teenage fiction and non-fiction. Publishes both German and international authors including Stephenie Meyer, J.K. Rowling and Philip Pullman. Publisher of the *Harry Potter* series. Imprint: Chicken House Deutschland. Age groups: preschool, 5–10, 10–15, 15+. Unsolicited MSS welcome but must include a sae for return. Do not follow up by phone or post. For illustrations, submit no more than three colour photocopies and unlimited b&w copies. Founded 1953.

dtv Verlagsgesellschaft mbH & Co. KG

Tumblingerstraße 21, 80337 Munich
tel +49 (0)89 38167282
email verlag@dtv.de
website www.dtvjunior.de
Facebook www.facebook.com/dtvVerlag
Twitter @dtv_verlag
Children's Publishing Director Susanne Stark

Fiction and non-fiction for children, teenagers and young adults. Authors include Kate DiCamillo, Kevin

Brooks, Colleen Hoover, Sarah J. Maas, Libba Bray, Eva Ibbotson, Sarah Dessen. Founded 1971.

Bold

Young general fiction. Authors include: Hank Green, Atticus, K.A. Tucker. Founded 2018.

Carl Hanser Verlag

Vilshofener Straße 10, 81679 Munich
tel +49 (0)89 998300
email info@hanser.de
website www.hanser-literaturverlage.de
Facebook www.facebook.com/HanserLiteraturverlage
Twitter @hanserliteratur
Instagram @hanserliteratur, @hanser.hey
Children's Publisher Saskia Heintz

High-quality hardback books for all ages from preschool to young adults. Board books, picture books, fiction and non-fiction. Age groups: 3–10, 10–15, 15+. Founded 1993.

Ravensburger Buchverlag

Robert-Bosch-Straße 1, 88214 Ravensburg
tel +49 (0)751 860
email buchverlag@ravensburger.de
website www.ravensburger.de

Activity books, novelty books, picture books, fiction for children 5–8 and 9–12 years, teenage fiction, series fiction and educational games and puzzles. Publishes approx. 450 titles each year and has 1,500 in print. Will consider unsolicited MSS for fiction only. Allow two months for response. Founded 1883.

ITALY

De Agostini Editore

Via Giovanni da Verrazano 15, 28100 Novara
tel +39 02-380861
website www.deagostini.it
Publisher Annachiara Tassan

Illustrated and children's books. Founded 1901.

Edizioni Arka srl

Via Milano 73/75, 20010 Cornaredo Milan
tel +39 02-4818230
email daisy.zonato@edizioniel.it
website www.arkaedizioni.it
Publisher Ginevra Viscardi

Picture books and some general fiction for preschool children and children up to 10 years.

Edizioni El/Einaudi Ragazzi/Emme Edizioni

Via J. Ressel 5, 34018 San Dorligo della Valle TS
tel +39 040-3880311
email edizioniel@edizioniel.it
website www.edizioniel.com
Children's Publisher Orietta Fatucci

Activity books, board books, picture books, pop-up books, non-fiction, novels, poetry, fairy tales, fiction. Age groups: preschool, 5–10, 10–15, 15+.

Giunti Editore S.p.A.
Via Bolognese 165, 50139 Florence
tel +39 055-50621
email info@giunti.it
website www.giunti.it
Facebook www.facebook.com/GiuntiEditore
Twitter @GiuntiEditore
President Sergio Giunti

Activity books, board books, novelty books, picture books, colouring books, pop-up books and some educational textbooks. Founded 1841.

Arnoldo Mondadori Editore S.p.A. (Mondadori)
Via Mondadori 1, 20090 Segrate, Milan
tel +39 02-75421
email stampalibri@mondadori.it
website www.mondadori.it

Activity books, board books, novelty books, picture books, painting and colouring books, pop-up books, how-to books, hobbies, leisure, pets, sport, comics, poetry, fairy tales, education, fiction and non-fiction. Age groups: preschool, 5–10, 10–15, 15+. Founded 1907.

Adriano Salani Editore S.p.A.
Via Gherardini 10, 20145 Milan
tel +39 02-34597624
email info@salani.it
website www.salani.it
Children's Publisher Simona Scandellari

Picture books, how-to books, comics, gift books, fiction, novels, poetry, fairy tales. Age groups: preschool, 5–10, 10–15, 15+. Founded 1862.

THE NETHERLANDS

Lemniscaat BV
Vijverlaan 48, 3062 HL Rotterdam
tel +31 10-2062929
email info@lemniscaat.nl
website www.lemniscaat.nl
Publisher Jesse Goossens

Well-known independent children's book publisher. Publishes picture books, juvenile novels and young adult literature. Founded 1963.

Rubinstein Publishing
Prinseneiland 43, 1013 LL Amsterdam
tel +31 20-4200772
email info@rubinstein.nl
website www.rubinstein.nl
Children's Publisher Mascha de Vries

Independent publisher specialising in audiobooks for children. Also produces novelty books. Founded 1985.

Van Goor/Van Holkema & Warendorf
PO Box 23202, 1100 DS Amsterdam
tel +31 20-2364200
website www.de-leukste-kinderboeken.nl, www.bestofyabooks.nl

High-quality picture books, learn-to-read books, middle grade and (literary) fiction and non-fiction, young adult. Founded 2009.

NEW ZEALAND

*Member of the New Zealand Book Publishers' Association

Block Chook Books*
PO Box 137, Waimauku, Auckland, 0842
email info@blackchookbooks.co.nz
website www.blackchookbooks.co.nz
Facebook www.facebook.com/blackchookbooks
Publisher Martin Bailey

Publishes children's fiction, specialises in board books. Founded 2020.

Cengage Learning New Zealand*
Unit 4B, Rosedale Office Park, 331 Rosedale Road, Albany, North Shore 0632
Postal address PO Box 33376, Takapuna, North Shore 0740
tel +64 (0)9 415 6850
Vice President, Higher Education Paul Petrulis, *Vice President, School Division* Nicole McCarten

Educational books. Founded 2007.

Edify Ltd*
Level 1, 39 Woodside Avenue, Northcote, Auckland 0627
tel +64 (0)9 972 9428
email mark@edify.co.nz
website www.edify.co.nz
Ceo Adrian Keane

A publishing, sales and marketing business providing its partners with opportunities for their products and solutions in the New Zealand educational market. Exclusive representatives of Pearson and the New Zealand based educational publisher, Sunshine Books. Founded 2013.

Gecko Press*
PO Box 9335, Marion Square, Wellington 6141
tel +64 (0)4 801 9333
email office@geckopress.com
website www.geckopress.com
Publisher Julia Marshall

Children's books: picture books, junior fiction and non-fiction. Translates and publishes award-winning children's books from around the world and a small number of own titles. Selects books strong in story, character, illustration and design. See website for submission guidelines. Founded 2005.

HarperCollins Publishers (New Zealand) Ltd*

Unit D, 63 Apollo Drive, Rosedale, Auckland 0632
tel +64 (0)9 443 9400
email publicity@harpercollins.co.nz
Postal address PO Box 1, Shortland Street, Auckland 1140
website www.harpercollins.co.nz

General literature, non-fiction, reference, children's. HarperCollins New Zealand does not accept proposals or MSS for consideration, except via the Wednesday Post portal on its website. Founded 1989.

McGraw-Hill Book Company New Zealand Ltd

Level 8, 56–60 Cawley Street, Ellerslie, Auckland 1005
Postal address Private Bag 11904, Ellerslie, Auckland 1005
tel +64 (0)9 526 6200
website www.mcgraw-hill.com.au

Educational publisher: higher education, primary and secondary education (grades K–12) and professional (including medical, general and reference). Division of the McGraw-Hill Companies. Always looking for potential authors. Has a rapidly expanding publishing programme. See website for author's guide. Founded 1974.

Mākaro Books

Level 6, 138 Wakefield Street, Te Aro, Wellington 6011
email makaropress@gmail.com
Publishers Mary McCallum, Paul Stewart

Fiction, as well as poetry, children's books, memoir, biography and journalism. Founded 2013.

New Zealand Council for Educational Research

Box 3237, Education House, 178–182 Willis Street, Wellington 6140
tel +64 (0)4 384 7939
email info@nzcer.org.nz
website https://www.nzcer.org.nz
Publishing Manager David Ellis

Education, including educational policy and practice, early childhood education, educational achievement tests, Māori education, schooling for the future, curriculum and assessment. Founded 1934.

Penguin Random House New Zealand Ltd*

Private Bag 102 902, North Shore, Auckland 0745
tel +64 (0)9 442 7400

email publishing@penguinrandomhouse.co.nz
website www.penguinrandomhouse.co.nz
Facebook www.facebook.com/PenguinBooksNewZealand
Publishing Director Debra Millar, *Head of Publishing* Claire Murdoch

Adult and children's fiction and non-fiction. Imprints: Penguin, Vintage, Black Swan, Godwit, Viking, Puffin Books. Part of Penguin Random House. Founded 2013.

SOUTH AFRICA

Member of the Publishers' Association of South Africa

Cambridge University Press, Africa*

Lower Ground Floor, Nautica Building, The Water Club, Beach Road, Granger Bay, Cape Town 8005
tel +27 (0)21 773 0147
email capetown@cambridge.org
website www.cambridge.org
Publishing Director Johan Traut

Textbooks and literature for sub-Sahara African countries, as well as primary reading materials in 28 African languages. Founded 1534.

Educat Publishers Pty Ltd

4 Clifford Street, Ottery, Cape Town
tel +27 (0)21 697 3669
email takeeducat@gmail.com
website www.educat.co.za

Educational products including science and maths, product designs for schools and retail, as well as mass markets. Age groups: preschool, 5–10, 10–15, 15+.

Human & Rousseau

12th Floor, Naspers, 40 Heerengracht, Roggebaai 8012
tel +27 (0)21 406 3033
email nb@nb.co.za
website www.humanrousseau.com

General Afrikaans and English titles. Quality Afrikaans literature, popular literature, general children's and youth literature, cookery, self-help. Founded 1959.

Macmillan Education South Africa

4th Floor, Building G, Hertford Office Park, 90 Bekker Road, Vorna Valley, Midrand 1685
tel +27 (0)11 731 3300
Postal address Private Bag X19, Northlands 2116
website www.macmillan.co.za
Managing Director Preggy Naidoo

Educational titles for the RSA market. Founded 1843.

NB Publishers (Pty) Ltd*

12th Floor, Media24 Centre, 40 Heerengracht, Cape Town 8001

tel +27 (0)21 406 3033
email nb@nb.co.za
website www.nb.co.za

General: Afrikaans fiction, politics, children's and youth literature in all the country's languages, non-fiction. Imprints: Tafelberg, Human & Rousseau, Queillerie, Pharos, Kwela, Best Books and Lux Verbi. Founded 1950.

New Africa Books (Pty) Ltd

Unit 13A, Athlone Industrial Park,
10 Mymoena Crescent, Cape Town 7764
tel +27 (0)21 467 5860
email info@newafricabooks.co.za
Postal address PostNet, Suite 144, Private Bag X9190, Cape Town 8000

An independent publisher of picture books, fiction, non-fiction and comics with South African content in all South African languages. Award-winning writers and illustrators include Sindiwe Magona, Richard Rive, Lebohang Masango, Paddy Bouma, Nicolaas Maritz, Lorato Trok and Xolisa Guzula. Founded 1971.

Oxford University Press Southern Africa*

Vasco Boulevard, N1 City, Goodwood,
Cape Town 7460
tel +27 (0)21 596 2300
email oxford.za@oup.com
Postal address PO Box 12119, N1 City,
Cape Town 7463
website www.oxford.co.za
Managing Director Hanri Pieterse

One of the leading educational publishers in South Africa, producing a wide range of quality educational material in print and digital format. The range includes books from Grade R to Grade 12, as well as TVET textbooks, textbooks, school literature, dictionaries and atlases. Founded 1586.

Pearson South Africa*

4th Floor, Auto Atlantic Building,
Corner Hertzog Boulevard and Heerengracht Boulevard, Cape Town 8001
Postal address PO Box 396, Cape Town 8000
tel +27 (0)21 532 6008
email pearsonza.enquiries@pearson.com
website https://za.pearson.com/

Pearson South Africa provides learning materials, technologies and services for use in schools, TVET colleges, higher education institutions and in home and professional environments. Founded 2010.

Shuter and Shooter Publishers (Pty) Ltd*

110 CB Downes Road, Pietermaritzburg,
KwaZulu-Natal 3201

tel +27 (0)33 846 8700
email sales@shuters.com
Postal address PO Box 61, Mkondeni, KwaZulu-Natal 3212
website www.shuters.co.za
Ceo Primi Chetty

Core curriculum-based textbooks for use at foundation, intermediate, senior and FET phases. Supplementary readers in various languages; dictionaries; reading development kits, charts. Literature titles in English, isiXhosa, Sesotho, Sepedi, Setswana, Tshivenda, Xitsonga, Ndebele, isiZulu and Siswati. Founded 1925.

Via Afrika Publishers

11th Floor, 40 Heerengracht, Cape Town 8001
Postal address PO Box 5197, Cape Town 8001
tel +27 (0)21 406 3528
email customerservices@viaafrika.com
website www.viaafrika.com
Ceo Christina Watson

Educational materials for South African schools and FET colleges, for all learning areas and subjects at all grades/levels: in all official languages of South Africa. Imprints: Acacia, Action, Afritech, Afro, Atlas, Bateleur Books, Collegium, Idem, Juta/Gariep, KZN Books, Nasou; Stimela, Van Schaik (literature), Via Afrika. Founded 1949.

SPAIN

Grupo Anaya

C/Juan Ignacio Luca de Tena 15, 28027 Madrid
tel +34 913 938 800
website www.anaya.es

Non-fiction: education textbooks for preschool–15+. Part of Hachette Livre. Founded 1984.

Editorial Cruilla

C/Roger de Llúria 44, 4th, 08009 Barcelona
tel +34 902 123 336
email editorial@cruilla.cat
website www.cruilla.cat

Activity books, novelty books, fiction for children 5–8 and 9–12 years, teenage fiction and poetry. Publishes approx. 120–130 titles each year. Successes include *El Vaixell de Vapor* (series), *Vull Llegir!* and *Molly Moon Stops the World/Molly Moon's Incredible Book of Hypnotism*. Subsidiary of Ediciones SM. Founded 1984.

Destino Infantil & Juvenil

Carrer de Llull 51, 60–4A, 08005 Barcelona
email info@librosdelzorrorojo.com
website www.librosdelzorrorojo.com
Children's & Young Adult Director Marta Bueno Miró

Fiction for children 6–16 years. Picture books, pop-up books, fiction and some unusual illustrated books.

Books

Libros del Zorro Rojo

Carrer de Llull 51, 6–4, 08005 Barcelona
email rights@librosdelzorrorojo.com
website www.librosdelzorrorojo.com
Editorial Director Fernando Diego García

Independent publisher specialising in children's and illustrated young adult books. Main focus is picture books for young children and classics with high-quality illustrations for young readers. Founded 2004.

Editorial Libsa

C/ Puerto de Navacerrada, 88, Pol. Ind. Las Nieves, Madrid
tel +34 916 572 580
email libsa@libsa.es
website www.libsa.es
President Amado Sanchez, *Children's Books Editor* Maria Dolores Maeso

Publisher and packager of highly illustrated mass market books: activity books, board books, picture books, colouring books, how-to books, fairy tales.

Penguin Random House Grupo Editorial

Luchana 23, 1A, 28010 Madrid
tel +34 915 358 190
website www.penguinrandomhousegrupoeditorial. com

Preschool activity, novelty and picture books through to young adult fiction. Also a packager and printer. Part of Penguin Random House. Founded 2013.

Vicens Vives SA

Avenida Sarriá 130–132, 08017 Barcelona
tel +34 932 523 700
email rrhh@vicensvives.es
website www.vicensvives.com

Activity and novelty books, fiction, art, encyclopedias, dictionaries, education, geography, history, music, science, textbooks, posters. Age groups: preschool, 5–10, 10–15, 15+. Founded 1960.

USA

*Member of the Association of American Publishers Inc.

Abingdon Press

810 12th Ave South, Nashville, TN 37203
tel +1 800-251-3320
website www.abingdonpress.com
Facebook www.facebook.com/AbingdonPress
Twitter @AbingdonPress
President & Publisher Neil Alexander

General interest, professional, academic and reference, non-fiction and fiction, youth and children's non-fiction and Vatican Bible School; primarily directed to the religious market. Imprint of United Methodist Publishing House with tradition of crossing denominational boundaries. United Methodist Publishing House founded 1789.

Harry N. Abrams, Inc.

195 Broadway, 9th Floor, New York, NY 10007
tel +1 212-206-7715
email abrams@abramsbooks.com
website www.abramsbooks.com

Art and architecture, photography, natural sciences, performing arts, children's books. Imprints include: Abrams, Abrams Appleseed, Abrams Books for Young Readers, Abrams ComicArts, Abrams Image, Abrams Noterie, Abrams Press, Amulet Books, Amulet Paperbacks, Cernunnos, Magic Cat, The Overlook Press. Founded 1949.

Abrams Books for Young Readers

tel +1 212-519-1200
website www.abramsyoungreaders.com

Fiction and non-fiction: picture books, young readers, middle readers, young adult. For picture books submit covering letter and complete MS, for longer works and non-fiction send query and sample chapter with sase.

Aladdin Paperbacks – see Simon & Schuster Children's Publishing Division

All About Kids Publishing

PO Box 159, Gilroy, CA 95021
tel +1 408-337-1152
email lguevara@allaboutkidspub.com
website www.allaboutkidspub.com
Publisher Mike G. Guevara, *Editor* Linda L. Guevara

Fiction and non-fiction picture books and chapter books. Successes include *Don't Let the Dead Bugs Bite!* by Stephen Zmina (picture book) and *Cold Waves, Cold Blood* by Patrick Doherty (teen novel). See website for submission guidelines. Founded 2000.

Astra Publishing House

19 West 21st Street, #1201, New York, NY 10010
email info@bmkbooks.com
website www.boydsmillsandkane.com
Facebook www.facebook.com/BMKbooks
Twitter @kanepress
President Leying Jiang

Activity books, picture books, fiction, non-fiction and poetry for 18 years and under. Publishes 80 titles each year. Check website for submission guidelines. Imprints: Astra House, Astra Young Readers, Calkins Creek, Hippo Park, Kane Press, minedition US, Toon Books, Word Song. Founded 1991.

Atheneum Books for Young Readers – see Simon & Schuster Children's Publishing Division

AV2

276 5th Ave, Suite 704 #917, New York, NY 10001
tel +1 866-649-3445
website www.av2books.com

Educational publisher: children's non-fiction titles. Successes include *The AV2 Collection* (av2books.com). Founded 1979.

Avon – see HarperCollins Publishers

Barefoot Books
23 Bradford Street, Concord, MA 01742
tel +1 617-576-0660
email publicity@barefootbooks.com
website www.barefootbooks.com
Facebook www.facebook.com/barefootbooks
Twitter @BarefootBooks
Editorial Director Emma Parkin

Currently not accepting MS submissions or queries. Accepts illustrator samples via mail only. Please mail samples (no original artwork) for the attention of the editor. Successes include *Mindful Kids* by Whitney Stewart, illustrated by Mina Braun; and *The Barefoot Book of Children* by Kate DePalma and Tessa Strickland, illustrated by David Dean (3–7 years, picture book). Length: 500–1,000 words (picture books), 2,000–3,000 words (young readers). US branch founded 1998.

Bloomsbury Publishing USA*
1385 Broadway, New York, NY 10018
tel +1 212-419-5300
email Contact-USA@bloomsbury.com
website www.bloomsbury.com/us
President Adrienne Vaughan, *Publishing Director* Mary Kate Castellan

Supports the worldwide publishing activities of Bloomsbury Publishing Plc: caters for the US market. For submission guidelines see website. Established in 1998 as an American subsidiary of Bloomsbury Publishing Plc. Founded 1986.

The Blue Sky Press – see Scholastic, Inc.

Calkins Creek Books – see Astra Publishing House

Candlewick Press
99 Dover Street, Somerville, MA 02144
tel +1 617-661-3330
email bigbear@candlewick.com
website www.candlewick.com
President & Publisher Karen Lotz, *Creative Director & Associate Publisher* Chris Paul, *Executive Editorial Director & Associate Publisher* Liz Bicknell, *Editorial Director & Director of Editorial Operations* Mary Lee Donovan

Books for babies through teens: board books, picture books, early readers, first chapter books, novels, non-fiction, novelty books, poetry, graphic novels. Publishes 70 picture books, 40 middle readers and 30 young adult titles each year. Founded 1991.

Candlewick Entertainment
Group Editorial Director Joan Powers
Media-related children's books, including film/TV tie-ins.

Charlesbridge Publishing
9 Galen Street, Watertown, MA 02472
tel +1 617-926-0329
email development@charlesbridge.com
website www.charlesbridge.com

Fiction and non-fiction board books, picture books and middle grade books for preschool–14 years. Young adult novels for readers 14+. Dedicated to diversity and new voices across genres. Non-fiction list specialises in nature, concept, history and science. Publishes roughly 60% non-fiction, 40% fiction. Send full MSS; no queries; electronic submissions only (childrens.submissions@charlesbridge.com). Responds to MSS of interest. For illustrations, send art postcards or electronic query with samples, pdf or jpg portfolio, and website URL (design.submissions@charlesbridge.com). Founded 1980.

Chicago Review Press
814 North Franklin Street, Chicago, IL 60610
tel +1 312-337-0747
email frontdesk@jpg.com
website www.chicagoreviewpress.com
Publisher Cynthia Sherry

General publisher. Non-fiction activity books for children. Imprint Zephyr publishes professional development titles for teachers. Interested in hands-on educational books. See website for submission guidelines. Founded 1973.

Chronicle Books*
680 Second Street, San Francisco, CA 94107
tel +1 415-537-4200
email hello@chroniclebooks.com
website www.chroniclebooks.com, www.chroniclebooks.com/titles/kids-teens
Facebook www.facebook.com/chroniclekidsbooks
Twitter @ChronicleKids
Instagram @chroniclekidsbooks
Chairman & Ceo Nion McEvoy, *Publisher* Christine Carswell

Traditional and innovative children's books. Looking for projects that have a unique edge – in subject matter, writing style or illustrative technique – that will add a distinctive flair. Interested in fiction and non-fiction for children of all ages as well as board books, decks, activity kits and other unusual or 'novelty' formats. Publishes 60–100 books each year. Also for adults: cooking, how-to books, nature, art, biographies, fiction, gift. For picture books submit MS. For older readers, submit outline/synopsis and three sample chapters. No submitted materials will be returned. Response approx. three months. Founded 1967.

Books

Clarion Books – see Houghton Mifflin Harcourt

Clear Light Books

823 Don Diego, Santa Fe, NM 87505
tel +1 505-989-9590
website www.clearlightbooks.com

For adults: art and photography, cookbooks, ecology/ environment, health, gift books, history, Native America, Tibet, Western Americana. Non-fiction for children and young adults: multicultural, American Indian, Hispanic. Looking for authentic American Indian art and folklore. Send complete MS with sase.

David C Cook

4050 Lee Vance View, Colorado Springs, CO 80918
tel +1 719-536-0100
website www.davidccook.com
Ceo John Aden

Christian education resources for preschool to teenagers. Founded 1875.

Cooper Square Publishing – see Rowman & Littlefield

Dawn Publications

P.O. Box 4410, Naperville, IL 60567-4410
tel +1 800-432-7444
website www.sourcebooks.com/dawn-publications.html
Publishers Carol Malnor, Bruce Malnor

Dedicated to inspiring in children a deeper understanding and appreciation for all life on Earth. The aim is to help parents and teachers encourage children to bond with the Earth in a relationship of love, respect and intelligent cooperation, through the books published and the educational materials offered online. Dawn Books is an imprint of Sourcebooks eXplore, the children's non-fiction division of Sourcebooks. Founded 1979.

Dial Books – see Penguin Young Readers

Tom Doherty Associates, LLC

120 Broadway, 22nd Floor, New York, NY 10271
tel +1 212-388-0100
email enquiries@tor.com
website www.torforgeblog.com
Facebook www.facebook.com/tordotcom
Twitter @tordotcom

Fiction and non-fiction for middle readers and young adults. Publishes 5–10 middle readers and 5–10 young adult books each year. Successes include *Hidden Talents, Flip* by David Lubar (fantasy, 10+ years), *Briar Rose* by Jane Yolen (fiction, 12+ years), *Strange Unsolved Mysteries* by Phyllis Rabin Amert (non-fiction). For adults: fiction – general, historical, western, suspense, mystery, horror, science fiction, fantasy, humour, juvenile, classics (English language);

non-fiction. For both fiction and non-fiction, submit outline/synopsis and complete MS. Responds to queries in one month; MSS in six months for unsolicited work. For illustrations, query with samples to Art Director. Responds only if interested. Imprints: Tor Books, Forge Books, Orb Books, Starscope, Tor Teen. Founded 1980.

Forge

Publishes general fiction, both contemporary and historical; thrillers, mysteries and suspense novels; westerns and Americana; military fiction and non-fiction.

StarScape

Award-winning science fiction and fantasy for middle grade readers ages 10 and up (grades 5 and up). All titles are age- and theme-appropriate. Some editions include reader's guides and other supplemental materials.

Tor

Science fiction and fantasy published in hardback and paperback.

Tor Teen
website www.torteen.com

Science fiction and fantasy for children 12+ years.

Doubleday – see Penguin Random House

Dover Publications, Inc.

31 East 2nd Street, Mineola, NY 11501
tel +1 516-294-7000
website https://store.doverpublications.com/
Facebook www.facebook.com/doverpublications
Twitter @doverpublications

Activity books, novelty books, picture books, fiction for children 5–8 and 9–12 years, teenage fiction, series fiction, reference, plays, religion, poetry, audio and CD-Roms. Also adult non-fiction. Will consider unsolicited MSS but write for guidelines. Founded 1941.

EDCON Publishing Group

9316 East Raintree Drive, Suite 120, Scottsdale, AZ 85260
tel +1 800-826-4740
email info@edconpublishing.com
website www.edconpublishing.com

Supplemental instructional materials for use by education professionals to improve reading and maths skills. Includes early reading, *Classics* series, *Easy Shakespeare*, fiction and non-fiction, reading diagnosis and vocabulary books. Founded 1970.

Eerdmans Publishing Company

4035 Park East Court SE, Grand Rapids, MI 49546
tel +1 616-459-4591
website www.eerdmans.com
President & Publisher Anita Eerdmans

Independent publisher of a wide range of religious books, from academic works in theology, biblical studies, religious history and reference to popular titles in spirituality, social and cultural criticism and literature. Founded 1911.

Eerdmans Books for Young Readers
website www.eerdmans.com/youngreader
Picture books, biographies, and middle reader fiction and non-fiction. Publishes 18–22 books a year. Stories that celebrate diversity, stories of historical significance and stories that relate to current issues are of special interest. Accepts unsolicited submissions. Send to Acquisitions Editor; responds in four months only to submissions of interest. For illustrations, send photocopies or printed media and include a list of previous illustrated publications. Send to Art Director. Samples will be kept on file; they will not be returned.

Enchanted Lion Press
248, Creamer Street, Studio 4, Brooklyn, New York NY 11231
website https://enchantedlion.com/
Facebook www.facebook.com/enchantedlion
Twitter @EnchantedLion
Publisher Claudia Zoe Bedrick

An independent children's book publisher based in Brooklyn, New York, publishing illustrated books from around the world. Founded 2003.

Encyclopaedia Britannica Inc.
325 North La Salle Street, Suite 200, Chicago, IL 60654-2682
tel +1 312-347-7159
email contact@eb.com
website www.britannica.com

Encyclopedias, reference books, almanacs, videos and CD-Roms for adults and children 5–15+ years. Founded 1999.

Enslow Publishers, Inc.
29 East 21st Street, New York, NY 10010
tel +1 800-398-2504
email customerservice@enslow.com
website www.enslow.com
Owner Roger Rosen

Provides fiction and non-fiction content across the K-12 space. Aims to inspire readers to become lifelong learners. Founded 1976.

Evan-Moor Educational Publishers
18 Lower Ragsdale Drive, Monterey, CA 93940
tel +1 800-714-0971
email marketing@evan-moor.com
website www.evan-moor.com
Founder & Ceo William E. Evans

Educational materials for parents and teachers of children (3–12 years): activity books, textbooks, how-to books, CD-Roms. Subjects include maths, geography, history, science, reading, writing, social studies, art and craft. Publishes approx. 50 titles each year and has over 500 in print. Less than 10% of books are by first-time authors. Query or submit outline, table of contents and sample pages. Responds to queries in two months; MSS in four months. See website for submission guidelines. For illustrations, send résumé, samples and tearsheets to the Art Director. Primarily uses b&w material. Founded 1979.

Farrar Straus Giroux Books for Young Readers
175 Fifth Avenue, New York, NY 10010
website https://us.macmillan.com/publishers/farrar-straus-giroux#FYR/

An imprint of Macmillan Children's Publishing Group. Books for toddlers through to young adults: picture books, fiction and non-fiction for all ages, and poetry (occasionally). Publishes 70 hardcover originals plus ten paperback reprints each year and has approx. 500 titles in print. Approx. 10% of books are by first-time authors. No unsolicited MSS. Founded 1946.

The Feminist Press
365 Fifth Avenue, Suite 5406, New York, NY 10016
website www.feministpress.org
Facebook www.facebook.com/feministpress
Twitter @feministpress

Publishes books that ignite movements and social transformation. Publishes 12 to 15 books a year and specialises in an array of genres including cutting-edge fiction, activist non-fiction, literature in translation, hybrid memoirs and children's books. Founded 1970.

Flux
2297 Waters Drive, Mendota Heights, MN 55120
tel +1 888-917-0145
email publicity@northstareditions.com
email submissions@northstareditions.com
website www.fluxnow.com
Facebook www.facebook.com/FluxBooks
Twitter @FluxBooks
Managing Editor Mari Kesselring

Children and young adult. See website above for submission guidelines. Accepts electronic submissions only. Flux is an imprint of North Star Editions, Inc. Founded 2006.

Flux Books (imprint)
email submissions@northstareditions.com
website www.fluxnow.com
Young adult: fiction for ages 12+ in all genres. Particularly interested in books that tell the stories of young adults in unexpected or surprising situations around the globe. Flux is an imprint of North Star Editions, Inc.

Books

Free Spirit Publishing

6325 Sandburg Road, Suite 100, Golden Valley,
MN 55427
tel +1 612-338-2068
email help4kids@freespirit.com
website www.freespirit.com
Facebook www.facebook.com/freespiritpublishing
Twitter @freespiritbooks
President Judy Galbraith

Award-winning publisher of non-fiction materials for
children and teens, parents, educators and
counsellors. Specialises in self-help materials for kids
and teens which empower young people and
promote positive self-esteem through improved social
and emotional health. Topics include self-esteem and
self-awareness, stress management, school success,
creativity, friends and family, peacemaking, social
action and special educational needs (i.e. gifted and
talented, children with learning differences).
Publishes approx. 18–22 new products each year,
adding to a backlist of over 200 books and posters.
Free Spirit authors are expert educators and mental
health professionals who have been honoured
nationally for their contributions on behalf of
children. Founded 1983.

Fulcrum Publishing

3970 Youngfiled Street, Wheat Ridge, CO 80033
tel +1 303-277-1623
email orders@fulcrumbooks.com
website https://fulcrum.bookstore.ipgbook.com/

Publishes a wide variety of educational non-fiction
texts and children's books, also books and support
materials for teachers, librarians, parents and
elementary through middle school children. Subjects
include: science and nature, literature and
storytelling, history, multicultural studies and Native
American and Hispanic cultures. Founded 1965.

Gale Cengage Learning*

27555 Executive Drive, Suite 350, Farmington Hills,
MI 48331
tel +1 248-699-4253
website www.gale.com

Education publishing for libraries, schools and
businesses. Serves the K–12 market with the following
imprints: Blackbirch Press, Greenhaven Press,
KidHaven Press, Lucent Books, Sleeping Bear Press,
UXL. Founded 1954.

Greenhaven Press

29 East 21st Street, New York, NY 10010
website https://greenhavenpublishing.com/
High-quality non-fiction resources for the education
community. Publishes 220 young adult academic
reference titles each year. Successes include the
Opposing Viewpoints series. Approx. 35% of books
are by first-time authors. No unsolicited MSS. All
writing is done on a work-to-hire basis. Send query,
résumé and list of published works. Founded 1970.

KidHaven Press

Non-fiction references for younger researchers.

Lucent Books

Non-fiction resources for upper-elementary to high
school students. Successes include *Women in the
American Revolution* and *Civil Liberties and the War
on Terrorism*. No unsolicited MSS. Query with
résumé.

Sleeping Bear Press

email sleepingbearpress@cengage.com
website www.sleepingbearpress.com
High-quality picture books.

Gibbs Smith

570 N Sportsplex Drive, Kaysville, UT 84037
tel +1 801-544-9800
email info@gibbs-smith.com
website www.gibbs-smith.com

A Utah-based publisher. Its trade and special interest
division publishes home reference, cookbook and
children's titles. The Gibbs Smith Education division
is the nation's leading publisher of state history
programs. All unsolicited queries, submissions and
correspondence should be via email. Responds only
to projects of interest. Founded 1969.

Greenhaven Press – see Gale Cengage Learning

Gryphon House, Inc.

PO Box 10, 6848 Leon's Way, Lewisville, NC 27023
tel +1 800-636-0928
email info@gryhonhouse.com
website www.gryphonhouse.com
President Jennifer Lewis, *Executive Editor* Stephanie
Roselli

Early childhood (0–8 years) resource books for
teachers and parents. Looking for books that are
developmentally appropriate for the intended age
group, are well researched and based on current
trends in the field, and include creative, participatory
learning experiences with a common conceptual
theme to tie them together. Send query and/or a
proposal. Founded 1971.

Hachai Publishing

527 Empire Boulevard, Brooklyn, New York,
NY 11225
tel +1 718-633-0100
email info@hachai.com
website www.hachai.com

Jewish books for children 0–8+ years. Welcomes
unsolicited MSS. Specialises in books for children 2–4
years and 3–6 years. Looking for stories that convey
the traditional Jewish experience in modern times or
long ago, traditional Jewish observance and positive
character traits. Founded 1988.

Hachette Book Group*

1290 Avenue of the Americas, New York, NY 10104
tel +1 212-364-1100
website www.hachettebookgroup.com

Publishing groups: Grand Central Publishing; Hachette Audio; Hachette Nashville; Little, Brown and Company; Little, Brown Books for Young Readers; Orbit; Perseus Books; Workman Imprints: Grand Central: Balance; Forever; Forever Yours; Legacy Lit; Twelve; Vision. Hachette Nashville: Center Street; Ellie Claire; FaithWords; Worthy Books; WorthyKids. Little, Brown and Company: Back Bay Books; Little, Brown Spark; Mulholland Books; Voracious. Little, Brown Books for Young Readers: Christy Ottaviano Books; JIMMY Patterson; LB Kids; LBYR+; Poppy. Orbit: Redhook. Perseus Books: Avalon Travel, Basic Books; Black Dog & Leventhal; Bold Type Books; Hachette Books; Hachette Go; Moon Travel; Rick Steves; RP Studio; Running Press; Running Press Kids; PublicAffairs; Seal Press. Founded 1996.

Handprint Books

413 Sixth Avenue, Brooklyn, New York, NY 11215–3310
tel +1 718-768-3696
email cmf@handprintbooks.com
website www.handprintbooks.com
Publisher Christopher Franceschelli

A range of children's books: picture and story books through to young adult fiction. Imprints: Handprint Books, Ragged Bears, Blue Apple. Welcomes submissions of MSS of quality for works ranging from board books to young adult novels. For novels, first query interest on the subject and submit a 7,500-word max. sample. Accepts MSS on an e-submission basis only. Artwork should be sent as small jpgs; artists' website addresses may also be submitted. No series fiction, licensed character (or characters whose primary avatar is meant to be as licences), 'I-Can-Read'-type books or titles intended primarily for mass merchandise outlets. Founded 2000.

HarperCollins Publishers*

195 Broadway, New York, NY 10007
tel +1 212-207-700
website https://corporate.harpercollins.com/us/
President & Ceo Brian Murray

For children, publishes fiction (literary, juvenile poetry) and non-fiction (education, history). No unsolicited material; all submissions must come through a literary agent. Founded 1817.

History Compass LLC

25 Leslie Road, Auburndale, MA 02466
tel +1 617-332-2202
email info@historycompass.com
website www.historycompass.com

Publishes the history of the USA presented through the study of primary source documents. Also historical fiction for younger readers. Successes include *Get a Clue!* (grades 2–8) and *Adventures in History* series (grades 4–8). Other series include *Perspectives on History* (grades 5–12+) and *Researching American History* (8–15 year-olds and ESL students). Founded 1990.

Holiday House, Inc.*

120 Broadway, New York, NY 10271
tel +1 212-646 5025
email submissions@holidayhouse.com
website www.holidayhouse.com

General fiction for children. Publishes 35 picture books, 10 young reader, 15 middle reader and eight young adult titles each year. Successes include *Lafayette and the American Revolution* by Russell Freedman. Approx. 20% of books are by first-time authors. Send entire MS. Only responds to projects of interest. Will review MS/illustration packages from artists: send MS with dummy and colour photocopies. Founded 1935.

Houghton Mifflin Harcourt*

3 Park Avenue, Floor 19, New York, NY 10016
tel +1 212-598-5730
website www.hmhco.com

Reference, fiction and non-fiction for adults and young readers. Also educational content and solutions for K-12 teachers and students. Founded 1832.

Houghton Mifflin Harcourt Books for Young Readers

website www.hmhbooks.com

Picture books, fiction, poetry and non-fiction for children, preschool through to high school. Successes include *The Testing* by Joelle Charbonneau and *Sleep Like a Tiger* by Mary Logue and illustrated by Pamela Zagarenski. Imprint: Clarion Books. For fiction, submit complete MS. For non-fiction, submit outline/synopsis and sample chapters. Responds only if interested. For illustrations, query with samples (colour photocopies and tearsheets). Responds in four months.

Houghton Mifflin Harcourt/Clarion Books

Picture books, fiction, poetry and non-fiction for children, preschool through to high school. Successes include *Mr. Wuffles!* by David Wiesner. For fiction and picture books, send complete MS. For non-fiction, send query with up to three sample chapters. Founded 1965.

Hyperion Books for Children*

237 Park Avenue, New York, NY 10017
tel +1 212-633-4400
website www.hyperionbooks.com

Board and novelty books, picture books, young readers, middle grade, young adult, non-fiction (all subjects at all levels). Successes include *Don't Let the Pigeon Drive the Bus*, written and illustrated by Mo Willems, *Dumpy The Dump Truck* series by Julie Andrews Edwards and Emma Walton Hamilton (3–7 years) and *Artemis Fowl* by Eoin Colfer (young adult novel). Imprints include Michael di Capua Books, Jump at the Sun, Volo. Approx. 10% of books are by first-time authors. Only interested in submissions via literary agents. For illustrations, send résumé, business card, promotional literature or tearsheets to be kept on file to Art Director. Founded 1990.

Impact Publishers Inc.

5674 Shattuck Avenue, Oakland, CA 94609
tel +1 805-466-5917
email customerservice@newharbinger.com
website www.newharbinger.com/about-us/impact-publishers

Psychology and self-improvement books and audio tapes for adults, children, families, organisations and communities. Imprint of New Harbinger Publications. Only publishes non-fiction books which serve human development and are written by highly respected psychologists and other human service professionals. Rarely publishes authors outside of the USA. See website for guidelines. Founded 1970.

Incentive Publications by World Book

180 N. LaSalle, Suite 900, Chicago, IL 60601
tel +1 888-482-9764
website https://incentivepublications.com/

Produces supplemental resources for student use and instruction and classroom management improvement materials for teachers. Specialises in supplemental resources for middle grade students and teaching strategies for grades K–12. More than 300 titles are available. Send a letter of introduction, table of contents, a sample chapter and sase for return of material. Acquired by World Book in 2013. Founded 1969.

Jolly Fish Press

2297 Waters Drive, Mendota Heights, MN 55120
tel +1 888-417-0195
email publicity@jollyfishpress.com
email submit@jollyfishpress.com
website www.jollyfishpress.com
Facebook www.facebook.com/JollyFishPress
Twitter @JollyFishPress

Dedicated to promoting exceptional, unique new voices in middle grade fiction and jumpstarting writing careers. See website above for submission guidelines. Accepts electronic submissions only. Imprint of North Star Editions, Inc. Founded 2011.

Just Us Books, Inc.

395 Pleasant Valley Way, Suite B, West Orange, NJ 07052
tel +1 973-672-7701
email info@justusbooks.com
website https://justusbooks.com/
Publishers Cheryl Hudson, Wade Hudson

Publishers of Black-interest books for young people, including preschool materials, picture books, biographies, chapter books and young adult fiction. Focuses on Black history, Black culture and Black experiences. Imprint: Sankofa Books. Currently accepting queries for young adult titles, targeted to 13–16 year-old readers. Work should contain realistic, contemporary characters, compelling plot lines that introduce conflict and resolution, and cultural authenticity. Also considers MSS for picture books and middle reader chapter books. Send a query letter, 1–2pp synopsis, a brief author biography that includes any previously published work, plus an sase. Founded 1988.

Kaeden Books

PO Box 16190, Rocky River, OH 44116
tel +1 800-890-7323
email info@kaeden.com
website www.kaeden.com

Educational publisher specialising in early literacy books and beginning chapter books. Accepts samples of all styles of illustration but is primarily looking for samples that match the often humorous style appropriate for juvenile literature. Vocabulary and sentence structure must be appropriate for young readers. No sentence fragments. See website for complete guidelines. Founded 1986.

Kane Press – see Astra Publishing House

KidHaven Press – see Gale Cengage Learning

Alfred A. Knopf – see Penguin Random House

Lee & Low Books, Inc.

95 Madison Avenue, Suite 1205, New York, NY 10016
tel +1 212-779-4400
email general@leeandlow.com
website www.leeandlow.com
Editorial Director Cheryl Klein

Children's book publisher specialising in multi-cultural literature that is relevant to young readers. The company's goal is to meet the need for stories that children of colour can identify with and that all children can enjoy and which promote a greater understanding of one another. Focuses on fiction, non-fiction and poetry for children 5–12 years, and for middle graders and young adults 13–18 years. Of special interest are realistic fiction, historical fiction and non-fiction with a non-white protagonist, a distinct voice or unique approach. Does not consider folktales or animal stories. Offers two writing contests per year for debut picture book writers and novelists. Writers of colour and/or of Native nations are especially encouraged to submit. Imprints: Lee & Low, Lee & Low Games, Bebop Books, Cinco Puntos Books, Tu Books, Children's Book Press, Dive Into Reading, Shen's Books. Please visit website to see current guidelines and needs. Potential authors will be contacted by email or phone within six months if interested. Founded 1911.

Lerner Publishing Group

241 First Avenue NorthMinneapolis, MN 55401
tel +1 800-328-4929
email info@lernerbooks.com
website www.lernerbooks.com
Publisher Adam Lerner

Independent publisher of high-quality children's books for K–12 schools and libraries: picture books, fiction for children 5–8 and 9–12 years, teenage fiction, series fiction and non-fiction. Subjects include biography, social studies, science, sports and curriculum. Publishes approx. 300 titles each year and has about 1,500 in print. Publishing Group includes: Carolrhoda Books, Carolrhoda LAB, Darby Creek, ediciones Lerner, First Avenue Editions, Graphic Universe, Kar-Ben Publishing, Lerner, Lerner Classroom, Lerner Digital, Millbrook Press, Twenty-First Century Books, Zest Books. Publishing Group Partners include: Anderson Press, Big & Small, Cheriton Children's Books, Creston Books, Full Tilt Press, Gecko Press, Hungry Tomato, JR Comics, Lantana Publishing, Live Oak Media, Lorimer Children's & Teens, Maverick Arts Publishing, New Frontier Publishing, Page Education Foundation, Quarto Library, Red Chair Press, Ruby Tuesday Books, Souring Kite Books, We Do Listen. No unsolicited submissions for any imprint. Founded 1959.

Little, Brown & Company

1290 Ave of the Americas, New York, NY 10104
tel +1 212-364-1100
email lbpublicity.Generic@hbgusa.com
website www.littlebrown.com
Facebook www.facebook.com/littlebrownandcompany
Twitter @littlebrown
Senior Vice President & Publisher Bruce Nichols

General literature, fiction, non-fiction, biography, history, trade paperbacks, children's. Founded 1837.

Little, Brown Spark

Publishes books for young people and adults that spark ideas, feelings and change. Looking for authors who are experts and thought leaders in the fields of health, lifestyle, psychology and science.

Lucent Books – see Gale Cengage Learning

Margaret K. McElderry Books – see Simon & Schuster Children's Publishing Division

McGraw-Hill Professional*

2 Penn Plaza, 12th Floor, New York, NY 10121
tel +1 212-904-2000
website www.mhprofessional.com

Divisions include: Business, Education and Test Prep, International Marine and Ragged Mountain Press, Medical, Open University Press. To find individual editorial contacts check website. Founded 1966.

Macmillan Publishers, Inc.

120 Broadway, New York, NY 10271
tel +1 646-307-5151
email press.inquiries@macmillanusa.com
website https://us.macmillan.com/

Publishers: Celadon Books; Farrar, Straus and Giroux; Flatiron Books; Henry Holt and Co.; Macmillan Children's Publishing Group; Macmillan Audio; St. Martin's Publishing Group; and Tor/Forge. Founded 1843.

Marshall Cavendish

99 White Plains Road, Tarrytown, NY 10591
email customerservice@marshallcavendish.com
website http://mcdebooks.pdn.ipccublishcentral.com/

Non-fiction books for young, middle grade and young adult readers. Subjects include: American studies, the arts, biographies, health, mathematics, science, social studies, history, world cultures. Non-fiction subjects should be curriculum-related and are published in series form. Length: 1,500–25,000 words. Send synopsis with one or more sample chapters and sample table of contents. Founded 1968.

Marshall Cavendish Children's Books

99 White Plains Road, Tarrytown, NY 10591
email customerservice@mceducation.com
website http://mcdebooks.pdn.ipublishcentral.com/

Picture books and novels for middle grade and teens. Does not accept submissions via email. Imprint of Marshall Cavendish Corporation. Founded 1968.

Mitchell Lane Publishers, Inc.

2001 S.W. 31st Avenue, Hallandale, FL 33009
tel +1 800 223 3251
email customerservice@mitchelllane.com
website www.mitchelllane.com
President Phil Comer

Non-fiction titles for young readers, middle readers and young adults. Founded 1962.

Mondo Publishing*

501 Grant StreetUnion Trust Building, Suite, 1075 Pittsburgh, PA 15219
tel +1 877-401-2527
email info@mondopub.com
website www.mondopub.com

Classroom materials and professional development for K–5 educators. Part of Carnegie Learning. Founded 1986.

Thomas Nelson Publisher

PO Box 141000, Nashville, TN 37214
tel +1 800-251-4000
email publicity@thomasnelson.com
website www.thomasnelson.com

Bibles, religious, non-fiction and fiction general trade books for adults and children. Acquired by HarperCollins in 2012. Founded 1798.

NorthSouth Books

600 Third Avenue, 2nd Floor, New York, NY 10016
tel +1 917-699-2079
website www.northsouth.com
Publisher Herwig Bitsche, *Associate Publisher* Andrew Rushton, *Editor* Beth Terrill, *Managing Director* Riky Stock

Publishes 45 titles a year. Publishes fresh, original, fiction and non-fiction with universal themes that could appeal to children 3–8 years. Accepting agented picture book submissions from US authors and illustrators. Guidelines on submissions: accepts picture book MSS (1,000 words or less); typically, does not acquire rhyming texts (although have been exceptions for simple/original text); authors do not need to include illustrations. Illustrators can send work for consideration via postcards/PDFs emailed to: submissions@northsouth.com. Successes include *The Rainbow Fish* by Marcus Pfister, *Little Polar by Hans de Beer, Einstein – The Fantastic Journey of a Mouse Through Space and Time* by Torben Kuhlmann, *Peace* by Baptiste Paul, Miranda Paul, and Estelí Meza, *The Field* by Baptiste Paul and Jacqueline Alcántara, *Frida Kahlo and Her Animalitos* by Monica Brown and John Parra, and *Surf's Up* by Kwame Alexander and Daniel Miyares. Founded 1961.

Orchard Books – see Scholastic, Inc.

Richard C. Owen Publishers, Inc.

PO Box 585, Katonah, NY 10536
tel +1 914-232-3903
website www.rcowen.com
Publisher Richard C. Owen

Books for grades K–6. All work must be submitted as hard copy. Books for young learners: Seeks high-interest stories with charm and appeal that children 5–7 years can read by themselves. Interested in original, realistic, contemporary stories, as well as folktales, legends and myths of all cultures. Non-fiction content must be supported with accurate facts. Length: 45–1,000 words. Also beginning chapter books up to 3,000 words.

Pearson Education*

One Lake Street, Upper Saddle River, NJ 07458
tel +1 201-236-7000
email communications@pearsoned.com
website www.pearsoned.com

Educational secondary publisher of scientifically researched and standards-based instruction materials for today's Grade 6–12 classrooms. Subjects include: arts, mathematics, modern and classical languages, science, social studies, careers and technology. Part of the Curriculum Division of Pearson Education, Inc. Founded 1966.

Pelican Publishing

990 N. Corporate Drive, Suite 100, New Orleans, LA 70123
tel +1 504-684-8976
email editorial@pelicanpub.com
website www.arcadiapublishing.com
Publisher & President Scott Campbell

Gulf South children's books. Also biographies, holiday books, local cookbooks, history. Email a query letter, outline if chapter book, and résumé. No unsolicited MSS for chapter books. Most young children's books are 32 illustrated pages when published; their MSS will be 1,100 words maximum. Proposed books for middle readers (8+ years) should be at least 90pp. Brief books for readers under 9 years may be submitted in their entirety. Founded 1926.

Penguin Random House*

1745 Broadway, New York, NY 10019
tel +1 212-782-9000
website www.penguinrandomhouse.com
Ceo Madeline McIntosh

Consists of 300 independent imprints and brands, more than 15,000 new print titles and close to 800 million print, audio and ebooks. Committed to publishing adult and children's fiction and non-fiction print editions, and is a pioneer in digital publishing. Its book brands include storied imprints such as Doubleday, Viking and Alfred A. Knopf (USA); Ebury, Hamish Hamilton and Jonathan Cape (UK); Plaza & Janés and Alfaguara (Spain); and Sudamericana (Argentina); as well as the international imprint DK. Founded 2013.

Penguin Young Readers*

1745 Broadway, New York, NY 10019
tel +1 212-366-2000
website www.penguin.com/children
Facebook www.facebook.com/penguinkidsbooks
Twitter @penguinkids
President Jen Loja

A leading children's book publisher in the USA. The company owns a wide range of imprints and trademarks including Dial Books, Dutton, Grosset & Dunlap, Kathy Dawson Books, Kokila, Nancy Paulsen Books, Penguin Workshop, Philomel, Puffin, G.P. Putnam's Sons, Razorbill, Speak, Viking and Frederick Warne. Penguin Young Readers is a division of Penguin Group LLC, a Penguin Random House company. Founded 1935.

Puffin – see Penguin Young Readers

Simon Pulse Books – see Simon & Schuster Children's Publishing Division

Quarto Publishing Group – Walter Foster Publishing Jr.
100 Cummings Center, Suite 265D, Beverly, MA 01915
tel +1 978-282-9590
email walterfoster@quarto.com
website www.walterfoster.com
Group Publisher Anne Landa, *Senior Managing Editor* Karen Julian

Imprint of The Quarto Group. Instructional art books for children and adults. Also art and activity kits for children. A division of Quarto Publishing Group US. Founded 1976.

Random House Children's Books*
1745 Broadway, New York, NY 10019
tel +1 212-782-9000
website www.rhcbooks.com,
www.randomhouse.com/teachers
President & Publisher Barbara Marcus

An English-language children's trade book publisher. Creates books for preschool children through young adult readers, in all formats from board books to activity books to picture books, graphic novels, novels and non-fiction. Imprints: Dragonfly, Ember, Laurel-Leaf, Little Golden Books, Make Me A World, Princeton Review, Random House Books for Young Readers, Random House Graphic, Rodale Kids, Schwartz & Wade Books, Sylvan Learning, Wendy Lamb Books, Yearling Books. Part of Penguin Random House (page 58). Founded 1925.

Razorbill – see Penguin Young Readers

Roaring Brook Press
120 Broadway, New York, NY 10271
tel +1 646-600-7861
website https://us.macmillan.com/publishers/roaring-brook-press/
Publisher Jennifer Besser

Picture books, chapter books, novels and graphic novels in fiction and non-fiction for young readers, 0–18 years. Publishes about 70 titles a year. Division of Holtzbrink Publishers. Part of Macmillan Children's Publishing Group. Does not accept unsolicited MSS or submissions in print or digital. Founded 2002.

Rowman & Littlefield
4501 Forbes Boulevard, Suite 200, Lanham, MD 20706
tel +1 301-459-3366
email customercare@rowman.com
website www.rowman.com
Facebook www.facebook.com/rowmanuk
Twitter @rowmanuk
President & Ceo James E. Lyons

An independent publisher specialising in academic publishing in the humanities and social sciences, government and official data and educational publishing. Founded 1925.

Running Press Book Publishers
2300 Chestnut Street, Suite 200, Philadelphia, PA 19103
tel +1 215-567-5080
email perseus.promos@perseusbooks.com
website www.runningpress.com
Facebook www.facebook.com/runningpressbooks
Twitter @running_press

General non-fiction, science, history, children's fiction and non-fiction, cookbooks, pop culture, lifestyle, illustrated gift books, Miniature Editions. Imprints: Running Press, Running Press Miniature Editions, Running Press Kids, Running Press Adults. Member of the Perseus Books Group. Successes include *You Are a Badass* by Jen Sincero, *Ripe* by Cheryl Sternman Rule, *Cats in Hats* by Sara Thomas and *Slow Beauty* by Shel Pink. Founded 1972.

Running Press Kids
Picture books, activity books, young adult fiction. Successes include the *Doodles* series.

Sasquatch Books
1904 Third Ave, Suite 710 Seattle, WA 98101
tel +1 206-467-4300
email custserv@sasquatchbooks.com
website www.sasquatchbooks.com
Facebook www.facebook.com/SasquatchBooksSeattle
Twitter @sasquatchbooks

Publishes a variety of non-fiction books, as well as children's books under the Little Bigfoot imprint. Will consider queries and proposals from authors and agents for new projects that fit into the company's West Coast regional publishing programme. Founded 1986.

Scholastic, Inc.*
557 Broadway, New York, NY 10012
tel +1 212-343-6100
email news@scholastic.com
website www.scholastic.com
Facebook www.facebook.com/scholastic
Twitter @scholastic

The world's largest publisher and distributor of children's books and a leader in education technology and children's media. Divisions: Scholastic Trade Publishing, Scholastic Book Clubs, Scholastic Book Fairs, Scholastic Education, Scholastic International, Media, Licensing and Advertising. Imprints include: Arthur A. Levine Books, The Blue Sky Press, Cartwheel Books, Chicken House, David Fickling Books, Graphix, Orchard Books, Point, PUSH, Scholastic en español, Scholastic Focus, Scholastic Licensed Publishing, Scholastic Nonfiction, Scholastic Paperbacks, Scholastic Press and Scholastic Reference.

In addition, Scholastic Trade Books includes Klutz, a highly innovative publisher and creator of 'books plus' for children. Founded 1920.

Scholastic Trade Books, Children's Book Publishing

Award-winning publisher of original children's books. Publishes over 600 new titles a year including bestselling brands such as *Harry Potter*, *Captain Underpants*, *The Hunger Games*, *Clifford The Big Red Dog*, *I Spy* and *The Magic School Bus*.

Scholastic Education*

557 Broadway, New York, NY 10012
tel +1 212-343-6100
website www.scholastic.com

Educational publisher of research-based core and supplementary instructional materials. A leading provider in reading improvement and professional development products, as well as learning services that address the needs of the developing reader – from grades pre-K to high school. Publishes 32 curriculum-based classroom magazines used by teachers in grades pre-K–12 as supplementary educational materials to raise awareness about current events in an age-appropriate manner and to help children develop reading skills. Scholastic Education has also developed technology-based reading assessment and management products to help administrators and educators quickly and accurately assess student reading levels, match students to the appropriate books, predict how well they will do on district and state standardised tests and inform instruction to improve reading skills. Founded 1923.

Scholastic Library Publishing

90 Sherman Turnpike, Danbury, CT 06816
tel +1 203-797-3500
website www.scholastic.com

Online and print publisher of reference products.

Simon & Schuster Children's Publishing Division*

1230 Avenue of the Americas, New York, NY 10020
tel +1 212-698-7200
website www.simonandschuster.com/kids
President & Publisher Jon Anderson

Preschool to young adult, fiction and non-fiction, trade, library and mass market. Imprints: Aladdin Paperbacks, Atheneum Books for Young Readers, Beach Lane Books, Little Simon, Margaret K. McElderry Books, Salaam Reads, Simon & Schuster Books for Young Readers, Simon Pulse, Simon Spotlight, Paula Wiseman Books. Division of Simon & Schuster, Inc. Founded 1924.

Aladdin Books

Vice-President & Publisher Valerie Garfield

Publishes commercial middle-grade fiction with an emphasis on adventure, fantasy and humor. Accepts query letters with proposals for middle-grade series and single-title fiction, middle grade and commercial non-fiction. Send MS for the attention of the Submissions Editor.

Atheneum Books for Young Readers

Vice-President & Publisher Justin Chanda

Picture books, chapter books, mysteries, biography, science fiction, fantasy, graphic novels, middle-grade and young adult fiction and non-fiction. Covers preschool–young adult. Publishes 20–30 picture books, 4–5 young readers, 20–25 middle readers and 10–15 young adult books each year. Approximately 10% of books are by first-time authors. No unsolicited MSS. Send query letter only. Responds in one month.

Margaret K. McElderry Books

Vice-President & Publisher Justin Chanda

Picture books, easy-to-read books, fiction (8–12 years, young adult), poetry, fantasy. Covers preschool to young adult. Publishes 10–12 picture books, 2–4 young reader titles, 8–10 middle reader titles and 5–7 young adult books each year. Approximately 10% of books are by first-time authors. No unsolicited MSS. Responds in three months. Samples returned with sase.

Simon & Schuster Books for Young Readers

Vice President & Publisher Justin Chandu

Publishes a wide range of contemporary, commercial, award-winning fiction and non-fiction that spans every age of children's publishing. Seeking challenging and psychologically-complex young adult novels; also imaginative and humorous middle-grade fiction. No unsolicited MSS. Send query letter only. Responds in two months.

Paula Wiseman

email paulawiseman@simonandschuster.com
Vice-President & Publisher Paula Wiseman

Publishes award-winning and bestselling books, including picture books, novelty books and novels. The imprint focuses on stories and art that are childlike, timeless, innovative and centered in emotion. Approx. 10% of books are by first-time authors. Submit complete MS. Length: picture books – 500 words; others standard length. Considers all categories of fiction. Will review MS/illustration packages from artists. Send MS with dummy.

Sleeping Bear Press – see Gale Cengage Learning

Sourcebooks, Inc.

PO Box, 4410, Naperville, IL 60567-4410
website www.sourcebooks.com
Editorial Director Todd Stocke

A leading independent publisher in a wide variety of genres including fiction, romance, children's, young adult, gift/calendars and college-bound. E-commerce businesses include *Put Me In the Story*, the number one personalised books platform. Imprints include: Cumberland House, Dawn Publications, Little Pickle Press, Poison Pen Press, Simple Truths, Sourcebooks, Sourcebooks Casablanca, Sourcebooks Fire, Sourcebooks Kids, Sourcebooks Landmarks. Founded 1987.

Sourcebooks Kids

Publishes notable fiction and non-fiction projects including board books, picture books, chapter books and middle-grade works with the hope of engaging children in the pure fun of books and the wonder of learning new things.

Tachyon Publications

1459 18th Street, #139, San Francisco CA 94107
tel +1 415-285-5615
email Tachyon@tachyonpublications.com
website https://tachyonpublications.com/
Facebook www.facebook.com/Tachyon-Publications
Twitter @TachyonPub
Publisher Jacob Weisman

A publisher of smart science fiction, fantasy and horror, as well as occasional mysteries, memoirs, young adult and literary fiction. Founded 1995.

Teacher Created Resources

12621 Western Ave, Garden Grove, CA 92841
tel +1 800-662-4321
email custserv@teachercreated.com
website www.teachercreated.com

Educational materials. See website for guidelines. Founded 1977.

Union Square & Co.

33 East 17th Street, New York, NY 10003
tel +1 800-367-9692
email editorial@sterlingpublishing.com
website www.unionsquareandco.com

Adult non-fiction and children's board books, picture books and non-fiction. Imprints include: Union Square & Co., Union Square Kids, Sterling Ethos, Puzzlewright Press, Flashkids, Hearst Books. Founded 1949.

Viking – see Penguin Young Readers

Walker Books US

99 Dover Street, Somerville, MA 02144
tel +1 617-661-3330
website www.walkerbooksus.com,
www.candlewick.com
Facebook www.facebook.com/CandlewickPressBooks
Directors Susan Van Metre (editorial), Maria Middleton (art)

Great storytelling and instant reader appeal in fiction, graphic novels and illustrated non-fiction. Titles range from young adult to picture books, with emphasis on middle grade and young adult works. Walker Books US is a division of Candlewick Press (page 51). Founded 2017.

Albert Whitman & Company

250 South Northwest Highway, Suite 320, Park Ridge, Illinois, IL 60068
tel +1 847-581-0033
email mail@awhitmanco.com
website www.albertwhitman.com

Books that respond to cultural diversity and the special educational needs and concerns of children and their families (e.g. divorce, bullying). Also novels for middle-grade readers, picture books and non-fiction for children 2–12 years. For submissions guidelines see website. Founded 1919.

Paula Wiseman – see Simon & Schuster Children's Publishing Division

Wordsong – see Astra Publishing House

Workman Publishing Company*

225 Varick Street, New York, NY 10014
tel +1 212-254-5900
email info@workman.com
website www.workman.com
Publisher & Editorial Director Susan Bolotin

General non-fiction for adults and children. Calendars. Acquired by Hachette Book Group in 2021. Founded 1968.

World Book, Inc.

180 North LaSalle Street, Suite 900, Chicago, Illinois 60601
tel +1 800-729-5800
email international@worldbook.com
website www.worldbook.com
Facebook www.facebook.com/WorldBook
Twitter @worldbookinc

A leading publisher of authoritative, age-appropriate and reliable print and digital educational and reference materials for children and adults. Trade companies include children's book publisher Bright Connections Media and Incentive Publications which specialises in supplemental resources for children and teachers. Founded 1917.

WorthyKids

6100 Tower Circle, Suite 210, Franklin, TN 37067
email IdealsInfo@hbgusa.com
website www.worthykids.com
Facebook www.Facebook.com/worthykidsbooks

An imprint of Hachette Book Group. Picture books and board books for young children (1–8 years). Email to request submission guidelines. Digital submissions not accepted. Due to the large volume of submissions, the company only responds to those that are of interest to the publishing program. Potential authors should become familiar with current books before submitting. Agents welcome. Founded 1944.

Yen Press

Hachette Book Group, 1290 Avenue of the Americas, New York, NY 10104

email yenpress@hbgusa.com
website www.yenpress.com
Facebook www.facebook.com/yenpress
Twitter @yenpress

Graphic novels and manga in all formats for all ages. Currently not seeking original project pitches from writers who are not already working with an illustrator. For submission guidelines, see under Contact on website. Division of Hachette Book Group (page 55). Founded 2006.

Children's audio publishers

Many of the audio publishers listed below are also publishers of print and electronic books.

Audible
email partners-uk@audible.co.uk
website www.audible.co.uk
Twitter @audibleuk

Producer and seller of digital audio entertainment, including fiction and non-fiction audiobooks for adults and children. Publishers interested in exploring business opportunities with Audible may email the address above, or find out more about turning print books into audiobooks at www.acx.com. Founded 1995; acquired by Amazon 2008.

Audiobooks.com
email acquisitions@audiobooks.com
website www.audiobooks.com
Facebook www.facebook.com/audiobookscom
Twitter @audiobooks_com

Subscription audiobook service, offering a wide range of fiction and non-fiction genres, as well as some children's titles. Publishers interested in having their titles included in the company's library may get in touch via the email address above.

Barrington Stoke – see page 23

BookBeat
email info@bookbeat.com
website www.bookbeat.com/uk
Twitter @BookBeatUK

Digital streaming service for adult and children's audiobooks across a variety of fiction and non-fiction genres. Monthly subscription model. Owned by Bonnier. Founded 2017.

Canongate Audio Books
14 High Street, Edinburgh EH1 1TE
tel 0131 557 5111
email info@canongate.co.uk
website www.canongate.co.uk
Twitter @canongatebooks

Classic children's literature such as *Just William*, *Billy Bunter* and *Black Beauty*; also adult, classic and contemporary literary authors. Founded 1991 as CSA Word; acquired by Canongate 2010.

Cló Iar-Chonnacht Teo
Cheardlann, Spiddal, Co. Galway, Republic of Ireland
tel +353 (0)91 593307
email eolas@cic.ie
website www.cic.ie
Twitter @CloIarChonnacht
Ceo Micheál Ó Conghaile

Predominantly Irish-language children's books with accompanying audio of stories/folklore/poetry. Founded 1985.

Dref Wen
28 Church Road, Whitchurch, Cardiff CF14 2EA
tel 029-2061 7860
website www.drefwren.com
Directors Roger Boore, Anne Boore, Gwilym Boore, Alun Boore, Rhys Boore

Welsh-language and dual-language children's books. Founded 1970.

The Educational Company of Ireland
Ballymount Road, Walkinstown, Dublin D12 R25C, Republic of Ireland
tel +353 (0)1 4500611
email info@edco.ie
website www.edco.ie
Chief Executive Martina Harford

Irish language CDs. Trading unit of Smurfit Kappa Group – Ireland. Founded 1910.

HarperCollins Publishers
The News Building, 1 London Bridge Street, London, SE1 9GF
tel 020-8285 4016
website www.harpercollins.co.uk
Twitter @HarperCollinsUK
Audio Publishing Director Fionnuala Barrett

Publishers of award-winning fiction and non-fiction audiobooks for adults and children. Founded 1990.

W. F. Howes Ltd
Unit 5, St George's House, Rearsby Business Park, Gaddesby Lane, Rearsby, Leicester LE7 4YH
tel (01664) 423000
email info@wfhowes.co.uk
website www.wfhowes.co.uk

Audiobook and large-print publisher, distributing its content through consumer and library vendors. Author catalogue lists over 30,000 writers, including Danielle Steel, Val McDermid, Dan Jones and V. E. Schwab; children's authors include David Walliams, Greg James and David Baddiel. UK subsidiary of RBmedia. Founded 1999.

Books

Kobo
website www.kobo.com/gb/en
Twitter @kobo

Audiobook streaming service, for a monthly fee. Offers fiction, non-fiction, adult, children's and young adult titles.

Naxos AudioBooks
5 Wyllyotts Place, Potters Bar, Herts. EN6 2JD
tel (01707) 653326
email info@naxosaudiobooks.com
website www.naxosaudiobooks.com
Twitter @NaxosAudioBooks

Managing Director Anthony Anderson

Recordings of classic literature, modern fiction, non-fiction, drama and poetry. Founded 1994.

Penguin Random House UK Audio (Children's)
Penguin Studios, One Embassy Gardens, Nine Elms Lane, London SW8 5BL
website www.penguinrandomhouse.co.uk
Studio Manager Kate MacDonald

Contemporary and classic literature for younger listeners. Authors include Malorie Blackman, Charlie Higson, Roald Dahl and Eoin Colfer.

Children's book packagers

Many illustrated books are created by book packagers, whose particular skills are in the areas of book design and graphic content. In-house editors match up the expertise of specialist writers, artists and photographers who usually work on a freelance basis.

Aladdin Books Ltd

PO Box 53987, London SW15 2SF
tel 020-3174 3090
email sales@aladdinbooks.co.uk
website https://simonandschusterpublishing.com/aladdin/
Editorial Director Kristin Gilson

Full design and book packaging facility specialising in children's non-fiction and reference. Part of Simon & Schuster (page 38). Founded 1980.

Nicola Baxter

16 Cathedral Street, Norwich NR1 1LX
tel (01603) 766585 / 07778 285555
email nb@nicolabaxter.co.uk
website www.nicolabaxter.co.uk
Director Nicola Baxter

Full packaging service for children's books in both traditional and digital formats. Happy to take projects from concept to finished work or supply bespoke authorial, editorial, design, project management or commissioning services. Produces both fiction and non-fiction titles in a wide range of formats, for babies to young adults, and experienced in novelty books and licensed publishing. Founded 1990.

Brown Bear Books Ltd

Unit 1/D, Leroy House, 436 Essex Road, London N1 3QP
tel 020-3176 8603
website www.windmillbooks.co.uk
Children's Publisher Anne O'Daly

Specialises in high-quality illustrated reference books and multi-volume sets for trade and educational markets. Opportunities for freelancers. Imprint of Windmill Books. Founded 1967.

John Brown Group – Children's Division

10 Triton Street, Regents Place, London NW1 3BF
tel 020-7565 3000
email andrew.hirsch@johnbrownmedia.com
website www.johnbrownmedia.com
Director Chris Dicey (business development)

Creative development and packaging of children's products including books, magazines, teachers' resource packs, partworks, CDs and websites. Founded 2000.

Global Blended Learning Ltd

Singleton Court, Wonastow Road, Monmouth NP25 5JA
tel (01993) 706273
email info@hlstudios.eu.com
website www.globalblendedlearning.com

Primary, secondary academic education (geography, science, modern languages) and co-editions (travel guides, gardening, cookery). Multimedia (CD-Rom programming and animations). Opportunities for freelancers. Founded 1985.

Graham-Cameron Publishing & Illustration

59 Hertford Road, Brighton BN1 7GG
tel (01273) 385890
email enquiry@gciforillustration.com
Alternative address The Art House, Uplands Park, Sheringham, Norfolk NR26 8NE
tel (01263) 821333
website www.gciforillustration.com
Partners Helen Graham-Cameron, Duncan Graham-Cameron

Offers illustration and editorial services for picture books, information books, educational materials, activity books, non-fiction and reference books. Do not send unsolicited MSS. Founded 1985.

Hart McLeod Ltd

14A Greenside, Waterbeach, Cambridge CB25 9HP
tel (01223) 861495
email jo@hartmcleod.co.uk
website www.hartmcleod.co.uk
Director Joanne Barker

Primarily educational and general non-fiction with particular expertise in illustrated books, school texts, ELT and electronic and audio content. Opportunities for freelancers and work experience. Founded 1985.

Hawcock Books

242 Bloomfield Road, Bath BA2 2AX
tel 07976 708720
website www.hawcockbooks.co.uk
Twitter @DavidHawcock

Designs and produces highly creative and original pop-up art and three-dimensional paper-engineered concepts. Most experience is in developing, providing editorial assistance, printing and manufacturing pop-up books and novelty items for the publishing industry. Also undertakes demanding commissions from the advertising world for model-making, point-of-sale and all printed three-dimensional aspects of major campaigns.

Little People Books

The Home of BookBod, Knighton,
Radnorshire LD7 1UP
tel (01547) 520925
email littlepeoplebooks@thehobb.tv
website www.littlepeoplebooks.co.uk
Directors Grant Jessé (production & managing)

Packager of audio, children's educational and textbooks, digital publications. Parent company: Grant Jessé UK.

Orpheus Books Ltd

2 Hewlett Place, Cheltenham, Glos. GL52 6DQ
tel (01993) 774949
email info@orpheusbooks.com
website www.orpheusbooks.com, www.Q-files.com
Executive Directors Nicholas Harris, Sarah Hartley

Produces children's books and ebooks for the international co-editions market: non-fiction and reference. Orpheus Books are the creators of Q-files.com, the online educational resource for schools and libraries. Founded 1993.

The Puzzle House

Ivy Cottage, Battlesea Green, Stradbroke,
Suffolk IP21 5NE
tel (01379) 384656
email puzzlehouse@btinternet.com
website www.thepuzzlehouse.co.uk
Partners Roy Preston, Sue Preston

Editorial service creating crossword, quiz, puzzle and activity material for all ages. Founded 1988.

Toucan Books Ltd

Cannon Street Business Centre, Albert Buildings,
49 Queen Victoria Street, London EC4N 4SA
tel 020-7250 3388
website www.toucanbooks.co.uk

International co-editions; editorial, design and production services. Founded 1985.

David West Children's Books

11 Glebe Road, London SW13 0DR
tel 020-8876 1405
email lynn@davidwestbooks.com
website www.davidwestchildrensbooks.com
Proprietor David West, Partner Lynn Lockett

Packagers of highly illustrated children's non-fiction books. Specialises in science, art, geography, history, sport and flight. Produces 20 titles each year. Opportunities for freelancers. Founded 1986.

Working Partners Ltd

9 Kingsway, 4th Floor, London WC2B 6XF
tel 020-7841 3939
email enquiries@workingpartnersltd.co.uk
website www.workingpartnersltd.co.uk
Managing Director Chris Snowdon

Children's and young adult fiction series: animal fiction, fantasy, horror, historical fiction, detective, magical, adventure. Successes include *Rainbow Magic*, *Beast Quest* and *Warriors*. Unable to accept any MSS or illustration submissions. Pays advance and royalty; retains copyright on all works. Selects writers from unpaid writing samples based on specific brief provided. Always looking to add writers to database: to register details visit website. Founded 1995.

Children's bookshops

The bookshops in the first part of this list specialise in selling new children's books and are good places for writers and illustrators to check out the marketplace. Most of them are members of the Booksellers Association and are well known to publishers. A list of secondhand and antiquarian children's bookshops follows. Independent Booksellers Week usually takes place each year in June or July, but check online for further information (https://booksellers.org.uk/Campaigns/independentbookshopweek).

The Alligator's Mouth
2A Church Court, Richmond, Surrey TW9 1JL
tel 020-8948 6775
email info@thealligatorsmouth.co.uk
website www.thealligatorsmouth.co.uk
Facebook www.facebook.com/alligatorsmouth
Twitter @alligatorsmouth

Independent children's bookshop stocking works for all ages from babies to teenagers. Runs regular story-time sessions, book clubs and author events. Nominated for Children's Bookseller of the Year in *The Bookseller* Industry Awards 2018.

Bags-of-Books
1 South Street, Lewes BN7 2BT
tel (01273) 479320
email bagsofbooks@bags-of-books.co.uk
website https://bags-of-books.co.uk
Twitter @BagsofBooks
Instagram @bagsofbookslewes
Proprietor Rachel Givertz

Independent children's bookshop situated within a 16th-century building. Extensive selection of fiction and non-fiction from babies up to age eighteen. Hosts author visits and runs a books-for-schools programme.

Bert's Books
54 Goodwin Court, Swindon SN1 4BB
email bert@bertsbooks.co.uk
website https://bertsbooks.co.uk/
Facebook www.facebook.com/BertsBooks/
Twitter @BertsBooks
Founder Alex Call

Online bookshop with a focus on diversity. Offers books in monthly bundles, including young adult titles. A bricks-and-mortar shop opened in May 2022. Founded 2019.

Blackwell's Bookshop
Blackwell's Bookshop, 50 Broad Street, Oxford OX1 3BQ
tel (01865) 333694
email oxford@blackwell.co.uk
website https://bookshop.blackwell.co.uk/bookshop/home
Facebook www.facebook.com/blackwellbooks

Children's department of Blackwell's flagship bookshop stocks over 10,000 titles for children of all ages and holds a regular events programme, including author visits to schools.

The Blue House Bookshop
10 Bootham, York YO30 7BL
tel (01904) 927838
email karen@thebluehousebookshop.co.uk
website https://thebluehousebookshop.co.uk
Facebook www.facebook.com/bluehousebookshop
Twitter @bookishkids
Instagram @thebluehousebookshop
Proprietor Karen Walker

Independent children's bookshop in the historic heart of York. Offers a range of fiction and non-fiction to young readers. Supplies books for schools and can advise on book choices. Supporter of the Yorkshire Dales Millennium Trust. Founded 2019.

The Book Burrow @ Aardvark Books & Café
The Bookery, Manor Farm, Brampton Bryan, Bucknell SY7 0DH
email aardvaark@btconnect.com
website www.aardvark-books.com
Facebook www.facebook.com/AardvarkBooks
Twitter @AardvarkEthel
Instagram @aardvarkbookscafe
Proprietors Sheridan and Sarah Swinson

Book and play space with a castle, enchanted forest, pirate cabin and princess seat. Extensive range of books, mostly new but some secondhand and rare. Children's events throughout the year. BA member.

Book Corner
24 Milton Street, Saltburn-by-the-Sea TS12 1DG
tel (01287) 348010
email jenna@bookcornershop.co.uk
website www.bookcornershop.co.uk
Facebook https://en-gb.facebook.com/Book-Corner-Saltburn-1506322029595573/
Twitter @BookCornerShop
Proprietor Jenna Warren

Independent bookshop with dedicated children's section, stocking books for all ages from babies to young adults. Also stocks fiction and non-fiction for adults, and hosts author visits.

The Book Den
125 High Street, Hythe CT21 5JJ
tel (01303) 264639
email info@thebookden.co.uk
website https://thebookden.co.uk
Instagram @thebookden

Family-run independent children's bookshop and toy store. Stocks books for readers from their earliest years up to young adult. Founded 2018.

The Book House
93 High Street, Thame, Oxon OX9 3HJ
tel (01844) 213032
email office@thebookhousethame.co.uk
website www.thebookhousethame.co.uk
Instagram @the_book_house
Proprietor Brian Pattinson

Specialises in children's books alongside a wide range of titles for all ages. Established in the community for over 50 years, the Book House holds its own literary festival every October.

The Book Nook
First Avenue, Hove BN3 2FJ
tel (01273) 911988
email info@booknookuk.com
website www.booknookuk.com
Twitter @booknookhove
Proprietors Vanessa Lewis, Julie Ward

Specialist children's bookshop set in a child-friendly environment with author events, daily story-time, café and pirate ship. Previous winner of Children's Bookseller of the Year category at *The Bookseller* Industry Awards.

Booka Bookshop and Café
26–28 Church Street, Oswestry, Shrops. SY11 2SP
tel (01691) 662244
email hello@bookabookshop.co.uk
website www.bookabookshop.co.uk
Facebook www.facebook.com/bookabookshop
Twitter @bookabookshop
Proprietors Carrie and Tim Morris

Independent bookshop and café offering a wide range of books, cards and gifts. Hosts a regular programme of author talks and signings, organises themed events, runs bookclubs and works with schools and the local library. Previous winner of Independent Bookshop of the Year category at *The Bookseller* Industry Awards.

Bookbugs and Dragon Tales
41 Timberhill, Norwich NR1 3LA
tel (01603) 964022
email leanne@bookbugsanddragontales.com
website https://bookbugsanddragontales.com
Facebook www.facebook.com/Bookbugs-and-Dragon-Tales-683095175486432
Twitter @Bookbugsdragon1
Instagram @bookbugsdragontales
Proprietors Dan and Leanne Fridd

Independent bookshop offering a wide range of books and events for children and their families. An events space that hosts bookclubs, classes and other interactive opportunities is also available. Founded 2019.

The Broadway Bookshop
6 Broadway Market, London E8 4QJ
tel 020-7241 1626
email books@broadwaybookshophackney.com
website www.broadwaybookshophackney.com
Proprietor Jane Howe

General independent bookshop specialising in literary fiction with a strong selection of children's books for all ages.

Browns Books For Students
5 Redcliff Road, Melton, East Yorkshire HU14 3RS
tel (01482) 384660
email enquiries@brownsbfs.co.uk
website www.brownsbfs.co.uk
Facebook www.facebook.com/BrownsBFS
Twitter @BrownsBFS
Instagram @BrownsBFS

Supplier of books and educational resources across the UK and internationally. Offers next-day delivery, an extensive eBook catalogue, in-house stock selection team and shelf-ready book servicing.

Chicken & Frog
30 Crown Street, Brentwood, Essex, CM14 4BA
tel (01277) 230068
email info@chickenandfrog.co.uk
website https://chickenandfrog.com
Twitter @chickenandfrog
Instagram @chickenandfrog
Proprietors Jim and Natasha Radford

Independent children's bookshop and tuition centre. Weekly rhythm and rhyme, creative writing and handwriting sessions. Regular events for children and families, book clubs (in person and online), school supply and consultation.

The Children's Bookshop – Hay-on-Wye
Toll Cottage, Pontvaen, Hay-on-Wye, Herefordshire HR3 5EW
tel (01497) 821083
email sales@childrensbookshop.com
website www.childrensbookshop.com
Twitter @childrnsbkshop
Proprietors Judith and Colin Gardner

Second-hand and antiquarian children's books.

Children's Bookshop (Huddersfield)
37–39 Lidget Street, Lindley, Huddersfield,
West Yorkshire HD3 3JF
tel (01484) 658013
email hello@childrensbookshuddersfield.co.uk
website www.childrensbookshuddersfield.co.uk
Twitter @Lindley_Books
Contact Nicola Lee

Independent bookshop stocking a wide selection of titles for children, from picture books to YA. Also offers services to schools.

Children's Bookshop (Muswell Hill)
29 Fortis Green Road, London N10 3HP
tel 020-8444 5500
email admin@childrensbookshoplondon.co.uk
website www.childrensbookshoplondon.com
Facebook www.facebook.com/
ChildrensBookshopLondon
Twitter @childrensbkshop
Instagram childrensbookshoplondon

Specialist children's bookshop. Stocks approximately 12,000 titles and 25,000 books for children from babies to teenagers. Also offers services for schools and individuals. Founded 1974.

DRAKE The Bookshop
26–27 Silver Street, Stockton-on-Tees TS18 1SX
tel (01642) 909970
email books@drakethebookshop.co.uk
website www.drakethebookshop.co.uk
Twitter @drakebookshop
Proprietors Richard Drake, Melanie Greenwood

Independent bookshop with strong children's offering, as well as events and initiatives aimed at young readers and schools. The shop runs three children's book groups (Teen Readers, High-Rise Readers and Young Bookworms) and offers a selection of dyslexia-friendly titles. Founded 2015.

ebb & flo bookshop
12 Gillibrand Street, Chorley, Lancs. PR7 2EJ
tel (01257) 262773
email diane@ebbandflobookshop.co.uk
website www.ebbandflobookshop.co.uk
Facebook www.facebook.com/ebbandflobookshop
Twitter @ebbandflobooks
Proprietor Diane Gunning

Small independent bookshop stocking books for children and adults, plus toys, cards and gifts. Supplies books to local schools, including library restocks and topic boxes. Organises author visits. Hosts a weekly story-time for preschool children as well as regular author events and holiday workshops.

The Edinburgh Bookshop
219 Bruntsfield Place, Edinburgh EH10 4DH
tel 0131 447 1917
email mail@edinburghbookshop.com
website www.edinburghbookshop.com
Facebook www.facebook.com/EdinBookshop
Twitter @EdinBookshop
Proprietor Marie Moser

Three-time Scottish Independent of the Year winner. Events programme includes author visits, book clubs and a twice-weekly story-time for the under 5s. Founded 2007.

Far from the Madding Crowd
20 High Street, Linlithgow EH49 7AE
tel (01506) 845509
email sally@maddingcrowdlinlithgow.com
website www.maddingcrowdlinlithgow.com
Facebook www.facebook.com/
FarFromTheMaddingCrowdLinlithgow
Twitter @Furtherfrom

Independent bookshop with eclectic range of titles, including children's and preschool in the dedicated Little Owl's section. Strong influence from Scottish publishers. Free story-telling on Fridays at 3pm: tickets must be booked in advance.

Foggie Toddle Books
18 North Main Street, Wigtown DG8 9HL
tel (01988) 402896
email hello@foggietoddlebooks.co.uk
website https://foggietoddlebooks.co.uk
Facebook www.facebook.com/FoggieToddleBooks
Twitter @FoggieToddler
Instagram @foggietoddlebooks
Proprietor Jayne Baldwin

Independent children's bookshop and publisher named after the Scots word for bumblebee. Stocks new, second-hand and vintage books for age groups from babies to young adults. Also available: local art and crafts; a different artist or crafter is featured every month. Member of the Booksellers Association.

Ginger and Pickles
51 St Stephen Street, Edinburgh EH3 5AH
tel 0131 285 8069
email hello@gingerandpicklesbookshop.com
website www.gingerandpicklesbookshop.com
Facebook www.facebook.com/
gingerandpickleschildrensbookshop
Instagram @gingerandpicklesbookshop

Independent children's bookshop catering for young readers from birth to teenage years. Also offers professional advice to schools on stocking and ordering key titles. Currently preparing events programme and a schools department. Founded 2020.

Glowworm Books & Gifts Ltd
Unit 2, 5 Youngs Road, East Mains Industrial Estate, Broxburn, West Lothian EH52 5LY
tel (01506) 857570
website www.glowwormbooks.co.uk

Specialises in supplying books for children, especially those who find reading difficult due to physical or special educational challenges.

Golden Hare Books

68 St Stephen Street, Edinburgh EH3 5AQ
tel 0131 225 7755
email mail@goldenharebooks.com
website www.goldenharebooks.com
Twitter @GoldenHareBooks
Owner Mark Jones

Stocks books for readers of all ages. Holds regular Sunday story sessions for children and author events. Previous winner of Independent Bookshop of the Year at the British Book Awards.

Harbour Bookshop

2 Mill Street, Kingsbridge, Devon TQ7 1ED
tel (01548) 857233
email hello@harbourbookshop.co.uk
website www.harbourbookshop.co.uk
Twitter @HarbourBookshop
Proprietor Jane Fincham, *Manager* Louise Sanders

Well-established independent bookshop with an extensive range of children's books for all ages. Next-day delivery available. Also works with primary and secondary schools and holds children's book events and celebrations.

Heath Educational Books

Willow House, Willow Walk, Whittaker Road, Sutton, Surrey SM3 9QQ
tel 020-8644 7788
email orders@heathbooks.co.uk
website www.heathbooks.co.uk
Proprietor Richard Heath

Supplies books to schools and teachers throughout Europe. Large showroom.

Jacqson Diego Story Emporium

444 London Road, Westcliff on Sea, Essex SS0 9LN
tel (01702) 344262
email stories@jacqsondiego.com
website www.jacqsondiego.com
Facebook www.facebook.com/jacqsondiego
Twitter @jacqsondiego
Instagram @jacqsondiego

Independent bookshop offering fiction and non-fiction for children and young people. Regular events include bookclubs and writing groups. Also runs bespoke book-related services for schools and nurseries, including author visits, library audits, consultancy and workshops. BA member.

Madeleine Lindley Ltd

Book Centre, Broadgate, Broadway Business Park, Chadderton, Oldham OL9 9XA
tel 0161 683 4400

email books@madeleinelindley.com
website www.madeleinelindley.com
Twitter @teacher_books

Supplies books to schools and nurseries, provides information services and runs open days and training courses for teachers. Hosts author/publisher events for teachers and children.

The Little Bookshop

47 Harrogate Road, Chapel Allerton, Leeds LS7 3PD
tel 0113 212 3465
email hello@thelittlebookshopleeds.co.uk
website www.thelittlebookshopleeds.co.uk
Facebook www.facebook.com/
thelittlebookshopleedskids
Instagram @thelittlebookshopleeds
Proprietor Cheryl Duffield

Independent bookshop specialising in books for children; also stocks some adult titles. Carries a wide range of diverse and inclusive books and also provides subscription service for readers of all ages. Holds storytimes every Friday at 11am outside of school holidays. Offers services for schools, including creating and ordering book lists, as well as arranging author events and book fairs. Founded 2017.

The Mainstreet Trading Company

Main Street, St Boswells, Scottish Borders TD6 0AT
tel (01835) 824087
email info@mainstreetbooks.co.uk
website www.mainstreetbooks.co.uk
Facebook www.facebook.com/
Mainstreet.Trading.Company
Twitter @mainstreethare
Instagram mainstreethare
Proprietors Rosamund and Bill de la Hey

General bookshop with a particular focus on children's books. Previous winner of Independent Bookseller of the Year category at the *The Bookseller* Industry Awards.

Moon Lane Ink CIC

300 Stanstead Road, London SE23 1DE
tel 020-3489 7030
email info@moonlaneink.co.uk
website www.moonlaneink.co.uk
Facebook www.facebook.com/moonlaneink
Twitter @moonlaneink
Instagram @moonlaneink

Community-interest company dedicated to raising equality in children's books; equality of access, representation and roles in the publishing industry. In addition to a bookshop, runs enterprise workshops for children as well as a range of events. Founded 2018.

Nickel Books

9 Merlin Close, Sittingbourne ME10 4TY
tel 07731 152089

email enquiries@nickelbooks.co.uk
website www.nickelbooks.co.uk
Twitter @NickelBooks
Instagram @nickelbooks
Proprietor Andrea Don

Mail-order, school books supply, visits, fairs, fetes and events. Specialises in children's books, from birth to teenage; also books for parents.

Norfolk Children's Book Centre

Church Lane, Alby, Norwich NR11 7HB
tel (01263) 761402
email marilyn@ncbc.co.uk
website https://ncbc.co.uk
website https://uk.bookshop.org/shop/NorfolkCBC
Facebook www.facebook.com/NorfolkCBC
Twitter @NorfolkCBC
Instagram @NorfolkCBC

Independent bookshop established for over 35 years, specialising in books for children and teachers. Offers storytelling and school booksales within East Anglia, and nationwide conference book displays and mail order. Other services include school library assessment and rejuvenation, and topic-based approval collections.

Octavia's Bookshop

24 Black Jack Street, Cirencester, Glos. GL7 2AA
tel (01285) 650677
email info@octaviasbookshop.co.uk
website www.octaviasbookshop.co.uk
Twitter @octaviabookshop
Proprietor Octavia Emanuel

Independent bookshop in which more than half the stock is dedicated to children's titles, from buggy books to teen fiction and classics. Previous winner of Children's Independent Bookseller of the Year category at the *The Bookseller* Industry Awards.

The Oundle Bookshop

13 Market Place, Oundle, Peterborough PE8 4BA
tel (01832) 273523
email oundlebookshop@colemangroup.co.uk
website www.colemans-online.co.uk/oundle-bookshop.html

General bookshop with extensive children's selection.

Owl and Pyramid

10 Fore Street, Seaton EX12 2LA
tel (01297) 598030
email owl.pyramid@yahoo.com
website www.owlandpyramid.co.uk
Facebook www.facebook.com/owlpyramid
Twitter @OwlPyramid
Instagram @owlandpyramidbookshop

Independent children's bookshop stocking fiction and non-fiction for young readers from babies to teenagers. Also runs four book clubs for different age groups. Small but growing section of adult fiction and non-fiction. Founded 2014.

Peters Ltd

120 Bromsgrove Street, Birmingham B5 6RJ
tel 0121 666 6646
website www.peters.co.uk
Facebook www.facebook.com/
Petersbooksbirmingham
Twitter @petersbooks
Instagram @petersbooks

Specialist supplier of children's books and library furniture to schools, nurseries, academies and public libraries, with a book and furniture showroom, online ordering facilities and ten specialist children's librarians. Also provides a library design and installation service and book-related promotional material. Peters are sponsors of the CILIP Carnegie and Kate Greenaway Shadowing Awards, and also host regular professional development events for teachers and librarians, featuring speakers, authors and illustrators.

Pickled Pepper Books

10 Middle Lane, Crouch End, London N8 8PL
tel 020-3632 0823
email info@pickledpepperbooks.co.uk
website www.pickledpepperbooks.co.uk
Twitter @pickledbooks
Proprietors Urmi Merchant, Steven Pryse

Family-run specialist children's bookshop with a café and weekly programme of events for under 5s including story-times, art and craft, music groups, Spanish and French sing-alongs and NCT coffee mornings. After-school events include book groups for 9–12 year olds and teens' creative writing and illustration clubs. Also hosts regular interactive author events, as well as innovative theatre and puppet shows. A pop-up shop opened in 2021 as part of the Culture Palace in Enfield; see website for details and events. Founded 2012.

The Rocketship Bookshop

5 Bridge Street, Salisbury SP1 2ND
tel (01722) 237172
email info@rocketbookshop.co.uk
website https://rocketshipbookshop.co.uk
Facebook www.facebook.com/rocketshipbookshop
Twitter @rshipbshop
Instagram @rocketshipbooks

Independent bookshop catering predominantly for children and young people, although a specially curated selection of adult titles is also available. Host author events and supports Salisbury International Arts Festival.

Books

Round Table Books
97 Granville Avenue, Brixton Village,
London SW9 8PS
email bookshop@roundtablebooks.co.uk
website www.roundtablebooks.co.uk
Facebook www.facebook.com/RoundtableBookshop
Twitter @BooksRound
Instagram @roundtablebooks

Inclusive children's bookshop, launched by the
Knights Of an independent children's publisher that
champions authors and illustrators from diverse
backgrounds. Founded 2019.

Seven Stories – see page 334

Seven Stories Bookshop
30 Lime Street, Ouseburn Valley,
Newcastle upon Tyne NE1 2PQ
tel 0300 330 1095
email bookshop@sevenstories.org.uk
website www.sevenstories.org.uk
Twitter @7StoriesBooks

Independent children's bookshop and part of the
National Centre for Children's Books. School
accounts are available, as is advice on library stock.

Simply Books
228 Moss Lane, Bramhall, Cheshire SK7 1BD
tel 0161 439 1436
email enquiries@simplybooks.info
website www.simplybooks.info
Twitter @simplybooksNo1

Independent bookshop with strong children's
selection, as well as regular events and reading groups
for adults and children readers.

Storytellers, Inc.
7 The Crescent, St Anne's on Sea, Lytham St Anne's,
Lancs. FY8 1SN
tel (01253) 781690
email info@storytellersinc.co.uk
website www.storytellersinc.co.uk
Twitter @storytellersinc
Proprietors Carolyn Clapham, Katie Clapham

Independent bookshop with dedicated children's
section. Supplies books to local schools. Regional
winner (North) in the Independent Bookshop of the
Year category at *The Bookseller* Industry Awards 2015.

Tales On Moon Lane
25 Half Moon Lane, London SE24 9JU
tel 020-7274 5759
email info@talesonmoonlane.co.uk
website www.talesonmoonlane.co.uk
Twitter @talesonmoonlane
Proprietor Tamara Macfarlane

Specialist children's bookshop which runs yearly
children's literature festivals in February and
October, as well as weekly story-telling sessions for
preschool children.

Through the Wardrobe Books
2 Nettleton Road, Mirfield, West Yorks. WF14 9AA
email hello@throughthewardrobebooks.co.uk
website www.throughthewardrobebooks.co.uk
Facebook www.facebook.com/
throughthewardrobebooks
Twitter @WardrobeBooks
Founders Leanne Yeomans, Samantha Ward

Specialist children's and young adults bookshop.
Open Monday to Saturday. Founded 2019.

West End Lane Books
277 West End Lane, London NW6 1QS
tel 020-7431 3770
email info@welbooks.co.uk
website www.welbooks.co.uk
Twitter @WELBooks

Independent family-owned bookshop, carrying
fiction and non-fiction books and stationery. Offers
twice-weekly story-time sessions for preschool
children. Hosts regular author talks and book groups,
and also offers a children's personal shopper service.

Winstone's Hunting Raven Books
10 Cheap Street, Frome, Somerset BA11 1BN
tel (01373) 473111
email winstonebooks3@gmail.com
Facebook www.facebook.com/HuntingRavenBooks
Twitter @HuntingRavenBks
Instagram @huntingravenbooks
Proprietor Wayne Winstone, *Manager* Tina Gaisford-
Waller

Award-winning independent bookshop with
extensive range of books and gifts for all ages and a
strong children's section. Holds events and signings
throughout the year. South-West Independent
bookshop of the year 2020. Other Winstone's
bookshops can be found in Sidmouth and Sherborne.

Wonderland Bookshop
64 Carolgate, Retford DN22 6EF
tel (01777) 948580
email hello@wonderlandbookshop.co.uk
website https://wonderlandbookshop.co.uk
Facebook www.facebook.com/WonderlandBookshop
Twitter @Wonder_Bookshop
Instagram @wonderlandbookshop
Proprietor Helen Tamblyn-Saville

Specialist children's bookshop stocking titles for
readers from birth to teens (also curated selection of
adults' titles). Includes dyslexia-friendly and
LGBTQI+ shelves. Also offers services for schools,
including library advice, author visits (in person or

online) and school wishlists. Named independent Bookshop of the Year (Midlands region) 2022 at the British Book Awards. Founded 2019.

BOOKSELLERS FOR COLLECTORS

Blackwell's Rare Books
48–51 Broad Street, Oxford OX1 3BQ
tel (01865) 333555
email rarebooks@blackwell.co.uk
website www.blackwell.co.uk
Facebook www.facebook.com/blackwellrare
Twitter @blackwellrare

Deals in early and modern first editions of children's books, among other subjects.

Bookmark Children's Books
Fortnight, Broad Hinton, Swindon, Wilts. SN4 9NR
tel (01793) 731693 , *tel* 07788 841305
email leonora.f.smith@gmail.com
Contacts Leonora Smith, Anne Excell

Mail-order bookseller, specialising in books for collectors, ranging from antiquarian to modern. A wide range of first editions, novelty and picture books, chap-books, ABCs, annuals, etc. Also a selection of vintage toys, games, greetings cards and illustrated postcards, dolls and nursery china. Book-search service available within this specialist area. Member of PBFA, exhibiting at PBFA book fairs in London, Bristol, York, Bath, Brighton and Oxford. Established 1973.

Henry Sotheran Ltd
2–5 Sackville Street, Piccadilly, London W1S 3DP
tel 020-7439 6151
email rh@sotherans.co.uk
website www.sotherans.co.uk
website https://sotherans.co.uk/blogs/latest-posts
Facebook www.facebook.com/sotherans
Twitter @Sotherans
Instagram @sotherans_piccadilly
Contact Rosie Hodge

Large showroom with hundreds of important children's books spanning two centuries, specialising in first editions and illustrated works by pivotal artists. Opening hours: Mon–Fri 9.30am–6pm. Two specialist catalogues issued annually, available free on request.

Stella & Rose's Books
Monmouth Road, Tintern,
Monmouthshire NP16 6SE
tel (01291) 689755
email enquiry@stellabooks.com
website www.stellabooks.com
Twitter @stellarosebooks

Specialists in rare, out-of-print children's and illustrated books, also carrying a large and varied general stock (over 25,000 books in stock). Stock available for sale via website. Specialist lists issued regularly. Open seven days a week; see website for opening hours. Single items or collections purchased. Founded 1991.

Books, sites and blogs about children's books

These listings include some of the best print and online resources about children's books for readers, writers and illustrators.

BOOKS

The Oxford Companion to Children's Literature
Edited by Daniel Hahn
Published by Oxford University Press (2015, 2nd edn)
ISBN 978-0-1987-1554-2

An indispensable reference book for anyone interested in children's books. Over 900 biographical entries deal with authors, illustrators, printers, publishers, educationalists and others who have influenced the development of children's literature. Genres covered include myths and legends, fairy tales, adventure stories, school stories, fantasy, science fiction, crime and romance. This book is of particular interest to librarians, teachers, students, parents and collectors.

The Reading Bug – and how you can help your child to catch it
by Paul Jennings
Published by Penguin Books (2004)
ISBN 978-0-1413-18400

Paul Jennings is a well-known children's author. This book explains, in his unique humorous style, how readers can open up the world through a love of books. He cuts through the jargon and the controversies to reveal the simple truths, which should enable adults to infect children with the reading bug.

Sticks and Stones: The Troublesome Success of Children's Literature from Slovenly Peter to Harry Potter
by Jack Zipes
Published by Routledge (2002)
ISBN 978-0-4159-38808

Jack Zipes – translator of the Grimm tales, teacher, storyteller and scholar – questions whether children ever really had a literature of their own. He sees children's literature in many ways as being the 'grown-ups' version' – a story about childhood that adults tell kids. He discusses children's literature from the 19th century moralism of Slovenly Peter (whose fingers get cut off) to the wildly successful *Harry Potter* books. Children's literature is a booming market but its success, this author says, is disguising its limitations. *Sticks and Stones* is a forthright and engaging book by someone who clearly cares deeply about what and how children read.

1001 Children's Books You Must Read Before You Grow Up
Edited by Julia Eccleshare
Published by Cassell Illustrated (2009)
ISBN 978-1-8440-36714

This aims to provide an introduction to the best of children's literature, ranging from international classics to contemporary writers. Reviews of each book are accompanied by line drawings and artwork from the books themselves. A number of authors including Michael Morpurgo and Jacqueline Wilson also write about their favourite books. The reviews are ordered according to the book's publication date, from past to present, and age range of the reader.

The Ultimate Book Guide
Edited by Leonie Flynn, Daniel Hahn and Susan Reuben
Published by A&C Black (2009)
ISBN 978-1-4081-04385

Over 600 entries covering the best books for children aged 8–12, from classics to more recently published titles. Funny, friendly and frank recommendations written for children by their favourite and best-known authors including Anthony Horowitz, Jacqueline Wilson, Celia Rees, Darren Shan, David Almond and Dick King-Smith. Plus features on the most popular genres.

The Ultimate First Book Guide
Edited by Leonie Flynn, Daniel Hahn and Susan Reuben
Published by A&C Black (2008)
ISBN 978-0-7136-73319

Comprehensive reference to help children aged 0–7 with their first steps into the world of books. Covers board books and novelty books, through to classic and contemporary picture books, chapter books and more challenging reads. It includes recommendations and features from top authors and experts in the field of children's books, including former Children's Laureate Michael Rosen, Tony Bradman, Malachy Doyle and Wendy Cooling. There are also special features on a variety of topics and themed lists, and a selection of cross-references to other titles children may enjoy.

The Ultimate Teen Book Guide
Edited by Daniel Hahn and Leonie Flynn
Published by A&C Black (2010, 2nd edn)
ISBN 978–1–4081–04378

Listings of over 700 books that might interest teenage readers, recommended and reviewed by authors such as Melvin Burgess, Anthony Horowitz, Meg Cabot, Eoin Colfer and Philip Pullman. Reviews cover the classics to cult fiction, and graphic novels to bestsellers, and each is cross-referenced to other titles as suggestions of what to read next. The book also contains essays on areas of teenage writing including *Race in Young Adult Fiction* by Bali Rai and *Off the Rails* by Kevin Brooks. There are also the results of a national teen readers' poll, plus reviews from teen readers.

ONLINE

Armadillo
www.armadillomagazine.co.uk

An online magazine about children's books, including reviews, interviews, features and profiles. New issues are posted at the end of March, June, September and December. It was founded in 1999 by author Mary Hoffman as a review publication for children's books.

BBC Bitesize
www.bbc.co.uk/bitesize

Information about UK schools' curriculum. Useful for those wishing to write for educational publishers but also for keeping abreast of curricular topics.

The Bookbag
www.thebookbag.co.uk

A UK-based website focused on great reviews about children's books, there are also booklists and information about book awards, as well as articles and author interviews.

Books for Keeps
http://booksforkeeps.co.uk

Featuring a quarterly online magazine for children's books including book reviews and features.

The Bookseller
www.thebookseller.com

A magazine for the publishing industry, sharing news on author deals, book launches and industry features to subscribers. Some content is available for free, including the fortnightly *Chapter and Verse: The Art of Selling Children's Books* podcast.

BookTrust
www.booktrust.org.uk

Dedicated children's reading charity, this is a useful site for professionals working with young readers. Information on events, prizes, books, authors, etc.

BookTrust Great Books Guide
www.booktrust.org.uk/books-and-reading/our-recommendations/great-books-guide/

BookTrust's independent annual 'pick of the best' in children's paperback fiction published in the previous calendar year. It is designed to help parents and those interested in children's reading to select books for children, from babies to teenagers.

Branford Boase Award
www.branfordboaseaward.org.uk

The website for the annual children's book award dedicated to debut children's writers and their editor. Includes a writing competition for young people.

CBBC
www.bbc.co.uk/cbbc

Website of the CBBC channel with games, activities and news for children.

The Children's Book Council
www.cbcbooks.org

The Children's Book Council in the USA is dedicated to encouraging literacy and the enjoyment of children's books. The website includes reviews of children's books published in the USA, forthcoming publications and author profiles. A good site for checking out the US marketplace.

Children's Laureate
www.booktrust.org.uk/what-we-do/childrens-laureate

Official website of the Children's Laureate with resources and activities for children.

Children's Literature
http://childrenslit.com/

US website of the Children's Literature Comprehensive Database (CLCD), a subscription database with over 100,000 reviews of children's books. Plus links to US author and illustrator websites.

CILIP Carnegie & Kate Greenaway Medals
http://carnegiegreenaway.org.uk

This website follows the only UK children's book award where the winners are selected by specialist

The Federation of Children's Book Groups

http://fcbg.org.uk/

The FCBG runs an annual children's book award, judged by children, and a network of local groups for those interested in finding out more about children's books and authors. See page 337.

Good Reads for Children

www.goodreads.com/genres/childrens

The Amazon-owned website supports consumer reviews about books for children that can be researched by categories including middle grade and picture books, etc.

The Horn Book

www.hbook.com

US website hosting *The Horn Book Guide Online*, a comprehensive, fully searchable database of over 70,000 book titles and reviews for children and young adults. Also includes a regular newsletter sharing an interview with an author or illustrator, *Authors & Illustrators talk with Roger*, and and a monthly e-newsletter for parents, *Notes from the Horn Book*.

House of Illustration

www.houseofillustration.org.uk

The brainchild of author and illustrator Quentin Blake, the House of Illustration celebrates all forms of illustration, runs regular talks and events and supports schools-based activities.

National Literacy Trust

www.literacytrust.org.uk

The organisation is focused on developing literacy among adults and children and its website documents its activities. See page 339.

Picture Book Den

http://picturebookden.blogspot.com

An independent website created by professional children's authors based in the UK and Ireland where they share their passion for picture books, with blogs on getting published and creating picture books.

ReadingZone.com

https://readingzone.com

A magazine-style website, created with Arts Council support, dedicated to children's books including monthly book reviews by teachers and librarians as well as children, chapters to download, author interviews, news, activities and a regular newsletter. There are distinct areas for teachers, librarians, families, children and teenagers.

Scottish Book Trust

www.scottishbooktrust.com

Information on books for children of all ages in Scotland plus a national programme of events with children's writers: author tours, festivals, writing competitions and exciting activities.

Seven Stories

www.sevenstories.org.uk

The Seven Stories National Centre for Children's Books, based in Newcastle, provides regular events and exhibitions dedicated to children's literature which are highlighted on its website. See page 334.

The Story Museum

www.storymuseum.org.uk

Stories from around the world to watch, hear, read and tell.

Toppsta

https://toppsta.com/

A children's book review website that invites children and adults to review books for children and teenagers.

Words & Pictures

www.wordsandpics.org

The online magazine of SCBWI, a worldwide organisation of writers and illustrators of children's books, with advice on writing, illustrating, news, blogs and activities. See page 330.

Who Next ... ?

www.whonextguide.com

Writers of children's fiction are listed with suggestions of other authors who write in a similar way, together with key book and series titles. There is a small annual subscription fee for accessing the information.

World Book Day

www.worldbookday.com

Providing a range of resources for children and teenagers, from writing and illustration masterclasses to quizzes, activities and reading ideas.

Inspiring writers

Making a writer

Sarah Crossan describes what led her to take her writing seriously, put her secret dream of being a writer into practice and – with time and resolve – achieve her goal.

I never thought a person like me could be a writer. I was an incredibly ordinary child, have become an even more ordinary adult and believed many untruths about writing and writers. Firstly, I didn't come from a family connected to the literati, which I perceived as a major problem, though at the time I probably hadn't even come across the word 'literati'. Secondly, I wasn't privately educated and didn't have anything close to a BBC newsreader's accent – grand drawback. Finally, and perhaps most importantly, I didn't own a serious-looking scarf. You know the ones. All proper artists own them.

When I went to university, to study Philosophy and Literature, my fears about what went into making a writer were compounded as I carefully stalked the creative writing students: they all seemed aloof, important and occasionally sad, hanging out in the humanities building, wearing oversized jumpers and, yes, their scholarly scarves.

After my undergraduate degree, convinced writing wasn't for me (and secretly hating all those creative writing students who'd spent three years smugly impersonating Margaret Atwood), I went off to study teaching. It was a way to make books a part of my daily life. And I was actually really good at it. The students fell in love with words and sentences, with poems and novels. I even convinced a class of hardened Shakespeare haters (one of whom offered to steal my car for £50 so I could pick up the insurance money!) to perform scenes from *Romeo and Juliet*, as well as partake in some Renaissance dancing. I loved teaching – my job was about books and kids, words and relationships.

Then came an afternoon that changed everything – a lesson that had an outcome missing from my planning notes. I was teaching poetry, encouraging students to write about their dreams, their hopes, how they saw their lives developing. I believed in those kids. I knew they could be anything they wanted to be if they just puffed out their chests and did some hard work. They wrote wonderful poems. They wrote moving poems. And then, at the end of the lesson, one child put up his hand and asked a question: 'Have you always wanted to be an English teacher, Miss?'. Now, a more sensitive person might have read some subtext into this, namely '*Why are you a teacher, Miss? You're terrible at your job.*' But I don't think that's what he meant. He genuinely wanted to know whether or not I'd lived my dreams, so shyly I explained that, as well as being a teacher, I wanted to be a writer, a poet and a novelist, but that I didn't think I quite had what it took. The boy frowned, as did a few other students, and angrily replied, 'Well you have a bit of cheek then, don't you, telling us to live our dreams when you haven't even done it yourself. Have you even tried?'

Despite being young, I was a strict teacher; I never tolerated rudeness, but in that moment I was dumbstruck – because he was right. Who was I to lecture them on bravery and risk when I had never taken myself nor my own desires seriously? Instead of asking him to leave the room, where I could speak to him about his tone of voice, I quietly said, 'You're right. I've been too afraid to try.'

On the basis of that very bald conversation, I applied to go back to university and study creative writing – which I did the very next year, annoying the head teacher who had to find a replacement for the next academic year at short notice.

And so I began to write. And I began to take my writing seriously. Rather than going to the cinema when friends asked, I started to say, 'Sorry, I can't. I'm writing.' When they seemed irritated by my resolve, I didn't care. If I wanted to achieve my dream of writing for a living, I had to believe in myself, otherwise no one else would. I found a way out of my shame and into a pattern of work that I loved.

That doesn't mean a contract came quickly; it didn't. It was another ten years of graft and fine-tuning my skills before I found an agent, listed in the *Writers' & Artists' Yearbook* in the children's section, who seemed to fit the bill. I sent her my book and astonishingly she took me on within days. We are still together, for better or for worse, and when I start to flounder and find myself wondering if I should pack it all in, she reminds me that I don't need anything to succeed except a dash of self-belief and a bit of hard work. Oh, and my serious writerly scarf, of course. Everyone needs one of those!

Sarah Crossan is the award-winning author of the young adult novel *One* (Bloomsbury 2015) which won the CILIP Carnegie Medal, the YA Book Prize, the CBI Book of the Year Award and the CLiPPA Poetry Award in 2016. Also published by Bloomsbury, her books *The Weight of Water* (2011) and *Apple and Rain* (2014) were both shortlisted for the CILIP Carnegie Medal. Sarah's other children's novels are *Breathe* (2012), its sequel *Resist* (2013), *We Come Apart* (co-authored with Brian Conaghan 2017) and the free verse novel *Moonrise* (2017), which was shortlisted for the Costa Children's Book Award, the YA Book Prize and the CBI Book of the Year Award. Her latest books are *Toffee* (Bloomsbury 2019), a free verse novel for adults *Here is the Beehive* (Bloomsbury Circus 2020) and a collection of contemporary and classic poetry *Tomorrow is Beautiful* (Bloomsbury 2021). Sarah was Laureate na nÓg, the Irish Children's Laureate, from 2018-20.

Books

Finding your voice and point of view

Anna Wilson looks at the importance of finding your own distinctive voice as a writer and at the impact and technical considerations involved in choosing a particular point of view to tell your story. She shows how much this choice of viewpoint influences your reader's perceptions, enabling you to 'be the director of your own movie'.

When, as a teenager, I asked someone what it would take to become a writer, they said rather grandly, 'You need to find your voice'. This felt like an important pronouncement, so I nodded sagely, having absolutely no idea what they meant or how I was going to be able to do this for myself. I thought that finding my voice must go hand in hand with having a Muse, or Inspiration, or Life Experience. These were all things I had read that writers should have – and all things which seemed far out of reach to a grammar school kid living in suburbia, where the most exciting thing ever to happen was when Deirdre-next-door got ideas above her station and had a conservatory built.

What I didn't realise was that, to be a writer, I didn't need to do anything other than to write, and I had been doing that ever since I could pick up a pencil. I still have some of my early scribbles – drawings of people, mostly, to whom I would chatter endlessly, creating conversations and adventures for them; these soon morphed into cartoons influenced by my love of the *Beano*, and from there I started writing my own 'proper stories'. By the time I had reached my early teens I had already filled innumerable notebooks with angsty thoughts and records of what I had been up to at school and elsewhere. And I was becoming conscious, through my obsessive reading, that 'becoming a writer' was something that I could aspire to. Yet how to achieve this? How on earth was I to 'find my voice'?

We all have a voice. And if we all started out doing as the great scriptwriter Russell T. Davies does – 'writing how you speak', each of us would soon see our own voice appearing on the page straight away. One of the first mistakes emerging writers tend to make (I include my younger self in this) is that they try too hard to nail down a voice, and end up writing something that rings false. Looking back at my journals, I can see I had a distinctive voice emerging then: the cadence and rhythm of my writing is 100% me, and it has found its way into so much of my children's fiction via characters who bear a striking resemblance to that bored suburban kid who lived in her head and dreamed of better things.

In writerly terms, 'voice' is the combination of **what** is said and **how** it's said. Anyone reading this will be able to think immediately of books with a voice so real it leaps off the page and keeps on talking inside your head long after you've stopped reading. I am thinking of Lauren Child's *Clarice Bean* series (1999–) or Louise Rennison's inimitable Georgia Nicolson in her teen books such as *Angus, Thongs and Full-Frontal Snogging* (Piccadilly Press 1999) or McKay Tambo in Alex Wheatle's *Crongton Knights* trilogy (Little, Brown 2017–). In picture books, voice will come through as strongly in the illustrations as it does in the text. Think of the way the mouse looks out from the pages of *The Gruffalo* (Macmillan 1999); Axel Scheffler's illustrations make sure that the mouse is saying as much with his eyes as Julia Donaldson's words have him say with his mouth.

Much of what constitutes voice will come down to 'point of view', which can often be another minefield. In fact, this seems to get emerging writers into more of a tangle than almost any other technical issue, and it's certainly something that I struggle with every single time I sit down to write a new book. Should I write in the first person and thereby show the whole story through one immutable lens? Should I step back and have an omniscient narrator who can move silently and god-like through my story and have a finger in every pie, a foot in every room, an eye in every meeting-place? Or should I choose one character to take my reader through the story, but keep a pace behind them by writing in third person whilst also staying close to their experiences? In other words, where am I allowing the narrator to stand? From which point of view am I allowing my reader to see things?

All books are written by people, about people – even when they're apparently about animals: any child reading *The Gruffalo* will recognise the power of the mouse's cunning over the other animals' fear and stupidity, and thus the mouse is really a human in disguise. And any being, human or otherwise, can perceive certain things through their senses – and not perceive others. As visual animals we talk about 'view', but good writing in fact uses all the senses, not only sight. Therefore, 'point of view' will necessarily include all the senses. We can't physically see behind our own heads, but we can smell the bakery behind us. We can't see someone six floors up, but we might hear, from the open window, the music they are playing. In writing, as in the rest of life, this idea of what a particular being can and can't perceive widens to include how they understand it, how it makes them feel, what else they know about the world, what they think of it all, what they say, and – crucially – what they don't say about it. All of this is point of view.

When I was writing my *Vlad the World's Worst Vampire* series (Stripes Publishing 2017–), I wanted to keep close to Vlad's experiences. He was going out into the human world for the first time and discovering that it was very different from the terrifying pictures his parents had painted of it. I wanted the reader to see things through his eyes and to taste human food as he tasted it, to see human school and human relationships as he saw them. I therefore chose to write the stories in 'close third', rather than from the perspective of an all-seeing, all-knowing, distant third-person narrator. I could have chosen first person, of course, but I rejected this as I didn't want to use such a limited viewpoint that my reader had only Vlad's voice in their heads. Also, as this is a series for confident young readers who are just becoming adept at reading alone, I didn't want to stray too far from the storytelling voice that they would be used to from most picture books and early readers. So I had many considerations in mind when choosing this 'close third' point of view.

However, I knew there were some things to be aware of in choosing this slightly limited viewpoint: the reader could only ever know what Vlad knew, could only ever see what Vlad saw; and I risked letting him stay in his thoughts too long if I left him on his own for any length of time. This led to me to invent a character who was nearly always with him – his pet bat, Flit. Flit acted like Vlad's own conscience, helping him work through problems or challenging him when he was about to do something stupid (pets can be useful like that in children's fiction, even if they don't actually speak!).

A final note on point of view: whichever voice you choose, and from whichever standpoint you prefer to allow your characters to speak, try to 'vary the camera angles' in your writing. By this I mean, don't always be showing your reader an intense close-up where we are so inside the character's head that we have lost sight of what is going on outside it – this can be a very claustrophobic experience for the reader. Equally, don't swamp the reader with continual long 'wide-angle' shots that give pages and pages of scene-setting;

Books

these can take the reader away from the action and from what the characters are thinking, saying and doing in the moment. Think of yourself as the director of your own movie, particularly when it comes to editing. Ask yourself: has my character spent too long walking down that path wondering what they are going to have for dinner? Or: has the narrator spent too long sitting in a car looking out of the window on the way to their auntie's, taking in the scenery and describing the whole, boring journey beat by beat? Remember that the reader needs to see only the things that matter. Think of how a director uses 'jump-cuts' to move us from one scene to the next. As the American writer Colum McCann says in his wonderful book *Letters to a Young Writer* (Random House 2017):

It is a good trick to assume that you have a number of changeable lenses. Be fish-eye. Be wide-angle. Be telephoto. Zoom in. Zoom out. Distort. Sharpen. Divide. Imagine yourself into the actual camera. Find the words that are glass and shutter both.

It's all about the degree to which we are inside a character's head. And the choice of which 'person' we choose to write in, or which point of view we choose, will have an impact on how close in we are, right from the off. In first person we are clearly right in the thick of things – we are, as McCann says, 'glass and shutter both'. In third person, there is an immediate element of detachment, but there are degrees of closeness too; you only have to think of how Hilary Mantel writes from the point of view of Thomas Cromwell in *Wolf Hall* (Fourth Estate 2009) to see that 'he' can easily transubstantiate into 'I'.

If all this sounds like too much, and you still have no idea how to find your voice or which point of view is right for your work in progress, step away from the manuscript and give yourself a little exercise to loosen things up. Think yourself into your main character's shoes. If you've been writing in the first person, swap to third – close or omniscient, it's up to you. If you've been using third person, swap to first. Now have a think about a scene that you're struggling to inject some energy into; maybe your character is too much in their head, or they seem to be taking an age to get from A to B and frankly, even you, their creator, is feeling pretty bored with them now. Flip the point of view and see what happens. Has it brought you closer to a character you were struggling to bring alive on the page? Has it given you a perspective that has shown your character in a startling new light? Do you prefer this new piece written from this point of view, or has your writing become stodgier? Why do you feel the way you do about these shifts of perspective?

Above all, have fun! It is in constantly trying things for size that we improve and grow as writers. And it is in playing around like children chattering to their first made-up scribbled pictures, that we learn to find our voice.

Anna Wilson is the author of over 50 books for children, including novels, non-fiction, poems, short stories, picture books and early readers. Her books include *The Parent Problem* (2016) and *The Family Fiasco* (2017), both published by Macmillan Children's, and *Spook-tacular Surprise* (Stripes Publishing 2019), the latest in her *Vlad the World's Worst Vampire* series. Her most recent picture book for children is *The Wide, Wide Sea* (Nosy Crow 2021). She produces an annual children's almanac *Nature Month-by-Month* (Nosy Crow/National Trust). Anna runs creative workshops for the Arvon Foundation. She is an RLF Fellow at Exeter University from 2022. Read her blog on acwilsonwriter.wordpress.com. Follow her on Twitter @acwilsonwriter.

Parent your inner child: what kind of writer are you?

Lucy van Smit explores how to thrive as a writer in uncertain times and overcome anxiety, self-doubt and self-criticism. She explains how to apply four key principles of parenting to help you understand, boost and nurture your inner writer.

Your shadow is what you don't know about yourself

Heads up, I'm a dyslexic author who didn't know I had ADHD until after publication. And what should have been the best of times became months of Dark Nights, until my shiny, writerly soul forced me to stop and listen to my life. Luckily, I did, before a virus flipped our world inside out with a pandemic.

What has this to do with your writing career?

As an author, I wish I'd seen overwhelm coming. I was unprepared for the anxiety that infected me and my writing friends. Do you struggle to soothe yourself when fear, rejection, procrastination and writer's block strike? Writers need to be able to regulate their emotions. Here's the kicker: maybe you don't see yourself as anxious? I didn't. I am cheerful, friendly, witty, clever, spiritual; I love life. And I'm tough. Really tough. After all, I'd been a successful TV producer who made documentaries on famous authors. I survived ten miscarriages, the stillbirth of our darling Luke; I'm an expert at getting a seriously dyslexic boy through pushy London day schools; a wife of 30 years … an artist … a writer … top friend … a great mother (something I didn't learn growing up – sorry Mum, but you were rubbish).

Pre-publication oblivion

Neuro-diversity shines at outwitting problems. In TV, I applauded myself for working 20-hour days, in the Philippines living on chocolate and orange juice for six weeks – classic shadow, ADHD behaviour. Gabor Maté says what you admire is often what kills you. Niceness disguises suppressed feelings. Overworking is labelled success.

Speed forward a decade or three, in the run-up to publication; already an insomniac, I had several nights a week with no sleep. I still didn't get it. Eventually, at the awesome age of 60, it occurred to me that my insomnia, since childhood, was anxiety. My niece sniggered when I told her my revelation. The thing is, unlike you lovelies, we didn't have the word 'anxiety' when I was growing up. We self-medicated with alcohol and distraction; from love affairs to careers.

Older, wiser, I read more. Energy Medicine (yes, my teenage son scoffed too, until the virus), Yoga, Flow Psychology, Nutrition, Spirituality, Podcasts, Writing Workshops. Bought loads more books. The arrogance of a conceptual brain – you try everything … except talking to your intuitive self.

When *Writers'* & *Artists'* asked for a YA workshop

I wanted to share skills from the Family Links Parenting Programme I ran at my son's school. Its focus is emotional intelligence for otherwise cerebral, articulate, ambitious parents, whose kids behaved in mystifying ways. Who knew rebellion is a child's response to feeling powerless? Maybe procrastination is our rebellion against powerlessness in the publishing industry? Four parenting tools are great for writers:

1. Know yourself

I am so busted. Did you know that Socrates ridiculed you if you studied any subject before you took the time to have a good hard look at yourself? In his *Four Quartets*, T.S. Eliot got it: 'We shall not cease from exploration./And the end of all our exploring./ Will be to arrive where we started./And know the place for the first time.' To be a good author, you need to know what makes you tick.

What don't you know about yourself?

As writers, not knowing your shadow shows up in blurting out mean words to yourself, or your perfectionism sabotaging your dreams by never finishing that book.

Mystical, archetypal patterns of power help me decode the excuses I make. What archetype is pulling *your* strings? Are you playing your Victim card? Your Prostitute card? Do you negotiate survival on any terms? We all share four Survival Archetypes. Everyone has a Child Archetype – but which one? The Nature Child? The Wounded Child? The Abandoned Child? We are unconscious of how often we abandon ourselves. Writers can abandon their own voice: you write what others want; you rate others' approval above your own. This is central in understanding young adults; teenagers often abandon themselves to fit in with their peers. It was the core theme for my debut YA novel, *The Hurting* (Chicken House 2018). Abandoned as a baby by her mother, Nell abducts baby Ulv Pup to win a boy's approval. Redemption comes when her greatest flaw becomes her greatest strength; Nell must choose between the damaged Lukas, the love of her life, or saving the abandoned baby from wolves on his wild Norwegian mountain. She must learn that No Boy is Worth Your Soul.

You know the power of words

Do you notice how you speak to yourself? For instance, using words like 'blame', 'I don't deserve this' or 'I'm entitled' is the language of your Victim Archetype. Author Caroline Myss advises editing shame words out of your vocabulary. And Goethe knew that, once you 'decide', the universe steps in behind you. Intention is everything.

Are you a conceptual or an intuitive writer?

Know your inner writer. Are you an intuitive or a conceptual one? We veer towards one or the other, and ignorance is an obstacle to getting your work to a publishable standard. Have you ever been told your writing is beautiful, and wondered why you're not signed? Do your characters sing off the page with originality? Do agents love, love, love your voice, but don't snap you up?

Maybe, often, it's because the promise of your voice sputters out. Your story rambles; agents give up, confused. Somehow your right brain can't seem to fix your story problem; you add more events to add a bit of structure, only to make the narrative flat, linear. You struggle with the dynamics of drama, conflict. But everyone loves your characters, you wail. You brought them to life. They're so real. Of course. You poured your soul into them. But still … your story doesn't sell.

A conceptual writer is the exact opposite

You've read every writing craft book going. You can hit the Inciting Incident on page one – hey, you can hit it in the opening paragraph. You can write a mesmerising Hook. You nail your story in a 25-word logline (one-sentence summary) and have all those important beats, conflict, climax, rising tension, a great ending. You know exactly what happens to your protagonist at Midpoint. You know her 'flaw' and her basic 'need'. But you don't get snapped up. Why? Maybe, often, agents don't care enough about your characters. Readers don't feel for them, because *you* didn't feel anything when you wrote them. You can't access emotion from your left brain.

We tend to play to our strengths and hide weaknesses, which makes them worse. Learn to use both sides of your brain, but not at the same time. This is why you don't stop to edit when you write your first draft. Editing is a left-brain activity. Switching between two brain hemispheres is a skillset every writer can learn.

Screenwriting guru, Corey Mandell, calls the process 'creative integration'. He advocates an arduous training; conceptual writers are not allowed to structure or plot, for months! Intuitive writers must stop creating dialogue (ouch) until you can crack structure. I don't buy Mandell's theory that your *corpus callosum*, the bit facilitating communication between brain hemispheres, can't work them both at the same time, nor that it takes ages to re-train writers. Practice builds neural pathways, so write. Stop avoiding what you don't like to do – outlining, for instance. Think of it as eating your greens as a kid. A little goes a long way, and there are new tools to help. My favourite tool is 'energy medicine' – brilliant for connecting both sides of your brain, fast. It works by crossing and strengthening the energy pathways in your body. I practise Donna Eden's Daily Energy Routine (https://edenenergymedicine.com/donnas-daily-energy-routine) before I start to write. It calms even a bonkers brain like mine.

Music is another activity that uses both parts of the brain simultaneously. Conceptual writers, try meditating before you start: dance, create a sacred space, breathe, focus on your body, set an intention that tunes you into your creative right brain. You know, by the language you use, which part of the brain you are firing.

As a general principle, intuitive writers do best if they outline first. Keep it simple. Sketch, map it out, just so you know where you're going. Think … what is best for your story? Best for your characters? And best for you to write? When that all aligns, it feels like flow … fun! But conceptual writers, hold off planning. Play first, and discover your characters, before you work on your brilliant plot. Make us *care* first.

2. Empathy

To be a good parent, you need the ability to empathise with your child and put yourself in their shoes. Pixar have a formula to enable conceptual writers to write emotion for their protagonist:

$$EC = EM (R+P^2) +H +A +ES +(MS)$$

Don't panic … it's easier than it looks!

To create Empathy (EM) with your reader you need to find the Emotional Core (EC) of your character. What drives them? Fear? Love of a sister? Pixar creates empathy through Recognition (R) of heaping obstacles, so we pity the Protagonist (P^2), makes them Human (H) and gives them a skill for us to Admire (A), like bravery. Also create high Emotional Stakes (ES) … what happens if your protagonist fails? The final element (MS) stands for Meaning: the 'why' of your story. Make readers care what happens to your characters and empathise with what they desperately want or need.

3. Appropriate expectations

The third principle of good parenting. Do you have Appropriate Expectations of your inner writer? (What? ... I hear you say.) How long have you been writing? Ten years? Two? Do you assume your inner writer should behave with the maturity of your chronological age – even if you've only been writing for a year or two?

Inappropriate Expectations cause a lot of unnecessary stress. Would you say to a toddler, 'Get up, you Dummy!' when they fall down? But you say that to yourself all the time. There's a reason why Enid Blyton locked her kids away – so she could write. And why Barbara Hepworth dumped her triplets on friends – so she could sculpt. Do you work? Do you have a young family? Or elderly parents? Do you have Appropriate Expectations of what you can get done ... or of where you think your writing career should be? My simple rule is: if you are stressed, your expectations are inappropriate. As a writer, have compassion for yourself. Rest.

4. Positive discipline

Positive Discipline means praise. We praise children in order to focus on what they are doing right. Good teachers praise. Constant self-criticism doesn't help you perform better or love writing more. We forget how to praise ourselves. Practise. Praise your inner writer for showing up. Praise switches off that constant inner critic that says you're not good enough at this writing malarkey.

You can't praise and criticise yourself at the same time. So praise yourself – when you think like a writer, when you read as a writer, when you sit down to write. We don't compare our children, so don't compare yourself to published authors. Praise yourself for just being you, not for doing more or achieving more. Success will happen naturally, joyfully. Play more. Fun breeds success.

While it's useful to think of parenting your inner writer child, don't take it as an excuse to baby yourself, to have unlimited duvets days, or to 'snowflake', as my teenager calls it. Writing needs a lot of self-discipline to sit down and write. When it gets tough, finish what you have started. Breathe. Exercise. Play. Journal. Know what kind of writer you are before you even think about getting published. I promise that knowing yourself better helps you write better. And when you do send your work out, don't wait to hear back; write something new, don't wait for approval. End of story.

Former TV producer and artist, **Lucy van Smit's** latest book is *A Writer's Journal Workbook* (Bloomsbury 2021). Lucy won the Bath Children's Novel Award with her debut novel, *The Hurting* (Chicken House), pitched as 'Nordic Noir Wuthering Heights'; she is currently working on *The Hurting* film script. She has a BA Hons in Fine Art and received a Distinction in her MA in Creative Writing. She offers one-to-one creative recovery coaching and workshops. Follow Lucy on Twitter and Instagram @Lucyvansmit.

If at first you don't succeed...

Frances Hardinge describes the steps she took, as a hopeful young writer, to brave rejection, persevere and grow in confidence, and the friends and resources that helped her find where her writing belonged and gain that first momentous book contract.

I was in my teens when I bought my first copy of the *Writers' & Artists' Yearbook*. Back then, the *Children's Writers' & Artists' Yearbook* didn't exist. But in those days I wasn't an adult writing children's fiction, I was a teenager trying my hand at adult fiction.

Buying the book felt significant – a little intimidating, in fact. I sensed that I was making a promise to myself. I wouldn't keep my stories safely hidden away. I would send them off to be judged, and expose my fragile, iridescent bubble-dreams to the jagged edges of the real world. In effect, I had *bought* some of my cowardly excuses into non-existence: '*I can't send my work off, I don't know where to start!*'; '*I don't know what to send, or where!*'. Well, now I did.

And whenever I let schoolwork or other commitments eat up all my time, I'd spot the *Yearbook* on my shelf, fire-engine red. A silent, insistent reminder of my promise to myself. A gentle but much-needed boot in the rear.

I meticulously typed out my stories on the roaring, ill-tempered electric typewriter I'd bought from my sister for five pounds. Every time I made an error and had to perform Tipp-Ex surgery, I agonised over it and considered typing the whole page again.

And all the while I was gripped by a crippling fear that my first submission might be my only chance, and that if I messed it up badly all would be lost. The submissions editor would look coldly at my clunkiest metaphor, or scowl at my Tipp-Ex, and then stride away to the dark chamber where the editor collective kept the Terrible Tome of Authors We Must Never Publish. They would add my name to the list, and from that moment all my other submissions would be doomed. Prospective editors would consult the book, see my name in blood-red letters, shake their heads and throw my manuscript in the bin.

Only after a few trembling submissions did I start to suspect that the Terrible Tome didn't actually exist. Rejection slips arrived in the post, but didn't bring the apocalypse with them. Occasionally there was an actual rejection letter. (My favourite of these effectively said: 'We rather liked your story, and we wish we knew what it was about.') Eventually I realised that I had nothing to lose but the cost of two stamps and a spoonful of pride. If I was turned down it didn't matter. All that mattered was that I kept trying.

By my twenties, I was subscribing to *Writers' News* and *Writing Magazine* to supplement the *Yearbook*. I now typed my stories on a little Franken-puter that my boyfriend had cobbled together from parts of discarded, elderly computers. My friends and I set up a small writers' group, which gave me a regular deadline to keep me writing. With their feedback I became more confident, and less precious about editing my work.

And one day, after sending a short story to a little independent magazine, I received an answer that wasn't a 'no'. This was the first in a series of 'not-no' responses. However, when I received my first book contract a few years later, it was thanks to my good friend Rhiannon Lassiter. She realised something I hadn't – that my peculiar dark fairy tales were actually children's fiction. Rhiannon persuaded me to try writing a children's novel, then wrested my first five chapters from my unwilling hands and marched off with them to her editor.

The *Children's Writers' & Artists' Yearbook* would have been invaluable to me as a young, aspiring children's writer, if I'd had the sense to realise that that was what I was. The latest editions of the *Yearbook* are even richer and more useful than those I bought in my teens and twenties, with more information on agents, prizes, courses, conferences, digital publishing and self-publishing, and a wealth of essays, articles and advice.

Even now, when I look at the *Writers' & Artists' Yearbook*, I still recall everything it symbolised for me. It looks too heavy for the shelf, packed to the binding with hunger, trepidation, determination and hope. It's still a little intimidating. Opportunities often are.

Frances Hardinge is the award-winning author of *Fly by Night* (Macmillan Children's Books 2005), winner of the 2006 Branford Boase Award, *Twilight Robbery* (Macmillan Children's Books 2011), shortlisted for the Guardian Children's Fiction Prize, and *Cuckoo Song* (Pan Macmillan 2014), which won the Robert Holdstock Award for Best Novel at the British Fantasy Awards 2015. *The Lie Tree* (Macmillan Children's Books 2015) won the Costa Book of the Year 2015 award, the 2016 UKLA Book Award (12–16 category), the 2016 *Boston Globe* Horn Book Fiction Award and the 2016 *Los Angeles Times* Young Adult Literature Prize and was also shortlisted for the Independent Booksellers Week Award 2015, the *Guardian* Children's Fiction Prize 2015 and the 2016 Carnegie Medal. The sequel, *A Skinful of Shadows* (Pan Macmillan 2017), won the Dracula Society's Children of the Night award. Her other books include *Gullstruck Island* (Macmillan Children's Books 2009) and *A Face Like Glass* (Pan Macmillan Children's 2012). Her latest book is *Deeplight* (Macmillan 2019). She was nominated for the 2021 Astrid Lindgren Memorial Award. Find out more at http://www.franceshardinge.com/.

How stories shape you as a writer

Patrice Lawrence reflects on how she found her voice through the stories she read.

I'm writing this in rather unexpected circumstances. I had originally planned a few paragraphs about my love of reading and how privileged I feel now that my own books are on the shelves of libraries and shops and in the hands of readers. I do still feel incredibly privileged, but as we're coming to understand the long-term global impact of the covid-19 virus, it's impossible not to reflect further.

Like many full-time writers, I smiled knowingly in the early days of the pandemic lockdown. Stay inside? That's what we do anyway, isn't it? Hanging around in our pyjamas, staring mystically into space and occasionally tapping a laptop. But, actually, for me that's just a small part of the story. Many of my books are set in London – a city crammed full of history. If I look up, I see Hercules taming horses on the Royal Mews, a pterodactyl on the Natural History Museum and angels on the Apollo Theatre. When I look down, I see clay pipe stems on the Thames foreshore and fragments of pottery that were held by hands hundreds of years ago. So many stories, waiting to be collected and assembled. London also – usually – vibrates with the clamour of many different voices. There are moments of drama happening everywhere. And when I'm not eavesdropping and scribbling notes, I'm visiting schools, learning from the children and young people I write for and about.

It has been an uncertain, frightening time, but what has become clear is the absolute importance of stories. Writers and illustrators have been sharing their stories online; children and young people encouraged to tell their own tales. Struggling to write or even read fiction, I've lost myself in audiobooks, finding comfort in books being read to me.

Stories, though, have shaped me for as long as I can remember. I'm part of the first generation of Caribbean-heritage people to be born in the UK. I have lived in households that were often different from those around me – multi-ethnic, or lone parent, or in a private foster arrangement. I've never lived in a family where we're all the same colour. I was a passionate reader from very young, but there were never stories featuring families like mine.

I started writing. I wrote and illustrated stories about a giant purple rabbit for my toddler brother. I delivered my Year 7 history homework about the Saxons in rhyming couplets (thank you, Mr Mann, for the A). When I was 13, I hit pay dirt when my poem published in the *Brighton Evening Argus* earned me a £1 postal order. At sixth-form college, my 1980s version of *The Wizard of Oz* was performed on stage, complete with Michael Jackson-esque Thriller zombies with releasable arms!

During my 20s, I fell in love with short stories. I managed to get a couple of stories published in teenage romance magazines, greatly helped by the *Writers' & Artists' Yearbook*; I'd read every listing for UK magazines, every detail of every agent, and wondered how on earth I could ever be part of that world. As a young person growing up in Sussex suburbia, it seemed impossible.

Three things happened that inadvertently propelled me into the world of children's publishing. Firstly, I moved to London in my late 20s to be a mature student at Goldsmiths' College. London seemed unfathomable and terrifying for a long time, but gradually I realised I was inside an endless whorl of stories and started noting down vignettes and

Books

ideas. Prompted by one of those scraps, I submitted a short story to a competition for unpublished writers and it was included in a high-profile anthology. Although it was adult writing, my characters were teenagers and it led me to my wonderful agent, Caroline Sheldon.

Secondly, I joined a writing group. It was brutal and empowering and, through critiquing and being critiqued, I am an infinitely better writer. We supported and commiserated with each other, we even ran continual professional development sessions to up our game. Last of all, and most important for me, I found my voice. At that time there were no working-class, multi-ethnic British families in children's books – and only a few in adult books. I internalised the message that I was not allowed to write from my own perspective.

Then, one winter afternoon in 1999, I turned on the TV and discovered Malorie Blackman. It was the BBC adaptation of her novel *Pig Heart Boy* (Doubleday 1997). A story about a black family who weren't the Cosbys or in *The Fresh Prince of Bel-Air*? A story set in England? A door opened for me and I stepped through ... and eventually wrote *Orangeboy* (Hodder Children's Books 2016). It was shortlisted for the Costa Children's Award and won other prizes. But, do you want to know a secret? It was the fifth book I'd actually written. It took a while!

So, keep at it. Write. Find your voice. Keep improving and, like me, you'll get there.

Patrice Lawrence MBE is an award-winning writer of fiction both for adults and children. Her books for young adults have won many prizes including the YA Prize, the Waterstones Prize for Older Children's Fiction, the Crimefest YA Prize twice and the inaugural Jhalak Prize for Children and Young People. *Elemental Detectives*, the first in a fantasy series set in Georgian London, is published by Scholastic in September 2022.

My way into a different world

Sally Green describes how, in middle life, she found herself hooked on the creative process of writing and, by applying hard work and good advice, made her way into the world of the professional writer.

I remember the beginning of my writing career quite clearly. It was a sunny afternoon in June 2010, I was 48 years old and doing housework and I had an idea for a story. I'd never written anything before (no diary, no dabbling in short stories, no childhood dreams of being an author), but what did I have to lose other than a few hours of my time? Anything had to be more interesting than hoovering, and no one would ever read the story but me, so I sat down and wrote.

At school I'd learnt the basics of grammar and punctuation, but I always felt inhibited about my writing and that I lacked imagination. Now I realize that everyone has imagination, but being brave and comfortable enough to risk expressing it is the hard thing. By June 2010 schoolgirl inhibitions were a distant memory, although learning wasn't, as the previous year I'd begun to study Social Sciences with the Open University. Because of the OU course I had developed the habit of writing – I had to produce regular assignments and I enjoyed closing the door on the outside world and immersing myself in a new topic. I loved the process of putting ideas and words together and creating something, even if it was only a rather poor essay on politics.

So that June afternoon, with no more essays to write, I repeated the procedure but instead of an essay I began a short story about a girl who didn't know that she was a witch. I didn't have much of a plan – I just wrote, and I continued the next day and the next. After two weeks of this I had to admit to myself that the story wasn't that short; in fact I was probably writing a novel, and it was now taking up all my time. I was hooked. Possibly I was in love too – with my characters. I was obsessed with them, thinking about what they'd do and how, and why. I carried on writing and by September 2010 my story was complete and definitely not short (136,000 words). It wasn't atrocious but there were things wrong with it, though I wasn't even sure what those things were (the narrative point of view was jumping all over the place). I was desperate to improve and so I switched my OU course to Creative Writing, studying hard and all the while working on my manuscript.

I never really believed I'd be a published writer – it seemed less likely than winning the lottery – but I believed in my story. I wanted to try to get it published, but I had a problem: I didn't know a thing about the publishing world. However, I had heard about the *Writers' & Artists' Yearbook* and I found a rather battered copy at my local library. As soon as I started leafing through it I knew I'd found a book I could trust. I devoured its advice. It became my Bible, a source of knowledge and comfort. It was my way into a different world – the world of the professional writer.

I decided to try the traditional route of getting an agent who would then help me find a publisher, and so I listed the agents who accepted manuscripts for YA books, googled them and chose a few I thought might be interested in my story. I submitted to eight agents and within a few months received five brief replies saying 'No' (though the non-replies were fairly clear No's too). However, one reply was different: it was still a 'No', but the agent said she liked my writing style though the story 'didn't have the necessary edge for today's market'. I was delighted. OK – it was a rejection, but an agent from a prestigious London literary agency liked my writing style! I was over the moon. Better yet, I was fired up – I knew I could do edgy better than most people, and I knew that I could improve on the manuscript that I'd sent out. My mindset, once I decided I'd try to get published, was that I would write at least three novels before I'd give up, so starting again didn't daunt me. I gave myself a year to rewrite the story and immediately set to work. Best of all, I'd been released from the cage that I hadn't realised I was still in; I'd been told to be edgy, and to do that I had to let go of my writing inhibitions and make the story mine.

A year later I was back in the library with the *Writers' & Artists' Yearbook*, following its advice about covering letters and synopses (much better advice than the, often American, tips I'd seen online) for what turned out to be my first published novel.

I would have been lost without *Writers' & Artists' Yearbook* to guide me, and I'm delighted there is now this *Children's Writers' & Artists' Yearbook*. It's a wonderful resource – it's *the* resource for writers.

Sally Green is the author of an internationally acclaimed trilogy of young adult fantasy novels, *Half Bad* (2014), *Half Wild* (2015) and *Half Lost* (2016), published by Penguin. *Half Bad* (2014), which was Sally's debut novel, was named Waterstones Best Book for Teenagers 2015 and was shortlisted for the YA Book Prize 2015 and for the 2015 Branford Boase Award. Sally's latest fantasy series published by Penguin includes, *The Smoke Thieves* (2018), *The Demon World* (2019) and *The Burning Kingdoms* (2020).

See also...
• *Writing for teens*, page 277

How do you do it?

After more than two decades as a published author William Sutcliffe has only one answer to the often-asked question 'How do you do it?'. He shares the most important piece of advice he has to offer and reminds writers to enjoy every step of the long journey they are embarking upon.

In the 24 years that I have been writing and publishing books I have been to scores of literary events, both as a speaker and an audience member. If I had to agglomerate all the questions I've heard put to authors into one overarching meta-question, it would be this: 'How do you do it?'. Sadly, my agglomerated meta-answer to that question would have to be 'I don't know.' Every published writer frequently gets asked for advice, and most of them have only one truly essential tip to offer: buy the *Writers' & Artists' Yearbook*. The key turning point in every professional writer's life is when writing shifts from being a hobby or a dream into a source of income. For making that transition, this book is the Bible.

To get published, you don't have to know someone; you don't have to know someone who knows someone; you don't have to live in Hampstead; and you don't need a degree in English literature. You do, however, need to understand that publishing is a business and that, like every other business, it operates in a way that seems obvious and transparent to insiders, but is opaque and confusing to outsiders. This is what makes the *Writers' & Artists' Yearbook* an essential reference book for everyone who hopes to make a living as a writer. Trying to get published without it is like setting off on a hike without a map.

When put to a writer, the question 'How do you do it?' can mean two things. If it means 'How do you get published?', you are holding the answer in your hands right now. Not everyone who hopes to find a publisher will achieve that, not by a long shot, but if you want to give your work in progress the best possible chance of finding an agent and ultimately a publisher, all the answers you need are right here. Of course, the other thing that question often means is 'How do you write a good book?'; and for that one, there are no clear-cut answers. Moreover, when it comes to key questions such as getting started, editing, plotting, characterisation and getting unstuck when you are stuck, for every writer there is a different solution. There is a right and a wrong way to make a submission to an agent; there isn't a right and a wrong way to write a novel. Everyone finds their own method.

The fascinating essays in this volume contain a wealth of experience from many of Britain's finest children's authors. You will find Jacqueline Wilson on 20 years of perseverance before her big breakthrough; J.K. Rowling on rejection letters; Michael Rosen analysing who children's writers write for; and many more fascinating pieces. None of these essays will tell you how to write like those authors, but they will open your thoughts onto how you should write – how to get your personality onto the page; how to tell a unique story in an original way; how to navigate your own path through the craft of writing. These essays are the second-best resource there is for hearing the secrets of good children's writing. The best resource, of course, is the novels themselves.

Read them. Read them once as a reader, then again as a writer – which is to say with the eyes of a hyena. Pull the books to pieces. Think about the word choices, the structure, the characterisation, the pacing, the world-building. Read the books you love ruthlessly and critically. Read the books you don't love in the same way, and hone your sense of where your literary taste sits. There is no objective scale of good and bad. You need to make your own. This gimlet-eyed reading is essential, because only when you have done it to others will you be able to do it to your own prose. To write for children you have to tap into a playfulness in your imagination, but when it comes to editing and rewriting you have to be brutal. Any word or sentence that isn't doing a useful job has to go.

This book is filled with practical and creative advice for writers at every stage of a writing career, but I would like to leave you with the simplest and most important advice there is: enjoy it. When you write, pour yourself into the work. Think of the blank page not as a scary place but as a path to freedom. Writing can take you anywhere. If you really apply yourself to the task, whether you get published or not, that journey will be worthwhile.

William Sutcliffe writes for adults, young adults and children and is the author of 12 novels, including three titles in his *Circus of Thieves* series, published by Simon & Schuster Children's: *Circus of Thieves and the Raffle of Doom* (2014), *Circus of Thieves on the Rampage* (2015) and *Circus of Thieves and the Comeback Caper* (2016). His YA books are *The Wall* (2014) which was shortlisted for the CILIP Carnegie Medal, *Concentr8* (2016), shortlisted for the YA Book Prize, *We See Everything* (2017), *The Gifted, The Talented and Me* (2019) and *The Summer We Turned Green* (2021), all published by Bloomsbury. William's novels for adults include the international bestseller *Are You Experienced?* (Hamish Hamilton 1997), *New Boy* (Penguin 1996), *Bad Influence* (Hamish Hamilton 2004) and *Whatever Makes You Happy* (Bloomsbury 2008), which was adapted into a Netflix film with the new title, *Otherhood*, in 2019. He is also a screenwriter. His work has been translated into 28 languages. Follow him on Twitter @Will_Sutcliffe8.

A jobbing writer's lot

Joanna Nadin describes the challenges, rewards, satisfaction and financial sense of taking on a variety of work, in different genres and for different ages, in order to make a successful and creative living from writing.

Nineteen years ago, I was called into the office of my soon-to-be agent, Sarah Molloy – an agent I'd found in the pages of the *Writers' & Artists' Yearbook*, a dog-eared and annotated copy from our local library. There, in a small, book-lined office, at the top of a skew-whiff staircase on St Martin's Lane in London, I was given two sage, salient pieces of advice: (1) don't cut off your hair, and (2) don't give up your day job until your advance is three times your salary.

The first I ignored and had my Shirley Temple curls shaved defiantly short. The second I have followed doggedly, and it has served me well. Firstly, it has kept me financially safe. I was working in politics at the time and, though hardly in the higher echelons, paid comfortably enough that no advance to this date has ever come close to one year's salary. Secondly, it denied me false hope, which I fear is all too prevalent in a world whose stock-in-trade is fiction and fairy tales.

What Sarah said made it patently clear to me that, if I wanted to make a living from writing, banking all my hopes on one big hitter was a fool's errand. For one thing, those deals are almost as rare as a ticket to a chocolate factory. For another, if they are laid on the table they may turn out to be a poisoned chalice, piling on pressure that a new and possibly novice writer doesn't need: if you don't earn your advance out, your publisher may view you as a disappointment. On top of which, the next advance, if you get one, is almost certain to be a lot smaller.

Debut novelists can be particularly prone to these 'golden hellos'; who wouldn't turn down a life-changing cheque, after all? But what I have found is that it can pay, in the long run, to work on building a reputation as a reliable freelancer. 'Be good, be nice, be on time,' I was once told by another clever fellow. And that is exactly what I try to be – working with both my agents (my style and savings adviser Sarah retired eventually) to find a variety of work that keeps me busy, and keeps the big, bad wolf from the door.

I write for all ages – from picture book up to adult – and across genres too. Alongside my own original trade fiction, I write for specialist publishers on school reading programmes, conjuring up exciting adventures for early readers or retelling traditional tales with a contemporary twist. These deals are often arranged by the publishers directly with authors (usually those who have worked with them on trade titles) rather than through agents, but they are also something I ask to be actively put forward for by my agent. They do usually require working within strict subject guidelines and to strict word counts – sometimes as few as 50 words – and with limited lexicons as well. I see this not simply as a challenge, but also as an opportunity to help hone my storytelling and make it spare and succinct – a skill that can be put to excellent use elsewhere. On top of which, while initial advances for these deals are low, if there are royalties in the contract, these can mount up quickly as books are sold in class-size packs and around the world, meaning you earn out fast and earn several times your advance within five years.

Thanks to a Finnish publishing deal that brought me to the attention of a games company out there, I've written tie-in novels under another name. These are on a flat fee basis, and were agreed after a synopsis and sample chapters met approval. But these hoops proved worth it for me, financially and creatively. While, again, this can mean your characters are already painted and your parameters set before you even begin to think about plot (since the people and world you're being paid to play with is likely to have featured in prequels, a film, a TV series or, as in my case, a gaming app), I saw this as an opportunity to be freed of that part of the process.

I ghostwrite, too, working on a ten-book fiction series with the Olympian Sir Chris Hoy – a collaboration that has inspired and stretched my imagination, as I've helped to bring someone else's distinct vision and mission to life. Aimed at 5-8 year-olds, the *Flying Fergus* series (Piccadilly) has been a process of intense toing and froing between Chris and I as we conjure up the ideas, bringing our editor in once I've sketched them out on paper. Working in this way requires you to park your ego to an even greater extent than the usual editorial process, accepting that you may not even get your own darlings in the text in the first place to kill them off! But it is enormously rewarding, and having someone else come up with storylines in such a long-running series is almost a relief.

I also co-wrote the YA novel *Everybody Hurts* (Atom 2017) with Anthony McGowan, each of us taking one side of the story and playing ping-pong with chapters in a giant game of consequences. This requires patience – again, an effacing of one's own ego – as well as the ability to handle a complete curveball, when your partner decides to take the tale not just left-field but completely out of the park!

Finally, I've written three-minute-long TV scripts for puppet worms, presenting the links between programmes on the kids' TV channel Nickelodeon. The invention required to bring to life all-singing, all-dancing, but ultimately armless annelids is not to be underestimated.

I am, to all extents and purposes, a writer for hire, willing and able to turn my hand to most things. It helps, of course, that I have a background in journalism and politics. Not only did these worlds teach me to write tight copy to tighter deadlines, they also taught me never to work for nothing, and that writers' block is a luxury afforded only to those who don't use words to pay their bills. That's not to say writing isn't sometimes difficult, but it is never impossible.

The relative anonymity of my past employment has also served to satisfy me that these books aren't in some way worth less because they're series, or because my name isn't on the cover. They still allow me to flex my writing muscle, to show off (and, importantly, improve) my skills, and to plunder the soup of story that swirls in my head. This approach hasn't precluded commercial or critical success either. There have been awards, TV deals, places on bestseller lists, if only for a week or two.

Eighty-seven books later, and I'm still not J.K. Rowling or Jacqueline Wilson; you may not even have heard of me. But, do you know what? That's fine. Because, for the last decade, I've earned a living doing what I love – which is a rare privilege in itself.

Working like this does have its drawbacks – you have to be disciplined, organised and able to multitask, including switching between stories on a daily basis at times. And I still haven't entirely given up the day job, at least for one day a week. While I am passionate about publishing, it is a precarious profession and, besides, I am as happy writing scripts and speeches as I am short series or standalone thrillers. I also now hold a PhD in Creative Writing, I lecture on the acclaimed Masters course at Bath Spa University, I give workshops at festivals and events around the country, I visit schools. In other words, I have made words – rather than one or two books – my career. A career that allows me to spend days, weeks, months on end exploring new worlds, playing dress up and let's pretend, trying on new lives for size.

I am a jobbing writer, and I can't think of a better way to live.

Joanna Nadin worked as a journalist and in politics before becoming an award-winning writer. She has written more than 80 books for children, teenagers and adults including the Carnegie-nominated YA novel *Joe All Alone* (Little, Brown 2015), which is now a BAFTA-winning and Emmy-nominated BBC drama series. Joanna is also a senior lecturer in creative writing at University of Bristol. Her latest book for adults is *The Talk of Pram Town* (Mantle 2021), and her latest book for children is the third instalment in *The Worst Class in the World* series (Bloomsbury 2020). For more information visit her website https://joannanadin.com. Find her on Facebook @joannanadinauthor and Twitter @joannanadin.

Writing and translating children's fiction

Clémentine Beauvais explains the special satisfaction, pleasure and value to be found in translation, with its concentrated focus on language. She urges all writers to use translation to develop and re-energise their reading and writing skills.

This article is about writing children's fiction and translating children's fiction, and the peculiar kinds of pleasure and knowledge that arise when you do both. Let's start by stating the obvious: there shouldn't be any stark distinction between 'writing' and 'translating' children's fiction. Translating is an act of writing. Some translators actually prefer to call themselves 'writers of translations'. As Kate Briggs puts it beautifully, translated texts 'come to us twice-written'. Aren't we lucky, as readers of translations, that not just *one*, but *two* writers, gave their time and applied their talent to that text?

I was a children's writer long before I became a literary translator, and these days I spend roughly half of my time doing 'my' writing and half of my time translating – namely, redoing someone else's writing. Many people are surprised that I would choose to halve what they see as my 'real writing' time, a thought which you could well translate as: 'Surely translation is something you only do when you can't *really* write?'

My view, of course, is that you should translate only if you can *really* write. And only if you can *really* read. And the more you do it, the more it transforms your writing and reading. I want to convince you that if you wish to be a writer, you should *absolutely* write translations. Even if you don't speak another language fluently. Even though it will never bring you fame or money. Even if no one ever reads your translations. Translate. Do it for yourself, for your writing. Do it as a secret pleasure. Do it as a way of learning to write and read better. Here's why.

Translating is writing, rewriting and rewiring your writing

Translating forces you to focus on language, and only on language. I shiver to write this, because of course there's no such thing as 'only' language: it is literally the *only* stuff literature is made of. But when you write a whole novel, you need to keep a million things in mind at the same time: narrative structure, characterisation, audience considerations, chapter length, ideological aspects, the logistics of seriality. And that's even before the editorial dance starts.

When you're translating, you have one task: language. The story's in place, the characters are there; you have a global view of them, in their finished form. Your task is to focus on the words, and to make sure that, in the target language, each of them does the job of propping up this whole fictional world. By 'each of them' I do mean each word, and this is why translating is close to the purest kind of writing: rarely in one's writerly life does one get the luxury of 'angsting' so much over every single word. You think about every word at least twice – in the source language, and in the target one – when the equivalence is obvious. But it seldom is. So you think of each word many times. It is precision work, a series of micro-decisions, adjusting and tweaking language. That's your only job and it's a colossal one.

Doing so will show you two things that are crucial to developing your writing. Firstly: you are never an expert in your native language. All my qualms about writing in English collapsed when I realised I was working from an erroneous assumption – that I knew French. French fails me just as often as English does. We can never write perfectly in any language, nor even approach perfection. Those little failures of language, of any language, are literature.

Secondly: translating changes your writing by forcing you out of your writerly reflexes. My writerly self is lazy. There are certain character types, certain places, certain genres or certain voices it doesn't write because it can't be bothered to venture out of its comfort zone. And my writerly self is ignorant – it doesn't write about things it doesn't know. My translating self cannot afford such whimsicality. It needs to write a text full of those things my writerly self usually avoids or simply doesn't know about. When I translated Sarah Crossan's *Moonrise* (Bloomsbury Children's 2017), I had to write a whole novel about the American prison system; I ended up having, effectively, written it. I never knew anything about it before; I have now learnt not just facts but a way of writing them. Translating is one of the most enlightening acts of writing you can do, because it forces you into the writerly reflexes and comfort zones of someone else.

And it changes your writing, of course, because there's no way you can survive the experience and not acquire new practices, a new way of looking at structure, at character, at style. It inspires you and re-energises your writing. It gives you a glimpse of what your writing-from-scratch could be like if you tried out something entirely different.

Translating is reading, rereading and learning to read

At the same time, translating is also an act of reading – arguably one of the most reverent, attentive and generous acts of reading. I was, so to speak, a professional reader before I became a translator – as an academic specialising in children's fiction – and those skills are evidently useful when reading-for-translation; it's helpful to be able to notice and name the literary devices, and know roughly what the equivalent ones would be in the other language. For instance, I know that an iambic pentameter in English is like the French twelve-footed alexandrin; both are the classic, solemn rhythms at which the hearts of those cultures beat.

Those reading skills, however, are activated not just for analysis and description, but in close relation with writerly decisions. If I'm looking for equivalence of *effect*, the TaDAM TaDAM TaDAM TaDAM TaDAM of my English iambic pentameter could become the tadadadadaDAM tadadadadaDAM of the French alexandrin. It is equivalently lulling, pleasant and familiar. But wait – perhaps I want my French reader to feel that English beat, to be slightly puzzled by that poetic rhythm from beyond the sea? And there I'll wrench my French into an awkward five-footed line.

I decide. I'm in charge. When you're reading-for-translation, you're exercising your critical reading skills and making that interpretation matter for writing. Thus translating teaches you a special kind of reading practice. You read with the eyes of a critic and a creator. Of course, all writers should read as widely as possible in their chosen genres and beyond, but when we say this we generally mean that they should do this for their own edification and/or for pleasure. Reading for translation adjusts a different kind of lens to your readerly eye; this is active reading, in the sense of reading activated by the writing that must come next.

So when I translated Meg Rosoff's minuscule novel *Moose Baby* (Barrington Stoke 2013), I needed to understand how she packed so much humour in so little space, and it was a free lesson in the mechanics of humour in literature. I learned to spot exactly where funny dwells, at the level of sentence, paragraph, page. But it was no academic exercise; none of this would have mattered unless I also thought about where to reinject that humour in the French rewriting. This is more than close reading – it's intimate reading: you reread the same sentence many times, holding in your head analytical considerations of literary devices, writerly considerations of effect and your own sensitivity as a reader. In so doing, you learn to read better, and more precisely, as you start to develop a sense for the composition and aesthetics of even the tiniest units of text.

So go away and translate

So please: go away and translate. If you're lucky enough to have another language, use it for your writing. Write translations. Pick a book you love in the other language and translate it into your own. Not for money, not for networking, not for any kind of profitability as measured by normal standards. No one will thank you for it; you probably won't be paid for it. But it will teach you so much about reading and writing. It will teach you the amazing focus on language that only translating can afford – the aesthetic epiphanies brought about by the most minute of tweaks; the fact that so much in a good piece of literature depends on the right word; character, plot and the way words pull them in this direction or that. The intense attention to words is a lesson you'll never learn better than when translating.

If you are unlucky enough to be monolingual, learn another language. I'm serious – do it. How can you claim to see what your own language can do if you can't watch it from the vantage point of another? All writers, if they really care about words and language – which is the stuff their work is made of, and therefore a professional requirement – should yearn to feel that estrangement, that distancing which brings understanding, knowledge and the destabilising sense that you can't say everything in your own language.

Careful – I'm not saying 'go away and become bilingual'. Fun fact: not all translators are fluent in the languages they translate *from*. Many can't actually hold a conversation. Translating is an act of writing and reading, not dazzling everyone with your perfect accent. Anyway, even bilinguals don't speak two languages perfectly. Even monolinguals don't speak their one language perfectly. Learn another language precisely, *because you'll never speak it perfectly.*

Start small. Pick up a picture book in whatever language you did at school, ages ago. Translate a few lines, painstakingly, using dictionaries and the internet. From that ugly literal translation, make a beautiful literary one. There you go. It's at the same time much more and much less difficult than it sounds.

People are awed by translators because they think 'they're really good at languages', whereas they should really be awed by thinking 'they're really good at writing'. You're good at writing, and that's all that matters: go and write translations. The more you do it, the more you'll develop that superpower and the better you'll write and the better you'll read. And one day you, too, will join that underground league of people who secretly think: 'Hey, writers. We know our stuff ... *and* yours. Here we are, in your writing, taking your words, making them our words. No one's read you like we have. No one's rewritten you like we have. You are mine now.'

Clémentine Beauvais is a Senior Lecturer in English in Education at the University of York. She is also a writer for children and young adults in French, and a literary translator from English to French. Her books written in English include the *Sesame Seade Mysteries* series (Holiday House), *The Royal Babysitters* series (Bloomsbury Children's), *Piglettes* (Pushkin Press 2017, self-translated from the French) and *In Paris With You* (Wednesday Books 2019, translated by Sam Taylor). Her translation of J.K. Rowling's children's book, *The Ickabog*, was published in French as *L'Ickabog* (Gallimard 2020). She is also the French translator of Sarah Crossan, Elizabeth Acevedo and some works by Meg Rosoff. For more information visit www.clementinebeauvais.com/eng.

Writing for different genres and markets

Writing books to read aloud

Bestselling author Anne Fine looks at why and how books are read aloud to children.

The first thing to say about writing books to read aloud is that they should be as much of a pleasure to read alone silently as any other story. Indeed, at first it's difficult to see where any differences might lie. Certainly when it comes to stories for the very young we tend to have a picture in our heads of the exhausted parent inviting the child to 'clean your teeth, hop into bed, and I'll read you a story'. And since all days are long for a parent, nobody wants their offspring to be worked into a frenzy all over again. So, in the classic bedtime stories for the younger child, there's very often a softer humour and a gentler tone, and a satisfactory and fulfilling ending.

And for the older child, there often isn't.

So, same old story really. No rules (or having to face the fact that rules appear to be there only for some other writer to irritate you intensely by making a fortune breaking them). But there are always the basic guidelines.

Keep things as simple as they can be for your particular story. With picture books you can of course assume that the child is propped up beside the reader, sharing each illustration as it comes along. But by the time the child is six, maybe they would prefer to snuggle down and shut their eyes to listen. So do you really have to take half a dozen sentences to describe the rigging, and the number and nature of the sails, and exactly how the ship was armed? Couldn't you just refer to it as 'the most magnificent galleon that ever sailed the seas' and leave it at that? After all, if those cannon ever come to be fired, we'll hear about it later.

Listeners are easily distracted. One minute they're all ears; the next, they're actually more interested in tracking the progress of a fly across the ceiling. Of course they're not going to admit they've lost the thread of the story, in case the parent snatches the opportunity to suggest they're too tired to listen and makes for the door, or the teacher decides it's time to move on to the workbooks. But their attention does stray. So it is best to try (as ever) to order your tale so you can start at the beginning and move on in sequence, steering clear of flashbacks.

On this matter of keeping things simple, does it sound mad to say that plots can be overrated? And never more so than in books designed to be read aloud to the young. In my own very short chapter book, *It Moved!*, Lily takes a stone in for Show and Tell and claims it sometimes moves, and we just get to see who in the class believes her and who doesn't, and how they all react over a day of watching it. In the *Stories of Jamie and Angus*, Jamie is an amiable child of about four in a perfectly normal household. His favourite soft toy is a little Aberdeen Angus bull. In the first story, Angus ends up in the washing machine when he's supposed to be 'dry clean only'. In another, the pair sort out the books in their bedroom according to their own rather strange shelving preferences. In yet another, they do little more than draw 'angry eggs'. The stories almost couldn't be more plain and domestic, and yet we still run through joy, misery, jealousy, anxiety, distress, fear, empathy, generosity, self-sacrifice, fury, resentment – the entire mercurial gamut of preschool emotions. So do be confident that, especially for the very young, a tremendous amount can be forged from what seems, at first sight, not very much at all. With writing – just as with practically everything else in life – it's not what you do but the way that you do it.

Children, like adults, have to *care* about what's being read. We adults tend to ask the 'Can I be *bothered* with these people?' question before returning a book, half-read, to the library. It's a test even harder to pass when you're writing for young ones. Remember Robert Browning:

If you want your songs to last
Base them on the human heart

because children love to identify with someone or something in the story – it doesn't really matter what. It could be another child, or a puppy, or even a lost pebble. But they do have to care. So perhaps it's best to make sure that, all the way through, your listener knows what your character (or puppy, or pebble) is feeling. And make sure that these are thoughts and emotions they will recognise. A child of six isn't 'disappointed that the weather is unpleasant'. It's all far more immediate. He feels the tears pricking because his socks are wet and his woolly hat is itching and his coat's too tight under his armpits. Ever heard them moan?

Joan Aiken once remarked that anyone who writes for the young 'should, ideally, be a dedicated semi-lunatic'. But you can go too far. The problem is one of differing – and shifting – levels of sophistication. What makes one child hoot with laughter will cause another to sneer, and there is in any case an entirely undefinable line between cashing in on a child's acceptance of the unlikely or the magical, and offering them something they think of as simply being 'stupid'. You might, for example, get away with the idea that the horse the child rescued from its cruel owner is being secretly kept in the garage, only to find your young readers baulking at the suggestion that Mum could walk in to fetch a screwdriver and not even notice it.

Avoid being arch. Of course there are differing levels at which many shared books can be read. The older reader often gets a sly chuckle out of things that sail right over the head of somebody smaller. But the joke does usually have to be at least potentially inclusive, so that, the tenth time around, out comes the thumb, down comes the chubby hand to stop you turning the page, and out comes the question: 'Daddy was just teasing them, really, wasn't he?' 'Mum *really* wanted to get back to reading the paper, didn't she?' In the benighted language of the National Curriculum, the child's already 'drawing inferences from text' (or, as we used to call it back in the good old days, 'reading').

Does it help to read your work aloud to children to see how it goes down? Not really, no. For one thing most children are notoriously polite and gentle with people they love, or strangers who come into class. And the sheer joy of having their opinions canvassed can send them haywire. One says, 'I liked this bit!' You beam, and all the other hands shoot up. 'I liked that bit!' 'And I liked that bit!' Everyone wants to have a go at the pleasure of shouting out to the visitor.

So trust your own judgement. You are the writer, after all. Try reading it aloud to an imaginary son or daughter or class. You'll soon notice which bits you're rushing through because they're tiresome, and which of the sentences you're tripping over because they're too clumsy or long. You'll realise that, yes, you *can* put that rather ambitious word into a story for four year-olds because the very context and the way in which it will be read out will make its meaning transparent.

Are there some subjects best avoided in books to be shared between adults and children? Again, it's hard to say. Some parents will read anything the child demands. Others, like teachers, will beach up on things like 'pottymouth' poetry ('Well, *you* just said bogey! And you just said poo *twice*!'). Or books that appear to encourage the child to relish – or, worse, be amused by – cruelty and the infliction of pain. I watched as at least 30 parents with small children trooped out of a book fair when one enthusiastic author read out a passage from one of his history books about red hot pokers being driven up people's bottoms. (I wondered, frankly, why the others stayed.) He may justifiably argue that he's sold hundreds of thousands of copies, but I would guess that few of them have been read aloud by squeamish parents to imaginative children before the lights go out. So use your sense.

What about *how* a book is read aloud? Should that make a difference to how you write it? I don't see how it can. After all, some readers treat the words in the old-fashioned way, and simply speak them with intelligence and inflections sympathetic to the meaning. They read, in short, as if it were a *book*. Others go half-mad, acting out every sentence, doing all the voices in different accents, shouting the yells and whispering the quiet bits. They treat the pages in front of them pretty well as a script for a stage performance. Like every other author whose work has been professionally recorded, I've shuddered through one actor's butchering of my work with his frantic showing off, and also been startled to find tears pricking as another has used her skills to mine a poignancy I had forgotten about or never even realised was there. It's their own voice that most writers hear in their head as they put down the words, so go along with that.

And that's the root of all writing, when it comes down to it. Your own voice. Children are strange. Ralph Waldo Emerson defined them as 'curly dimpled lunatics'. They assume that they're immortal. (Why else do adults have to step in so smartly and often, simply to keep them alive?) And children are at one with eternity. (When did you last see a nine-year-old glance at a clock and say, 'My God! It's three already! And I've got nothing done!') Their lives may change immeasurably. See how the language of their stories has moved so seamlessly over the centuries from tumbledown cottages in dark forests, through secret gardens and kind governesses, to the babysitter and the stepbrother. But in their essential nature – however individual and various those natures may be – children have barely changed at all.

So the successful children's authors will always be those who can best make their work chime in with the child's capacity to understand and enjoy it. And since, like Walt Whitman, all children 'contain multitudes', that gives the writer enormous scope to get it very, very wrong or very, very right.

Anne Fine OBE, FRSL is one of the best-known and most popular writers for children of all ages and was Children's Laureate 2001–3. She has twice won both the Carnegie Medal and the Whitbread Children's Book of the Year Award and at the Galaxy British Book Awards has twice been voted Children's Author of the Year. She has also won the *Guardian* Children's Fiction Prize and dozens of other awards in the UK and abroad. Her work is translated into more than 45 languages. Her latest book for older readers is *Aftershocks* (Old Barn Books 2022) and for younger readers is *Scared of a Rainbow* (Collins Big Cat 2022). Anne also writes for adults. Her website is www.annefine.co.uk.

Finding new readers and markets

Tom Palmer shows how, by seeking out unexpected working partnerships, a children's author can open up mutually rewarding and productive markets and draw in new young readers.

I have managed to make a living as a full-time children's author for 14 years. As everyone who has tried it knows, it is not easy to earn enough money to live on from being a writer. You're forever in fear. Forever asking yourself questions … How long will people want to buy your books? Will school events dry up as finances tighten and the political landscape changes? There is little respite, even if you are living the dream. Which I am.

That's why I spend a lot of time trying to think of ways I can attract interest to my books, so that people will continue to buy and borrow them. And so schools will keep paying me to visit. One of the most successful ways I have found to do this is to *give*.

Looking for partnerships

There are a lot of organisations, charities and companies who would benefit from working with a children's author. But who are they? What can you give them? And, what can they give you? I have developed relationships with several organisations – large and small – giving and taking. In partnership. As a result of those partnerships, I have boosted my longevity as a children's author.

Each partnership is different and each evolves in its own unpredictable way. But it usually starts with a series of questions that I ask myself, and which I suggest you ask *yourself*. Here is a plan of action:

- Think about what you've written. List subjects, settings, themes, ideas. And dig deep. Text your friends and family. Your readers. Ask them what *they* think you write about.
- Now look at your list. Are there natural partners for your work? (For instance, Beatrix Potter might have chosen the RSPCA, a pet shop chain or *Animals & You* magazine. Or she might not.)

> ### How to approach potential partners
> 1 The more you know about the possible partner the better. That includes researching the right person to contact.
> 2 Offer to do as much of the set-up and admin work as you can. They are likely to be under massive time-pressure with their job already.
> 3 When you meet for the first time, try to make it open and creative. Set it up as a thinking/sharing session, not just a blast of ideas from you.
> 4 You probably have to be willing to give first, to do stuff for free to demonstrate that your partnership could help them. Then, as your relationship evolves, the balance will tip back in your favour.

- Suss out one or more partners whose work is linked to what you write about. Again, stretch it. Brainstorm; be creative. Have ideas that are stupid. Cross them out. Have more. There might be one that fits.
- Think carefully about those potential partners. Go to their website. Watch them. What do they do? What do they want to achieve? Can you help them?
- Now think about what you could ask for from *them*. How can they help you to promote your books? Or, how can your link with them help you to promote your books?

Case studies

Over the last decade I have worked successfully with the RAF Museums, England Rugby, the Premier League, Divine Chocolate, Leeds Schools Library Service, Leeds United, the

Anne Frank Trust and many others. Below are three different examples. They could help you see how to identify suitable partners that fit the writing and themes of your own books.

Fair trade chocolate

I was writing a book about football and fair trade for Puffin. It's called *Off Side* and includes storylines relating to the trafficking of young African footballers and to fair-trade cocoa bean farming. I needed help to write it. A lot of help. From people who knew about football and chocolate in Africa.

So I did a bit of research. In fact, my wife did. She came up with Divine Chocolate who work with fair-trade farmers so that the likes of us can give them a fair wage for what they farm. I identified the Right to Dream football academy in Ghana. They look after gifted young child footballers and help protect them from being exploited by corrupt football agents. I contacted both, suggesting that I could help raise awareness of what they do. Could they explain it to me? Could they help me research and write a meaningful book? They said they could.

I went to Ghana at my own expense. I saw everything I needed to see. It was amazing. When I got home I promoted Divine and Right to Dream and the great work they do through writing my story. And my book continues to sell well because it was properly researched and I knew what I was talking about. Job done.

But relationships evolve. When *Off Side* was published, Divine wanted me to tell the story of how fair trade makes a difference. They gave me a PowerPoint. I used it as part of my talk in schools. I did this for free, of course. But it enhanced my school events, made them more meaningful. As a result, more schools wanted to book me to go in and talk to their pupils, meaning my book became better known in schools with fair-trade status and beyond. More book sales. More paid school events. And the raising of awareness of very important issues.

Ask yourself:
– *Does my book deal with an issue or a cause?*
– *Which charity or campaign group might be interested in working with me?*
– *How can I help that cause through my book and events?*

The Royal Air Force

I was writing a series about children going back in time to fly famous RAF aeroplanes. I approached three organisations to ask if they'd like to work with me. Two did not reply. The RAF Museums did.

The RAF Museums have some amazing artefacts in their collections at Hendon and Cosford: tiny kite-like planes from the First World War; terrifying giants like the Vulcan bomber. But the RAF Museums are always looking for ways to bring those planes to life. For ways to tell the story behind them, and about the men and women who flew them. That was what they needed. A way of telling more stories. That's what I could give.

I volunteered to do a school event for them for free, to see if we could work together. It was a success, and they offered to pay me for the next one. Six months later, they had a new exhibition called 'First World War in the Air'. They asked me how we could work together to tell a story about the pilots. One of their exhibits is of the possessions of a 19-year-old pilot, Kevin Furniss, who was killed on his second sortie. His gloves. His shaving equipment. His Bible. His pipe. Letters home. These items were poignant enough on their own, but I suggested writing a story about Furniss using those objects before his fateful flight. The museum then used the story in schools to attract visitors. And I was paid for the story.

Now I am the museum's Children's Writer in Residence. I do four school and public events a year for them, based around the three important planes from their collections that I have since – with their help – written books about: the Sopwith Camel; the Spitfire; and the Eurofighter Typhoon. My book is on sale in their shops. They promote my events and books to the many RAF and aeroplane interest groups that they work with. We bring schools into their museum and run writing workshops based around their aircraft and artefacts.

Ask yourself:
– *Is there subject matter in my books that relates to a museum, gallery, festival, interest group?*
– *Which ones should I research and what might they be interested in from me?*
– *How could I or my book help them?*
– *Can we work together?*

England Rugby

I had a trilogy of rugby stories published in 2015 by Barrington Stoke (*Rugby Academy: Combat Zone*; *Rugby Academy: Dead Locked*; and *Rugby Academy: Surface to Air*). We timed their publication to tie in with the Rugby World Cup, hosted in the UK that year.

I contacted the education people at England Rugby, the RFU, in the hope that I could apply for money to create literacy interventions. With the RFU as a partners, I'd have a good chance. I suggested that the RFU and I apply for money to tour an event at the library near each of the 13 Rugby World Cup venues. I also suggested a set of literacy resources linking rugby to reading for pleasure and writing. And I said that I could write a live story to be read in schools as the Rugby World Cup was on. Would they be interested?

They were. My ideas met their needs because the RFU are keen to get into schools. They want to use the interest in the game to encourage children to read and write. They want to spread the culture of their five core values. And they want to start more rugby teams in schools to help create players for the future. So they offered to pay for it all direct, with no need to apply for funding.

I now work regularly with the RFU, performing events, creating resources and writing stories that they publish on their website. This has led to my *Rugby Academy* series becoming very well-known in rugby circles. Which goes a long way to explaining how all three sold out their advance within a year of publication.

Ask yourself:
– *Is there an activity or interest at the centre or on the margins of my book?*
– *Does a national or regional body administer that interest?*
– *Who can I work with? Who would be interested in my book?*

Working with partners has been a massive boon for my career. If I had not sought out those partners, I think that my full-time writing career may well have ground to a halt. In addition, I have been able to promote the joys of reading for pleasure to children and families I might not have reached without the help of those partners. And that is deeply satisfying and very much on my agenda. One downside could be that – in always working with partners – I am a slave to *their* agenda. I try to overcome that by making sure the books I write with partners always meet whatever my obsession of the moment is. Also, the good money I make from working with partners buys me time to write other work that is 100% what I want to do.

Tom Palmer is the author of 56 books for children. He has been published by Puffin, Barrington Stoke and others. *Foul Play* was shortlisted for the 2008 Blue Peter Book Award. His recent books, *Armistice Runner* (2018), *After the War* (2020) and *Arctic Star* (2021), were each nominated for the Carnegie Medal. *Armistice Runner* (2018) and *D-Day Dog* (2019) both won the UK Children's Book Award in 2019 and 2020. Tom is Children's Writer in Residence at the RAF Museum and Leeds United FC. Tom was awarded the Ruth Rendell Award for his contribution to literacy in 2019. Find out more at http://tompalmer.co.uk, and follow him on Twitter @tompalmerauthor.

The learning curve: writing for the children's educational market

Rachel Bladon shares her experience of writing children's educational books and describes the appeal and value of this sector, with its broad range of content and skills, and the satisfying creative challenges and rewards it offers a writer.

Any kind of children's writing involves putting yourself in a young person's shoes and viewing the world through their eyes – that is one of the key attractions and challenges of working for this age group. But for writers like me, who are pitching our stories at the educational rather than trade market, there are quite a lot of extra considerations to take on board. It's not just a question of how old your readers are likely to be, but also what level they are working at, what kind of setting they are learning in, and above all, if you write for international markets, where in the world they are.

Children's educational publishing takes many forms. There are textbooks for every subject in UK schools, of course, plus a multitude of extra resources in print, digital and audio format; and, as any parent who's had to support their child with reading will know, there's also an abundance of literacy schemes out there. Then there's the home-learning market, and the sector I have ended up in: ELT (English Language Teaching) publishing, with its vast array of materials for the world's 1.5 billion English language learners.

The appeal of the role

Having your name on a textbook probably doesn't give quite the same hit a writer gets from seeing their lovingly crafted children's story make its way onto the shelves of a bookshop. But for me, this highly market-driven kind of publishing has always had a draw. I'd started out as a writer of information books with a well-known children's publisher, and it was a fun and vibrant place to work. I would sit at my desk writing a children's guide to beginner's German, of which I spoke not a word, while colleagues around me emerged occasionally from heaps of wool, crepe paper, straws and plasticine to write the next spread of a bestselling craft guide or a children's book on science experiments. I loved making a living from crafting words, surrounded by a buzz of creativity, but there was something missing for me in this desk-based existence, and in the broadness and freedom of the brief – which amounted to whatever notes you scribbled down during a short, white-knuckled meeting at the start of every project with the formidably capricious director, in his office on the top floor.

When I became aware of the thriving publishing industry that exists around ELT, something I'd got a qualification in and spent a year earning money from in France when fresh out of university, I realized I'd found something that really appealed to me. What better than travelling the world (and I really did), observing classes, talking to teachers and trying to get under the skin of a different country's education system, then coming home and writing books that would one day be used in those classrooms to help children learn English and thus access a wider world? I became an editor in children's ELT publishing at first, so not officially writing – but the authors of the books I was editing were often teachers with a reputation in their respective countries who had little writing experience, so there was always a lot of rewriting involved. Once I had a family and decided to go freelance, it was easy to make the hop across from editing into actually writing myself. I've always relished, and still do, the many different elements of my role: needing to understand the particular market I'm writing for; applying a particular methodology to the structure of the material; and researching and creating a wide range of content – from topical texts about issues of the moment, 'realia' (concocted newspaper articles, etc used to expose learners to 'real English') and self-contained stories to activities, exercises and tests, as well as scripts for audio and video (and now, of course, digital) components. And then there's the visual side: with the complexity of a textbook and its many constituent parts, the design is absolutely key, so collaborating closely with designers, artists, picture researchers and photographers is an essential part of the job.

Cultural sensitivities

As an ELT author and xenophile, one of the things I love most about writing for international markets is what you learn about the different cultures you are tailoring your materials for. There was a furore in the British press a few years ago when it was unearthed that we in the ELT world abide by a code of taboos called PARSNIPs, which denotes the various things we avoid at all times in our writing: Politics, Alcohol, Religion, Sex, Narcotics, 'Isms' (such as Communism), and Pork. In actual fact, there's a host of other things that we steer clear of, and in the course of my career I've been asked to avoid everything from ghosts and magic to aardvarks and crows. I never got to the bottom of what it is about aardvarks that makes them off-limits, but fortunately that particular taboo has never constrained me too greatly!

Critics have said that, by keeping these things out of our books, we're sanitising them and stifling opportunities for debate, discussion and the broadening of minds. But, while I would draw the line at anything that ventured into the realm of censorship, it has always seemed obvious to me that in books that are going to be used in the classroom, cultural sensitivity is essential. Partly this is a commercial necessity: in many countries, textbooks won't sell unless they are included in approved ministry lists, and anything that's seen as breaching cultural norms is not going to make the grade. But it also seems to be common sense, if you're creating a book for students in another part of the world, to show respect for their culture. In the same way that we'd be unlikely to show a child spitting in the street or smoking in a UK textbook, so teachers in China don't want to see pets in the kitchen (which they consider unhygienic), and a class of children in the Middle East will balk at a picture of someone showing the soles of their feet.

Graded readers

These days, I generally find myself writing for a global market that might typically include Brazil, Poland, Spain, Italy, Japan and Egypt. I've wiggled my way down into a particularly narrow niche in the world of ELT, writing 'graded readers' for students who are learning English. These are simplified storybooks, with the language and vocabulary carefully controlled so that an English language learner can read them fluently, at any level from beginner to advanced, consolidating and expanding their language skills as they do. One of the best things for me about writing graded readers is the freedom to write across different literary genres, and for a wide range of age groups. I've written everything from original fiction for pre-schoolers and adaptations of modern and classic titles for children aged 6-12, to non-fiction for teens and young adults – and in the past few years my smorgasbord of writing work has included new stories based around the TV characters *Dora the Explorer* and *Paw Patrol*, a book about the life and diaries of Anne Frank, an adaptation of the story of Don Quixote, and a young person's guide to the global issues of the 21st century.

For the 'grading' itself, I have a syllabus and vocabulary list on my desk at all times, bespoke for every different series; these tell me exactly what language I can and can't use at any particular level. Some writers might find it limiting and frustrating to work within such constraints, but I love the extra challenge, and I often feel there's something of the cryptic crossword about it – you think of the word that you need to convey a particular thought or idea, but if it doesn't fit your other criteria (in this case the syllabus) you then have to find some other way of saying what you want … it gives the brain a good stretch. The grading comes very much on top of all the requisites for any piece of storytelling; our number one priority is to engage and captivate the reader, so – as for all good stories – the prose needs to be sharp, the dialogues need to flow naturally, the characters have to jump out of the page, and there needs to be a clearly defined story arc. For adaptations, which are a big component of the graded reader library, there are the added challenges of deciding what from the original can be cut or condensed, and of trying to retain the author's original voice in simplified form.

The value and rewards

Writing for children in any format is intrinsically rewarding, of course, but a definite advantage of educational publishing is that the benefits are quantifiable. Research into the effectiveness of graded readers has shown what a huge impact they can have on language learning, and I've been really humbled on the occasions when I've actually seen my books in use in the classroom – this is quite a powerful reminder of the need to get things right and to put together the very best story you possibly can, in the hope of engaging a disaffected student or passing on the tiny nugget that might ignite something in a young mind.

Educational writing is also a lot easier to find a way into than the trade market, I think, especially if you're coming from a teaching background. Most practising teachers are too busy or exhausted to write new materials and, unless you have teaching experience or are a very engaged parent, you're unlikely to have a clear picture of what kind of resources are needed – or might work well – in a classroom setting. So if you do have the background, and the ideas, and are able to get them down on paper well, publishers might be very interested in what you can offer, particularly if you have some standing in your segment of the educational sector. There's also the advantage that sales can be quite substantial, because schools will usually buy class sets; this means every adoption might mean an order of tens or even hundreds of copies, still more if it's made by a big educational chain. Royalties are quite hard to come by these days, at least in the ELT world, but if you can secure them they're likely to hold up reasonably well. The world's bestselling ELT course-book, *Headway* (Oxford University Press), has sold more than 70 million copies, and is still going strong in its fifth edition!

Some might see educational writing for schools as the poor cousin of children's fiction, but I've found it a field with plenty of scope for creativity, in which you can foster a broad range of writing skills and dip your toe into other sides of the publishing process, like marketing and design. If, like Nelson Mandela, you believe that education is 'the most powerful weapon which you can use to change the world', you might just feel that as an educational writer, you're doing something that has value too.

Rachel Bladon is an EFL editor and writer, the author of more than 80 graded readers for adults and children, including *White Fang* (Macmillan Readers 2008), *Mulan* (Oxford Classic Tales 2017) and *The Life and Diaries of Anne Frank* (Oxford Bookworms 2018), winners of the ERF (Extensive Reading Foundation) Language Learner Literature Award. She is series editor of the *Oxford Bookworms Library*. For more information see www.linkedin.com/in/rachelbladon.

Writing adventures in the real world: children's non-fiction

Isabel Thomas explores the exciting world of children's non-fiction, and shares her tips for writing the perfect pitch.

Why write non-fiction?

Children's non-fiction is so much more than 'books with facts'. It's a different way for writers to reach young readers, to take them on a journey that makes them laugh, or cry, or bubble over with enthusiasm. It inspires children to explore their world – and to change it.

Recent years have seen an exciting renaissance in the genre. Dozens of new children's non-fiction imprints have been launched, and publishers are investing in lavish illustrations and large formats. Bookshops and libraries have reconfigured their shelves to make space for titles big enough to dive into. Children's non-fiction titles appear in bestseller charts, award shortlists and festival programmes. Readers – and their families – are demonstrating a huge appetite for bold and beautiful adventures in the real world.

It's an exciting time to be writing and illustrating children's non-fiction, and the scope for creativity is huge. I've written picture books, graphic texts and biographies where text and illustrations play together on the page. I've created educational books for libraries and classrooms, activity books packed with paper engineering, and hands-on crafts and experiments.

A good children's non-fiction book is nothing like a textbook. It's an opportunity to tell a complete story that helps children connect bite-sized facts with the bigger picture.

Where do I begin?

Find something that excites YOU, and then work out the best way to pass that excitement on to young readers. For me, it's science and nature.

My first book was about blue and purple foods. Educational non-fiction is often published in series, and the mainstream colours had already been covered! As debuts go it was low key. But it gave me the confidence to offer my services as a science writer to other publishers. Finding your niche is useful in winning that first commission, but it's not enough to know your subject area in depth. To make a topic irresistible to children, you need to know your readers too.

Spend time with children and immerse yourself in their world. Not just literature, but TV, films, apps and playground trends. Children's non-fiction competes with all of these things. I volunteer as a school governor and STEM Ambassador, roles that keep me in touch with curriculum change, and the influences that shape children's lives. I also read at libraries and run school events. 160 books into my career, I've become an expert in thinking like an eight-year-old.

Finding your angle

The value of a non-fiction book lies not just in the information delivered – which must of course be accurate and up-to-date – but in the way it's presented. How will you hook your reader, so that your book educates *and* entertains? Play with ideas, make connections and take your readers on a journey. It might be through humour, adventure or quirky details. Or it might be by making a complex topic simple enough to give a child that 'wow' moment.

An original angle is essential if your book is to stand out on a crowded shelf. Instead of listing facts about space, weave them into an alien's guide to the solar system, or a book of rocket science for beginners. If you're writing about life cycles, how about a zookeeper's handbook, or a hypothetical battle of lion versus tiger?

Developing your idea

At this point, a fiction author would write the first draft, ready to polish to perfection. The advice for non-fiction is rather different: don't write the book!

Children's non-fiction is usually a team effort, combining the author's ideas with those of talented editors, illustrators and designers to create something extraordinary. Unless you are pitching a picture book, there is usually no need to write the entire manuscript up front. Instead, develop a proposal and a few sample spreads, and make these as polished as you can. Once your idea has been commissioned, the editor will work with you to refine the approach, perfect the pacing of content and finalise the text features.

Don't forget to visit bookshops and libraries as you develop your idea. Holding the latest children's non-fiction books in your hands is much more revealing than looking at covers online. Get a feel for the typical extent and word count for each age group. How will you build knowledge and understanding over 48, 64 or 96 pages? Will you write a picture book with 20 words per page, or a reference book with 200? Read as many examples as you can to absorb the language level. Make a note of the page features that non-fiction writers use to break up the text into manageable chunks.

Writing a proposal – dos and don'ts

Children's non-fiction authors work with publishers in several different ways. The first will be familiar if you already write fiction. Pitch an original idea and negotiate an advance and royalty. Some non-fiction authors work with literary agents; others, like me, pitch directly to publishers and use the excellent Society of Authors (see page 323) for advice on contracts. When I worked as a non-fiction commissioning editor, I was equally happy to hear from both.

Editors also come to me with a subject in mind and ask for a text treatment – a fresh new approach that will work for their market. In this case, the remuneration may be a one-off fee, higher than the advance for a similar title. Either way, my first task for each new title is to write a concise and engaging proposal to make the case for my idea.

Begin with an **overview** that showcases your style and tone. It should be good enough to become the back-cover blurb (and it often does). Follow this attention-grabbing introduction with a longer **description**. Explain why the book is timely, perfect for the target age group and why you are the best person to write it. There's no need to send the whole manuscript (unless you are writing a short picture book). Instead provide a **breakdown of the structure**, showing how you build engagement and understanding. Finally, include two or three pages of **sample text** to bring the idea to life.

DO:

• **Explain why you are pitching to this publisher**. Visit bookshops and scour catalogues, including the rights catalogues that publishers produce for book fairs. Find out what makes their books special. Then show why your idea and their list are a perfect match.

• **Come up with an attention-grabbing title** that hints at both subject matter and approach. Humorous and irreverent or lyrical and atmospheric? Hands-on activities or narrative adventure?

• **Point out anything that might drive sales**, such as anniversaries, curriculum links or exhibitions. Remember to work at least 18-24 months ahead – illustrated non-fiction takes around a year to journey from manuscript to shelf.

• **Showcase your voice.** Ten years ago, children's non-fiction often had a formal tone, edited to match house style. Today, a unique voice will help you stand out.

DON'T:

• **Claim that there is no competition.** More often than not, this points to a lack of research. Competition can prove that a topic is in demand. Publishers will always offer books on dinosaurs, space and animals, and are hungry for creative new approaches to these popular themes. Compare your idea to existing titles – ideally successful ones! Explain why your approach will be different (and better).

• **Include illustrations.** Unless you're an author-illustrator, it's the publisher's role to find an illustrator that the audience will love (often, but not always, with your approval). Instead, note down ideas about the type of illustrations you think would work well, as part of your overall vision for the book.

• **Mention how much your family and friends like the idea.** Publishers get many proposals saying 'tested on my kids'. It's better to present the skills and experience that make you an expert in your subject area or target audience – or both!

Writing the book – three golden rules

1. Research is key

One of the best things about writing for a living is the chance to dive into a subject. You might be writing for ten-year-olds, but you'll need to understand your topic in much greater depth. To avoid introducing errors, track down original sources. If you read an interesting article, find the original research too. Better still, interview the author. Insist on two sources for every fact (and never make one of those sources Wikipedia). And be warned – when you're interviewing stuntwomen, scientists or astronauts, job envy is an occupational hazard!

2. Play on the page

Hooking the audience doesn't end with a creative angle. Every page, paragraph and sentence must work hard to weave in the information you'd like to cover, while keeping readers engaged.

Make good use of text features, such as infographics, charts, text boxes and quotes. They can help you to bring interesting facts to the fore, enticing a reader to explore the rest of the page. They also help to pace the flow of information, making complex topics or arguments easier to follow.

Resist the temptation to include everything. First drafts are often double the length of the final text, and the real work comes in deciding what to leave out.

3. Think visually

Illustrations are a key ingredient in children's non-fiction. Sourcing these illustrations (whether buying photographs or commissioning illustrators) is the job of the publisher. But briefing them is the job of the author.

Think like an art director – how will information be broken up into chunks and displayed on the page? What diagrams will help you to explain a difficult concept? Will you include cartoons and visual jokes? An information book might need simple photo briefs, while a graphic text demands detailed descriptions of every panel. Create a wish list, to be realized by a talented illustrator and designer.

Building a writing career

Children's non-fiction authors develop valuable skills: the ability to carry out in-depth research, to write at just the right level for a certain age group, and to build a story that educates and entertains. These skills are in demand outside book publishing – by companies, charities and organisations that want to create outreach resources, by children's magazines, museums and science centres, and by producers of educational websites, blogs and vlogs. Writing other types of non-fiction content helps you keep your voice and ideas fresh. It can also be another way to reach your audience if you have an idea that's close to your heart, but find that there is no commercial demand for it in book form.

As a non-fiction author, you are well placed to **design and run events** linked to your writing. For example, pitch yourself to local schools, museums and festivals; run craft sessions in bookshops and libraries; help children unleash their own non-fiction writing power in an interactive workshop. Events are a direct way to keep in touch with your readers, and you'll come away with dozens of ideas for new books.

Nothing beats the feeling of discovering something wonderful for the first time. Whether I'm writing a biography, an activity book or a picture book, I aim to give readers the same feeling. If I can encourage children to pick up a book, think 'wow', and keep reading, I know I've done a good job. But if they read something that encourages them to close the book, head outside and explore the world ... well, then I know I've done a *great* job.

Where will your next non-fiction adventure take you?

Isabel Thomas has written more than 160 non-fiction titles for young audiences, published by Bloomsbury, What on Earth? Books, Oxford University Press, Puffin, Laurence King, Ladybird, Collins, Pearson, Phaidon, DK, Rising Stars, Raintree, QED, Wren & Rook and Welbeck in the UK, and translated into more than 30 languages around the world. Her narrative non-fiction picture book *Moth: An Evolution Story* (Bloomsbury 2019) was awarded the 2020 AAAS Subaru Prize for Excellence in Science Books. Isabel's most recent publications include *The Bedtime Book of Impossible Questions* (Bloomsbury 2022), *Scientists* (DK 2021), *Fox: A Circle of Life Story* (Bloomsbury 2020) and *Exploring the Elements* (Phaidon 2020), a *New York Times* and Waterstones Book of the Year. Isabel's short course in developing and pitching non-fiction for young audiences is available via Domestika. Find out more at www.isabelthomas.co.uk and follow her on Twitter @isabelwriting and Instagram @isabelthomasbooks.

See also...

Connecting with your readers

Clare Povey explores how a writer can reach out and grow valuable connections with a wider readership. She shares her tips on how best to establish and maintain a strong author–reader relationship, through web content, social media, teachers, schools, libraries and bookshops.

Books

Every writer wants to be read. I believe that every writer writes the book that they want to read themselves. Why else would we spend hours of our lives typing or scribbling away, with no guarantee that anyone other than ourselves (and a few lucky family members or friends) will get to see it? Connecting with your readers has to start with yourself. It's essential that you, the writer, find the story that you are most passionate and excited about because, without this, you will struggle to engage with your readers. Believe me, children can sniff out insincerity.

The first proper story I wrote was one I absolutely wanted to read. For full disclosure, it was my own take on *Holes* (Bloomsbury Children's 2015) by Louis Sachar. In my version, a girl character named Clara (we'll ignore how this is one letter off my own name) is sent to Camp Green Lake and shakes things up. It was my very own fan fiction; I reread it until the pages started to wear thin and tear. Since then, I have carried that same energy into all the stories I've written. So, although my first piece of advice seems simple, I can assure you that being genuine is a starting point for any meaningful author–reader relationship.

How do you successfully reach beyond your one-person audience and find wider readers for your work? Every writer – whether agented or un-agented, whether they have published with a large or an independent publisher, or have self-published – can find this task overwhelming. But the advice in this article should be relevant.

My debut middle-grade book *The Unexpected Tale of Bastien Bonlivre* (Usborne) was published in September 2021. While bookshops were open then (thankfully), there were still certain restrictions in place. I wasn't able to get into schools immediately, and I also work full-time, so it was a challenge to organise school events to promote the book. This meant that, for the first six months of my book being out in the world, I had to find and use different ways of connecting with potential readers.

Promotional disclaimer

I must acknowledge, at this point, that I was lucky enough to receive the September 2021 slot for Waterstones Children's Book of the Month. This promotional opportunity definitely helped my book reach a really wide audience in its early days – the size of audience that any author, especially a debut author, would dream of. It meant that my book sat in the window of every Waterstones bookshop across the UK (all 283 of them), as well as being clearly placed on tables and displayed next to the till for a whole month. It was an opportunity that I will be forever grateful for, but I appreciate that it is also something that a writer has no control over; your publisher pitches your book to Waterstones and the head team of retail experts decides which story gets the coveted slot.

But, as a writer, establishing connections and maintaining them is something you need to grow for a lifetime, not just a single month. So much of the publishing world is out of your control, so it is important to focus on the things that you can do and take accountability for yourself. How, then, can you connect with your readers? Beyond summoning the bookish child inside you and demanding an answer, here are my five top tips on how you can connect and communicate best with your readers. All of these tips are interconnected, but I've broken them down into five separate points for clarity.

1. Create and organise your own content

A writer does not necessarily need a website (it's something you will have to pay for, as well as maintain and update), but you do need to build up a bank of content. By content, I mean blogs, articles, Q&A features, short videos or audio clips … anything that can be used for promotional purposes. Having a variety of content available to offer to teachers, librarians and parents is a great way to expand the scope of your book. I have a Resources area on my website that allows me to put worksheets, links to articles and blogs, reading lists, historical facts and much more all in one place. Teachers can directly download resources for their classrooms, as well as access the first chapter of my book. I'm planning to record a series of videos about different aspects of the writing process that I can share with interested teachers.

You don't need to be an expert video editor or design whizz to create content. I use the free versions of Canva (www.canva.com) and Clipchamp (https://clipchamp.com) and am learning as I go. But I do keep my publishers in the loop about what I'm up to. I created a 'villain' worksheet for my school events (see section on School visits below) and the Usborne marketing and design team redesigned it into something much more professional looking. Communication is key – because, even though I love learning new skills, I'm not an expert designer or video editor. If you need help, ask for it.

2. Find your corner of Twitter

Social media isn't for everyone. If you're reading this and thinking 'Nope, not going anywhere near that cesspool,' that's your choice. But, be aware that the online children's fiction writing and book community contains some of the most supportive people you could ever hope to meet. I have met so many writers, book bloggers, booksellers, librarians and teachers through Twitter. I'll go into more detail about each one of these communities below, but I cannot overstate how useful and rewarding it has been to connect with others digitally. I have found my own tiny corner of Twitter that is generous, kind and supportive.

While you might not be reaching your main readership through Twitter, especially if you are writing for children up to the age of 12, you will still connect with the people who buy books for your younger readers. Other children's fiction writers are not your competition, but your co-workers. They will support your book and recommend you to their own readers, and in turn you can shout about their writing and make friends for life.

3. Reaching out to teachers and librarians

There are so many brilliant primary school teachers and librarians who are incredibly engaged with the children's publishing world. They truly care about making sure that every single child feels seen. I've met a number of teachers, mainly through Twitter, who are passionate about literacy and want authors to get involved. Here are some ways that have allowed me to connect:

• Ask if any schools would like to enter an author pen-pal correspondence with you. You could contact a local school or even get in touch with your old primary school.

• Go to your local library to discover what reading resources are especially useful for children. Accelerated Reader (www.renaissance.com/products/accelerated-reader), for example, is a great programme that is used in many schools to encourage reading for pleasure.

• Get involved in online chat and keep an eye out for hashtags such as: #teachertwitter, #edutwitter, #primaryschoolbookclub.

4. The brilliance of bookshops and booksellers

It's well worth calling up or going into your local bookshop(s) and introducing yourself. It's hypocritical of me to tell you not to be shy because, even after visiting dozens upon dozens of bookshops, I still quietly mutter, 'My name's Clare and I wrote that book over there…' (*points ambiguously to a shelf in the distance*). Bookshops can't stock every single book that has been published (unless they're a Tardis in disguise). I guarantee they will want to hear from you and, if they don't have copies of your book in store, be assured that they will be ordering after your visit.

Once you connect with a bookseller, you can ask whether they might be interested in running an event with you or organising a signing. For all of the big glossy promotions and huge marketing and publicity campaigns, bookseller recommendations are still one of the most useful selling tools. How many times have you walked into a bookshop, only planning to buy just one book on your list, and then left with a dozen new recommendations from a friendly bookseller? Booksellers help your books to live a long and happy life, and to be read by new readers time and time again.

5. School visits

A school visit is one of the most direct ways to connect with your readers. In the *Writers' & Artists' Guide to Writing for Children and YA* (Bloomsbury 2019), author Linda Strachan has written a comprehensive guide for writers on how to navigate school visits. I do implore you to get that book and read it, so you can make the most out of any school visits you organise.

I am writing this article a few days after my first ever World Book Day Week in March 2022 as an author. I visited five different schools over the course of four days; I led assemblies on writing and the author life, as well as classroom workshops on creating authentic villains in a responsible way. Villains are a big part of my book and I always give a reading of my main villain – the bestselling author Olivier Odieux – and then immediately follow it up with a 'Guess the Villains' quiz, where I include villains from other books, films and TV shows. Think about what strands of your story would work best for a school event and how this will relate to your readers.

Not every writer is able to visit schools in-person, but there are still other ways of connecting with schoolchildren. Virtual workshops and Q&As are more popular than ever, and this is a great way to reach your readers from your home office desk or kitchen table. Alternatively, if you don't have time in your working day to offer virtual school visits, creating pre-recorded videos – whether it's a five-minute creative writing exercise challenge or a much longer workshop session – is another great way to maintain a connection with schools. You can also reuse any recordings as content for other schools or organisations, or upload it to your website.

A note to remember:

You can do as much or as little of this as you want. You might agree to write a blog for free; you might offer a visit to a school in a low-income area that would love to have an author visit but just doesn't have the financial means. As an author, you are in control of what you say 'Yes' and 'No' to. You never have to do anything you feel uncomfortable with. I always remind myself that connecting and growing readers is a marathon, not a sprint. Focus on what you can control and enjoy it – because, when you're having fun, your readers will too.

Clare Povey is an author and the editorial and communities manager of the *Writers' & Artists'* website. She fell in love with France as a child, inspired by the stories in her local Barking & Dagenham Library, and by discovering the vocabulary in Usborne's *First Thousand Words in French* (1995). The magic of speaking another language eventually led to her living and working in France, and writing her debut series, the Paris-based *The Unexpected Tale of Bastien Bonlivre* (Usborne 2021). For more information see www.clarepovey.com. Follow her on Twitter @ClareFPovey.

See also...
- *Finding new readers and markets*, page 107
- *Why teachers make great children's writers*, page 225

Keeping going: the ups and downs of being a published writer

Theresa Tomlinson shares the emotional and creative highs and lows, opportunities and hurdles an author may encounter during a long writing career. She tracks the course of her career – through finding and losing a trusted editor, writing fiction for children, adults and YA, and moving from traditional publishing to self-publishing.

As a child I had no ambitions to write, but I loved reading and delighted in magical escapes to Narnia. I failed the eleven-plus, and rather struggled at my convent boarding school, but discovered I had some facility for drawing and painting. I spent two years at Hull Art College but left without completing my graphic design course. Unsure of what to do next, I trained to be an infant teacher and it was in that role that I discovered the sheer joy of storytelling (in those days both children and teachers could look forward to a blissful story session at the end of each day).

Later, as the mother of three young children, I started to put together simple picture books, initially focusing on the artwork rather than the words. As time passed the stories grew longer; my interest in the artwork faded and I began to write somewhat obsessively. Visits to the local library provided huge inspiration as I discovered new and exciting children's writers; it was almost like finding a new version of Narnia. Discovering Jane Gardam was a revelation – not only did I love her humour, sensitivity and clear writing style, but I recognised many of the settings based on the part of the north-east coast where I grew up. I knew every street, garden and house in the background of *A Long Way from Verona* (Abacus 1997), heard familiar cadences in the dialogue and experienced once again the familiar tang of steelworks built close to the sea. I began to feel that I, too, had stories to tell.

Having discovered a local writers' workshop, tutored by Berlie Doherty, I settled to work more seriously as a writer; five years of hard work followed, including three inspiring Arvon courses. There were many rejections, but things started to look up when I was awarded a Yorkshire Arts Bursary to help me finish a book in progress – *The Flither Pickers* (1987) – stories of fishing families set on the north-east coast, along with an offer of publication from John Killick of the Littlewood Press, based at Hebden Bridge. Although it was a limited print run, it meant that I had a well-produced example of my work to send to publishers. Fairly soon after that I got my first (modest) offer from a London publisher – for a magical children's story set in the industrial seaside village that I had lived in as a child. The offer came from Julia MacRae, a highly respected publisher with her own imprint within Walker Books and – best of all – she was Jane Gardam's publisher! I was thrilled.

Over the next 20 years, with the support of Julia and my fabulous editor, Delia Huddy, I flourished. One book followed another. Historical themes appealed to me and were appreciated by schools. Julia MacRae moved to Random House and took me with her, though happily Walker Books continued to publish my younger-age 'time-slip' books, which allowed modern children to slip magically back through time to experience an earlier period. I was hugely encouraged when *Riding the Waves* (1990) a more modern novel, set on the north-east coast, was recommended for the Carnegie Medal and my young adult novels were translated into several languages and sold in the USA. I was regularly shortlisted for the Sheffield Children's Book Award (Michael Palin memorably turned his back on me and folded his arms when I was called up onto the stage twice in an award ceremony!); it was such good fun.

Publishing contracts were now becoming rather complicated for me to deal with, so I looked for an agent; persuading Caroline Walsh of David Higham to take me on turned out to be one of the best things I ever did. Educational publishers were asking for more historical time-slip stories and when again one of these, *Meet Me By The Steelmen* (1997), was shortlisted for the Carnegie Medal, I thought my future was secure ... But then gradually things started to change: schools became short of funds and invitations to visit grew scarce, ebooks appeared on the scene and time-slip stories seemed to fall out of favour. However, I still had the backing of my editor and a sympathetic agent.

For some time I had longed to use Anglo-Saxon Whitby as a setting for a story so, having moved to Whitby, I set out to write a trilogy of YA mystery/adventures with Hild's famous monastery as the setting. The research process was sheer pleasure and it was inspiring to be living in sight of the location. *Wolf Girl* (Corgi Children's 2006) was the first book completed and we had almost finished the editing process when my editor Delia suddenly died. The book was published but it didn't sell widely and Random House concluded that readers were not interested in Anglo-Saxon settings, but by then I had become passionately interested in the period; my bookshelves were filled with studies of food, clothing, language and crafts of the time – I'd persuaded my husband that our travels must include Sutton Hoo, West Stow Anglo-Saxon village, Durham, Bede's World (now Jarrow Hall), Yeavering, Bamburgh Castle and Lindisfarne.

By then, fortunately, trying to earn a living by writing had become less of a priority, but it was a depressing time; I almost considered giving up altogether. A few months of ignoring the computer, though, made me realise that it would be even more depressing not to write; for my own wellbeing, I needed to do it. Hearing that Whitby had a writers' group, I went to join them. It was like starting at the beginning again, and there was something rather exciting about that.

I couldn't let my Anglo-Saxon obsession go and began work on an adult murder mystery with the same setting as my YA book and with a theme somewhat similar to Ellis Peters' Cadfael series, but with a 7th-century half-pagan herb-wife, rather than a monk. Creating a much older protagonist was something I'd wanted to try for a while and the character of Fridgyth was already present in *Wolf Girl*, waiting to step forward into the limelight. Whitby Writers Group provided practical criticism and friendly encouragement and my pleasure in writing returned. A difficult decision had to be made when the manuscript was completed: whether to try to get it published traditionally or go down the self-publishing route. I talked it through with my agent and it became clear that, although I'd had some success as a children's writer, that wouldn't mean much when tackling the competitive, adult, historical crime fiction market. Even acceptance by a traditional publisher might mean waiting years for publication.

I was then in my 60s and felt time might be running out, so I decided to experiment with self-publishing. My agent negotiated a contract with Acorn Independent Press. They provided discerning editing, and I enjoyed having lots of input into the cover design. The book was well produced as a print-on-demand (POD) and ebook edition and Acorn helped with marketing and distribution. *A Swarming of Bees* (2012) was put forward for an Amazon promotion and within a few weeks it reached number three in the historical bestsellers chart – I was briefly placed between Hilary Mantel and C.J. Sansom and couldn't have been happier. I recovered my costs fairly quickly and local bookshops still sell copies at a steady pace, which I supply them with.

I set about writing a sequel and I also had a straightforward historical novel published, *The Tribute Bride* (2014), this time with a 6th-century setting. Self-publishing seemed to be working for me, so I began to look at my backlist of out-of-print titles. Two of my short novels, *The Flither Pickers* and *The Herring Girls*, focusing on the harsh lives of the fishing families of the north-east coast, were published in a paperback edition in 2017, illustrated with atmospheric Victorian/Edwardian photographs by Frank Meadow Sutcliffe. York Publishing Services (www.yps-publishing.co.uk) produced the book and it was a real benefit to be able to discuss the project face to face before agreeing to go ahead and at any point during the production process. YPS produced a Kindle version that displays the photographs beautifully and the books are selling steadily in local shops. YPS suggested an initial print run of 250 copies and I'm now into my second run.

However, self-publishing hasn't been all plain sailing. When the manuscript for my 'herb-wife' sequel was finished, Acorn were happy to put the book together but had decided to withdraw from providing marketing services. Once again, my agent came to the rescue: Caroline negotiated a rather different contract with Acorn, and David Higham Agency agreed to take on the setting up and management of a Kindle version and POD facility themselves. *Queen of a Distant Hive* (2017) was produced and has gathered positive reviews – not least from fellow historical writers. I sense that there is more interest in the Anglo-Saxon period now and I have discovered a good community of support out there, especially from those writing in a similar genre. Bloggers invite me to appear as their guest and provide reviews – Annie Whitehead (http://anniewhiteheadauthor.co.uk), Helen Hollick (https://discoveringdiamonds.blogspot.com) and Carla Nayland (http://carlanayland.blogspot.com) are three active examples.

I haven't entirely given up on traditional children's publishing and am working on a YA novel set in Victorian Whitby. At the age of 72 my ambitions are modest. I have a small pension, a supportive husband and a loyal agent – it's a privileged position to be in. I'm grateful simply to be able to sit down at my computer and still spend a few magical hours in Narnia – or any other time or place that I fancy.

Theresa Tomlinson is known for her YA and children's historical novels, particularly those set on the north-east coast of England. Her books include *The Flither Pickers* (1987), *Summer Witches* (1991), and five *Time Slip* adventures including the republication of *Meet Me By the Steelmen* (Award Publications Ltd 2019), which was followed by a sequel, *Forged in Steel* (Award Publications Ltd 2020), shortlisted for the 2021 Sheffield Children's Book Award. Under her own imprint, The Old Print Workshop, she published her latest novel, *Dark Fortune* (2021), and in 2022 republished the *Forestwife* trilogy – *The Forestwife, Child of the May* and *Path of the She-Wolf*. Theresa's other books include the *Troy and the Warrior Women* series – *The Moon Riders* (2002) and *The Voyage of the Snake Lady* (2004). Theresa has been shortlisted twice for the Carnegie Medal and for the Sheffield Children's Book Award. For more information and Theresa's blog, see www.theresatomlinson.com.

How to write a picture book

Tessa Strickland highlights the enduring value of picture books, both educational and emotional, for young children in today's world, and offers advice for writers wishing to engage in the child's world on the process, practices, qualities and skills they will need to succeed.

A picture book is a child's first theatre. It's likely to be the first time a child experiences the drama of storytelling as the spoken word, accompanied by glorious illustration and skilful design. As on a theatre stage, several disciplines come together. The result is an art form whose impact on the imagination can extend well beyond childhood. I remain inspired by my favourite childhood picture books, among them Golden MacDonald's evocative Hebridean story *The Little Island* (Doubleday 1946), Kay Thompson's badass heroine *Eloise* (Simon & Schuster 1955) and Barbara Cooney's Caldecott-winning 1959 version of *Chanticleer and the Fox* (Crowell 1958). Decades later, the picture books that were my own children's favourites still take pride of place on the shelves of my family library.

Picture books are not just about entertainment: they play a crucial role in establishing basic literacy skills, emotional intelligence, acquisition of language, appetite for learning and enjoyment of art. Of course, the child is not reading the text, it is being read to her. But as she listens, she knows that the adult reader is decoding those curious black marks that run along the page. She knows too that these marks, these words, are the key to what is happening in the illustrations. So, the heart of the picture book is this marriage between the text and the illustration – each depends on the other.

Where to start

The starting point is the story. Picture books are short (publishers typically require a text of less than 1,000 words), so it's dangerously easy to think that they are easy to write. In fact, the opposite is the case. Writing a picture book presents the same challenges as writing a poem. Your aim is to achieve a sense of balance and harmony between the story as music and as meaning. Small children will experience the storytelling as sound first, sense later. As long as the sound of the language is congruent with its meaning, they will happily let themselves be carried along by the emotional momentum of the narrative.

If you want to have a go at picture book writing, it is a very good idea to spend dedicated time with children under five. You may have children of your own; you may teach in an early-years setting; you may simply like the idea of storytelling for this enthusiastic and receptive age group. Consider volunteering to read aloud at your local preschool, primary school or library. This will help you to get a sense of what stories the children enjoy listening to AND what kind of stories you most enjoy telling. Notice what the children are doing and saying when they play (children come into the world knowing instinctively that play is work. This is how they learn, and their interactions reveal their major interests and preoccupations).

As well as engaging with the child's world, try to remember what you felt like as a child. Get these feelings into your storytelling. This will make your writing authentic. Children see straight through sentimentality, yet an alarming number of adults shy away from the intensities and terrors of childhood and try to sugar-coat it. This won't work.

Practice and peer groups

Write as often as you can. If it's not possible for you to write every day (for many of us, it isn't), then choose at least a couple of hours a week and make this your personal, un-interruptable writing time. Writing is a craft and, like any craft, the more you practise, the better you get. Look for a supportive writing group – the excellent Society of Children's Book Writers & Illustrators (see page 330) has many local chapters and there are also all kinds of courses online and masterclasses at literature festivals (see *Children's writing courses and conferences*, page 380). Peer support groups can be transformative and you will learn a lot, not only about your potential as a writer but also about how to give and receive feedback. Very few of us can write to please everyone. So, like any professional writer, one of your challenges will be how to decide what to retain because you instinctively believe that it works, and what to revise or discard based on other people's feedback.

Finding your thread

Aristotle was right when he said that a story needs a beginning, a middle and an end. When you have an idea for a story, you may be surprised by how difficult it is to start, to get a beginning that really *is* a beginning.

Once you *have* started, it can be tricky to tell the story you thought you were going to tell. Don't worry! This is a good sign. Writing is a creative act. Your characters may well take on lives of their own and decide they are going to get up to all kinds of antics you had not predicted. Be prepared to fool around for a good many drafts, to get to know the characters you are writing about, to give them a back story. The back story won't necessarily appear on the page, but by creating it you will ground your narrative and make it more convincing than it would otherwise be.

Some writers start with their characters and go from there. What ages are they? What are their strengths and weaknesses, likes and dislikes? What do they need or crave? Try writing about two strongly contrasting characters: exaggerate their traits and explore the different ways in which they communicate. You may surprise yourself, and if you do this in a group, you will be fascinated by the different ways in which this one-to-one exchange can be unpacked.

Other writers prefer to start with a situation and then decide who they are going to conjure up to resolve it. This is also a sound strategy and every good story needs a problem. If your characters live in a trouble-free dream world or a happy-ever-after hedgerow, your readers are going to be bored and unconvinced, because life is not like this. So, to engage your young audience, you need a situation which quickly becomes problematic. Then you need a way of resolving the problem that is transformative for your main character. The problem may be internal (for example, your character may be afraid of something) or it may be external (for example, a storm is coming). And you may well find that solving one problem leads to another ... learning how to find your thread AND hold onto it will require you to redraft and redraft.

Staying true to life

The infant's journey from birth to the age of five is the most formative in its entire life. As babies grow into toddlers and then into children, they live among giants, with adults and perhaps older siblings, looming above them and exerting tremendous power. This is why stories about larger-than-life characters resonate so powerfully in young children's minds.

Books

There is something of a trend in contemporary children's publishing to avoid scaring children. In my view, this is a mistake. Fear and rage, pain and sorrow are as familiar to children as cornflakes at breakfast. They are often scared or infuriated and by hearing stories in which scary things happen and are successfully dealt with, they learn that there are ways of navigating and mastering their feelings. Often, successful children's writers tackle these feelings through symbol and metaphor; territory in which most children are naturally at ease.

Using humour

One of the most valuable resources in the picture book writer's toolkit is humour. It is like medicine, and it can take many forms: it may be dry; it may be quiet; it may be outrageous. Understatement can go a long way with children. By contrast, irony and sarcasm tend to be too sophisticated for little ones. So, if you are using humour, keep it straightforward. It can be tempting, as the writer, to introduce layers of tongue-in-cheek humour that are evident to the adult, who is also, after all, the one who is likely to have paid for the book in the first place, and this can be wonderful. Just be careful that it is not at the expense of the child for whom you are writing.

Writing in verse

Aspiring writers can find themselves utterly bewildered by conflicting advice about whether or not to write in verse. My experience both as a publisher and as a writer is that verse is hugely popular. However, it's a common misperception among beginners that verse means no more than having a rhyme scheme. To write in verse, you need to have an ear for metre and for the relationship between metre, tone and meaning. The rhyme is secondary. It is certainly valuable in all kinds of ways – children and adults alike take enormous pleasure in guessing and remembering the word that completes a rhyming couplet, and unexpected rhymes are particularly delightful. But without a convincing metre, verse becomes flat-footed. If you want to write in verse, read and decode the masters, and be prepared to do a lot of re-writing to get it right. One false note will kill your endeavour.

Going to market

You have been diligently writing for a year or two and you now have three or four man-uscripts you are happy with. It is time to gird your loins and pitch your work to an agent or a publisher. It is certainly not essential to have an agent, but if you do go this route, a good agent will know what different publishers are looking for and be able to negotiate terms on your behalf. Also, the UK children's publishing industry is a small world. Agents who do well on behalf of their clients do so because they keep up to date on changing trends and know who is looking for what.

You don't need to find an illustrator; the publisher will do this. You just need to have a selection of short manuscripts that are skilfully crafted, that surprise and delight the editor who will read them first and that show you have a distinctive voice. Before you make your submissions, check what is on the market and make sure someone else hasn't already had your idea (you will be surprised by how often this happens). Check the agent's or publisher's website, so that you have a sense of what kind of taste they have and what their successes are.

Be professional. Follow the agent's or publisher's submission guidelines and keep your cover letter brief. You will not help your cause by saying that your children or grandchildren love your writing. Of course they do, but they are not the ones taking the commercial risk.

Persist. Many of the most successful picture book writers have endured years of rejection. They have succeeded not only because they are talented but also because they have been prepared to work very hard and to persevere.

The international picture book market

Picture books are expensive to develop. This is one of the reasons why only a few new picture books appear on UK publishers' lists each year. The expense of sourcing and commissioning artwork, then paying for full-colour origination and printing, quickly runs well into five figures. To recover this investment, UK publishers typically seek out publishing partners overseas, from the USA to China. Economies of scale mean that the more copies a publisher prints, the lower the unit cost. Because the UK market is a small one, publishers here usually seek to sell co-edition licences to as many partners as possible before they go to press.

This process takes time. So, do not give up your day job! The period between having your manuscript accepted and seeing it in the world as a printed book can be anything between one and three years.

Writing in a Global Pandemic

The coronavirus pandemic has drastically changed all of our lives. This includes the lives of everyone involved in children's literature: writers, designers, publishers, printers, educational suppliers, librarians, booksellers, teachers. It's been a period that has brought great suffering for many. For those of us fortunate enough not to have been left jobless or to have lost loved ones, it has been a time of adaptation and reflection. For many - including me - it has prompted a lot of soul-searching about what matters most and what kind of future we want for ourselves and our children. The enforced seclusion of successive lockdowns has not all been gloom and doom. Numerous parents and carers of small children have turned to picture books as fantastic resources for storytelling, sharing and discussion. Publishers with a strong online presence have flourished, often magnificently supported by booksellers who have risen to the challenge of selling in new ways. Those publishers whose sales have to date been more through the shops of public spaces such as art galleries, museums and airport shops have fared less well. There's definitely a sense that we are caught in the wheels of massive change. And because supply chains have been disrupted, there is a bit of a backlog in many publishers' calendars. However, my agent has sold five picture book texts for me in the past couple of years and it's been an enormous pleasure to witness more and more emergent picture book writers secure their first, second or third contracts. As restrictions lift at long last and we regain the freedom to take off our masks, visit friends and family and have new adventures, I am glad that sales of children's picture books have held their own and I am optimistic that they will continue to do so!

Tessa Strickland is the co-founder and advisory editor of independent children's publisher Barefoot Books. As Stella Blackstone, she has written many internationally acclaimed picture books and her writing has been translated into over 30 languages. Tessa also offers one-to-one mentoring and short group courses for picture book writers. Contact tessa@challiscombe.com for details.

Writing short stories for children

Julia Green describes the power and the pleasure of a well-written children's short story, and its essential attributes. She encourages aspiring short story writers to read, study, practice, experiment and aim high.

Primary School. I'm maybe eight or nine. We're reading a short story in class, from an ancient hardback collection of stories and poems illustrated with line drawings, with a faded blue and green cover. I can't remember the title of the anthology, but I do remember one story, about a lonely man making sand sculptures on the beach – Weymouth, in my memory. And the atmosphere – slightly melancholy, a sense of loss, the way that I often felt as a child when it was time to leave the beach – the tide coming in, late afternoon, the beach emptying out. The man walks away, the sea washes in and erases the sculptures... Later on, aged 13 or 14, in an English lesson we read Ted Hughes' short story *The Rain Horse*, which is all atmosphere – a field, the rain, the threatening horse, a young man's sense of terror.

Why have these particular short stories stayed in my mind over so many years, out of all the others we read as children? Perhaps it's the strong sense of place, the use of vivid detail to create a landscape and a moment in time through the appeal to all the senses. And a strong *feeling*: sadness, sense of loss, fear. It's partly in what is *not said*; an effective short story doesn't waste words. It leaves a space for the reader to imagine, to fill in the gaps. We enter into the story world, stay a short time, and leave again – but as a reader, we're left with the sense that something has changed forever. We've glimpsed something, felt something, of lasting significance. The short story as 'an arrow in flight', as the Irish writer Mary Lavin described it.

We are talking here about **the short story as a form in itself**; not a short book for children, like a picture book, or an illustrated story for young children which is short in length but is in essence a short novel – though much of what I am saying here would apply to these forms of story, too. And we are thinking of the **audience** as children aged from about four, when a child might be listening to the story being read aloud rather than reading for themselves, to about 12. Publishers and booksellers classify readers older than that as 'teen' or 'young adult' rather than children. It is helpful for a new writer to be aware of this. Writing for a four- or five-year-old is obviously very different from writing for someone of 9-12 years. Think about how appropriate the theme or experiences and emotions in your story would be for the age group you want to write for. Alternatively, first write the story you want to write, and *then* think about that question of audience. The problem for many new or unpublished writers is a mismatch between the style/language/content of the story and the age and interest of the 'audience': the child reader. Of course there are many notable exceptions to this, but as a *beginner writer* it's helpful to think about making the age of your main character just a little older than the age of your readers. You will need to be aware of the language and style, too, to make it appropriate for the intended audience.

If you want to write short stories for children, the important thing, of course, is to *read* many! Immerse yourself in the form. You might reread stories you enjoyed as a child, to re-experience them with your adult 'writer' mind, namely reading as-a-writer, alert to the way the story has been written. Examine closely: 1) the language, the way words and sentences work, how much or little description there is, how dialogue is used, how much or how little 'action' or 'plot'; 2) the pace (how quickly do things move along?); 3) what the story is actually 'about'; 4) the form of the short story, studying this is the best way of learning how to do it yourself (not so that you write in exactly the same way – we can only ever write authentically as ourselves – but to help you think about the different options open to you, and the tools of your trade). Make notes for yourself in a notebook.

Read contemporary short stories for children, too, to see what is being published now. Fashions change. Haunt bookshops and libraries. Look at anthologies of short stories published for children, such as *Moonlight Magic* (Stripes 2016) or *My Kind of School* (A&C Black 2008), edited by Tony Bradman; collections for different age groups, such as *The Puffin Book of Stories for Five-Year-Olds* (Penguin 1996) edited by Wendy Cooling, or *Funny Stories for 5-Year-Olds* (Pan Macmillan 2016), edited by Helen Paiba. These contain stories by different writers, new and old.

Read collections of short stories by individual authors, too. These are usually by established authors (it is very rare for a brand-new writer to have a collection of stories accepted for publication):
• Nicola Davies' *Up on the Hill* (Walker 2008) consists of three separate short stories about children who live in the country.
• Michael Morpurgo wrote a memorable collection, published as *The White Horse of Zennor and other stories* (Mammoth 1982).
• Leila Berg's wonderful *Little Pete Stories* (Methuen) for very young children written in the 1950s were groundbreaking in their time for the way she showed 'real' children, feeling strong emotions including anger.
• Emma Carroll's *When We Were Warriors* (Faber 2019) contains three short stories linked to her popular historical novels for children.
• David Almond's collection *Counting Stars* (Hodder Children's 2000) illustrates the richness of the short story form in the hands of a master storyteller. These layered, rich, strange and beautiful stories are based on his childhood in Felling in the North-East of England and transcend the usual publishing boundaries of 'age groups'. Almond wrote them before he wrote the prize-winning *Skellig* (Hodder Children's 1998), but they weren't published until after he was established as a successful novelist for young people.

Read these stories and then, as a 'writing exercise' in your writing notebook (of course you have one of these!), take real incidents or experiences from your own childhood as the material for a short story, so as to get in touch with the real, raw emotions of childhood and to help you find an authentic voice in your writing. (Note: this might end up as a short story 'about childhood' as distinct from a story 'for children', two subtly different things.)

One of the great satisfactions of writing a short story is that sense of having the complete story in your hand, so you can 'see' it all at once, with its beautiful, honed shape. You can polish and perfect it, and learn much that will help you with all your writing, particularly about precision and brevity, voice and tone, and about the significance of endings. Aim high. Only the very best writing is good enough for children.

As children's writers, we have other things to consider as well as mastery of the short form. A contemporary short story for children is likely to be commissioned by an editor, via an agent, on a particular theme, to be published alongside other stories by other writers on that same theme. For example, I have been asked to write stories about children and animals suitable for several 'winter' anthologies, about the experience of primary school and on the theme of friendship for children of primary school age (up to age 11). The challenge is to write a story that will be original and different enough from the others in the collection, that will appeal to the age group, be accessible, reflect the diversity of the world we live in and be enjoyable and engaging. The story needs to feel complete, to give the reader that satisfaction of a happy (or happy/hopeful *enough*) ending. It needs to take the reader into its world and introduce the main character (in my case always a child) swiftly and immersively, and to do this within a word limit (in these examples, 1500 words).

So, like a novel but in very condensed form, the story has to establish a character, a setting and a situation. It must take the reader on some kind of 'journey' with ups and downs, as the character does things (takes certain actions) to try to resolve the 'situation' (problem/issue). And then it must swiftly reach an ending – in such a way that the situation you established at the beginning is either resolved or changed in some way. You might ask yourself these questions: What does my character want? What do they DO, to try to get it? How does it all work out? (Do they get what they wanted ... or something else, unexpected?)

In a story for children, it is usually a good idea to put the child at the centre of the action, to make them ACTIVE (rather than passive, having things done TO them). **Write from the child's perspective**. Find a voice that feels fresh and authentic and contemporary. Experiment with first person or close-up third person as a way of bringing your child reader close to the action. Children want to immerse themselves in the story.

I write realistic stories, but a short story might be in any genre: fantasy, science fiction, supernatural, funny, historical. It can be a good way to **try out something new**, in terms of style or genre, before committing to a longer project. And some ideas just come as 'short'; you know that's the form they need to take. After I'd written a commissioned short story about a girl and a seal pup, I went on to write a novel, *Seal Island* (OUP 2014). The short story had led me into a longer story in a similar setting with a similar central character, but with more incidents, more characters, more developed themes and the longer time-frame that a novel allows.

When we are learning, nothing we write is ever wasted, whether it gets published or not. We write first and foremost for ourselves. **Practising the short story form will improve all your writing.** There are short story competitions which can give you the benefit of a deadline, and sometimes a subject or theme, too. Having the constraints of a word count can be strangely liberating. Set yourself a deadline, a word count, and a subject, and see what magic happens. The mind plays games. A character will arrive, and a place – all stories have to happen somewhere – and before you know it, the story will start to emerge. Keep asking questions: *What if...? Supposing she....* Write it, one word, one sentence at a time. Write the first draft, fast. Then – cut, cut, cut! Polish. Make it beautiful. Make it the best story it can be. Write the story only *you* can write.

Julia Green is the author of more than 20 novels and short stories for young people. She is Emeritus Professor in Writing for Young People at Bath Spa University and founded the MA Writing for Young People, which has launched the careers of more than 65 writers for children and young adults. Her most recent novels for children are *The House of Light* (2019) and *The Children of Swallow Fell* (2020), both published by OUP Children's, and a picture book *The Boy Who Sailed the World* (David Fickling Books 2022). She is currently writing a collection of short stories and a new novel for young people. For more information see www.julia-green.co.uk.

Writing ghostly stories

Cornelia Funke describes the adventure of writing ghost stories for children. She highlights the questions writers can ask themselves when creating in this genre and considers how scary the stories can be for children.

I am not sure whether I liked ghost stories as a child. I know that at some point I loved Oscar Wilde's *Ghost of Canterville* (and now think it is the most touching ghost story ever told). But the first one I remember was written by a German, Otfried Preussler, whose *Satanic Mill* is an unforgettable tale: Preussler's ghosts were bowling with their own heads, as far as I recall.

Different types of ghosts

The funny ghosts who try to be scary and are not scary at all. We meet them in fairy tales, myths and Hollywood movies. They are slimy and loud, easily frightened by human heroes and, of course, are the most obvious choice for a ghost story written for children.

The first ghost I wrote about was that kind of ghost: Hugo, an ASG (Averagely Spooky Ghost), to be precise. I created him when an editor friend asked me many years ago to write a ghost story for 8–12 year-olds (don't we love it when publishers put our audience in cleanly separated boxes?). The story became a series of books, *Ghosthunters*, about a boy who is very afraid of ghosts but becomes a famous ghost hunter, with the assistance of the ASG. I had immense fun writing about COHAGs (Completely Harmless Ghosts), FOFIFOs (Foggy Fug Ghosts) and GHADAPs (Ghosts with a Dark Past). Interestingly, with every book my ghosts became darker and scarier.

My young readers became quite obsessed with the series and sent me lots of suggestions for ghost types. I heard from teachers that boys who despised reading had stolen *Ghost-hunters* books from their tables to secretly devour them. My stories invited readers to play with fear – to make fun of it, hunt it, destroy it.

Ghosts are perfect for that. They are the impersonation of our greatest fears – the fear of the night, of death and what may await us on the other side. Not only that – they impersonate guilt, redemption, sadness that can't even be cured by death, they can bear witness to unspeakable crimes and the inescapable heritage of the past.

Heavy themes.

Nothing suitable for children?

Oh yes, they are. All of them.

Children take life very seriously. Life, death, pain, loss … they still face the big questions, because they haven't learned to look away. We can develop quite a skill in that as grown-ups. Children want to look at the dark because they know that what they fear becomes even more frightening when they turn their back on it or lock it away.

Young readers often don't have emotional memories attached to the themes of death, loss and guilt, which makes them much tougher when they play with them. But they've heard about them, the great monsters waiting … and they love to encounter them on the safe grounds of a printed page. As for the children who do know – we so easily forget that many know quite a lot about death and loss, even guilt – they long for stories that help them to cope with the dark by asking questions about it or maybe even give meaning to it. For them, stories can be both shelter and comfort, without looking away, and ghosts can be the perfect travel companions into realms that know about pain and fear.

It was a long journey through life for me between *Ghosthunters* and *Ghost Knight*. During that period, I learned some things about death and loss, about human nature, good and evil – all this apart from the fact that I had always been completely obsessed with knights. (*The Once and Future King* by T.H. White is still my favourite book).

Serious ghosts

The ghosts I found for *Ghost Knight* were not funny. If you intend to write a ghost story that walks on the darker side of this genre I recommend that you find your heroes in real places. Children love the enchantment of fiction that makes them discover reality. The ghosts I found in Salisbury, Lacock and Kilmington were human, and shadows of ourselves. They take my young readers on a journey into their own future as grown ups, but they also tempt them to travel into the past, to Salisbury Cathedral, Lacock Abbey and Kilmington Graveyard. These are all places where they can touch and breathe times gone and lost and follow in the steps of those who have lived before them.

I will never forget the reading I did at Salisbury Cathedral late at night, surrounded by children and parents. It took place, of course, next to the tomb of William Longespee, the man who had inspired my ghostly hero and incarnated my dreams about knights, and who at the same time allowed me to bow to what Oscar Wilde taught me about the sadness of ghosts.

Writing a ghost story

So, as you see, a ghost story is not just a ghost story. Maybe that is especially true for one written for children. There are so many paths to take. A good story always starts with the right questions. Ghost stories like to hide from us, dress themselves in a dozen veils. In readings I always try to explain this by comparing them to a labyrinth. Each one is full of traps and surprises, full of characters that hide between the hedges and love to jump at the poor writer who is trying to find his way through. There are whispers. A story likes to keep its secrets, but it also likes to be chased, found out, hunted and tamed. So it teases you by giving you hints and wrong tracks. And there you are, a pen in your hand (well, as in my case, you may write using a computer), a Moleskine notebook under my arm (well, once again, you may just carry your laptop … be careful though, there's nowhere to plug in in the labyrinth). You are stumbling down the narrow paths, looking for the one that is exactly right – the one that won't be so long and windy that it bores your readers to death; the one that shows all the secrets, all the characters hiding and whispering … It is the greatest adventure to find the heart of a story. And it's true storyline. Of course this endeavour is especially scary when you are looking for a ghost story! You may only find out after turning several corners that you are dealing with a scary ghost. Did I give you the impression that you choose whether it will be funny or scary? I apologise. The story chooses, once you enter its labyrinth. So make sure you ask the right questions before you decide on the one you enter. What do you want the labyrinth to grow for you?

Do you want your readers to love the ghost whose story you'll tell? Do you want them to pity it? Or fear it? Once again – you may answer all these questions and then find that a completely different story emerges. It has happened to me. Many times.

What age group do you intend to tell your story for? Once again, this is a good question and it needs to be asked. But be ready to change your answer if the story demands it.

The setting. Once you've decided on where the story will be set it will be hard to change it, especially if you choose an existing location. With an imagined one you leave most decisions to the labyrinth (which can be interesting!). With a real place, you walk in with a map, with your research and knowledge guiding you. A real place, with all its history, can be like a bag of provisions for your writer's journey. It can be your main character, all the food you need. It will tell you about landscapes, weather, buildings – even characters – and your readers will be able to follow your tracks in their own world, making a wonderful adventure. I still receive photos showing children in Venice who have followed the tracks of my book, *The Thief Lord*. And I heard about a boy who knelt in front of Longespee's tomb in Salisbury Cathedral after meeting him in *Ghost Knight*.

Oh – one more question: who will you be? The hero? Somebody who watches him/her and all the others, a narrator who knows everything? The god of the story? (Well, ghosts don't accept these gods but try, if you want to.) Most likely, you will be all of them. That's the joy of being a writer. You can live a thousand lives and take a thousand shapes.

Yes, go and write ghost stories! And write them for children! Even the dark ones, soaked in tragedy and the shadows of death – maybe those especially. Children are the most magical audience. They slip into a story like a fish into water. Without hesitating. Without asking how deep it is and where you got it from. They will travel the past on their printed wings. They will face their fear of gravestones and shadows moving in the dark. They will consider the possibility that life may not end in death and wonder why it scares them to see proof of it. They'll remember those who came before them and may even get a glimpse at the never-ending circle of life. And if all that gets too scary, just let them chase the ghosts – to save the good ones and send the bad ones to hell.

Hurrah for ghost stories!

Cornelia Funke (pronounced Foon-ke) is a multiple award-winning author of children's fiction and has sold over 20 million copies of her books worldwide. She was brought to the attention of Barry Cunningham at Chicken House (see page 25) when a young German girl living in England asked him why her favourite author's books were not available in English. Chicken House published her latest title at that time in English translation, *The Thief Lord* (2006), and it stayed at No. 2 on the *New York Times* bestseller list for 25 weeks. It was followed by the *Dragon Rider* series, the *Inkheart* trilogy, *Ghosthunter* series and the *Reckless* series. The fourth installment in the *Reckless* series, *Silver Tracks*, was published in Autumn 2021 (Pushkin Press).

See also...
• *Spotting talent*, page 1

Writing magic into fiction

Kiran Millwood Hargrave recommends the techniques she uses to feed and inspire her magical stories, and guides us through each stage of the process that allows a writer's fantastical ideas to come to fruition.

All fiction is a kind of magic: a conjuring. From your imagination, you are building whole people, whole worlds, making them so vivid and tangible your reader will be able to touch them, see them, wish they lived in your stories – but how do you layer magic upon magic and introduce a fantastical strand to your story? Perhaps you call it fabulism, perhaps magical realism, perhaps fantasy. They are all branches of the same enchanted tree, and here are my experiences of reading – and rooting my own stories in – magic.

Roots

My earliest love was the *His Dark Materials* trilogy by Philip Pullman. Read first when I was ten, much of it admittedly flew over my head, but I didn't mind because *how* it flew! Like witches on yew twigs, like swan daemons swirling, like angels stirring the clouds. I believe we all have 'books of power', as I term them, often discovered when we are young, that are keystones for the sort of stories we wish to write.

When I look at my own 'books of power', they largely fall into what I used to call magical realism. This was incorrect, as I've recently learned magical realism refers to those writing in the South American tradition, which addresses issues of colonialism. The better term is fabulism. Alongside Pullman's epic trilogy are: *Skellig* by David Almond, the *Chrestomanci* books by Diana Wynne Jones, *The Wolves of Willoughby Chase* by Joan Aiken, *Journey to the River Sea* by Eva Ibbotson and the ubiquitous *Harry Potter* series by J.K. Rowling. All hold very different, varying systems and approaches to 'magic', and often my first task when writing a novel is to decide where I want my book to sit within that spectrum. My debut, *The Girl of Ink & Stars* (Chicken House 2016), plunges into fully-fledged fantasy; my second novel, *The Island at the End of Everything* (2017) finds magic in nature, and my third, *The Way Past Winter* (2018), is folkloric in its telling and so sits on the border of fabulism.

My first challenge to you is to ask: what are your 'books of power'? Do they tell you about the sort of books you love, and give you an insight, as I believe, into the sort of books you should probably be writing? Some of you will be fantasy fans, while others may prefer that world to be recognisable but knocked slightly ajar to let some magic in. I like to keep my 'books of power' on my desk throughout my current writing project (the books change from project to project). It's an excellent procrastination exercise, but also an inspiring one.

Shoots

Your books of power are on your desk; perhaps you're listening to a film soundtrack (Enya is my writing jam); maybe you have a scented candle wafting snatches of 'Mystical Forest' towards you – and now you're ready to write. It's all possibility ... like new shoots of green life emerging in spring. Some of you will plunge straight in, others will plan your narrative to within an inch of its life, but as a self-confessed 'pantser' (as in by-the-seat-of-your-pants vs 'planner') I wholly condone the former. There is nothing more exciting to me than plunging into the adventure alongside your characters and, as they take on more life, letting them make the decisions.

That said, I started my writing life as a poet; a bit of structure has always helped me and I give this to myself in the form of a map. This piece of advice is probably most useful to those of you writing a quest narrative – something where the characters travel through landscape – but I've also worked on maps of houses, or schools or streets. As soon as the perimeters of the places your characters will inhabit are solid, your imagination can run wild. Often these places also help to define the sort of magic you'll encounter in your world: if it's rife with mountains and dragons, you're probably reaching for an alternate universe, the rules of which you get to decide; if it's a secret door in an otherwise ordinary garden, you've got a beautiful set-up for fabulism. But my main advice at this stage is not to worry about labelling *what* sort of magic you're choosing. Let your story tell you what will work.

When I say 'draw a map', it does not need to be a work of art. My map for *The Girl of Ink & Stars* was a clumsily drawn circle with childish landmarks, with the routes of my characters plotted through the landscape in different colours for each. The plan for *The Way Past Winter* was even more basic: a house, some trees, some mountains, the sea and an arrow pointing 'North'. Think of it as storyboarding, as they do for films. You have your whole story on one piece of paper – and you can always rip it up and start again.

Rings

I can only speak to describe my own experience of writing – and everyone is different – but I like to charge through my first draft, full pelt towards the conclusion. This results in very short, fast-paced first drafts, but it means that the fear of the blank page is conquered. Something is easier to improve than nothing, so I would encourage you to write your first draft quickly, too. Then, the real work begins.

A tree grows rings as it ages, and so too will your story. These next drafts are for firming up its core, and finding the confidence to set down more firmly what you perhaps only gestured at in first drafts. I would argue this is not the time for brutal editing. Rather, luxuriate in bringing your story more fully into being. If you've written a fantasy, full of mermaids and talking animals, give them their back stories. If you've written in magical objects that transport your character into parallel worlds, think about how they feel, smell, look, where they came from. Put in all those details you would want as a reader: colour your world in. Check that your characters' names suit them and the world they inhabit. Research any asides that observant readers will appreciate and think how clever you are. Enjoy playing around, giving credence to ideas that may not quite be working, but that you think *could* – with just one more draft (or three).

This stage takes the longest for me, but it is also the most fun. It's when I experiment and learn the most about myself as a writer, and about what I want this story to do, and what I want a reader to take from it.

Branches

This next stage may appear to be misleadingly titled, as it implies growth when actually it's very likely that your manuscript will shrink – but editing really *is* like growing branches; it's also a little bit about hacking off the weaker ones.

As a reformed poet, editing holds a special place in my heart. I love it, because finally I know what my story is, and editing will help me get it there. But I know not everyone shares my enthusiasm for hacking at sentences or scenes that took weeks/months/years to write. So my advice to you is this: look at it as *giving* your story something, not taking something away. Only by editing can you find the sub-plots worth growing, and those that need pruning. Only by editing can you find the heart of your story, and make it sing.

Buds

Now you're ready to submit (I hugely dislike this word: when I was on 'submission' to agents I made a spreadsheet to keep track of where/when/who and my husband changed all the headings to things like 'date soul delivered' to denote when I sent out the manuscript, and 'poop or not poop?' to indicate whether I got a full request or a meeting/rejection ... humour helps!). Speaking from experience, the waiting is possibly the worst bit of all. Even when you're waiting to hear from, and often being rejected by, publishers, at least you and your agent are in it together. So hang in there, and give yourself the best possible chance of success by taking special care when choosing which agents you send to.

I made a list from the *Children's Writers' & Artists' Yearbook* and thoroughly researched this shortlist, breaking it into a top-tier I wanted to send to first, and then a second to help me get straight back on the horse if those initial queries bore no fruit. Look at those who represent the writers of your 'books of power', and pop them on the list too. Aim high. I did, and I ended up with my first choice of agent. But there was something I did not do right, and that I would urge you to do – that is to classify what exactly I had written.

I've mentioned that one of my 'books of power' was *His Dark Materials* by Philip Pullman, but another was *One Hundred Years of Solitude* by Gabriel Garcia Marquez and a third was *The Border Trilogy* by Cormac McCarthy. If that sounds like a confused list, it was, and it made for a confused manuscript. Fraught with long descriptions of landscape, and far too much pathetic fallacy, I wasn't sure what I had written. This showed in my query letter, which announced *The Girl of Ink & Stars* (then *The Cartographer's Daughter*) as a 'magical-realist YA/crossover adventure story'... Yes, I really did write all that down, and press 'send'. Luckily, my wonderful agent saw past it, but you can help yourself enormously by really pinning down what sort of book you've written. This is the only point at which this really matters, I would argue. Until you send your book to agents, just follow your instincts and write in whatever way your story needs you to write it. Once you have an agent, they can help you nail down what exactly you've written. We sent *The Girl of Ink & Stars* out as an adventure story and let the fantasy element come as a surprise.

That's why I've called this section 'buds' – it's about making your story look as appealing as possible, making it impossible for them *not* to want to represent you, and showing that you really know what you're talking about and are taking this seriously. So, finesse what you call your book. Perhaps it's a 'YA coming-of-age story with magic', like Harry Potter, or a 'fast-paced action adventure story' like Percy Jackson. Comparisons to other successful books on the market are always a good idea, but you should highlight how your book differentiates itself too.

Know that you are not alone in your fear and trepidation ... or your big dreams. I look forward to reading your no-doubt magical stories.

Kiran Millwood Hargrave is an award-winning writer and poet. Her children's books include *The Girl of Ink & Stars* (2016), winner of the British Book Awards Children's Book of the Year and the Waterstones Children's Book Prize 2017; Costa and Blue Peter Book shortlisted *The Island at the End of Everything* (2017); *The Way Past Winter* (2018), winner of Blackwell's Children's Book of the Year 2018; and *A Secret of Birds & Bone* (2020), which was a Waterstones, *Guardian*, and Big Issue Book of the Year (all published by Chicken House). *Julia and the Shark* (Hachette Children's Group 2021), illustrated by Tom de Freston, won the Waterstones Children's Gift of the Year 2021. YA Book Prize shortlisted and Carnegie longlisted *The Deathless Girls* (Hachette Children's 2019) was her debut for YA readers. For adults, she has written the *Sunday Times* bestselling *The Mercies* (Picador 2020) and *The Dance Tree* (Picador 2022). For more information see www.kiranmillwoodhargrave.com. Follow her on Twitter @Kiran_MH.

Reinventing old stories for new readers

Deirdre Sullivan shares her fascination for retellings of fairy tales and the possibilities that arise from looking with fresh eyes at these stories, reworking their age-old power to inspire, influence and connect with young adult readers.

I think we all remember the first stories that spoke to us – however we encountered them, from the mouths of teachers or caregivers or by ourselves. Different voices speak to different readers, and Hans Christian Andersen's *The Little Mermaid* and Oscar Wilde's *The Nightingale and the Rose* spoke to me. I had learned to expect a 'happily ever after', in the way we all do, so these melancholy stories defied my expectations and lodged themselves in my heart, like a shard of the Devil's mirror.

In college I was introduced to the work of Jack Zipes and his anthology, *Don't Bet On The Prince* (Gower 1987) by a friend (to whom the book is dedicated), and I became acquainted with a greater breadth of fairy-tale retellings, in female voices. I had encountered feminist fairy tales before (a small Irish publisher, Attic Press, had published a children's series of these that I used to hunt for in libraries and secondhand bookshops), but revisiting them at the tail end of my adolescence was as potent as a poisoned comb to the skull. Fairy tales have always had what Marina Warner calls a 'suspect whiff of femininity', but I had been raised on stories told by men. Soon I was discovering Madame Leprince de Beaumont and Dortchen Wild. Female tellers had been there all along, it seemed, if you only took the care to look more closely. From then on, fairy-tale motifs wound themselves through my writing, both subtly and explicitly. I became hungry for more fairy-tale retellings, and devoured stories by the likes of Emma Donoghue, Robin McKinley, Neil Gaiman, Aimee Bender, Francesca Lia Block, Isabel Allende and Margaret Atwood.

In the summer of 2015 my publisher, Little Island, approached me about publishing a collection of my fairy-tale retellings. I was instantly excited about it. It felt right. I dusted off some old stories and began work on some new ones. As the collection progressed, though, I ended up writing 12 brand-new retellings, to ensure the themes and voice felt uniform. It wasn't a hardship. When I write, I feel like I am in conversation with myself and with the stories I have been told about the world around me. I run my hands over their edges, and I try to notice new details I am drawn to. I write what I know, but also what I fear and what I love.

Tangleweed and Brine (Little Island 2017) is a book that centres the female experience of the world within the fairy-tale realm. I wanted to write about bodies, and how terrifying and messy they can be. I wanted to talk about being a woman in a society built by and for men. I wanted to talk about fear, but also anger. I wanted to write about the lessons that the world teaches girls, drip by drip or all at once. I was 12 when the last Magdalene laundry closed, and until 2018, I had lived my whole life in the shadow of the eighth amendment. My country was structured in a way that let me know, that let us all know – over and over again – how little women's lives mattered. That casts a shadow, and when I began to piece together the stories for the collection it was largely women in the shadows I was drawn to

– women with bodies that didn't fit societal expectations, women used as pawns for political gain, women who try to find the right thing in a wrong world. It is a sad book, and an angry book, but there are moments of freedom there as well.

… Because there is a witchcraft to being female. From the whisper networks to tampons slipped underneath a cubicle by some kind hand, we find support in each other. There's a shared struggle that binds us. And no one knows that more than a teenage girl. Adolescence can be a very dangerous and lonely place, but there is a power in it, too, an alchemy: changing bodies, fluctuating emotions, the dawning realisations; it's a heady time, and an intense one. It's that mixture of dependence and independence, of forging your own path and being guided along the one envisioned for you. It is a time in my life I remember sharply, and a time that will continue to inspire me. I facilitate creative writing workshops for teenagers, and they are incisive and passionate readers who can enjoy books while recognising their faults. Recently someone asked me when I would write a book 'for adults'; this happens every now and then and is generally framed as a compliment. I brush it off quietly, saying things like 'Oh, you never know', but I'm fairly sure I do know. I write for young adults because I want to, and for the same reason that I tell the stories I do – because they inspire me.

I'm aware that *Tangleweed and Brine* came out at an opportune moment. There was something of a fairy-tale zeitgeist in the air, as well as increased discussion of feminism with the #MeToo movement started by Tarana Burke gaining traction in 2017, when the book had just been published. People, and young people in particular, were becoming increasingly comfortable confronting and unpacking previously unspoken things, looking at the way the world worked and articulating why that wasn't good enough. Whispers were becoming shouts. And my book was not alone – around that time Melissa Albert, Sarah Henning, Louise O' Neill and Daniel Lavery also had books out that reworked or built on old stories and turned them into something of their own. There was something in the air that made writers look at the tales they had been told and hold them up to the light with fresh eyes. And each of us saw something different and built something that was our own from that. There may be a lot of talk about trends in YA but we are all living in the same world; we experience a lot of similar things, consume a lot of the same media, hear the same news headlines. The same inspiration can take two people on very different journeys … I love that.

My advice for someone who wants to rewrite fairy tales would be to be aware of what is out there – to read and reread to give you a sense of what can be done and has been done. Then to listen to yourself. In tarot readings, there are the prescribed meanings of the cards, but sometimes a reader will find themselves drawn to a detail or a symbol; they may not know why, but something about it calls to them. That sense of moving away from what a story is supposed to be towards what it could become for you in this moment – that little, precious space is inspiration. And it's worth worrying at those details like a dog, until you've chewed it into something that's yours alone. With old stories, the more familiar people are with them, the more of a shorthand you can use; a shoe, a wolf, an apple becomes symbolic. Whatever world you put it into, the old story will be humming underneath like a familiar tune. The reader will sense it pulling at them, making them remember when it first spoke to them and all the ways it has spoken to them since. When you retell a fairy tale, you are invoking something very old and very powerful; there's a responsibility to get it right, but a satisfaction when something clicks.

I had two big 'clicks' of this kind when writing *Tangleweed and Brine*. One of them came from years of trying and the other came to me in a dream. The second way was far easier, but I think the first was more satisfying. I had put a lot of 'Little Mermaids' into the collection at first, as it's a story I'm drawn to time and time again. As someone who feels like they spend a lot of time on the outside wondering how people work, I found the mermaid character spoke to me. I grew up beside the ocean, and the tang of salt air was never far away when I was small. The story of *The Little Mermaid* brought me my first sad ending and my first Disney princess, and both of those left small dents on my heart. I had to cull a fair few mermaids as I drafted *Tangleweed and Brine*, but I remember sitting in a café thinking that I could just have my mermaid kill the prince and return to the ocean, and feeling so happy for her. I'm not normally in favour of murder, but I wanted that little tongueless girl – who'd walked on glass for love – to choose herself. And so, in my story, I asked her to do that – and she did. The child I was when I first encountered that story wouldn't have been fond of it ending in a stabbing, but it made sense for me to follow the path not taken in the Andersen story … and to send my mermaid home. The second magic click came with *Bluebeard*. I didn't know what to do; I'd written what was turning into a tender little love story, but the fairy tale demanded a roomful of murdered wives and I just didn't think the *Bluebeard* I had written would do that (#notallbluebeards). I worried and wondered about it for ages, tweaking other stories while I did (one of my favourite things to do when I get blocked on a project is to start something else, even a ridiculous thing; it provides the distance you need to stand back and see what must be done to set things right). It took a dream to point me in the right direction. I woke up with an image seared into my brain: a room full of dead men. And that gave me the key I needed to unlock my version of the story, where the secret is not the things that Bluebeard has done, but who he is and what he has survived.

I care a lot about these old stories. I have tried to inhabit them respectfully, but my experience is only one experience, and that's not enough for such an intricate world. The stories we tell matter. They can and should change. Your voices matter. I look forward to the next retelling and the next one – the same old story, through a different lens, a different heart.

Deirdre Sullivan is the award-winning author of the Primrose Leary trilogy: *Prim Improper* (2010), *Improper Order* (2013) and *Primperfect* (2014), the YA novel *Needlework* (2016) and three books in the *Nightmare Club* series under the name Annie Graves; all published by Little Island. Her collection of fairy-tale retellings comprises *Tangleweed and Brine* (Little Island 2018), *Perfectly Preventable Deaths* (Hot Key Books 2019) and *Savage Her Reply* (Hot Keys Books 2020). A sequel to *Perfectly Preventable Deaths*, *Precious Catastrophe*, was published in 2021. Her short story collection for adults, *I Want To Know That I Will Be Okay*, was published by Banshee Press in 2021. Follow her on Twitter @propermiss.

Books

Journey to publication: the summit is worth the climb

M.G. Leonard shares the obstacles she faced on her journey to publication, how she overcame them and what she learnt about the requirements for middle-grade novels along the way.

To me, the feat of becoming a published author was as daunting as climbing Mount Everest ... people say they want to do it but the odds of getting to the top are slim and the probability of getting hurt is high. Few people try and even fewer succeed.

Stage One of my ascent was to have the idea for my book – and it crawled into my brain on six legs with an exoskeleton and two pairs of wings. My story was going to be about beetles, an ecological entomological adventure, and so I enthusiastically began researching the bugs – which I thought would take a couple of weeks but actually took six years, because there are over 400,000 known species of beetle and I hadn't known that.

Stage Two was to write the book. During this time, I bought the *Writers' & Artists' Yearbook* and put it on a shelf beside my desk. I would flick through the pages inhaling the smell of an industry I longed to be a part of. Foolishly, I didn't read it. Including false starts and real-life obstacles to creativity, like getting divorced and being a single working mum, it took me four years to complete a draft of my manuscript.

Finally, I was moving to Stage Three of the climb – getting an agent! I'd fantasised about finding my literary best friend, the Clyde to my Bonnie, who would belay for me on the toughest part of the ascent – submitting to publishers. But then I got the fear. What if I sent my book to every single agent in the *Writers' & Artists' Yearbook* and they all hated it? I would crash to earth, a failure (cue sad music). I chose procrastination as my avoidance technique: I took the *Yearbook* and went through every agent, putting the ones I thought looked good (all of them) into a spreadsheet; I typed out all their details into columns (there was absolutely no need to do this), including their submission preferences. Then one day I'd completed my long list of possible agents ... there was nothing else I could do other than submit.

At this point, I must confess that I presumed my book about a 13-year-old boy and a sentient giant rhinoceros beetle was for adult readers. I have no defence for this other than I thought: I am an adult, the story came out of my brain, so it must be for adults. As you might guess from this assumption, I hadn't got a clue about how the publishing industry worked. Despite spending a large percentage of my life in libraries and bookshops, I hadn't considered the categories books are sorted into or where my story might fit amongst them. I hadn't thought about what happened after you got an agent. I figured my agent would tell me that. This was an error.

I submitted to four agents on my list. Three rejected me with no feedback. I added a column to my spreadsheet in which to put insults about agents who rejected me. The fourth agent asked for the full manuscript and I sent all 120,000 words of it to them, only to receive a swift reply telling me my book was middle grade (I didn't know what this meant) and that they only represented adult fiction and YA (I didn't know what this meant either). They informed me a middle-grade debut shouldn't exceed 60,000 words and politely suggested I do some market research and edit my book accordingly.

I fell to the ground with a sickening thud. But I'm not a quitter, and a year later, on maternity leave, I began submitting again. This time I'd bought a copy of the *Children's Writers' & Artists' Yearbook* and focused my attention on understanding the rock face I was climbing. I read the whole book, cover to cover, learning about the business and drawing courage from author essays about their journey to publication. It's rare to find a book that's as useful as it is inspiring, but this book is essential reading for aspiring children's authors. Equipped with new knowledge, I began my second ascent, able to see the hand- and footholds that others had used before me.

Once again, I submitted to four agents; once again, three of them rejected me. One said a book on beetles wouldn't sell. Another was rude about my protagonist. I was rude about both of them in my spreadsheet. However, I took on board the agent's concerns about my protagonist and revised my opening chapters. The fourth agent requested my full manuscript. I submitted my 60,000-word book, with a more likeable protagonist, and held my breath … Eventually, I was rewarded with a real-life phone call! Unfortunately, I had a six-month-old baby, so it went to voicemail.

I can still remember repeatedly listening to that voicemail. It was surreal, like getting a message from the other side. The agent said they liked my beetle book and that I could write, but that the manuscript needed work; it had a flabby fourth act and a problematic ending. They told me to call the Golden Egg Academy. This was not the news I'd been hoping for, but it was a crevice into which I could insert my fingers and heave myself a little further up the mountainside. At the Golden Egg Academy, I discovered I'd written a middle-grade book with a YA ending and got a lesson in story structure. I edited my book again. Finally, I had a manuscript fit for submission, and the Golden Egg Academy helped me find both my agent and my first publishing deal.

My journey to publication would have been easier and quicker if I'd read the *Children's Writers' & Artists' Yearbook* before I began my epic climb, but I got here in the end. So, dear climber, put this book in your backpack and don't just smell it, read it from cover to cover. Heed the advice you're given, only be rude in spreadsheets, and don't give up. See you at the top.

M.G. Leonard is the bestselling, award-winning writer of children's books *Beetle Boy* (2016), *Beetle Queen* (2017) and *Battle of the Beetles* (2018), published by Chicken House, the *Adventures on Trains* series with Sam Sedgman (Macmillan Children's 2020-22) and *The Twitchers* series (Walker Books 2021-). Her books have been translated into 40 languages and *Beetle Boy* is being developed as a live-action series for TV. *Beetle Boy* won the Branford Boase Award (2017), and was shortlisted for the Waterstones Children's Book Award and longlisted for the Carnegie Medal. *The Highland Falcon Thief* (Macmillan Children's 2020), the first in the *Adventures on Trains* series, won the Books Are My Bag Readers Award 2020 for Children's Fiction and the Children's Fiction Book of the Year 2021 in the British Book Awards. The second book in the series, *Kidnap on the California Comet*, was nominated for an Edgar award. *Twitch* (Walker Books 2021), the first in *The Twitchers* series, won the Sainsbury's Fiction Children's Book Award in 2021 and was nominated for the Carnegie Medal. Find out more here https://www.mgleonard.com/ and follow M.G. on Twitter @MGLnrd.

Plotting: how to keep your YA readers reading

Sarah Mussi spells out the function and importance of plot in driving your story along to a gripping climax, and provides a sure-fire plotting route-map you can follow to ensure your readers stay reading.

When I was a child I loved playing chess. I loved the feel of the pieces and the way each one had its own character. My brother, four years my senior, used to challenge me to a daily best of three. I loved obscure openings and mad middles – all those heads that rolled! I adored setting the board up and the names of the pieces – rook and pawn, bishop and knight – but I hardly ever lasted long enough to experience endings. My brother wiped the board with me. At last, one day, he took pity on poor, beaten, eight-year-old me: he said, 'Thing is, sis, chess is a game of strategy – you've got to plot out your moves and, unless you learn how to do that, you're never ever going to win.'

I got a lot better at chess very quickly. I woke up from the dream of touch and name. Part of the magic was gone and I never really enjoyed the game in the same way. But now I won as often as I lost and, in time, the calculations of strategy brought their own pleasures.

Plotting a novel is much the same. In the good old days, I'd start at the beginning and meander through the story at whim, following errant characters and getting so excited about their lives. Somewhere around the middle, just as in those early games of chess, I'd come a cropper and do all I could to salvage the story. Then I'd send it out and cross my fingers … and get nowhere.

Now I plot. I plot to keep my YA readers thrilled, to keep my publishers coming back, and to succeed at the important craft of storytelling.

So what is a plot?

I think of plot as a journey, and very specific to the story I am setting out to tell. As for any successful journey, there are some basics I need to know, such as where I'm going, and the route; above all I need to know *why* I'm going at all. If the plot, then, is the journey, the structure is the *way* I tell you about it. Blow by blow, or after the event? Or perhaps framed by me sitting up in a hospital bed, in a way designed to raise your curiosity about how I ended up there? How I tell you about my journey is key to engaging your interest, manipulating your emotions, helping you and my teen readers relive the fun and feel the despair.

I believe every story is an emotional journey, and plot is therefore soul food, catharsis and relief from the seemingly random ravages of life. That is the true function of plot, and why it's so important to work hard at delivering it.

Setting the route

When considering any journey, it's a good idea to see who has made that journey before and whether they left a map. Luckily, since ancient Greek times, writers of story have charted many maps, among them the ubiquitous five-act structure of Shakespearean drama and Greek tragedy (six for comedy), which later inspired the three-act structure of modern storytelling and film. All share important features, but the key to delivering the story is in capturing causality. Without causality, the structure of the story starts to descend into happenstance, with random events taking over – a bit like in real life. One thing I have learned is: never let real life get in the way of a good story!

The key to causality lies in setting up a *character-driven plot*. The action can be driven by either the protagonist or the antagonist. The only difference is that in the former, a protagonist-driven narrative, the protagonist acts from his/her own desire to achieve a goal whereas in the latter, an antagonist-driven narrative, the protagonist reacts often in order to survive. The narrative equation I like to establish, in either case, before embarking on my story journey is:

character + goal (*desire/survival*) – obstacles + solutions = climax and catharsis

Therefore the key, in tying character and events together to form a balanced plot, is in *character motivation*. This drives the action and creates cause and effect. So one key question I ask both my protagonist and my antagonist is: what is motivating you?

Setting out on the journey

When I finally put fingers to keyboard, I want to know how the opening of my story will draw the reader in. The initial setting out (I prefer this term to 'setting', which risks being static) of the story must reveal the everyday life of my hero and establish reader identification with them. I check to make sure my hero is indeed heroic. I'd hate to go on a long car journey with a miserable moaning teenager – and I feel the same is true in story. I have to be selective about what to include about their backgrounds. Exposition is always clunky, so I work on a strictly need-to-know basis. If the reader doesn't need to know any bit of information, I don't tell them.

Being guided by the principal that every character needs a *purpose* (and a purpose in a story forms the foundations of plot), I try to always have my characters wanting something, even if it's just a glass of water. Then I make sure they don't get the water easily. Being mean to my characters is paramount.

The most useful story goal is one that is dramatic, for example your character receiving a gold medal as opposed to wanting to win. If I find my protagonist being driven to act by too much internalised feeling I stop and ask myself what would that look like? And jot the answer down under the section entitled: Planning the climax.

However, journeying towards a destination is not going to be momentous unless something is at stake. If the mission fails, there needs to be some consequence. Any journey could soon be aborted if nothing would be lost by doing so. I like to think of the stakes as the negative goals. Many a hero might have said, 'Oh heck to this, I'm going home,' when presented with the first obstacle – unless there was no home to go back to. The higher the stakes the better, too. If I can fix it so that the existence of the universe hinges on the achievement of the quest, then I know I've got a page-turner.

Understanding why the hero sets out to achieve their goal at all is key. Very early on I like to introduce the inciting incident – maybe even on the first page – sometimes even before that. I present my hero with an irresistible opportunity to start them on their journey.

I like to try and fill in a through line, just to be sure I'm staying on track, for example:

_____(*story title*)_____ is about _____ (*character/characters*) _____who set(s) out to _____ (*the goal*) ____because _____ , but all does not go smoothly because _____ (*the problem and stakes*) _____so he/she/they end(s) up _____ (*the solution*).

Story beginnings are hard to get right. I personally like to be tutored by the ancients. I like to begin, as they did, *in medias res* (in the middle of things). Sometimes, of course, you have to work up to that and, like slicing the crust off a loaf to get to the yummy bit, you have to slice off your first few chapters. I console myself that my initial opening work will not be lost: after the story gets going and I head towards my first set piece, I can cut the characters enough slack to drip-feed in those key bits of background I had worked on initially.

Setting up the set piece

I consider a set piece to be a big scene and describe it as a set piece because it needs setting up. So, after 'setting out' comes 'setting up': I start by mentioning the event, then foreshadowing it. I remind the reader that 'something is coming'.

The set piece, like all set pieces when it arrives (Oh, that moment when Lucy and her siblings actually go through the wardrobe together …), should deliver a twist or a turning point. It should reverse the fortunes of the protagonist.

When it comes to a turning point, I love the word 'volte-face'. It reminds me to make sure my character comes out of the scene drastically changed by that experience. For example in *Snow White*, after the inciting incident (that unwelcome message from the mirror) the huntsman takes Snow White into the woods to be slaughtered. The fact that he spares her doesn't change the volte-face. She goes from being rich to penniless, from a princess to a beggar, from being alive to dead (in the reported sense).

So how do I deliver this? Well, I think it should be dramatic (i.e. a big scene) and pose a dilemma. It should leave the protagonist in a situation that is directly at odds with the one they were in when they entered the scene. The dilemma posed by the set piece needs to force the protagonist to act in a way that they had probably never considered before.

Middle or muddle?

Now the story has got punch. Each event can trigger the next and so on, upping the stakes as they occur, until the point of no return is reached.

And then what does your character do? Well, hopefully they make things a lot worse. Why so? Because no story is gripping without tension. So your character during Act Two must struggle onwards and fail, until nearly overcome by the challenges. For as Oscar Wilde said: 'The suspense is terrible, let's hope it will last.'

The setting (or the antagonist) can provide the challenges, as can the inner demons of the protagonist themselves. Like God testing Job on his rubbish tip, our job as gods in our narratives is to test our heroes by making things truly appalling.

But how do we deliver this? Well, plotting a downhill path for the hero means remembering that for every challenge the protagonist needs to formulate a solution. Each solution should not solve the problem, but instead *cause* the next problem. Inside every solution should be that built-in flaw. Each flawed solution might tap into the protagonist's main tragic flaw.

Using conflict in this way, I build until we reach the most serious volte-face, which reverses the fortunes for my hero so drastically that the darkest hour – the well of despond or last straw – is reached.

As the protagonist sits on his rubbish tip (à la Job) or feels despair in his cave (Robert the Bruce) or lies slaughtered upon the stone table (Aslan), it is worth considering the position of the antagonist and refreshing the readers' memory as to what the antagonist's motivations are, and especially what is their Achilles' heel. Think Smaug's loose scale or the White Witch's failure to study the Deep Magic. For therein lies the moment of truth, when the hero can search inside themselves and act from their inner essence to exploit their antagonist's vulnerability and reverse their own fortunes for the last time. Then they can go into the final set piece, the Act Three volte-face, the obligatory scene, the ordeal, the shoot-out at OK Corral, the climax of the plot, *and win*.

Setting the question

Several things must occur at the climax of the story: firstly, the hero must face their biggest obstacle or it will be an anticlimax. They must determine their own fate and the story goal must be resolved once and for all.

Hopefully during the climactic scene, as in a good pantomime, all of my key characters will appear. Hopefully I will have foreshadowed the setting, and visited it already early in the story, as this will avoid me engaging in any distracting description. I might have paired the scene with an earlier one as well, to mirror the action; I can't help thinking of Steinbeck when I plot out my climaxes – his so superbly plotted *Of Mice and Men* is a master class in how to deliver climaxes.

All that remains now is to enable my protagonist to: stay on a collision course with the antagonist; win by losing (to be kept heroic); undergo a 'seeming' death only to be reborn (without it all getting too B-movie). At the very end, I like to narrow things down to one simple action (the pull of a trigger as in *Of Mice and Men*; the dropping of a ring in *Lord of the Rings*); this focuses me and gives an elegance to the ending.

However, no story ends precisely with the resolution of the hero's objective. Readers want to know what happens afterwards; they want to know everyone gets their just deserts. I usually try to keep this as short as possible. Whilst readers do want to know, they don't want to know much. After a penalty shoot-out everyone wants to head home. So I keep it short and head home myself.

Writing a novel does indeed mean plotting out your moves. But I'll leave the last word on that to Wilkie Collins, a far greater master of it than myself:

'*Make 'em laugh. Make 'em cry. Above all, make 'em wait.*'

Sarah Mussi's first novel *The Lion Skin Rug* was shortlisted for the BBC Worldwide Children's Talent Fiction Award and her second novel, *The Door of No Return* (Hodder Children's 2007) won the Glen Dimplex & Irish Writers' Children's Book of the Year Award and was shortlisted for the Branford Boase Award. Other books include *The Last of the Warrior Kings* (Hodder 2009), *Angel Dust* (Hot Key Books 2012), *Siege* (Hodder 2013), *Breakdown* (Hot Key Books 2014), *Riot* (Hodder Children's 2014) which won the Lancashire Book Award, *Bomb* (Hodder Children's 2014), the Snowdonia Chronicles trilogy: *Here Be Dragons, Here Be Witches* and *Here Be Wizards* (Vertebrate Publishing 2015 & Shrine Bell Publishing 2017 and 2020) and *Room Empty* (published by Oneworld 2017). Her most recent YA title, *You Can't Hide*, was published by Hodder Children's Books in 2019. Sarah has recently taken a detour into LitRPG (literary role playing games) with *Golem Dungeon* published by Portal Books in 2021. See her website www.sarahmussi.com.

Plotting and pace in your middle-grade adventure

Christopher Edge understands the highs and lows, twists and turns that are needed to hold the attention of middle-grade fiction readers with a thirst for adventure. Here he shares valuable advice on how to structure a plot and drive forward an emotionally engaging storyline that has all the essential elements.

'Adventure is just bad planning.' So said the great Norwegian explorer, Roald Amundsen, who was the first man to reach both the North and South poles but who, as far as I know, never wrote a single word of children's fiction – so I really wouldn't go listening to him when it comes to planning your middle-grade adventure.

But what is a 'middle-grade adventure'? Well, the first part is easy to define, as middle-grade is the term the publishing industry uses to describe novels for children aged 9–12. Now, I'm a subscriber to C.S. Lewis's dictum that the best children's books which can be enjoyed at the age of ten are equally worth reading at the age of 50 and beyond, so when we talk about middle grade we're definitely not talking about fiction that is any way middle-of-the-road or second-rate. These are the stories that can shape young readers' lives, opening doors into new realities, allowing them to escape into other lives, and inspiring them to step boldly forward to mark their own place in the world. And as for adventure, I'd argue it's not so much a genre but more an attitude that's woven into the fabric of children's fiction. Whether it's fantasy, mystery, historical, contemporary, science fiction or even comedy, from Lewis Carroll's *Alice's Adventures in Wonderland* (Macmillan 1865) to *Rowley Jefferson's Awesome Friendly Adventure* by Jeff Kinney (Penguin Random House 2020), the drumbeat of adventure can always be heard as we turn the pages of the novels we find on the bookshelves labelled 'Fiction 9–12'.

This is certainly true of my own fiction. I find it difficult to pin the stories I write down to a single genre, but adventure is an 'ever-present'; from *The Many Worlds of Albie Bright* (Nosy Crow 2016) where Albie climbs inside a cardboard box to travel to parallel universes in search of his mum, to *The Infinite Lives of Maisie Day* (Nosy Crow 2018) where Maisie's adventures are contained within the four walls of her home after the universe outside her front door disappears. In children's fiction there are no hard-and-fast rules about where adventure can be found and, in stories such as *The Longest Night of Charlie Noon* (Nosy Crow 2019) which begins, 'Once upon a time, three kids got lost in the woods', I've enjoyed twisting familiar tropes into unexpected new shapes. But why do readers of middle-grade fiction have such a thirst for adventure? In surveys about children's reading habits, such as Scholastic's biennial *Kids & Family Reading Report*, children aged 9–12 respond that they want books that have characters that look like them; this reaffirms the need for all readers to find themselves represented in the fiction they read, but also that they want characters they wish they could be like because they're smart or strong or brave. So this thirst for adventure could be viewed as a form of wish fulfilment, as young readers seek out stories in which they can see idealised reflections of themselves, placed in exciting and dangerous situations. For these readers, reading can be role-play, their identification with the heroes and heroines of middle-grade fiction offering them a vicarious agency they might not be able to find in their everyday lives.

I think another reason why such a rich thread of adventure runs through middle-grade fiction can be found in the world-view of its readers. Still shaping their understanding of the world around them, these are curious readers who read with fearless eyes. Their tastes aren't fixed in the same way that an adult readers often are. This isn't a jaded audience, but it is an audience with high expectations who will only keep turning the pages of a story if it delivers on its promise of adventure. So how can you craft a middle-grade adventure that will keep these readers turning the pages? The first thing to consider is plot. Now plot is just another name for story – it's the sequence of events that take place in a narrative. And the plotting stage is where you decide exactly what these events will be and the best way to structure them. This is a stage of writing that I love. For me, stories rarely land in my brain fully formed. The initial spark of inspiration might arrive in the form of a character, a situation, or a setting. For *The Infinite Lives of Maisie Day*, I had an image of a girl opening her front door to find an infinite darkness outside. Like any spark of inspiration, this image initially existed in what Russell T. Davies dubs 'the quantum state of Maybe' – with seemingly infinite possibilities it could spawn in terms of the story sparking in and out of existence inside my mind. Through a process of asking questions, researching ideas, and making connections, I started to shape these possibilities into a definitive storyline.

But how could I be sure that the plot I was building was taking the right shape? Lots of theories about story structure come from the world of film. From the three-act structure of set-up, confrontation and resolution, with key scenes that tip the story from one act to the next, to mythic structures such as the 'Hero's Journey' where a protagonist heeds a call to adventure, faces tests, trials and challenges before seizing their reward, screenwriting formulas seemingly offer a short cut to crafting the perfect plot. However, I must admit I don't consciously hold any theories like these in the front of my mind when plotting my adventures. For me, the plot always grows from character or, more accurately, plot and character grow together.

Stories are about change and change is driven by character. Examining your protagonist's motives can help you to build your plot, as you consider the actions they might pursue as they try to attain their goal. In *The Many Worlds of Albie Bright*, the motive that spurs Albie to set out on his adventure is his desire to see his mum again, with this goal fuelling his creation of the Quantum Banana Theory – the invention that enables him to travel into parallel worlds. Handily, this universe-hopping device also gave me a skeleton structure for the story, as Albie journeys through these alternate universes in search of the one where his mum is still alive. Now if your protagonist achieves their primary goal straight away, there's not much of a story – so you need to think about what's going to stand in their way. This could be an antagonist whose own motives and goals place them in conflict with your protagonist. In every adventure there needs to be obstacles, complications and confrontations which your protagonist has to navigate to get closer to their goal. Some scenes might shine brightest in your mind at this point, but thinking about the cause-and-effect of these key moments can trigger ideas for other scenes and help you start to sequence these into a coherent plot. I sometimes draw a flow chart to plot the action of the story – this helps me to visualise the links between different events and keep track of how characters develop.

Every scene should have a purpose that drives the plot forward; deciding what this is can help you to focus on the details that matter when you start writing. Begin each scene as far into the action as possible and as soon as the purpose is achieved that should be your signal to end the scene. Each scene should contain the seeds of the next and, as the story moves forward, you want to keep raising the stakes – but you also need to vary the rhythm of the story so that it doesn't become predictable for the reader. Think about the rhythm you want to create, perhaps balancing action-packed scenes with quieter moments of description and dialogue that slow the narrative pace and give the reader a chance to catch their breath.

Now every adventure must come to an end. Some authors only discover the ending of a story through the act of writing it, but I usually find mine before I even write the very first line. At the outset I have a clear picture in my mind of the opening scene and also the climax of the story, with these two moments tracing the emotional arc of my protagonist's adventure. In *The Many Worlds of Albie Bright*, Albie's journeys through different parallel worlds show him the alternative lives he could have lived, and these experiences change Albie and help him to come to an understanding of what he's really searching for as the story reaches its climax. An adventure isn't just an action-packed sequence of events but an emotional journey too, as characters make discoveries, find out things about themselves, and are changed by their experiences.

Writing itself can be an adventure, so don't be afraid to follow your own path. There will be trials and challenges along the way, and you may even feel lost at times as you hack through the thickets of a first draft – but always try to take pleasure in the journey. And when you make it to the end, the reward you find can be greater than any treasure hoard: it's the sight of a young reader turning the pages of your story, their eyes shining with excitement as they escape into a world of adventure.

Christopher Edge is an award-winning author whose novels for children include *Twelve Minutes to Midnight* (2012), *The Black Crow Conspiracy* (2014), *The Many Worlds of Albie Bright* (2016), *The Jamie Drake Equation* (2017), *The Infinite Lives of Maisie Day* (2018) and *The Longest Night of Charlie Noon* (2019), all published by Nosy Crow. His latest novel is *Space Oddity* (Chicken House 2021). He also is an experienced teacher, the author of guides to creative writing for children and teenagers, *How to Write Your Best Story Ever!* (OUP 2015) and *How to be a Young #Writer* (OUP 2017), and a freelance publisher and education consultant. For more information see his website www.christopheredge.co.uk. Follow him on Twitter @edgechristopher.

See also...
- *Plotting: how to keep your YA readers reading*, page 144
- *Writing mystery and adventure stories*, page 154

Creating your cast of characters

Aisling Fowler considers the power of fictional characters to engage young readers, and gives advice on how to know and develop your characters fully, in a way that draws readers with them on an emotional journey.

The breadth of children's literature is enormous, but no matter what type of book a child loves to read, one thing remains constant: it's the characters that take our young readers by the hand to lead them through the story. Authors hope that their fictional characters will engage a reader emotionally, compelling them to devour chapter after chapter. But how, as writers, can we create characters who feel *real* enough to do this? I think there are two parts to this: 1) not to think of your characters purely as made-up creations, but as people just as real as anyone you might know – with all the depth, complexity and contradictions that go along with that; 2) getting to know those characters inside out, so their authenticity sings off the page when you write them.

In my case, it was the main character of the *Fireborn* series (HarperCollins 2021-), Twelve, who was the first spark of the story for me. She sprang into my imagination with her axes in hand and full of a fiery anger that took me by surprise. She immediately felt strong – but getting to know her thoroughly took a while. I started by asking her questions such as: Why are you so angry? Where is your family? What are those axes for? Through this, Twelve's personality, back story, and many features of the fantastical world of Ember pulled into focus.

When I started writing my first draft, I thought I knew Twelve well. But by the end she was vastly different – not purely because of the journey she'd been on, but also because I'd got to know her better through the act of writing her story. She was no longer abstract; I'd seen her in a variety of situations and discovered her responses to different characters. She felt more complete, more authentic, more three-dimensional. I was delighted – until I realised this meant rewriting how she was portrayed earlier in the book.

For some of us, perhaps those who lean more towards being 'pantsers' (seat-of-the-pants types) than plotters, this is how we ultimately get to know our main characters: we write them and discover them on the page. For those more organised individuals who want to have a clearer idea before they begin, though, there are a multitude of possible methods. You could interview your character, or write test scenes – which is particularly useful, in my opinion, for working out group dynamics. How about reading your character's horoscope, writing diary entries for them, or even giving them the Myers–Briggs personality test? Your imagination is the limit here … anything goes. This will all help you discover your character's strengths and weaknesses, their personality and backstory. But to identify what truly drives them, their goals and motivations for behaving the way they do, you will have to go even deeper, and ask trickier questions: What do they want most? Or even, what do they *think* they want but what do they *actually* want? What do they need (whether acknowledged by them or otherwise)?

Once you've achieved this deep knowledge of your main character, it's time to start thinking about their story arc through your book. How will their experiences change them? How will they grow? This might be immediately obvious or take some careful thought, but your character's emotional journey is every bit as important as their physical one. It's

Books

worth thinking about it in conjunction with your plot to make sure these two crucial aspects of the story are working together to draw your reader ever onwards. In *Fireborn*, Twelve is haunted by her past, tormented by the guilt of what happened to her family and obsessed with thoughts of revenge. I knew almost immediately that her arc needed to be a journey towards acceptance and self-forgiveness, one that would allow her to open up enough to allow friendship to blossom. In a way, her entire quest to rescue a kidnapped girl is a vehicle which lets that emotional shift take place in her. Many of the decisions I made about the plot were informed by how Twelve would react and whether that reaction moved her closer to or further from the goals of greater inner peace and friendship.

I can't think of many children's books (or any?) where there is a single, solitary character. At some point, you'll need to consider the wider cast, those sidekicks who'll be beside your main character on their journey. It's definitely worth getting to know these secondary characters just as well as you know your protagonist. Ideally, each of them needs to feel entirely distinct, with their own desires and story arcs through the book – these might end up being important subplots. As you did for your main character, identify their personalities and back story as well as their goals and motivations. Ask yourself how they differ from the main character and from each other. What sets each character apart?

In any group, real or imagined, there are usually complex dynamics at play. The chances are that this is true in your story too. Does everyone get on equally well, or are some closer than others? Does anyone feel left out? Do your characters bring out the best in each other, or the worst? Does one of them compensate for a lack of a particular trait in another? These are things worth thinking about carefully and I'll illustrate this with a couple of examples from *Fireborn*. Twelve has almost-impenetrable defensive walls around herself and is very prickly towards the other characters. I wanted the story to end with her having made friends, but it was very clear to me that Twelve herself would not be building any bridges. That meant I needed at least one of the other characters to be both kind and persistent enough to do that for her. These ended up being key traits in a secondary human character called Six. Another example involves Twelve's pet squirrel, Widge. I was worried that, because of those walls I mentioned, a reader would find Twelve unlikeable. I wanted to show there was more to her than raw anger. The solution came through Widge, who at the start of the story is her only friend. Early on, it's only through him that we see a different, softer side to Twelve. As he was a non-human character, I didn't feel I was compromising the coherency of Twelve's determination to remain alone – he's a squirrel: different rules apply than to the human characters.

In both examples, the sidekicks are compensating for flaws in my main character, working under cover to make her more relatable, while also (hopefully) staking their own claim on the reader's affections. It's important to remember that, with each new character, there's another chance to engage your young reader – another opportunity for them to find something they relate to, something that speaks to them and makes them care about your characters on a deeper, emotional level. It's this that can make a story utterly compelling. We can probably all think of a book that kept us up way past our bedtime, one that we couldn't stop reading because we had to know what happened to the characters we cared about so much. But, as writers, how do we invite this degree of connection? My take on it is this: we can like a character for their strengths and admire them for their triumphs, but to *love* them, to root for them with every fibre of your being, to cry for them, you need to see their vulnerabilities, their fears, their moments of weakness and the way they face adversity. Almost inevitably, this means putting them in difficult situations. Although this article is about creating characters, don't forget that it's your plot which showcases them. The two things can (and perhaps should) develop in tangent. Don't be afraid to think something like: 'My character is brave – how can I use the story to show this?'.

Let's take a step back. You now have your cast of characters and you know each of them well. It's time to consider how they can be portrayed clearly on the page. Remember that, particularly in the early chapters, their every word and action should be reinforcing who they are, drawing a clear, defined picture in your reader's mind. Consider what you know about each character: how will those things affect the way they speak, the language they choose to use? What about the way they dress, or their attitude towards others? Perhaps even the names you choose for them can help show who they are. This doesn't mean your characters can't have hidden depths, or behave surprisingly, but you need coherence in terms of who you know they are and the journey they're on, both individually and together. From the very first page, you want every character – but especially your main character – to feel as three-dimensional as possible.

In early drafts of *Fireborn*, I found differentiating subsidiary characters difficult. This was because I didn't know them well enough and needed to spend more time with them one-on-one. Later, to make each one feel more unique, I gave them habits or quirks unique to them. For example, one of my characters has a stutter, another constantly uses 'obviously' in his sentences, Twelve bites her lip when she's nervous, and Widge nibbles her hair. These are small things, but if you choose the traits carefully in a way that is authentic to the character, they can act as a shorthand which builds a clearer picture for your reader.

Creating believable characters is at the very heart of what we do as writers for children. Through your characters, young readers will experience ways of thinking and living that are different to their own – and perhaps, through that lens, they'll make more sense of their own lives and beliefs. Maybe your characters will even encourage young readers to question the world around them, show them that they can make a difference, empower them to be the people they want to be. The characters *you* create can do this. So, create them with love, don't be afraid of making them deep or complex and, above all, enjoy the process.

Aisling Fowler is the author of *Fireborn: Twelve and the Frozen Forest* (HarperCollins 2021), her debut novel. *Fireborn: Phoenix and the Frost Palace*, the second book in her middle-grade fantasy trilogy, is due out in Spring 2023. Aisling worked as a support worker and then as a nurse, before rediscovering her childhood love of writing. Follow her on Twitter @fowler_aisling and Instagram @aislingfowler.

Writing mystery and adventure stories

H.L. Dennis shares her own imaginative method of creating and refining a story, and bringing adventures and emotions fully to the page, using the structure and inspiration of a film-maker's craft.

I'm going to tell you a secret. I'm not a writer at all … actually, I'm the Chief Executive of my very own Imagination Headquarters. It's a game I play, and it makes writing such an adventure that I'm going to let you in on the mystery of how it works. Not everyone will like this method, but you just might … so I hope you'll enjoy it too.

I've never been to film school – but being the Ceo of Imagination HQ is like being an entire studio working on a film. After all, a good book plays like a film inside our heads. We watch as characters experience triumph and despair, happiness and pain. And, if the story is a good one, we feel those emotions too. That's my aim: to generate emotion in the reader, to make them laugh, gasp or cry. I want readers to feel, to believe, to remember. I hope they'll adventure with me, racing through the pages of my story as the mystery unfolds.

So now let me show you how it works – in Imagination HQ – as I try to achieve this.

Time for popcorn …

It begins with the 'popcorn stage'. This is a time that fuels my spirit – when I'm reminded of the power of good stories. I watch film and TV avidly, re-watching sections, trying to understand the storyteller's craft. I analyse moments when I'm on the edge of my seat, and I break down scenes where I'm sobbing or screaming at the screen. I try to establish exactly how the lighting, music and camera angles make me feel. Then I use exactly the same close analysis on my favourite books; I reread extracts over and over, in precisely the same analytical way. I immerse myself in adventures and mysteries well told. Only then am I ready to start work myself.

Stage One: Development

1. Find the theme – First of all, your story needs to get the 'green light'. You must know why this story needs telling and why it's you who needs to tell it. The theme is the light that guides all the decisions later. It's why the story is emotionally significant. Your job isn't to preach, but to explore a theme that matters to you

My series *Secret Breakers* (Hodder Children's 2012-) was about children's hidden potential. Working as a teacher at the time, I was concerned about how education rated some skills more highly than others. You, too, need to find an area that fascinates, angers, worries or intrigues you. Find something that makes you *feel*; this will become the 'why' that lights your way.

2. Choose your story world – In *Secret Breakers* I wanted to celebrate the abilities of children to do more than adults thought possible. The world of code-cracking was a perfect fit. You might choose to explore the theme of fairness, for example, through the world of sport or science, theatre or space travel. So find a world where you can explore your theme. Ground your adventure in this particular, chosen world.

Books

3. **Prepare the trailer** – Film trailers pare back films to their basic elements. Trailers give us a sense of the story's 'palette'. They prepare us for high octane, thrilling action or quiet, sinister mystery. We know what to expect because trailers sell us emotions the film promises to deliver. Your adventure could be created in a range of different tones, so establish the emotional impact you want by analysing film trailers. Then attempt to write a basic summary of a story, noting what you want the reader to feel as they read.

Stage Two: Pre-production

1. **Select your locations** – If you can set your story anywhere – real or imagined – be purposeful and selective about every single location you use. In my *River of Ink* series (Hodder Children's 2017-) I explored the theme of what makes a life worth living. I chose the world of alchemy to do this and, as the elixir of life was central to this theme, I focused on river locations for my adventure. You need to make every location work to support the story. Choose contrasting locations, intriguing locations, locations that will provoke emotion! Work as a 'location scout', visiting places you can't visit in reality – via guidebooks or the internet.

2. **Cast the characters** – We care about stories because we care about characters. Make sure you rigorously audition every member of your cast, to be certain they're worthy of screen time. The hero of an adventure becomes such after she is tested and because of the difficult choices she makes. We must feel for the characters – even the villains. Make us cheer on an underdog, empathise with the lost soul, root for the character who is scared just like us.

You need characters who give elements of contrast to your theme. In *River of Ink*, a girl with a life ruled by schedules would learn the value of spontaneity. Characters must change as a result of their adventures, so think about how you'd like your character to be in the final stage of your story, then work backwards to create your character at the beginning. Audition a cast of contrasting characters and show us what they're truly like, through their actions and interactions, decision-making and discoveries.

*I like to set up Pinterest boards at this stage – with pictures of locations, sketches of characters and quotes that support my theme. This helps create a sense of tone and sets me up for the more technical stages ahead.

Stage Three: Production

1. **Prepare the shooting schedule** – You can now begin to sketch out the major arc of an adventure. Think about: an inciting incident; times of crisis when all hope seems lost; then the ultimate life-changing climax. Why is the mystery your characters are trying to solve so important? What obstacles are in the way? What is there to gain or lose? Just as you didn't settle for mediocre locations or cast, make sure the stakes are as big as possible, as meaningful as they can be and the most likely to provoke emotion. We need our characters to be scared about losing everything in order for the adventure to mean everything to us.

2. **Compose the storyboard** – By this I don't mean a drawn storyboard (although this might be just your thing); take the schedule and break it into scenes. It's important, particularly in mysteries, to work out what needs to be revealed when and in what order. You might also have an idea about some key set pieces, and indeed the finale which you're working towards. I envisioned one particular scene, at the end of *Secret Breakers* Book Six, before I ever wrote the words 'Book One: Chapter One'. I was always striving towards this

culmination of the adventure – a point when the characters were at their most desperate, and the risk of making the wrong decision the most intense. I could see the weather in the scene, and even hear the musical soundtrack in my head. Here my characters' emotions were at their most raw (and hopefully the reader's would be too!).

The big reveal of the mystery must be worth the pay-off, so give the finale a massive amount of your time, energy and thought. Your ending must deliver all the emotional punch you planned from the trailer stage. Be sure to build anticipation as your storyboard develops; keep the adventure moving, the characters changing, and the stakes increasing.

3. Rehearse the scenes – Now I've worked out the gist of what will happen in each scene and, finally, I get to rehearse. A film director might shoot the same scene many times – you can too.

Don't offer your reader your first thoughts about how to show that scene. Try lots of different ways of 'staging' it. For this, I find the 'record card' system really satisfying: on record cards, jot down how variations of each scene could look. Experiment by changing camera angles and focusing on one character more than others or elevating one emotion over another. Try different ways of revealing character through dialogue and actions. The aim of these rehearsals is to choose a version of the scene that will best generate the suspense, worry, fear or elation in the reader you hoped for. Don't settle. Be the director who demands the ultimate take.

4. Make a rough cut – By this stage I've worked through all the angst of how best to show something; I've built up tension by heightening anticipation; I've put characters through the very worst situations they (or I) could imagine. So now I cut together the ultimate version of each scene and begin to type them out in a document labelled 'My Book'. This is my Director's Cut – and now it's ready for editing.

Stage Four: Post-production

1. Add effects – Every single scene must be worthy of the reader's time. So I cut, I tighten, I search for the most powerful phrase, the truest character reaction, the most poignant beat to build emotion. You can speed up shots or change the lighting to get closer to the characters and show their emotions more clearly. It's fun to scrutinise every page, every paragraph and every sentence, to make sure it's the best it can be.

2. Check continuity – Now I ask whether the whole thing hangs together as one seamless piece. Does the internal logic of the whole adventure make sense? Does the mystery unfold without stuttering or confusing? It's time to ask if you've done everything you promised the reader you would. The record cards are packed away and it's time to focus on the whole story you've created, splicing together the joins so no-one can see the technicalities of your craft!

Stage Five: Distribution

Release – This is it. You've created a story. You've written an adventure full of emotion, twists, turns and cliffhangers, which all build to the solution of your mystery and the emotional punch you guaranteed! Now, at last, it's time to grab your copy of the *Children's Writers' & Artists Yearbook* and – if you have any of those record cards left – use them to jot down a list of agents to approach. It's time to send your story out into the world to find its audience.

Time for popcorn again

And now you wait …

Remember though – some people might dislike my suggestions about how to create a story; some fear that such a technical approach might clutter the magic of creation. There's also a chance your story might not resonate with all who read it, but that is part of the adventure – the mystery of the power of words. I personally believe magic *can* come from design, emotion from knowing direction and a powerful story through purposeful attention to detail.

So, if at every stage of the operation of Imagination HQ you've worked hard and refused to settle for mediocre, then you need to relax now and trust in your process. You *will* find an audience. The right reader is waiting. Just enjoy another bowl of popcorn, while your story makes its way out into the world to find them.

Helen Dennis is the award-winning author of the *Secret Breakers* six-book series and the *River of Ink* quartet, both published by Hodder Children's Books. *Secret Breakers: The Knights of Neustria* (2013) was nominated for the Carnegie Medal and the series has been optioned for a live action TV series. *River of Ink: Genesis* was selected as a BookBuzz book by BookTrust 2016 and included in their Deaf Awareness Week Recommendation List 2019. Helen worked for 20 years as a junior school teacher before becoming a full-time writer. She has an MA in Creative Writing Education and the Arts from Sussex University. For more information see www.helendennisbooks.com and www.hldennis.com. Follow her on Twitter @HLDennisauthor.

World-building in your fantasy fiction

L.D. Lapinski explores the creative art of world-building, with its imaginative potential and hidden depths, and has advice on how writers can bring their fantasy worlds, and the characters that navigate through them, to life in a way that engages and absorbs young readers.

World-building is such a strange and magical thing: using just your mind, you are bringing entire populations, places and universes almost to life. Creating a new reality that can feel as precious and vulnerable and enticing as the one we live and breathe in is a fantastic exercise, and one that – given how little we have been able to travel recently due to the global pandemic – seems increasingly tempting. The world you build is not an empty set; it can have as much character as your hero, or as much menace as your villain. The world you create takes your reader on a journey which can be as close to home or as far flung as you desire.

I have always created imaginary places and worlds. Reading and writing have been my creative escape for as long as I can remember (and possibly even further back than that), and I have very fond memories of spending a rainy holiday in a caravan hunched over, drawing a detailed map and plotting a vast history for 'The World of Bunny Rabbits'. The real world wasn't appealing right then, so I made my own. And I'm still doing it. My first novel for children 9+, *The Strangeworlds Travel Agency* (Orion Children's 2020), arrived in bookshops at the start of the pandemic and, though it was a very unexpected baptism, I hope it offered an escape to young readers looking for ways to get away from our world and into others.

However, simply hurling a new world at a reader does not a story make. Novels are, at their very heart, entertainment. The story needs to seize us by the wrist and drag us along a journey, not simply abandon us, mapless, in a new place with no sense of direction. Any world you create is there to work with and for your characters – it is a backdrop that you can change to fit and make the most impact in your story and, although your characters may navigate it with ease, the world they explore and tell the reader about still needs to be strong and 'real' enough to support their narrative journey. And this support is quite a literal concept when it comes to fantasy worlds!

Picture a penguin. Add the David Attenborough narration, if you like, as the camera pans back to reveal that the tiny penguin has hitched a ride on the top of an iceberg, and the iceberg drops deep into the depths below, far more of it below the waterline than above it. This iceberg, and the penguin, is your world-building. As you might expect, there is always so much more going on below the surface when writing fantasy books, but in this analogy what's really important for you to focus on isn't the iceberg at all. It's the penguin. As the writer, that tiny wee penguin is the amount of world-building you're actually going to have the space and words to include in your children's book. The iceberg above the surface is the amount and detail that you, your editor, and your agent will know. And, sadly, that huge mass below the surface is everything that not one other person will ever, ever, see. You might not even write it down.

Then surely we can get rid of it? Well, you could do. Take the iceberg away and the penguin would be able to swim for a bit. But it wouldn't be able to keep it up forever, and eventually it would get eaten by a sea leopard. The iceberg, even the unseen and unwritten part, protects and supports the penguin on its journey. In the same way, your characters and their journey could not carry on for very long without the supporting detail and facts of your world-building.

Tell me again how a world should feel

In *The Strangeworlds Travel Agency* series so far, Flick and Jonathan have travelled to 14 different worlds in the space of two books. Hardly a great feat for them, given that there are 743 magical suitcase-portals in the travel agency, but certainly a challenge for me to keep a handle on when writing. Such a plethora of worlds could rapidly have felt overwhelming and difficult to keep track of, but – rather than begin an encyclopaedic collection of notes – I consciously crafted the worlds so that each one would appear distinct, without having to deep-dive into the history of each one, particularly since some of the characters' visits are rather fleeting.

I designed each individual world to evoke a specific emotional reaction from both the characters and the reader, and in such a way that each reaction would not be deliberately repeated. I created one world written to be deliberately frightening, another to be innocently joyful, one to be calm and soothing, and so on. In doing so, I was able both to show off the vast potential of *The Strangeworlds Travel Agency*'s magical suitcases, and to ensure that each of the worlds visited by the reader would be memorable. Even if the name of the place was forgotten, a younger reader might remember that one world was 'the scary one' and another 'the funny one', because they will relate to the world in the same way that Flick and Jonathan do. The characters' emotional reaction would be tied to the setting and what happened there, and will be mirrored by the reader, who wants to find out more and find out what will happen next.

Fantasy rules! Okay...?

Who runs the world? Well, you do! The great thing about fantasy world rules is you get to make them up. And they can be as 'normal' or as outlandish as you like. They don't even have to serve a purpose beyond being entertaining! If everyone has to stand on their chair and shout 'WAHOOEY!' after eating, you can make that a rule. Perhaps this is never explained – and that's completely fine too. But how many of those rules you want to include is dependent on several factors: firstly and most importantly, your readers (and probably your characters) are children. Whether they are visiting this world for a brief visit like in *Strangeworlds*, or they live there full time, they are only going to focus on the aspects of their world that are the most pressing and interesting to them – the parts of their world that are driving their story, and their journey, forward. And if this element is shouting WAHOOEY, your characters might not bother mentioning the complex political systems of their world. Thinking again of the penguin atop the iceberg of world-building and how aware it may be about what's going on below it, remember that, however much you might know your fantasy world inside and out, your reader wants your characters to navigate the world you have built, not to read a travel guide about it.

Secondly, the amount of description you have space to include will always be restricted by the word count. There's nothing wrong with having enough world-building potential to fill a 500,000-word book, but editors and agents generally prefer shorter books (and it helps to keep printing costs down!). Tell readers what they need to know straight away, and use the rest of your imagined rules as iceberg-style unseen support for the story. It's still important, it's just out of sight.

Books

Think fast!

Anyone familiar with video games will know that at the start of a game there is often a video, less than three minutes long, in which the world of gameplay is introduced – a few minutes of speedy world-building for games that can take dozens of hours to complete. I checked a few of these out, and on average an introductory video accounts for about 0.1% of total gameplay time. That's like doing all your introductory world-building in the space of a paragraph that takes up about one third of a page. That sounds pretty extreme, doesn't it?

Actually, no. A decent chunky paragraph at the start of a book can work extremely hard, just as the intro to a video game might. That initial chunk of world-building description introduces what sort of world this is, whether there's anything readers can recognise and relate to, whether there's magic or not, and it sets the scene for other, smaller bits of world-building which can be 'confettied' through the rest of the story. A first world-building paragraph has to be enticing; it may be the deciding factor as to whether someone carries on reading your book or not, having picked it up in a shop to browse through. The first impressions the reader of your fantasy world receives need to be rich, engaging … and brief. Readers should want, nay *need*, to know how your characters are going to navigate this wonderful or terrifying new place. They may even have an initial idea about the sort of problems they may encounter or the fun they might have. That early paragraph of world-building is advertising the journey your characters are about to go on; show off the best bits, and leave the details for later. And if, as in *The Strangeworlds Travel Agency*, the concept of your world is what you want to showcase rather than a description of a place, remember to hint at the richness of its potential but leave the reader hungry for more. Your character's journey is to get from A to B (whether this is physically or emotionally), but your reader's journey is to find out the details and to get thoroughly lost in your new world of fantasy and magic.

To be able to build a world for young readers to explore is a wonderful thing. Whether or not we can ever throw open the doors to our fantasy worlds completely, by writing them down at all we are inviting readers to wander within, to make up their own minds about the potential dangers or excitements – and inspiring them to create escapes of their own.

L.D. Lapinski is the author of *The Strangeworlds Travel Agency* (2020) and the sequels *The Edge of the Ocean* (2021) and *The Secrets of the Stormforest* (2022), all published by Orion Children's Books. They have worked as a primary school teacher and have an MA in Creative Writing from Nottingham Trent University. For more information see www.ldlapinski.com. Follow them on Twitter @ldlapinski.

See also...
• *Writing magic into fiction*, page 136

Dealing with tough issues in YA fiction

Holly Bourne shares advice for YA authors on how to deal with sensitive and difficult issues through fiction in a responsible, truthful and supportive way that provides 'a safe space for teenagers to explore the dark'.

The YA author has an undeniable influence on their readers, which is why it is vital that they write sensitively and responsibly. I believe that the right book given to a teenager at the right time can change – maybe even save – their life.

Puberty is a pretty ruthless stage in life; it is when weird things happen to your body, a time of first love and first heartache, of first-time sex, and maybe when bullying, loneliness, exam stress or mental illness cast a shadow over your life (75% of people who develop mental illness in their lifetime do so before the age of 18). In short, it is a period when you are grappling with your sense of identity, trying to figure out *who you are*. Being a teenager can be exhausting, exhilarating and terrifying, and I believe fiction can offer both refuge and respite during this time. The best stories don't only provide a gripping plot but also help young readers to make sense of their lives or to feel less alone.

As a YA writer, you must convey essential truths about the teen experience for your stories to have any hope of connecting with your readership. Teenagers are not naive about the hardships of their existence. I travel to schools all over the country to talk about books and mental health and I'm always blown away by how sensitive teenagers are to emerging social issues. There's not much darkness they're not already hugely aware of or personally wrestling with. They're hugely grateful to have books that shed light on the concerns that preoccupy them. Remember that teenagers are legally children and therefore, as a YA writer, you have a responsibility to tell the truth *safely*; you must ensure your story is truthful but not harmful. This delicate balancing act is something it can be tricky to get right.

Before I became a full-time author, I spent five years working as an advisor for young people at a charity called The Mix. This experience gave me a concrete understanding of teen issues and how to engage with young people about their problems within a rigorous safeguarding framework. This has provided me with an invaluable background to my fiction career, in which I feel able to tackle the darkest subject matter in a way I know is as safe for readers as possible. In my novels I've tackled suicide, self-harm, abusive relationships, rape and sexual assault, obsessive compulsive disorder, alcoholic and neglectful parents and many other 'tough issues'. If you research your topics intensively and remember any safeguarding training you have had and expert advice at all times, there are no limits to how dark you can go in your fiction. In fact, teenagers may be grateful that you have.

This safeguarding underpinning must be there at all times. Never let your writerly ego, or the thrill of writing the more dramatic bits on the page, seduce you away from your responsibility to provide a safe space for teenagers to explore the dark. Whatever issues you decide to tackle, you'll need to research them more vigorously than simply reading this article, but I hope the following guidelines will be a useful starting point. Now, where's the torch?

Writing suicide safely

I'm starting at the very darkest of where the dark can go. That's because it's a hugely common theme running through YA books and one that can have literally fatal consequences if tackled insensitively. Unfortunately, many YA books that have handled this topic dangerously have gone on to achieve huge publishing success. Rather than making it a free-for-all, we need to learn lessons from this – educating ourselves and trying to do better. Any author who wants to explore this issue should research its copycat nature and how getting it wrong can cost someone's life. For instance, Google searches for 'how to commit suicide' rose by 26% after Netflix released the first season of *13 Reasons Why*.

Strong starting-points for research include the Samaritans guidance for covering suicide, as well as the World Health Organization's media guidelines for preventing suicide. Here are some of the most important guidelines:

• Try not to include any detailed suicide methodology

Leave out any technical details about how a character may take their own life, such as how many pills to take, and never discuss the 'success rate' of any method. Never imply there's any quick or painless way of completing suicide.

• Never show suicide as a solution to a problem

I once heard suicide described as 'a very permanent solution to a temporary problem.' Even if that is what's going on in a character's head, avoid glamorising the fatal notion that suicide is an 'answer' to life's hardships. Instead perhaps strive to show a character who overcomes this suicide idealisation, gets help and goes on to enjoy happiness. This is something I did in my novel *Are We All Lemmings and Snowflakes?* (Usborne Publishing 2018) which opened with my protagonist Olive in a suicidal state, but ended with her in a much better place. I was also careful to focus mostly on Olive's suicidal 'feelings' rather than showing her detailed thoughts.

• Avoid giving characters who have completed suicide 'notoriety'

The element of notoriety that may result when someone takes their own life is something that can glamorise it and cause copycat behaviours, which young people are particularly susceptible to.

• Suicide is never triggered by just one thing

It's is a hugely complicated behaviour, with no $a + b = c$ formula behind it, so it's important not to give a reason 'why' a character was triggered to take their own life.

The right book can save someone's life. Suicide is certainly not a subject to avoid; just ensure you take the time and consideration to write about it safely – there can be catastrophic consequences if you don't.

What is 'triggering'? And how to avoid it

Triggering is a word with a huge amount of misunderstanding and stigma attached to it. Currently we're seeing a backlash against so-called 'sensitive snowflakes' who demand 'trigger warnings' in art. To some extent it is true that you cannot produce any art that doesn't trigger someone, somewhere, somehow, but the term 'triggering' does actually relate to known psychological responses to trauma which it is important to write about safely. No, you can't keep every reader safe from being triggered, but the following guidelines will certainly minimise any unintentional harm in your writing:

• Self-harm

This is a behaviour that, like suicide, can have a copycat element to it, and reading descriptions of it can 'trigger' people to self-harm. Try to keep any description of self-harm off the page, focusing instead on the *feelings* rather than the behaviour itself. Certainly never describe the method a character uses to harm themselves, and avoid graphic descriptions of bleeding.

• Disorder eating

When writing about someone who overeats or under-eats, never actually state that character's specific weight or dress size. This can cause the reader to compare themselves with that character, triggering shame and further disordered eating. The same goes for calories consumed and calories burned by a character's exercise regime – giving these specifics can be very unhelpful, especially as they're so easily avoided.

• PTSD

The phenomenon most commonly associated with the word 'trigger' is when something triggers a devastating flashback in somebody suffering with Post Traumatic Stress Disorder. A memory of trauma is not stored in the brain in the same way as other memories and therefore, for a PTSD sufferer, reading something similar to what they've been through can cause a flashback. A flashback is when the victim essentially feels like they're reliving their trauma in the present moment, which is obviously hugely upsetting. Although people may be triggered by many different things, I feel it's wise at least to try and minimise graphic descriptions of violence, and especially sexual violence, in your writing. Sadly, many young people are living with trauma and sexual trauma – one in thirteen young people have PTSD by the age of 18 – so keep that in mind when writing about these subjects. You don't need to explicitly 'go there' in order for your story to be powerful. If you get published, do flag the parts of the book you're worried about with your editor. They can then hire a sensitivity reader to check the manuscript, as well as putting a trigger warning on the cover. This is something we've decided to do in my book *The Places I've Cried in Public* (Usborne 2019) which has an off-page rape in it. My publisher hired a psychologist specialising in sexual violence triggers to go through the manuscript and the tweaks she suggested didn't impact the narrative in any way.

Remember mental illness does not exist in a vacuum

Recently there's been a welcome shift away from a simplistic biological explanation for mental illness. The World Health Organization has stated that it is inexplicably linked to human rights issues, and leading experts are campaigning for us to ask people 'What happened to you?' rather than 'What's wrong with you?'. The causes of mental illness might be environmental, socioeconomic or biological, so make sure your character's illness makes sense in the context of the wider world they live in. This is what I tried to explore in *Am I Normal Yet?* (Usborne 2015) about a girl called Evie who has OCD. The book explored both mental illness and gender inequality, making links between the two. I was careful to make sure Evie was never just characterised by her mental illness but was depicted as a fully rounded character who happened to have a mental illness.

An issue isn't a story

Just as a character is not merely representative of a single attribute or one defining feature, a single 'issue' is never a good substitute for an engaging, well-structured plot. It's completely natural that, when writing for and about teenagers, you should want to include tough issues, simply a realistic interpretation of a teenager's life, but the fundamentals of successful storytelling must not be lost.

Always offer hope

I feel a responsibility as a children's writer to ensure my novels have a hopeful tinge, especially when dealing with the tougher stuff. Though I'm careful never to perpetuate unhelpful fantasies such as *Love can cure mental illness*, I do want teen readers who see aspects of themselves in my characters to believe that light can emerge from the darkness. Whether that's through caring parents, the power of good friendships or showing positive experiences of teenagers using mental health services, I believe a YA writer should always offer hope, and that your book should be a light that guides them towards it.

Holly Bourne is a bestselling author whose YA books, all published by Usborne Publishing, include the award-winning *Spinster Club* series: *Am I Normal Yet?* (2015), *How Hard Can Love Be?* (2016), *What's a Girl Gotta Do?* (2016) and *And a Happy New Year?* (2016). Her other books include *Soulmates* (2013), *It Only Happens in the Movies* (2017), *Are We All Lemmings & Snowflakes?* (2018) and *The Places I've Cried in Public* (2019). Her latest books are *The Yearbook* (Usborne 2021) for young adults and *Pretending* (Hodder & Stoughton 2021) for adults. Holly has worked as a news journalist, an editor, relationship advisor and 'agony aunt' for The Mix, a youth charity which helps young people with their relationships and mental health. She is an ambassador for Women's Aid. Follow her on Twitter @holly_bourneYA.

See also...

• *Writing about love and loss for children,* page 168

Writing hopeful climate fiction

Bestselling author and self-confessed literary activist Lauren James has advice for writers on how to promote climate awareness and avoid potential pitfalls when dealing with climate change and the planet in children's fiction.

From the beginning of my writing career, I've wanted to write about climate change. But my writing is focused on character and story. It's funny and romantic. For a long time, writing a book about a topic that is discomforting at best and soul-crushing at worst felt impossible.

The turning point came when I realized that I could focus on characters who are actively working to slow climate change. I'm not interested in dark dystopias about a climate-ravaged planet. We know the dangers already – and I feel strongly that in children's and YA literature we should not be telling a generation that their future is broken. I want to read – and write – inspiring, optimistic stories. After all, the books that reach the widest audiences, that have the best chance of spreading awareness, are enjoyable ones.

After seven years of writing, my sixth novel, *Green Rising* (Walker Books 2021), was the result. It centres on teenagers who can grow plants from their skin. These 'Greenfingers', as they are called, use their powers to rewild the planet, and stand up to profit-hungry corporations. The novel shows how positive environmental changes – involving kelp forests, peatlands, reforestation – can help store carbon in huge quantities. I expected the writing process to be depressing. But, in fact, immersing myself in the climate debate helped me to stop feeling helpless. Instead of trying desperately to ignore the monster looming in the corner of my vision, I was facing it head-on. I was doing something.

Writing the novel, and another climate novella, *The Deep-Sea Duke* (Barrington Stoke 2021), led me to setting up the Climate Fiction Writers League. I was inspired in part by the Women Writers Suffrage League, a UK-based awareness-raising organization, founded in 1908 and disbanded in 1918 after the UK granted (some) women the right to vote. The League's prospectus asserted that 'A body of writers working for a common cause cannot fail to influence public opinion'. This has become our own League's guiding principle. Fiction is one of the best ways to inspire passion, empathy and action. We also partner with many other climate activism groups at events and panels, and by publishing essays and interviews.

Researching the climate crisis

I'm not great at reading scientific publications – it feels too much like homework. But I am good at wasting time on social media. So I tricked myself into researching climate change through online resources although, often, the science has been obscured by politics or disinformation campaigns. Take geoengineering – slowing the global temperature increase by, for instance, using a solar mirror in space, or spraying chemicals into the atmosphere to reflect light away from the planet. These ideas are supported by the fossil fuel industry, which wants to be able to continue selling its products while ostensibly supporting climate action. However, we have no firm idea what knock-on effects geoengineering might have on the planet.

I wanted to explore *Juliana v. US* – an ongoing legal case in which young plaintiffs have argued that the US government has violated their constitutional rights by failing to act on climate change. I'm interested in the way youth activist groups like Extinction Rebellion are treated by the press – as extremist terrorists and moral heroes standing up for the planet, often simultaneously. I also wanted to investigate how billionaires are investing money in accessible space tourism, rather than fixing Earth, and how the new, trendy NFT (non-fungible token) art and bitcoin use huge amounts of power to create cryptocurrency. I wanted to highlight the issues related to carbon emissions, like metal poisoning from coal ash, microplastics and the garbage patches in the ocean. And I wanted to do it all in a positive way, in a book for teenagers. It was a lot to tackle.

Representing all views

I tried to look at both sides of the debate, because the way that climate deniers talk about the topic can often be really helpful for creating narratives. (Why not let them do the hard work of being creative with arguments?) The CEO of an oil company, a billionaire trying to launch a space mission or a politician with investments in fossil fuels don't see themselves as the 'bad guys'. To them, they're community-builders, providing jobs and energy to keep the world running. I tried to put myself in their shoes so I could write characters who felt the way they might. For example, space-race billionaire Elon Musk recently tweeted that he didn't want to pay tax on his companies' profits because: 'My plan is to use the money to get humanity to Mars and preserve the light of consciousness'. In my novel *Green Rising*, space-race billionaire Edgar Warren uses a similar justification in an argument with the novel's teenage protagonist Theo.

I also subscribed to a very niche geoengineering forum. Eavesdropping on scientists' highly technical bickering gave me a lot of insight into the people working at the forefront of this issue, on both sides of the equation.

Making science engaging

In the writing, I tried not to get bogged down in the science. Story always has to come first. I looked for ways to tie science into other fields, like archaeology or linguistics. In *Green Rising*, for instance, my characters plan to use their 'Greenfingers' powers of growing plants to launch an illegal protest against fossil fuel companies, power plants and vehicle manufacturers. I wrote extracts from their online discussions in an activists' forum, dramatising their doubts concerning the science of such topics as solar seeding.

I keep an eye out for interesting, well-known science stories that might provide a way to talk about something more complicated, and for debunked or disproven theories from the past that tell us a lot about people's knowledge level – and motivations – at the time. I also try to think about big concepts in terms of historical events. How can we look at archaeology to get a new perspective on climate change? How might the present day look from a far-future or far-past point of view? Has something like this ever happened before on Earth? What might a climate disaster look like in a far-future world set on another planet? In my novella *The Deep-Sea Duke*, butterfly-like aliens are forced to flee their planet after burning fossil fuels has raised the temperature too high for their caterpillar offspring to survive. Problems arise when the planet they migrate to has the wrong type of environment (fully oceanic) and the butterflies introduce an invasive species to their new home (a rambunctious ferret pet). The book is aimed at ages 8+, and uses this humorous lens to comment on real-world issues.

Should fiction be political?

Ultimately, climate change is a political topic. It's unavoidable. The end of the world is profitable. From trading stock market futures on water scarcities, to increased crop yields in extreme weather, business will thrive as the planet collapses. My characters are angry they're being told to reduce their climate footprint, that they're being made to feel guilty about their personal pollution when industry is responsible for the vast majority of emissions.

From a legal perspective, there were things I couldn't do – I wasn't allowed to mention real life companies or people by name, and had to create fictional versions of certain things. But in *Green Rising*, I tried to capture the feeling of being part of the ongoing green revolution, to show what it feels like to grow up in a time of unprecedented existential fear. I wanted to write about young people who are turning that fear into hope and action, pushing against the enormous weight of the existing establishment.

Writing advice

My top tips for writers who want to include climate change in their work:
• Read climate fiction in a variety of genres, not just science fiction and fantasy.
• Consider the activism going on outside the very vocal UK/US groups. Activists from the countries most affected by climate change are often ignored in the media.
• Inspire activism – but be aware that readers don't want to be made to feel guilty.
• Convey the seriousness of the situation without making action seem futile.
• Show how climate change is no longer a long-term issue but something happening right now.
• Use your frustration in your writing – but be aware that most people don't want to read an angry book.
• Remember that hope and optimism will inspire more action than anything else. Fiction can inspire a huge amount of empathy, which is a force that can be used collectively to inspire change on a global level.

Hopeful climate fiction reading list

A Cloud Called Bhura: Climate Champions to the Rescue by Bijal Vachharajani (Speaking Tiger 2019)

Amara and the Bats by Emma Reynolds (Simon & Schuster 2021)

Beauty and the Bin by Joanne O'Connell (Pan Macmillan 2021)

How to Save the World with a Chicken and an Egg by Emma Shevah (Chicken House 2021)

The Summer We Turned Green by William Sutcliffe (Bloomsbury 2021)

The Tale of a Toothbrush by M.G. Leonard (Walker Books 2020)

A version of this piece first appeared in *The Author*, the journal of the Society of Authors (Spring 2022 Vol. 133.1).

Lauren James is the bestselling author of many YA novels, including *Green Rising* (2021), *The Reckless Afterlife of Harriet Stoker* (2020), *The Quiet at the End of the World* (2019) and *The Loneliest Girl in the Universe* (2017), all published by Walker Books. Lauren is a Royal Literary Fund Royal Fellow, freelance editor and screenwriter, and founder of the Climate Fiction Writers League. For more information see https://laurenejames.co.uk. Follow her on Twitter @Lauren_E_James.

Writing about love and loss for children

Natasha Farrant considers the responsibility shouldered by authors who write about love and loss for children and teenagers and how such novels can be a valuable opportunity for young readers to explore challenging emotions and life experiences.

Years ago, when I started out working in children's publishing and before I was published myself, I went to a lecture given by Anne Fine. A member of the audience asked her what the difference was between writing for children and writing for adults. She replied that you could write about all the same subjects, whatever the age of your readers, but that you would tell the story differently. It was all a question, she said, of the angle at which you shone the light. I want to explore that question here in relation to writing about loss and love, because these are subjects I have returned to again and again in my own books.

Even as I write this, I read in *The Bookseller* that authors John Boyne, Malorie Blackman and Sam Copeland, presenting their titles at the Penguin Random House Children's Showcase, 'spoke of transgender issues, experiences of psychosis and how to cope with anxiety as a small child'. And this focus on difficult themes is by no means new to children's literature. From *The Railway Children* to *The Secret Garden*, *Matilda* to *Journey to the River Sea* and *Harry Potter*, authors have dealt with parental imprisonment, poverty, bereavement, loneliness, persecution, child neglect – all huge issues; all, one way or another, connected with loss.

'Struggle and hardship are the essential ingredients of narrative', writes Trisha Lee, theatre director and founder of MakeBelieve Arts, in *Princesses, Dragons and Helicopter Stories* (Routledge 2015). She goes on to quote Kieran Egan in *Teaching as Storytelling* (University of Chicago Press 1989) who believes that it is our desire to explore global concerns with binary opposites – good and evil, fair and unfair, cruel and kind – that engages us with fiction. This is true whatever age the reader. It's up to us, the reader, to make that exploration as engaging, accessible and, dare I say it, as age-appropriate as possible.

My first book for young people, *The Things We Did For Love* (Faber 2012), is a Second World War love story based on the massacre which took place at Oradour-sur-Glane, near Limoges in South West France, in 1944. Years later, a friend still hasn't got over my writing this: 'A children's book! About a massacre!' Well, it wasn't a children's book, as was made clear by the cover. I have no desire to give it to a child – frankly, there are gentler ways for them to learn about man's brutality to man. But teenagers are a different matter. The novel deals with subjects most teens I know are familiar with: sex and desire, jealousy, shame, the awareness that although they long to do the right thing they often feel coerced by social pressure to do the opposite. Most teenagers, by dint of the online world we live in, do know about war. My book offers them a chance to reflect further on what it means.

What, though, makes it a book for teens, and not for adults? It's a tricky question. A book for young people doesn't mean adults can't enjoy it too. It doesn't mean it can't have adult characters. It doesn't mean, for example, that the characters can't have sex. Sex! How often have I heard book pitches along the lines of 'It's a love story, but don't worry, it's for teens so it doesn't have sex in it' – as if teenagers didn't have sex! In *The Things We Did For Love* my teenage protagonists Arianne and Luc have sex. In fact, Arianne uses sex, rather naively thinking that if she sleeps with Luc, he won't join the Resistance and leave her. I don't show them having sex. I show rose petals leading up to a door (corny, but I couldn't resist), and I show that door closing. But we know perfectly well what is happening, and it's the sort of device that's used in plenty of grown-up fiction.

So again, if I can show torture and I can (sort of) show sex, what makes this a book for teens rather than adults? How have I shone the light? Well, there's the characters, I guess – three of the main protagonists are teenagers; one is a child (and one is a fully-grown man, but we'll put that to one side). They have teen and childhood preoccupations, like falling in love and doing homework. Arianne is trying to fill the gap left by her dead mother and her imprisoned father. She believes she may have found her answer in Luc. She believes she can use her love for him to keep him from harm. And the unnamed teenage narrator, after the massacre, writes that the lovers will be together forever. As adults, we suspect that this is unlikely. As teenagers, it's important (I think) to believe that it is true. Maybe that is the key – that belief in the redemptive power of love.

One of my golden rules, when writing for young people, is this: do not leave the reader without hope. Do not destroy that belief that the world can do better. It's difficult, if you're writing about certain subjects. Climate change is a classic example. But I would suggest that if you see no future for humanity yourself, then perhaps writing for young people is not for you. There are various forms of redemption to be found in *The Things We Did For Love*. They were hard to find, in the bleakness of that event, but the focus of the book (and indeed its inspiration) is the small acts of heroism I discovered in the course of my research and which give the book its title. Because writing for children comes with a certain responsibility.

Scientific research has shown that 'when we connect with a story, parts of our brain related to a particular emotion or action light up, and our neurons start firing as if we were engaged in the activity ourselves' (Kieran Egan; *Princesses, Dragons and Helicopter Stories*). And what is true for us as adults is even more true for a child, during the plastic years of brain formation. Philip Pullman writes about his experiences of playing at Davy Crockett in the suburbs of Adelaide when he was growing up: 'When we children play at being characters we admire, doing things we value, we discover areas and depths of feeling it would be hard to reach otherwise. Exhilaration, heroism, despair, resolution, triumph, noble renunciation, sacrifice: in acting these out we experience them in miniature or, as it were, in safety' (*Daemon Voices: Essays on Storytelling*, David Fickling Books 2017). He goes on to write that, through play, he was 'building patterns of behaviour and expectation into my moral understanding'.

As children play, so they read. They *live* the books they love, and these books offer tremendous opportunity to learn about love and loss and everything in between. They will shape their young readers and make them who they are. And yet, remember this. When you are writing for children, know that you are writing for some of the toughest, most critical readers there are, who will not suffer unnecessary babble. Know that that babble includes you pontificating on love and loss, on how sad your heroine is, or how hard she is crying, or how slowly time is passing. Never forget that other golden rule: 'Show don't tell.' *Show* the loss. *Show* the emotion. *Show* the redemptive love. Use every writing trick at your disposal – metaphor, imagery, leitmotiv – to make them come to life. They're never going to live your book if they're bored.

My middle-grade book *The Children of Castle Rock* (Faber 2018) traces the grief of the main protagonist, Alice, as she mourns the death of her mother. The book opens as she prepares to leave her family home forever. Rather than linger on Alice's emotions, I choose to focus on her refusal to leave without taking her mother's commemorative rosebush, which is dug up and squished into the car. The rosebush then reappears periodically – on a balcony, as a watercolour and eventually in a new garden – in a way which shows the reader without spelling it out that Alice, without forgetting, is nevertheless learning to move on.

As I wrote the story, I asked myself these questions: What has Alice lost? What does she want? What does she need? These are the questions which drive the plot. Alice has lost her mum, her dad is completely unreliable and her home is sold. She needs to rebuild a sense of family, she wants her dad to do this for her but she needs to understand that he never will. These are the questions which give the novel emotional depth and a sense of purpose. They are not what make it an exciting read, though. The excitement comes from the fact that, in her pursuit of these needs, Alice runs away from boarding school, camps on a Scottish beach, almost drowns, breaks into a house and gets chased onto a stack of rocks by a bunch of Italian gangsters, where she gets cut off by the tide … and in the end conquers both her fear of losing her dad and her fear of heights by abseiling down a cliff.

Even as I write this, I'm aware how complex this question of responsibility is. It is absolutely not about watering down difficult subjects, but it's about rendering them in such a way that a child can explore them – as Pullman writes in the quote I cited earlier – in safety. Children, like all readers, will take what they can and what they need from a story. A child who has experienced severe loss will be alive to Alice's grief. A child with less experience of loss may simply enjoy the adventure. The story may lead to greater understanding; it may simply entertain. All forms of reading are valid.

In *The Children of Castle Rock*, as in all my other books, I have tried to acknowledge that bad things do happen, that the people you love are not always reliable, but that there are others who love you if you can open your eyes and heart to them. I have also tried to fulfil my other responsibility as a writer, which is to make my story as cohesive, exciting and as good as I possibly can. But there my task as a writer is finished. Alice's story is in the world, to be completed in as many ways as there are readers. Which is just as it should be.

Natasha Farrant is a writer and literary scout. Her books include *The Children of Castle Rock* (Faber 2018) and *Eight Princesses and a Magic Mirror* (Zephyr 2019) as well as *The Things We Did for Love* (2012) and four titles in her popular children's series *The Diaries of Bluebell Gadsby*: *After Iris* (2013), *Flora in Love* (2014), *All About Pumpkin* (2015) and *Time for Jas* (2016), all published by Faber & Faber. Her latest books are *Voyage of the Sparrowhawk* (Faber 2020), which won the Costa Children's Book Award, and was *The Times* Children's Book of the Year, and *The Girl Who Talked to Trees* (Zephyr 2021). For more information visit www.natashafarrant.com, and follow her on Twitter @NatashaFarrant1.

Series fiction: writing as part of a team

Writer Lucy Courtenay spills the beans on the profitable world of series fiction: its fictional authors, the publishers and packagers, and the skilled teams of editors and writers that create and produce it.

Once upon a time, a group of editors sat around a table, brainstorming ideas for a new children's series for girls aged 6–9. It needed to be collectable with a strong series identity. One editor put up her hand. 'I had an idea for a series when I was seven years old,' she said. 'It was about seven fairies. One for each colour of the rainbow.'

The series, *Rainbow Magic* by Daisy Meadows, has since spawned over 200 titles. There are mini-series of four or seven interconnected titles within the overarching series which share common themes: the rainbow, the weather, the ocean, popstars and parties and animals, to give a few examples. Sales of the series currently stand at over ten million copies worldwide.

You might assume, on those statistics, that *Rainbow Magic* has made its author rich. It has, but not in the way you might imagine. If you remember, it was an editor's idea. Daisy Meadows herself doesn't exist. She is an amalgamation of dozens of different writers and editors, all of whom have taken a share of her profits. She is successful because she is the product of professional, dedicated teams who know how to produce books that children love. The same is true of Lucy Daniels – whose *Animal Ark* series could be said to have started the whole series fiction phenomenon in the 1990s – and Adam Blade, more recently of the *Beast Quest* series. There are plenty of other examples, but these are perhaps the best known. When people first learn this, they are often surprised and baffled. What is the point? Why do publishers produce books in this way? Shouldn't they be supporting original talent, promoting original authors?

A fictional author has no rights over a series, which makes that series more flexible and profitable for a publisher or a packager. A fictional author can also write six or more books at the same time, which does wonders for a publisher's production line and (you've guessed it) profits. A fictional author can be designed to fit a niche in the market. They can be given an alphabetically appropriate name to meet a browser's eye level or queue-barge on to the shelf ahead of the direct competition. They can be designed to fit as many commercial platforms as possible, should opportunity present: clothing, online games, stationery. They can also enjoy lives far more exotic than those of real authors. Adam Blade's biography charmingly gives him a pet capuchin monkey called Omar, while Lucy Daniels apparently lives in Yorkshire with Russian Blue cats.

If this seems hard-nosed and commercial, it is. Publishing is a business, and it has to think like a business in the current climate where books fight to be heard above the clamour of YouTube. And, as if the competition weren't tough enough, publishing is an industry with very low margins. A book is cheap compared to a games console; it's cheap compared to a pair of decent socks. In order to turn a profit these days, publishers need to sell a lot of books. A title ideally needs to shift around 10,000 copies a year. More if it's an expensive full-colour book.

Adam Blade, Daisy Meadows and friends sell in these quantities. Their success bankrolls the quieter titles, the books that publishers love but which won't set a financial spreadsheet alight: the standalones, the ones with sad endings and quirky illustrations and unusual production values, the literary prizewinners and the poetry, and all the things which keep a publishing list energised and wide-ranging.

There are dozens of well-known authors now established in their own right who have written packaged series fiction at some point in their careers. Advances aren't high, but the steady stream of royalties and the great and glorious mysteries of PLR income (see *Public Lending Right*, page 396) often mean that the projects are worthwhile. It is a dependable source of income in an unreliable industry. Or 'gas-bill money', as literary agent Lesley Hadcroft once put it.

Publishers are wise to the series-fiction juggernaut and regularly design their own series, commissioning authors and illustrators. But series fiction also originates with packagers. Packagers are an intermediary business. They produce ideas and source writers. But they still have to pitch those ideas to publishers for publication and distribution. In that respect, they are in the same boat as the author rapping on doors to get a commissioning editor's attention. However, publishers take packagers with good track records more seriously than they might a first-time author. Working Partners, for example, has produced some of the biggest series in recent years, including *Rainbow Magic* and *Beast Quest*.

Packagers employ teams of highly experienced editors who have regular meetings to exchange ideas for series, like the meeting described in my opening paragraph. When an idea has been agreed, they will either find a publisher to take it on the strength of the idea (a rare Holy Grail) or, more often, they will ask writers to produce some sample material to fit the concept before presenting it to publishers. The writer is given character names, scenes and complete chapter breakdowns by the packager, with express instructions to fill out the characters and develop the scenes as energetically as possible. There is no fee for sample material, but writers are usually happy to oblige in the knowledge that a little free work can sometimes net a paid project. In terms of cold hard cash, there is usually a small advance if the project is accepted, with around one-third of the royalty charged by the packagers going to the writers.

And here's the good news. Commercial fiction packagers don't need established names to write for them. They simply need writers who can write, and who are able and happy to follow a detailed brief. What's more, they actively recruit them. Go to the website for Working Partners (www.workingpartnersltd.co.uk) and it's hard to miss the great big button shouting APPLY NOW! There are forms to fill in regarding experience and interests, and you are asked to submit some sample writing. Not everyone will make the cut, but if you can turn a phrase and hold a story together, you have as good a chance as anyone else.

It's important to note that packagers are not interested in your magnificent idea about a talking wombat. They are only interested in the mechanics of your writing. In the world of team fiction, it is up to them to produce the ideas. Your job is to fill in the gaps as fluently and excitingly as you can. As such, writing as part of a series team can be a humbling exercise. You might produce your best joke or most moving sentiment in years, but if it doesn't fit the flavour of the series you are writing for, it will be binned as swiftly and unthinkingly as old yoghurt. A successful team writer is the person who can produce writing that fits seamlessly into the whole, not the person with the individual edge.

If your ego can take it, writing series fiction is an incomparable crash course in how to write. I learned a vast amount at the coalface as Lucy Daniels/Adam Blade (yes, I'm both) about pacing, plotting, cliffhangers, world-building, character development and all those other building blocks of successful storytelling. You work closely – often line by line – with expert industry editors, whose practical advice and guidance can feel like a creative writing course without the fee. Instead, miraculously, you are the one who gets paid. There's even a published book to show for your efforts at the end of it all. Writing in this way can be a valuable apprenticeship for the big bad world of author-led fiction that all writers hope lies in their future. Bring an open mind and a flexible pen to the process, and you will find that the craft of writing will lose several of its many mysterious layers.

You will note that producing series fiction in this way is about the writer, not the illustrator. Illustration and design for this type of series fiction lies strictly with the publisher who buys the concept. If you are an illustrator or author-illustrator, the series-fiction route probably isn't for you. If you are a writer: Hello, opportunity!

Lucy Courtenay has been writing children's fiction for over 20 years, working as a team writer on series such as *Animal Ark* and *Beast Quest*. She has several series under her own name, most recently *Mermaid School* (2020–22) for Andersen Press with illustrator Sheena Dempsey, and has also written contemporary teen romances for Hodder Children's. She is the Managing Editor for Fiction at Farshore, a freelance editor of children's fiction for Cornerstones Literary Consultancy and Curtis Brown Creative, and the author of *Get Started in Writing an Illustrated Children's Book* for the *Teach Yourself* series (John Murray 2016). She tweets @LucyCourtenay1.

The long and winding road to publication

Paul Stewart tells how he achieved his childhood dream of becoming a writer, championing illustrated books for children, and shares his experience of the submission process, rejection and success, and finding the ideal collaboration.

When I was at school, other boys in my class wanted to be footballers or train drivers. One wanted to be an astronomer. Me, I didn't have a clue. Possibly a singer in a band. Then, when I was eight, I was given a prize by a music teacher. Her husband worked for Collins and the prize was a book: *The Phantom Tollbooth* by Norton Juster, with illustrations by Jules Feiffer (Collins 1962). She apologized that it was an uncorrected proof, but thought I would love it. She was right. The novel took me to somewhere wonderful and, from that moment on, I knew I wanted to be a writer.

I started work on my own children's novel – as well as drawing the pictures to accompany it. I soon discovered two things: writing was more difficult than I'd thought, while illustrating was beyond me. I abandoned the project, but I never lost that new-found enthusiasm for my future career.

At university I studied English, choosing Lancaster because they offered a unit in Creative Writing. Then I applied for a (then almost unknown) writing MA at UEA, run by Malcolm Bradbury and Angela Carter. By the end of the course I had a folder of 20 short stories and an idea for a novel. One of those stories – a reimagining of Andersen's *The Snow Queen*, called *Ice* – was published in a literary magazine, *Bananas*. I still remember the thrill of reading their letter of acceptance: '… we'd like to use it in the next issue due out at the end of this month.' It was my first short story in print. I'd arrived.

I hadn't, of course. The other 19 stories – separately and as a collection – were not published, and the novel remained an idea. I decided that if it was indeed true that you should write about what you know, then I needed to know more. It was time to go travelling.

This was back before computers. Up until then I had been writing on an olive-green Olympia SM3 – allegedly a portable typewriter, but Charles Atlas would probably have had problems lugging it about. So I bought a lightweight Olivetti Lettera 32 and, following Malcolm's parting comment – 'I don't have the address but it is, like all the other addresses, in the *Writers' & Artists' Yearbook*' – got hold of a copy. Then I set off.

I lived in Greece, Germany and Sri Lanka; I travelled through Europe, India, parts of the Far East, Australia, the US, Kenya. I had numerous jobs – factory packer, security guard, fork-lift truck driver, bank operative, translator, EFL teacher, you name it – and I wrote something every day. The typewriter went everywhere I went, and each time I completed a piece of writing, I would search through the *Yearbook* for an appropriate publication. A growing number of magazines and publishers in the UK received examples of my work.

Most, to their credit, were kind in their rejections. Many offered advice. I always tried to match the manuscript to the publication, though not always successfully. A leading women's magazine responded to one story with the comment: 'The idea was ingenious but ... we do try to keep death out of our stories.'

I also discovered that I was receiving letters from people I'd actually heard of: Robert McCrum, Bill Buford, Paul Samwell-Smith (ah, yes ... still nurturing dreams of singing in a band, I'd also submitted a cassette of songs for appraisal). The thrill of communicating with famous people was tempered by the fact that they were sending me rejection letters – one after the other they arrived, enough to paper my walls, and I was feeling increasingly disheartened, though unable to stop writing.

It was this optimistic response from Tom Maschler of Jonathan Cape that set me back on track: 'The above said [i.e. the inevitable rejection], I don't like to lose sight of you because frankly I am convinced that you will make it as a serious writer, and think it likely that we would want to publish you in the future if we had the opportunity.'

I was in Sri Lanka in the '80s when civil war broke out. The school I'd been teaching in was closed, and I returned to England to find that the adult novel I'd almost completed over there suddenly seemed flippant and superficial. So I went back to the children's book I'd been musing over for more than two decades and, three months later, *The Thought Domain* was finished. Published by Viking in 1988, it was my first children's novel in print. For a second time, I'd arrived.

Largely on the strength of that published book, I was taken on by a literary agent. This took a lot of the hard work – and inevitable heartache – out of the process of trying to find a home for my scribblings. I now had someone to do it for me. Three years later, a deal was secured for a book I'd been researching. Based on a true story I'd stumbled upon in Kenya, it was accepted by – yes – Jonathan Cape. In 1991, my first adult book, *Trek*, was duly published. I'd *arrived* ...

Apart from that one book (and even *Trek* itself reads like a *Boy's Own* tale of gung-ho misadventure), it was children's literature that I pursued. I liked the discipline of writing for a younger audience, as well as the rigour, clarity and sincerity it demands. My early books were our-world-but-with-a-twist fantasies, often starting with a simple What if...? premise. What if there was a dimension where our thoughts were stored? What if a child was born able to communicate with animals? What if a video machine could record our nightmares?

After the publication of *The Thought Domain*, I submitted fresh proposals in the form of the first three chapters of the new work, a rough outline of the entire novel and a working title, in order to gauge whether my primary editor thought it had legs. If he didn't, my agent would send it to other publishers. I had, by this time, given up teaching EFL to devote myself to writing full time. I did not intend to return to the classroom. Not only did I generate my own stories, but I also started taking on commissions – writing to order, following briefs. I wrote football stories, puzzle adventures books, graded readers, horror and fantasy novels; I had short stories published in themed anthologies.

All these pieces of work, even the ones for older children, were illustrated. I considered this a good thing; I still do. There is, I believe, something perverse about using pictures to lure children into the world of books and then, when they've cracked reading, to remove them. It feels almost like a punishment. If I'd been able to I would have illustrated my own texts but, since I wasn't good enough, the next best thing was to find an illustrator I could work closely with.

Books

This proved far from easy. Publishers often keep authors and illustrators apart. An American editor once explained that this was company policy, as authors 'tend to bully illustrators'. A likely story! Had there been closer cooperation between me and my various illustrators, however, maybe a scene I'd written about a boy on a bike being attacked by a slavering dog wouldn't have been depicted by an old bicycle leaning up against a wall. I mentioned my disappointment to my editor and was given a new illustrator – based in Tasmania …

It was at a publisher's party in London that I first got talking to Chris Riddell. Beforehand, we had seen each other at the nursery our two sons went to, but we'd never spoken. On our train journey home that evening we talked about working together and, after a couple of false starts, produced a picture book about a rabbit and a hedgehog: *A Little Bit of Winter* (Andersen Press). It was my first picture book and my first collaboration.

The year was 1998, and that wasn't the only work we had published … Working together on *Rabbit and Hedgehog*, we'd both realized how much we enjoyed the collaborative process. Chris drew me a fantasy map entitled The Edge: 'Here's the world,' he said. 'What happens in it?'. It was at this stage that we tested our ability to work together to the max. This wasn't a 12-page spread picture book; it would be a long novel for 11-year-olds, illustrated throughout. There were times when we both wondered whether it would ever be completed, but finally, 15 months later, *Beyond the Deepwoods* (Doubleday 1998) – the first of what would become a 13-part fantasy series, *The Edge Chronicles* – was on the shelves. I'd arrived. Again!

Oddly, the series nearly didn't happen. I'd spoken to my editor at the time about the idea. She thought pictures would make the fantasy look too young. 'Not Chris's pictures', I assured her and, though unconvinced, she suggested I send in the proposal. In the usual way, I printed up the three chapters we'd completed, plus a rough synopsis of the book and outline of the world, and included a wad of Chris's pictures. The envelope came back return of post. Being a writer with a string of rejections under his belt, I naturally assumed they'd dismissed it out of hand as a rubbish idea. It was two days later when a tentative phone enquiry revealed that a youngster on a Youth Opportunities scheme had decided to tidy up the office and sent back all the manuscripts that were lying around – ours included. I've often fantasized about other novels that might have been rejected in the same batch …

Chris and I have written and illustrated more than 40 books together to date. One of us will come up with a very general idea, then we talk, talk, talk. If that initial idea starts to fly, we set about building a self-contained world – with maps, characters, names, back histories – for the two of us to immerse ourselves in; a place where we discover the stories that will turn into books. A flying box containing an ominous warning became the first *Far-Flung Adventure* – *Fergus Crane* (Doubleday 2004); a Victorian delivery lad with an insight into the supernatural became the *Barnaby Grimes* novels; a trio of aliens on a spurious mission to Earth became *The Blobheads*; humans versus killer robots – *Scavenger*; cowboys and dragons – *Wyrmeweald*.

Since Chris and I come to a piece of work from different perspectives, the text itself goes through many revisions. Although it is immensely enjoyable working with someone else – the writing, the events, the festivals, plus the fact that 'writer's block' is impossible if two of you are working together on a piece – collaboration is never easy. If we had tried working together when we'd first left college, it might not have worked. By the time we did start, I think we were both old enough to realize that the finished item was of far more importance than our individual egos. And certainly, none of the books we produced together could have been done by either of us alone.

Looking back on my writing career, it seems to have been so arbitrary. I kept thinking I'd arrived, only to discover that it was not my final destination – that there was always somewhere else to go to. All I know is that, ever since first realizing that 'I wanted to be a writer', everything has been geared towards making that a possibility. Publishing is currently changing. It is interesting to see that in the latest *Children's Writers' & Artists' Yearbook* there is a section on 'self-publishing'. I wonder where I will arrive at next …

Paul Stewart is a bestselling author of children's and adult books. He is co-creator (with Chris Riddell) of the *Edge Chronicles* series, the *Far-Flung Adventures* series including *Fergus Crane* (Gold Smarties Prize winner), *Corby Flood* and *Hugo Pepper* (both Silver Nestlé Prize winners), as well as the *Barnaby Grimes* series (published by Penguin Random House), and the *Free Lance, Wyrmeweald* and *Scavenger* trilogies. His other books include two *Muddle Earth* adventures and the *Blobheads* series (for younger readers), published by Macmillan Children's, and the *Rabbit and Hedgehog* picture books (Andersen Press). *Brian the Brave* (Otter-Barry Books 2019), the second picture book he has worked on with illustrator Jane Porter, won the 2020 Derby Children's Book Award. Barrington Stoke has re-issued both the *Free Lance* trilogy and his *Football Mad* series. Paul has written six titles for OUP's *Hero Academy* series and a biography of footballer Alex Oxlade-Chamberlain (Scholastic 2021). For more information see www.edgechronicles.co.uk.

Murderous inventions

Robin Stevens reveals how her murder mystery books, written for her 12-year-old self, have tapped into children's fascination for the nasty parts of life. When so much of a writer's career depends on chance, she stresses the value of following your instinct and of finding exactly the right agent and editor to share one's vision and passion.

It's probably not surprising that I'm an author. I grew up in a family that believed in books, and there's never been a moment of my life that I haven't told stories. I have always known with absolute determination that I wanted to have those stories published – but as a child I also wanted to own a zoo, be a wizard and live inside an Eva Ibbotson novel, and all of those ambitions seemed about as likely as each other. So no, it's not surprising that I'm an author – but all the same, I still wake up delighted every single morning by my bewildering good fortune, because *Murder Most Unladylike* (Corgi 2014) was not supposed to be the book that got me published.

I wrote the first draft of it in 2010, during NaNoWriMo (National Novel Writing Month). I really want to stress that I did not have even the smallest insight into the children's book market at the time. The simple fact was that there was no story that made more sense to me. I had discovered Agatha Christie's murder mysteries aged 12 and was then sent to Cheltenham Ladies' College aged 13. Detective stories and boarding schools are in my blood, and so deciding to write a murder mystery set at a boarding school was as obvious as falling in love – a feeling of: ... *Oh, of course it's you.*

Murder Most Unladylike let me work through all my confused memories of a boarding-school life that was neither as good nor as bad as Enid Blyton had promised it would be. The structure of its detective story felt like a reassuring arm around my shoulders in an adult world which was turning out to be far less organised that I had been expecting. I knew no one else would want this story, but I realised that I really needed it.

That sounds like a fairy tale, but of course the truth of writing an actual book is not a fairy tale at all. I wrote the first 50,000 words in a wild rush unlike anything I'd done before. I had a full-time job at the time, and so I had to hammer out my word count during lunch breaks, early in the morning and late at night. Daisy and Hazel were the only characters who had names, and they spent long scenes just chatting emptily to each other because I didn't know what was supposed to happen next. I wrote that first draft in 30 days, but I spent two years heavily working and reworking my text before I felt confident enough to actually send the book out to agents.

Once I'd decided to do that, though, I truly realised that I had no idea how to go about it. How did people find agents for their books? And, for that matter, what *was* my book? It was about children who solved a murder – so did that make it for children, or for adults? The only thing I did know was that when I thought about my favourite authors, they wrote for children. So off I marched to a bookshop, bought a copy of the *Writers & Artists' Yearbook 2012* (I still own it) and began to randomly pick children's agents from its pages.

I know now that this was a terrible idea. I should not have just been looking for an agent who works on children's books. I should have looked for children's agents who had specific experience in the type of book I had written. I *should* have been seeking out agents with a specialty in adventurous crime stories that centre on female characters. Hindsight is obviously a wonderful thing, but I wish I could take my younger self by the hand and gently explain to her that genres are important, that picture books are not the same as children's fiction which is not the same as YA fiction, that there are differences between commercial books and prize winners.

Of course, I got a lot of rejections – partly because what I was pitching was a murder mystery for kids, but mostly because I was approaching the wrong people. I have learned since that this is really the cause of almost every 'No' you'll ever get: the people rejecting you are not stupid, or cruel, or wicked – they are simply not obsessed with what you have written. An agent doesn't just need to *like* your book, they need to *love* it with every fibre of their being. They need to be able to spend five, or ten, or twenty years of their lives so wild about it that they will collar random strangers at parties to tell them how brilliant it is. As an author, you shouldn't want an agent that isn't perfect for you – and I was lucky enough (it really was the most incredible luck) to find the perfect agent in Gemma Cooper.

One day I stumbled on a blog post Gemma had written about how much she loved shows like *Murder She Wrote* and *Poirot*, and how she'd love to find a book like that for children – and I suddenly realised where I'd been going wrong. I sent my manuscript to her, not as a random children's agent but as a lover of murder mysteries who understood the children's book market. And it worked. Gemma met me and bowled me over with her enthusiasm for my book and her keen business sense. I signed with her a week later and she helped me trim my flabby and chaotic 80,000-word manuscript (this word count makes me wince to remember it) into a 60,000-word crime novel squarely aimed at children. We sent the book out to UK publishers in the spring of 2013.

Again, we got a lot of rejections. I want to stress that if any author tells you no one ever rejected them, they are either lying or the luckiest human on the planet. *Everyone gets rejected.* J.K. Rowling got rejected *repeatedly*, and the publishers who rejected J.K. Rowling were not idiots. They were just *not the right publishers* for J.K. Rowling. If one of them had bought *Harry Potter*, they would not have cared about it with enough passion to propel it higher into the bestseller charts with every title. It would not have become the global phenomenon that it is, and other authors would not have to spend so much time explaining to their friends and family why they are not as rich as J.K. Rowling.

Only Random House offered for *Murder Most Unladylike*, because only my editor Natalie Doherty was right for my book. She was besotted with it nine years ago, and she's still wild about it today, which is how I know this is true. She believed so passionately that a children's book about murder would sell that she convinced her publicity team and sales team, and they convinced booksellers, and then … the book sold.

I need to be very honest here and say that I was not expecting *Murder Most Unladylike* to do this well. By the time it came out, in June 2014, I was working in children's publishing myself. I knew the size of the market, and I was realistic about a debut author's chances. Most books – and aspiring authors should prepare themselves for this – sell about 1,000 copies. If you are selling more than 100 books a week you are doing very well indeed. If you sell more than 300 copies a week your publishers will have a small party at their desks in your honour. There are a lot of books on the market, and most of them get lost in the noise. And that was what I was prepared for. I'm still pinching myself that this is not what happened.

I was helped by a lot of things that I had nothing to do with: I had a great cover; I got a few nice reviews; my second book was chosen as the Waterstones Children's Book of the

Month in February 2015; and then I won the Waterstones Prize for Younger Fiction in March. I could not have influenced those events, but I'm not sure I would have been able to write a nine-book series today if even one of them had not occurred. A lot of what happens to an author happens outside their orbit – all you can do is react as calmly as possible to the news in your inbox every morning. This lack of control is slightly horrific, and it's a lot to take on board. In fact, what I have realised is that there is only one aspect of my writing career that is within my control – as it is in the control of every writer in the world: the books I write. And I think the content of those books certainly helped me, because the truth is that children *love* thinking about murder.

As adults (or at least, as the good sort of adults), we work very hard to keep children safe. The world is a horrible, stressful place that we struggle to deal with ourselves, and so we put a lot of effort into making sure children do not realise how awful it is until they are grown up and it is too late. Children, on the other hand, spend pretty much every waking hour trying to work out everything they can about the nastiest parts of life. Children are *desperate* to know what adults do to each other, why they behave the way they do, why bad things happen and what those bad things look like.

When you write for children, you have to stop being an adult and remember what it's like to be a child. Children want to understand and explore the darkest places in the universe, and as authors we can let them do that. (We always make sure that we leave behind invisible safety trails, of course, but they're more for us than for our audience). And children also want to be shown that sometimes small is powerful; that kids can be strong and brave and save the day, even when they feel weak and scared; that sometimes adults are good, and sometimes adults are bad; and that it's possible to work out the difference.

I didn't consciously know I was doing all of this when I wrote *Murder Most Unladylike*, of course I didn't. I'm not that clever. But watching how children respond to my series, I've realised this is the key to its success, and to the success of every good children's book ever written. I thought I didn't know who I was writing for, but of course I was lying to myself. I wrote for that 12-year-old Robin who was very grown up but also not grown up at all, who wanted life to be okay and worried that it wasn't, who cared very deeply about crime and justice. This is the only key to success as a children's author that I can pass on to you. *So* much is down to chance and circumstance. You can't hope to give the market what it wants. All you can do is write the book that would have set your younger self's world on fire, and trust that we're all very similar underneath.

Robin Stevens is the author of the *Murder Most Unladylike* mystery series (these include *Murder Most Unladylike* (2014), *First Class Murder* (2016) and *Death Sets Sail* (2020), all published by Puffin), and five *Wells and Wong Mysteries*, reissued by Simon & Schuster. She is also the author of *The Guggenheim Mystery* (Puffin 2017), from an idea and characters by Siobhan Dowd. Her latest books are a collection of *Murder Most Unladylike* short stories, *Once Upon a Crime* (Puffin 2021), and the first book in a new series *The Ministry of Unladylike Activity* (Puffin 2022). Born in California, Robin came to live in England at the age of three. She worked as an editor in children's publishing before becoming a full-time writer. For more information see https://robin-stevens.co.uk, and follow her on Twitter @redbreastedbird.

Self-publishing

An indie's journey to award-winning success

Setting aside the idea of her novel being published traditionally, Griselda Heppel found the high standards and professionalism of a self-publishing company gave her the best of both worlds.

It used to be so simple. Aspiring writers had two options: to land a contract with a traditional publishing house or, failing that, pay for publication themselves, thus earning the undying scorn of the literary world for anyone resorting to the so-called 'vanity press'. A book not published in the usual way must, the argument went, by definition be badly written, poorly edited and have no appeal to anyone but the writer and their own loyal family.

Well, if that was true once it isn't anymore. In today's competitive publishing world it is extremely hard for unknown authors to be taken on by traditional firms. Where once an editor might have had time to nurture a new talent, now financial realities demand strong projected sales that makes such slow-burn methods increasingly unlikely. The new book and the new author have to be winners from the word go and that is a big ask, especially if your book does something no one has ever tried before. Like creating a children's version of Dante's *Inferno*, for instance.

I've always loved stories that draw on great myths and epics: *The Iliad* and *The Odyssey*, Greek and Roman legends, Norse sagas, King Arthur and Robin Hood. Classical works provide rich narrative material and form the basis for many of the best books ever written for children. Yet the *Inferno*, in which Dante imagines himself descending into ever darker circles of Hades, having to deal with Cerberus, Harpies, Minotaur, Furies – a gold mine of fantasy and adventure if ever there was one – seems to have been neglected in this respect, and I was determined to put that right. Dante became 12-year-old Ante (Antonia) who finds herself plunged on this hellish journey, accompanied by her arch enemy, Florence, and a mysterious 13-year-old boy called Gil (Virgil – a reference to the Roman poet who is Dante's guide).

When I sent the completed manuscript to publishers and agents, it attracted some interest but ultimately no offers. Some of the rejection letters contained useful feedback, for which I was grateful. Others told me my story was too complicated for children; they'd be confused by the combined themes of Hell, mythical creatures and the First World War (an important element in *Ante's Inferno*). I knew they were wrong about this. My book had already been read by 40 or so children, aged 9–16 years, not one of whom had any difficulty in understanding it, and the fact that young people's abilities can still be so underestimated frankly puzzled me.

It struck me that however much I rewrote *Ante's Inferno*, as an unknown author I'd never get past this conservative view from mainstream publishing companies. I realised that if I wanted to see my book in print, I'd have to get on with it myself. I knew it would be hard but there were advantages: how and when the book was published would be up to me, I could commission my own cover illustration and I'd have the final say on design, print and production. I'd be in control.

Books

The rapid growth in recent years of ways in which to self-publish has opened up a number of choices to authors. I was determined that *Ante's Inferno* should be a top-quality book, well-designed with high production values. There'd be an ebook version, of course, but for children the act of holding, feeling, smelling a book is a vital part of their enjoyment (actually, it is for me too); *Ante's Inferno* should be a pleasure to pick up in bookshops, where it wouldn't look out of place among all the traditionally published titles, and retailers should be able to order it from their wholesalers in the usual way. In short, what I needed was an established publishing company that would do a professional job.

Google 'self-publishing' and you'll come up with a bewildering array of companies offering services. Some of these are very basic and very cheap and, not surprisingly, their books look it. But there are others whose high standards mean their products can compete with the best of any published books. I settled on Matador, which, as an imprint of trade publishing company Troubador, offers partnership services to authors supported by professional expertise in copy-editing, design, production, marketing and distribution fields. 'For authors whose work we are happy to publish,' says Matador on its home page, 'we will undertake as much or as little of the publishing process as required.'

And there you have it: the gulf between self-publishing and the low quality control associated with the vanity press. Submitting your manuscript to Matador does not guarantee publication. Matador may offer partnerships in which authors take on financial risk, but they will only do so if they consider the books to be of a high enough standard. If not, an author will be advised to rework the manuscript, perhaps after undergoing a critical assessment from a literary consultancy or a professional editor. A significant proportion of all books offered to Matador are rejected in this way.

This brings me to the heart of getting your book published by whatever method, traditional or independent: the quality of the book itself. I rewrote *Ante's Inferno* many times, responding to feedback from literary agents, editors and writing mentors, before sending it to Cornerstones Literary Consultancy for a critique. Their editorial report was tough and hard-hitting. It was difficult criticism to take on board but it proved invaluable, enabling me to resolve structural issues and tighten up the writing. By the time I submitted *Ante's Inferno* to Matador, it had already gone through a rigorous editorial process and was a much better book as a result.

Once taken on by Matador, I could have left it all to them but I didn't want to. For the cover, I commissioned Hilary Paynter, a top wood engraver, to create a dark and menacing image of the path down to Hell, reminiscent of the haunting illustrations of Dante's *Inferno* by Gustave Doré. Designer Pete Lawrence used the wood engraving to create an atmospheric, eye-catching cover. With my publisher, I had input, too, the page design and typeface used but was glad for them to take charge of production, printing, distribution and marketing. I had no illusions that bookshops throughout the UK would instantly stock *Ante's Inferno* – the thousands of new children's titles that appear every year are all fighting for the same space, after all – but Matador would present them with every opportunity to do so.

Next came the hard bit: promotion. Unless you have the full weight – and budget – of a large firm's publicity department, it is extremely difficult to get your book noticed by the media. Even authors signed by traditional publishing companies can be disappointed to find the funds allocated to publicising their book are relatively small. Increasingly they are expected to promote themselves, in a way not demanded before (and often contrary to their nature – not all authors are confident extroverts!). It's not enough just to write books, it seems; you need to establish an online presence by blogging, tweeting and updating Facebook and website pages with amusing snippets (not just sales pitches) to charm and entertain potential readers. All this can be fun, but it's also time-consuming, not to mention stressful (am I tweeting/blogging/facebooking enough?).

I entered this world of social media with some trepidation but found it a great way of connecting with other writers, readers, agents and editors and making new friends, as well as spreading the word about *Ante's Inferno* and garnering a good number of reviews. In addition, my publishers ran a publicity campaign which achieved a decent amount of press coverage – local, mainly, but also some on a national level – on radio programmes, in newspapers and magazines. Eager to share my interest in Dante with children, I put to-gether an illustrated talk about the themes that inspired *Ante's Inferno*. This goes down extremely well in schools (Years 5–8) and I fit in a few school visits every term.

It was a wonderful feeling when *Ante's Inferno* won a Silver in the Wishing Shelf Awards (www.thewsa.co.uk), swiftly followed by – even more exciting – the Children's category of the People's Book Prize (www.peoplesbookprize.com). Both competitions are judged exclusively by readers: the Wishing Shelf Awards by schoolchildren alone, and the People's Book Prize by any member of the public, either online or through their local library. For me it was a solid endorsement, not just of *Ante's Inferno*, but of the independent publishing method I'd gone for.

There are downsides, however. Partnership publishing has been a terrific experience but there's no disguising the amount of time and effort it takes up, arguably leaving less of both for the writing itself. A well-known, mainstream firm can inevitably give a book wider exposure than *Ante's Inferno* has achieved (though selling out its first 1,000 copy print run in eight months isn't bad).

Still, I have a tried and trusted model that I know works. With my next book, *The Tragickall History of Henry Fowst* (Matador 2015) I engaged the same dream team of Hilary Paynter and Pete Lawrence to come up with a brilliantly spooky cover for this tale of a 13-year-old boy who – somewhat unwisely – makes a pact with a demon. They also created the jacket for *The Fall of a Sparrow* (Matador 2021), its warm, summery atmosphere deftly hinting at a dark mystery lurking just below the surface.

With each new title, the thrill of seeing my vision for the book translated into reality remains as strong as ever. So strong in fact that, while as a writer I'll always be open to the possibility of mainstream publishing, it would take a very good offer to tempt me.

Perhaps even a Faustian pact.

Hm, now there's an idea …

Griselda Heppel read English at Cambridge and worked in publishing before moving to Oxford with her husband to bring up their four children. Her first book, *Ante's Inferno* (Matador 2012) won the People's Book Prize and a Silver Wishing Shelf Award. Her other novels include *The Tragickall History of Henry Fowst* (2015) and *The Fall of a Sparrow* (2021), both published by Matador. *The Fall of a Sparrow* was a finalist in the International Page Turner Awards and the Wishing Shelf Independent Book Awards. Read Griselda's blog at https://griseldaheppel.wordpress.com/; or visit her on Twitter @GriseldaHeppel and Instagram @heppelgriselda.

See also...
● *Editorial services and self-publishing providers*, page 193

How to hire a freelance editor

Jenny Bowman has helpful advice for the self-publishing author on how to set about hiring the ideal editor. She clarifies what is involved in the editorial process, what to look for in an editor and why their role is essential in ensuring your book is perfectly polished and ready for publication.

Self-publishing has become a widely accepted avenue for publishing children's books, from picture books to young adult novels. In contrast to the traditional way of publishing a book, self-published authors can bypass the need for an agent, as well as maintain complete creative control of their manuscript from start to finish. Self-publishing can be particularly attractive to picture book authors who prefer to select and collaborate with their illustrators.

There are many reasons an author might decide to self-publish their book: maybe they have researched the traditional route and decided it's just not the path they want to take; they might be writing to fill a need for a specific audience; or they may plan to write just one book. Being clear on motivation for self-publishing is important and will guide you through every step of the process. Since self-published books forgo the rigorous editing performed when a book is acquired by a publisher, hiring a freelance editor is a must. It's important to understand the different types of editorial services available to authors, and the order in which they are typically employed.

Types of editing

1. Developmental editing

Developmental editing is the first editing step; it is a comprehensive process that reviews the major backbone of a manuscript while also looking at the details, and then at how it all works together. Developmental editors will evaluate your manuscript as a whole and will offer relevant writing advice, constructive criticism and – if they're good – words of encouragement. Developmental editors typically evaluate:

• the book's core intentions and goals;
• the underlying premise and the story;
• character development and dialogue;
• narrative voice;
• the book's overall pacing, style and language;
• the age of the readership in relationship to themes and category.

Look for someone who is willing to offer a fluid working relationship and who will communicate openly on major changes. Out of all the editors you may hire, you will do the most rigorous revisions while working with your developmental editor.

2. Copy-editing

A copy-editor will check your manuscript making sure the syntax is smooth and the writing adheres to the conventions of grammar. They will spot minor inconsistencies in plot and story or character development, and comment on readability. They will bring your manuscript to a professional level before you format your book in preparation for a proofread and print. Copy-editors typically evaluate:

• overall readability;
• grammatical conventions and punctuation;

• consistency in content layout, such as chapters or sections, and content delivery;
• syntax and sentence structure;
• overall style and tone of the manuscript.

3. Proofreading

A proofreader is the detail-oriented, 'fan-of-the-red-pen' person whose job it is to make sure your book is error-free. Both you and your editor will know your manuscript inside and out; this means that errors such as simple grammar, formatting and spelling mistakes might easily be overlooked. Hiring a proofreader is an absolute must for authors wishing to self-publish. Many self-published authors even hire two proofreaders before going to print. Proofreaders typically:

• evaluate and correct grammar, typos and punctuation;
• ensure the document is error-free and consistent in style;
• review formatting and ensure that the book is ready for print.

Hiring an editor

There are hundreds of children's book editors available, and the range of editorial services is wide. With so many editors available, how do you know which one to choose? To start, select an editor who specialises in writing for children. You want someone who understands the complex category systems within the umbrella of children's books. This is especially important when you are at the developmental stage, or if you are unsure which category your children's book falls within. Are you writing a picture book, chapter book or easy reader? Is your book for middle-grade readers or young adults? How many words should your book have in order to be age-appropriate? What themes or topics are typically relevant? These are some of the more generalised questions your developmental editor can answer for you.

Where to start

A Google search for a children's book editor is the best place to start. Look for an editor who is specialised, or who has edited books similar to your own. An easy way to do this is to open a few of your favourites in tabs and check out each editor's website and 'About me' section. Take a look at their testimonials; see if any stand out to you.

Another resource to check out are the acknowledgements in your favourite children's book. For example, if you're writing a middle-grade novel, hop to the back of your most recent read and see who the author thanked. Even traditionally published authors hire freelance editors, and they often return to these same editors time and again. This is a fantastic way to narrow your search down stylistically.

Check out the Editorial Freelancers Association (EFA) – a vetted, members-only organisation. The EFA website (www.the-efa.org) has a user-friendly search tool for narrowing down your selections, and provides information such as years worked in editing and editor bios, all in one place. The UK equivalent is the Chartered Institute of Editing and Proofreading (CIEP), which includes a Directory of contacts, www.ciep.uk/directory (see page 346). Use the *Children's Writers' & Artists' Yearbook*, or *The Book* from the Society of Children's Book Writers and Illustrators (SCBWI; see page 330). Both publications have listings for editorial services.

What to look for in an editor

Once you have a list of prospective editors, study their websites to narrow down your choices. Some qualifications you might look for are:
• How long have they been editing?
• Have they edited books similar to your own?
• What do their testimonials say?
• What are their rates, if published online?
• Besides a list of services, does their website offer helpful resources for new and emerging authors?
• Is there helpful information about self-publishing children's books?

When to contact an editor

Once you have narrowed down your options to a few editors, get in touch with them. If they have a contact form on their website, use it to submit the information they need to offer a quote on services, rates and timeline. If not, send your core questions via email. You might ask the following:
• What editing services will you provide?
• Do you have experience of editing books in my category and/or genre?
• What are your rates?
• What is your turnaround time and when are you available to start?
• Do you offer an opportunity for a follow-up call?

Communicating via email is often enough to get your questions answered. If not, find out if the editor is willing to talk with you about your project before being hired. Most editors will include the opportunity to chat at some point during the process. Be mindful of the time you are requesting; if you have a 500-word manuscript that needs a copy-edit, it's unrealistic to ask a freelance editor to attend an hour-long interview before getting hired.

Key points to remember

Budget

Be up-front about your budget. Most freelance editors publish their fees online, so you can get a sense of what you'll be spending. If you find that your dream editor, and their rates, are out of reach, think twice before asking for a discount, as this may come across as devaluing the freelancer's qualifications and expertise. Rather, be proactive. Ask if the editor will consider a payment plan, or look for another editor who fits your budget.

Timing

Plan ahead. Many freelance editors are booked well in advance. If you have a tight deadline, or you have prearranged other services such as illustrations, or have a launch date goal in mind, be sure to get your editor booked. Expect to wait a month or more once you find your editor.

About sample edits

The editor's web presence, testimonials and credentials should be enough to qualify them for hire. It's unrealistic to ask for a sample edit. Sample edits are not reflective of the multiple manuscript reviews, suggested rewrites, inline edits and comments that are part of a full edit. It's equally unrealistic to ask an editor to send a sample of something they've previously edited, since most editors work under an agreement of confidentiality with their authors.

What to expect after hire

Typically, editors will outline the process – from hire to project completion – by email. After you initiate hire, you should receive a comprehensive contract that outlines the entire process. Most editors do line edits using 'track changes' in MS Word. Certainly with a developmental edit, and sometimes with a copy-edit and proofread, you will receive an editorial assessment of the document as well; this will review any problem areas, with steps to tackle revisions, and will also point out the areas that are really strong and working well. While editing your manuscript, editors will reach out if any pressing questions come up. When editing is complete, they will provide an in-depth review of their recommendations and answer any questions you may have.

Special considerations for picture book writers

• Picture books take a surprising amount of work – every word matters. The overall structure of the book, as well as specific placement of each word or sentence, each refrain, really matters. You will want to hire an editor who has unique experience in editing picture books.

• Is your book in rhyme? If so, hire an editor who is an old hand with poetry. Your rhyme and metre will need to be deliberately crafted with purpose. Today's market is choosy when it comes to rhyming picture books; there is definitely an art to writing a successful one.

• Hire your editor *before* you commission illustrations. Quality illustrations are pricey. How heartbreaking it is when an author completes illustrations, only to realise during the editing process that major changes are needed to their book which make those illustrations obsolete. Hire your illustrator when all editing, apart from the final proofread, is complete.

Finding an editor to collaborate with is an essential step in producing a polished and complete book for publication. It can also be a rewarding learning experience, especially at the developmental stage, when it comes to the craft of writing for kids. Self-publishing your children's book is an exciting path to follow, with one of the most satisfying endings – the joy of holding your first printed book, and then revisiting that feeling every time someone reads your story. Happy writing!

Jenny Bowman is a creative writer and children's book editor with experience editing books on the *New York Times* bestseller list, and books with international acclaim. Having edited over 100 books for children to young adults, Jenny is well-versed in all genres of children's literature. She is an active member of the EFA, the Society for Children's Books Writers and Illustrators, the Children's Literature Association, and participates annually in both the 12x12 Picture Book Challenge and Inked Voices. Her website is www.jennybowman.com.

The hybrid author: you can do it all – your way!

Shelli R. Johannes explains what it is to be a hybrid author, explores the pros and cons of traditional publishing and self-publishing, and describes how an author can enjoy the best of both worlds.

My journey

When I was a little girl, I never believed there was only one way of doing things. So I grew up trying to accomplish things in a different way. As you can imagine, my parents weren't always thrilled about me 'thinking outside the box'. Years later, nothing has changed. I feel the same way about publishing. As a writer, I was always told there was a right way and a wrong way to break down walls in the secret society of publishing. Like many writers, I stood outside the closed doors to publishing, banging my head against invisible barriers. If I couldn't find my way in, I decided I would carve my own passage.

In 2011, when I first decided to self-publish, it was considered 'taboo' in the publishing industry. To many, taking that route meant I was cheating the system – that maybe I wasn't good enough to barge through the front door of traditional publishing. In my heart, I knew that wasn't true. I had an agent who loved my writing. My books had made it to acquisitions at several publishing houses. But as many of you know, writing is like any art – it's subjective and it's competitive. There are hundreds of other manuscripts vying for that same opening at a publishing house at any given time. I started thinking that self-publishing was the way in.

To date I have sold over 250,000 ebooks of my *Nature of Grace* series. I have self-published five novels to date and plan to continue. Not only did I sell well, but I also loved the whole process – the control in creating my own covers, the excitement of watching my sales numbers, choosing where and when I wanted to publish. It was like nurturing my own books. However, although I loved it, I still wanted to publish traditionally because I wanted the experience of working with a big publisher. Again, I was told I had to choose – it was one way or the other. In addition to self-publishing, I have sold eighteen children's picture and chapter books to Greenwillow Books, HarperCollins Children's Books, Philomel and Capstone.

Until recently, there wasn't a word or even a title for authors who straddled both sides of the great divide. Now, we call it *hybrid publishing*.

What is a hybrid author?

A hybrid author is someone who publishes through many different media. For example, hybrid authors can self-publish some books while selling other books to a traditional publisher. I realized publishing doesn't have to be one way or the other. I wavered between playing them all at once or deciding which one to play first for a long time. With so many pros and cons to each channel, everything was exciting and new.

So, what are the pros and cons of being a hybrid author? A hybrid author generally benefits from the traditional advance, professional editing, distribution and marketing. But they also get the self-publishing benefit of creative control, flexible pricing, and the opportunity to write and publish timely titles for immediate earnings (see box: *Traditional publishing: pros and cons*).

How to be a successful hybrid author

As authors, we have no reason to stay in one lane. We can do it all. But an author must understand what they are getting into and how to do it right. Before diving into hybrid publishing, it's crucial to research – do your homework and seek advice. Here are a few points to keep in mind when preparing your action plan:

1. Write an amazing book

Always have a book in your queue. I like to write for my agent first because the traditional path tends to be much slower than the self-publishing channel. Once my book is on submission or in my agent's

Traditional publishing: pros and cons
PROS
• advance
• team makes the book
• mass print distribution
• validated
• access to TV, film, etc
• access to reviewers
CONS
• sells rights
• little marketing
• lower royalty
• slower to market
• risk averse regarding the type of book published
• decreasing revenue

hands, I develop my novels for self-publishing. This way, I'm always working on something that can move my career forward. It's also critical to 'go for high-quality' in all your writing. Every piece of work should be your absolute best. Being a hybrid author isn't a short cut to writing; it's a different path to market. So, write the best book possible and *then* figure out how to publish it. Bad writing doesn't sell in *any* market or channel – no matter how you publish.

2. Be prepared to run a business

To be a successful hybrid author, you must be prepared to manage your writing as a business. You will have to juggle many different processes at the same time. Traditional publishing will include the basics in editing and marketing; in self-publishing, you do those things too, but self-publishing also demands a business acumen and an entrepreneurial spirit to keep everything moving forward. You will be expected to learn about and manage the book's production (covers, editing, jacket copy, etc), plus the business side of publishing such as inventory, sales, distribution, finances, marketing and more. Some people don't mind this part – but it can be overwhelming at times. It also takes away from your writing time, so you need to be efficient and organised. Find out what works for you. Being a hybrid author requires a different business mindset from traditional publishing because you have to juggle simultaneous processes across multiple channels. Don't be scared – it can be done, but it is a challenging process. You will have to try new things, not be afraid of failing and take risks. It's all part of the process.

3. Do yourself a favour and get an agent!

If you think you are going to be a hybrid author, I still believe you need an agent. Agents can help you determine which books are best for each publishing path. They know the market. They can also help you navigate other tasks, like contract negotiation and managing other rights – foreign, subsidiary, etc. Of course, you need an agent who believes in the hybrid model. You must find the right agent/agency that truly believes there are viable sales on both publishing paths. Make sure they are experienced in digital publishing and open to all opportunities that arise. Nine years ago, I was lucky enough to find my agent Lara Perkins at Andrea Brown Literary Agency at a conference. She understood and valued the possibilities of the self-publishing model. You need someone on your side, and someone who has your best interest and career in mind. Trust me, agents are worth their 15%, and then some! (see box: *How an agent can help you succeed*).

> **How an agent can help you succeed:**
>
> • **Channel management** – Helps decide which path is best for your books.
>
> • **Contract negotiation** – Reviews any issues that might surface.
>
> • **Editorial advice** – Provides manuscript revisions and edits.
>
> • **Market knowledge** – Gives insight into the various markets/channels.
>
> • **Networking** – Has access to a variety of resources.
>
> • **Rights management** – Can facilitate the sale of other rights.
>
> • **Trusted partner** – Offers advice on whole career and portfolio.

Books

4. Make a book plan

Decide which books you want to publish traditionally and which ones you want to keep for yourself. My agent helps me choose the best path for each book idea we discuss. Because let's face it, self-publishing doesn't work for all books, and traditional publishing doesn't work for everything either. For example, my picture books (such as *Cece Loves Science*) and chapter books on submission are currently better suited for traditional publishing. In contrast, some of my YA material based on a timely topic (such as *ReWired*) or that may target a niche audience (such as the *Nature of Grace* wilderness thriller series), may be better geared toward self-publishing. So decide what you want to write and then figure out what the best channel to market; consider time, topic and level of control.

5. Always keep writing

The indie world is very fast paced while the traditional model is much slower. Doing both can bog you down in tasks, project management and marketing. But it's essential to always keep writing. This is the best way to build a portfolio. When one book is in edits, work on a new idea. When one manuscript is in your agent's or critique partner's hands, outline your next book. Never sit and wait for something to happen. Make something happen. It's all worth it in the end!

I want to continue with my hybrid career because I love both the traditional and self-publishing options for very different reasons. I value the flexibility and control that self-publishing offers. BUT I also enjoy the collaborative process of working with an editor at a publishing house. As I develop as a writer, I want to remain open to ANY writing opportunity or path available. I want to pave my own way in this exciting, frustrating, wonderful and challenging industry. Because at the end of the day, I just want to write great books and reach people of all ages with my words. I'm proud to be a hybrid author – one who publishes my work, my way.

Remember, there is no right way to make this journey; there's only *your* way!

Shelli R. Johannes is the co-author of the nine-part science picture book series, *Loves Science* (Greenwillow/ HarperCollins). She is also the author of the forthcoming picture book series *Theo Thesaurus* (Philomel/ Viking) and *Shine Line a Unicorn* (HarperCollins Children's 2021) and *Penny, The Engineering Tale of the Fourth Pig* (Capstone). Shelli writes middle grade and YA, and has self-published five books, selling over 250,000 ebooks. After earning an MBA specialising in Marketing and working in corporate America as a senior vice president, Shelli traded in her heels and suits for flip-flops and jeans to follow her passion for writing. For more information visit www.srjohannes.com and follow her on Twitter or Instagram @srjohannes.

See also...
• *An indie's journey to award-winning success,* page 182

Editorial services and self-publishing providers

This is a selection of the expanding list of companies that offer editorial, production, marketing and distribution support predominantly (but not exclusively) for authors who want to self-publish. As with all the organisations mentioned in the *Yearbook*, we recommend that you check carefully what companies offer and their fees; also be aware of any minimum commitment requirements. Note that in the entries below, 'POD' refers to 'print on demand'. A longer list of companies and individuals who provide similar services is included in our subscription service: www.writersandartists.co.uk/shop/subscriptions.

Amolibros
Loundshay Manor Cottage, Preston Bowyer, Milverton, Somerset TA4 1QF
tel (01823) 401527
email amolibros@aol.com
website www.amolibros.com
Director Jane Tatam

Services include print and ebook design, production, copy-editing and distribution through online retailers. Sales and marketing services include design and production of adverts, leaflets, author websites, distribution of press releases and direct mail campaigns.

Blue Falcon Publishing
The Mill, Pury Hill Business Park, Alderton Road, Towcester, Northants NN12 7LS
tel 07955 002040
email books@bluefalconpublishing.co.uk
website www.bluefalconpublishing.co.uk
Facebook www.facebook.com/bluefalconpublishing
Twitter @bluefalconpub
Instagram @bluefalconpub

Small independent company publishing children's fiction books with a focus on high-quality, personal service. Services include: editing; typesetting; publishing and ebook production. Prices start from £450 for the basic service.

Bookollective
email hello@bookollective.com
website www.bookollective.com
Facebook www.facebook.com/bookollective
Twitter @bookollective
Contacts Esther Harris (editorial), Aimee Coveney (design), Helen McCusker (publicity)

Award-winning team offering a range of publicity, promotion and marketing options, editing services, book-cover design and website creation. Works alongside publishers, industry professionals and direct with writers. Also hosts regular networking events and literary areas within festivals.

BookPrinting UK
Remus House, Coltsfoot Drive, Woodston, Peterborough PE2 9BF
tel (01733) 898102
email info@bookprintinguk.com
website www.bookprintinguk.com
Twitter @BookPrintingUK

Offers colour and b&w printing and POD books in a range of bindings. Can provide custom illustration and interior layout options, as well as typesetting. Supplies templates for formatting manuscript files before sending. Can also distribute print books direct to customers. Prints bookmarks, posters and flyers.

eBook Versions
27 Old Gloucester Street, London WC1N 3AX
website www.ebookversions.com
Proprietor John Ransley

Offers ebook, paperback and hardback self-publishing and distribution through online retailers and trade wholesalers including Amazon Kindle Direct Publishing, Gardners Books and more than 300 independent high street booksellers. Fees begin at £95 for ebook conversion of a manuscript of up to 100,000 words. POD paperback and hardback pre-press production is available from £295. OCR scanning of hardbacks, paperbacks and typescripts is also offered.

Frank Fahy Publishing Services
5 Barna Village Centre, Barna, Co. Galway, H91 DF24, Republic of Ireland
tel +353 (0)86 2269330
email frank.fahy0@gmail.com
website https://frankfahypublishing.wordpress.com/

Specialises in preparing manuscripts for book production, either as printed books or digital ebooks. This can include, as required, copy-editing and/or proofreading, or preparing presentations for submission to publishers. Estimates are free of charge and authors' individual requirements discussed. Publishing projects of all kinds considered, from individuals, institutions or businesses. Founded 2007.

Grosvenor House Publishing

Link House, 140 The Broadway, Tolworth,
Surrey KT6 7HT
tel 020-8339 6060
website www.grosvenorhousepublishing.co.uk
Founder Kim Cross

Publishes across a range of genres including
children's and non-fiction in colour, b&w, POD,
paperback, hardback and ebook formats. Offers a
£795 publishing package which includes typesetting
and five free print copies as well as an ISBN, and
print and ebook distribution via online retailers.
Marketing services include producing posters and
postcards, and website set-up from template with two
years' hosting. Ebook publishing costs £195 if the
print edition of the book has been produced by the
company and £495 otherwise. Print costs and
royalties depend on book specification. A
proofreading service is offered at a rate of £5 per
1,000 words. See website for full list of costs.

Jelly Bean Self-Publishing

Candy Jar Ltd, Mackintosh House,
136 Newport Road, Cardiff CF24 1DJ
tel 029-211 57202
email submissions@jellybeanselfpublishing.co.uk
website www.jellybeanselfpublishing.co.uk
Twitter @Jelly_BeanUK
Director Shaun Russell

Self-publishing imprint of the award-winning Candy
Jar Books. Services include, but are not limited to,
editing, typesetting, illustration, cover design, website
design, audiobook production and marketing
support. Can accommodate authors of every genre,
budget and timetable. Welsh Self-Publisher of the
Year 2020. Founded 2012.

Kindle Direct Publishing

website https://kdp.amazon.com
Facebook www.facebook.com/KindleDirectPublishing
Twitter @AmazonKDP

Ebook self-publishing and distribution platform for
Kindle and Kindle Apps. Its business model offers up
to a 70% royalty (on certain retail prices between
$2.99–$9.99) in many countries and availability in
Amazon stores worldwide. POD options are also
available. Note that KDP Select makes books
exclusive to Amazon (which means they cannot be
sold through an author's personal website, for
example), but authors can share in the Global Fund
amount every time the book is borrowed from the
Kindle Owners' Lending Library.

Kobo Writing Life

email writinglife@kobo.com
website www.kobo.com/gb/en/p/aboutkobo
Facebook www.facebook.com/KoboWritingLife
Twitter @kobo

Ebook self-publishing platform where authors can
upload manuscripts and cover images. These files are
then converted into ebooks before being distributed
through the Kobo ebookstore. Authors are able to set
pricing and DRM territories, as well as track sales.
Royalty rates vary depending on price or territory;
enquire directly. Free to join. Owned by Rakuten.

Little Steps

Vicarage House, 58–60 Kensington Church Street,
London W8 4DB
email info@littlestepspublishing.co.uk
website www.littlestepspublishing.co.uk
Facebook www.facebook.com/littlestepspublishinguk
Instagram @littlestepspublishinguk

Provides a complete service for the aspiring children's
author, including printing, design, marketing, editing,
proofreading, public relations, production and
distribution. Authors invest financially in their own
books, entitling them to receive majority royalties.
Founded in the UK 2019; has been operating for over
10 years in Australia.

Manuscripts & Mentoring

25 Corinne Road, London N19 5EZ
tel 07973 300276
email manuscriptmentoring@gmail.com
website www.genevievefox.com
Twitter @genevievefox21
Contact Genevieve Fox

Helps both fledgling and experienced writers of
fiction, non-fiction, memoir and YA fiction get from
first draft to finished manuscript. Primary services
include editing, manuscript overviews as well as
advice on structure, plot, themes and
characterisation. One-to-one tutoring, mentoring and
coaching, writing plans, ghostwriting; and creative
writing courses also available.

Matador

Troubador Publishing Ltd, Unit E2,
Airfield Business Park, Harrison Road,
Market Harborough, Leics. LE16 7UL
tel 0116 279 2299
email books@troubador.co.uk
website www.troubador.co.uk/matador
Facebook www.facebook.com/matadorbooks
Twitter @matadorbooks
Managing Director Jeremy Thompson, *Operations
Director* Jane Rowland

Self-publishing imprint of Troubador Publishing.
Offers POD, short-run digital- and litho-printed
books as well as audiobooks and ebook production,
with distribution through high-street bookshops and
online retailers. Also worldwide ebook distribution.
Author services include all book, ebook and
audiobook production, trade and retail marketing,
plus bookshop distribution and sales representation
by Star Book Sales. Founded 1999.

MJV Literary Author Services

71–75 Shelton Street, London WC2H 9JQ
email authors@mjvliterary.com
website www.mjvliterary.com
Contact Matt McAvoy

Offers professional proofreading, copy-editing and beta-reading services for self-published and traditionally published authors of all genres, including fiction, non-fiction and children's books, as well as a popular ebook and KDP-ready Kindle-book creation service, at $49. As part of the company's #ReturnToRealBooks campaign, KDP-formatted print-ready typesetting is offered free with all proofreading and copy-editing instructions. Other services include translation into English with full copy-editing, for non-English language authors. Editing services start from $6.95 per 1,000 words, and all instructions include two human editor passes and software checks as standard.

Peahen Publishing

tel 0117 427 0126
email info@peahenpublishing.com
website www.peahenpublishing.com
Twitter @peahenbooks
Instagram @peahenbooks
Contact Carly Corlett

Small, independent publisher specialising in children's books that raise awareness. Produces a range of titles, from picture books to rhyming books, YA novels to short story collections. Authors are guided through the publishing process, from initial manuscript consultation to illustration, from paper and font selection to delivering bookshelf-ready books. Founded 2015.

PublishNation

Suite 544, Kemp House, 152 City Road, London EC1V 2NX
email david@publishnation.co.uk
website www.publishnation.co.uk
Publisher David Morrison

Offers POD paperback and Kindle format ebooks, available through Amazon. Publication in both print and digital formats costs £325 or £175 for Kindle format. Images may be included from £3.95 each. A range of book sizes is available, as are free template book covers. Enhanced cover design costs £40. Marketing services include creation of a press release, social media accounts and author website. Standard proofreading is £8 per 1,000 words, while an 'express' option from £125 focuses on the beginning of the manuscript. Editorial critique reports range in price from £99 for manuscripts of up to 15,000 words to £219 for manuscripts of up to 120,000 words.

SilverWood Books

14 Small Street, Bristol BS1 1DE
tel 0117 910 5829
email enquiries@silverwoodbooks.co.uk
website www.silverwoodbooks.co.uk
Twitter @SilverWoodBooks
Publishing Director Helen Hart

Offers a complete self-publishing service for adult and children's books (including picture books), from manuscript feedback to editing and proofreading, professional cover and page design, typesetting, ebook hand-formatting and conversion, b&w and colour POD, short-run and lithographic printing, one-to-one support and coaching. Distributes to bookshops via wholesalers and to online retailers including Amazon. See website for price information.

WRITERSWORLD

2 Bear Close Flats, Bear Close, Woodstock, Oxon OX20 1JX
tel 0800 1214966
email enquiries@writersworld.co.uk
website www.writersworld.co.uk
Founder & Owner Graham Cook

Specialises in self-publishing, POD books and book reprints. Also issues ISBNs on behalf of authors, pays them 90% of the royalties and supplies them with copies of their books at print cost. Worldwide book distribution. Founded 2000.

Books

Poetry
Writing poetry for children

Rachel Rooney reflects on how she re-engaged with a childhood passion and sought out valuable educational and competitive opportunities and challenges to sharpen her poetic skills. With advice for new poets, she sees how both serendipity and tenacity played their part on her path to publication and award-winning success.

I fell in love with poetry twice – once as a bookish child and again, much later, as a middle-aged woman. Maybe it was the 27-year hiatus that fuelled my desire to become a poet for young people, an urge to pick up from where I'd left off. With my third son starting school, and while taking a short break in my teaching career, I signed up to a weekly Writing for Children course run by Roger Stevens, the founder of the online children's website The Poetry Zone (https://poetryzone.co.uk). It ran over three terms, with the main focus on fiction writing, but it quickly became clear that my strengths lay in poetry. I rediscovered a pleasure in its rhythms, rhymes and patterning, and found a natural tendency to condense ideas rather than expand on them.

Soon I became hooked and began to experiment with different forms and styles. I read widely for inspiration, from childhood favourites such as Christina Rossetti and Charles Causley through to contemporary poets. Then I sought out the winning collections from the CLPE Poetry Award (now named the CLiPPA Award; see page 362) as well as those from its predecessor, The Signal Poetry Award. While admiring playful, sharp wordplay and well-crafted light verse, I was also drawn to the 'adult poets' such as Matthew Sweeney, Philip Gross and Carol Ann Duffy, those who turned their skills to the writing of subtle, weighted poems for a younger audience. The scope of children's poetry was opening up to me – from early infant lullabies through to teen/adult crossover free-verse, and I was keen to embrace it all.

It was at this time I first had a poem published in an anthology, which had been submitted as part of a challenge organised by the tutor. The early 2000s was a barren era for single-poet collections, but there was a proliferation of anthologies for children and, as an emerging poet trying to get a toehold in the publishing industry, it was perfect timing. My details were soon passed to other anthologists who keep informal lists of poets to contact when calling for submissions. The submission briefs sent out tend to be specific in nature, targeting a particular age-range and dictating the subject matter to be covered. While this can feel a little restrictive at times, it serves well as a homework-type exercise and a handy writing prompt. Assuming that the most obvious angles and poetic forms would be covered, I learned to submit poems from slant, unusual perspectives, increasing the likelihood they'd be chosen. The fee offered is low – for as long as I can recall it has mysteriously remained at an average of £50 per poem. As the saying goes, there's no poetry in money and no money in poetry. But I gained a fairly decent strike rate and soon became an established contributor.

By now I had a notion to publish a collection for children, but this was overshadowed by a desire to learn more about the art itself. I felt driven to explore 'adult' poetry, with all its nuance, variations and complexities. So, while juggling a return to special needs teaching, motherhood and a crumbling marriage, I attended a year-long evening class, followed by a part-time two-year Creative Writing certificate at University of Sussex, both under the excellent tutorage of the poet and novelist Ros Barber. Her rigorous teaching helped sharpen up my technical skills and deepened my appreciation of the art. Workshopping poems taught me to accept critical feedback and to constructively critique the writing of others. And in the process I developed supportive relationships with those at a similar stage in their writing careers, some of which continue to this day. After completing the certificate, I refocused on children's poetry. I entered the Belmont Prize, which at the time was the only national poetry competition for a single children's poem. Getting shortlisted in this was an early highlight and gave me reassurance that I was on the right path. The Belmont is now sadly defunct, but two other national single-poem competitions have taken its place: the Caterpillar Prize (see page 361), run by the children's magazine *The Caterpillar*, and the YorkMix Poems for Children Competition (https://yorkmix.com/yorkmix-poems-for-children-competition). There may also be other local and regional competitions to be found.

I'd accumulated a healthy number of poems over four years, but had come to a frustrating impasse. While I was confident I had the basis of a decent collection, I was at a loss to know how to proceed. Most publishers weren't willing to accept unsolicited manuscripts and securing an agent as an unknown poet was unlikely, especially as there was little demand for single-poet collections back then. But I was determined to be published – why, I'd even written 'Win CLPE Poetry Award' on my list of Things I Must Do, hadn't I? To keep myself buoyant, I splashed out on an Arvon residential course (see page 207), Writing Poetry for Children, run by Carol Ann Duffy. These courses don't come cheap but spending five full days (and evenings) immersed in all things poetic, free from real-life distractions and with the perfect tutor, was a magical and productive experience.

Despite Carol Ann's encouraging response to my writing, I fell back into a despondent personal place. So I decided to channel this feeling into a rhyming picture book text titled *A Patch of Black* – a night-time lullaby about fear of the dark. I made multiple submissions to publishers I thought might suit; although none were taken up I did receive a few positive-sounding rejections and this spurred me on to source a mentor, the late Gerard Benson, whose poetry I admired. Having contacted him through his publisher Smith-Doorstop, I sent him a selection of my poems to see if we'd be a 'good fit' and he agreed to critique my work for a reasonable fee. Gerard was a perceptive reader and an assured editor. We developed an email correspondence over several months and met up at a few poetry events. At one event – a children's poetry showcase at The Society of Authors – he introduced me to a few industry employees including Suzanne Carnell, then the Editorial Director at Macmillan Children's Books. Gently prompted by Gerald, I mentioned that I'd submitted *A Patch of Black* but hadn't heard anything back. Suzanne gave me her business card and suggested I contacted her directly, which I duly did. Though I wasn't aware at the time, I had just engaged in what some might term 'networking', thanks to Gerard's generous manoeuvres.

Eventually, *A Patch of Black*, illustrated by Deborah Allwright, was taken up by Macmillan and was to be published in 2010. Now, the hunt for an agent was on. I had no idea where to begin, so I rifled though the *Writers' & Artists' Yearbook* and selected several potential agents to contact. I was delighted to eventually be taken up by Caroline Walsh at David Higham and we've worked together happily ever since. I struck lucky here; after all, poets aren't the most lucrative clients to take on. And, again, the timing was good – Janetta-Otter Barry at Frances Lincoln (now Quarto) was setting up a rare single-poet poetry list and was looking to launch new poetry voices. My agent pitched my work, and *The Language of Cat* was published by Frances Lincoln in 2011, along with a wonderful endorsement from Carol Ann Duffy herself. It was longlisted for the Carnegie Medal and also went on to win the CLPE Prize. Two more poetry collections have followed, both shortlisted for the CLiPPA, with one winning the North Somerset Teachers' Award. *Hey, Girl!*, a collection for young teens, will be published by Otter-Barry Books in August 2021 and a picture book, *The Fears You Fear* is currently in production – the last in a set of three rhyming stories based around emotions, illustrated by the wonderful Zehra Hicks.

My publishing journey reads like a dream come true, and in retrospect I think it has been. However, that isn't the whole story – or poem, if you will. There have been real challenges along the way. Many times it has felt like an uphill struggle, a salutary lesson in remaining tenacious. As in the careers of most published writers, there has been an element of serendipity at play, of chance meetings and fortuitous timings. Unfortunately, you can never be factor these in when you set out. In recent years, the publishing landscape has altered somewhat. Children's poetry is inhabiting a more central position, and social media platforms such as Twitter and Instagram provide visibility and exposure for newcomers and established writers alike. Online courses and readings are now commonplace and accessible to most. And the children's poetry world is a relatively small and welcoming one, especially when raw talent is spotted.

So, what advice might I give a poet starting out? I remember once meeting an editor who told me she had real difficulty sourcing new poets for her list. When I asked her why, she told me it was because writing children's poetry is deceptively difficult and most people think it an easy thing to do. With this in mind, my foremost advice is to focus on the craft itself; if your poetry is strong enough, it's sure to get noticed eventually. Good luck!

Rachel Rooney is a trained teacher in Primary and Special Education. Her first poetry collection *The Language of Cat* (re-published by Otter-Barry Books 2021) won the CLPE Poetry Award and was longlisted for the Carnegie Medal in 2011. Her other collections, *My Life as a Goldfish* (Quarto 2014) and *A Kid in My Class* (Otter-Barry Books 2018) have both been shortlisted for the CLiPPA Award. Her latest collection, *Hey, Girl!* (Otter-Barry 2021) was nominated for the Carnegie Medal. She performs at festivals and for The Children's Bookshow. In 2017 she was the Chair of Judges for the CLiPPA and has judged the Betjeman Poetry Prize. Rachel visits schools for workshops and lives in Brighton. See her website www.rachelrooneypoet.com for more information and follow her on Twitter @RooneyRachel.

See also...

Poetry

Flying the poetry flag

Poet and anthologist John Foster explains the difficulties faced by aspiring children's poets and offers practical advice on writing poetry for children.

Once upon a time, there was a teacher who enjoyed sharing poems with the children she taught. As well as reading them poems from books in the class library, she read some of the poems she had written herself. She was encouraged by their response and decided to see if she could get the poems published. She looked in publishers' catalogues and found that there were numerous anthologies of poetry for children, as well as a number of single author collections.

She chose a publisher and sent them her poems. The publisher liked the poems. But as she was unknown they did not think they could risk a single author collection. However, they thought her poems showed promise, so they forwarded them to one of their anthologists. Although the anthologist liked the poems too, they did not fit into the anthology that he was currently working on. But he added her to the list of contacts to whom he sent details of new anthologies, specifying the subject of the collection and the types of poem he was looking for. When he next did an anthology, she submitted a number of poems for consideration and the anthologist chose three of them to be included.

She managed to track down other anthologists and they sent her details of the anthologies they were compiling. She became a regular contributor to anthologies and an established name in the children's poetry world, and gave up full-time teaching so that she could accept invitations to visit schools to read her poems and run poetry workshops. She struggled to find a publisher to do a single author collection. But eventually she managed to get a collection published and it sold well on her school visits. She didn't make a fortune from writing children's poetry, but her success and the obvious enjoyment children got from her poems was gratifying.

That was how it was in the late 1980s, throughout the 1990s and in the early 2000s, when children's poetry was in fine fettle. How lucky she and the rest of us children's poets were then and how times have changed. Whereas in those days there were plenty of poetry books for children published annually, now there are only a few and new anthologies are a rarity.

Briefly, in 2010/11 it looked as if children's poetry might be making a comeback. Writing in the summer 2011 *Carousel* magazine, Brian Moses heralded what he hoped was a new spring for children's poetry, spearheaded by the launch of a new poetry list by Salt Publishing and a new imprint from Frances Lincoln. However, the Salt Children's Poetry Library has failed to make an impact and, despite the best efforts of Macmillan, A&C Black and Frances Lincoln, children's poetry publishing remains in the doldrums.

What explains the dearth of new children's poetry books? There are a number of factors involved. But it has nothing to do with children's attitudes towards poetry. Children enjoy reading poetry as much as they did in the boom years of the 1990s. Children's poets are as in demand at Book Weeks in schools as they have always been. They perform their poems to rapt audiences, who go on to get their parents to buy whatever poetry books they have managed to get publishers to publish or, in desperation, have self-published.

So why has children's poetry publishing declined? It is partly due to the attitude of booksellers. They argue that poetry books don't sell. Of course they don't, if they don't stock them. Walk into the children's section of a bookshop today and you'll find a handful of poetry books, often hidden away on the bottom shelf, alongside the joke books. In the past, you'd find a shelf full of poetry books at eye-level.

In the eyes of the book buyers, who control what is stocked in bookshops, children's poetry isn't fashionable at present. This has a knock-on effect. The publisher's sales team report back that poetry books don't sell, despite the evidence to the contrary from the travelling poets, who sell hundreds of pounds' worth of their books during their school visits. So the publishers only publish a fraction of the poetry books that they used to. It's a vicious circle.

And the economic climate doesn't help. A full-colour poetry book aimed at younger children is like a picture book in terms of how much it costs to produce. But poetry doesn't translate in the way that stories do, so it isn't possible to sell foreign rights as a way of recouping the costs of production. It can be hard for a commissioning editor to convince the publishing committee to back a poetry project that will not make much money on the first printing.

Nevertheless, while many of the mainstream children's book publishers still shy away from publishing poetry, smaller independent publishers, such as Martin West at Troika and Janetta Otter-Barry at Otter-Barry Books, are producing an increasing number of poetry books. But the number remains very small when compared to the number of children's novels that are published annually.

Consequently, the aspiring children's poet faces a daunting task. There aren't the anthologies that it was possible to contribute to in the past and it is even harder these days to get a single author collection accepted. But if you are determined to write children's poetry, here are a few tips.

Get inspired by children

Starting with the most obvious, get to know children's language. If you are writing about an experience from a child's point of view, you must get the language right. It is, perhaps, not surprising that many of the most successful children's poets are from a teaching background – for example, Tony Mitton, Wes Magee, Judith Nicholls, Paul Cookson and Brian Moses. Teachers not only know what children's interests are, but they also know how children think and how they express themselves. Steep yourself in children's language, not just the language of your children and those of your friends, but of children from all sorts of backgrounds and cultures.

Try to arrange to visit schools in different areas. But always go through the correct channels with a letter to the literacy coordinator, copied to the headteacher, explaining the reasons you would like to visit. Schools these days are, quite rightly, very security-conscious.

If you are visiting a school, you can offer to run a writing workshop. You have the opportunity to try out your poems too. There's nothing like a deafening wall of silence greeting that punchline which you thought they would find so amusing to let you know that, in fact, the poem doesn't work!

Visiting schools is also worthwhile because you can bring yourself up to date with how poetry is being used in the classroom. For example, the new curriculum requires that pupils learn poems by heart. Literacy co-ordinators will therefore be on the lookout for new performance poems. There is an educational as well as a trade market for children's poems and it is worth knowing what the educational publishers might be looking for.

Schools are also a good source of ideas. Many a poem comes from a child's tale or a teacher's comment. In one school, I met a girl called Alison, who told me what had happened when she tried to pull a loose tooth out with a piece of string. So I went home and wrote this poem, 'When Allie Had a Loose Tooth':

When Allie had a loose tooth
She did as her dad said.
She went into the kitchen
And found a piece of thread.
She tied it round the tooth.
She tied it to the door.
But when she slammed the door shut,
The knob fell on the floor.

Appealing to the reader

Visiting schools will also give you an idea of what interests children have and what subjects to write about. Then it's up to you to think of something that will appeal to them. But a word of warning: be careful of being risqué just to appeal to the reader. Avoid being rude for the sake of it, and especially don't be crude. Besides, you could easily get yourself labelled! During a performance in Glasgow, I included two poems which made references to 'bottoms' and 'knickers', getting the usual delighted response from the audience. However, I was taken aback when I asked them to suggest why publishers won't allow me to illustrate my poetry books. Instead of giving me the expected – and correct – answer that my drawings are no good, the first boy that I asked said: 'Because your poems are dirty!'

You want your poems to stand out for some reason, so try to come up with something that is different. One way of making your poem stand out is to write it in a more unusual form. For example, say you are going to write a poem about St George and the dragon, instead of writing it in couplets, you could write it in the form of an encyclopedia entry, as a series of entries in St George's diary or even as a text message. Try experimenting with forms, not just haiku and cinquains but triolets, villanelles and univolics. You can find examples in *The Works – Every shape, style and form of poem that you could ever need for the Literacy Hour* (Macmillan 2009).

Children enjoy the ridiculous and the bizarre, but getting an idea can be hard. If you are stuck for a humorous idea, one way of trying to find one is to look through a book of jokes. I was racking my brains to think of an idea for a new poem to include in a book of magic poems, when I came across this joke: Why are the ghosts of magicians no good at conjuring? Because you can see right through their tricks! This led to:

The ghost of the magician said:
'I'm really in a fix.
The trouble is the audience
Sees right through all my tricks!'

I learned a great deal about how to write children's poetry by being an anthologist. So study the work of established children's poets and learn, for example, about how to play with words by reading Roger McGough's poems and about how to write story-poems as dramatic monologues by reading Michael Rosen's poems. You can get ideas, too, from researching what established poets have written. Two of my nonsense poems, both of which are well received in schools, 'The Land of the Flibbertigibbets' and 'On the Clip, Clop Clap' were inspired by Spike Milligan poems – 'In the Land of the Bumbley Boo' and 'On the Ning Nang Nong'.

If you get the opportunity, go along to a school, library or festival at which a children's poet is performing. In addition to listening to what they have to say, you may be able to talk to them afterwards. But don't expect them necessarily to be prepared to look at your poems and to give you a free tutorial on how to write children's poetry.

It's also worth looking at the websites of established writers. One particularly useful website is The Poetry Zone (http://poetryzone.co.uk), set up by the poet Roger Stevens. It consists of articles about writing children's poetry, as well as reviews and interviews with children's poets. The children's section of the Poetry Archive (https://poetryarchive.org/) is worth visiting too.

Getting into print

So how does the aspiring children's poet get published? As I've explained, it's far harder now than it used to be, in the days when there were lots of anthologies being published. One way is to do it yourself. Self-publishing is not as expensive as it used to be. You can get 500 copies of an A5 booklet printed for around £500 and, if you get onto the school circuit, you can sell them directly yourself and more than cover your costs.

Then, there's the internet. You can post your poems on a website. You won't, of course, make any money from doing so and once the poems are out there, then there's the danger that someone else will copy them and claim to have written them. But at least they'll be there for people to read.

You can also consider publishing your poems as an ebook. But there are so many other books available as ebooks that you probably won't sell many copies.

It's not easy for the aspiring children's poet to get recognised at present and you certainly won't make a fortune. But children's poetry is far from dead, as the enthusiastic audiences that greet visiting poets in schools show. So good luck! Keep writing. Visit schools and fly the poetry flag. Join the campaign for a national poetry month, such as exists in the USA. Children's poetry may not be as fashionable as it once was, but it's far from finished!

John Foster's collected poems *The Poetry Chest* (2007) is published by Oxford University Press. His other books include *Eggs with Legs* (Troika 2018), illustrated by Korky Paul, and *Oxford Children's Rhyming Words* (Oxford University Press 2021). His anthologies *Fantastic Football Poems*, *Dragon Poems* and *Dinosaur Poems*, also illustrated by Korky Paul, have been reissued by Oxford University Press.

See also...
● *Poetry organisations*, page 204

Poetry organisations

Below are some organisations which provide budding poets with opportunities to develop their skills, perform and engage with audiences and other poets. Many poetry events are once more happening in person, but there may be an online component to some: please check websites for details.

WHERE TO GET INVOLVED

A range of organisations – from local groups to larger professional bodies – exists at which emerging and established poets can access support or learn more about others' work. A concise selection appears below.

Literature Wales

Glyn Jones Centre, Wales Millennium Centre, Bute Place, Cardiff CF10 5AL
tel 029-2047 2266
email post@literaturewales.org
website www.literaturewales.org

National company for the development of literature in Wales. Working to inspire communities, develop writers and celebrate Wales' literary culture. Activities include the Wales Book of the Year Award, the Children's Laureate Wales and Bardd Plant Cymru schemes, creative writing courses at Tŷ Newydd Writing Centre, writer's bursaries and mentoring, and the National Poet of Wales initiative. The organisation is a member of the Arts Council of Wales' Arts Portfolio Wales.

The Poetry Book Society

Milburn House, Dean Street, Newcastle Upon Tyne NE1 1LF
tel 0191 230 8100
email enquiries@poetrybooksociety.co.uk
website www.poetrybooks.co.uk
Facebook www.facebook.com/poetrybooksoc
Twitter @poetrybooksoc

Book club for readers of poetry founded in 1953 by T.S. Eliot. Every quarter, expert poet selectors choose one outstanding publication (the PBS Choice), and recommend four other titles; these are sent to members, who are also offered discounts on other poetry books. The PBS also produces the quarterly membership magazine, the *Bulletin* (available to all members), which contains the poet selectors' reviews of the Choice and Recommendations, interviews with international poets, reviews and listings. Also offers a range of educational memberships for secondary school libraries with expert teaching tips and posters to inspire students with a love of poetry.

The Poetry Business

Campo House, 54 Campo Lane, Sheffield S1 2EG
tel 0114 438 4074
email office@poetrybusiness.co.uk
website www.poetrybusiness.co.uk

Publishes pamphlets by young poets between the ages of 17 and 24 under The New Poets List imprint; runs the literary magazine, *The North*. Also organises a national pamphlet competition for young poets between the ages of 17 and 24, writing days, and residential courses.

Poetry Ireland

11 Parnell Square East, Dublin D01 ND60, Republic of Ireland
tel +353 (0)1 6789815
email info@poetryireland.ie
website www.poetryireland.ie

Organisation committed to achieving excellence in the reading, writing and performance of poetry throughout the island of Ireland. Poetry Ireland receives support from The Arts Council / An Chomhairle Ealaíon and The Arts Council of Northern Ireland and enjoys partnerships with arts centres, festivals, schools, colleges and bookshops at home and abroad. Its commitment to creating performance and publication opportunities for poets at all stages of their careers helps ensure that the best work is made available to the widest possible audience. Poetry Ireland publishes the well-regarded journal, *Poetry Ireland Review*.

The Poetry Society

22 Betterton Street, London WC2H 9BX
tel 020-7420 9880
email info@poetrysociety.org.uk
website www.poetrysociety.org.uk

A leading voice for poets and poetry in Britain. Founded in 1909 to promote a more general recognition and appreciation of poetry, the Society has nearly 4,000 members. With innovative education, commissioning and publishing programmes, and a packed calendar of performances, readings and competitions, the Society champions poetry in its many forms.

The Society also publishes education resources for teachers and educators; organises high-profile events including an Annual Lecture and National Poetry Day celebrations; runs Poetry Prescription, a critical appraisal service; and provides an education advisory service, INSET packages for schools and networks of schools, a poets in schools service, school membership, youth membership and a website.

Competitions run by the Society include the annual National Poetry Competition, with a first prize of £5,000, and the Foyle Young Poets of the Year Award.

Tower Poetry

Christ Church, Oxford OX1 1DP
tel 07849 625906
email tower.poetry@chch.ox.ac.uk
website www.chch.ox.ac.uk/towerpoetry
Facebook www.facebook.com/towerpoetry/
Twitter @towerpoetry

Exists to encourage and challenge everyone who reads or writes poetry. Funded by a generous bequest to Christ Church, Oxford, by the late Christopher Tower, the aims of Tower Poetry are to stimulate an enjoyment and critical appreciation of poetry, particularly among young people in education, and to challenge people to write their own poetry.

WHERE TO GET INFORMATION

Your local library is a good first port of call, and should have information about the poetry scene in the area. Many libraries are actively involved in spreading the word about poetry as well as having modern poetry available for loan.

Alliance of Literary Societies (ALS)

email allianceoflitsocs@gmail.com
website www.allianceofliterarysocieties.org.uk
Facebook www.facebook.com/
allianceofliterarysocieties/
Twitter @alliancelitsocs
Instagram @alliancelitsocs
Chair Marty Ross

Umbrella organisation for literary societies and groups in the UK. It provides support and advice on a variety of literary subjects, as well as promoting cooperation between member societies. Its publications include a twice-yearly members' newsletter, *Not Only But...*, and an annual journal, *ALSo*. ALS holds an AGM weekend which is hosted by a different member society each year, moving around the UK, or online. Founded 1973.

Arts Council England

tel 0161 934 4317
email enquiries@artscouncil.org.uk
website www.artscouncil.org.uk

National development agency for the arts in England, providing funding for a range of arts and cultural activities. It supports creative writing including poetry, fiction, storytelling, spoken word, digital work, writing for children and literary translation. It funds a range of publishers and magazines as well as providing grants to individual writers. Contact the enquiries team for more information on funding support and advice.

Arts Council of Wales

Bute Place, Cardiff CF10 5AL
tel 0845 8734 900
email information@arts.wales
website www.arts.wales

Independent charity, established by Royal Charter in 1994. It has three regional offices and its principal sponsor is the Welsh Government. It is the country's funding and development agency for the arts, supporting and developing high-quality arts activities. Its funding schemes offer opportunities for arts organisations and individuals in Wales to apply, through a competitive process, for funding towards a clearly defined arts-related project.

Manchester Poetry Library

Manchester Poetry Library,
Manchester Metropolitan University,
Grosvenor Building, Cavendish Street,
Manchester M15 6BG
email poetrylibrary@mmu.ac.uk
website www.mmu.ac.uk/poetrylibrary
Twitter @mcrpoetrylib
Instagram @mcrpoetrylibrary
Director Becky Swain

Sets out to expand access to poetry and to encourage the writing of it at all levels, from primary school to professional standard. Its core collection includes 19th- to 21st-century poetry in English from around the world, as well as poetry in translation. Audio and print versions available. Runs events that celebrate the role of local communities and languages in the process.

National Association of Writers' Groups

Old Vicarage, Scammonden, Huddersfield HD3 3FT
email info@nawg.co.uk
website www.nawg.co.uk

Aims to bring cohesion and fellowship to isolated writers' groups and individuals, promoting the study and art of writing in all its aspects. There are many affiliated groups and associate (individual) members across the UK.

National Poetry Library (Children's Collection)

Level 5, Royal Festival Hall, Southbank Centre, London SE1 8XX
tel 020-7921 0943
email info@poetrylibrary.org.uk
website www.nationalpoetrylibrary.org.uk
Facebook www.facebook.com/NationalPoetryLibrary
Twitter @natpoetrylib
Instagram @nationalpoetrylibrary

Comprises thousands of items for young poets of all ages, including poetry on CD and DVD. The library has an education service for teachers and writing groups, with a separate collection of books and materials for teachers and poets who work with children in schools. Group visits can be organised, allowing children to interact with the collection in various ways, from taking a Poetry Word Trail across Southbank Centre, to exploring how the worlds of science and poetry interact, engaging with war poetry via the Letters Home booklet, or becoming a Poetry Library Poetry Explorer. Nursery schools can also book a Rug Rhymes session for under-5s. Children of all ages can join for free and borrow books and other materials. A special membership scheme is available for teachers to borrow books for the classroom. Contact the library for membership and opening time details.

Northern Poetry Library

The Chantry, Bridge Street, Morpeth, Northumberland NE61 1PD
tel (01670) 620391
email mylibrary@northumberland.gov.uk
website www.northernpoetrylibrary.org.uk
Twitter @nplpoetry

Largest collection of contemporary poetry outside London, housing over 15,000 titles and magazines covering poetry published since 1945. Founded 1968.

Scottish Poetry Library

5 Crichton's Close, Canongate, Edinburgh EH8 8DT
tel 0131 557 2876
email reception@spl.org.uk
website www.scottishpoetrylibrary.org.uk

Houses over 45,000 poetry-related items: books, magazines, pamphlets, recordings and the Edwin Morgan Archive (featuring rare works by Morgan and others). The core of the collection is contemporary and classic poetry written in Scotland – Scots, Gaelic and English – but classic Scottish poetry as well as contemporary works from almost every part of the world are also available. All resources, advice and information are readily accessible, free of charge. The SPL has its own shop and holds regular exhibitions and poetry events, including reading and writing groups and out-reach projects throughout the nation, details of which are available on the library website. Closed Saturday and Sunday. Founded 1984.

ONLINE RESOURCES

There is a wealth of information available for poets at the click of a mouse: the suggestions below are a good starting point.

The Children's Poetry Archive

website https://childrenspoetryarchive.org

World's premier online collection of recordings of children's poets reading their work. Visitors to the website may listen, free of charge, to the voices of contemporary English-language poets and of poets from the past. Featured poets include Allan Ahlberg, Michael Rosen and Valerie Bloom, but the Archive is added to regularly. The website has a range of search options, so that users can search by theme, poet name, lyric, and so on.

LoveReading4Kids.co.uk

website www.lovereading4kids.co.uk/

Independent literature recommendation site designed to inspire and inform parents about the best new reads in children's publishing from toddlers to YA, including poetry. Features include: categories broken down by age range and theme; downloadable opening extracts of featured books; like-for-like recommendations for discovering new authors; exclusive online book reviews by children's books experts including Julia Eccleshare, Andrea Reece and Joanne Owen; and authentic reader reviews from children across all relevant age groups. Includes book price comparison linked to a wide range of affiliates and Bookshop.org. A wide variety of content produced every month, making it easy to find a child's next favourite book and encourage reading for pleasure. Also offers The Book Box by LoveReading4Kids – a gift and book subscription service for children.

LoveReading4Schools.co.uk

website www.lovereading4schools.co.uk/

Independent literature recommendation site designed to support teachers, school librarians and parents to inspire and inform about the best new reads in children's publishing from toddlers to YA, including poetry. Features include: categories broken down by Key Stage, year group and theme; downloadable opening extracts of featured books; like-for-like recommendations for discovering new authors; exclusive online book reviews; and authentic reader reviews from children across all relevant age groups.

Also included are updated reading lists for every year group which are refreshed for the beginning of each academic year. Experts also curate other reading lists to map many key curriculum areas like The Stone Age, Mythology and Ancient Greece, The Victorians, The Great Fire of London, Awesome Earth and many others. Members are able to order books directly from the site from the site's exclusive supplier, Browns Books.

The Poetry Kit

email info@poetrykit.org
website www.poetrykit.org
Twitter @thepoetrykit

Collates a wide variety of poetry-related information, including events, competitions, courses and more for an international readership.

Poetry Space

email susan@poetryspace.co.uk
website www.poetryspace.co.uk

Specialist publisher of poetry and short stories, as well as news and features, edited by Susan Jane Sims. Operates as a social enterprise with all profits being used to publish online and in print, and to hold events to widen participation in poetry. Submissions of poems, stories, novel extracts, photographs and artwork accepted all year for Young Writers' and Artists' Space (18s and under; work by under 16s particularly welcomed).

Seven Stories – National Centre for Children's Books

email info@sevenstories.org.uk
website www.sevenstories.org.uk
Twitter @7Stories
Interim Chief Executive Wendy Elliott

Seven Stories is the only place in the United Kingdom dedicated to the art of children's books. Its website features a blog and online catalogue that may be of use to researchers and authors.

Teachit: English Teaching Resources

website www.teachitenglish.co.uk
Twitter @TeachitEnglish

Resource website for teachers, with over 20,000 pages of classroom worksheets, PowerPoint presentations and activities that have been written and edited by experienced English teachers. The website offers free pdfs as well as teaching packs, classroom posters and books designed for Key Stages 3, 4 and 5.

Write Out Loud

email info@writeoutloud.net
website www.writeoutloud.net

Poetry news, features and reviews, with comprehensive listings of poetry events, publications, festivals and competitions. Members may post poems, join discussions, add their profile, etc. 50,000+ monthly users.

WHERE TO CELEBRATE POETRY

Festival information should be available from Arts Council England offices (see page 342). See also *Children's literature festivals and trade fairs* on page 374.

The British Council

British Council Customer Service UK, Bridgewater House, 58 Whitworth Street, Manchester M1 6BB
tel 0161 957 7755
email uk-literature@britishcouncil.org
website https://literature.britishcouncil.org
Twitter @litbritish

See website for information on events, authors and projects.

Imagine: Writers and Writing for Children

Southbank Centre, London SE1 8XX
tel 020-7960 4200
website www.southbankcentre.co.uk/whats-on/festivals-series/imagine-childrens-festival
Twitter @southbankcentre
Takes place February

Annual festival celebrating writing for children featuring a selection of poets, storytellers and illustrators.

Ledbury Poetry Festival

The Master's House, St Katherine's, Bye Street, Ledbury HR8 1EA
tel (01531) 636232
email director@poetry-festival.co.uk
website www.poetry-festival.co.uk
Artistic Director Chloe Garner
Takes place July and throughout the year

The UK's biggest celebration of poetry and spoken word, attended by poets from all over the world. Established and upcoming talents take part in a wide variety of events, from masterclasses, walks, talks and films through to breakfasts, music, exhibitions and bike rides. International Poetry Competition launches every February.

WHERE TO WRITE POETRY

Arvon

Lumb Bank – The Ted Hughes Arvon Centre, Heptonstall, Hebden Bridge, West Yorkshire HX7 6DF
tel (01422) 843714
email lumbbank@arvon.org
Totleigh Barton, Sheepwash, Beaworthy, Devon EX21 5NS
tel (01409) 231338
email totleighbarton@arvon.org
The Hurst – The John Osborne Arvon Centre, Clunton, Craven Arms, Shrops. SY7 0JA
tel (01588) 640658
email thehurst@arvon.org
website www.arvon.org

Hosts residential creative writing courses and retreats in three rural writing houses. With the opportunity to live and work with professional writers, participants transform their writing through workshops, one-to-one tutorials, time and space to write. Five-day courses and shorter courses are available in a wide range of genres, including writing for children and young adults, fiction, poetry, theatre, creative non-fiction. An online programme of writing courses, masterclasses and live readings also runs year-round. Grants and concessions are available to help with course fees. Founded 1968.

Poetry

Poetry

City Lit

1–10 Keeley Street, London WC2B 4BA
tel 020-7831 7831
email writing@citylit.ac.uk
website www.citylit.ac.uk
Twitter @citylit

Offers classes and courses (online and in-person) on poetry appreciation, as well as a wide range of other topics.

The Poetry School

Somerset House, Strand, London WC2R 1LA
tel 020-7582 1679
website www.poetryschool.com

Teaches the art and craft of writing poetry, with courses in London and around the UK, ranging from evening classes, small seminars and individual tutorials, to one-day workshops, year-long courses and an accredited MA. Activities for beginners to advanced writers, with classes happening face-to-face and online. Three termly programmes a year, plus professional skills development projects and CAMPUS, a social network for poets.

Tŷ Newydd Writing Centre

Llanystumdwy, Cricieth, Gwynedd LL52 0LW
tel (01766) 522811
email tynewydd@literaturewales.org
website www.tynewydd.wales

Tŷ Newydd, the former home of Prime Minister David Lloyd George, has hosted residential creative writing courses for writers of all abilities for over 30 years. Open to everyone over the age of 16. Courses cover everything from poetry and popular fiction to writing for the theatre, developing a novel for young adults. No qualifications are necessary. Staff can advise on the suitability of courses, and further details about each individual course can be obtained by visiting the website, or contacting the team by phone or email. Tŷ Newydd also offers courses for schools, corporate courses and away days for companies. Tŷ Newydd is also home to Nant, the writers' retreat cottage located on site. Tŷ Newydd Writing Centre is run by Literature Wales, the national company for the development of literature in Wales.

HELP FOR YOUNG POETS AND TEACHERS

National Association of Writers in Education (NAWE)

Tower House, Mill Lane, off Askham Fields Lane,
Askham Bryan, York YO23 3FS
tel 0330 333 5909
email admin@nawe.co.uk
website www.nawe.co.uk

National membership organisation which aims to further knowledge, understanding and enjoyment of creative writing and to support good practice in its teaching and learning at all levels. NAWE promotes creative writing as both a distinct discipline and an essential element in education generally. Its membership includes those working in Higher Education, the many freelance writers working in schools and community contexts, and the teachers and other professionals who work with them. It runs a national database of writers, produces a weekly opportunities bulletin, publishes two journals – *Writing in Education* and *Writing in Practice* – and holds a national conference (this was online in 2022). Professional membership includes public liability insurance cover.

Poetry Society Education

The Poetry Society, 22 Betterton Street,
London WC2H 9BX
tel 020-7420 9880
email educationadmin@poetrysociety.org.uk
website www.poetrysociety.org.uk

An arm of The Poetry Society aiming to facilitate exciting and innovative education work. For over 30 years it has been introducing poets into classrooms, providing comprehensive teachers' resources and producing accessible publications for pupils. It develops projects and schemes to keep poetry flourishing in schools, libraries and workplaces, giving work to hundreds of poets and allowing thousands of children and adults to experience poetry for themselves.

Through projects such as the Foyle Young Poets of the Year Award and Young Poets Network, The Poetry Society gives valuable encouragement and exposure to young writers and performers.

Schools membership offers a range of benefits, including quarterly Poetry Society publications, books and posters, and free access to the Poets in Schools placement service. Youth membership is also available (for ages 11–18; from £20 p.a.) and offers discounts, publications, poetry books and posters.

Young Poets Network

email educationadmin@poetrysociety.org.uk
website https://ypn.poetrysociety.org.uk
Facebook www.facebook.com/YoungPoetsNetwork
Twitter @youngpoetsnet

Online resource from The Poetry Society comprising features about reading, writing and performing poetry, plus new work by young poets and regular writing challenges. Open to anyone under the age of 25.

YOUNG POETRY COMPETITIONS

Children's competitions are included in the competition list provided by the Poetry Library: this is free online at www.nationalpoetrylibrary.org.uk/write-publish/competitions. Further information on literary prizes can be found on the BookTrust website (www.booktrust.org.uk/what-we-do/awards-and-prizes/).

Foyle Young Poets of the Year Award

The Poetry Society, 22 Betterton Street, London WC2H 9BX
tel 020-7420 9880
email fyp@poetrysociety.org.uk
website https://foyleyoungpoets.org/
Facebook www.facebook.com/thepoetrysociety
Twitter @PoetrySociety

Annual competition for writers aged 11–17. Prizes include publication, mentoring and a residential writing course. Deadline 31 July. Free to enter. Founded 2001.

Christopher Tower Poetry Competition
Christ Church, Oxford OX1 1DP
tel (01865) 286591
email tower.poetry@chch.ox.ac.uk
website www.chch.ox.ac.uk/towerpoetry
Twitter @TowerPoetry

Annual poetry competition (open from November to March) from Christ Church, Oxford, aimed at students aged between 16 and 18 in UK schools and colleges. The poems should be no longer than 48 lines, on a different chosen theme each year. Free to enter. Prizes: £3,000 (1st), £1,000 (2nd), £500 (3rd). Every winner also receives a prize for his or her school.

FURTHER READING

See also...
• *Flying the poetry flag*, page 200

Further reading

Addonizio, Kim, *Ordinary Genius: A Guide for the Poet Within* (W.W. Norton and Co. 2012)

Bell, Jo, and Jane Commane, *How to Be a Poet: A 21st Century Guide to Writing Well* (Nine Arches Press 2017)

Bell, Jo, and guests: *52: Write a Poem a Week – Start Now, Keep Going* (Nine Arches Press 2015)

Chisholm, Alison, *A Practical Guide to Poetry Forms* (Compass Books 2014)

Fairfax, John, and John Moat, *The Way to Write* (Penguin Books, 2nd edn revised 1998)

Greene, Roland, *et al.*, *Princeton Encyclopedia of Poetry and Poetics* (Princeton University Press, 4th edn 2012)

Hamilton, Ian, and Jeremy Noel-Tod, *The Oxford Companion to Modern Poetry in English* (Oxford University Press, 2nd edn 2014)

Kowit, Steve, *In the Palm of Your Hand: A Poet's Portable Workshop* (Tilbury House, 2nd edn 2017)

Maxwell, Glyn, *On Poetry* (Oberon Books 2017)

Oliver, Mary, *Rules for the Dance: Handbook for Writing and Reading Metrical Verse* (Houghton Mifflin 1998)

Padel, Ruth, *52 Ways of Looking at a Poem: A Poem for Every Week of the Year* (Vintage 2004)

Padel, Ruth, *The Poem and the Journey: 60 Poems for the Journey of Life* (Vintage 2008)

Roberts, Philip Davies, *How Poetry Works* (Penguin Books, 2nd edn 2000)

Sampson, Fiona, *Poetry Writing: The Expert Guide* (Robert Hale 2009)

Sansom, Peter, *Writing Poems* (Bloodaxe 1993, repr. 1997)

Whitworth, John, *Writing Poetry* (A&C Black, 2nd edn 2006)

Poetry

Literary agents
What do agents *do* for their commission?

Generally, literary agents take 15% of their clients' earnings as their commission. Julia Churchill explains what she does in her role of literary agent in return for that percentage.

My role as a literary agent is to help my authors have successful careers. I endeavour to make money in as many rights streams as possible (with an eye on the long term), and enable an easier professional life for my clients so that they can focus on writing. My job involves spotting talent, helping to develop it and selling it.

Some of my clients came to me as established authors wanting to take their careers up a gear, but most have come via my slush pile, as debut writers. I get well over 100 submissions a week, and I may take on a new writer every few months (if I'm lucky). Spotting talent is often where my job starts. I think I have good taste, and I know that my taste isn't unique. If I love a book, it is likely that there are others who will love it too.

I tend not to follow trends, but I am aware of them. There are two markets to consider, and a good agent will have a clear understanding of both. The first is what I focus on when I sell books to publishers. The editor is the buyer and I need to think about their enthusiasms and needs for their list. Then there's the real market, which is reflected in what people are buying from booksellers right now. Both these markets change constantly and part of my job is to keep up to date with trends, and the preferences of individual editors. This knowledge feeds into my decision-making when considering new authors and guidance for my existing clients, although there are also many opportunities outside of obvious trends. To some extent I'm looking for what's fashionable, but more than anything I'm looking for what may be evergreen.

What I am looking for

When I read a manuscript, I'm looking to connect with a voice, a concept, a character and a story, a book with something to say. I'm looking for clarity and intent in the storytelling, and to be taken somewhere new.

Most debut manuscripts that arrive in my office are not yet ready to sell to a publisher, and I may work with the author to focus on what's best about the character(s) and story. Every edit is different. We may sit down together with a cup of tea and talk through the book, exploring such questions as: What does the writer do best? Where does the story lose focus? How can we keep raising the stakes? Why does this section not work? Is it needed? Is the story pulling in too many directions? What is the book about, in the small ways and the big ways?

Before I offer to represent an author, I'll talk them through the work that I think their manuscript needs. I want to be sure, for the author's sake as well as my own, that we're pointed in the same direction and in sync with our ambitions. It's my job to help the author bring out what is best in the manuscript. Sometimes these conversations are about the architecture of the book, and at other times just the interior design. I do what's necessary to maximise the chance of achieving a book deal and the value of that deal.

When I'm satisfied that the book is ready, I submit it to editors. On occasion, I may approach just one editor, and one publishing house, if there is a very specific reason why this would be the best possible outcome for the author. This is matchmaking. More often, I send out the manuscript widely in order to find the publisher with the most passion for the book and the best plan for it.

Selling the book

My favourite aspect of being a literary agent is seeing talent before the rest of the world does. The publishing business relies on having champions for books and an agent is the first professional champion. The agent shares their passion about a book with editors, who in turn pass it on to sales and marketing experts, publicists, reviewers, bloggers, librarians, booksellers and then finally readers.

Sometimes it takes just a few days to sell a book and for other books it can take months – on occasion it has taken years. An auction is lively, but more than anything it's a logistical challenge and requires being organised and systematic. Auctions provide an opportunity for the agent and author to see each publisher's vision, and they give maximum leverage for the best possible deal. Although the idea of an auction may sound exciting, I probably get as much professional satisfaction from humbly selling a book that's been very tough to place as I do from an eight-publisher auction that takes days to tie up.

Looking at contracts

Being a literary agent is not all about passionate pitches, editorial chats over cups of tea and champagne celebrations. There is some glamour to our business, but in many ways an agent's job is quite mundane and is taken up with working on contracts between publishers and authors. A contract has a long life and it requires rigour and experience to convert a publisher-friendly contract into one that is author-friendly. Negotiating contracts is not confined to increasing the advance and pushing for the best royalty and high discount rates, although that is where an agent is likely to show the most immediate value. It's also about ensuring that the author gets their rights back if the book stops selling above a certain level, that the pay-out is staggered in a way that favours the author, that certain sub-rights revert if they are unexploited, that the delivery and acceptance terms are favourable, that in a multi-book deal the books are accounted separately, that the split of sub-rights are as good as they possibly can be, that there is total clarity on what electronic rights the publisher has and that they don't cut across the author's reserved rights. The list of considerations is long: there is a lot to cover in a contract.

An agency will often sell translation rights, and television and film rights. Some of my clients make more money in Brazil or Norway than they do in the USA or UK. And while some markets shrink, others thrive, so for books with reach, it's important to have a strong international team and relationships with film scouts and production companies.

As in any career, a writer is faced with opportunities and decisions to make. Some are small and possibly of little consequence, and some are big and important to get right. Every now and then, there are huge forks in the road which require bravery, clear-minded counsel and an ally. The role of an agent is to be informed and to guide each of their authors to make the best decisions. On behalf of the author, an agent is responsible for talking through grievances, ensuring that publishers deliver what has been promised, feeding into conversations about strategy regarding their work, saying 'no' when it's appropriate, finding work and pushing back.

While everyone concerned in the publishing process wants a book to succeed, my interests as an agent are the same as those of my client. Publishers' interests obviously dovetail with those of the author, but they aren't identical. This is why we generally find ourselves harmonious and in accord with the process, but occasionally in conflict with it. It's my job to have the necessary conversations to look after my authors, to do everything I can to ensure they have the career they want. We are in it together.

Julia Churchill is the children's agent at A.M. Heath Ltd. She is always on the lookout for new writing talent and considers the slush pile to be the greatest place on earth. She is looking for debut and established authors with storytelling magic, from picture book texts through to young adult fiction. Follow her on Twitter @JuliaChurchill.

See also...

Submission to a literary agent (the when, what and how...)

Hannah Sheppard offers practical advice on the process of submitting your finished work to a literary agent and provides top tips and inside knowledge on how to find the representation that might be right for you.

Congratulations! You've finished your novel. This is a huge achievement – not everyone manages to see the task through to completion (I know this from experience ... twice). But, what should you do next?

At the risk of being a complete bore – unless you've already done this, now you need to *get back to work and start editing*.

Honing your final manuscript

The first rule of submitting to literary agents is: ***don't* submit your first draft**. It's time to read your work objectively. Where does the pace drop? Where do the characters do things that don't fit with their motivations? Remember that section you really love but know, if you're honest, isn't moving the plot forward? Cut it.

Find a critique partner (Twitter and local writers' groups can be a good place to start); read and give feedback on their novel in return for feedback on your own. You'll learn as much from exercising your inner editor on someone else's work as you will from the feedback they give you.

Go back and re-write. Do it again. Do it until, hand on heart, you cannot see another thing that might need changing. Then print your freshly edited story in a font you haven't seen it in before (alternatively stick the manuscript on your e-reader or phone, or read it aloud to yourself); this will help you see the words with fresh eyes and make it easier to spot any lingering typos, word repetitions or slightly awkward sentences, so you can fix those. Only now are you ready to start thinking about submitting to a literary agent, and first, you'll need to decide who to submit to.

Making your agent list

The second rule of submitting to literary agents is: ***don't* send your work to everyone**. Agents have different tastes and specialisms and there's enough information out there to help you narrow down a list of those who might be suitable for your manuscript. The amount of time authors spend waiting for a response to submissions would be a lot shorter if everyone stuck to this rule!

Luckily, you currently have in your hand the fount of all knowledge when it comes to literary agents – well done. Make your way through the *Children's Writers' & Artists' Yearbook* (but not yet, finish reading this first) looking for agents who represent your genre, and make yourself a longlist. Then look these agents up online – nearly all will have a website, many will also have Twitter accounts, and if you keep hunting you might find articles they've written and also their manuscript wish lists. All of this will give you some clues as to whether each agent might be right for you and your work.

It's also worth thinking about what's important to you when it comes to this relation-ship. Do you want someone who is a cut-throat dealmaker who is all about the business side of publishing, or someone a little more approachable? (If I'm honest, they're all pretty lovely – I haven't met many of the first kind.) Do you want someone who will be hands-on editorially or do you feel like you've got that covered? My top piece of advice is to find someone you can ask basic questions to without feeling stupid ... because there are going to be a lot of those. Quite honestly, there's no reason you *should* know all about how this industry works. Publishing can be flummoxing at times – even for someone who's been working in it for over 15 years.

After researching everyone on your longlist, put them into some sort of order – from those who feel like the closest fit in terms of their list and who you think you might gel with personally, down to those who could be a bit of wild card but are not completely beyond the realms of possibility. But if an agent says they don't represent your genre, it's unlikely they're going to start doing so just because of *your* book; this is about their publishing contacts as much as anything – and you want an agent who knows the right editors to sell your work.

Putting together a submission package

After selecting the agents to approach, you'll need to prepare your submission package, and the third rule of submitting to literary agents is: **always follow their guidelines.** As well as your *manuscript* (usually the first three chapters or 10,000 words, and always from the beginning of your manuscript), the submission package should generally include a *synopsis* and a *cover letter*. But it's important to check exactly what each agent wants and how they want it sent. These may be different for every agent on your list. Yes, that may be tiresome, but the guidelines are there to enable your chosen agent to get through their inbox as fast as possible (they've worked out a system that works for them) and get an answer to you. And if an author appears to think they're above following the guidelines, I ask myself – why would I want to work with someone who doesn't respect me? Could I feel confident promoting them to editors I have good working relationships with? The harsh truth is, I don't even need to read the material in these cases.

There's a lot of great advice online about writing a synopsis (see for example, www.writersandartists.co.uk/advice/synopsis) but, in short, this should be one page of A4, size 12 font (typically Times New Roman or something similarly readable), single-spaced. Don't play with the margins or shrink the font; think about the person who has to read it – if it's tiny, densely packed text, you've probably lost them. White space on the page is always good.

A synopsis should be a very functional overview of your protagonist's emotional journey. This isn't about trying to wow an agent with your style (but be sure to proofread – try using the different font trick mentioned above). You don't need to include every plot point or introduce every character, but agents do need to know the cause-and-effect structure of your plot – all of it. We *want* the spoilers here please. An agent needs to know that the mechanics of your story work; from this they can see where there might be structural issues to address.

For your cover letter, it's good to strike a professional yet personable tone. This isn't a casual approach, but an agent does want to see some of your personality, to judge whether you're someone they might work well with. Overleaf is the kind of letter I like to see – the focus is very much on the character and story, rather than themes or why the author wrote it.

① Dear Hannah/Ms Sheppard

② I'm writing to submit *Romeo and Juliet*, a tragic love story for YA readers, complete at 75,000 words.

③ When Romeo Montague and Juliet Capulet fall in love, it enrages their feuding families. Can they find a way to be together before Juliet is married off to someone else?

④ Juliet can't even remember what started the argument between her family and the Montagues, it's been going on so long, and as a result she hasn't seen her childhood friend Romeo for years. But when fate brings them together at a school dance which Romeo and his friends have gate-crashed, the connection is immediate. They are meant to be together. Surely their families will see that? But they don't. And in an effort to keep Romeo and Juliet apart, Juliet's family arrange a marriage between Juliet and a friend of her father. Horrified, Romeo and Juliet hatch a plan to escape together, but a series of mixed messages and missed connections lead to disaster.

⑤ *Romeo and Juliet* will appeal to readers of *Othello* and *Antony and Cleopatra* and fans of Christopher Marlowe.

⑥ I am a debut writer who has …

⑦ I am submitting to you because …

⑧ Yours sincerely/Regards …

① I'm happy with either style. Some agents prefer more formality … but, above all, spell it correctly.

② Clearly state your title, target market and word count.

③ This is your short elevator pitch – it's great to have something like this prepared for chance encounters with an agent, but also for post-publication when you're at promotional events in front of an audience and you're asked to introduce your book. A useful structure is: When A (inciting incident) happens, B (protagonist) must do C (action) otherwise/before D (stakes) happen.

④ This gives you a chance to expand a little on the story. You want to focus on the main story line and the emotional journey of your protagonist, making sure that the stakes are clear – knowing what the character stands to lose is important for emotionally engaging your reader. Think of this paragraph a little like the blurb on the back of a book; you want to make me care about the character and intrigue me. The synopsis is where you give the full story.

⑤ This is your chance to position your work within the market and demonstrate that you understand the area you're writing into. Try not to include only the mega-sellers, as that suggests you don't read widely in the market – and it's important that you do.

⑥ We don't need a huge amount of information about you at this point, but try to include anything pertinent, e.g. have you joined SCBWI; are you part of a writers' group; have you completed a writing course or won a writing competition? None of this is essential, but anything you have done will show how seriously you're taking your writing. My top tip here is **keep it positive**. So, for example, if you haven't won any writing competitions, just don't mention them.

⑦ Show that you've done your research and understand a little about the particular agency and agent you're submitting to. Have you read an article in which I talked about my love for the type of story you've written? Does it fit with something my agency has mentioned on its manuscript wish list? Are you a huge fan of one of our existing clients and feel your mutual fandom of that body of work suggests we might like yours too?

⑧ Polite sign off … Use your actual name, not just initials or a pseudonym, even if that's what you want to write under. The agent is going to have a working relationship with you.

A few final top tips:

• Use your own, professional email address – almost all submissions are via email now. My agency, DHH Literary, no longer accepts hard copy submissions, and many agencies have the same policy. Don't use an email address you share with your partner or one that was funny when you were a student. Email accounts are easy and free to set up, so have a separate one for your work.

• Make attachment file names as useful as possible... 'synopsis for Hannah' is not very helpful (I receive hundreds with a similar description). Instead include your name and the title of your book.

• Try testing the water by contacting four or five agents initially, to see what response you get. That will give you the chance to tweak your submission. Maybe start midway down the list you drew up of those to contact. If you start getting positive reactions, you can always quickly send the submission to the agents at the top of the list too.

• Brace yourself for a long wait. Agents don't do this to torture you; we're very busy and we use our office time working for our existing clients. This means reading submissions happens in the evenings and at weekends. I typically receive ten submissions a day.

• Start writing your next book, so that you're not focused solely on the fate of the first one you send out. This should ideally be something new rather than a sequel, just in case your first submission doesn't work out.

• Usually a gentle nudge is fine if you haven't heard back within the time stated on the agent's website, but always stay polite. Definitely update an agent if you've had a full manuscript request elsewhere or have been offered representation, and withdraw the submission if you accept that representation.

• If you get feedback, take it seriously. I'm so busy that I rarely give personalised feedback and only when I think there's something easy to fix which would make a significant difference to an author's chances.

• Remember that rejections are part of the process. They don't always mean your book or your writing is bad; they can simply mean that yours wasn't the right book for that agent at that time. There's a lot of luck and serendipity involved here too.

• If all you are getting are standard rejections, take some time out to think about whether you need to do more work. Perhaps you should get a professional assessment on your manuscript? Or maybe it's time to begin a different project (luckily you followed my earlier tip and have already started one, right?).

• Keep an open mind, the right agent for you might not be the person you initially put at the top of your wish list. How you get on at a personal level when you chat with an agent will be important.

So that's it ... you're ready to start submitting. Good luck, hold your nerve and keep trying.

Literary agent and development editor **Hannah Sheppard** worked as an in-house editor with Macmillan Children's Books and Headline Publishing Group before joining the DHH Literary Agency in 2013. She represents authors from across children's fiction (middle grade, teen and young adult) and adult fiction (crime/thriller and women's fiction). For more information see www.dhhliteraryagency.com/hannah-sheppard.html. Follow Hannah on Twitter @YA_Books.

Choosing the right agent

Literary agent Gill McLay describes some of the differences between big and small agencies, and identifies some of the ways you can discover which might be the right one for you to approach and to sign up with if you are offered representation.

After completing my marketing and publishing degree I moved to London and went straight into my first publishing job. Over 25 years later I am still in publishing. I have worked for small, independent publishers and large global publishers, always on the publicity, marketing and sales side of the business. Then, about 15 years ago, I decided I wanted to work for myself. One of the many things I did was to set up the Bath Festival of Children's Literature, the largest festival in Europe devoted exclusively to books, authors, illustrators and readers of children's books – from picture books right up to young adult. I knew it had to start big if it was to compete in the already vibrant and well-developed literary festivals calendar. After our success with the festival, we have evolved again to establish, Events of Wonder (www.eventsofwonder.com) which stages events for children in Bath, Bristol and beyond. Creating these magical moments for children and families remains very close to my heart and having a wider range of partners has meant we can now reach so many more people. It has also allowed us to stage art exhibitions, other festivals and develop clubs that ensure we work at a truly grassroots level.

It was while I was working more closely with authors, through the festival, that I started to be asked for publishing advice. I would frequently recommend agents that fledging writers could approach and was repeatedly asked why I didn't offer an agent service myself. Being an agent is an all-encompassing job and I knew it would need me to be full-time, so I decided that when my son started school I would do it!

At the time, I was running media training courses for authors and was always surprised by the questions they asked (or hadn't dared or thought to ask). I decided that if I was to be an agent, I would manage careers rather than projects and I would allow authors to become a fully engaged part of my agency. For me, part of surviving in this tough and competitive business is to help my clients be prepared, and to share my knowledge of why decisions are made and how. As well as showing respect for my authors' writing and other creative work, I set out to establish working relationships based on mutual respect, understanding and gratitude for the respective skills of both author and agent; from such close links, greater successes emerge. *Teams* of people create books, and I wanted to put this team spirit right at the heart of my agency.

The Bath Literary Agency is a relatively small company that offers a very hands-on style of management for writers and illustrators of children's books. We are one of many small literary agencies based outside London, the main publishing metropolis, and we like to think that we offer authors something different to what a larger agency provides. The agency is now ten years old and continues to go from strength to strength, due to my clients who work incredibly hard to deliver saleable books. Together we are always working on our next project.

How can *you* find the right agent?

I believe that having an agent is essential. Once you are lucky enough to find your publishing home, it makes a big difference if you can focus on the creative side and let your agent focus on the business aspects of your writing.

This doesn't mean you don't get involved. You *must* be involved. It does, however, mean that you can talk through things with your agent and ask all the questions you like without fear of asking the wrong thing – which might not be the case if you were talking directly to a publisher. It also gives you a greater understanding of which things to challenge and which to accept, both contractually and creatively. There is a huge difference between writing for yourself and writing to be published; an agent can help you navigate this fine line.

What are the differences between small and large agencies?

Bigger agencies, London-based agencies, multimedia agencies and small boutique agencies (with only one or two agents, say) all offer different things. They each have their strengths and weaknesses; the most important thing for you, as a new author, is to get the right agent for *your* books and *your* needs.

The size of the agency is actually irrelevant in many ways, because everything comes down to the relationship you have with one person: your own agent.

That relationship should be symbiotic, with writer and agent coming together to make the strongest possible offering to a publisher, and thus ultimately to your readership or market. Your respective strengths and weaknesses should complement each other.

This is why you need to know your agent's experience. Agents come from all

> **In a nutshell**
>
> **Know what you want:**
> • Do you want to be a big fish in a small pond?
> • Do you write across several genres; if so, does the agent represent them all?
> • Do you want an agent with editorial skills to help shape your writing?
> • Do you want personal support or purely business/commercial help?

sorts of different backgrounds, which can make a huge difference to their individual approach. Many have been editors, some move over from selling rights in publishing houses to agenting and others have come from the sales and book-buying side of publishing. Each set of skills and experience has its own strengths.

My background is in sales and marketing. As a result, I approach things from a very commercial angle and spend almost as much time scouting for new opportunities as I do creating them. When I advise my clients, we talk about long-term objectives and career progression. The individual books are important, but I am always keen to find out what else an author can do and where they want to be.

An agent with an editorial background, however, may focus more on the individual manuscript. For some authors this is essential and they need this support, but others may already have confidence and feel secure in their writing, but they may need help to understand the market and publishing process and to pitch their story to the right audience and gatekeepers (i.e. publishers).

Part of this writer-development process, fostering authors of tomorrow, comes from the other professional hats I wear. Media training for authors, Events of Wonder and the festival I have run has given me a real insight into the life of a successful author today. Gone are the days of being able to write, send your script to an agent, sell your book and then start writing again. An author needs to promote and reach their audience. The first book you sell to a publisher will be the last before you add the role of juggler to your CV, as you tackle the balancing act of writing *and* promoting!

Literary agents

A larger agency will often have staff who specialise in rights, contract, legal, accounts and admin support. A smaller agency is more likely to have only a couple of these specialists, and sometimes they will have none; the agent may coordinate all aspects of the process. Which you prefer and works best for you is completely personal. Do you want to work with one person who answers everything, or do you wish to work with a team? Larger agencies may also be able to offer you other focused advice. For example, if you wish to write for adults, write plays or film scripts, they may have people on hand to advise or represent you beyond, for example, your initial work in young adult fiction. Smaller agencies can sometimes do this too, but tend to be more specialised.

Ideally, you should meet agents from both large and smaller agencies – that's if you are lucky enough to be offered representation by more than one agency. This will help you make an informed decision. It is in no one's interest for you to be with the wrong agent. Choosing the right agent is a balance of gut instinct and information; do your research before you contact them with your initial submission, and then again when they have shown interest in representing you.

One thing that everyone needs is an agent who is nice to work with, but also one who is an effective and strong dealmaker. When selecting your agent, there are some **key things to consider**:

1. How many clients do they have and who are they? If you feel that you will need and want a lot of hands-on support with your writing, a large agency may not be for you. If you are a confident writer and want someone who has big agency presence, then maybe the children's agent in a bigger agency would suit you.

2. Do they have clients that write in the same genre as you? This is a great indicator that they have strong contacts with the right commissioning editors and can sell this genre. But if they have lots of authors in this field, will you be competing with other clients within their agency? The balance needs to be right. So do look at their client list.

3. Where are they based? These days this seems to matter less and less but, if they are not near you, how often could you and they travel to a mutually sensible location (e.g. London)?

4. What sort of agent are they? Do you want an editor or commercial management? Do you have one book that you need an agent to sell, or do you have multiple ideas that you want someone to help you develop?

5. Can you relax and feel comfortable with them? You need to be able to communicate well with your agent. Is this someone you can work with? The relationship will become really important as you set off on the rollercoaster ride of getting published; you need to be yourself and have complete trust in your agent.

Always trust your gut instinct. If this is the agency and person you can imagine working with, then take the next step and sign up. Getting published is a long process, success doesn't come overnight, so who you share your journey with is important. Big agency or small agency, it's all about best fit and only you can decide which is right for you.

Gill McLay runs the Bath Literary Agency (www.bathliteraryagency.com) which specialises in children's books. She is co-founder of the annual Bath Festival of Children's Literature. She runs Events of Wonder (www.eventsofwonder.com) with her husband John McLay.

Finding an agent for your picture book

Jodie Hodges explains the opportunities and options for aspiring picture book authors and illustrators, sharing her experience and essential advice on how to find representation and build a successful career in this creative sector.

I've been a literary agent for nearly 15 years; apart from a post-university six months as a bookseller, it is the only adult job I've ever known. Every day I count myself lucky that I was second choice for a position as assistant to Rosemary Canter at Peters, Fraser & Dunlop, one of the only children's literary agents at the time, and that her first choice turned down the job! Working with Rosemary, the agent of children's book luminaries like Giles Andreae, William Nicholson and Benjamin Zephaniah, was a privilege that gave me an incomparable grounding in the job of literary representation. We moved to United Agents in 2007 and when Rosemary died in 2011 I inherited her list, combining it with my own fledging group of authors and illustrators of children's books. Working equally with new and established talent affords me a perspective on building careers – allowing me to see how things have changed and what remains the same, and I'm lucky enough to represent a fantastically varied list of creators across all age groups in children's publishing.

I love working with picture book creators; I enjoy the variety, the creativity, the collaboration. Picture book authors and illustrators in the children's market are in a particularly fortunate position, having the opportunity to publish multiple books (strategically managed by a good agent, of course!) and therefore to give themselves several chances of having a hit. I choose to represent both authors and illustrators of picture books, which gives me a full picture of this area of the market and the chance to work on lots and lots of different books (... I so enjoy doing this job, so why wouldn't I want to work on as many books as I can?).

So what is a picture book?

When I say 'picture books', I'm mainly talking about colour illustrated books of around 12 double-page spreads with a text of about 500 words, aimed at a shared reading experience for adult and child under seven. Traditionally these would be fictional stories but, increasingly, narrative non-fiction is also published in this format. There are longer picture books, of course, and baby books, but the vast majority of picture books fall within that definition.

Picture books can be created by one person, an author-illustrator, such as Rob Biddulph. They can also be collaborations between an author and an illustrator, such as *The Littlest Yak* (Simon & Schuster Children's UK 2020) written by Lu Fraser and illustrated by Kate Hindley. When a picture book is a collaboration, it's usually the case that the publisher has acquired the text first and then searches for a suitable illustrator, commissioning them to bring the text to life visually. More rarely, a book might start from an illustrator's image or character which a publisher then commissions a writer to create a text for – as with *Dogs in Disguise* (HarperCollins Children's 2021) written by Peter Bently and illustrated by John Bond. Each collaborator is contracted separately – for most deals this will be an advance and royalty – and the royalty rate is usually split 50/50 between author and illustrator, although their advances are likely to vary as the illustrator has months of artwork to produce. The story may have started with the text, but it becomes a book when the illustrator comes on board – a true collaboration.

An illustrator's essentials

If you want to get started as an illustrator of picture books, it's vital to have a really strong, targeted, market-specific portfolio, even if you only intend to illustrate your own stories. What sort of things come up in picture books? Animals, toddlers, dragons, friendship … a varied mix. To give you some ideas for images, try going into a bookshop to take a look at the tables of new picture books, and making a list of their subjects, themes and settings.

Equally important is to find a stylistic voice of your own that also marries commercially with the market. Here again, research and inspiration are key. I think around 20 pages of work is about right for your portfolio, with a mixture of vignettes and spreads that allow you to show characterisation and how you would put a scene together. When your portfolio is ready, you can use this *Yearbook* to look up suitable agents to send it to (see the listings starting on page 235). There are literary agents and also illustration agents; it's wise to think about which of those might be right for you. As a literary agent, I represent my illustrators for their book work only, whereas an illustration agent might cover many other areas. Make a list of agents and then look them up on their websites, social media and trade press – who do they represent? Are they doing plenty of deals? Do you like the cut of their jib? Follow each agent's submission guidelines and hopefully someone will connect with your work and want to progress a conversation. If things go well, this might lead to representation.

Advice for the picture book author

For authors of picture book texts, my first piece of advice is to embrace prolificacy. Write, write and write some more. Have lots of texts and lots of ideas. This is important for several reasons. Firstly, I assume you'd like to earn some money from your writing; advances for picture book texts are at the lower end of the scale, so selling and publishing multiple books each year is a way to increase your income.

Secondly, the picture book market moves quickly and is extremely focused on the new. You might have a text about a fussy-eating unicorn, but if your agent sends it to a publisher who has just bought a text about a fussy-eating dinosaur, or a unicorn with bad manners, then they're unlikely to have room for yours. It's not the fault of the text, but simply timing and elements that are out of your agent's control and yours. So, what do you do? Move on. Hopefully you've already got some other texts ready, and you try those.

The third reason to be prolific – which is also relevant to illustrators working on collaborative books – is that every new book, every new combination of text and illustration, is a new opportunity for a bestseller or an international success. The publishers use their market expertise to give the books the best possible chance, but sometimes it's simply alchemy. For example, the magical combination of Rachel Bright's words with my client Jim Field's illustrations in their bestselling series of books beginning with *The Lion Inside* (Orchard Books 2015) has meant both UK commercial success and many international partner publishers. We might have hoped for that – but it's never a given.

I would always advise an aspiring picture book author looking for an agent to use the same strategy they will need when they're published: if you submit some stories to agents and they're not picked up – press on and write some more. Use feedback, read, research, and go again. The next one might be the one. And then you'll need another one.

If an agent connects with your work, be it texts or illustrations, it's vital you feel able to have an honest, open, productive relationship with them. Meet them, ask all the questions you have in mind; if you're offered representation, take some time to mull over your meeting before making your decision. We all hope an agent-client relationship is going to be long-term, so don't rush into it.

Dos and don'ts for authors and illustrators:

• If you're a picture book author, you **don't** need to find an illustrator yourself to be able to approach an agent. Have plenty of stories, make sure you're sending to agents representing picture book authors, and follow their guidelines – that's it.

• If you're an illustrator, you **don't** need to write a story. If you want to, and you've created a package that you feel could be a commercial picture book, that's great – but it's possible to have a very successful career as an illustrator who doesn't write.

• **Do** try to write your text with the book format in mind. It's good practice to write it out labelling the spreads 1-12. That way you can pace your story correctly and work with the page-turns to add jeopardy or humour.

• **Don't** provide extensive illustrative notes on your texts. If there's a visual joke that isn't spelt out in the text itself then, of course, mention it, but the reason a picture book royalty is split 50/50 is that the illustrator is equally as important as the author. I've seen projects completely transform when the illustrator takes the story to a different setting or casts it in a way the author just wouldn't have thought of. There will always be consultation; no one wants the author to be part of a book they don't recognise as their story any longer. More often than not, though, it's an extremely positive process.

• **Do** think about working outside the field of picture books. The skills used in writing and illustrating picture books can very often be transferred into other types of children's books – young fiction, chapter books, illustrated middle grade and young adult, non-fiction. It's thrilling to see creators branch out, with books like Rob Biddulph's *Peanut Jones* series (Macmillan Children's), or Jenny Løvlie illustrating both *The Boys* picture book (Caterpillar Books 2021) and the *Kitty* young fiction series (OUP 2019–). Once you've found an agent, you can talk about diversifying your writing or illustrating, or perhaps if you're struggling to find an agent with your picture book work, think about creating submissions for a different area of the market.

• **Don't** get carried away imagining the animated series and theme park of your picture book – even if you're lucky enough to have it published. It's natural, and desirable, to have ambitions, but expectation management is an undervalued and essential part of the publishing process and the life of an author and illustrator.

Submission rules

I want to assure you the 'slush' pile is a friend of the aspiring picture book creator. An agent can read the texts, or look through portfolio work, much more quickly than they can read a novel. So use that to your advantage by making your submission as easy to navigate as possible. For me this means a clear, short covering email, and separate attachments for each text or a single PDF portfolio I can scroll through. Submitting in the good old-fashioned way is your best chance of finding an agent – I've taken on countless clients this way. So don't imagine there's a shortcut. No good agent is ignoring their submissions – we want to find gold in there. I hope I might see some of your work in my own inbox soon.

Jodie Hodges is an agent with United Agents, representing children's illustrators and authors of picture books, middle grade, teenage and young adult, including Rob Biddulph, Jim Field, Smriti Halls, Sophie McKenzie, Jamie Smart and Harriet Muncaster. She began working with Rosemary Canter at Peters, Fraser & Dunlop in 2006, becoming an agent in 2010. For more information see www.unitedagents.co.uk/jhodgesunitedagentscouk. Follow her on Twitter @jodiehodges31.

See also...
- *Being an illustrator* and *a writer*, page 259
- *Choosing the right agent*, page 218
- *Eight great tips to get your picture book published*, page 268

Why teachers make great children's writers

Kate Scarborough shares her thoughts on how a teacher's experience and skills can empower and benefit them as a children's writer, as well as the essential advice, tools and tips she can offer new writers since setting up her own agency.

If you are thumbing through this book wondering whether your dreams of becoming a published writer can become a reality, my story and practical advice might be useful. By giving you a little background into how and why I set up my literary agency – Tyild's Agency – in 2021, I hope to help you on that journey. (In the best teacherly tradition, I'll mark up in bold type the bits that are particularly pertinent to you, the aspiring writer).

Writers often talk about suffering from 'Imposter Syndrome' and, in this new post-pandemic publishing life I have created for myself, it's a condition I understand. As I dive deeper into the publishing world, I see fledgling writers revealing their unease through nervous tweets, published authors writing articles on how they can't believe they have been published, agents trying to find the next big thing, and publishers never being sure that a book they adore is going to fly on the open market. But amid all that self-doubt, I take comfort from accepting that **none of us really know for sure what makes a successful book and that the route to success is laced with huge amounts of luck**.

That said, it is easy to forget that **experience, planning, perseverance, persistence and craft account for a great deal**. I was an editor, writer and publisher in children's publishing for the first 14 years of my working life. I had a fabulous time, being creative, coming up with ideas, pitching them, putting them together and selling them, and ultimately being responsible for a team of people doing the same. Following a different dream, I then moved to teaching. Ironically – because I was always a bit of a rebel as a pupil, and *not* the teacher's favourite – I adored going back to the classroom, and loved planning ways to enthuse children about learning and especially about reading. The chance to use books in the classroom, find out what children particularly enjoy, and study how those books are written, was invaluable.

But upheavals, such as the pandemic, can have a dramatic effect on personal priorities. Like many, I found myself asking: What do I really want to do? What do I love doing? How do I make the most of my experience? I have always loved books and the creative process, and I know how to put them together. I love teaching and inspiring readers of all kinds. My wonderful colleague and friend for many years, Frances McKay (a successful illustrator's agent), gave me a nudge. Why not use these experiences to become an agent? There are many experienced, dynamic agents out there who have been digging out and nurturing writers for years. What could I bring to this market that would make my experience count? It had always struck me that **so many of our top children's authors previously worked in the classroom**. An agency that championed all those aspiring teacher writers might be exactly what I should do. And so Tyild's Agency was born.

Starting from scratch is daunting. I had to publicise my credentials and persuade authors to join the agency before I could begin to approach publishers with news that the agency was live. It is not easy to promote yourself – I had to work hard to remember that I was, in fact, qualified to do this job. However, this self-promotion is really important, and it is equally so for you, as authors. **In your covering letters to agents and publishers**, make sure you **mention all your training and your writing successes so far**. I had to spend a lot of time making connections through Twitter, LinkedIn, Facebook and Instagram. I could not have found my authors and developed the business without these tools. Teachers are one of the most communicative and vibrant communities online; they support and encourage one another across all these platforms and welcome newcomers with enthusiasm. And teacher writers are the best of these. I found that word spread quickly and, in no time, I had an inbox bulging with hopes and dreams.

Choosing authors to represent is extremely difficult, as there are so many talented writers out there. I have been fairly ambitious in my scope, in that I represent authors of picture books, chapter books and middle-grade titles. Most of the authors I have taken on, however, are keen to work across the age ranges, which is something I do look out for. Versatility and imagination are key, but it all starts with the initial email. And – forgive me – but if the email from a potential author is not addressed to me but has clearly been lumped in with a mailshot to lots of other agents, I tend not to prioritise it. **An agent will work very closely with an author and striking a good relationship right at the start is vital**. I check to see if an email shows that the sender has done their research and that they have followed my guidelines. The tone and style of the email also helps me to judge whether or not I should spend time reading the submission. When I started the agency, I had such high hopes of reading every word of each submission and of being able to give thoughtful feedback. I now know that this is absolutely impossible, given everything I need to do. And the same applies for all agents and publishers – so give yourself a head start, **do your research, follow the guidelines**, and **make it personal**.

Being a start-up, I am very conscious that the writers who have signed up with me are taking a gamble, and I speak to every potential writer to make sure that they understand this. It is a risk that is not for everyone and I understand that. The agency is in its infancy and each milestone – taking on new authors, meeting publishers, getting those first contracts signed – is fantastic, but (with a small child and a dog to support) I still have to earn in order to follow this dream. So, I am **not giving up the day job** … yet. I tutor children in English, which I love because it ties in so well with the agency work. It means I am reading, studying and critiquing books with the target market, which provides the perfect insight.

But why do I feel so strongly that teachers can be great writers for children? And what can we learn from their experience to help our own writing? Some of the biggest names in children's publishing started in teaching – J.R. Tolkien, C.S. Lewis, Philip Pullman, Eva Ibbotson, David Almond, Michael Morpurgo – even J.K. Rowling and Julia Donaldson dabbled. On a Twitter exchange, **Philip Pullman** explained his journey by revealing that in class '…I told stories (not my own – myths, folk tales) because I thought it was a good thing to do. **I learned to tell [stories] by doing it.**' And **David Almond**, who said that teaching is central to his life as a writer, explained that in his lessons, he '…**wrote stories with the children**, inspired their own stories, dramatised stories with them. [This] helped me explore the varieties of form, and a connection to voice/movement.'

When writing for children, you need to **know your audience** in so many ways, from the practical (**what are they *able* to read**) to the inspirational (**what do they *want* to read**). A teacher works with children in the classroom, helping them to become readers. They can witness first-hand the impact stories have on young readers. The teacher will see which stories open eyes, widen horizons, encourage questions, unlock imagination and switch on light bulbs in their heads! Teachers also come to **know the book market** pretty well, especially those who take a professional interest in it. Most teacher writers will try out their own fledgling books on their class – who are always a willing audience. This can have a very direct effect, in that the teacher writer is able to edit on the fly and they quickly, even sometimes painfully (George, don't do that…), **learn how to hold a reader's attention, how to build suspense, how to move them and how to make them laugh.**

It can seem that, as adults, we forget what it is like to be a child, but the teacher hopefully never forgets. Teachers are part of children's daily lives, and are there to share their joys, successes, struggles, battles and humour. This awareness of their audience that results from working with children means that teachers **never underestimate their reader**. Teaching children to write also lays bare the creative process for teachers. Every teacher writer that I work with writes with their pupils, and there is nothing more powerful than modelling writing for children, sharing what is good and exploring the difficulties. If children can see you struggle, change your mind, make mistakes and self-edit, then it is fine for them to do it. This **constant practice in editing helps hone a writer's craft.**

I spend a huge amount of my teaching time **exploring inference and empathy**. These are the skills you need to be a good reader (indeed, person), and which frankly give the child reader such a fantastic head start in life. As a writer, you need to know how to encourage inference and empathy in your reader, but you also must understand when your carefully crafted inference will go sailing right over the top of your reader's head. **Pitching it right for your reader** with enough to stretch children, and enough to help them begin to see it, is a delicate skill and the teacher writer has a distinct advantage with their insider knowledge. Good teachers **never stop learning**. There is so much help and support out there for writers, both of the teacher variety and others. My authors have writing groups, critical partners, go on courses for writing, attend conferences about the industry, join communities (see *Children's writing courses and conferences*, page 380 and *Societies, associations and organisations*, page 341). Using this book will help you to find those communities, as will the *Writers' & Artists'* website (www.writersandartists.co.uk; see *More than a book*, page ix).

Once your book is published you will need to do **school visits, festivals and presentations to children in order to market your work**. These are uplifting experiences, but can be extremely nerve-racking. Although – dare I say it – not to a teacher. Most teachers are more than happy to show off in front of children (any excuse) and know exactly how to manage that crowd so they don't lose them in the excitement. Not all great writers are teachers and not all teachers are great writers – but, if you talk to any writer who *has* taught, they will tell you the experience was invaluable. So, try to **get into a classroom and meet teachers**; they will be your strongest allies.

My own journey has really only just begun, and I hope the agency, which has been warmly welcomed by the publishing community, will flourish. I am and will go through the same highs and lows that everyone has in this industry. **It is not easy, but it is worth it.** It is worth it for so many different reasons: you get to meet wonderful people; you share your creative vision; and ultimately, if all goes well, you get to inspire the next generation. You will feel what all teachers feel – that sense of vocation.

[With thanks to these teacher writers who shared their thoughts on Twitter: Gaynor Andrews, Barbara Henderson, Mark Smith, Catherine Bruton, Lindsay Galvin, David Almond and Philip Pullman.]

Kate Scarborough is the founder of Tyild's Agency, a literary agency particularly for teachers who write for children. She has, over the last thirty years, been an editor, writer, publisher and teacher and now combines all this experience and enthusiasm into promoting teacher writers whose talent crosses over from the classroom to the page. For more information see www.tyildsagency.co.uk and follow on Twitter @TyildS.

CBC
CURTIS BROWN CREATIVE

THE CREATIVE WRITING SCHOOL FROM THE
MAJOR LITERARY AGENCY

Learn how to write or illustrate brilliant stories for children and young adults

160+
former students with
publishing deals

'I cannot overstate
the huge impact the
course had on my
writing'

Jenny Pearson
*The Super Miraculous
Journey of Freddie Yates*

'The CBC course was
where my career as a
children's author all
began'

Rachael Davis
I Am NOT A Prince

'Having the chance
to meet with industry
professionals was
hugely helpful'

Struan Murray
Orphans of the Tide

Start your story with an online course
www.curtisbrowncreative.co.uk

STORYMIX

THE INCLUSIVE FICTION STUDIO

WITH YOUR HELP AND TALENT STORYMIX CREATES INCLUSIVE CHILDREN'S FICTION FOR PUBLISHERS

WE'RE LOOKING FOR CREATIVES WHO:

- Are keen to write or illustrate for children;
- Can work collaboratively and to a brief;
- Are from a Black or Minority Ethnic background.

Fewer than 2% of published authors and illustrators in the UK are British people of colour.

Storymix imagines differently.

We work with agented and unagented, published, self-published and unpublished creatives to make heroes for all kids.

STORYMIX.CO.UK/WRITE-FOR-US

faber
academy

Manuscript
Assessment

Just finished a new draft? Getting ready to submit to agents? Or looking for an honest, professional steer on your work-in-progress? Our experienced readers provide constructive, comprehensive reports to help your manuscript stand out from the crowd.

A message for under-represented writers: We Want You

Davinia Andrew-Lynch knows that, as well as a good story, agents and editors are also on the lookout for talented writers from groups and communities currently under-represented in the world of children's publishing. She has advice for marginalised writers on how to find the representation, confidence and support they need.

Despite the increasing number of children's books published each year, many budding authors find the world of publishing daunting. And, for those of you from under-represented groups (including, but not limited to, minority ethnic/religious, LGBTQ+ and working-class communities), this London-centric industry can seem wholly unwelcoming.

Things are changing, however. The vital importance of youngsters seeing themselves reflected in the books they read has become an issue more frequently recognised by 'gate-keepers' across the industry. The inclusion of these different narratives is not only good for society; it is also good for the health of our business. So, let's get practical. Whilst this book contains a plethora of information to get you on your way, the advice offered highlights how you, as an under-represented writer, can kick-start your career and get noticed.

When submitting to agents, always *do your research*. Does the agent you're looking at represent picture books, middle grade, young adult or all of these? What genres do they favour? Are they newer agents actively on the hunt for talent? Studying an agent's existing list will answer many of your questions, but Twitter can also provide you with extra up-to-date information. You never know, an agent's simple #MSWL (Manuscript Wish List) alert may just equate to the very book you've written. And check out #DVPit (strapline 'A Twitter Pitching Event for Marginalized Voices'); it's a great *free* opportunity.

At the same time, do not be deterred from approaching an agent whose list *doesn't* seem obviously inclusive. Time and time again I have met authors who have not submitted work to an agency because they didn't feel that they were reflected by an agent's existing clientele. And, do you know what? Often agents will say that they're just not hearing from marginalised writers, and that they don't understand *why*. Clearly there's a bit of a catch-22 situation going on here, because I for one know that you exist. Remember that agents are essentially looking for a good story and, granted, it is their job to look for talent in (and from) all forms and places; by not submitting your work, you are limiting your chance of discovery. If your story has the elements of a potential success, then the right agent will give you that chance of representation. So, if you like the look of an agent and think your work may appeal, type that email and hit Send!

If you are not yet ready to submit your manuscript, an extensive satellite industry of advice and support has developed to provide authors with the tools to navigate the world of publishing. And, now more than ever, many of these programmes are actively looking to reach out to those who may not have previously believed or found publishing to be a welcoming space. Often you will find events giving you access to many of the individuals on the 'inside', and these insiders (including agents and editors) want to hear from *you*. Understand, these gatekeepers are not wanting to pay lip service to a fad; they are driven by the satisfaction of finding and supporting genuine talent.

Literary agents

Writers' conferences and festivals can often be a good place to start. Yes, they can be an expense, but they can also be a worthwhile investment. Not only are they a vast source of information but, by giving you a couple of days to immerse yourself in a space which celebrates and encourages your writing, they can be the perfect boost for your confidence. You will have the opportunity to attend specific workshops, panel events, hear keynote speeches and often you can book a one-to-one appointment with an agent or editor. For many authors, these one-to-ones can be particularly valuable, and in fact I met one of my current clients at the Winchester Writers' Festival in this way. One of the most prominent such events, focusing on children's content, is hosted by SCBWI, a worldwide members network (see page 330). Their conference offers all of the above, but it also gives you access to a community of like-minded authors, and this can be a particular draw and comfort.

Do check the conference listings in this *Yearbook* (which start on page 380). As you will see, there are a number of them taking place around the country, at different times of the year and sometimes focusing on a specific area of publishing. But do understand, it is not about attending as many as possible. Assess your situation; consider what it is that you want to know about the industry and then do your research. If you are making the choice to spend your money in this way, then you should ensure that it is cash well spent – you want to leave that conference feeling better equipped to deal with what will, hopefully, be a future career. If the idea of a conference feels too much, then consider the many evening salons, day workshops and afternoon panel sessions offering more tailored advice. There really are events aplenty, and sometimes these are more affordable financially and timewise.

How do you find out about these events? Check out your local regional literary organisations, for instance, New Writing North/South, Writing West/East Midlands and Spread the Word (London) are a few of the most prominent (see *Societies, associations and organisations* section, starting on page 341). Each of these bodies work tirelessly to support new writers – and particularly those who may have to overcome varying barriers due to a, frankly, institutional bias (however unintentional). Not only do these organisations host their own events but they will often highlight and promote worthwhile external opportunities. A good example of this is the Free Reads Scheme organised by The Literary Consultancy (one of the largest editorial services companies in the country). In conjunction with the Arts Council, the scheme works with local literary organisations to find authors who may require and appreciate a subsidised manuscript assessment service. It is a brilliant opportunity which acknowledges that the choice to write is not necessarily an affordable one – a fact which in itself makes publishing seem as though it should only be for the privileged few. And, on the issue of expense, you may find that some of these services will offer bursaries for specific groups of people. They are there to help, not isolate. Do not hesitate to get in touch with those who are organising such events and ask whether there is anything you can apply for.

Do also keep an eye out for upcoming competitions; industry magazine the *Bookseller* often announces the most notable of these. While many are open to all writers, it is also worth investigating the increasing number which specifically target under-represented groups. These competitions may not land you with the hallowed publishing deal or representation but, depending on the scheme, they may offer the opportunity for you to get a foot in the door. For instance (and please excuse the personal plug here, ahem ahem ...): the FAB Prize (see page 363) was set up by Faber Children's and ANDLYN, looking specifically for un-agented and un-published BAME writing/illustrating talent. The individual category winners are awarded with mentoring, and an anthology of their work and the work of the runners-up is circulated around children's literary agents. Since the Prize's inception, a number of entrants have gone on to gain representation and get published. The prize was a *platform*, but these writers reached their goal off the back of their own merit. Be sure to use these opportunities – that is what they are there for.

I would be remiss not to mention the Arts Council (see page 342) in this context. Easily forgotten, but open to all, it has a number of grant schemes which provide writers with the time and space to focus on their writing. It has to be said that, particularly within children's publishing, the body is incredibly keen to help address the imbalance of marginalised voices. As mentioned, the financial implications of wanting to be a writer stretch far and wide; if this applies to you, see whether there is a grant for which you may qualify.

Having dealt with the practical side of pursuing your writing career, here's my take on how our identities can enrich the stories we tell. Children's publishing has always been synonymous with the idea that its stories and literature can teach children about the society in which they live. Yet statistics (most recently those led by BookTrust and CLPE – the Centre for Literacy in Primary Education – on multicultural diversity) show that there is a serious dearth of stories featuring characters from under-represented backgrounds. In my conversations with authors, the word 'diversity' seems to have inadvertently given way to the suggestion and/or impression that diverse stories should be 'issue'-led, that they should highlight the barriers or difficulties of 'other' lives. And, because there are so few novels in the market featuring minority groups and/or marginalised characters within a British context, it has become all too easy to associate particular kinds of stories with the different under-represented groups.

This means that, to some extent, an element of stereotyping has come in to play. But why? We can learn about each other within the framework of a simply entertaining and *mainstream* story. Your idea, *not* your identity, should be your USP. Remember you want (and deserve) to be measured on the same scale as any other author and, with that, there should be a freedom to write any kind of story. If you want to create an epic 'through the wardrobe'-style adventure, a young adult rom-com, or a rather left-of-centre comedy, then you must. Saying that, if you want to write a gritty issue-led tale, feel free to do that too! For those working within the industry, your ability to produce an excellent narrative is the attraction, but when your stories reflect you, your community, your *rarely seen world* – that is refreshing, and frankly a bonus.

There are many individuals within children's publishing who actively want to change the landscape so that its output is more inclusive. It cannot be denied, however, that our intentions are often left rattling around an echo chamber and that this message of inclusivity isn't necessarily being received on the 'outside'. So I am saying this very clearly now: as an industry we need your stories but, more importantly, we want you … *all of you, not just your demographic.* We look forward to hearing from you soon!

Davinia Andrew-Lynch founded the literary agency ANDLYN in 2015, where she specialises in children's and young adult fiction and content. She previously worked as an associate agent at the Dench Arnold Agency, a film/TV agency, and as a freelance children's fiction editor and reader. For more information see www.andlyn.co.uk. Follow Davinia on Twitter @nocturnalreader.

See also...
● *Opportunities for under-represented writers*, page 371

The life and works of a literary scout

Sophie Clarke explains just what a literary scout's role and life entails, with its varied and challenging workload and often all-consuming pace, the buzz of staying well-informed and well-connected, and the satisfaction that comes from matching the right book to the right client.

Entitling this article 'the life and works of a literary scout' seems unusually apt because, as with many jobs in publishing, trying to separate the personal from the professional in the career of a literary scout is nigh on impossible. It is a job that relies on forming, maintaining and nurturing connections, assessing the industry with a finely-honed eye to see which way the winds are blowing, and on reading accurately and critically at speed. Your role is to deliver professional judgement with a personal touch to your clients, who need guidance or advice to help them find the books which will work best for them. You are, in effect, a literary matchmaker. The clients of a literary scout are foreign publishers seeking to buy titles originally published in one language in order to translate them into their own, for publication and sale in their territory or market. Scouts can work across a range of languages, for example all literature from the Scandinavian countries, or in one language, such as just the UK or USA.

The information game

Literary scouts, unlike agents and editors, do not work directly with authors. They trade in information, gossip, industry buzz and foreign-market knowledge. A good scout has their finger on the pulse of the market they are scouting. They know which books are out on submission from agents to editors and, of those, which are making noise and going up for auction or being pre-empted. They are aware of which editors are moving between publishing houses, going on parental leave or sabbatical, or looking to acquire specific types of titles. They stay up-to-date on which new authors an agent might be representing; announcements on Twitter are particularly helpful for this. Before titles go on submission (the process where agents send manuscripts to editors for them to sign-up or 'buy' for publication), scouts actively check in with agents about any titles which sound particularly interesting, or any which might be particularly suited to specific clients of theirs.

In order to gather this information, at least half of the scout's role is to talk – and to as many people as possible. Scouts are in contact day-to-day with primary agents (representing authors), rights agents (selling titles internationally) and publishing editors (acquiring titles and working with authors) via email and WhatsApp, as well as via video, phone and in-person meetings. These conversations allow scouts to build up a picture of what is currently going on in UK publishing. The wider and warmer a scout's network of contacts, the better the overall picture they can provide, and the better informed their clients will be – ideally ahead of competitors – and thus able to make decisions faster. A scout's network is more than a directory of contacts. Most become friends or – at the very least – valued acquaintances. It's almost impossible not to build up a close relationship; a scout may talk to a client once a day in peak season to check in on a title that's moving quickly and being acquired widely. Over the course of many meetings and emails, both parties get to know each other well. But of course, the core aspect of the relationship requires that, however kindly one might think of a contact personally, each has professional duties to the other.

Reading ... with a difference

The other half of a scout's role is to read, and to read quickly, professionally and widely in the area they scout in. Some scouts cover all genres; some specialise, for example in children's and young adult, like me. Reading and reporting on titles – providing a brief summary of the plot, information on the author and any notable facts or sales for the title – must be prioritised. Often, it must be done at speed. When titles are submitted for acquisition and begin to gather buzz domestically and/or internationally, translation sales begin to fall like dominoes in the right territories. A scout's reading does not always take place in the office or within office hours; with their clients in a variety of different time zones and territories, scouts must always be prepared to support and respond at any time of the day or night. As titles begin to move, auctions (multiple publishing houses bidding and offering on a title) and pre-empts (making an offer so convincing that the title is bought quickly and exclusively without the hassle of an auction) can happen overnight or even within a matter of hours from submission. This means that speed of reading, re-sponding and reporting to clients is of the essence. You may be reading several manuscripts at one time, especially if you cover a broad range of titles. It's not uncommon for an individual scout to read between seven and ten titles a week – sometimes even more, around the busy book-fair seasons. You read with several different hats on, as there are many considerations: Will this title work in the UK market? Will it work in any of my client markets? Will any of the client's editors like it, even if it might not seem to be something for their market? Is it, objectively, any good? Do you, personally, like it – and would you be willing to recommend it, based on your own tastes, despite any other minor flaws to it? Addressing such questions, while reading to tight deadlines before reporting back to clients on a title, turns a seemingly simple task into one filled with nuance that requires a scout's expertise and professional knowledge.

Networking nous

Networking, as with the reading, isn't entirely limited within office hours either. Scouts are a regular fixture at parties, book launches and other publishing industry events – in fact anywhere where it's possible to hobnob and mix with the widest possible number of people and have the most wide-ranging conversations, gleaning titbits of gossip and in-formation. Breakfasts, lunches, coffees, dinners and drinks meetings all feature regularly in scout life as well – meaning that we're extremely well-fed, as well as well-informed! As a scout, you quickly become very comfortable with walking into events where you might only know a few people, and leaving having befriended at least a few more. This skill comes in particularly useful at the international trade book fairs. These happen throughout the year, but the main ones are in Frankfurt in the autumn, London and Bologna in the spring. Bologna is specifically focused on children's and young adult titles. Editors, agents and rights agents from a multitude of countries gather to buy, sell and discuss titles. Scouts are at the heart of it – talking to their clients, meeting with editors and rights agents from outside their home territory and attending as many events as possible to meet the maxi-mum number of people. Rights fairs are key for rights sales and for getting material, authors and passion in front of editors' noses. A scout's enthusiasm for a particular title, and their awareness of information ahead of it being public knowledge, can create excitement and help their publisher clients strike deals.

Literary agents

Author's friend

Indirectly, a scout is helping an author, even though they'll probably never meet and an author may be unaware of a scout's role across the publishing process. Across the course of many weeks, months or years, a scout may constantly re-flag an author's work or a specific title to their clients, demonstrating the momentum that a book or author is gathering both in their home territory and across other territories too. Sometimes, a book moves very quickly and there are swift acquisitions in the UK, the USA and a host of international territories – that's the dream scenario. But often books and authors take time to garner success and recognition and, as each building block of that process is achieved (e.g. sales figures, prize-shortlisting or -winning, accrued rights sales), a scout can be instrumental in reminding their clients of a title, seeing whose publishing list or taste might have changed enough to acquire it now, even if they passed over it previously.

To be a successful scout involves a high level of networking and reading, but of course there is far more to it than that. It also involves a huge volume of email traffic, lots of administration to stay on top of contacts – their changing roles and keeping up-to-date on correct territory contacts at each publisher and agency, organising meeting schedules for the book fairs, and reporting regularly to clients. All of this builds up to an ever-changing and shifting role – which is precisely what makes it one of the most exciting jobs in publishing. Scouts come from a variety of different backgrounds: some have started as interns at scouting agencies and worked their way up; others have previously worked at a publisher in rights or in editorial; others have come from a literary agency and are able to employ their already keen understanding of the industry. Most have some knowledge of a foreign language and culture, although almost all communication between scout and client is in English, and all reading is done in English too. Regardless of how they entered the industry, the key element a scout must have is a passion for, and deep knowledge of, the area of literature they are working in – no matter how broad or narrow that patch. Also helpful are the enthusiasm and energy to work more than occasional long hours, a curiosity about foreign markets, a desire to be well-informed about as much as possible, and the ability to read and network and manage emails beyond the office. And you need to be prepared – at peak book-fair season, when the pace becomes frenetic and the pressure to remain ahead of competitors becomes high – to be almost consumed by the job!

Reading back through this, I'm afraid I may have made scouting sound far too serious, when actually it's the most fun job I've ever had. There's a lot of stress, to be sure, but there also is a lot of laughter and camaraderie in the team as everyone works so closely together to deliver a great service to their clients. It's nigh on impossible to complain (and I certainly wouldn't now, amidst the pandemic) about drinks events and book launches and parties and trips to the book fairs, even if they are outside office hours. You read books months and even years before the general public sees them. It's fair to say that scouting, in both little and big ways, shapes your life because it dictates the structure of your social and professional weeks, months and seasons; but it also shapes the lives of authors. For a scout, when a client acquires a title that you loved – one that has the potential to be successful for them and you also know the deal will be wonderful for the author – it really is the best feeling. Literary match … made.

Sophie Clarke is a scout for children's and young adult books at Daniela Schlingmann Literary Scouting (https://schlingmann.co.uk). She has previously worked at the publisher Penguin Random House Children's and at the literary agencies Curtis Brown and Bell Lomax Moreton.

Children's literary agents UK and Ireland

The *Children's Writers' & Artists' Yearbook*, along with the Association of Authors' Agents and the Society of Authors, takes a dim view of any literary agent who asks potential clients for a fee prior to a manuscript being placed with a publisher. We advise you to treat any such request with caution and to let us know if that agent appears in the listings below. Agents may charge additional costs later in the process but these should only arise once a book has been accepted by a publisher and the author is earning an income. Authors should also check agents' websites before making an enquiry and should familiarise themselves with submission guidelines, agent preferences and manuscript formatting.

*Member of the Association of Authors' Agents
sae = self-addressed envelope

The Agency (London) Ltd*
Closed
24 Pottery Lane, London W11 4LZ
tel 020-7727 1346
email childrensbooksubmissions@theagency.co.uk
website https://theagency.co.uk/childrens-books/childrens-home/
Twitter @TALLChildrens
Children's Book Agents Hilary Delamere, Jessica Hare

Works in conjunction with overseas agents. The Agency also represents screenwriters, directors, playwrights and composers. Represents picture books, including novelty books, fiction for all ages including teenage fiction and series fiction. *Commission* Home 15%, overseas 20%. Submission guidelines on website. *Founded* 1995.

Aitken Alexander Associates Ltd*
291 Gray's Inn Road, London WC1X 8QJ
tel 020-7373 8672
email reception@aitkenalexander.co.uk
website www.aitkenalexander.co.uk
Twitter @AitkenAlexander
Instagram @AitkenAlexander
Agent Amy St Johnston

Children's and YA fiction. Handles fiction for 9+ to young adults. *Commission* Home 15%, overseas 20%. Email preliminary letter with half-page synopsis and first 30 pages via agency website or to submissions@aitkenalexander.co.uk. No picture books. *Founded* 1977.

Darley Anderson Children's Book Agency Ltd*
Unit 19, Matrix Studios, 91 Peterborough Road, London SW6 3BU
tel 020-7385 6652
email childrens@darleyanderson.com
website www.darleyandersonchildrens.com
Twitter @DA_Childrens
Instagram @da_childrens
Contacts Darley Anderson (Managing Director), Camilla Bolton (Director), Clare Wallace (Director and Senior Agent), Lydia Silver (Agent), Becca Langton (Agent), Sheila David (TV and Film Rights), Chloe Davis (Junior Agent), Mary Darby (Head of Rights), Kristina Egan (Rights Agent), Georgia Fuller (Rights Agent)

Children's fiction and non-fiction (for all ages from picture book to middle grade through to YA and crossover). For illustrators, please refer to the Darley Anderson Illustration Agency (see page 273). *Commission* Home 15%, USA/translation 20%, film/TV/radio 20%. Send covering letter, short synopsis and first 3 chapters by email. No scripts or screenplays.

Clients include Gina Blaxill, Cathy Cassidy, John Connolly, Kate Foster, Martyn Ford, Stewart Foster, Lindsay Galvin, A.M. Howell, Polly Ho-Yen, Rachel Ip, Rachel Morrisroe, Beth Reekles, Dave Rudden, Nick Sheridan, Rashmi Sirdeshpande, Deirdre Sullivan, Efua Traoré. *Founded* 1988.

ANDLYN
Closed
tel 020-3290 5638
email submissions@andlyn.co.uk
website www.andlyn.co.uk
Twitter @AndlynLit
Founder & Agent Davinia Andrew-Lynch

Represents authors of picture books, middle-grade, YA and crossover fiction – all genres. Also represents adult fiction and non-fiction. *Commission* Home and audio 15%; USA, foreign/translation, film/TV, multi-platform and online media rights 20%. See website for submission guidelines.

Clients include Malcolm Duffy, Bex Hogan, Julie Middleton, Annabelle Sami. *Founded* 2015.

ASH Literary

email info@ashliterary.com
website www.ashliterary.com
Twitter @ashliterary
Instagram @ashliterary
Literary Agent Alice Sutherland-Hawes

Children's and YA focused agency representing authors and illustrators covering picture books to YA titles, including graphic novels. All genres represented except horror and sci-fi. *Commission* Home 15%, translation and dramatisation 20%. Send first 3 chapters and synopsis through QueryManager. Does not handle adult fiction or non-fiction.

Clients include Kereen Getten, Alex Falase-Koya, Radiya Hafiza, Jess McGeachin, Poonam Mistry, Úna Woods. *Founded* 2020.

Bath Literary Agency*

5 Gloucester Road, Bath BA1 7BH
email submissions@bathliteraryagency.com
website www.bathliteraryagency.com
Twitter @BathLitAgency
Instagram @bathlitagency
Contact Gill McLay

Specialist in fiction for children and young adults. Also accepts submissions in picture books, non-fiction and author illustrators. *Commission* UK 15%, overseas 20%, film/TV 20%. For full submission details, refer to the website.

Clients include Lou Abercrombie, Fox Benwell, Conor Busuttil, Philippa Forrester, Dr Jess French, Tweedy, Joe Haddow, Demelsa Haughton, Harry Heape, Laura James, Pippa Pixley, Dr Shini Somara, Tessa Strickland, Anna Terreros Martin, Chris Wakling. *Founded* 2011.

The Bell Lomax Moreton Agency*

Suite C, Victory House, 131 Queensway, Petts Wood, Kent BR5 1DG
tel 020-7930 4447
email agency@bell-lomax.co.uk
website www.belllomaxmoreton.co.uk
Twitter @BLM_Agency
Executives Paul Moreton, Lauren Gardner, Jo Bell, Katie Fulford, Justine Smith, John Baker, Lorna Hemingway, Soraya Bouazzaoui, Julie Gourinchas, Rory Jeffers, Sarah McDonnell

Will consider most fiction, non-fiction and children's (including picture books, middle grade and YA) book proposals. Submission guidelines on website. Physical submissions should be accompanied by an sae for return and an email address for correspondence. Does not represent poetry, short stories or novellas, education textbooks, film scripts or stage plays. *Founded* 2000.

The Bent Agency*

17 Kelsall Mews, Richmond TW9 4BP
email info@thebentagency.com
website www.thebentagency.com

Agents Nicola Barr, Jenny Bent, Victoria Cappello, Gemma Cooper, Claire Draper, Louise Fury, Molly Ker Hawn, James Musterlier, Zöe Plant, John Silbersack, Laurel Symonds, Desiree Wilson

Full-service literary agency with offices in the UK and USA. Represents a diverse range of genres including history, humour, lifestyle, inspiration, memoir, literary fiction, children's and commercial fiction. Only accepts email queries. See website for detailed query and submission guidelines.

Clients include Faridah Abike-Iyimide, Sophie Anderson, P.G. Bell, Dhonielle Clayton, Stephanie Garber, Alwyn Hamilton, Hilary McKay, Mo O'Hara, Sibeal Pounder, Robin Stevens, Angie Thomas, Jessica Townsend. *Founded* 2009.

The BIA

website www.the-bia.com
Twitter @blindingbks
Agents Ben Illis, Rachel Hamilton

Children's and YA fiction specialist literary agency, with several notable prize-winning writers on the books. No picture books, fiction for under 7s or educational books. Submissions open twice a year in Spring and Autumn. Electronic submission only via website; send the first 50 pages and a synopsis for fiction or a detailed proposal for non-fiction. *Founded* 2013.

The Blair Partnership*

PO Box 7828, London W1A 4GE
tel 020-7504 2520
email info@theblairpartnership.com
website www.theblairpartnership.com
Twitter @TBP_agency
Founding Partner Neil Blair, *Agency Director* Rory Scarfe, *Associate Agent* Jordan Lees, *Agents* Hattie Grünewald, Rachel Petty

Represents a range of writers internationally from debut to established, with a strong focus on TV/film alongside literary publication. Considers fiction and non-fiction across YA, middle grade and below. Will consider unsolicited MSS. Fiction: email a covering letter, a one-page synopsis and the first 3 chapters. Non-fiction: email a proposal document and writing sample. Picture books: email your query and full project. Not currently accepting screenplays, short stories or poetry.

Clients include Bana Alabed, JJ Arcanjo, Dawn Coulter-Cruttenden, Helena Duggan, Emma Farrarons, Sir Chris Hoy, Frank Lampard, Kieran Larwood, J.K. Rowling, Nicki Thornton. *Founded* 2011.

The Bravo Blue Agency*

email charlotte@bravoblue.co.uk
website www.bravoblue.co.uk
Contact Charlotte Colwill

Boutique literary agency. Children's fiction and non-fiction, including picture books. Also literary fiction, narrative non-fiction, category fiction, lifestyle, health and history. Send first five pages, synopsis and covering letter via email.

Authors include Bill Swiggs, Megan Vickers, Cecily Blench, Brian Schofield, Gianni Washington, Jacob Avila, Rupal Patel, Stephen Jackley, Andrew Lane. *Founded* 2018.

The Bright Agency*

103–105 St John's Hill, London SW11 1SY
tel 020-7326 9140
50 West Street, C12, New York, NY 10006
tel +1 646-578-6542
website https://thebrightagency.com/uk
Contacts UK: Founder Vicki Willden-Lebrecht, *Director* Arabella Stein, *Managing Agents* Susan Penny, Freddie Dawson, Robyn Newton, *Senior Agents* Lucie Luddington, Helen Biles, *Agents* Amy Caplin, Leah Dever; *US: Managing Agents* James Burns, Anne Moore Armstrong, Alex Gehringer; *China: Agent* Ilaria Vigilante

A full-service global creative agency that represents and nurtures artists, animators, authors and brands. Areas of representation include: children's publishing (picture books, children's fiction and non-fiction, activity books, novels, pre-school), educational, advertising and design, animation, editorial film & television rights management, greetings & gift, illustration, art licensing, toys & games, home & gift and brand development and management. See website for full submission requirements. No submissions by post.

Authors include Benji Davies, David Litchfield, Jarvis, Yasmeen Ismail, Fiona Woodcock, Laura Hughes, Galia Bernstein, Mechal Roe, Maddie Frost, Zoe Perisco, Aura Lewis, Karl James Mountford. *Founded* 2003.

Jenny Brown Associates*

31 Marchmont Road, Edinburgh EH9 1HU
tel 0131 229 5334
email childrens@jennybrownassociates.com
website www.jennybrownassociates.com
Contact Lucy Juckes

Writing and illustration for children, fiction and non-fiction. Has a preference for working with writers or illustrators based in Scotland. *Commission* Home 12.5%, overseas/translation 20%. A small agency which only reads submissions at certain points in the year; always check website before sending work.

Clients include Christopher Edge, Keith Gray, Helen Kellock, Emily MacKenzie, Jonathan Meres, Alison Murray. *Founded* 2002.

Felicity Bryan Associates*

2A North Parade, Banbury Road, Oxford OX2 6LX
tel (01865) 513816
email agency@felicitybryan.com
website www.felicitybryan.com

Translation rights handled by Andrew Nurnberg Associates; works in conjunction with US agents. Fiction for children aged 8–14 and YA, and adult fiction and general non-fiction. *Commission* Home 15%, overseas 20%. All submissions and queries through website. No sci-fi and fantasy, horror, erotica, romance, self-help, graphic novels, scripts or poetry.

Children's authors include David Almond, Katya Balen, Matt Burton, Jenny Downham, Sally Gardner, Natasha Farrant, Clare Furniss, Liz Kessler, Annabel Pitcher, Meg Rosoff, Alom Shaha, Lauren St John, Chris Vick, Lisa Williamson, Lucy Worsley. *Founded* 1988.

C&W Agency*

(previously Conville & Walsh)
Haymarket House, 28–29 Haymarket, London SW1Y 4SP
tel 020-7393 4200
website www.cwagency.co.uk
Twitter @CWAgencyUK
Instagram @CWAgencyUK

A boutique and very select list of fiction for 5–8 and 9–12 year-olds, teenage fiction, series fiction and film/TV tie-ins. Also handles adult literary and commercial fiction and non-fiction. *Commission* Home 15%, overseas 20%. Submissions welcome: first 3 chapters, cover letter and synopsis by email. Part of the Curtis Brown Group of Companies; simultaneous submission accepted. Not taking on picture books.

Children's authors include Katie Davies, Matt Haig, P.J. Lynch, Josua Mowll, Paula Rawsthorne, Nicky Singer, Piers Torday, Steve Voake, the Estate of John Burningham. *Founded* 2000.

Georgina Capel Associates Ltd*

29 Wardour Street, London W1D 6PS
tel 020-7734 2414
email firstname@georginacapel.com
website www.georginacapel.com
Agents Georgina Capel, Rachel Conway, Simon Shaps, Irene Baldoni, Philippa Brewster

Children's and YA; literary and commercial fiction, history, biography; film and TV. *Commission* Home/overseas 15%. Postal submissions preferred, but do accept email. Include a covering letter, synopsis and first 3 chapters. *Founded* 1999.

The Catchpole Agency

53 Cranham Street, Oxford OX2 6DD
tel 07789 588070
email james@thecatchpoleagency.co.uk
website www.thecatchpoleagency.co.uk
Proprietor James Catchpole

Agents for authors and illustrators of children's books from picture books through to YA novels, with a specialism in editorial work. See website for contact and submissions details.

Authors include Polly Dunbar, SF Said, Michelle Robinson, Emer Stamp, Sean Taylor. *Founded* 1996.

Anne Clark Literary Agency*

email submissions@anneclarkliteraryagency.co.uk
website www.anneclarkliteraryagency.co.uk
Facebook www.facebook.com/anneclarkliterary
Twitter @AnneClarkLit
Contact Anne Clark

Specialist in fiction, non-fiction and picture books for children and young adults. *Commission* Home 15%, overseas 20%. Submissions by email only. See website for details.

Clients include Mike Barfield, Anne Booth, Moira Butterfield, Lou Carter, Patricia Forde, Leah Mohammed, Pippa Goodhart, Miriam Halahmy, Cath Howe, Mike Jackson, Penny Joelson, Rebecca Patterson, Jason Rohan, Lucy Rowland. *Founded* 2012.

Creative Authors Ltd

11A Woodlawn Street, Whitstable, Kent CT5 1HQ
email write@creativeauthors.co.uk
website www.creativeauthors.co.uk
Twitter @creativeauthors
Instagram @creativeauthors
Director Isabel Atherton

Children's fiction, picture books, YA, graphic novels and illustrators. Also fiction and non-fiction for adults. *Commission* Home 15%, overseas 20%. Only accepts email submissions.

Authors and illustrators include Guojing, Ged Adamson, Coll Muir, Bethany Straker, Lucy Scott, Colleen Kosinski, Jules Miller, Megan Tadden, Cassie Liverside. *Founded* 2008.

Rupert Crew Ltd*

Southgate, 7 Linden Avenue, Dorchester DT1 1EJ
tel (01305) 260335
email info@rupertcrew.co.uk
website www.rupertcrew.co.uk
Managing Director Caroline Montgomery

International representation, handling accessible literary and commercial fiction and non-fiction for adult and children's (8+) markets. *Commission* Home 15%; overseas, TV/film and radio 20%. No unsolicited MSS: see website for current submission guidelines. No picture books, plays, screenplays, poetry, journalism, sci-fi and fantasy or short stories. *Founded* 1927.

Curtis Brown*

Haymarket House, 28–29 Haymarket,
London SW1Y 4SP
tel 020-7393 4400
email cb@curtisbrown.co.uk
website www.curtisbrown.co.uk
website www.curtisbrowncreative.co.uk
Twitter @CBGBooks

Twitter @cbcreative
Children's Agents Stephanie Thwaites, Isobel Gahan (Associate)

Children's fiction ranges from picture books to YA novels across all genres. Represents prominent writers, from debut authors to established prize winners and bestsellers. Actively seeking talented new writers, particularly for books aimed at 8–12 year olds, adventure, fantasy, gothic stories and humour. Manages the international careers of authors with strong relationships in translation and US markets. *Founded* 1899.

DHH Literary Agency*

23–27 Cecil Court, London WC2N 4EZ
tel 020-7836 7376
email enquiries@dhhliteraryagency.com
website www.dhhliteraryagency.com
Facebook www.facebook.com/dhhliteraryagency
Twitter @dhhlitagency
Agents David H. Headley, Broo Doherty, Hannah Sheppard, Harry Illingworth, Emily Glenister, Tom Drake-Lee

Children's fiction and YA fiction. Also adult fiction, women's commercial fiction, crime, literary fiction, science fiction and fantasy; and non-fiction including history, cookery and humour. *Commission* UK 15%; overseas 15% where a sub agent is not used, 20% where a sub agent is used. Send informative preliminary email with first 3 chapters and synopsis. Consult website for correct email addresses for each agent. New authors welcome. No picture books, plays or scripts, poetry or short stories.

Authors include Matthew Crow, Phyllida Shrimpton, James Goodhand, Abi Elphinstone, Keris Stainton, Gabrielle Kent, Kate Mallinder, Darren Charlton, Amy Beashel. *Founded* 2008.

Diamond Kahn & Woods Literary Agency*

Top Floor, 66 Onslow Gardens, London N10 3JX
tel 020-3514 6544
email info@dkwlitagency.co.uk
email submissions.ella@dkwlitagency.co.uk
email submissions.bryony@dkwlitagency.co.uk
website www.dkwlitagency.co.uk
Twitter @DKWLitAgency
Agents Ella Diamond Kahn, Bryony Woods

Children's, YA and crossover fiction; literary and commercial fiction (including all major genres) and non-fiction. Interested in new writers. *Commission* Home 15%, USA/translation 20%. Email submissions only. Send 3 chapters and synopsis to one agent only.

Clients include Virginia Macgregor, Nicole Burstein, David Owen, Sharon Gosling, Sylvia Bishop, Sarah Baker, Katherine Orton, Dan Smith, Jamie Russell, Tom Huddleston, Caroline O'Donoghue, Daisy May Johnson. *Founded* 2012.

Eddison Pearson Ltd*

West Hill House, 6 Swains Lane, London N6 6QS
tel 020-7700 7763
email enquiries@eddisonpearson.com
website www.eddisonpearson.com
Contact Clare Pearson

Small, personally run agency. Children's and YA books, fiction and non-fiction, poetry. *Commission* Home 10–15%, overseas 15–20%. Enquiries and submissions by email only; email for up-to-date submission guidelines. May suggest revision where appropriate.
   Authors include Valerie Bloom, Sue Heap, Caroline Lawrence, Robert Muchamore, Mary Murphy, Megan Rix. *Founded* 1997.

Fraser Ross Associates

6 Wellington Place, Edinburgh EH6 7EQ
tel 0131 553 2759/657 4412
email agentlmfraser@gmail.com
email kjross@tiscali.co.uk
website www.fraserross.co.uk
Facebook www.facebook.com/fraserrossassociates
Twitter @FraserRossLA
Instagram @fraserrossassociates
Partners Lindsey Fraser, Kathryn Ross

Represents writers and illustrators. See website for submission guidelines. *Founded* 2002.

The Good Literary Agency*

email info@thegoodliteraryagency.org
website www.thegoodliteraryagency.org
Twitter @thegoodagencyuk
Instagram @thegoodagencyuk

Represents authors from backgrounds under-represented in UK publishing including writers of colour, working class writers, disabled writers, LGBTQ+ writers and anyone who feels that they or their stories are under-represented. Children's and YA (all genres in fiction and non-fiction for readers 8+). Also adult fiction and non-fiction. For detailed submission guidelines, visit the website.
   Authors include Nicola Garrard, Judy Hepburn, Lizzie Huxley-Jones, Raj Kaur Khaira, Thomas Leeds, Jade Mutyora, Musa Okwonga, Clare Weze. *Founded* 2018.

Annette Green Authors' Agency

5 Henwoods Mount, Pembury,
Tunbridge Wells TN2 4BH
tel (01892) 263252
email annette@annettegreenagency.com
website www.annettegreenagency.co.uk
Partners Annette Green, David Smith

Fiction: literary, general and teenage fiction. Non-fiction: popular culture, history and science. *Commission* Home 15%, overseas 20–25%. Preliminary letter, synopsis, sample chapter and sae

essential. No picture books, dramatic scripts, poetry, sci-fi or fantasy. *Founded* 1998.

The Greenhouse Literary Agency

tel 020-7841 3958
email info@greenhouseliterary.com
website www.greenhouseliterary.com
Twitter @sarahgreenhouse
Twitter @chelseberly
Director Chelsea Eberly, Agent Kristin Ostby

Children's fiction and nonfiction: illustrators who write picture books, middle grade through to teen/YA novels, and graphic novels. Some women's fiction. Will suggest revision. Represents both US and UK authors. *Commission* USA/UK 15%, translation 25%. Submissions via QueryManager only; see website for submission guidelines. No poetry or film scripts.
   Authors include Gavin Aung Than, Sarwat Chadda, Winifred Conkling, Andrea Contos, Alexandra Diaz, Bill Doyle, Theanne Griffith, Michelle Lam, Rebecca Mock, Kelis Rowe, Ali Standish, Emily Thiede, Ngozi Ukazu. *Founded* 2008.

Marianne Gunn O'Connor Literary, Film/TV Agency

Morrison Chambers, 32 Nassau Street, Dublin 2, Republic of Ireland
email submissions@mariannegunnoconnor.com
website www.mariannegunnoconnor.com
Contact Marianne Gunn O'Connor

Represents children's books, middle grade, YA, new adult and crossover fiction; as well as literary fiction, upmarket fiction and non-fiction for adults. No screenplays. *Founded* 1996.

Hardman & Swainson*

S106 Somerset House, London WC2R 1LA
tel 020-3701 7449
email submissions@hardmanswainson.com
website www.hardmanswainson.com
Twitter @hardmanswainson
Directors Caroline Hardman, Joanna Swainson

Literary and commercial fiction, crime and thriller, women's, accessible literary, YA and middle-grade children's fiction. Non-fiction, including memoir, biography, popular science, history and philosophy. *Commission* Home 15%; USA/translation, film/TV 20%. Submissions by email only; check the website for details. Will work editorially with the author where appropriate. No poetry, screenplays or picture books.
   Clients include Alex Bell, Justin Davies, Fiona Sandiford, Maria Kuzniar. *Founded* 2012.

Antony Harwood Ltd

103 Walton Street, Oxford OX2 6EB
tel (01865) 559615
email mail@antonyharwood.com
website www.antonyharwood.com

Contacts Antony Harwood, James Macdonald, Jo Williamson

General and genre fiction; general non-fiction. *Commission* Home 15%, overseas 20%. Will suggest revision.

Children's authors include Tamsyn Murray, Jennifer Gray, Peter Bunzl. *Founded* 2000.

A.M. Heath & Co. Ltd*
6 Warwick Court, London WC1R 5DJ
tel 020-7242 2811
email enquiries@amheath.com
website www.amheath.com
Twitter @amheathltd
Contact Julia Churchill

Children's fiction and non-fiction from picture books to YA. Also handles adult literary and commercial fiction and non-fiction. *Commission* Home 15%, USA/translation 20%, film/TV 15–20% by agreement. Digital submission via website. No screenplays, poetry or short stories except for collections.

Authors include Nicholas Allan, Sam Copeland, Sarah Crossan, Conn Iggulden, Pip Jones, Michelle Harrison, Sarah Lean, Jenny McLachlan, Joanna Nadin, Amy Sparkes, Patricia Toht, Holly Webb and the estates of Noel Streatfield, Joan Aiken, Christianna Brand. *Founded* 1919.

Sophie Hicks Agency*
email info@sophiehicksagency.com
website www.sophiehicksagency.com
Twitter @SophieHicksAg
Agents Sophie Hicks, Sarah Williams

Fiction for 9+. Also handles adult fiction and non-fiction. *Commission* UK/USA 15%, translation 20%. Email submissions only, see website for guidelines. No poetry or scripts.

Authors include Herbie Brennan, Anne Cassidy, Lucy Coats, Eoin Colfer, Andrew Donkin, Kathryn Evans, Emerald Fennell, Padraig Kenny, Sarah Mussi, Siobhan Parkinson, Alexander Gordon Smith, Kate Thompson, Shamim Sarif, Sif Sigmarsdóttir, Kia Thomas. *Founded* 2014.

David Higham Associates Ltd*
6th Floor, Waverley House, 7–12 Noel Street, London W1F 8GQ
tel 020-7434 5900
email dha@davidhigham.co.uk
website www.davidhigham.co.uk
Managing Director Anthony Goff, *Books* Veronique Baxter, Anthony Goff, Caroline Walsh, Christabel McKinley, *Children's Rights* Allison Cole, Olivia Hickman, *Film/TV/Theatre* Nicky Lund, Clare Israel, Penelope Killick

Children's fiction and non-fiction. 35% of the agency's list is for the children's market. Represented in all foreign markets. Also represents illustrators for

children's book publishing. Handles novelty books, picture books, fiction for 5–8 and 9–12 year-olds, teen and YA fiction, series fiction, poetry, plays, film/TV tie-ins, non-fiction and audio. Also handles adult fiction, general non-fiction, plays, film and TV scripts. *Commission* Home 15%, USA/translation 20%, scripts 10%. See website for submissions policy.

Clients include Martin Brown, Emma Chichester Clark, Cressida Cowell, Roald Dahl, Nicola Davies, Anna Kemp, Geraldine McCaughrean, Tom McLaughlin, Michael Morpurgo, Kate O'Hearn, Liz Pichon, Catherine Rayner, Nick Sharratt, Jonathan Stroud, Jenny Valentine, Jacqueline Wilson. *Founded* 1935.

Johnson & Alcock Ltd*
Bloomsbury House, 74–77 Great Russell Street, London WC1B 3DA
tel 020-7251 0125
website www.johnsonandalcock.co.uk
Contact Anna Power, Ed Wilson

All types of YA and teen fiction, particularly graphic novels. *Commission* Home 15%, USA/translation/film 20%. Send first 3 chapters (or 50 pages), full synopsis and brief covering letter with details of writing experience. For submission guidelines see website. Return postage essential. No short stories, poetry or board/picture books. *Founded* 1956.

JQ Literary Agency
17 Carlton House Terrace, St James's, London SW1Y 5AH
tel 07396 344505
email joey@jq-agency.co.uk
website www.jq-agency.co.uk
Director Joey Quince

Actively looking for debut children's middle-grade fiction brimming with magic, fantasy, adventure and heart. Represents children's middle-grade, YA and fantasy fiction. Email in first instance with a summary of the book and an author biography. *Founded* 2019.

Kane Literary Agency*
2 Dukes Avenue, London N10 2PT
tel 020-8351 9680
website www.kaneliteraryagency.com
Twitter @YasminKane3
Director Yasmin Kane

Interested in discovering new writers and launching the careers of first-time writers. Children's fiction: middle grade to YA. No picture books. Also handles literary and commercial fiction for adults. *Commission* Home 15%, overseas 20%. Send submissions by email only; no submissions by post. Send first 3 chapters and synopsis (one side of A4). No picture books.

Authors include Sarah Harris, Andrew Murray. *Founded* 2004.

Lambs to Lions Literary Agency

Centurion House, Leyland Business Park,
Centurion Way, Farington, Leyland PR25 3GR
tel 07546 415403
email info@lambstolions.co.uk
website https://lambstolions.co.uk
Managing Director Anthony Sergeant, *Ceo* Jake
Pilkington

Aims to encourage a respect for the natural world
through books. Supports authors right through from
original manuscript, to polished, published and
promoted books. Children's fiction, middle grade,
picture books, adventure, speculative fiction and
non-fiction. Email in first instance using the form on
the website regarding submission.

LBA Books*

91 Great Russell Street, London WC1B 3PS
tel 020-7637 1234
email info@lbabooks.com
website www.lbabooks.com
Twitter @LBA_Agency
Agents Luigi Bonomi, Amanda Preston, Louise
Lamont, Hannah Schofield

Fiction and non-fiction. Keen to find new authors
and help them develop their careers. Works with
foreign agencies and has links with film and TV
production companies. YA and children's fiction, as
well as adult fiction and non-fiction. *Commission*
Home 15%, overseas 20%. Send preliminary letter,
synopsis and first 3 chapters. No postal submissions.
No poetry, short stories or screenplays.
  Authors include Virginia Bergin, Anna Carey,
Rebecca Cobb, Julia Gray, Helen Hancocks, Rachael
Lucas, Anne Miller, Ben Miller, Nazneen Ahmed
Pathak, S.A. Patrick, Lucy Strange, Tamsin Winter,
Laura Wood, Katherine Woodfine, Emma Yarlett.
Founded 2005.

Lindsay Literary Agency*

East Worldham House, Alton, Hants GU34 3AT
tel (01420) 831430
email info@lindsayliteraryagency.co.uk
website www.lindsayliteraryagency.co.uk
Twitter @LindsayLit
Director Becky Bagnell

Specialists in children's fiction and non-fiction, teen/
YA, middle grade and picture books. *Commission*
Home 15%, translation 20%. Send first 3 chapters,
synopsis and covering letter by email. No
submissions by post. Will suggest revision.
  Authors include Pamela Butchart, Christina Collins,
Donna David, Sam Gayton, Sital Gorasia Chapman,
Ruth Hatfield, Larry Hayes, J.M. Joseph, Giles Paley-
Phillips, Sharon Tregenza, Rachel Valentine, Sue
Wallman, Joe Wilson. *Founded* 2008.

The Literary Office

71-75 Shelton Street, London WC2H 9JQ
tel 07910 267336
email jenny.todd@theliteraryoffice.com
website www.theliteraryoffice.com
Founder Jenny Todd

Literary agent and publishing advisor representing
quality literary and commercial fiction, non-fiction,
YA, film and TV. Drawn to works of originality by
inventive, relevant and multi-faceted writers and
artists, and committed to developing long-term
strategies for their careers. *Commission* Home 15%,
overseas 20%. Submissions via website. Send covering
letter, synopsis and 3 sample chapters. *Founded* 2021.

Luithlen Agency

88 Holmfield Road, Leicester LE2 1SB
tel 0116 273 8863
email penny@luithlenagency.com
website www.luithlenagency.com
Agents Jennifer Luithlen, Penny Luithlen

Children's fiction, all ages up to YA. *Commission*
Home 15%, overseas 20%, performance rights 15%.
See website for submission information.
Founded 1986.

Eunice McMullen Ltd

Low Ibbotsholme Cottage, Off Bridge Lane,
Troutbeck Bridge, Windermere, Cumbria LA23 1HU
tel (01539) 448551
email eunice@eunicemcmullen.co.uk
website www.eunicemcmullen.co.uk
Director Eunice McMullen

Specialises exclusively in children's books, especially
picture books and older fiction. Handles novelty
books, picture books, fiction for all ages including
teenage, series fiction and audio. *Commission* Home
15%, overseas 15%. No unsolicited scripts. Telephone
or email enquiries only.
  Authors include Ross Collins, Emma Dodd, Alison
Friend, Charles Fuge, Cally Johnson Isaacs, Sarah
Massini, James Mayhew, David Melling, Angela
McAllister, Angie Sage. *Founded* 1992.

Andrew Mann Ltd*

6 Quernmore Road, London N4 4QU
tel 020-7609 6218
email tina@andrewmann.co.uk
website www.andrewmann.co.uk
Twitter @AML_Literary
Contacts Tina Betts

Currently closed to new submissions. *Founded* 1975.

Marjacq Scripts Ltd*

The Space, 235 High Holborn, London WC1V 7DN
tel 020-7935 9499
website www.marjacq.com
Twitter @MarjacqScripts
Contact Catherine Pellegrino (children's and YA);
Sandra Sawicka (YA only)

Handles all rights. In-house legal, foreign rights and
book-to-film support. All genres represented.

Commission Home 15%; overseas, film 20%. See website for submission guidelines.

Clients include James Campbell, Rose Edwards, Roopa Farooki, Steve Feasey, Gemma Fowler, Nick Garlick, Finbar Hawkins, T.C. Shelley, Claire Waller, Harriet Whitehorn. Founded 1973.

MBA Literary and Script Agents Ltd*
62 Grafton Way, London W1T 5DW
tel 020-7387 2076
website www.mbalit.co.uk
Twitter @mbaagents
Children's Book Agent Sophie Gorell Barnes, Film & TV Agent Diana Tyler

Fiction, non-fiction, children's books. Foreign rights handled by Louisa Pritchard Associates. Commission Home 15%, overseas 20%, TV/theatre/radio 10%, film 15%. See website for submission guidelines.

Clients include Sufiya Ahmed, Sita Brahmachari, Christopher William Hill, Mark Wheeller. Founded 1971.

Madeleine Milburn Literary, TV & Film Agency*
The Factory, 1 Park Hill, Clapham, London SW4 9NS
tel 020-7499 7550
email childrens@madeleinemilburn.com
website www.madeleinemilburn.co.uk
Facebook www.facebook.com/MadeleineMilburnLiteraryAgency
Twitter @MMLitAgency
Instagram @madeleinemilburn
Contacts Madeleine Milburn, Giles Milburn (Directors), Liane-Louise Smith (Rights Director), Chloe Seager (Children's & YA Agent), Georgina Simmonds (Rights Agent), Hannah Ladds (Dramatic Rights Agent)

Special interest in launching the careers of debut authors and illustrators. Represents a dynamic and prize-winning range of children's and YA fiction and non-fiction. Also award-winning and popular fiction including fantasy, real life/contemporary, YA thrillers, mystery, action, historical, sci-fi, romance, coming of age and film/TV tie-ins.

Represents British, American, Canadian and international authors. Handles all rights in the UK, US and foreign markets including film/TV/theatre/radio (for clients with book deal in place only) and digital. Areas include picture books, 6–8 years, 9–12 years, 12+, teen, YA, new adult and books appealing to both children and adults. Commission Home 15%; USA/translation, film 20%. No submissions by post. See submission guidelines and agency news on website. Works editorially with all clients.

Authors include Holly Bourne, Anna Fargher, Kathryn Foxfield, Kate Weston, Lara Williamson, Ben Oliver, Danielle Jawando, Benjamin Dean, Lex Croucher, Katie Kirby, Jen Carney, Helen Rutter, Maisie Chan. Founded 2012.

Miles Stott Children's Literary Agency Ltd*
East Hook Farm, Lower Quay Road, Hook, Haverfordwest, Pembrokeshire SA62 4LR
tel 07855 252043
email nancy@milesstottagency.co.uk
email mandy@milesstottagency.co.uk
email victoria@milesstottagency.co.uk
website www.milesstottagency.co.uk
Twitter @milesstott
Instagram @milesstott
Director Nancy Miles, Associate Agents Victoria Birkett, Mandy Suhr

Specialist in children's novelty books, picture books, fiction for 6–9 and 10–12 year-olds, YA series fiction and non-fiction. Commission Home 15%; overseas, film/TV 20%. Fiction submissions by email only to fictionsubs@milesstottagency.co.uk including covering letter, brief synopsis and first 3 chapters. Picture book submissions by email only to picturebooksubs@milesstottagency.co.uk including covering letter, complete text and/or pdfs of sample artwork.

Authors include Kirsty Applebaum, Atinuke, Rachel Bright, Stacy Gregg, Frances Hardinge, Caryl Hart, Gill Lewis, Tom Percival, Tom Pollock, Mark Sperring. Founded 2003.

Morgan Green Creatives Ltd
157 Ribblesdale Road, London SW16 6SP
email kirsty@morgangreencreatives.com
website www.morgangreencreatives.com
Founder Kirsty McLachlan

Actively looking for fresh talent and to be challenged with new ideas, inspired and moved by great writing, and to find unique and distinct voices with compelling stories to tell. Represents fiction, non-fiction and children's book writers. Submission by email which includes a covering letter within the body of the email, plus 30 pages of your work attached. Founded 2020.

Paper Lion Ltd
13 Grayham Road, New Malden, Surrey KT3 5HR
tel 07748 786199, (01276) 61322
email katyloffman@paperlionltd.com
email lesleypollinger@paperlionltd.com
website www.paperlionltd.com
Agents Katy Loffman, Lesley Pollinger

A cross-media literary agency. The client list includes award-winning authors, literary estates and publishers. Has a strong focus on the exploration of digital opportunities and expertise in solving complex copyright, dramatic rights and literary issues from the present and past.

Clients include Max Allen, Michael Coleman, Vince Cross, Cordelia Feldman, Fiction Express, Catherine Fisher, Dave Gatward, Bruce Hobson, Saviour Pirotta and the estates of authors including Gene Kemp and Gwynedd Rae. *Founded* 2017.

Redhammer Management Ltd
website www.redhammer.info
Vice President Peter Cox

A boutique literary agency providing in-depth management for a restricted number of clients. Specialises in works with international book, film and TV potential. Participates in Pop-Up Submissions every Sunday; submit a title, brief description and first 700 words of the work. No radio or theatre scripts.

Rogers, Coleridge & White Ltd*
20 Powis Mews, London W11 1JN
tel 020-7221 3717
email info@rcwlitagency.com
website www.rcwlitagency.com
Twitter @RCWLitAgency
Instagram @rcwliteraryagency
Managing Director Peter Straus, *Directors* Sam Copeland, Stephen Edwards, Natasha Fairweather, Georgia Garrett, Laurence Laluyaux, Zoë Waldie, Claire Wilson, *Agents* Cara Jones, Jon Wood

International representation for all genres of fiction, non-fiction, children's and YA. *Commission* Home 15%, USA 20%, translation 20%. See website for submissions information.
   Clients include David Baddiel, Frank Cottrell Boyce, Cerrie Burnell, Catherine Doyle, Lissa Evans, Anna James, Femi Fadugba, Alice Oseman, Katherine Rundell, A.F. Steadman, Holly Jackson, Katie and Kevin Tsang. *Founded* 1967 as Deborah Rogers Ltd, 1989 as Rogers, Coleridge & White Ltd.

Elizabeth Roy Literary Agency
White Cottage, Greatford, Stamford, Lincs. PE9 4PR
tel (01778) 560672
website www.elizabethroy.co.uk

Children's fiction, picture books and non-fiction – writers and illustrators. *Commission* Home 15%, overseas 20%. Send preliminary letter, synopsis and sample chapters with names of publishers and agents previously contacted. Return postage essential. *Founded* 1990.

Caroline Sheldon Literary Agency Ltd*
71 Hillgate Place, London W8 7SS
tel 020-7727 9102
email info@carolinesheldon.co.uk
website www.carolinesheldon.co.uk
Twitter @CarolineAgent
Contact Caroline Sheldon

Represents in all areas of children's fiction, whether picture book, middle grade or YA. Looks for strong concepts, wonderful characterisation and excellent story-telling and compelling non-fiction. Also represents leading illustrators of children's books.

Works closely with a media agent on film, TV and other opportunities. All genres of children's writing including fantasy, humour, contemporary life, thriller, stories set in schools and non-fiction. *Commission* Home 15%, USA/translation 20%, film/TV 20%. To submit work send an introductory email: in the subject line write: Proposal and the title of the work; at the head of the email include a 3-line synopsis; give further full information in the email about the work and yourself. Authors – send the first 3 chapters or equivalent length. Illustrators – attach work or include a link to your portfolio. *Founded* 1985.

Dorie Simmonds Agency Ltd*
email info@doriesimmonds.com
website https://doriesimmonds.com/
Twitter @Dorie_Simmonds
Contact Dorie Simmonds

Children's fiction, general non-fiction and commercial fiction. *Commission* Home 15%, USA 15%, translation 20%. Send a short synopsis, 2 to 3 sample chapters and a CV including writing/publishing background. Does not represent poetry or screenplays. *Founded* 1997.

Skylark Literary Limited
19 Parkway, Weybridge, Surrey KT13 9HD
tel 020-8144 7440
email info@skylark-literary.com
email submissions@skylark-literary.com
website www.skylark-literary.com
Facebook www.facebook.com/SkylarkLiteraryLtd
Twitter @skylarklit
Directors Joanna Moult, Amber Caraveo

Specialists in children's and YA fiction. All genres considered. *Commission* Home 15%, overseas 20%. Keen to support new and established authors. Will consider unsolicited submissions. Agents have editorial backgrounds and will work closely with clients on their manuscripts to increase chances of publication. Submissions by email only. Will suggest revision where appropriate. No adult fiction/non-fiction.
   Clients include Amy Wilson, Simon James Green, Alyssa Hollingsworth, Rachel Burge, Nizrana Farook, Lesley Parr, Em Lynas, Lily Dyu. *Founded* 2014.

The Soho Agency Ltd*
(previously LAW/Lucas Alexander Whitley Ltd)
16–17 Wardour Mews, 2nd Floor, London W1F 8AT
tel 020-7471 7900
website www.thesohoagency.co.uk
Twitter @TheSohoAgencyUK
Managing Director Rowan Lawton, *Agent* Philippa Milnes-Smith

Novelty books, picture books, fiction for 5–8 and 9–12 year olds including series, YA, film/TV and non-fiction. Special interests: projects with cross-media potential, diverse voices, visual storytelling and innovative non-fiction. *Commission* Home 15%, overseas 20%. Representation in all markets. Unsolicited and debut work considered. See website for further information about the clients and genres represented and essential information on submissions. No postal submissions.

Clients include Lauren Child, Steve Cole, Linda Chapman, Gillian Cross, Emily Gravett, Chris Judge, Sophie Kinsella, Philip Reeve, Chris Riddell, Niamh Sharkey, Sarah Webb. *Founded* 1996.

SP Literary Agency

email info@sp-agency.co.uk
website https://sp-agency.co.uk/
Facebook www.facebook.com/sp.literary.agency
Agents Philippa Perry, Abigail Sparrow

Represents authors and illustrators across children's, YA and adult fiction and non-fiction. Email submissions are preferred; attach a synopsis and the first 3 chapters to a covering email. Children's or YA submissions should also be clearly marked in the subject line.

Abner Stein*

China House, Suite 137, 100 Black Prince Road, London SE1 7SJ
tel 020-7373 0456
email info@abnerstein.co.uk
website www.abnerstein.co.uk
Contacts Caspian Dennis, Sandy Violette

Fiction, general non-fiction and children's. *Commission* Home 15%, overseas 20%. Not taking on any new clients at present.

Rochelle Stevens & Co

2 Terretts Place, Upper Street, London N1 1QZ
tel 020-7359 3900
email info@rochellestevens.com
website www.rochellestevens.com
Twitter @TerrettsPlace
Directors Rochelle Stevens, Frances Arnold

Scripts for TV, theatre and radio. *Commission* 10%. Send preliminary letter, CV, short synopsis and opening 10 pages of a drama script by post (sae essential for return of material). See website for full submission guidelines. *Founded* 1984.

Sarah Such Literary Agency

38 Church Road, Barnes, London SW13 9HN
tel 020-8741 2107
email info@sarah-such.com
website https://sarahsuchliteraryagency.tumblr.com
Twitter @sarahsuch
Instagram @sarahsuch1
Director Sarah Such

High-quality literary and commercial non-fiction and fiction for adults and children. Always looking for original children's and YA writers and projects.

Translation representation by The Buckman Agency. Film/TV representation by Lesley Thorne, Aitken Alexander Associates Ltd. Particular focus on debut YA novels, topical middle-grade non-fiction, children's fiction series, picture books and graphic novels. *Commission* Home 15%, TV/film 20%, overseas 20%. Will suggest revision. Submit synopsis and three sample chapters (as a Word attachment by email) and an author biography. No postal submissions unless requested. No unsolicited MSS or telephone enquiries. TV/film scripts for established clients only. No radio or theatre scripts, poetry, fantasy, self-help or short stories (unless full collections).

Authors include Matthew De Abaitua, Jeffrey Boakye, Kit Caless, Maxim Jakubowski, Antony Johnston, Amy Lankester-Owen, Louisa Leaman, Vesna Maric, Heather Martin, Rachel Pashley, John Rowley, Caroline Sanderson, Nikhil Singh, Sara Starbuck. *Founded* 2007.

Two Piers Literary Agency

email hello@twopiersagency.com
website https://twopiersagency.com/
Facebook www.facebook.com/TwoPiersAgency
Twitter @TwoPiersAgency
Instagram @twopiersagency
Agent Rufus Purdy

Represents fiction and non-fiction, including children's (from 7+) and memoir. Submissions through form on website. For fiction, submit the first 3 chapters and synopsis; for non-fiction, send 3 chapters and proposal. Submissions must include a covering letter. *Founded* 2021.

Tyild's Agency

email submissionstotyildsagency@gmail.com
website www.tyildsagency.co.uk
Twitter @tyilds
Agents Kate Scarborough, Frances McKay

A children's literary agency, set up particularly for teachers who write. Represents authors of picture books, young readers and middle-grade fiction, as well as non-fiction. Actively looking for new voices - wonderful storytellers with an innate understanding of children. *Commission* Home 15%, overseas 20%. See website for more details on how to send in submissions. *Founded* 2020.

United Agents LLP*

12–26 Lexington Street, London W1F 0LE
tel 020-3214 0800
email info@unitedagents.co.uk
website www.unitedagents.co.uk
Agents Jodie Hodges, Emily Talbot

Fiction and non-fiction. *Commission* Home 15%, USA/translation 20%. See website for submission details. *Founded* 2008.

Jo Unwin Literary Agency*
West Wing, Somerset House, London WC2R 1LA
email info@jounwin.co.uk
website www.jounwin.co.uk
Twitter @jounwin, @rachelphilippa, @MillyReilly
Agents Jo Unwin, Rachel Mann

Represents authors of literary fiction, commercial women's fiction, non-fiction, cookery, YA fiction and fiction for children aged 5+ (picture books only accepted if written by established clients).
Authors include Wibke Brueggemann, Jack Meggitt-Phillips, Sarah Moore Fitzgerald, Hayley Scott, Nadia Shireen, Emma-Jane Smith-Barton, Lucy Cuthew, Bethany Rutter. *Founded* 2016.

Watson, Little Ltd*
Suite 315, ScreenWorks, 22 Highbury Grove, London N5 2ER
tel 020-7388 7529
email office@watsonlittle.com
email submissions@watsonlittle.com
website www.watsonlittle.com
Twitter @watsonlittle
Managing Director James Wills, *Agents* Laetitia Rutherford, Megan Carroll, *Rights Director* Rachel Richardson

Offers a full service to its clients across all aspects of media. Handles a wide range of fiction and non-fiction for adults and children and works in conjunction with US agents and selected film and TV associates. YA and middle-grade fiction, picture books and children's non-fiction in all genres. *Commission* Home 15%, USA/translation 20%. Send informative preliminary letter, synopsis and sample chapters by email only. No poetry, TV, play or film scripts.
Authors include Tom Clempson, Rebecca Elliott, Tim Hall, Richard Joyce, Lynne Reid Banks, Margaret Mahy. *Founded* 1970.

Whispering Buffalo Literary Agency Ltd
97 Chesson Road, London W14 9QS
tel 020-7565 4737
email info@whisperingbuffalo.com
website www.whisperingbuffalo.com
Director Mariam Keen

Commercial and literary fiction and non-fiction, children's and YA fiction. Special interest in book-to-screen adaptations; TV and film rights in novels and non-fiction handled in-house. *Commission* Home 15%, overseas 20%. Only accepts submissions by email. Will suggest revision. *Founded* 2008.

Eve White Literary Agency Limited*
15 Alderney Street, London SW1V 4ES
tel 020-7630 1155
email eve@evewhite.co.uk
email ludo@evewhite.co.uk
website www.evewhite.co.uk
Twitter @EveWhiteAgency
Contacts Eve White, Ludo Cinelli

Boutique agency representing young, middle grade, teenage and YA fiction, picture books and film/TV tie-ins. Also handles adult commercial and literary fiction and non-fiction; 35% of the list is for the children's market. *Commission* Home 15%, overseas 20%. Will suggest revision where appropriate. See website for up-to-date submission requirements. No submissions by post.
Clients include Andy Stanton, Rae Earl, Tracey Corderoy, Abie Longstaff, Elli Woollard, Sarah Naughton, Iona Rangeley, Alex Barclay, Alexia Mason, James Bishop, Sarah Coyle, Ivan Brett. *Founded* 2003.

Alice Williams Literary*
tel 020-7385 2118
email submissions@alicewilliamsliterary.co.uk
website www.alicewilliamsliterary.co.uk
Twitter @alicelovesbooks
Contact Alice Williams

Specialist literary agency representing writers and illustrators of picture books, children's fiction, teen/YA fiction and children's non-fiction. *Commission* Home 15%; USA/translation, film/TV 20%. By email only; attach full typescript and synopsis, two or three picture book texts or illustration portfolio. See website for further guidelines and submission openings.
Clients include Lauren Beard, Jo Clarke, Fiona Danks and Jo Schofield, Rachael Davis, Rachel Delahaye, Lara Hawthorne, Meg McLaren, Natelle Quek, Rose Robbins, Fabi Santiago, Suzy Senior, Ciara Smyth, Cat Weldon, Clare Helen Welsh, Pete Williamson. *Founded* 2018.

Susan Yearwood Agency*
2 Knebworth House, Londesborough Road, London N16 8RL
tel 020-7503 0954
email submissions@susanyearwoodagency.com
website www.susanyearwoodagency.com
Twitter @sya_susan
Contact Susan Yearwood

Children's fiction 9+ and YA. *Commission* Home 15%, overseas 20%. Send submission with covering letter and brief synopsis via email. Submissions not accepted by hand or post. Tends not to read sci-fi and fantasy in adult fiction, short stories or poetry.
Authors include Suzanne Snow, Fil Reid, Rosa Temple and Sarupa Shah. *Founded* 2007.

Children's literary agents overseas

This list includes only a selection of agents across the English-speaking world. Before submitting material, writers are advised to visit agents' websites for detailed submission guidelines and to ascertain terms.

AUSTRALIA

ALM: Australian Literary Management
tel +61 (02) 9818 8557
email alphaalm8@gmail.com
website www.austlit.com

For full details of genres represented and submission guidelines, see website. Does not consider TV or film scripts of any kind, poetry, self-help, sci-fi and fantasy or books for children by unpublished authors. Does not accept self-published work or previously published works, including ebooks, or writing by non-Australian authors.

The Authors' Agent
PO Box 577, Terrigal, NSW 2260
email briancook@theauthorsagent.com.au
website www.theauthorsagent.com.au

Specialises in children's books and represents Australian citizens only. Accepts submissions by email. For detailed guidelines, see website.

Sarah McKenzie Literary Management
email submissions@smlm.com.au
website www.smlm.com.au

Provides advice, advocacy and representation for Australian authors, helping them to shape and polish their writing projects, negotiate the best possible terms in their contracts and identify and create opportunities to build a writing career. Actively seeks established and emerging authors of fiction, non-fiction and children's fiction. Does not represent works that have been previously self-published in any form. Submissions via email only.

CANADA

CookeMcDermid
email admin@cookemcdermid.com
website https://cookemcdermid.com
Agents Dean Cooke, Sally Harding, Martha Webb, Suzanne Brandreth, Ron Eckel, Rachel Letofsky, Stephanie Sinclair, Paige Sisley

CMD represents authors of literary, commercial and science/fantasy fiction; a broad range of narrative non-fiction; health and wellness resources; and middle-grade and YA books. Sells Canadian and American rights directly. Cooke International represents UK and translation rights, in conjunction with a network of co-agents around the world. CMD also sells film and TV rights directly, in addition to working with associates in New York and LA. Submission via online form. *Founded* 2017.

Transatlantic Agency
2 Bloor Street East, Suite 3500, Toronto, Ontario M4W 1A8
tel +1 416-488-9214
website www.transatlanticagency.com
Facebook www.facebook.com/TransLitAgency
Twitter @TransLitAgency

Represents more than 700 American, Canadian and internationally bestselling and award-winning clients, with a team of 20 experienced agents based in cities across North America. Offers a full spectrum of career representation to authors (adult, children's and YA, and illustrators) and storytellers (speakers, industry leaders and influencers) across all genres and formats for book, content development, speaking and TV & film. *Founded* 1993.

NEW ZEALAND

Delaney Worner International
email info@delaneyworner.com
website www.delaneyworner.com
Contacts Joseph Delaney, Linda Worner, Joanne Delaney

Specialises in children's, teen and YA books but will consider all types of fiction. While the agency does not seek non-fiction or poetry submissions, it welcomes picture books which use rhyme as the text narrative. Submit the first 3 chapters and a synopsis. *Founded* 2016.

Frances Plumpton Literary Agency
PO Box 15061, New Lynn, Auckland 0640
tel +64 (0)9 827 6785
email submissions@francesplumpton.com
website www.francesplumpton.com
Facebook www.facebook.com/Frances-Plumpton-Literary-Agency-685680644791804/

Represents picture books, junior and YA fiction and children's non-fiction by New Zealand writers and/or illustrators. No poetry or short stories. Submissions should be sent as an attachment (Word or pdf) with the manuscript title in the subject line. See website for submission guidelines. *Founded* 2012.

USA

Member of the Association of American Literary Agents

Adams Literary*

7845 Colony Road, C4 Suite 215, Charlotte,
NC 28226
tel +1 (704) 542-1440
email info@adamsliterary.com
website www.adamsliterary.com
Facebook www.facebook.com/adamsliterary
Twitter @adamsliterary
Agents Tracey Adams, Josh Adams

Exclusively children's from picture books to YA
novels. Submissions through website: authors send a
pdf of your complete manuscript; illustrators send a
pdf sample of your work or a link to your website.
Founded 2004.

Bradford Literary Agency*

5694 Mission Center Road, Suite 347, San Diego,
CA 92108
email queries@bradfordlit.com
website www.bradfordlit.com

Currently looking for picture books, chapter books,
middle grade and YA in both fiction and non-fiction
categories. Query by email only. For detailed
submission guidelines, see website.

Andrea Brown Literary Agency*

website www.andreabrownlit.com
Facebook www.facebook.com/AndreaBrownAgency
Twitter @andreabrownlit
President Andrea Brown, *Agents* Laura Rennert,
Caryn Wiseman, Jennifer Laughran, Jennifer Rofé,
Kelly Sonnack, Jamie Weiss Chilton, Jennifer
Mattson, Kathleen Rushall, Lara Perkins, Saritza
Hernádez, Jennifer March Soloway, *Associate Agents*
Jemiscoe Chambers-Black, Paige Terlip

Exclusively all kinds of children's books. Represents
both authors and illustrators. Email and form
submissions only. See website for guidelines.
Founded 1981.

Maria Carvainis Agency Inc.*

Rockefeller Center, 1270 Avenue of the Americas,
Suite 2915, New York, NY 10020
tel +1 212-245-6365
email mca@mariacarvainisagency.com
website www.mariacarvainisagency.com
President & Literary Agent Maria Carvainis

YA fiction. Also handles adult fiction and non-fiction.
Commission Home 15%, overseas 20%. Send a query
letter, a synopsis of the work, first 5–10 pages and a
note of any writing credentials. See website for full
submission guidelines. *Founded* 1977.

The Chudney Agency

72 North State Road, Suite 501, Briarcliff Manor,
NY 10510
tel +1 201-758-8739
email steven@thechudneyagency.com
website https://thechudneyagency.com
Contact Steven Chudney

Represents authors of children's books and adult
fiction. Does not accept sci-fi, non-fiction, plays,
screenplays or film scripts. Submissions via email.
Founded 2002.

Curtis Brown, Ltd*

228 East 45th Street, Suite 310, New York, NY 10017
tel +1 212-473-5400
email info@cbltd.com
website www.curtisbrown.com
Twitter @CurtisBrownLtd
Instagram curtisbrown.ltd
Ceo Timothy Knowlton, *President* Peter Ginsberg,
Vice President Elizabeth Harding, *Executive Vice
President* Ginger Knowlton, *Contacts* Sarah Gerton,
Jonathan Lyons, Jazmia Young, *Film & TV Rights*
Holly Frederick, *Translation rights* Sarah Perillo

Fiction and non-fiction, juvenile, film and TV rights.
No unsolicited MSS. See individual agent's entry on
the Agents page of the website for specific query and
submission information. *Founded* 1914.

Liza Dawson Associates*

121 West 27th Street, Suite 1201, New York,
NY 10001
email lwu@lizadawson.com
website www.lizadawsonassociates.com
Twitter @LizaDawsonAssoc
Ceo Liza Dawson

A full-service agency which draws on expertise as
former publishers. YA and middle grade: thrillers,
mysteries, romance, historical fiction, sci-fi and
fantasy, contemporary. See website for submission
guidelines and email contacts. *Founded* 1996.

Sandra Dijkstra & Associates*

PMB 515, 1155 Camino Del Mar, Del Mar, CA 92014
tel +1 858-755-3115
website www.dijkstraagency.com
Contacts Sandra Dijkstra, Elise Capron, Jill Marr,
Thao Le, Andrea Cavallaro, Jessica Watterson,
Jennifer Kim

YA science fiction, fantasy and contemporary;
middle-grade fiction and non-fiction; picture books
by author/illustrators only. *Commission* Home 15%,
overseas 20%. Works in conjunction with foreign and
film agents. Email submissions only. Please see
website for the most up-to-date guidelines.
Founded 1981.

Dunham Literary Inc.*

email query@dunhamlit.com
website www.dunhamlit.com
Contact Jennie Dunham, Leslie Zampetti

Children's books: handles picture books, fiction for 5–8 and 9–12 year-olds and teenage fiction. Also handles adult literary fiction and non-fiction; 50% of list is for the children's market. *Commission* Home 15%, overseas 20%. Send query by email including a synopsis and first 5 pages in the body of the email. *Founded* 2000.

Dystel, Goderich & Bourret LLC*
1 Union Square West, New York, NY 10003
tel +1 212-627-9100
website www.dystel.com
Facebook www.facebook.com/DGandB/
Twitter @DGandBTweets
Contacts Michael Bourret, Jim McCarthy, Stacey Glick, John Rudolph, Lauren Abramo, Michaela Whatnall

Children's fiction: handles picture books, fiction for 5–8 and 9–12 year-olds, teenage fiction and series fiction. Looking for quality YA fiction. Also handles adult fiction and non-fiction. *Commission* Home 15%, overseas 19%. See website for submission guidelines. *Founded* 1994.

The Ethan Ellenberg Literary Agency*
155 Suffolk Street, Suite 2R, New York, NY 10002
tel +1 212-431-4554
email agent@ethanellenberg.com
website www.ethanellenberg.com
President & Agent Ethan Ellenberg, *Senior Agent* Evan Gregory, *Associate Agent* Bibi Lewis

Fiction and non-fiction. Interested in all types of children's fiction: new adult, YA, middle grade, chapter books and picture books. Will consider all genres: literary, mystery, romance, fantasy and sci-fi, humorous. Will consider other illustrated works. *Commission* Home 15%, overseas 20%. No scholarly works, poetry, short stories or screenplays.

Accepts unsolicited MSS and seriously considers all submissions, including first-time writers. For fiction, submit synopsis and first 3 chapters. For shorter children's works, send complete MS. Illustrators should send a representative selection of colour copies (no original artwork). Unable to return any material from overseas. *Founded* 1983.

Flannery Literary
email jennifer@flanneryliterary.com
website www.flanneryliterary.com
Contact Jennifer Flannery

Specialises in children's and YA, juvenile fiction and non-fiction. *Commission* Home 15%, overseas 20%. *Founded* 1992.

Folio Literary Management*
The Film Center Building, 630 9th Avenue, Suite 1101, New York, NY 10036
website www.foliolit.com
Twitter @FolioLiterary

Represents both first-time and established authors. Seeks upmarket adult fiction, literary fiction, commercial fiction that features fresh voices and/or memorable characters, and narrative non-fiction. Folio Jr is devoted exclusively to representing children's book authors and artists. Consult agents' submission guidelines on the website before making contact.

Barry Goldblatt Literary LLC*
594 Dean Street, Brooklyn, NY 11238
website https://bgliterary.com
Contact Barry Goldblatt

Represents YA and middle-grade fiction, as well as adult sci-fi and fantasy. No non-fiction. Has a preference for quirky, offbeat work. Query only. See website for full submission guidelines. *Founded* 2000.

The Greenhouse Literary Agency*
4114 Legato Road, 5th Floor, Fairfax, VA 22033
tel +1 571-758-5615
website www.greenhouseliterary.com
Director Sarah Davies, *Agent* Chelsea Eberly

Children's fiction from picture book authors/illustrators through to teen/YA. Occasional non-fiction projects and women's fiction will also be considered. Represents both US and UK authors. *Commission* 15% USA/UK, elsewhere 25%. No poetry or film scripts. Will suggest revision. See website for submission guidelines.

Authors include Andrea Contos, Tami Lewis Brown, Sarwat Chadda, Elle Cosimano, Alexandra Diaz, Bill Doyle, Ashley Elston, Tae Keller, Dawn Kurtagich, Cori McCarthy, Joanna Meyer, Megan Miranda, Mae Respicio, Ali Standish, Kat Yeh, Allen Zadoff, Brenna Yovanoff. *Founded* 2008.

John Hawkins & Associates Inc.*
80 Maiden Lane, Suite 1503, New York, NY 10038
tel +1 212-807-7040
email jha@jhalit.com
website www.jhalit.com
Agents Moses Cardona (President), Warren Frazier, Anne Hawkins

Fiction and non-fiction; YA. *Founded* 1893.

kt literary*
9249 S. Broadway 200–543, Highlands Ranch, CO 80129
tel +1 720-344-4728
email contact@ktliterary.com
website https://ktliterary.com
Twitter @ktliterary
Instagram @ktliterary
Agents Kate Testerman, Sara Megibow, Hannah Fergesen, Renee Nyen, Hilary Harwell, Kelly Van Sant, Jas Perry, Karl Sutherland, Chelsea Hensley, Aida Z. Lilly

Primarily middle-grade and YA fiction and graphic novels. Some picture books and select narrative non-fiction for children. Queries are accepted via QueryManager. No postal submissions.

Clients include Maureen Johnson, Stephanie Perkins, Matthew Cody, Ellen Booraem, Trish Doller, Amy Spalding, Jaleigh Johnson, Casey McQuiston, Rebecca Roanhorse, Stefan Bachmann. *Founded* 2008.

Gina Maccoby Literary Agency*

PO Box 60, Chappaqua, NY 10514
tel +1 914-238-5630
email query@maccobylit.com
website www.publishersmarketplace.com/members/GinaMaccoby/
Contact Gina Maccoby

Looking for high-quality upmarket fiction and non-fiction for adults and children. An engaging narrative voice and strong premise are most important; across all forms the agency is looking for compelling stories and fresh perspectives. Children's, YA, middle grade and picture books of writers/illustrators only. Non-fiction areas of interest include history, biography, popular science and narrative journalism. No unsolicited submissions. Query first: query@maccobylit.com. Due to the volume of submissions received, will only reply if interested. *Founded* 1986.

McIntosh & Otis Inc.*

207 E. 37th Street, Suite BG, New York, NY 10016
tel +1 212-687-7400
email info@mcintoshandotis.com
website www.mcintoshandotis.com
Head of Children's Department Christa Heschke

Board books, picture books (fiction and non-fiction), fiction for 5–8 and 9–12 year-olds, teenage fiction, series fiction, poetry and non-fiction for children. No unsolicited MSS for novels; query first via email, see website for instructions. *Founded* 1928.

Erin Murphy Literary Agency

824 Roosevelt Trail, Suite #290, Windham, ME 04062
website https://emliterary.com
President Erin Murphy, *Senior Agents* Ammi-Joan Paquette, Tricia Lawrence, *Agents* Tara Gonzalez, Kevin Lewis, Miranda Paul

Children's books: fiction, non-fiction, picture books, middle grade and YA. *Commission* Home 15%, overseas 20–30%. No unsolicited queries or submissions; considers material only by referral or through personal contact such as at conferences or online pitch event requests. Some agents have submissions forms on QueryTracker. *Founded* 1999.

Olswanger Literary LLC*

email anna@olswangerliterary.com
website www.olswanger.com
Contact Anna Olswanger

Specialises in representing author-illustrators of picture books and graphic novels. Clients have won the Newbery Medal, Asian Pacific American Award for Literature, Flora Stieglitz Strauss Award for Non-fiction, Orbis Pictus, PEN/Steven Kroll Award for Picture Book Writing, Parents Choice Gold Award, Bank Street College of Education Best Children's Book, Sibert Award and the Ezra Jack Keats Book Award, and have been on the *New York Times* bestseller list.

Alison Picard, Literary Agent

PO Box 2000, Cotuit, MA 02635
tel +1 508-477-7192
email ajpicard@aol.com

Adult fiction and non-fiction, children's and YA. No short stories, poetry, plays, screenplays or sci-fi and fantasy. *Commission* 15%. Please send query via email (no attachments). *Founded* 1985.

Pippin Properties Inc.

110 West 40th Street, Suite 1704, New York, NY 10018
tel +1 212-338-9310
email info@pippinproperties.com
website www.pippinproperties.com
Facebook www.facebook.com/pippinproperties
Twitter @LovethePippins
Contacts Holly McGhee, Elena Giovinazzo, Sara Crowe, Cameron Chase, Ashley Valentine, Rakeem Nelson

Focuses on children's book authors and artists, including picture books, middle grade, graphic novels and YA novels, and adult trade books on occasion. *Commission* Home 15%, overseas 25%. Query by email. *Founded* 1998.

Rodeen Literary Management

email submissions@rodeenliterary.com
website www.rodeenliterary.com
Facebook www.facebook.com/RodeenLiterary/
Twitter @RodeenLiterary

Open to submissions from writers and illustrators of all genres of children's literature including picture books, early readers, middle-grade fiction and non-fiction, graphic novels, and YA fiction and non-fiction. Submit the first 50 pages of a novel (authors), a portfolio (illustrators) or a picture book dummy via email. *Founded* 2008.

Susan Schulman Literary Agency LLC*

454 West 44th Street, New York, NY 10036
tel +1 212-713-1633
email susan@schulmanagency.com
Twitter @SSchulman

Agents for negotiation in all markets (with co-agents) of fiction and general non-fiction; for picture books, middle-grade and YA markets; and associated subsidiary rights including plays, TV adaptation and film. *Commission* Home 15%, UK 7.5%, overseas 20%. Return postage required. Email enquiries to queries@schulmanagency.com.

Stimola Literary Studio, Inc.*

tel +1 508-696-9353
website www.stimolaliterarystudio.com
President & Founder Rosemary B. Stimola, *Vice President & Agent for Graphic Novels* Peter K Ryan, *Senior Agent* Erica Rand Silverman, *Agents* Adriana Stimola, Allison Hellegers, *Associate Agent* Allison Remcheck

Children's fiction and non-fiction, from preschool to YA; adult fiction, non-fiction, cookbooks and lifestyle. *Commission* Home 15%, overseas 20%. Most clients come via referral. *Founded* 1997.

WME

11 Madison Avenue, 18th Floor, New York, NY 10010

tel +1 212-586-5100
website www.wmeentertainment.com

Worldwide talent and literary agency with offices in New York, Beverly Hills, Nashville, Sydney and London. Represents bestselling authors, critically acclaimed literary writers, award-winning thought leaders and up-and-coming talent.

Writers House LLC*

120 Broadway, 22nd floor, New York, NY 10271
tel +1 212-685-2400
website www.writershouse.com

Fiction and non-fiction, including film and TV rights. Send a query letter and a synopsis of your work addressed to one agent. *Founded* 1973.

Illustration
Notes from a successful children's author and illustrator

Lauren Child describes how *Clarice Bean, That's Me* came to be published and shares her experiences of taking advice from publishers and editors.

My first attempt at writing a children's book was when I was 18 – my friend Bridget and I had an idea. Everything seemed simple – we were going to write a book, get it published and get on with something else. Almost immediately, and by sheer fluke, we had an interested publisher. We were invited along for a 'working lunch' to discuss the story development. The editor made some suggestions for improvement which we were quite happy about – we really had no objection to rewriting; we were happier still with the business lunch and were fuelled by the confidence of youth that life would always be this easy. We did nothing, of course, and the whole thing fell through which, with hindsight, was a relief – I think we would both be squirming now. It was a number of years later before I even thought to write anything else.

Please yourself

The next time I learnt the hard way, by trekking around uninterested publishers with my portfolio – something it would be almost impossible to do now, as no one wants to see unsolicited work. I used any contacts I had, however distant. I forced myself to phone complete strangers in order to get appointments and advice, which I hated doing. When I met with publishers they seemed to have very set views on what a children's book should be. I listened to their advice and always tried to write the book they wanted me to write. But, whenever I went back to them with my work, there was always something missing – I could never write the book they had in mind.

So, unable to interest publishers, no matter how hard I tried to give them what they said they wanted, I forgot about the whole project and got on with other things. One day, having reached a rather low point in my life, and having looked at every possible career path, a friend suggested that I leave my portfolio of designs, drawings and ideas with her so she could show it to her business manager who had created and managed various successful companies. When I met with this woman, I mentioned I had an interest in film and animation and also designing products for children. Although I had no relevant training, she suggested that I try to write a children's book because, hopefully, it would prove I could create characters and invent a world for them. I think that I was just at a point where I was ready to listen – perhaps because she was very successful, perhaps because it made sense, perhaps because she was a complete stranger.

I started to write the odd sentence, then draw a character, then write a bit more … there was no order to it, no plot structure. I wasn't even sure what I was writing, all I knew was that I was interested when I hadn't been before. I think it helped enormously that I wasn't

Illustration

fixated on creating the perfect children's book – it was merely a means to an end, a way to get into something else. I stopped being self-conscious about what I was doing and stopped trying to please everyone else. When I took this book – *Clarice Bean, That's Me* – to publishers, the difference was very obvious – they were all interested! However, no one was willing to take it on – they all thought it was unpublishable and told me so. But I had written something that had at least got their attention.

Listening to publishers

Nearly every publisher made suggestions of what I should change in order for this book to be published, some of them quite fundamental. I was told to drop the illustrations and simplify the text. I was told that varying fonts and integrating text and pictures was too complicated, that it would confuse young readers. I listened to them all; I considered what they had to say, but I knew they were all wrong – I knew they were wrong because I knew I wouldn't be happy with the end result. Because I had written something which felt right to me, it seemed better not to be published at all than to publish a book that wasn't really mine. After four or so long years, I eventually found a publisher who was willing to take the book on pretty much as it was.

And I think this is one of the most important things to know – how far will you go, how far *should* you go to be published? When it comes to this you have to follow your gut instinct. Despite my experience, I do think it is important to listen to what publishers have to say – it is always wise to listen, but it is not always right to take it on board. In the end, they can give you the benefit of their experience, but they cannot write the book for you, and you cannot write the book for them. As the writer, the book has to come from you. Of course, if more than one or two people pick up on the same thing then it may be worth following that advice, but for me it is never worth making a change when, after much consideration, it still feels wrong.

Know who you are writing for

When it comes to the question of writing for the 6–9 year-old market, I would say there is no formula. I don't write for 6–9 year-olds, I write for myself. My books are for anyone who wants to read them. For me, writing young fiction is less about writing for a particular audience or age group and more about telling a story that interests me. I have never thought 'Is this a book for 6–9 year-olds?' or 'Is this a book for 8–12 year-olds?'. I feel the same when writing picture books; they are there to be enjoyed by both adults *and* children because while the child looks at the pictures, it is the adult who usually reads the story.

How does a writer come up with the interesting ideas in the first place? As an adult writing a children's book, is it helpful – even necessary – to have children of your own? My own view is that it is simply irrelevant. First, we have all been children and anyone who wants to write for children must have strong feelings from his or her own childhood to draw upon. But more importantly, good fiction writing is not about imitation – it is about imagination. Just as having children does not mean you have anything to say to them in book form, so not having children is no bar to writing in a manner to which they will respond. Writing for anyone is about having something to say – a point of view. Writing for children is no different. When it comes to writing fiction, I think that any good writer will see children as people first, and as children second. Of course the context of childhood experiences is different from those of adults, but there is no emotion experienced as a child which is not felt equally in adult life.

At the more practical level, I do not believe that there are any fixed rules. I know that many writers plot a book out before they start, and I had always been told that I needed to plot my books and understand where they were going if I was to write successfully. But I never begin writing a book knowing how it is going to end. I never normally know how it is going to start either. I generally just begin with a sentence taken at random. For me, it is all about an idea taking hold, and the writing tends to be more about a feeling than anything. *Clarice Bean, Don't Look Now* began as a book about love and ended up being a book more about loss than anything else. I wrote a few sentences about Clarice's inability to sleep and from that the whole mood of the book was determined. I started to write about insomnia and then wondered why Clarice might experience this, which led to thinking about her worries, which in turn led to the idea that she might be feeling very insecure and start questioning things around her. So, in a way, a few sentences shaped the whole plot because they reflected something that I felt personally at the time. I didn't try to force a story that I wasn't interested in writing; instead it became a book about Clarice's anxieties, her inability to explain the world to herself and some recognition on her part that not only is life something which cannot be controlled, but it's also something which can only be imperfectly understood.

I write a lot of material and read it over and over, until I see what themes are emerging and then I look for a way to hang it all together. Once it has a solid plot, I start to cut. Writing picture books is a very good discipline for writing novels because with just 800 or so words to play with, you have to decide what is important and what isn't: what exactly is this book *about*? Writing picture books makes you much less frightened of editing out the bits that you love. You really can't be indulgent, and have to pare your writing down to the essence of what that story is about. Although, of course, a novel gives you much more freedom – *Don't Look Now* was 42,000 words – I still consciously try to make sure that every chapter is pushing the story forward and has something to say.

A good editor

That brings me on to another important part – your editor. I really have to trust who I am working with. I rely so much on my editor because of the patchwork way I work. A good editor will let you debate back and forth until you've finally reached a point where you know that you can't make something any better. You do have to trust them because it is so easy to lose your perspective about your own work. You may think it's great and not listen to criticism, but more often than not you will get doubtful and think it's all rubbish, and that's where an editor can keep you believing in your work.

If there's a single piece of advice I could offer for writing fiction, it would be to write from the heart. When I wrote *Clarice Bean, That's Me*, I became passionate about what I was writing and found it exciting. If you're bored when you're writing, you will write a boring book. And no matter how hard you find the early stages, keep going. You just need to write and write until you've written the imitation stuff out of you. It is hard but it is very rewarding too. Writing is one of the best things in the world – a licence to discuss ideas – even if it's just with yourself.

Lauren Child's picture books have won many awards, including the Kate Greenaway Medal in 2000 for *I Will Not Ever Never Eat a Tomato* (Orchard Books 2000); the Smarties Gold Award in 2002 for *That Pesky Rat* (Orchard Books 2002); and the Smarties Bronze Award for *Clarice Bean, That's Me* (Orchard Books 1999); *Beware of the Storybook Wolves* (Hodder Children's Books 2000); and *What Planet Are You From, Clarice Bean?* (Orchard Books 2001). In 2002 she published *Utterly Me, Clarice Bean* (Orchard Books), the first of three Clarice Bean novels. Three animated TV series of *Charlie & Lola* have been shown on CBBC and on channels around the world, and the series has won four BAFTAs. From 2011–16 she wrote the *Ruby Redfort* novels (HarperCollin's Children's Books), a six book adventure series for young teens and illustrated new editions of Astrid Lindgren's *Pippi Longstocking* series as well as P.L. Travis' *Mary Poppins* (HarperCollin's Children's Books). Her latest books are *The Goody* (Orchard Books 2020) and *Clarice Bean Think Like An Elf* (HarperCollins 2021). Lauren has written and/or illustrated over 50 books. She was Children's Laureate 2017–19, is a Fellow of the Foundling Museum and a trustee of the House of Illustration. Her websites are www.milkmonitor.me and www.staringintospace.me.

See also...
• *Writing books to read aloud*, page 104

The craft of the illustrator

Salvatore Rubbino describes how he finds inspiration by looking at the world around him with curiosity and wonder, and explains the exciting creative and collaborative process by which sketches and ideas are woven together into finished picture books.

Illustration

Looking is a wonderful thing

As a picture book illustrator, I spend my day drawing and thinking about stories. I love words – the music they make and the taste they leave behind in my mouth – but above all I think in pictures. My task is to shape a tangible graphic world where story events and characters can thrive, a world that the reader can believe in. Pictures are a perfect story-telling tool and stories help to give a context to experience and our lives. We simply can't live without them!

Looking at the world around me is where my ideas come from. Drawing roots me to the spot and turns an initial glance into a long hard stare. It connects me to my surroundings and reminds me how interesting and varied life can be. Looking and drawing is a process of discovery; it helps me to notice the 'overlooked' and feeds my imagination.

We live a good deal of our lives in the humdrum (punctuated every now and then, perhaps, with something extraordinary) but I find the 'everyday' and the tiniest events inspiring and full of poetry. I carry a notebook with me wherever I go, ready to capture those special moments; I have little books for drawing on crowded trains should I see a compelling face, and larger paper that I might lay out on the pavement for more sustained work. I like to collect characters – we are all interesting and everyone comes with a story, and I have certain themes that I often return to. Musicians give the city a rhythm; they perform to be noticed and I have pages full of expressive players, particularly accordionists, so I hope one day to weave my musical drawings into a tale.

I've overheard some astonishing phone conversations whilst out walking – albeit only one half of the exchange (if you're an illustrator you're allowed to be nosey!). We continue to be expressive, pulling faces and gesturing vigorously, even when we can't see the other person on the line, and this gives me the chance to record some wonderfully animated behaviour. I can never pass a group of gossiping ladies without straining to hear what they're talking about and capture them in a picture. To be an illustrator, it's also necessary to cultivate a sense of wonder. This starts with a willingness to look with curiosity and to train the eye to find meaning in everything around you. I'm still learning.

From observation to imagination

City life has always inspired me – almost any street corner will do, although the busier the better, a spot where I can watch little everyday dramas unfold. My first picture book was set in New York (*A Walk in New York*; Candlewick Press 2009) and describes a walk over the course of a day. It follows a real route that a family might attempt (importantly no more than 3km), with stops for lunch and cheesecake – and no doubt the loo, too. It was quite a rigorous process to join up landmarks and beautiful views to form a satisfying sequence. When I was thinking about the characters, I asked myself, 'Well, who do you know?'. In the end I decided to have a dad based on me (more dapper and taller, why not? – after all, anything is possible in a story) and the boy who was a version of my son. At the

Illustration

time my son was only six months old, but I imagined him as a boy aged about seven, in a striped T-shirt and occasionally dragging his tired feet, even though in real life he had not yet learned to walk. I showed both of us craning our necks to look up at the skyscrapers, just as I did on my visit to the Big Apple when collecting ingredients for the book.

As a Londoner, I was excited when asked to make my next walk and subsequent book, *A Walk in London* (Candlewick Press 2011), about 'my' city. When you've lived somewhere all your life it's easy to feel you know it, the challenge was to see the city with fresh eyes. So, I bought a very large sketchbook and set out to audition locations and landmarks for a role in the book. One of my favourite places is Trafalgar Square. There's something quite joyful about a spurting fountain, especially on a hot day when you can put your hand in the water to cool down. I can't think of many national landmarks that you're allowed to climb, but, as long as you're careful, no one actually tells you off if you decide to sit on one of the lions guarding Nelson's column at the heart of the Square.

I am a little embarrassed to admit that I had never seen the Changing of the Guard ceremony in front of Buckingham Palace until I chose to include it in my story. It's a spectacle of synchronised walking accompanied by an orchestra and a cheerful tune. It begins with military precision at 11.27 a.m., and I made sure I had a place in front of the palace in good time, as I knew it would get crowded. And then it happened – an elegant lady wearing a wide-brimmed hat walked out of a side door, accompanied by her entourage; she got into her car and drove away – it was, of course, the Queen! I was astonished, but the encounter triggered an idea. I introduced a 'spot the royals' game, with the royal car weaving its way through the book; it's not mentioned explicitly, but the characters (a girl and her mother this time) receive a royal wave on the last page. I doubt if I would have thought of the idea without this experience of 'meeting the Queen'.

My early visual thinking for all pages in the London book was a flat plan. It records a conversation I had with my publisher when we made decisions about what to include, what to say about London and how to organize everything into a coherent whole. There are crossing outs and several blank pages, so it is still a work in progress. Your publisher or editor may have different opinions, and – whilst it's important to have an honest discussion – it's worth remembering that they want to find the best treatment for the story too. Trust your creative instinct, but also be prepared to listen.

Marshalling your creativity

The text for a story arrives, via the publisher rather than directly from an author, in a compact form – usually a couple of sides of A4, accompanied by a few notes from the publisher ending with 'Please let me know if you're interested' (I'm always very interested!). By the time it reaches me the text has already undergone a rigorous process of rewriting, and has a well-crafted plot and clear point of view. Being invited to illustrate someone else's words is like collaborating with someone else's imagination – it's extremely exciting. I may sometimes meet the author and discuss the project, but our paths don't cross very often. Our relationship is via the publisher, who realises that I need to respond to the text in my own way.

I tend to start with a slow read-through of the story and then I reread it whilst busily scribbling first impressions all over the manuscript. These notes might be about mood, a sense of place, character or anything that's particularly vivid. I don't start work straight away. Instead I let the story sink in over the next few days. I will try to visit places or find aspects of the story that I can see and draw. I don't want to illustrate the text word for word (like a list) but instead I slide up to the story … sideways. I'm trying to find a way into the heart of the story. I'm looking for interesting things to describe, dramatic moments full of visual friction with the potential for mark-making or moments that might allow me to draw the things that I like and a chance to celebrate beauty.

My first drawing attempts for a book are usually quite unrefined. There is no process or formula an illustrator has to follow, or indeed that I follow, for each new project. In every case, I'm meeting the book's characters for the first time, getting to know them and the world they inhabit. I might simply respond to one line or phrase to begin with, until eventually I feel confident enough to start mapping a composition on the page. A book takes time.

I tend to approach a new book rather like a method actor learning a role. *A Book of Feelings* (Walker Books 2015) allowed me to be expressive and play with character in a way I had not tried before. I purchased a mirror so that I could practice a grimace or gesture, in order to draw myself and understand the way in which the child characters in the story might feel and behave and look – even doing a range of voices to help inhabit each emotional state I was depicting. The face has over 40 muscles, which makes it a fantastically elastic communication tool. I try to think about situations in my own life that relate to those described in a story, to provide me with creative inspiration.

What else can illustrators do?

If you are a commissioning editor reading this, I'd like to remind you that illustrators are resourceful people and good problem-solvers. Support them and help to celebrate images together. If you're an author, it's worth adding that illustrators make keen collaborators and will relish the chance to draw your story. And if you're an illustrator, why not consider sharing your appetite for creating pictures? Illustration can be a solitary business, but talking about pictures, running workshops or teaching can be very rewarding, as well as another way to support yourself financially. I'm often invited to take part in festivals and events and I like to cultivate this (time permitting). I also teach, as a visiting tutor, and regularly deliver activities at schools and museums.

I always find watching other people draw or demonstrate a technique quite magical. From humble beginnings something takes shape until it becomes more substantial, to form a face, an animal or a landscape full of life. We all seek to express ourselves, and drawing and creating is a perfect vehicle. People are keen to know 'how it's done' and as an illustrator you can take them on a behind-the-scenes tour.

The picture books I make often have a family at the heart of the story, doing things together; there's friction sometimes, but a good deal of understanding too. Running family activities allows me to observe how children and adults collaborate and eventually find a solution by working together, feeling proud of their achievements by the end of the task. One child might be busy cutting whilst their dad holds the card; another sibling is gluing, untroubled about sticky fingers, and at the same time mum or a grandparent may be helping to colour in. Explaining to others what I do, and thinking about pictures with others, makes me deeply aware of my own creative practice; at the same time it exposes me to lots of refreshingly different points of view – and so, whilst sharing, you never stop learning.

Salvatore Rubbino graduated from the Royal College of Art in 2005. His first picture book, *A Walk in New York*, was published in 2009 by Candlewick Press, followed by *A Walk in London* in 2011. His other books, all published by Walker Books, include *Just Ducks!* (2012) written by Nicola Davies, *A Walk in Paris* (2014), *A Book of Feelings* (2015), *Our Very Own Dog* (2016) written by Amanda McCardie and *Harry Miller's Run* (2015) by David Almond. His latest book is *Ride the Wind* written by Nicola Davies (Walker Books 2020). He received a Booktrust Best New Illustrators Award in 2011.

See also...
- *Finding your voice and point of view*, page 80
- *How to write a picture book*, page 126

Being an illustrator *and* a writer

Writer and illustrator of children's books, Liz Pichon, tells how persistence and hard work – and following the urge to create the kind of books *you* would have enjoyed as a child – can bring successful and very enjoyable results.

Illustration

I always loved drawing and writing stories, but it wasn't something I ever thought I could do for a living. I was a bit hopeless at spelling (and still am). My route to becoming an author came through being asked to work on other people's stories as an illustrator. I found it too stressful sitting around waiting for someone else to give me a job, so I had a go at writing my own picture book ideas to illustrate as well. I already had an agent for my illustration work in books (Caroline Walsh at David Higham Associates), who was very encouraging (and has stuck by me for over 16 years).

My first picture book, *Square Eyed Pat*, was published in 2004. This was followed by *My Big Brother, Boris*, which won the Smarties Book Prize Silver Award (0–5 Years) and gave me more confidence to keep writing and drawing.

This year is the 10th anniversary of my *Tom Gates* series and I have just published the 18th book. The series started life as a picture book idea. Publishers said they liked the format but didn't think there was sufficient story. So eventually, after rewriting it in different formats, I sat down and wrote afresh the first pages in a school exercise book. I imagined Tom writing about a rotten camping holiday he'd had with his family which included his teacher's comments as well as lots of drawings and doodles.

This was about the third (or fourth) go I'd had at it. But when Caroline sent out this version we got seven offers from seven different publishers within two weeks – which of course had NEVER happened to me before.

Here's my advice to anyone who wants to write or illustrate children's books:
• Be persistent. I know lots of people who have had their first efforts turned down or ideas rejected. But if the comments from publishers are positive, keep going and don't give up. Take feedback on board, especially if you're being told the same thing from different publishers. (However, some of my best ideas have lingered around for a while.)
• Think about what kind of books YOU really enjoyed reading when you were a child. I was crazy about a series about a bear called Mary Plain. Looking at them now, I realise that the main stories didn't really engage me, but Mary used to write letters with lots of drawings and doodles as part of them. I loved these bits so much that I would skip through the whole book to devour her letters. This is exactly why the *Tom Gates* books have so many doodles and drawings in them: I wanted to write a book that I would have enjoyed as a child.

The *Children's Writers' & Artists' Yearbook* is a fantastic source of information, STUFFED full of useful FACTS to help you get writing (and drawing). So be sure to make good use of it. And if you're lucky enough to get a book published – ENJOY it! Put together an event and do anything you can to help it along the way. I love going to schools and doing events now, although I found it tricky at first. It's really fantastic to be invited to talk about your books and meet the children and other people who are reading them. I often get ideas from going out and about.

As I look back on ten years of *Tom Gates* and am working on the next book in the series, I can honestly say I've never worked so hard on anything or enjoyed myself so much. So keep going and don't give up!

Here's my feet   not touching the ground

– because that's what has happened to me since *The Brilliant World of Tom Gates* was published in April 2011.

Liz Pichon is a writer and illustrator of children's books, including *A Tale of Two Kitties* (Scholastic 2006), *Bored Bill* (Little TigerPress 2008), *My Big Brother, Boris* (winner of the Smarties Book Prize Silver Award in 2004; Scholastic 2004), *The Very Ugly Bug* (Little Tiger Press 2004), *Spinderella* (Egmont 2002), *Square Eyed Pat* (Puffin 2003), *Penguins* (Gullane Children's Books 2008), *My Little Sister, Doris* (Scholastic 2008) and *The Three Horrid Pigs and the Big Friendly Wolf* (Little Tiger Press 2009). Her first standalone middle-grade title is *Shoe Wars* (Scholastic 2020). 2021 was the 10th anniversary of the *Tom Gates* series; it has sold over 11 million copies, has been a multiple No. 1 children's bestseller and has been translated into 45 languages. The latest title in the series is *Tom Gates: Ten Tremendous Tales* (Scholastic 2021). *The Brilliant World of Tom Gates* won the 2011 Roald Dahl Funny Prize (7–14 Years), the 2012 Red House Children's Book Award (Younger Readers) and the 2012 Waterstones Children's Book Prize (Best Fiction for 5–12s); *Tom Gates – Genius Ideas (Mostly)* won the 2013 Blue Peter Book Award for Best Story; and *Tom Gates – Epic Adventures* won the 2018 LOLLIES Laugh Out Loud Book Award. Liz co-wrote the script for *Tom Gates Live*, which toured around the UK and Ireland in 2019, and co-writes the scripts and songs and presents the DRAW IT section of the Sky Kids TV animated/magazine-style adaptation of *The Brilliant World of Tom Gates*. The first series won a Scottish BAFTA for Best Entertainment in 2021. Find out more on her website http://lizpichon.com/ and follow her on Twitter @LizPichon.

See also...

• *Notes from a successful children's author and illustrator,* page 251

Do judge a book by its cover

Thomas Taylor explains how a good cover can tell you, at a glance, just how it feels to read the book, and he describes the key, defining, attention-grabbing elements that, thanks to the skills of designer, publisher and marketing team, combine to sell your book to the reader.

Not its contents, of course – I would never suggest that the quality of someone's writing or their ability to tell a story can be fairly assessed by how the book appears; but do judge the book as an object – by how it looks on the shelf or feels in your hand – because a lot of effort went into making it that way.

When my middle-grade novel *Malamander* (Walker Books 2019) was being prepared for publication, I was eager to do the cover art myself. I am, after all, an illustrator, and my first published piece of illustration – straight out of art school – was the cover art for *Harry Potter and the Philosopher's Stone* (Bloomsbury 1997) by J.K. Rowling. Editor Barry Cunningham contacted me, after seeing some sample drawings I left at the offices of Bloomsbury, and invited me to make a painting for the cover of a debut book by an unknown author. The brief was simple: paint Harry beside the Hogwarts Express, on Platform Nine and Three Quarters, and then paint a wizard ('any wizard will do') for the back cover. After some to-ing and fro-ing with rough sketches, I produced the paintings, which were then whisked into book cover shape by a designer. At the time I had little inkling what this 'whisking' entailed.

Given this experience – and the years of working on picture books that followed – it seemed only natural that I would do the cover art for my own middle-grade novel too, and not just the incidental interior drawings and the map. Indeed, I'd doodled and sketched right through the process of writing *Malamander*, so I was ready to go. But that's not what happened.

One of the questions I get asked most by up-and-coming writers looking to break into traditional publishing and asking for guidance is: 'Do I need to find an illustrator before I submit to publishers?'. This comes up especially frequently with picture book writers, who correctly sense the importance images will have as a vehicle for their storytelling, but don't always know how to handle it if they're not doing the art themselves. Well, there's some good news. The answer to this is: you *never* need to find an illustrator. Not if you are following the traditional publishing route.

Selecting the right visual match for your writing and storytelling is a complex business, and one the publishers will definitely want to be in control of. Art directors bring enormous expertise to this process, as well as the contact details of some of the best cover artists and designers in the industry. Actually, be *glad* that they'll handle all this for you; querying an agent or prospective publisher as a double act will make you much harder to deal with anyway, and will throw up unnecessary complications that no editor wants to deal with.

When you have a publishing contract, you may get some say in the look of the book – probably further down the line, once the work has essentially been done. But this is likely to be a polite request for comment, rather than an invitation to send the designers back to the storyboard. Well-established writers may be able to exert more influence on the process, perhaps thanks to a clause they (or more likely their agent) were able to insert into the contract. Whether they *should* or not is a point for debate, though; an author may have strong feelings about how the book should look, but their preferences may not marry up with current trends or other marketing factors that could be crucial to a book's success in a highly competitive market.

Sometimes it can be hard when an author sees their cover for the first time and it is nothing like they imagined it would or should be. The publishing process can often appear mysterious and veiled, especially for new writers, who may feel that they are on the receiving end of arcane decisions made in secret conclave. But it's important to trust that the publishers know the market and how to position your book successfully in it, and to remember that they are on your side and have every interest in seeing your book succeed. This isn't to say you shouldn't use your chance to comment on the cover design, or that you should be shy of sharing your ideas. Just be aware that your voice is only one of many.

The first thing I noticed when the cover art for *Malamander* was being discussed was just how many people had input or a say in the process – from publishing and sales directors, through marketing and PR reps, to representatives of export sales, special sales, book club sales, etc. Oh, and designers of course. And that's before factoring in key account (bookshop chains, for example) managers and buyers who will have to actually sell the book, and who may well have strong views on what does or doesn't work on the shop floor. And yes, these views are sometimes strong enough to get a book cover design changed, in order to secure a substantial order.

This process has become more intense since my own experience of producing the cover art for *Harry Potter* back in 1996, due not only to ever-increasing competition in children's fiction but also to the rise of digital platforms. For example, the question of how a cover will display as a thumbnail is more important than ever, because that tiny postage-stamp-sized image that scrolls down an iPhone screen in a second may be the book's only chance to connect with potential readers. If the actual physical book benefits from a foil finish, or sprayed edges or embossed lettering, it still has to look good at just 107 pixels wide by 160 high (standard thumbnail dimensions), where all these flourishes will be invisible. Delicate typography might vanish altogether at that resolution, and subtle artwork become little more than a blob.

For similar reasons, the spine of a book – so often overlooked – might be the only side of your work a browsing reader sees as they scan the shelves. But a good designer can tell them the author's name, the title, the publisher and something of the flavour of the story – all in the narrow strip of paper that holds the book together. And in a way that catches the eye too.

Series recognition and author branding often rests entirely on how that author's books appear. Get this right from the beginning and you can create a graphic language that tells us, at a glance, that the new book by X is out. Often this is achieved simply by choosing (and sticking with) a distinctive font for the author's name and making this the dominating graphic element of the cover. Think Rankin, Ellroy and Le Carré, and now you know where the term 'Big Name author' comes from.

They say a good cover tells you how it will *feel* to read the book. So alongside the practical considerations of text hierarchy – the relative graphic importance of the title, author's name, and straplines and quotes – there are other, less literal design components at play. Photography, painted or decorative elements that conjure a sense of the story for the reader and entice them in, are complex considerations and easy to overdo. Clever font choice can straddle both of these fields, clearly communicating key information, whilst also hinting at the regional or temporal flavour of the story or summing up that elusive 'feel'.

There's only so much 'room' on a book cover. Doing a lot with font, for example, means you can't also add complex imagery without potentially overloading the design and creating a mess that the eye struggles to read at a glance. And when it comes to selling books by cover alone, a glance might be all you get.

What is or is not a good design is not entirely subjective. There are certain key elements that are usually combined to create a harmonious whole: what the book is called and who wrote it; how reading the story will make you feel; how the book can grab attention on displays; how the book cover fares when miniaturised to a thumbnail or glimpsed from across the street in a bookshop window. I now have a far greater appreciation for what designers do than I did when I painted those *Harry Potter* cover pictures way back at the start of my career.

I had my own lesson in the importance of the content of book cover art too, when the wizard I painted for the back cover of *Harry Potter* (the 'any wizard will do' wizard I mentioned at the start) became the subject of much fan speculation, and even consternation. With the rise of Pottermania, the identity of the wizard I originally painted there became the subject of debate – even some conspiracy theories. I was accused by some of having secret advance information about the then unwritten books, and of deliberately leaving clues and toying with readers. Nobody wanted to hear that the character I painted was just a generic wizard based on my own dad! Bloomsbury asked me, some years later, to paint a replacement picture – the image of Albus Dumbledore that most fans seemed to expect – and my father's brief career as an infamous magician came to an end.

In the ever-narrowing bricks-and-mortar retail space, and across the expanding and fiercely visual digital landscape, the appearance of your book has probably never been more important. So while it's still true that a good cover should tell you how it feels to read the book, these days it can't hurt if it also looks stunning on a coffee table, turns heads from across the street or launches a viral 'This was totally a cover buy, but …' Instagram wave.

I didn't do the cover art for *Malamander* in the end. I quickly became overwhelmed by how complex the process was, and how much editing and writing time it would take away. It was genuinely a relief to pass the task over to George Ermos, whose gorgeous art adorns the cover now – subtly suggesting the tone of the story within and how it will feel to read it, whilst also making a splash in a bookshop window. And yes, thanks to George, it also looks fabulous in an Instagram post.

Thomas Taylor is an author and illustrator. He has illustrated and contributed to dozens of books, and has also written and illustrated four of his own picture books, including *The Loudest Roar* (2003) and *The Biggest Splash* (2005), both published by OUP. His most recent books, in the *Legends of Eerie-on-Sea* series published by Walker Books for middle-grade readers, are *Malamander* (2019), *Gargantis* (2020) and *Shadowghast* (2021). For more information see www.thomastaylor-author.com; follow him on Twitter @ThomasHTaylor.

See also...
• *Being an illustrator* and *a writer*, page 259

Illustration

How to create a graphic novel

Isabel Greenberg has valuable advice for the would-be graphic novelist, provides tried-and-tested practical rules and tips for visual storytellers, and shares her knowledge of this creative and engaging medium.

Contrary to how they are often presented, graphic novels (or comics) are not a genre – like science fiction or fantasy or crime or historical fiction, but a medium – like film, poetry, interpretative dance or prose novels. They are a way of telling stories. I can introduce you to some of the conventions or 'un-conventional' aspects of this medium and talk you through my own process, but to instruct you in how to create a graphic novel in one short article is as impossible a task as instructing someone on how to write a novel or make a film. That said, what I can do is tell you how I make *my* graphic novels. I'll present you with some tips, pointers and thoughts that I think might be useful for anyone embarking on this creative route … for it is a mammoth undertaking.

Definitions

Whether you choose to call it a graphic novel or a comic book, or just a story told in pictures, is entirely up to you. For me, if it's the length of a novel, I call it a graphic novel. This doesn't mean its content is necessarily more 'highbrow' than your average comic; for me it simply denotes the length of the book. A short episodic periodical or a zine, regardless of its content, I would refer to as a comic. But hot debate surrounds this issue, with many comic fans feeling that the term 'graphic novel' has been used to make the medium more palatable to audiences who might balk at reading 'comic books'. I tend to feel that whether this is true or not doesn't matter, so long as it means more readers are willing to access this wonderful medium.

Where to start?

With your story of course – and how you begin to find this is up to you. For some writers, a character might be their catalyst; for others it's a plot or premise. This is a visual medium, however, so that is something worth thinking about. Much as a film-maker might struggle to make an arresting film that takes place entirely in a pitch-black room, so you, as a visual storyteller, might also (that being said, you may be up for a challenge!).

As with standard novels, graphic novels encompass a vast array of genres. You can read a graphic novel adventure, a thriller, horror, biography or history. And yes, there are graphic novels that feature superheroes! Autobiography is extremely popular too; the most well-known examples of the medium are *Persepolis* by Marjane Satrapi (Jonathan Cape 2003) and *Maus* by Art Speigelman (Pantheon Books 1991), to name two of the most seminal.

Many graphic novelists write and draw their own books. I am one of these. But if you are an aspiring writer who would like to team up with an artist, that is also possible. Some publishers may be willing to help facilitate this but, with such a visual medium, it is hard to pitch the project on words alone, and you might want to consider approaching an artist to work on the pitch with you. A note here: do not ask an artist to illustrate your graphic novel pitch free of charge, unless you are equally invested artistic partners in the project.

If you need someone to facilitate your vision, you must pay for this service. Illustrating a graphic novel is an extremely complex and time-consuming task.

For me, everything starts with the story. I would not even begin to sketch or imagine characters or setting until I had the bare bones of a premise to work upon. Even my first book, which was set in an imaginary world called Early Earth, started with a creation story, rather than the building of the world itself. Many people like to start by building the world, but this aspect can be addictive, and your world can swiftly become too huge to handle. Remember that you are sculpting a narrative; the richer your world, the better. Of course, you can and should know all the back stories and places that go on off the page – but keep your focus on the story you want to tell in your book.

My most recent graphic novel, *Glass House* (Jonathan Cape 2020), began with research, as it is part biography, part fantastical interpretation of the Bronte siblings' childhood world-building. Many graphic novelists write their words like a film script. I do this to some extent, but I often play with writing as prose, and I'll frequently break off from the script to draw little moments or scenes so I can see how they might play out.

Rules to break or keep

I won't tell you how many panels should be on a page, or how many words should be in a speech bubble. Some of my favourite graphic novels are totally silent, such as *The Arrival* by Shaun Tan (Hachette Children's 2007) and *Bad Island* by Stanley Donwood (Hamish Hamilton 2020), and some have so many words it's almost a challenge to separate them from the images, so of course these rules and conventions are there to be broken. But there are a few important maxims I do try to stick to:

• One action per panel

You cannot direct a character to cross a room and open a window in a single panel (writers who have written for film are often the worst culprits in this area). You are working with still images. A character may be pictured mid-stride, crossing a room in the first panel, and opening a window in the next.

• Communication is paramount

Test your story out on a reader at every point. If they do not understand what is happening, if your images are too oblique or you have too much going on, then you will need to adapt. I particularly like to test my work out on readers who are not familiar with, or do not read a lot of, this medium. If a reader does not understand what you want them to, then you need to rethink how you are telling the story. Writers who work with artists can sometimes assume that the images can clear up confusing motives or explain things they do not want to say in words. Sometimes this is the case, but remember that – unlike with film – you cannot control how long your reader lingers on a moment or panel, or puzzles over the expression and emotion of a character. If there is something important you want them to know, you must endeavour to communicate it. Above all, remember that if your reader doesn't understand something, this is not their fault; the responsibility is on you, as the creator, to convey your own message adequately.

• If a moment is important, make them stay

I just said above that you cannot control how long a reader lingers on a panel. This is quite true, but you can certainly try. If a moment is important, emotionally or as a crux to your story, let your reader know this. You could signify it with a full bleed spread for example (this is a single image that runs the entire width and height of your double page). It can create impact if not used too frequently in your story. This might be a point of emotional significance, or perhaps a scene-setting moment – to introduce a character's arrival in a certain setting, or to show a moment of excitement or action.

• The page-turn is powerful

Don't show a big reveal as the last panel on a spread or page. Your reader will first see the page as one image before their eye adjusts and they read it as panels. This means you cannot stop spoilers if you show them on the same page. If you have a surprise, let the reader discover it as they turn the page.

• If your picture is saying something, your words don't need to

If your images are showing or saying something, then there is no need for you to say it in words too. If your image shows a character looking into a beautiful sunrise, you do not need to say '[XX] looked at the beautiful sunrise'. But you might use your words to say something your image cannot convey, or to add another layer to the narrative: '[XX] had not seen a sunrise for nearly a year'. Or you may choose to let the image breathe, and speak for itself, letting your reader decide what your character is feeling at this moment of sunrise contemplation.

I tend to use narration in my work, rather than leaving the story to be told purely through dialogue and action. But this is a stylistic choice, and many writers and artists will try to avoid narration; it can seem like unnecessary, or obvious, exposition. I do use such exposition to capitalise on the humour of having an omniscient narrative voice.

• Consider keeping your text on a separate layer

Whether you are hand lettering or using a font, this is worth considering. In all likelihood, your editor may come back to you with tweaks or spelling and grammatical corrections. I found early on that if I kept my text on a separate layer to my artwork, this made shuffling and changing much easier. Furthermore, it meant that when the works went into foreign translation, I was able to easily provide my font (which I made from my own handwriting) when appropriate, and when it needed to be re-lettered (for different alphabets) my text was easy to remove.

Pitching

Most publishers will require a full synopsis and plot breakdown, as well as at least six to ten example spreads, showing your words and artwork together. Some will require even more of a completed script. When choosing your example spreads, pick a variety that can show your range. Perhaps you want some quiet, some dialogue-heavy spreads, and some action or full-page images, if your story will call for these, so that they can see the full visual scope of the story.

You may choose to approach an agent to represent you before approaching a publisher. Choose who you approach prudently. Not all publishers or agents will be right for your work. Pick a selection of graphic novels by writers or artists whose work you feel has a parallel with your own stylistically, and see who publishes or represents them. Remember you have to appeal to a publisher both visually and in terms of your story; one is no good without the other. Consider both of these things when deciding who to approach. Look through a publishers' back catalogue and see if they have a house 'style'. Don't attempt to change your work to fit that style, but do bear it in mind if you get a rejection – they just may not be the right place for you. An agent can advise you on this, and will guide you through the process of pitching, should you choose to get one.

Making graphic novels your profession

Be aware that even the most generous advance from a publisher is unlikely to be enough for you to live on entirely whilst you make your book. The market is neither as large, nor as lucrative, as regular fiction, and the advances publishers offer will sadly reflect this. Most graphic novelists and comic artists will have several strings to their bow. Some may also do children's books, freelance writing, commercial illustration, hire themselves out to be the artist on another writers' work or have another day job completely.

And finally ...

Good luck! Graphic novels are a mammoth undertaking. But they are also a unique medium in that you have the power to do absolutely everything: you are in charge of set design, lighting, script, costume and location. You are the director of your own world, and it can be created without having to source a million-dollar budget and deal with a staff of hundreds. This is a wonderful thing, so enjoy it.

Illustrator and writer **Isabel Greenberg** studied Illustration at the University of Brighton and completed an MA at the Royal College of Art in experimental animation. Her bestselling graphic novels, all published by Jonathan Cape in the UK, are *The Encyclopaedia of Early Earth* (2013), winner of the Best Book category at the British Comic Awards, *The One Hundred Nights of Hero* (2016), a *New York Times* Graphic Books Bestseller and *Glass Town* (2020). Her work also includes comics and illustration, animation and children's books. See www.isabelgreenberg.co.uk for more information, and follow her on Twitter @isabelgreenberg and @isabel_greenberg on instagram.

Eight great tips to get your picture book published

Tony Ross gives some sound advice for illustrators and writers of children's picture books.

I have always had the uncomfortable feeling that if I can get published, anyone can. A belief that being published is something that only happens to other people, holds some very good writers and illustrators back.

Assuming you have drawings – or a story – to offer, there are several ways to go about it. Probably the best way is to have a publishing house in the family! Failing that, all is not lost.

Work can be sent directly to a publisher's office. Most editors receive a good amount of unsolicited work, so be patient with them for a reply. A stamped addressed envelope for the return of postal submissions is always appreciated, bearing in mind that the majority of work submitted is refused. At the beginning of a career, refusal is quite normal and a great deal about yourself and your talent can be gleaned from this experience. Sometimes, advice gained at this stage can change your future.

Starting on a drawing career is an exciting time and I think it's a good idea to get yourself in perspective. Visit the library and some bookshops to look at all the styles that are around. Get a sense for what's out there: you don't want to regurgitate it, but to get a feel for the parameters. You can learn a lot, maybe more than you learned at art school, from looking at great artists such as Edward Ardizzone, E.H. Shepard, Maurice Sendak and Chris Van Allsburg.

Great Tip No. 1: Use black and white

There is great appeal in working in full colour but it's good to remember black and white. Sometimes a publisher may have a black and white project waiting for an illustrator, while all of the big interest is going into the colour picture book list. Some of the greatest children's books are illustrated in black and white – A.A. Milne and E.H. Shepard made one of the greatest partnerships with those tiny black ink drawings contributing so much to a great classic. Not a bad place to start, eh?

Ink drawing is simple in the hands of a master but not easy. That unforgiving fluid! Wonder at the uncomplicated, straightforwardness of the Pooh drawings. Consider Toad in *The Wind in the Willows*. When he applied to do the illustrations, Kenneth Graham said to Shepard: 'I have seen many artists who can draw better than you, but you make the animals live.' Can you learn anything from that? Look at Ardizzone's ability to draw mood. He can show both a summer afternoon and a cold November morning simply by using black ink. There is so much to look at, so much to learn from.

Try to include black and white work in your folder. Also include a series of perhaps 30 drawings, such as a fully illustrated story, where you show your ability to be consistent with the characters and the style, without repetition or irrelevance (like the radio programme *Just a Minute*).

It is a duty of an illustrator to be able to read, i.e. to try and understand the writer's aims, and to help them rather than to inflict a totally different angle onto the book (again, think of the Milne and Shepard partnership). Much of this comes down to being sensitive enough to recognise the tone of the writing, and skilful enough to draw in the same tone. So the importance of really taking an interest in the story cannot be overstressed. In the text, there will be either clues or blatant instructions to help the drawings gel. Be very aware.

Great Tip No. 2: Experiment

I have known illustrators who convinced themselves that they couldn't use black ink. Mostly this was because they were using the wrong ink, the wrong pen and/or the wrong paper. Types of black ink vary: waterproof behaves differently from water soluble. Fine nibs and broad nibs each give a totally different result, as does an old fountain pen or a sharpened stick. Try ten different inks, 50 different nibs, odd sticks and all the papers you can find: tracing, layout, calendered, five different cartridges, smooth and rough water-colour, handmade, wrapping paper, anything at all. It's a case of finding the combination that suits your hand and your intention. Your own genius, unrecognised at art school, could surprise you.

Many of the points I've made about black and white work also apply to colour. The marriage of image to text will be in your hands, but it must work.

Great Tip No. 3: Choose the right words

I am hesitant to give advice to writers. After all, there are few rules, and the next J.K. Rowling may read this. My own view is really quite simple, and rather obvious. I write mainly for under eight year-olds, so my stories are as short as I can make them. I feel that it is good to have a magnetic first sentence, and an ending that EXPLODES WITH SURPRISE. I think that the ending is the most important part of the story. The bit in the middle should waft the reader along, remembering that the *sound* of words and sentences can be a useful tool.

I like stories to be either funny or scary. *Very* funny, or *very* scary. To be dull is the worst thing in the world! That sounds so obvious, but it gets overlooked. If you are not excited with your work, maybe nobody else will be either.

A picture book has about 23 pages of text (but this can be flexible). I think those pages should have fewer than 2,000 words; 1,000–1,500 is good. One word per page would be great, if the one word was brilliant. As brilliant as the story. Don't be frightened of editing out surplus words. One brilliant one will work better than a dozen mundane ones.

Don't fall into the mindset that writing for children is easy. It has all the disciplines of writing for adults, with the added problem of understanding a child's mind and world. The great writers have a passport to a child's world – think of Roald Dahl. I have seen many brilliant ideas, with less than brilliant pictures, make wonderful books. I have seen a bad idea saved by wonderful illustrations. So, writing style apart, be your own concept's greatest critic. It is quite natural to be protective of your baby, of your story. But try to remember that there are a lot of good editors out there and it will be in your own interest to consider their advice. So don't be a young fogey: be flexible, listen, understand experienced points of view. This can be a good time to change for the better, and to start a relationship with one publishing house that may serve you for a lifetime.

Illustration

Great Tip No. 4: Choose what you draw

Don't plan huge drawing problems into your submitted roughs. They may be accepted, and the editor will expect the final art to be better than the roughs.

I illustrate my own writing. This appeals to me for all sorts of reasons, few of them noble. Firstly, I get all of the available fee and/or royalty because I don't have to let half or more go to a writer. Secondly, if there is something I don't like to draw, I don't write about it. For instance, most of my stories take place in the summer, because I prefer to handle trees with their leaves on.

Illustrations being worked on to be published is not the place to practise your drawing. *Practise, change, experiment* all the time, but not in a publishing project. Your finished illustrations must be as good as you can make them. I know an illustrator who won't draw feet, always hiding the ends of legs in grass, water, behind rocks, etc. This is okay if the text will allow; a well-drawn puddle is better than a badly drawn foot any day. It is better to think around a drawing problem, than just to go along with it.

Great Tip No. 5: Experiment with your main character

Before you start, try drawing your main character (the most important visual element of the story) in all sorts of ways. A day spent doing this can be so valuable. Getting the main character right can indicate ways to proceed with the whole book.

Great Tip No. 6: Think global

Remember that editors react well to stories with wide appeal, rather than niche interests. Foreign sales are in everyone's interest, so try to allow your work to travel. Rhyme is sometimes difficult to translate, as are unusual plays on words.

Great Tip No. 7: Plan the whole book

Do little mock-up books for yourself to plan what text goes on which page. This helps to get the story right throughout the book. A 32-page children's book (the most common extent for a picture book) includes covers, end papers, title and half-title pages. This leaves you 23–25 pages to play with. These little mock-ups are for your own use, not to be presented as roughs, so they can be quite workaday.

By working out what text goes on which page you will get some sort of an idea of which illustrations go where. Just as the drawings are creative, so is their use on the page. If you use a full double-page spread, another can be expected to follow it. But imagine the effect if the next page explodes with huge typography and tiny pictures? I am not suggesting you do this, only reminding you that pages of a book are there to be turned, and the turning can be unpredictable and adventurous. Book design is important, along with everything else.

Great Tip No. 8: Persevere

So much to do, so much to remember. The main thing is, every children's illustrator and writer I know who has kept trying has got there in the end and been published. But I've also seen great talents give up far too early. Remember that rejection is normal: it's only someone's point of view. Some great books have had long hunts for a publisher. Be open to change and always bear in mind that editors have the experience that you may lack and an editor's advice is meant to help you, not choke you off. However, not all of their advice may apply in your case, so try to recognise what applies to you. When I worked in advertising, I had an art director who said: 'Half of what I say is rubbish. Trouble is, I don't know which half.'

And a reminder
Don't waste time by sending work to publishers who don't publish material like yours. Libraries and bookshops are worth exploring to familiarise yourself with which publishing houses favour what types of work. Research of this kind is time well spent.

Try to show your work in person so that you get a chance to talk, and learn. Do not, however, just drop in. Make an appointment first and hope that these busy people have some time available.

There are also agents prepared to represent new talent (see *Illustrators' agents* on page 272). Of course, an agent will take a percentage of the fee for work sold, but as my dad used to say, '75% of something is better than 100% of nothing.'

I am troubled by giving advice. I can't help thinking of the young composer who approached the slightly older Mozart and asked, 'Maestro, how should I compose a concerto?' to which Mozart replied, 'You are very young, perhaps you should start with a simple tune'.

The young composer frowned and argued: 'But, Maestro, *you* composed a concerto when you were still a child!'

'Ah yes,' said Mozart, 'but I didn't have to ask how'.

Tony Ross is a renowned illustrator of international repute and the creator of such classics as *The Little Princess* and *I Want My Potty*. His first book was published in 1976 and since then he has illustrated around 3,000 books including titles by David Walliams, Astrid Lindgren, Francesca Simon, Roald Dahl and Jeanne Willis. His most recent books are *I Want a Bunny!* and *I Don't Want to Wash My Hands!* both published by Andersen Press in 2020.

See also...
- *Notes from a successful children's author and illustrator*, page 251
- *How to create a graphic novel*, page 264

Illustrators' agents

Before submitting work, artists are advised to make preliminary enquiries and to ascertain terms of work. Commission varies but averages 25–30%. The Association of Illustrators (see page 343) provides a valuable service for illustrators, agents and clients.

*Member of the Society of Artists Agents
†Member of the Association of Illustrators

Advocate Art Ltd
Suite 7, The Sanctuary, 23 Oakhill Grove, Surbiton, Surrey KT6 6DU
tel 020-8390 6293
email mail@advocate-art.com
website www.advocate-art.com
Director Edward Burns

Has seven agents representing 300 artists and illustrators. Bespoke illustration for children's books, greeting cards and fine art publishers, gift and ceramic manufacturers. For illustrators' submission guidelines see website. Animation, design and original content represented through LaB – Writers and Artists colLaBorate. Also original art gallery, stock library and website in German, Spanish and French. Founded 1996.

Allied Artists/Artistic License
tel 07971 111256
email info@allied-artists.net
website www.alliedartists-illustration.com
Contact Gary Mills

Represents over 90 illustrators ranging in styles from realistic through stylised to cute for all types of publishing but particularly children's illustration. Commission: 35%. Founded 1983.

Arena Illustration Ltd*†
31 Eleanor Road, London E15 4AB
tel 020-8555 9827
website www.arenaillustration.com
Contact Tamlyn Francis

Represents 27 artists. Average commission: 25%. Founded 1970.

The Art Agency
21 Morris Street, Sheringham, Norfolk NR26 8JY
tel (01263) 823424
email artagency@me.com
website www.the-art-agency.co.uk
Facebook www.facebook.com/illustrationagency

Provides non-fiction, reference and children's book illustration. Specialises in non-fiction illustrations across a wide variety of subjects and age groups. Submit up to six samples by email along with a link to your website. Founded 1990.

The Artworks†
64 Cranbourne Avenue, London E11 2BQ
email submissions@theartworksinc.com
website www.theartworksinc.com
Contacts Stephanie Alexander-Jinks, Alex Hadlow, Lucy Scherer

Represents 35 illustrators for design and advertising work as well as for non-fiction children's books, book jackets, illustrated gift books and children's picture books. Commission: 30% design and advertising, 25% publishing advances, 15% royalties, 25% book jackets. Founded 1983.

Astound US Inc
Suite 143, 61 Victoria Road, Surbiton KT6 4JX
tel 07465 772271
email contact@astound.us
website https://astound.us/publishing/
Director Vince Verma

A new kind of artist representation business based in New York City and London. Offers contemporary children's book illustration, and both licensing and commercial art from around the world.

Beehive Illustration
42A Cricklade Street, Cirencester, Glos. GL7 1JH
tel (01285) 644001
email enquiries@beehiveillustration.co.uk
website www.beehiveillustration.co.uk
Contact Paul Beebee

Represents 200 artists specialising in ELT, education and general children's publishing illustration. Commission: 25%. Founded 1989.

The Big Red Illustration Agency
tel 0808 120 0996
email enquiries@bigredillustrationagency.com
website www.bigredillustrationagency.com
Facebook www.facebook.com/thebigredillustrationagency
Twitter @big_red_author
Director Adam Rushton

Represents a number of professional illustrators. Over the years has developed strong relationships with a wide range of clients including children's book publishers, design agencies, greeting card companies and toy manufacturers. Founded 2012.

The Bright Agency

103–105 St John's Hill, London SW11 1SY
tel 020-7326 9140
US Office 50 West Street, C12, New York, NY 10006
tel +1 646-604-0992
email mail@thebrightagency.com
website www.thebrightagency.com
Founder (UK) Vicki Willden-Lebrecht, *Director*
Arabella Stein

Areas of representation include: children's publishing (picture books, children's fiction and non-fiction, activity books, novels, pre-school), advertising and design, animation, editorial film and television rights management, greetings and gift, art licensing, toys and games, fabric and apparel, home and gift and brand development and management. For submissions guidelines see website. No submissions by post. Clients include: Benji Davies, David Litchfield, Yasmeen Ismail, Chris Chatterton, Diane Ewen, Fiona Woodcock, Laura Hughes, Galia Bernstein, Mechal Roe, Zoe Perisco, Aura Lewis, Beatrice Blue, Karl James Mountford. Founded 2002.

Jenny Brown Associates – see page 237

The Catchpole Agency

53 Cranham Street, Oxford OX2 6DD
tel 07789 588070
email james@thecatchpoleagency.co.uk
email celia@thecatchpoleagency.co.uk
website www.thecatchpoleagency.co.uk
Proprietors James Catchpole, Celia Catchpole

Agents for authors and illustrators of children's books from picture books through to young adult novels, with a specialism in editorial work. See website for contact and submissions details. See also page 237. Founded 1996.

The Copyrights Group Ltd

3 Pancras Square, London N1C 4AG
tel 020-3880 0134
email info@copyrightsgroup.com
website www.copyrightsgroup.com
SVP UK Licensing & Retail Rachel Clarke, *SVP Brand
& International Licensing* Polly Emery, *VP Creative
Services* Demi Patel

Full-service international brand licensing company offering strategic worldwide brand development, licensing and retail expertise. Focuses on the long-term development of IP and quality merchandise programmes. Properties include *Paddington Bear, Mush-Mush and the Mushables, Father Christmas, Fungus The Bogeyman.* Founded 1984.

Darley Anderson Illustration Agency

Unit 19, Matrix Studios, 91 Peterborough Road, London SW6 3BU
tel 020-7385 6652
website www.darleyandersonillustration.com
Twitter @Illustration_da

Instagram @darleyanderson_illustration
Managing Director Clare Wallace, *Directors* Darley Anderson, Rosanna Bellingham

Represents bestselling and award-winning illustrators including Jo Brown, Harry Goldhawk, Zanna Goldhawk, Sojung Kim-McCarthy, Aleesha Nandhra, Lorna Scobie and Helene Weston. Works across all areas of publishing, from picture books to gift titles to graphic novels, across fiction and non-fiction, collaborating with both adult and children's publishers worldwide. Actively looking for new talent, especially illustrators from under-represented backgrounds. Commission: 20%. Submission guidelines: send an email with portfolio attached as a pdf or in the body of the email, along with information about yourself and links to social media channels used to display your work. Author-illustrators should send texts as pdf or Word attachments, along with a brief synopsis and illustration samples. Submissions should be made directly to the agent of choice. Founded 1988.

David Lewis Illustration Agency

3 Somali Road, London NW2 3RN
tel 020-7435 7762 / 07931 824674
email info@davidlewisillustration.com
Director David Lewis, *Associate* Lisa Britton

Representing approx. 25 illustrators creating different styles in varying mediums, mostly for all areas of children's publishing, including educational, merchandising and toys. Also considers complete picture books with text. Send A4 colour or b&w copies of samples with sae. Commission: 30%. Founded 1974.

Good Illustration Ltd

71–75 Shelton Street, Covent Garden, London WC2H 9JQ
tel 020-8123 0243 (UK) / +1 347-627-0243 (US)
email draw@goodillustration.com
website www.goodillustration.com
Directors Doreen Thorogood, Kate Webber, Tom Thorogood

Represents 50+ artists for advertising, design, publishing and animation. Send sae and samples. Commission: 25% publishing, 30% advertising. Founded 1977.

Graham-Cameron Illustration

59 Hertford Road, Brighton BN1 7GG
tel (01273) 385890
email enquiry@gciforillustration.com
Alternative address The Art House, Uplands Park, Sheringham, Norfolk NR26 8NE
tel (01263) 821333
website www.gciforillustration.com
Partners Helen Graham-Cameron, Duncan Graham-Cameron

Represents 37+ artists and undertakes illustration for publishing and communications. Specialises in educational, children's and information books. Phone before sending A4 samples with sae or email samples or link to a website. No MSS. Founded 1985.

David Higham Associates Ltd – see page 240

IllustrationX*†

4th Floor, Silverstream House, 45 Fitzroy Street, London W1T 6EB
tel 020-7720 5202
email hello@illustrationx.com
website www.illustrationx.com/uk
Facebook www.facebook.com/weareillustrationx
Twitter @illustrationx

Welcomes submissions from illustrators and animators whose work is distinctive and innovative. Only accepts applications from artists through submissions page: www.illustrationx.com/applications. Founded 1929.

Inky Illustration

483 Green Lanes, London N13 4BS
tel 0121 330 1312
email info@inkyillustration.com
website https://inkyillustration.com/
Facebook www.facebook.com/inkyillustration
Twitter @inkyillo

The range of illustrators have experience working with clients, on international advertising campaigns, publications and editorials, as well as commissions for smaller companies. Always happy to receive new work. New artists should fill out the form on the website or email: submissions@inkyillustration.com. Hard copies of work are accepted with a sae if the work is to be returned. Founded 2009.

B.L. Kearley Art & Antiques

Glebe House, Bakers Wood, Denham, Bucks. UB9 4LG
tel (01895) 832145
email christine.kearley@kearley.co.uk
website www.kearley.co.uk
Agent C.R. Kearley

Represents 30+ artists. Mainly specialises in children's book and educational illustration for the domestic market and overseas. Known for realistic figurative work. Specialises in the sale of original book illustration artwork. Commission: 25%. Founded 1948.

Kids Corner

1 Mailing Street, West Street, Lewes BN7 2NZ
tel 020-7593 0506
email claire@meiklejohn.co.uk
website www.kidscornerillustration.co.uk
Managing Director Claire Meiklejohn

Represents illustrators, from award-winning to emerging artists for children's publishing. Styles include fun, cute, stylised, picture book, young fiction, reference, graphic, traditional, painterly and digital. Founded 2015.

Lemonade Illustration Agency

Hill House, Suite 231, 210 Upper Richmond Road, London SW15 6NP
tel 07891 390750
email gary@lemonadeillustration.com
US office 347 Fifth Ave, Suite 1402, New York, NY 10016
website www.lemonadeillustration.com

Represents 180+ illustrators and character designers for all kinds of media from TV to children's books. Offices in London, New York, Sydney, Dubai and Wakefield. Works with leading children's, kidslit, ELT and educational publishers. Any submissions from illustrators by email must contain a website link (no attachments) or hard copies of samples can be sent by post with a sae to the London office. Cannot reply to all emails submissions received. Founded 2004.

Frances McKay Illustration

17 Church Road, West Mersea, Essex CO5 8QH
tel (01206) 383286
email frances@francesmckay.com
website www.francesmckay.com
Proprietor Frances McKay

Represents 15–20 artists for illustration mainly for children's books. For information on submissions please look at website. Submit email with low-res scans or colour copies of recent work; sae essential for return of all unsolicited samples sent by post. Commission: 25%. Founded 1999.

The Monkey Feet Illustration Directory

email enquiries@monkeyfeetillustration.com
website www.monkeyfeetillustration.com

Presents portfolios for artists creating work for children's book publishers, design agencies, greeting cards and toy companies. Founded 2012.

NB Illustration*

Home Farm, East Horrington, Somerset BA5 3EA
tel 07720 827328
email info@nbillustration.co.uk
website www.nbillustration.co.uk
Directors Joe Najman, Charlotte Dowson

Represents 50+ artists, 40% of whom produce children's material for picture books and educational publishing. For submission details see website. Commission: 30%. Founded 2000.

Plum Pudding Illustration Agency

Chapel House, St. Lawrences Way, Reigate, Surrey RH2 7AF
tel (01737) 244095

email letterbox@plumpuddingillustration.com
website www.plumpuddingillustration.com
Directors Mark Mills, Hannah Whitt

Represents 100+ artists and authors, producing texts and illustrations for children's publishing, advertising, editorial, greeting cards and packaging. See website for submission procedure. Commission: 30%. Founded 2006.

Sylvie Poggio Artists Agency
62 Ainsdale Road, London W5 1JX
tel 07775 894870
email sylvie-P@sylviepoggio.com
website www.sylviepoggio.com
Facebook www.facebook.com/Sylvie-Poggio-Artists-agency-700285410097943
Twitter @sylviepoggioart
Directors Sylvie Poggio, Bruno Caurat

Represents 40 artists producing illustrations for publishing and advertising. Founded 1996.

Elizabeth Roy Literary Agency
White Cottage, Greatford, Nr Stamford, Lincs. PE9 4PR
tel (01778) 560672
website http://elizabethroy.co.uk/

Handles illustrations for children's books. Only interested in exceptional material. Illustrators should research the children's book market before sending samples, which must include figure work. Send by post with sae; no CD, disk or email submissions. See also page 243. Founded 1990.

Caroline Sheldon Literary Agency Ltd
71 Hillgate Place, London W8 7SS
tel 020-727 9102
email info@carolinesheldon.co.uk
website www.carolinesheldon.co.uk
Twitter @CarolineAgent
Twitter @FelicityTrew
Contacts Caroline Sheldon, Felicity Trew

Represents leading illustrators working in a broad range of styles, selling their work throughout the world and in all media. All genres of illustration. Commission: UK 15%, USA/translation 20%, film/TV 20%. Submission guidelines: Send an introductory email with work attached or a link to your work. In the subject line write 'Proposal from Illustrator', and include information about yourself and your work in the email. Clients: represents prominent, award-winning and bestselling clients in all fields including books, illustration, audio, digital and theatre. Works closely with a media agent on

Film, TV and other opportunities. See al[...]
Founded 1985.

The Soho Agency Ltd
16–17 Wardour Mews, 2nd Floor, Londo[...]
tel 020-7471 7900
website www.thesohoagency.co.uk
Contacts Philippa Milnes-Smith

Illustrators for children's publishing for children 0–16 years. See website for submission requirements. Special interests: authors/artists creating their own projects, projects with cross media potential, illustrators from diverse backgrounds, original talent. Commission: 15% (20% overseas). Clients include Lauren Child, Emily Gravett, Chris Judge, Steve McCarthy, Jane Porter, Chris Riddell and Niamh Sharkey. See also page 243. Founded 1996.

Tallbean
tel (01728) 454921
email heather@tallbean.co.uk
website www.tallbean.co.uk
Founder Heather Richards

Provides specialist illustrators offering a range of styles. The team of well-established and creative illustrators is kept relatively small to ensure a close working relationship. Founded 1996.

Vicki Thomas Associates
195 Tollgate Road, London E6 5JY
tel 020-7511 5767
email vickithomasassociates@yahoo.co.uk
website www.vickithomasassociates.com
Twitter @VickiThomasA
Instagram @VickiThomasA
Consultant Vicki Thomas

Represents approx. 30 artists, 75% of whom produce children's material for all ages. Specialises in gift products and considers images for publishing, toys, stationery, clothing, decorative accessories. Email sample images, covering letter and CV. Commission: 30%. Founded 1985.

United Agents LLP
12–26 Lexington Street, London W1F 0LE
tel 020-3214 0800
email info@unitedagents.co.uk
website www.unitedagents.co.uk
Agents Jodie Hodges, Emily Talbot

Illustrators of children's books for all ages (commission: home 15%, USA/translation 20%). See website for submission details. Founded 2008.

Illustration

Magazines and newspapers
Writing for teens

Chloe Rhodes describes the possibilities, challenges and rewards of writing for today's teenage magazine market, explains what writers need to bear in mind to find that crucial, supportive connection with young readers, and provides essential tips on how to pitch your own ideas for features.

In a market that's often overly focused on looks, fashion and lifestyle, our magazine, *Teen Breathe*, gives attention to the fabric of readers' inner lives. It exists to provide a safe, reassuring and uplifting space at a time when many young adults are facing a crisis of confidence and experiencing worries that affect their physical and mental wellbeing. Published every seven weeks in print along with a digital edition, it's aimed at 11-14 year-olds (though some readers are as young as eight); its message is that *all* feelings and ways of being are valid, all questions readers might be asking themselves are normal, and that there are all kinds of ways to slow the pace and make meaningful connections in the world. Based on the experience I've had connecting with our readers (all 30,000 of them) at *Teen Breathe*, here is my advice on how to write for this demanding but rewarding market.

Pick 'n' mix

Teen Breathe tries, in myriad ways, to suggest that thinking about who you are, why you feel as you do, and how you experience the world can be enriching, especially during the formative teen years. That's not to say, however, that every feature has to offer profound insight or a therapeutic message. Creativity, humour and lightness are crucial ingredients too. Although they fall into the catch-all category of 'teens', our readers are as individual and unique as the rest of the population. Their family circumstances, cultural backgrounds, maturity levels, hobbies and interests vary wildly. As a result, we have no set list of subjects to constrain new contributors – just let the imagination flow! What the most powerful features we publish have in common is a) a curious approach, b) thorough, fact-backed research, and c) the sense that there might be something interesting for readers to glean … something that sheds light on themselves or the world they're beginning to explore.

For would-be contributors, choosing a subject can be liberating and fun. The young reader's thirst for knowledge means that things adults might take for granted, like pot plants, book groups or their sense of smell, can be approached with fresh wonder. In every issue we aim for a mixture of topics, so pieces might range from bullying to baking, grief to gardening, perhaps alongside a recipe for boba pearl ice-lollies and a DIY guide to building a wormery. But some areas are given a wide berth, including celebrity, romantic relationships, and losing or gaining weight (anything to do with how to sculpt the so-called 'perfect body' is *not* for us). We also avoid using the term 'teenagers' (readers know that's what they are) and usually sidestep anything that's self-consciously cool or edgy. On the whole, we also try to steer clear of using online trends as a starting point for features. While it's important, of course, to acknowledge the role social media plays in readers' lives, its impact on young minds is complex. We're careful to present a balanced and nuanced picture.

Tips on tone

While gentle guidance and suggestion is great, most readers, whatever their age, will baulk slightly if they feel they're being lectured – so we try hard to ensure content doesn't sound formal, condescending or overtly educational. Instead, we try to channel the voice of a supportive older sibling – chatty, warm, conversational – giving comfort and empathy while acknowledging that we're in it together in not having all the answers. The aim is to convey a positive message that no one needs to be perfect, and that most people sometimes experience uncertainty as well as happiness, self-doubt as well as confidence, loneliness as well as friendship. We remind them there's support available to help with sad or challenging issues, and that there are ways to learn from mistakes, and manageable methods which help bring balance and contentment.

Wise words

From a practical perspective, language is important. Pieces need to be accessible to 12-year-olds, so it's best not to use overly complex vocabulary – but it's fine to include two or three tricky words per piece if they flow in the text and are explained by the surrounding sentences. Examples, quotes and points of reference also need to be suitable for this age group. Paragraphs are generally kept short (35-40 words) and features run to approximately 850 words.

Pitch perfect

Every magazine will have its own submissions guidelines. At *Teen Breathe* we have a dedicated form for writers to use to send in a pitch (see www.teenbreathe.co.uk/contact-us). We welcome new voices and fresh perspectives, so please do get in touch if you'd like to collaborate with us on a feature. Follow these tips to give your idea the best chance of success:

1. Have at least one clear, age-appropriate idea for a feature you'd like to write. We receive a lot of enquiries from would-be writers who tell us how much they'd like to contribute to the magazine but forget to include a specific piece they have in mind. Links to websites or articles published elsewhere are useful background reading if your idea sounds promising, but you need to outline a **clear, concise and concrete proposal** that we can consider.

2. Give a **clear summary** of the piece. Ideally think of a title and write a sentence or two that could be used as a 'standfirst' – a compelling subheading that fills the reader in on what they can expect.

3. Do some **research**. We wouldn't expect you to have read every back issue, but being able to refer to a past article that you've enjoyed, or one that includes thematic parallels to your proposal, is helpful in two ways. Firstly, it tells us you know what kind of features work for a teen readership. Secondly, it allows us to imagine your piece alongside others we've commissioned.

4. If your subject matter would benefit from the inclusion of expert insight, make suggestions for **who you might interview**. Just a couple of pithy quotes from a professional in the relevant field can be invaluable and ensure the magazine is offering the right kind of help.

5. Provide suggestions for **how the piece might be presented**. We try to break up blocky text with subheadings, bullet points and panels, so include ideas for these, alongside exercises, writing prompts or activities that might complement the main article.

6. Include a brief outline of **your writing background** (with one or two links to previously published work, if appropriate) and any other relevant experience or subject-related qualifications. We'd like to know why you're the best person to write the piece.

Handle with care

One of the joys of writing for teens is they're often open-minded, curious and compassionate. This makes exploring subjects like neurodiversity, self-acceptance or care for the natural world all the more rewarding. The feedback we receive from young adults, plus their guardians and teachers – via email and through social media – is that there's a willingness to see things from different perspectives and an interest in the experiences of others that is refreshing and inspiring.

The other side of this coin, though, is the challenge presented by writing for such an open-hearted audience; the sensitivities of some readers might not at first occur to older writers. This means thinking carefully about word choice, subtext and potential triggers. Some of the messages we receive from readers reveal the struggles and vulnerabilities they're facing and the important role the magazine plays in dealing delicately with raw emotions. It's important to consider every possible interpretation of what you're saying, so that no one feels judged or hurt, and to avoid making assumptions of any kind.

Write for everyone

Teen Breathe has subscribers of all genders from all over the world, from the USA and Australia to Sweden and South Korea, so any activities suggested should be accessible and varied. It's impossible to cover every base, of course, but international examples should be in the mix. For example, local-interest stories, or features based on a project targeted only at girls in one part of the UK, could leave readers who don't fit into those categories feeling as though they're on the outside of things. It's important, too, that all our readers feel valued – which means seeing themselves on the page. We encourage all our writers to cast their net wide when sourcing case studies and professionals, and try to include as diverse, representative and authentic a set of voices as possible.

Consult your inner teen

There's one final point worth mentioning: writers sometimes think they need to have teenage children to write for the teen market. My own view is that – while that experience might equip you well to write parenting articles – the best preparation for writing for teens is simply to remember what it was like to *be* one. There's a gradual and natural loosening of the connection between the present version of yourself and the 'you' of your youth. But … if it's possible to re-inhabit that mindset for a little while, and even to let that teenage part of you pipe up with their ideas before you begin to write, you'll be better placed to get on readers' wavelength and connect with them more directly.

Chloe Rhodes is a commissioning editor at *Teen Breathe* (www.teenbreathe.co.uk). She is a former *Daily Telegraph* features commissioning editor and is also the author of several books on language and folklore, published by Michael O'Mara, and a series of reading books for children published by Oxford University Press. Her freelance work has been published in the *Guardian*, the *Sunday Times* and the *Independent*.

Magazines and newspapers for children

Listings of magazines about children's literature and education start on page 285.

AdventureBox

Bayard, PO Box 61269, London N17 1DF
tel 0800 055 6686
email contact@bayard-magazines.co.uk
website www.bayard-magazines.co.uk
Facebook www.facebook.com/
BayardPresseBoxMagazines
Twitter @BayardKidsMags
10 p.a. From £67 p.a.

Aimed at 6–9 year-old children starting to read on their own. Each issue contains a 44pp illustrated story plus games, a nature/science feature and comic strips. Specially commissions most material. Founded 1996.

Animals and You

D.C. Thomson & Co. Ltd, 2 Albert Square,
Dundee DD1 1DD
tel (01382) 575863
email animalsandyou@dcthomson.co.uk
website www.animalsandyou.co.uk
Twitter @animalsandyou
Every 4 weeks £3.99

Features, stories and posters for readers who love animals. Founded 1998.

Anorak

3rd Floor, 86–90 Paul Street, London EC2A 4NE
email anorakmagazine@gmail.com
website www.anorakmagazine.com
Twitter @AnorakMagazine
Editor Cathy Olmedillas
4 p.a. £7.50

Aimed at children aged 6+, and designed to encourage creativity. Founded 2006.

Aquila

Studio 2, 67A Willowfield Road, Eastbourne,
East Sussex BN22 8AP
tel (01323) 431313
email submissions@aquila.co.uk
email illustrators@aquila.co.uk
website www.aquila.co.uk
Facebook www.facebook.com/
AquilaChildrensMagazine
Twitter @AquilaMag
Instagram @aquila.magazine
Editorial Director Freya Hardy
Monthly £60 p.a.

Dedicated to encouraging children aged 8–13 to

reason and create, and to develop a caring nature. Short stories and serials of up to three parts. Occasional features commissioned from writers with specialist knowledge. Approach in writing with ideas and sample of writing style, along with sae or via e-mail (fiction and non-fiction pitches should be sent to the first email address above). Length: 700–800 words (features), 1,000–1,100 words (stories or per episode of a serial). Payment: by arrangement. Founded 1993.

The Astonishing Spider-Man

Panini UK, Brockbourne House, 77 Mount Ephraim,
Tunbridge Wells TN4 8AR
tel (01892) 500100
email astonspid@panini.co.uk
website https://comics.panini.co.uk
Facebook www.facebook.com/
MarvelCollectorsEditions
Every 2 weeks £4.50

52pp of comic strips, including both contemporary and classic stories.

BBC Doctor Who Magazine

Panini UK, Brockbourne House, 77 Mount Ephraim,
Tunbridge Wells TN4 8AR
tel (01892) 500100
email dwa@panini.co.uk
website https://doctorwhomagazine.com/
Twitter @DWMtweets
Editor Marcus Hearn
Monthly £6.99

Magazine for 6–12 year-old fans of *Doctor Who*. Readers are immersed into the world of the Doctor, taking them on an adventure into time and space, with monsters and creatures, excitement, action, adventure and humour. Founded 2006.

Beano

D.C. Thomson & Co. Ltd, 2 Albert Square,
Dundee DD1 1DD
email contactus@beano.com
website www.beano.com
Facebook www.facebook.com/BeanoOfficial
Twitter @BeanoOfficial
Editor John Anderson
50 p.a. £2.99

Comic strips for children aged 6–12. Series, 8–20 pictures. Artwork and scripts. Payment: on acceptance.

The Caterpillar

Ardan Grange, Milltown, Belturbet, Co. Cavan,
Republic of Ireland
tel +353 (0) 87 2657251
email editor@thecaterpillarmagazine.com
website www.thecaterpillarmagazine.com
Facebook www.facebook.com/thecaterpillarmagazine
Founders Rebecca O'Connor and Will Govan, *Editor*
Rebecca O'Connor
Quarterly €7, €28 p.a. (UK and Republic of Ireland),
€32 p.a. (RoW), including postage

Features original poetry and short stories written by
adults for children aged 7–11, alongside full-colour
artwork. Submissions from adults welcome, but
contributors should familiarise themselves with
magazine content first. Send no more than six poems
or two short stories (max. 1,500 words) by email or
post (sae). Also publishes *The Moth* and runs The
Caterpillar Poetry Prize (€1,000 for best poem written
for children by an adult). Founded 2013.

Cocoa Boy

Studio 210, 134–146 Curtain Road,
London EC2A 3AR
website https://cocoaboy.com
website www.cocoagirl.com/submissions
Instagram @cocoaboymag
Publisher and Creative Director Serlina Boyd
6 p.a. £3.99

The first UK magazine aimed specifically at young
Black boys. Includes empowering content aimed at
teaching children about Black culture and celebrating
role models. Actively encourages submissions from
children aged 7 to 11. Founded 2020.

Cocoa Girl

Studio 210, 134–146 Curtain Road,
London EC2A 3AR
website www.cocoagirl.com/submissions
Instagram @cocoagirlmag
Publisher Serlina Boyd, *Editor* Faith Boyd
6 p.a. £3.99

The first UK magazine aimed specifically at young
Black girls. Includes empowering content aimed at
teaching children about Black culture and celebrating
role models. Actively encourages submissions from
children aged 7 to 11. Winner of Launch of the Year
at the British Society of Magazine Editors' 2020
Awards. Founded 2020.

Commando

DC Thomson & Co Ltd., 2 Albert Square, Dundee,
DD1 1DD
email generalenquiries@commandomag.com
website www.commandocomics.com/submissions
Facebook https://m.facebook.com/C0mmandoComics
Twitter @CommandoComic
Instagram @commandocomics
8 per month (four new, four reprints) £2.25

Fictional stories set in time of war told in pictures.
Scripts: about 135 pictures. Synopsis required as an
opener. See website (address above) for submissions
information. Payment: on acceptance. Founded 1961.

DiscoveryBox

Bayard, PO Box 61269, London N17 1DF
tel 0800 055 6686
email contact@bayard-magazines.co.uk
website www.bayard-magazines.co.uk
Facebook www.facebook.com/
BayardPresseBoxMagazines
Twitter @BayardKidsMags
10 p.a. From £67

Voyage of discovery through nature, science and
history for children aged 9–12. Every issue contains:
animal topics, information about important historical
events, articles about the world, DIY activities, comic
strips, games and more. Founded 1996.

DOT

3rd Floor, 86–90 Paul Street, London EC2A 4NE
email anorakmagazine@gmail.com
website www.anorakmagazine.com/dot
Editor Cathy Olmedillas
4 p.a. £6

Ad-free magazine aimed at encouraging creativity
and learning in the under-5s.

Eco Kids Planet

Eco Kids Planet, 41 Claremont Road,
Barnet EN4 0HR
tel 0800 639 1365
email hello@ecokidsplanet.co.uk
website www.ecokidsplanet.co.uk
Facebook www.facebook.com/ecokidsplanet
Instagram @ecokidsplanetmag
Editor Anya Dimelow
11 p.a. £3.99

Aimed at 7–11 year-old children. Each issue is
dedicated to a different ecosystem and contains facts,
photographs, puzzles and projects. The magazine uses
fun, fictional characters in a story format to convey
facts about nature and the environment. It also
provides children with real-world examples of how
they can make a difference on the planet. Length:
500–1,200 words (themed articles). Requirements:
well-researched, up-to-date, informative articles,
creative approach and interesting language. Specially
commissions most material. Payment: by
arrangement. Founded 2014.

FirstNews

7 Playhouse Court, 62 Southwark Bridge Road,
London SE1 0AT
tel 020-3195 2000
email info@firstnews.co.uk
website www.firstnews.co.uk
Twitter @First_News

Editor-in-Chief Nicky Cox, *Managing Editor* Keilly Swift
Weekly Fri £2.35

Covers news and events in the UK and internationally for children aged 8–14. Founded 2006.

Girl Talk

Immediate Media Co. Ltd, Vineyard House, 44 Brook Green, London W6 7BT
tel 020-7150 5000
email hello@girltalkmagazine.com
Twitter @girltalkmags
Editor Kelly Wilks
Fortnightly £3.99

Magazine for children aged 7–12. Contains pop, TV and film celebrity features, personality features, quizzes, fashion, competitions and stories. Length: 500 words (fiction). Payment: by arrangement. All material is specially commissioned. Founded 1997.

Headliners

49–51 East Road, London N1 6AH
tel 020-7749 9360
email enquiries@headliners.org
website www.headliners.org
Twitter @HeadlinersUK
Chief Executive Ali Talbot

Award-winning journalism and multi-media charity, offering young people aged 8–18 the opportunity to write on issues of importance to them, for newspapers, radio and TV. Founded 1995.

KiCK!

Kennedy Publishing, Greenway Farm, Bath Road, Wick, Bristol BS30 5RL
tel (01179) 373003
email info@kennedypublishing.co.uk
Twitter @KiCKmagazine
Editor Ash Rose
13 p.a. £4.99

Football magazine for boys and girls aged 7–14. Reports on leading players and teams from a variety of divisions, including the Premier League; also includes puzzles, competitions and interviews.

Kids Alive! (The Young Soldier)

The Salvation Army, 101 Newington Causeway, London SE1 6BN
tel 020-7367 4911
email kidsalive@salvationarmy.org.uk
website www.salvationarmy.org.uk/kidsalive
Editor Justin Reeves, *Deputy Editor* Cara Mott
Weekly 50p

Children's magazine: scripts and artwork for cartoon strips, puzzles, etc; Christian-based articles with emphasis on education and lifestyle issues. Illustrations: half-tone, line and four-colour line, cartoons. Payment: by arrangement. Founded 1881.

Kookie

Missprint Media, PO Box 3500, Bristol, BS6 9QH
email hello@kookiemagazine.com
website www.kookiemagazine.co.uk
Twitter @kookiemagazine
Instagram @kookiemagazine
Editor Vivien Jones
4 p.a. £6.50

Award-winning, ad-free magazine for girls aged 7–12+. Features interviews with inspiring women and girls, original fiction, information on science, sports and IT as well as craft, book reviews and a problem page. Founded 2017.

Marvel Legends

Panini UK, Brockbourne House, 77 Mount Ephraim, Tunbridge Wells TN4 8AR
tel (01892) 500100
email astonspid@panini.co.uk
website www.paninicomics.co.uk
Facebook www.facebook.com/MarvelCollectorsEditions
Every 4 weeks £4.50

52pp of comic strips, including both contemporary and classic stories.

Match!

Kelsey Media, The Granary, Downs Court, Yalding Hill, Yalding, Kent ME18 6AL
email match.magazine@kelsey.co.uk
website www.matchfootball.co.uk
Twitter @matchmagazine
Group Editor Stephen Fishlock
Monthly £3.99

Aimed at teenage football fans. News, statistics and information on leading Premier League, Football League and Scottish Premier League teams.

Match of the Day

Immediate Media Co. Ltd, Vineyard House, 44 Brook Green, London W6 7BT
tel 020-7150 5111
email shout@motdmag.com
website www.motdmag.com
Weekly £3.50

Aims to bring football-crazy youngsters closer to their sporting heroes with interviews, facts & stats, the latest transfer gossip and results, posters and quizzes, as well as comic strips and funnies.

National Geographic Kids

Unit 10, Tomas Seth Business Park, Argent Road, Queenborough, Kent ME11 5TS
email kids@ngkids.co.uk
website www.natgeokids.co.uk
Facebook www.facebook.com/natgeokids
Twitter @natgeokidsuk
Instagram @natgeokidsuk
Editor Tim Herbert
Monthly From £39 p.a.

Fun facts, photos and features about animals, science, geography, history, the environment and popular culture, aimed at children aged 6–12.

The Official Jacqueline Wilson Mag

D.C. Thomson & Co. Ltd, 2 Albert Square, Dundee DD1 1DD
tel (01382) 223131
email contact@jw-mag.com
website www.jw-mag.com
Twitter @OfficialJWMag
Every 3 weeks £4.25

Based on the books and characters of award-winning author, Dame Jacqueline Wilson. Aimed at readers aged 7–12, content is tailored to encourage literacy and creativity across a range of reading abilities. Contains interactive features, art and writing projects, recipes and crafts; for less confident readers, educational benefits are presented in a fun and interesting format – e.g. story-starter games and writing prompts, design challenges and word puzzles.

Okido

1–5 Vyner Street, London E2 9DG
email info@okido.com
website www.okido.com
Facebook www.facebook.com/OKIDO.OFFICIAL
Twitter @okido.official
Monthly £5

Award-winning, eco-friendly illustrated science and arts magazine for children aged between 3–7. Created by scientists and educators to promote fun, immersive STEAM learning, with a new topic to explore every month. Each edition includes science experiments, activities, recipes, doodles and games. Founded 2007.

The Phoenix

29 Beaumont Street, Oxford OX1 2NP
email theeditor@thephoenixcomic.co.uk
website www.thephoenixcomic.co.uk
Twitter @phoenixcomicuk
Editor Tom Fickling
Weekly £3.25

32pp weekly anthology comic for boys and girls aged 7–14. Features serialised stories and one-off stories as well as non-fiction. Encourages reading for pleasure and children's critical thinking, creative writing and drawing skills. Contributors include Jamie Smart and Neill Cameron. Founded 2011.

PONY Magazine

DJ Murphy Publishers Ltd, Olive Studio, The Timber Yard, Grange Road, Tilford, Farnham, Surrey GU10 2DQ
tel (01428) 601020
email pony@djmurphy.co.uk
website www.ponymag.com
Twitter @PONY_mag

Editor-in-Chief Louise Kittle
13 p.a. from £3.99

Lively articles and short stories with a horsey theme aimed at readers aged 8–16. Technical accuracy and young, fresh writing essential. Length: up to 800 words. Payment: by arrangement. Illustrations: drawings (commissioned), photos, cartoons. Founded 1949.

Shout

D.C. Thomson & Co. Ltd, 2 Albert Square, Dundee DD1 1DD
tel (01382) 223131
email contact@shoutmag.co.uk
website www.shoutmag.co.uk
Facebook www.facebook.com/shoutmag
Twitter @shoutmag
Monthly £4.25

Magazine for 10–13 year-old girls. Includes fashion and beauty; celebrity gossip and interviews; TV and pop content; real-life stories; emotional and advice features with a teen focus. Length of article accepted: up to 1,000 words. Illustrations: links to online portfolios or websites welcome, but illustrations are commissioned on a feature-by-feature basis only. Payment: on acceptance. Founded 1993.

Storybox

Bayard, PO Box 61269, London N17 1DF
tel 0800 055 6686
email contact@bayard-magazines.co.uk
website www.bayard-magazines.co.uk
Facebook www.facebook.com/BayardPresseBoxMagazines
10 p.a. From £67

Aimed at 3–6 year-old children. Each issue presents a new, full-colour, 24pp story created by teams of writers and illustrators for laptime reading. A non-fiction section linked to a theme in the story follows, together with pages of games and craft ideas. Also includes games, an animal feature, science and a cartoon. Length: 500–1,000 words (stories). Requirements: rhyme, repetition and interesting language. Specially commissions most material. Payment: by arrangement. Founded 1996.

Storytime

61 Bridge Street, Kington HR5 3DJ
email hello@storytimemagazine.com
website www.storytimemagazine.com
website www.storytimeforschools.com
Facebook www.facebook.com/StorytimeMag
Twitter @StorytimeMag
Monthly From £38.99 p.a.

Illustrated bedtime story magazine for children aged 3–8. Accepting submissions from illustrators: see website for full submission guidelines. Calls for submissions from short-story writers also occur periodically; check online for details.

Teen Breathe

GMC Publications, 86 High Street, Lewes BN7 1XN
tel (01273) 477374
email hello@breathemagazine.com
website www.teenbreathe.co.uk/submissions
Publisher Jonathan Grogan
Bi-monthly £4.50

Tips, exercises and ideas on how to make mindfulness part of teenagers' lives so that they can stay positive and improve their wellbeing. Submissions welcomed from experienced or new writers, and from illustrators; see website for specific requirements for each type of potential contributor.

Top of the Pops

Immediate Media Co. Ltd, Vineyard House, 44 Brook Green, London W6 7BT
tel 020-7150 5123
email totpmag@totpmag.com
Monthly £4.99

Celebrity gossip and news, primarily aimed at girls aged 10–14. Founded 1995.

Toxic Magazine

Egmont UK Ltd, 2 Minster Court, London EC3R 7BB
email mpratt@euk.egmont.com
website www.toxicmag.co.uk
Twitter @ToxicMagUK
Editor Matthew Pratt

Every 3 weeks £4.50

Topical lifestyle magazine for 8–12 year-old boys. Includes competitions, pull-out posters, reviews and jokes. Covers boys' entertainment, sports, video games, films, TV, music, fashion and toys. Slapstick humour. Showcases latest products, events and trends. Payment: by arrangement. Founded 2002.

2000 AD

Rebellion Publishing, Riverside House, Osney Mead, Oxford OX2 0ES
website www.2000adonline.com
Twitter @2000AD
Weekly £3.25

Cult science fiction and fantasy comic. Submissions accepted by post only. Founded 1977.

The Week Junior

Future Publishing Limited, Quay House, The Ambury, Bath BA1 1UA
email hello@theweekjunior.co.uk
website https://theweekjunior.co.uk
Twitter @theweekjunior
Instagram @theweekjunior
Editorial Director Anna Bassi, *Editor* Felicity Capon
Weekly £3.25

Covers news and events in the UK and internationally for children aged 8–14. Companion publication focusing on science and nature also available.

Magazines about children's literature and education

Listings of magazines and newspapers for children start on page 280.

Armadillo

32 Cannon Court Road, Maidenhead SL6 7QN
tel (01628) 914516
email armadilloeditor@gmail.com
website www.armadillomagazine.co.uk
Facebook www.facebook.com/Armadillomag
Twitter @Armadillomag
Instagram @ArmadilloMagazine
Editor Louise Ellis-Barrett
4 p.a. Free

Online children's book review magazine including reviews, interviews, features, competitions, profiles and downloadable activities. Free weekly newsletter for subscribers. Weekly blog; daily social media posts; issues posted February, April, June, August, October, December. New reviewers and writers always welcome. Founded 1999.

Books for Keeps

30 Winton Avenue, London N11 2AT
tel 020-8889 1292
email andrea@booksforkeeps.co.uk
website www.booksforkeeps.co.uk
Twitter @BooksforKeeps
Editor Andrea Reece
Bi-monthly Free

Children's book review journal including features, reviews and news on the genre. Readership is both professionals and parents. Founded 1980.

The Bookseller

Floor 10, Westminster Tower,
3 Albert Embankment, London SE1 7SP
tel 020-3358 0369
email tom.tivnan@thebookseller.com
website www.thebookseller.com
Twitter @thebookseller
Editor Philip Jones, *Deputy Editor* Benedicte Page,
Managing Editor Tom Tivnan
Weekly £5.95

Journal of the UK publishing and bookselling trades. The *Children's Bookseller* supplement is published regularly and there is news on the children's book business in the main magazine. Produces the *Children's Buyer's Guide*, which previews children's books to be published in the following six months. The website features news on children's books, comment on the children's sector, author interviews and children's bestseller charts. Founded 1858.

Children's Bookshelf

Publishers Weekly, 49 West 23 Street, Ninth Floor,
New York, NY 10010, USA
tel +1 212-377-5500
email childrensbooks@publishersweekly.com
website www.publishersweekly.com
Facebook www.facebook.com/pubweekly
Twitter @PWKidsBookshelf
Children's Books Editor Diane Roback
Semi-weekly Free

E-newsletter about children's and young adult books. Published under the auspices of *Publishers Weekly*, which was founded in 1872. Children's book news, feature story ideas, new trends and pitches for author or illustrator interviews should be sent to the Editor. Visit website for PW's submission guidelines.

Educate

National Education Union, Hamilton House,
Mabledon Place, London WC1H 9BD
tel 020-7380 4708
email educate@neu.org.uk
website https://neu.org.uk/educate
Editor Max Watson
6 p.a. Free to NEU members

Articles, features and news of interest to all those involved in the education sector. Email outline in the first instance. Length: 500 words (single page), 1,000 (double page). Payment: NUJ rates to NUJ members.

Inis – The Children's Books Ireland Magazine

Children's Books Ireland,
17 North Great George Street, Dublin D01 R2F1,
Republic of Ireland
tel +353 (0)1 8727475
email jenny@childrensbooksireland.ie
website www.childrensbooksireland.ie
Editor and Deputy CEO Jenny Murray
3 p.a. €5

Solely devoted to children's books and the wider world of literature for young people. The three annual print issues each feature forty-four reviews of current or upcoming titles; the features section includes five-six articles, ranging from artist interviews, project overviews or a broader focus on a topic or theme. Each issue is printed in Ireland, distributed to Children's Books Ireland members and are available for individual purchase. Back issues become available online one year after print publication. The archive of back issues is available from childrensbooksireland.ie/our-recommendations. Founded 1989.

Literacy

UK Literacy Association, Room 9 c/o VAL, 9 Newarke Street, Leicester LE1 5SN
tel 0116 254 4116
website https://onlinelibrary.wiley.com/page/journal/ 17414369/homepage/forauthors.html
Editors Dr Diane R. Collier, Professor Natalia Kucirkova
3 p.a. Free to UKLA members or £717 p.a.

Official journal of the United Kingdom Literacy Association (see page 357), aimed at those interested in the study and development of literacy. Readership comprises practitioners, teachers, educators, researchers, undergraduate and graduate students. It offers educators a forum for debate through scrutinising research evidence, reflecting on analysed accounts of innovative practice and examining recent policy developments. Length: 2,000–6,000 words (articles). Illustrations: by arrangement. Formerly known as *Reading – Literacy and Language*. Founded 1966.

Nursery World

MA Education, St Jude's Church, Dulwich Road, London SE24 0PB
tel 020-8501 6693
email karen.faux@markallengroup.com
website www.nurseryworld.co.uk
Editor Karen Faux
Fortnightly From £11 per month

For all grades of primary school, nursery and childcare staff, nannies, foster parents and all those concerned with the care of expectant mothers, babies and young children. Authoritative and informative articles, 800 or 1,300 words, and photos on all aspects of child welfare and early education, from 0–8 years, in the UK. Practical ideas, policy news and career advice. No short stories. Illustrations: by arrangement. Payment: by arrangement.

Publishers Weekly

49 West 23 Street, Ninth Floor, New York, NY 10010, USA
tel +1 212-377-5500
email childrensbooks@publishersweekly.com
website www.publishersweekly.com
Facebook www.facebook.com/pubweekly
Twitter @PWKidsBookshelf
Children's Books Editor Diane Roback

International news magazine for the book industry. Covers all segments involved in the creation, production, marketing and sale of the written word in book, audio, video and electronic formats. In addition to reaching publishers worldwide, it

influences all media dealing with the acquisition, sale, distribution and rights of intellectual and cultural properties.

Children's books for review published in the U.S. market, from preschool to young adult, should be sent to Children's Books Reviews; note that all reviews are pre-publication. Also send story suggestions on children's publishing, new trends, author or illustrator interviews, etc for the semi-weekly *Children's Bookshelf* e-newsletter. Founded 1872.

The School Librarian

School Library Association, 1 Pine Court, Kembrey Park, Swindon SN2 8AD
tel (01793) 401154
email elizabeth.roberts@sla.org.uk
website www.sla.org.uk
Publications and Awards Officer Elizabeth Roberts
Quarterly Free to SLA members, £125 p.a. to others

Official journal of the School Library Association. Articles on news, best practice, education developments, school library management, literacy, publishing, developing reading, research skills and information literacy. Reviews of books, websites and other library resources from preschool to adult. Length: 1,200–1,800 words (articles). Payment: by arrangement. Founded 1937.

TES (The Times Educational Supplement)

26 Red Lion Square, London WC1R 4HQ
tel 020-3194 3000
email newsdesk@tes.com
email features@tes.com
website www.tes.com
Twitter @tes
Editor Jon Severs
Daily £15 per quarter

Education magazine publishing daily online. The latest news, analysis and teaching and learning research for those who work in schools. Specialist knowledge required and ideas should be emailed to the relevant sector editor. Payment: by arrangement. Founded 1910.

TESS (The Times Educational Supplement Scotland)

email henry.hepburn@tes.com
website www.tes.com/magazine
Twitter @TesScotland
News Editor Henry Hepburn
Updated daily; see website for subscription options

Online education magazine. Articles on education, preferably 500–600 words, written with special knowledge or experience. News items about Scottish educational affairs, especially those affecting schools. Payment: by arrangement. Founded 1965.

Screen and audio
Adapting children's books for stage and screen

Emma Reeves offers her experience of the challenges and rewards of adapting other people's literary creations for the television or stage, with practical advice on securing rights and successfully reimagining and reshaping a story you love in a way that works for the new medium.

If you are a working writer for stage, screen or radio, whether you're writing for children, adults or both, it's highly likely that adaptations will form a regular part of your work – and income. Audio drama, film, TV and theatre have a voracious appetite for valuable IP (intellectual property) and the rights to successful books are fought over ruthlessly. TV companies working in children's television are constantly reading and keeping up with the latest events in children's publishing.

CBBC's two biggest home-grown brands are probably *Horrible Histories* (based on the books by Terry Deary) and *The Dumping Ground*, evolved from *Tracy Beaker Returns* (created by Elly Brewer and Ben Ward), an original TV series which continued the story of Jacqueline Wilson's popular protagonist, Tracy Beaker, and introduced a whole new set of characters and problems. Tracy and her world have now been a vital part of the CBBC landscape for nearly 20 years – yet the CBBC development exec who initially championed Tracy's cause admits that it was an uphill struggle to get the powers that be to buy into the realistic story of a brutally neglected child who experiences bed-wetting, meltdowns, rages and attachment issues as an all-too-plausible result of a heartbreaking upbringing. In the end, Tracy's inimitable spirit – and 20 years of fierce audience loyalty – won the day; but it's worth keeping in mind that, when it comes to commissioning, nothing is ever really a 'no-brainer' – and if you truly believe in an idea, it's probably worth fighting for.

Book adaptations have a strong appeal for TV and theatre producers, who like to have a tangible idea of what they're getting before commissioning a new series or play. This can be frustrating for new writers who are desperate to get their own big new idea out there. It does mean, though, that producers are often looking for the 'right' writer to match with a project, which can be a shortcut to a paid commission. And artistically, it can give you the chance to experience the joy, fear and pain of taking control of a group of beloved characters in a rich, well-realised world.

Riding the highs and lows

The highs and lows of adaptation are dizzying. It's certainly not easier than original work. If you do happen to find it easier, I will sincerely try to be happy for you, but I enviously suspect that you're doing it wrong. In my personal experience, it doesn't hurt any less to fail as an adapter than as an originator – in fact, it's worse. You haven't just let yourself down, you've betrayed your original author, your guide, your travelling companion, maybe even your hero.

Of course, when things *do* work and people profess to love the resulting show, the Bad Voices in every writer's head lose no time in pointing out that *everything good is because of the original author ... everything bad is your fault*. And if those voices should ever abandon you (unlikely), there's always the internet ...

Which brings me to Rule One of adapting – no, Rule One of everything, ever: Never, *ever* search the internet. Just don't do it.

Rule Two: when you inevitably ignore my advice and search the internet – remember, they're just people, like you; maybe too much like you. As a child, I was an obsessive reader, and I still suffer from very strong 'fannish' tendencies. I know very well that there are certain books and authors of which no adaptation will ever satisfy me. The people who are hardest to please are the most devoted. If someone comes down hard on your adaptation, console yourself by imagining the review you'd give to any adaptation of *your* favourite book of all time.

The real high of adaptation is that you get to play inside someone else's incredible creation. And what could be better than that? As a stage adapter, I've been privileged to reimagine childhood favourites – *Little Women, Carrie's War, Anne of Green Gables, Sherlock Holmes, Cool Hand Luke, Doctor Jekyll and Mr Hyde* – and also to discover the work of a new generation of children's writers. I've written for *The Story of Tracy Beaker, Tracy Beaker Returns* and *The Dumping Ground* – all based on Jacqueline Wilson's work – and also worked on both the stage and TV versions of her *Hetty Feather*.

Every experience is different and brings its own challenges. Even within the same medium, there are different types of show. On TV, for example, at one end of the scale is the straight, closed-ended adaptation, where you are expected to more or less follow the story of the book. At the other end of the spectrum is the open-ended drama which may take nothing more from its source material than a few names and a situation, relying on the ingenuity of the script writers to come up with episodic plots. Most TV shows are somewhere in between – perhaps a novel may provide the protagonist's journey for series one, but then it's up to the writers to come up with new material.

Check out the rights

A lot of my adaptation work has come about through people approaching me. But what if you've fallen in love with an original work and you just have to adapt it or write a sequel? What should you do? Before you type your first words, make sure the rights are available and that you've got a realistic chance of getting them. The only exception is for out-of-copyright material (where the author has been dead for 70 years or more). Otherwise, anything you write without the blessing of the author or their estate is basically fan fiction; you may enjoy it, your friends may enjoy it, but you can never reach a mass audience, and certainly never make any money, unless you want a lawsuit on your hands. So, if you're serious about sharing your vision with the world, check out the rights before doing anything else.

If you have an agent, or an interested production company, they will be able to help you approach the rights-holders. If not, you can search online for the writer's agent or go through the publisher. Bear in mind that the latest hot properties and surprise hits will almost always be optioned already – but options lapse, so it's worth enquiring about the length of the option and trying again at the appropriate time. Read more obscure work in the hope of finding an un-optioned gem.

Despite all this, securing book rights is comparatively easy compared to getting the rights to adapt film or TV shows. This is particularly tricky for lone writers, as TV and film properties tend to have multiple owners and sorting out the various claims requires an army of showbiz lawyers. As a general rule, it's only worth pursuing if you have a major producing force on your side (both to give you credibility and to pay those lawyers' fees!), but there are always exceptions. If you're really passionate about a project and you think you can persuade the rights-holders, go for it. Our business is built on stories of those few lucky people whose tenacity and love for their project enabled them to break all the rules and succeed.

Reimagining the story

What happens next? A producer friend regularly chides me that he doesn't know why my scripts take so long, when all I have to do is copy down the book and cross out the description. Although I generally laugh bitterly at such comments, adaptation is a broad church and there are some gigs which are perhaps better described as abridging – such as when I worked out a three-hander version of *King Lear* and a four-hander version of *The Importance of Being Earnest* for a small touring company. Although you have to be a bit creative in situations like that, you're working within the intended medium and almost exclusively using the author's original text. At the other end of the scale of fidelity to the original work, I once worked on a children's TV show for two years before anyone informed me that it was actually based on a novel!

These two extremes aside, the job of the adapter is usually to reimagine the story in a way which works for the medium. For example, when I worked on the stage version of *Hetty Feather*, we started with Jacqueline's book and created the show in the rehearsal room with six actors. Using the wealth of material in the book, and even more which was generated by the actors, my job was to steer the story into a coherent structure which would fit into two hours' stage time, streamlining plot moments and making some tough calls about which brilliant bits to jettison. When I wrote episodes of the TV show, I had to come up with self-contained plots lasting half an hour. In the first case I had an overabundance of other people's material to deal with; in the second, it was up to me to tell new stories. People asked if I found it confusing but, to me, the worlds of *Hetty* the book, *Hetty* the stage show and *Hetty* the TV show were so different that I never struggled in that way. In some respects, the medium informs the writing experience possibly more than the original material does.

When you start to adapt a book, you are entering somebody else's world, and meeting their characters. In order to feel comfortable in that world, I always try to read as much of the writer's other work as I can. This may seem like obvious advice, but the benefits are so great that it's worth emphasising. If the author writes a lot about a specific time and place, that's useful for research and background colour. If they are preoccupied with certain ideas or social issues, you can get a greater understanding of where they were coming from when they wrote the book. I have actually transposed scenes from (out-of-copyright!) lesser-known works of authors, in order to illuminate important moments which I felt were glossed over somewhat in the work I was adapting. Cheeky perhaps, but it worked for me.

Creating the shape

So, you've got a handle on the world and the characters. Everything may be clearly set out for you, or you may need to fill the gaps – or change certain elements. You may discover what you need to change as you go along. At this stage, you take a step back from the source material (and its potentially seductive prose) and ask the normal questions of dramatic writing: Whose story is it? What do they want? Who is trying to stop them getting it?

A specific problem I have encountered is that many beloved books are episodic in nature: this happens, then that happens, then this happens ... In drama, stories tend to need ongoing hooks: this happens, SO that happens, SO that happens ... I find I need to work hard to create a sense of building drama and inevitability. Also, coincidence feels much harder to mask in drama than in novels. I find myself investigating plot conveniences – are they really just happenstance? Or did someone plan it? If you can decide that the events are the result of someone's plan, it immediately feels easier to dramatise plausibly.

You have to keep your characters active and keep your hooks dangling. Keep your protagonist pushing through to the end. When you're watching previews, or in the edit, try to resist the temptation to keep a 'good bit' in if your gut is screaming at you that it's slowing down the story and risks letting the audience's interest drop. Sometimes that comedy interlude just sits too awkwardly at a moment when the hero has to make a life-or-death choice and risk everything. Sometimes, it's time to stop piling torture, misery and despair on a character and let the audience know that they're ready to fight back. As an adapter, you need to take responsibility for the work as a whole – the shape is now up to you. And you may have to keep a mediocre bit at the expense of a good bit if, after a lot of consideration (and discussion with the director, editor or whoever), you realise that that's what the shape of the story needs.

Interestingly, not a word of the paragraph above couldn't also be usefully applied to original drama scripts.

So in summary: enjoy the highs, the fun and the privilege; appreciate the work that other people have done so you don't have to; but if something's not working, don't shrug it off as the original author's problem – look at it from all angles until you find a way to make it work for you. It's the very least that the author deserves. After all, it's probably their name that got you the gig.

Emma Reeves is a twice BAFTA-nominated writer whose credits include developing new versions of *The Worst Witch* and *The Demon Headmaster* for television. She also co-created an original science fiction show, *Eve*, for CBBC. Other TV credits include *The Dumping Ground*, *Tracy Beaker Returns*, *Young Dracula*, *Hetty Feather* and *The Story of Tracy Beaker*. West End stage adaptations include *The Worst Witch*, *Carrie's War*, *Little Women*, *Hetty Feather* and *Cool Hand Luke*. *The Worst Witch* won the Olivier Award for Best Family Show, while *Hetty Feather* (the stage show) was nominated for an Olivier Award and won the first ever CAMEO award for best page-to-stage adaptation. She is currently Chair of the Writers' Guild TV Committee. Follow her on Twitter @emmajanereeves.

See also...

Children's literature on radio, podcast and audio

The technologies for transmitting the spoken word to children are developing rapidly. Neville Teller describes the fast-changing world of radio, podcasting and audio, and explores what a writer for the microphone needs to know to break into this market.

'Read me a story' – one of childhood's perennial cries. Until radio arrived, parents found little relief from it (palming it off on grandma or auntie was perhaps the best bet). But from its very beginning, radio included in its schedules stories read aloud for children. So, for part of the time at least, the loudspeaker was able to provide a fair substitute for mummy or daddy by providing literature, specially prepared for performance at the microphone, read by professional actors.

Very early on, actors learned that performing at the microphone was a new skill – the techniques were specialised and quite different from those required on the stage. Writers, too, had to acquire a whole range of new skills in preparing material for radio. Two things quickly became apparent. First, the time taken to read a complete book on the air would be far too long to be acceptable, and in consequence most books would need to be abridged. Secondly, literature simply read aloud from the printed page often failed to 'come across' to a listening audience, because material produced to be scanned by the eye is often basically unsuited to the requirements of the microphone.

Today there are two main outlets in this country for aspiring writers for children in the radio/podcasting sphere: online radio/audio and audiobook publishers. How has this market reached its present position?

Radio/podcast

Children's radio in the UK came into existence in December 1922, just a few weeks after the BBC itself was born, and for some 40 years the daily 'Children's Hour' became an established and much-cherished feature of life.

However, in the 1960s the imminent death of radio was a generally accepted prognostication. Starting in 1961, in the belief that television was their preferred medium, children's radio was slowly but surely strangled.

The demise of children's radio naturally evoked a massive groundswell of protest. In response the BBC of the day did grant some sort of reprieve. *Story Time* – a programme of abridged radio readings – started life in the old Children's Hour slot with a strong bias towards children's literature. It was not long, however, before more general literature began to be selected, and finally, in 1982, that programme too was dropped. For the next 20 years the only regular children's programme left on BBC radio was *Listen with Mother*, the 15-minute slot for the under-fives.

Early in the new millennium, the BBC – moved, doubtless, by mounting evidence of the undiminished popularity of radio – decided to reintroduce a regular programme for children. All they could offer at the time was a 30-minute programme each Sunday evening on Radio 4 called *Go4It*, a magazine-type show which included a ten-minute reading, and I found myself abridging books for it like *The Lion, the Witch and the Wardrobe* by

C.S. Lewis and *The Wolves of Willoughby Chase* by Joan Aiken. Unfortunately, this renaissance was typically short-lived. *Go4It* was axed on 24 May 2009.

But the door had been pushed ajar, and in the autumn of 2002, when the BBC launched its new digital radio channel, BBC7, its schedules included, as a basic ingredient, daily programmes for children incorporating readings from children's literature, both current and classic. I prepared a considerable number of books for these programmes, including not only classical children's literature like *Robinson Crusoe* and *The Prince and the Pauper*, but also more general classics like *20,000 Leagues Under the Sea* and *Oliver Twist*. The programme for older children also featured up-to-the-moment favourites such as Anthony Horowitz's series about his boy secret agent, Alex Rider, the *Artemis Fowl* novels by Eoin Colfer, Terry Pratchett's *A Hat Full of Sky* and *The Amazing Maurice* and Jackie French's *Callisto* series. For younger listeners, I abridged books like the *Whizziwig* series by Malorie Blackman, the *Lily Quench* books by Natalie Jane Prior and Kaye Umansky's *The Silver Spoon of Solomon Snow*.

All seemed set fair, but towards the end of 2006 came news of major changes. The programme for younger listeners was converted into a radio extension of CBeebies, the BBC's digital television channel for the youngest children, while the BBC7 schedule included readings drawn from the programme's extensive archive, including my own abridgements of, among many others, *Bootleg* by Alex Shearer, *Stop the Train* by Geraldine McCaughrean, *Huckleberry Finn* by Mark Twain, *Slaves of the Mastery* and *Firesong* by William Nicholson, *Stig of the Dump* by Clive King, *The BGF* by Roald Dahl, *The Little House on the Prairie* by Laura Ingalls Wilder, *Dream Master* by Theresa Breslin and *Point Blanc* by Anthony Horowitz.

Nothing lasts for ever, and 2011 saw BBC7 transformed into BBC Radio 4 Extra. With the transformation came a new shape to children's radio – almost a return to the Children's Hour concept of yesteryear, *The Four O'Clock Show* always including abridged readings of children's literature. Among the specially commissioned readings I abridged Frank Cottrell Boyce's *Chitty Chitty Bang Bang Flies Again*, *Wonder* by R.J. Palacio and *Maggot Moon* by Sally Gardner.

Sadly, *The Four O'Clock Show* too succumbed to the rapidly changing technological needs of its audience. 30 April 2015 saw its final transmission. The axing of this hour of dedicated children's radio meant that there is no longer any children's programming on Radio 4 Extra, and its service licence has been amended to remove its commitment to the content.

However, the BBC is providing three online streams of children's programmes. CBeebies Radio is a daily web-based radio show for preschool children. They can either listen online on BBC Sounds through the CBeebies Radio Player or download and keep the podcast, choosing when and where is best for them to listen.

Meanwhile BBC Sounds has built up an impressive selection of radio programmes under its genre category 'Children', including readings and drama. Audio productions provided online to be downloaded and retained are now generally known as podcasts. Find BBC Sounds podcasts for children at www.bbc.co.uk/sounds/category/childrens. In addition, the BBC provides a dedicated online service for 3–5 year-olds via its School Radio programme. The range of podcasts available for download can be found at: www.bbc.co.uk/schoolradio/subjects/earlylearning.

In addition to the BBC, there is a national digital radio station dedicated entirely to children aged 6–12. Fun Kids is a nationwide 18-station digital multiplex whose content is also available via its website (www.funkidslive.com). Its podcasts and videos include stories, drama and educational material.

All these outlets require dedicated writers for children, prepared to adapt existing, or provide new, material in audio format specifically for young listeners.

Audiobooks

Audiobooks are literary works of all types, read by actors and available as CDs or as downloads from the internet. For some years, audiobooks had been the fastest growing area of consumer publishing in the UK. The coronavirus pandemic that locked people in their homes and shut down great swathes of the economy resulted in a further boom in audiobook sales. Nielsen prediction for 2020 was for audiobook revenue to increase by some 30%, reaching £115 million unit sales which would be an increase of nearly 16% on 2019. In comparison, Nielsen prediction for 2021 was for audiobook revenue to surpass £200 million. This can in part be attributed to lockdowns; the first six months of 2021 saw a 71% increase in audiobook sales compared with the same period in 2019 (the increase for ebooks was just 10%).

Audible dominates the audiobook market and its sales are booming, but it faces growing competition from newcomers such as audiobooks.com, Kobo and Bookbeat, as well as Google and Apple. Current estimates put the children's share of the market at 40% of the total.

The BBC's audio output, including the large and flourishing children's backlist, is now marketed through outlets such as Audible and Random House.

Nowadays, it is common for major publishers to launch a fair number of their new books, including books for older children, in printed and audiobook form simultaneously. Publishers of books for younger children often adopt the 'twin pack' concept – packaging book and audiobook together – so that children can read and listen at the same time. Such products are zero-rated for VAT. However VAT at 20% is still being charged on audiobooks; the UK book industry has mounted a campaign to have it removed.

How children listen

The ways in which children listen to the readings intended especially for them are multiplying at what seems an ever-increasing rate. In addition to online radio heard via digital radio sets, computers, smartphones and tablets, primary school teachers download BBC School podcasts and play them back in class.

Downloads are a growing method for children to access audiobooks especially for them. There are a range of online outlets, including Audible and Apple iTunes through its Audiobooks Store. Taken together, these DTO (Download to Own) providers have available an enormous and expanding list of children's books, and stories are proving a popular second-best to music for many children. Subscribers pay either a monthly fee for the right to download a specific number of titles or pay for downloads book by book. However, these days a surprising number of websites are offering free downloads of children's stories. One US website lists no less than 62 online sites from which children can download stories at no cost. The UK also has a fair number of such sites, including those run by the *Independent*, Storynory, Mashable, Oxford University Press and OpenCulture.

Screen and audio

Amazon has some 30,000 children's audiobooks available to be purchased and downloaded. Users can start listening within seconds, transfer the audiobook to a Kindle, computer, tablet, iPod or other device, or burn it to a CD. Other specialist providers of audiobooks for children include Children's Storybooks Online (www.magickeys.com/books) and the Story Home (www.thestoryhome.com). All commission new stories for children.

Young people are increasingly accessing not only their social networks via their smartphones, but also audiobooks. Google, Amazon and Audible are providing access to audiobooks via the mobile phone, and other providers are crowding into the marketplace.

Amazon's ebook reader, the Kindle, and its younger brother, Kindle Fire, which offers a colour touch-screen, have been runaway successes. The Kindle can download a book in about 30 seconds, either to be read on its 6-inch wide screen or to be read aloud to you (albeit in a somewhat robot-like voice). However audiobooks can also be downloaded, though the process is easier on the later versions of Kindle.

Kindle's biggest rival as a non-print reading device is Apple's iPad and iPad Mini, and its growing number of tablet competitors, all of which can download audiobooks speedily, and have loudspeaker and headphone facilities.

In-car MP3 playback, via the car radio, now widely available, is becoming increasingly popular as a means of keeping children happy on long journeys. Children's audiobooks are also now part of in-flight entertainment on long-haul flights.

A recent phenomenon is 'podiobooks', or podcast audiobook novels, released on the internet in instalments and for free. They are commonly offered together with a range of stickers, ringtones and wallpapers – all designed to appeal to the younger market. The pioneer is Scott Sigler, whose website (https://scottsigler.com) offers free audio fiction, together with videos, ebooks and blog posts via social media. The whole concept is aimed particularly at teenagers and young people.

The message of all this for writers is that the radio/audio/podcast market is mushrooming, and that burgeoning technological developments and innovations seem designed to appeal particularly to the internet-savvy younger generations. If you are keen to break into the rapidly changing world of children's literature on radio and audio, this seems as favourable and opportune a time to succeed as ever. For contact details for children's radio, see *Children's television and radio* (page 300) or search online for children's audiobook publishers, and offer your services. Do not be discouraged by initial rejection – that is often a writer's early experience. Persevere. As in all professional fields, the tyro is faced with the classic catch-22 situation: radio producers and audio publishers are reluctant to offer commissions to people without a track record, while it is of course impossible to gain a track record without having won a commission or two. The only advice is to keep plugging away, hoping for that elusive lucky break – and the only consolation on offer is that even the most experienced of today's professionals was once a complete novice.

Writing for the microphone

What of the techniques that need to be applied in converting material produced for the printed page into a script that can be performed by an actor with ease at the microphone, and bring real listening pleasure to the child at the other end?

Getting to grips with abridging books for the microphone requires, in the first instance, the application of some simple arithmetic. Take a book of around 70,000 words. CDs can accommodate some 70 minutes of airtime, which translates to about 10,500 words. So a 140-minute abridgement presented in the form of two CDs will allow the abridger about 21,000 words. Where the writer is called on to abridge specifically for download, the audiobook publishers will specify the length either in terms of time or wordage. Remember, an actor can normally get through about 2,200 words in 15 minutes.

What makes a good abridgement? To reproduce the sense of an original in fewer words while, in addition and quite as important, to retain the character of the original writing. That demands the capacity to respond sympathetically to the feel of an author's style and to be able to preserve it, even when large chunks of the original are being cut away.

How much liberty is the abridger allowed in translating the printed to the spoken word, while reducing the wordage? Some audiobook producers ask for the minimum of interference with the published text; some radio producers are content for the abridger to adapt the original freely, so as to enhance the actor's performance at the microphone. The different approaches reflect the fact that, in acquiring radio reading rights, the BBC retains editorial independence over the final product, while the granting of abridged audio rights is often conditional on the original writer's approval of the abridged text. So audio producers, reluctant to run the risk of rejection, sometimes allow the abridger very little freedom.

Nevertheless it is an undoubted fact that the requirements of eye and of ear do not always coincide, and that a message easily absorbed from the printed page can become surprisingly garbled if transmitted unamended at the microphone.

In crafting a radio/audio script, the needs of the listener must be one of the prime considerations. The needs of the actor who will read it at the microphone are another. The writer must keep in the forefront of their mind the fact that the script has to be performed. The words must 'flow trippingly off the tongue'. With audio the listener is in control, and can switch on or off whenever convenient.

It is essential that the abridger of children's books reproduces, as far as possible, the plot, atmosphere and character of the original. The aim must be to leave the listener with as complete a feeling of the original book as possible, given the technical limitations of time and wordage. It is, in short, an essential aspect of the radio/audio writer's craft to keep faith with the author.

Neville Teller MBE has been contributing to BBC radio for over 50 years. He is credited with over 250 abridgements for radio readings, 50 radio dramatisations and 300 audiobook abridgements. His publications include *5-Minute Bedtime Stories*, based on classic children's tales he wrote for BBC radio. His radio dramatisation of *Ozma of Oz* by Frank Baum, broadcast across the USA, was included in his book *Audio Drama: 10 Plays for Radio and Podcast*. Recent projects include his abridgement of *Bulldog Drummond* by Sapper, broadcast on BBC Radio 4 Extra, and his radio dramatisations of stories by Edgar Allen Poe and Zane Grey, broadcast across the States during the Covid-19 restrictions. They were included in his second book of radio plays published in 2021, *More Audio Drama: 10 More Plays for Radio and Podcast*. His own radio play *Little Boy Lost* is scheduled for broadcast during 2022. He is a past chairman of the Society of Authors' Broadcasting Committee and of the Audiobook Publishing Association's Contributors' Committee. He was made an MBE in 2006 for 'services to broadcasting and to drama'.

See also...
- *Children's audio publishers*, page 63
- *Children's television and radio*, page 300

Screen and audio

Writing for visual broadcast media

Jayne Kirkham shares her experience of writing for the ever-changing world of children's broadcast media, confident that the writer's role remains essentially unchanged: the writer needs to tell a story with characters and concepts that their audience will remember and love all their lives.

'Writing for kids' telly? Easy! I mean … how hard can it be?'

So says someone who doesn't write for children. For a start, are kids actually watching a telly? If you watch much children's content (and, if you're interested in writing for children, you should) you'll know they are more likely to be watching YouTube on a phone. Depending on what it is, you may be even more inclined to think 'No, seriously, how hard can it be?'. But what looks so simple has been put through a furnace of development: even a two minute TikTok, if money is involved somehow, will have been shaped, moulded, reshaped, possibly with a good deal of firing, before it is finally hammered into something that perfectly suits a broadcaster's or platform's particular audience. And that audience is very particular; children have all the myriad tastes and genre preferences of adults but with the different stages of a child's personal, social and physical development thrown in. Furthermore, the content has to be fun or, as kids in a 2019 report put it, 'amazing/cool/excellent' (*Social Media, Television and Children Report 2019: University of Sheffield, BBC Children's and Dubit*). Even the serious stuff must engage or children simply won't watch.

When I started writing for children's TV, it was a hugely competitive but fairly straightforward world to navigate, with only a handful of broadcasters and producers that commissioned shows. If you went to the Children's Media Conference (or Showcomotion, as it was called then), you could fit everyone you needed to meet into one room. Nowadays, if you go to the Children's Media Conference (and if you're interested in writing for children, you should), everyone you need to meet will still be there – but that 'everyone' covers not just TV but online, games, books, apps and toys! Changes in children's media policy, and advances in technology, mean that children and young people have never known anything but access to content (what used to be called 'programmes') whenever and wherever they like, and in all sorts of formats. They might watch something on TV while accessing extra information about it on their tablet and simultaneously playing along on their phone; what's more, they are making and broadcasting their own content.

To write professionally, this it looks like a much harder more bewildering world, to get into. But actually, whatever innovations arise and throw the industry into flux, for a writer the basics remain the same: know your audience and know how to tell a story, with characters and concepts that kids will remember and love all their lives. If you know your audience, you will know what they are watching and where. You will understand that they prefer to watch their content on YouTube rather than CBBC, and you will be aware of the growth of Disney+, Sky Kids, smart speakers and whatever new players are on the scene by the time you read this.

For a writer, things haven't changed as much as everyone would have us believe; children still enjoy drama, comedy, animation, game shows, documentaries and news made by professional media companies. Those companies need writers like you and me, but getting in touch with them can take a bit of detective work – and a decent pause button, so that you can read a programme's credits properly. Another source of information is the programme's entry on www.imdb.com (International Movie Database). Once you know the name of the production company, you can do an online search for their website where you can generally find contact details for particular producers and/or development departments. Before you contact anyone about writing for them, however, find out as much as you can about the producers, production companies and their intellectual properties (IP). What have they made in the past? What are they developing now? What do they want to develop? Remember, the show that you have just watched and enjoyed will probably have been written two years before; what are they doing now?

The children's channels or platforms also have websites you can explore. By 'platforms', I'm referring to online providers such as Disney+, Netflix, Amazon, Apple TV, Azoomee and Hopster, as well as the public service broadcasters (BBC, ITV, Channel 4 and Five) and the commercial digital channels (Nickelodeon, Pop, Cartoon Network, Disney, etc). To get beyond the shiny, public pages of games and fan chat, enter words like 'producer guidelines' or 'commissioning' into your search engine; you need to find the broadcasters' business pages which show what they are looking for. Remember, each channel/platform has its own brand identity, catering for a specific audience. Make sure you know the difference between a Nickelodeon and a Netflix show.

An easy way to compare and contrast the different platforms is to attend a trade event, such as the Children's Media Conference held in Sheffield every July (www.thechildrensmediaconference.com). There are other conferences and festivals, but the CMC is the best for UK children's media professionals; all the broadcasters attend and hold commissioning sessions where they explain what they want to produce in the next few years. It's also a great opportunity to meet producers and other professionals you may want to collaborate with or work for, with lots of time in the conference schedule for networking. While attending in person is best, it is possible to attend online if money and time are limited.

Having enjoyed a few years' respite from underfunding and lack of political support (thanks to the campaigning of organisations such as the Children's Media Foundation, and the WGGB (Writers' Guild of Great Britain; see page 326), children's media is now facing difficult times; government funds being cut, advertising restrictions and other threats to the public service broadcasters (BBC, ITV, C4 and C5) are making it increasingly difficult to finance content. If you've been watching the credits carefully (and if you're interested in writing for children, you should), you will have noticed that very few shows are the product of one producer and one broadcaster. With the multinational streamers and international co-production as the norm, this means the writing has to appeal to an international audience. It can also mean that you are competing not just with British writers but, writers from overseas. Rather than despair, let this open your eyes to other markets and territories. Countries like China, Brazil, India and many others have looked to the UK for writing talent in recent years. Annual international conferences, such as the Children's Media Conference here in the UK mentioned above, Mipcom Junior in Cannes (www.mipjunior.com) and Kidscreen in Miami (http://kidscreen.com), are great places to meet international companies face to face. Attending these can be costly and time-consuming – it's easier and cheaper to subscribe to their regular newsletters for excellent insider information that you can follow up.

Screen and audio

Working for an overseas company is one of the few reasons why a screenwriter might need an agent. I know a good number of non-agented writers working in the UK on existing shows; the contracts are generally straightforward and many follow WGGB guidelines. But when I have had overseas commissions, I've been grateful to have an agent used to dealing with other territories – not least getting the exchange rate and tax implications right.

It surely must be the dream of every screenwriter to get their own show produced. When the traditional broadcasters were the only players in town, new shows were generally commissioned from writers who had already proven themselves on other series. To get their ideas on screen, writers were dependent on the broadcaster's own producers or independent production companies and they often lost much creative control. The internet has created many more routes by which entrepreneurial writers can now reach their intended audience, for example, *Night Zookeeper* – now available on Sky Kids – started as a web-based teaching aid to encourage children to start writing their own stories.

However, no matter how you intend to get your idea in front of your audience, it needs to go through the same rigorous development process: interrogating the concept and the characters to make sure that it is age-appropriate and will engage the audience utterly, not just in its main format but also in different 'transmedia' guises (as an app, books, in social media, video game). And don't forget to consider toys and other merchandising, as appropriate. Different genres will, of course, have different opportunities and limitations. A drama like *The Dumping Ground* is unlikely to sell as many lunchboxes as, say, preschool animation *Paw Patrol*, but that doesn't mean it shouldn't get made. Just remember to allow the potential revenue returns to determine the budget. Rather confusingly, industry people tend to bandy the term 'genre' in their own special way, using it to describe animation, drama, preschool or comedy. If you watch enough kids' content, you will know that nearly all dramas have a lot of comedy, that animation covers everything from wacky shorts to sitcom to intense re-enactments for documentaries, and that preschool covers everything but in a way that's appropriate for the under-sixes. As I've mentioned, the specific requirements for each broadcaster/platform brand should be available on their websites.

Once you have sufficiently developed your idea – and in that development I would include writing some sample scripts to fully prove whether your idea works or not – and have researched the market, it is time to get it out there. Does your intended recipient give guidelines on submitting your intellectual property (IP)? They may ask you to use an online submission portal. If there are no guidelines, write a brief email introducing yourself and your project as succinctly as possible. Can you pitch it in one sentence? Can you explain the series on a single sheet of A4 paper? Do you have a decent sample script to show off your writing talents? Some producers are wary of unsolicited attachments, so you may want to start with just the email and then follow up when they have responded. Again, be led by their specific guidelines.

If you have the opportunity to pitch in person, practise! These are very busy people, so clarity and passion are essential for you and your idea to stand out. Show that you know your audience and any business or creative constraints: how easy would it be to animate your idea? Would young actors be able to deliver your stunts? The first time I pitched in person, I was a quivering jelly and just about as coherent. But – you know what? – I wasn't eaten, and the world didn't end. It sounds silly, but producers and commissioners are people and, in this industry, they're usually lovely people at that.

Being realistic, it is unlikely that your first project will get picked up. The thing to remember is that this is a business and your intellectual property is a commodity and your skills are a service for hire so don't take rejection personally. There is a lot to learn, so learn it; take feedback when it is offered and get better. It can feel galling to take what feels like a barrage of criticism from a 12 year-old 'executive', but that '12 year-old' will know better than you do what works on their platform. And they may well be in a position to offer you work on another show. It happens. There can be many reasons why an executive doesn't like your project, but that doesn't mean they don't like you or your style of writing. They may not get back to you. But then again, I was once called out of the blue by a producer who had rejected an idea of mine several years before; I ended up writing an animation series and a feature film (and, while the feature is in interminable 'pre-production', I still enjoy the residual fees from the international sales of the TV series).

The best advice I was ever given as a new writer was that you only fail when you give up. So keep on writing; keep on submitting; keep on keeping on.

Jayne Kirkham is a screenwriter and a script and development consultant. With over 30 years' experience working with and writing for children and young people, Jayne has worked on a wide range of theatre, film, TV, radio and online scripts, ranging in size from small conservation films in Africa to international feature films. Jayne taught at the Northern Film School for 14 years, and is a member of the board of directors of the Children's Media Foundation. See her website https://jaynekirkham.com for more information.

Children's television and radio

The information in this section has been compiled as a general guide for writers, artists, agents and publishers to the major companies and key contacts operating within the children's broadcasting industry. As personnel, corporate structures and commissioning guidelines can change frequently, please check the relevant websites for the most up-to-date information.

REGULATION

Advertising Standards Authority
Castle House, 37–45 Paul Street, London EC2A 4LS
tel 020-7492 2222
website www.asa.org.uk
Facebook www.facebook.com/adauthority
Twitter @ASA_UK
Chief Executive Guy Parker

The UK's independent regulator of advertising across all media. Its work includes acting on complaints and taking action against misleading, harmful or offensive advertisements.

Ofcom
Riverside House, 2A Southwark Bridge Road, London SE1 9HA
tel 020-7981 3000, 0300 123 3000
website www.ofcom.org.uk
Facebook www.facebook.com/ofcom
Twitter @Ofcom
Chief Executive Melanie Dawes

Accountable to parliament and exists to further the interests of consumers by balancing choice and competition with the duty to encourage plurality, protect viewers and listeners, promote diversity in the media and ensure full and fair competition between communications providers.

TELEVISION

BabyTV
Baby Network Ltd, 10 Hammersmith Grove, London W6 7AP
email info@babytvchannel.com
website www.babytv.com
Facebook www.facebook.com/BabyTVChannel
Twitter @BabyTVChannel

The world's leading baby and toddler network, for children under five and their parents, airing 24 hours a day and completely ad-free. BabyTV features top-quality shows created by child development experts, designed for child and parent to enjoy together.

The BBC
BBC Broadcasting House, Portland Place, London W1A 1AA

website www.bbc.co.uk
Director, Children's and Education Patricia Hidalgo Reina, *Head of Children's Content and Programming Strategy* Anna Taganov

The world's largest broadcasting organisation, with a remit to provide programmes that inform, educate and entertain. Established by Royal Charter, the BBC is a public service broadcaster funded by a licence fee. The Children's Director is responsible for the overall direction and management of all of the BBC's services for children, including CBeebies and CBBC channels and their websites.

Commissioning
CBeebies and CBBC are self-commissioning and self-scheduling, and proposals may be submitted at any time throughout the year. All submissions for TV and online should be made via Pitch. For further details and commissioning guidelines visit:
    www.bbc.co.uk/commissioning/childrens
    www.bbc.co.uk/commissioning/childrens/0-6
    www.bbc.co.uk/commissioning/childrens/7-12
    www.bbc.co.uk/commissioning/pitch
    https://pitch.bbc.co.uk

Television (genre commissioning)
Chief Content Officer Charlotte Moore

CBeebies
website www.bbc.co.uk/cbeebies
Twitter @CBeebiesHQ

Head of Commissioning & Acquisitions Kate Morton (0-6), *Commissioning Editors* Michael Towner, Julia Bond, *Assistant Commissioning Editor* Dan Flint, *Commissioning Executives* Joel Wilenius, Nick Hall

CBeebies offers mixed genre output for TV, online and radio and is specifically produced for a young audience using a variety of formats including live action and animation. Content covers drama, comedy, entertainment and factual, and the target audience is children aged 0–6 years. CBeebies is on air daily from 6am–7pm.

CBBC
website www.bbc.co.uk/cbbc
Twitter @cbbc

Head of Commissioning & Acquisitions Kate Morton (0-6), Commissioning Editors Michael Towner, Julia

Bond, Assistant Commissioning Editor Dan Flint, Commissioning Executives Joel Wilenius, Nick Hall

Offers mixed genre output for TV and online. Content covers drama, factual, comedy, entertainment, animation and news, and the target audience is children aged 6–12 years. CBBC is on air daily from 7am–7pm.

BBC Writersroom

email writersroom@bbc.co.uk

website www.bbc.co.uk/writersroom

Facebook www.facebook.com/BBCWriters

Twitter @bbcwritersroom

BBC Writersroom is a cross-genre department for scripted content, working with drama, comedy, CBeebies, CBBC, radio, online and others. It is the first port of call at the BBC for unsolicited scripts and new writers. Visit the website to discover:

• how and when to submit a script;
• new opportunities for writers;
• writing tips and success stories;
• interviews and top tips from writers;
• competitions and events.

The BBC Writersroom blog provides a wealth of behind-the-scenes commentary from writers and producers who have worked on BBC TV and radio programmes: www.bbc.co.uk/blogs/writersroom.

Channel 4

124–126 Horseferry Road, London SW1P 2TX
tel 0345 076 0191
website www.channel4.com
Facebook www.facebook.com/Channel4
Twitter @Channel4
Chief Executive Alex Mahon
Director of Programmes Ian Katz

A publicly owned television network that is freely available to all in the UK. Its commercially-funded, publicly owned structure enables all profit generated to be directly reinvested back into its public service remit. As a publisher-broadcaster Channel 4 commissions UK content from the independent production sector and currently works with over three hundred creative companies across the UK every year. It provides a digital streaming service, All 4, and a network of 12 television channels, aiming to create change by representing unheard voices and reinventing entertainment.

4Talent supports people to build their careers in the media industry across a range of disciplines. Visit https://careers.channel4.com/4talent.

Commissioning

Information about commissioning and related processes and guidelines can be found at www.channel4.com/info/commissioning. Email addresses for most individuals named below can be found on the relevant parts of the website under 4Producers.

Factual Entertainment

Head of Factual Entertainment Alf Lawrie, *Commissioning Editors* Ian Dunkley, Becky Cadman, Lee McMurray, Daniel Fromm, Tim Hancock, Vivienne Molokwu

Channel 5

17–29 Hawley Crescent, Camden Town, London NW1 8TT
tel 020-3580 3600
website www.channel5.com
Facebook www.facebook.com/channel5uk/
Twitter @channel5_tv
Director of Programming Ben Frow

Channel 5 brands include Channel 5, 5Star, 5USA and 5Select, and an on-demand service, My5. Channel 5 broadcasts over 24 hours of children's programmes every week under the Milkshake brand, which is aimed at children aged 2–5 years and airs daily from 6–9.15am (10am at weekends). Channel 5 commissions, co-produces and acquires preschool programming through a wide range of deals and arrangements.

Commissioning

Children's Programming: Milkshake!

Head of Children's Louise Bucknole

CITV

2 Waterhouse Square, 138–142 Holborn, London EC1N 2AE
website www.itv.com/citv
Facebook www.facebook.com/childrensitv/
Twitter @ChildrensITV
Chief Executive Carolyn McCall

ITV is the UK's largest commercial TV network. The ITV network is responsible for the commissioning, scheduling and marketing of network programmes on ITV1 and its digital channel portfolio including ITV2, ITV3, ITV4, ITVBe, ITV Encore and CITV, the commercial free-to-air children's channel. CITV airs from 6am–9pm daily, and CITV programming is aired on ITV from 6–8.30 am on weekends. CITV commissions and acquires a variety of programmes, including live action and animation, aimed at children up to age 12 years.

Commissioning

website www.itv.com/commissioning/articles/citv-nbdhkx05-ckc52cce

See website for information about commissioning and how to submit an idea.

Disney Channel UK

3 Queen Caroline Street, London W6 9PE
email help@disney.co.uk
website https://tv.disney.co.uk
Facebook www.facebook.com/DisneyChannel/

Screen and audio

Twitter @DisneyChannel

Channels run by the Walt Disney Company specialising in programming for children from preschoolers to teens. There are three channels: Disney Channel (9–17 years), Disney Junior (1–8 years) and Disney XD (6–11 years). They are available through the Disney + subscription streaming service.

Nickelodeon UK

17–29 Hawley Crescent, London NW1 8TT
email letterbox@nick.co.uk
website www.nick.co.uk
Facebook www.facebook.com/NickelodeonUK
Twitter @NickelodeonUK

Nickelodeon UK comprises three channels with a target audience spanning children aged approximately 2–12 years: Nickelodeon aimed at children aged 2–17 years, NickToons (www.nicktoons.co.uk) aimed at children aged 7–11 years and NickJr (www.nickjr.co.uk) aimed at children aged 2–5 years.

POP

Narrative Entertainment UK, 35 Inverness Street, London NW1 7HB
email info@popfun.co.uk
website www.popfun.co.uk

A free-to-air children's channel that broadcasts cartoons and live-action series for children aged 4–9 years. Has two sister channels.

Tiny Pop

email info@tinypop.co.uk
website www.tinypop.com
Twitter @TinyPopTV

Cartoons and live action series for children aged 3–7 years.

Pop Max

website www.popfun.co.uk/pop-max

Cartoons, sci-fi, action and anime for children aged 7–12 years.

RTÉ

Donnybrook, Dublin 4, Republic of Ireland
email info@rte.ie
website www.rte.ie
Facebook www.facebook.com/RTEjr
Twitter @RTEjr

RTÉ offers a comprehensive range of programmes for children and young people. RTÉjr broadcasts original and acquired live-action and animated content for children aged 2–7 years, airing each day from 7am–7pm. Additional content is made available on demand and online, as well as through RTÉjr radio. TRTÉ is aimed at children aged 7–15 and airs on RTÉ2.

Commissioning

Head of Children's & Young People's Content Suzanne Kelley, *Executive Producer* Eimear O'Mahony

website https://about.rte.ie/commissioning/commissioning-briefs/rte-young-peoples/

See website for information about commissioning and submitting proposals for children and young people.

S4C

Canolfan S4C Yr Egin, Carmarthen SA31 3EQ
tel 0370 600 4141
website www.s4c.cymru/en
Facebook www.facebook.com/S4C
Twitter @S4C

S4C is the world's only Welsh language TV channel, broadcasting programmes on sport, drama, music, factual, entertainment and culture. Cyw, a programming block for children aged 3–6 years, broadcasts every weekday from 7am–1.30pm. Stwnsh, a programming block for children aged 7–13 years, broadcasts every weekday from 4–6pm and on Saturdays from 9–11am.

ORGANISATIONS CONNECTED TO TELEVISION BROADCASTING

BARB

20 Orange Street, London WC2H 7EF
tel 020-7024 8100
email enquiries@barb.co.uk
website www.barb.co.uk
Twitter @BARBtelevision
Chief Executive Justin Sampson

The Broadcasters Audience Research Board is the official source of viewing figures in the UK.

Ipsos MORI

3 Thomas More Square, London E1W 1YW
tel 020-3059 5000
website www.ipsos.com/en-uk
Twitter @IpsosUK
Ceo Ben Page

One of the UK's leading research companies: conducts surveys for a wide range of major organisations (such as BARB and RAJAR), as well as for other market research agencies.

Pact

3rd Floor, Fitzrovia House,
153–157 Cleveland Street, London W1T 6QW
tel 020-7380 8230
website www.pact.co.uk
Twitter @PactUK
Ceo John McVay

The Producers Alliance for Cinema and Television is the trade association representing the commercial interests of UK independent TV, film, digital, children's and animation media companies.

Public Media Alliance
Room 02.101, Lawrence Stenhouse Building, University of East Anglia, Norwich NR4 7TJ
tel (01603) 592335
email info@publicmediaalliance.org
website www.publicmediaalliance.org
Twitter @PublicMediaPMA
Ceo Kristian Porter

World's largest association of public broadcasters. Provides advocacy, support, knowledge exchange, research and training opportunities for public media worldwide.

Royal Television Society
3 Dorset Rise, London EC4Y 8EN
tel 020-7822 2810
email info@rts.org.uk
website www.rts.org.uk
Facebook www.facebook.com/RoyalTelevisionSociety
Twitter @RTS_media
Ceo Theresa Wise

An educational charity promoting the art and science of television and is the leading forum for discussion and debate on all aspects of the TV community.

RADIO

BBC School Radio
website www.bbc.co.uk/schoolradio

BBC School Radio provides audio resources for primary schools including podcasts, downloads, audio and video clips, learning resources and teachers' notes that are curriculum-linked to Key Stages 1, 2, 3 and 4. Some Early Years Foundation Stage (EYFS) resources are also available.

CBeebies Radio
website www.bbc.co.uk/cbeebies/radio

CBeebies Radio is aimed at encouraging preschool children to develop their listening skills. In addition to radio output, the website contains games, songs, make & colour and story-time activities.

Fun Kids
website www.funkidslive.com

A British children's digital radio station (not national) providing programming to entertain children aged 7–12 years with a mixture of songs, stories, competitions and news. Available to listen via

the website or on DAB Digital Radio across London and south east England.

ORGANISATIONS CONNECTED TO RADIO BROADCASTING

Media.info
email info@media.info
website https://media.info/uk

This website provides detailed listings of UK radio stations alongside information about TV, newspapers, magazines and media ownership in the UK.

The Radio Academy
Suite 303, Pill Box Studios, 115 Coventry Road, London E2 6GH
tel 0800 044 3811
email info@radioacademy.org
website www.radioacademy.org
Facebook www.facebook.com/radioacademy/
Twitter @radioacademy
Chair Helen Thomas

The Radio Academy is a registered charity dedicated to the promotion of excellence in UK radio broadcasting and production. For over 30 years the Radio Academy has run the annual Audio and Radio Industry Awards (ARIAS), which celebrate content and creativity in the industry.

Radiocentre
15 Alfred Place, London WC1E 7EB
tel 020-7010 0600
website www.radiocentre.org
Facebook www.facebook.com/RadiocentreUK
Twitter @Radiocentre
Chief Executive Ian Moss

Radiocentre is the voice of UK commercial radio. Works with government, policy makers and regulators, and provides a forum for industry-wide debate and discussion.

RAJAR
15 Alfred Place, London WC1E 7EB
tel 020-7395 0630
website www.rajar.co.uk
Twitter @RAJARLtd
Chief Executive Jerry Hill

RAJAR – Radio Joint Audience Research – is the official body in charge of measuring radio audiences in the UK. It is jointly owned by the BBC and the RadioCentre on behalf of the commercial sector.

Screen and audio

Theatre
Writing for children's theatre

Writing plays for children is not a soft option. David Wood considers children to be the most difficult audience to write for and shares his thoughts here about this challenge.

'Would you write the Christmas play?' These six words, uttered by John Hole, Director of the Swan Theatre, Worcester, unwittingly changed my life, setting me off on a trail I'm still treading over 40 years later. It wasn't a totally mad question, even though I was then cutting my teeth as an 'adult' actor/director – and indeed I have managed to continue these so-called mainstream activities to a limited degree ever since. No, it had already struck me that children's audiences were important and, by doing magic at birthday parties since my teens, I had already developed an aptitude for and delight in entertaining children.

At Worcester I had organised Saturday morning children's theatre, inveigling my fellow repertory actors into helping me tell stories, lead participation songs and perform crazy sketches. And I was still haunted by the memory of seeing, a couple of years earlier, a big commercial panto in which the star comedian cracked an off-colour joke to a matinee house virtually full of children, got an appreciative cackle from a small party of ladies in the stalls, then advanced to the footlights and said, 'Let's get the kids out of here, then we can get started!'. In the dark I blushed and my hackles rose. How dare this man show such disdain for the young audience whose parents' hard-earned cash had contributed towards his doubtless considerable salary? It set me thinking about how few proper plays were then written and performed for children. There were traditional favourites like *Peter Pan* in London, the occasional *Wizard of Oz*, *Toad of Toad Hall* and *Alice in Wonderland* in the regions, but that was about it. Nothing new. Later I discovered my assessment had been too sweeping. There were several pioneers out there presenting proper plays for children, including Brian Way (Theatre Centre), Caryl Jenner (Unicorn), John Allen (Glyndebourne Children's Theatre) and John English (Midlands Arts Centre), but their work was not then widely recognised. Their contribution to the development of children's theatre in the UK cannot be overestimated. Also, in 1965, the Belgrade Theatre, Coventry, had created the first theatre-in-education company, touring innovative work into schools; and early in 1967, I had acted in the first production of the TIE Company at the Palace Theatre, Watford.

So writing *The Tinder Box* for Christmas 1967 seemed a natural opportunity and, although I don't think it was very good, it paved the way for me to write around 75 (so far) plays that try to trigger the imagination, make children laugh, cry and think, and hopefully lead them towards a love of theatre. The journey hasn't always been easy. It is frustrating that children's theatre is still often perceived as third division theatre; funding for it is less than for its adult counterpart, even though it often costs as much, sometimes more, to put on, and always commands a lower seat price; critics generally ignore it; and most theatre folk seem to think it is only for beginners or failures, a ridiculous belief, since children are the most difficult and honest audience of all – and yet the most rewarding when we get it right.

Let's pause briefly to talk terminology. The phrase 'children's theatre' means different things to different people. Whereas 'youth theatre' clearly implies that young people are taking part in the play, 'children's theatre' can mean not only children performing but also (more correctly, in my view) theatre produced by adults for children to watch. And, although I have occasionally, and enjoyably, written plays for children to perform (*Lady Lollipop*, from Dick King-Smith's book) or for children to take part in alongside adults (*The Lighthouse Keeper's Lunch*, from Ronda and David Armitage's book and *Dinosaurs and All That Rubbish*, from Michael Foreman's book), the vast majority of my plays have been written for professional actors to perform for children. Don't get me wrong. Participation by children is hugely beneficial and worthwhile, but I like to feel my plays might provide the inspiration to encourage them to want to do it themselves. I believe that children respond to exciting examples that inspire them. I also believe that children are more likely to, say, want to learn to play a musical instrument if they see and hear the best professional musicians playing in a concert. They are more likely to want to excel at football if they see – live or on television – the best professional teams displaying dazzling skills.

So any advice I can offer about children's theatre is mainly aimed towards writers who would like to create plays for grown-ups to perform for children. Having said that, it has always surprised me that several of my professionally performed plays have been subsequently put on by schools and youth groups who cope, showing tremendous flair and imagination, with tricky technical demands. I sometimes wish I could write more plays specifically for schools and youth groups, but I think I might be tempted to oversimplify (which would be patronising) or to try to write enough roles for a very large cast, which might dilute the content and fail to provide a satisfying structure.

Encouragingly, the professional children's theatre scene today is much healthier than when I started. There are many more touring companies (see page 318) large and small, producing high-quality work for all ages. There has been an exciting explosion in the amount of work for under-fives. And at last, we have three full-time children's theatre buildings – Unicorn, Polka and Hullabaloo – who put on their own plays as well as receive other companies' work. Unicorn and Polka are both in London, and Hullabaloo recently opened in Darlington. Hopefully there will in the future be many more such beacons in other cities and towns. Children are entitled to their own theatre, and creating theatre buildings especially for them, run by committed professionals, is the best way to improve the quantity, quality and status of the work. Alongside that, our major theatres, including the National and the Royal Shakespeare Company, should be setting an example by making children's theatre an integral part of their programming, rather than occasionally mounting a children's play as an optional extra. And this means more than coming up with an annual Christmas show.

Study the market

Go to see shows. Which companies are doing what? How many cast members can they afford? Are they looking for original plays as well as adaptations of successful books with big titles and box office appeal? Try to meet the artistic directors, to discuss what they might be looking for. What size spaces are the companies playing in? Studios? Large theatres? Do they have facilities for scene changes? Is there flying? Incidentally, restrictions on cast size and staging possibilities are not necessarily a bad thing. Well-defined parameters within which to work can be a help not a hindrance. I was asked to write a play for the Towngate, Basildon, a theatre that had no flying, not much stage depth and virtually no wing space. And I was allowed a cast of only six. At first I despaired but then managed to think positively and wrote *The Gingerbread Man*, which ended up paying the rent for 30 years! The play is set on a giant Welsh dresser. No props or scenery come on or off stage during the show – the basic set is self-contained. And the six characters are joined by the off-stage voices (recorded) of the 'Big Ones', the human owners of the dresser.

It may be putting the cart before the horse to worry about where and how your play might be performed – before you've written it! But it really is foolish to start before finding out what might be practical and realistic. Quite frankly, a cast of 20, or even a dozen, is going to be out of the question for most professional companies, so if your idea demands such numbers, maybe you should approach a school, a youth drama group or an amateur dramatic society instead.

Rather than rely on others, might you be in a position to create your own openings? Many children's theatre practitioners, including myself, have had to start by 'doing it themselves'. I, like Richard Gill, Vicky Ireland and Annie Wood (former artistic directors of the Polka Theatre) not only write but also direct. And Richard Gill, Tim Webb (Oily Cart), Guy Holland (Quicksilver) and I (Whirligig), went as far as to create companies to produce our own work, because we knew we were unlikely to get other companies to put it on. The TYA (Theatre for Young Audiences) website (see box) lists most of the companies currently in production, and is a useful first port of call to see the scope of the work.

What 'works' for children?

A good, satisfying story makes a helpful start, told with theatrical flair. By that I mean that we should use theatrical techniques to spark the imagination of the audience – scenery, costume, sound, lighting, puppetry, magic, circus skills, masks, mime, dancing and music. The physical as well as the verbal can help to retain the attention and interest of children. Page after page of two characters sitting talking are likely to prove a turn-off. It's better to see them do something rather than just talk about it. I try to introduce lots of 'suddenlies' to help keep the audience riveted to their seats, wanting to know what happens next. I've often said that my life's work has been dedicated to stopping children going to the lavatory. Suddenlies – a new character appearing, a sound effect, a lighting change, a surprise twist, a musical sting – can be a huge help. Compare it to the page-turning appeal of a successful children's book.

Play ideas can be found in fairy tales, myths and legends, traditional rhymes and popular stories. Be careful, however, not to waste time adapting books in copyright, unless you have got the necessary permission – no public performances, paid or unpaid, can be given without this. Approach the publisher or the author's agent to discover if the stage rights are available and, if they are, how much it might cost to acquire them for a year or two. Or you might use an incident from history, a pertinent modern social issue, such as conservation, or the real life of an inspirational or controversial person. Or you could explore a social problem especially relevant to children, like single-parent families or bullying.

In my book *Theatre for Children: A Guide to Writing, Adapting, Directing and Acting*, I identify useful ingredients for children's plays. They are really fairly obvious – things that we know children respond to. They include animals, toys, fantasy, a quest, goodies and baddies, humour, scale (small characters in large environments and vice versa), a child at the centre of the story. And justice – think *Cinderella*. Children, like adults, have a strong sense of fairness and will root for the underdog. Roald Dahl's stories, eight of which I have been lucky enough to adapt, all use this. Sophie (in *The BFG*), James (in *James and the Giant Peach*) and Boy (in *The Witches*) are all disadvantaged orphans whose strength of character leads them through immense difficulties to eventual triumph. They are empowered to succeed in an adult-dominated world, and children identify with them.

The use of audience participation is an option much argued about by children's theatre practitioners. Many hate it. For some plays, it would, indeed, be totally inappropriate. But for others it can be exciting and fun. I'm not talking about basic panto participation – 'he's behind you!' – though even this can be used on occasion with integrity. I'm talking about what I call 'positive participation', in which the audience contribute to the action by helping or hindering, by having ideas or by taking part in a 'set piece'. In *The Selfish Shellfish* they create a storm to fool an oil slick. In *The Meg and Mog Show* (for very small children), they make springtime noises and movements to encourage Meg's garden to grow. In *The See-Saw Tree* they vote on whether to save an ancient oak or allow it to be cut down to make way for a children's playground. In *The Gingerbread Man* they help catch the scavenging Sleek the Mouse under an upturned mug. Their contribution is crucial to the development and resolution of the plot. In *The Twits* the audience fools Mr and Mrs Twit by making them think that they, the audience, are upside down. They all remove their shoes, put them on their hands and stretch their arms up while lowering their heads! The sight of a thousand children all doing this, with joy and not a shred of cynicism, is pure magic to me.

I don't believe that a children's play has to have a moral, a self-improving message for the audience. But I do believe a children's play should *be* moral, presenting a positive attitude and an uplifting, hopeful conclusion. And I resent the notion that children's plays should always be written to tie in with the National Curriculum. Many do, but the educationalists shouldn't dictate our agenda – the tail shouldn't wag the dog.

Before you start

I strongly recommend that you create a synopsis, outlining the events in story order. This leads to clarity of storytelling, to the disciplined pursuit of a through-line, with not too many subplots that could end up as time-wasting, irrelevant cul-de-sacs. For myself, it would be foolish to think I had the brilliance to start a play with only an initial idea and just let my imagination lead me through uncharted waters. I find it far better to let the juices flow during the synopsis stage and, when it comes to writing the play, to conscientiously follow through my original instincts with not too many diversions.

Good luck with getting your first play produced. Getting it published may need determination. It was a very special day for me when Samuel French accepted (after initial rejections) *The Owl and the Pussycat Went to See...*, my second play, co-written with Sheila Ruskin. After its first production at Worcester, I beavered away to get it on stage in London and, thanks to several friends helping financially, managed to produce it at the Jeannetta Cochrane Theatre. To save money I directed it myself. We were lucky enough to get two rave reviews. I approached Samuel French again. They came to see it and, hallelujah, offered to publish it. Since then their loyalty has been more than gratifying – they still publish most of my efforts. There are now several specialist children's play publishers, many of whom also act as licensees of amateur performances. The National Theatre Bookshop and French's Theatre Bookshop stock a fair number of plays and, when searching for a publisher, it is worth checking out their shelves. The internet can help too. Tap in the names of successful children's playwrights, like Mike Kenny, Charles Way, Brendan Murray or the late Adrian Mitchell and see what comes up.

I find that the challenge of writing a play for children never gets easier, however many times I go through the process. It certainly isn't a soft option, i.e. easier than writing a play for adults. And it carries, I believe, a big responsibility. I always worry that I haven't the right to fail: the last thing I want to do is write something that might put children off theatre for life. I'm aware that many in the audience will be first-time theatre-goers, some of whom never asked to come! It's so important to get it right, to enthuse them so much they can't wait to return. And this is where the passion comes in. Most children's theatre practitioners are passionate about what they do, with an almost missionary zeal to stimulate and delight their audience. Also, we all know that, unlike adult audiences who tend to sit quietly and clap at the end, even if they've hated the play, our children's audiences won't be (and shouldn't be) so polite. It is palpably obvious when we 'lose' them. We are dedicated to using our experience and instinct to 'hold' them, to help them enjoy the communal experience of a theatre visit and willingly enter the spirit of the performance. The buzz I get from being in an auditorium of children overtly having a great time – listening hard, watching intently, reacting, feeling, letting the play take them on a special, magical, unique journey – is a buzz I constantly strive for. I suppose that's really why I do it.

Further reading

Bennett, Stuart (ed.), *Theatre for Children and Young People: 50 Years of Professional Theatre in the UK* (Aurora Metro 2005)

Maguire, Tom and Karian Schuitema (eds) with foreword by David Wood, *Theatre for Young Audiences: A Critical Handbook* (Institute of Education Press 2012)

Wood, David, with Janet Grant, *Theatre for Children: A Guide to Writing, Adapting, Directing and Acting* (Faber and Faber 1997)

Ireland, Vicky and Paul Harman (eds), *50 Best Plays for Young Audiences* (Aurora Metro 2016)

David Wood OBE has been dubbed 'the national children's dramatist' by *The Times*. His plays are performed regularly on tour, in the West End and all over the world. In 2006, for the Queen's 80th birthday party celebrations, he wrote *The Queen's Handbag*, which was broadcast live from Buckingham Palace Gardens and watched by eight million viewers on BBC1. Since 2008, his adaptation of Judith Kerr's *The Tiger Who Came to Tea* has toured the UK and abroad and played seven West End seasons. The production was nominated for an Olivier Award in 2012. David's grown-up musical, *The Go-Between* (co-written with Richard Taylor, adapted from L.P. Hartley's novel), won Best Musical Production in the Theatre Awards UK 2012 and in 2016 opened in the West End. His adaptation of Michelle Magorian's novel *Goodnight Mister Tom* won the 2013 Olivier Award for Best Entertainment and Family; it returned to the West End and toured in 2015/16. He has adapted the following Roald Dahl novels for the stage: *The BFG, The Witches, Fantastic Mr Fox, James and the Giant Peach, The Twits, George's Marvellous Medicine, Danny the Champion of the World* and *The Magic Finger*. *The See-Saw Tree* opened at the China National Theatre for Children in Beijing in 2019, and is still in their repertoire. In 2021, Methuen Drama published *David Wood Plays for 5-12 year olds*. His website is www.davidwood.org.uk.

See also...

● *Adapting books for the stage*, page 311

Adapting books for the stage

Stephen Briggs ponders the challenges and rewards of dramatising other people's novels.

Why me?

Stephen Briggs? Stephen Briggs? Who on earth is Stephen Briggs to write about adapting novels for the stage?

Well, many years ago I wrote a stage version of *A Christmas Carol* for my amdram group ... no, stick with me on this.... *Then*, a few years later I adapted two Tom Sharpe novels (these were for one-off productions and the scripts are now long gone). *However*, my overwhelming – and more recent – experience has been with dramatising the novels of the late Sir Terry Pratchett. I've now adapted 22 of Terry's books – four for Transworld/ Doubleday, three for Samuel French (now part of Concord Theatricals), three for Oxford University Press, six for Methuen Drama and three for Oberon Books (both now part of Bloomsbury), with three more being scheduled for publication as I type. These have been staged by amateur groups in over 20 countries from Zimbabwe to Antarctica (yes, really, Antarctica) and by professional groups in France and the Czech Republic. I also co-scripted the mini-dramatisations used by Sky One to promote their big budget television films of Terry's *Hogfather* and *Colour of Magic*.

I have been involved in amateur theatre since I left school. Not just acting, but also directing, choreography, set design/construction, costume design/construction – even brewing mulled wine for the audiences in our chilly medieval theatre. None of this makes me an expert, not by any interpretation of the word, but I was the one who had to make my scripts work on stage since I also directed them. I was also able to get useful and honest feedback from the original author. Hopefully I've learned a few lessons along the way, which I'm happy to pass on.

Dialogue

When you watch a film, a lot of screen time is taken up by fancy stuff – Imperial star cruisers roaring through space, ill-fated liners ploughing the waves, swooping pan shots over raddled pirate ships. In a play, you don't get any of that stuff. The dialogue has to drive the action.

The methods used to adapt a novel for the stage are as varied as the authors you try to adapt. Terry Pratchett, like Charles Dickens, wrote very good dialogue and the scenes already leap from the page. Other authors make greater use of narrative which the adapter has to weave into the play as well, if they are to keep to the spirit of the original work. Terry was well known for his use of footnotes and, for some of the plays, I even included the Footnote as a 'character' – a Brechtian alienation device, for those who want a more literary justification.

Keep it simple

Terry Pratchett wrote 'filmically' – his scenes cross-cut and swoop like a screenplay. On the silver screen, you can set a scene visually in a second. On the stage it can take longer, and you have to give the audience a chance to realise where they are if they are to have any possibility of keeping up with the – often quite complex – plot.

It's important to remember that a theatre audience doesn't have the luxury of being able to reread a page, or skip back to check a plot point – they (usually) get to see the play only once. It's vital, therefore, to ensure that important plot points are not lost along the way while one is tempted to keep in other favoured scenes from the much longer novel.

Keep it moving

Novelists are not constrained by budget – they can destroy cities, have characters who are 60-foot long dragons, write vital scenes involving time travel and other difficult concepts. These can initially appear to be a challenge for anyone without the budget of Industrial Light and Magic (www.ilm.com).

When I write, I have the good fortune to be writing for a theatre which has very limited space – on and off stage – and virtually no capacity for scenic effects. This makes staging the plays a nightma…, ahem… a challenge, but the benefit is that my adaptations can be staged virtually anywhere. I don't write them with essential big effects or big set changes. Of course, drama groups with huge budgets can go wild with all that – but the plays can work without it.

Plays which demand massive set changes or pose huge scenic problems are likely to put off many directors working to a tight budget. It's different if you're Alan Ayckbourn, of course … onstage swimming pool, floating river cruiser … no problem.

People say that radio has the best scenery. Allowing the audience to fill in the gaps can not only save on costly wood and canvas, but on occasions, can even be more effective than an expensive but stagey scenic effect. After all, Shakespeare's *Antony and Cleopatra* includes a sea battle between two great navies – all reported by two blokes standing on a hill.

The plays – like the books – have to keep moving. Scenes need to flow fairly seamlessly into one another. Set changes slow things down. I get to see large numbers of productions of my plays and the general rule is that the ones with frequent set-changes are the ones which plod.

Writing for schools

Three of my plays were written specifically for classroom use. I had to bear in mind that the plays were as likely to be used for reading in a classroom as for production on a stage. So I tried to keep the number of stage directions to a minimum because I know all too well from reading plays with my own amateur drama group that the need to read through huge chunks of explanatory stuff in italics, interspersed with snippets of uninformative dialogue, is very tedious. Here is an example (not, I hasten to add, an extract from a real play):

(As Smithers looks out of the window, Bert rushes downstairs, carrying an aspidistra in a brass bowl. He passes, but fails to notice, the gorilla. He trips and falls, dropping the plant and pot on Smithers' head)
SMITHERS: Oof!
(Smithers picks up a broom from the floor and chases after Bert. They run into the kitchen and out again, up the stairs and across the landing. Bert takes a wad of banknotes out of his pocket and throws them at Smithers)
BERT: Take that!

It was also important to avoid characters with just 'one line and a cough'. Nothing is worse in a read-through than to be given the role of 'King of France' only to find that the character speaks one line on page one and then is silent for the rest of the play. Except, perhaps, being allocated a role which contains dialogue that will invite ridicule from the rest of the class: 'Oh la, I am the prettiest person in the world; I do love to wander around wearing frilly pink underwear'.

I also try to ensure that whatever special effects are mentioned should be either easily achievable or not essential and, again, that the plays can be performed with the minimum amount of scenery.

Two of the three plays I wrote for OUP I would not be staging myself. It was really fascinating (and quite gratifying) to see the plays staged by schools and to find that they *worked*.

How do I start?

• **I read the book.** Then I read the book again. I then put it down, leave it for a week and write down all the main plot points I can recall, and a rough list of scenes. That should give me a rough shape for the play. Anything I've forgotten to include can probably go high up on the list of potential material to cut.

• **I write it.** I sit down and write the script. At this stage I don't try to keep to a specific length; I just adapt the book, making mental notes of any scenes that show potential for trimming, cutting or pasting into another as I go along. My overall plan is to keep the play to around two hours. If, when I get to the end, the play is too long, I then go back and look again at each scene and character to ensure they can justify their place in the script.

• **I dump it.** Reducing a 95,000-word novel into a 20,000-word play means that there will have to be an element of trimming. The trick, I suppose, is to ensure that the cuts will not be too glaring to the paying audience ('I reckon if we cut out the Prince of Denmark, we can get *Hamlet* down to an hour and a half, no problem'). Hopefully, there will be subplots, not vital to the main story, which can be excised to keep it all flowing. But even so, occasionally tough decisions have to be made once all the fat's been removed and one is forced to cut into muscle and bone (as it were). It's important to let stuff go – even if it's a favourite scene in the book, or a favourite character.

• **I share it.** It's good then to let someone else read it. It's all too easy to get so far into the wood that you can no longer see the trees. Being challenged on the decisions you made in adapting the book is a very good thing. I'd certainly recommend anyone adapting a book to have the script read by someone who knows the book well, and who can point out any important plot omissions. It is also good to have your script read by someone who does *not* know the book and who can ask the 'what on earth does that mean?' questions.

It's useful for me that many of my drama club are not *Discworld* 'fans'. Their outsider's view of the script is extremely useful. I also then have the luxury of amending the script in rehearsal to tidy up scenes, add in bits and take bits out. This means that the script which is submitted to the publisher is then fully tried and tested.

Some golden rules

It's difficult to be hard and fast about 'rules' for adapting books, but here are a few useful guidelines that I try to stick to:

• **Don't change the principle plot** – there's no point in calling a play *Bram Stoker's Dracula* if you're then going to have Dracula surviving at the end and starting up a flourishing law firm in Whitby.

• **Never sacrifice 'real' scenes in order to add in some of your own** – after all, you've chosen to adapt the author's work because, presumably, you admire their writing. If you think you can improve on their humour/drama/characterisation you should really be writing your own plots and not torturing theirs.

• **Use the author's dialogue whenever possible** – same as the above, really. Also try to attribute it to the right character whenever practicable.

• **Don't add characters** – stick to the ones the author has given you.

• **Don't be afraid to cut material** – after all, you're trying to squeeze a 300-page novel into a two-hour play; you just can't fit everything in, so don't try. Anything which does not advance the main plot should be on your list for potential dumping if your play overruns.

• **If it doesn't *need* changing – don't change it.**

As well as the 22 plays he mentions in his article, **Stephen Briggs** is the co-author, with Terry Pratchett, and illustrator of *Turtle Recall: The Discworld Companion* (Gollancz 1994), *The Streets of Ankh-Morpork* (Corgi Books 1993), *The Wit & Wisdom of Discworld* (Doubleday 2007) and a small raft of other publications emanating from Terry Pratchett's *Discworld* books, including their final collaboration, *The Ultimate Discworld Companion* (Gollancz 2021). He read the unabridged audio versions of Terry's books for Isis, HarperCollins and for Random House (in the USA). In 2005 he won an Audie Award (Audio Publishers Association, USA) for his reading of Terry's *Monstrous Regiment* (Corgi Books 2003) and in 2013 was nominated for his reading of *Dodger* (Doubleday 2012). He also won the Audible Audio Download Book of the Year 2008 for *Good Omens* (Gollancz 1990) and in 2009 received an Odyssey Award for his recording of Terry's *Nation* (Doubleday 2008) for Harper Audio. In 2010 he won two awards from *AudioFile* magazine for his recording of *Unseen Academicals* (Doubleday 2009), and in 2014 he won two more for *Raising Steam* (Doubleday 2013) and for *The Science of Discworld* (Ebury Press 1999). In 2021 his new Discworld-based show, *Terry Pratchett: Murder in Ankh-Morpork*, was staged, he published his dramatisation of *Dracula* (Amazon), and his adaptations of three more Pratchett books, *Hogfather*, *Lords and Ladies* and *The Shakespeare Codex*, were published by Bloomsbury.

See also...

• *Writing for children's theatre*, page 305
• *Theatre for children*, page 315
• *Adapting children's books for stage and screen*, page 287

Theatre for children

London and regional theatres are listed below; listings of touring companies start on page 318.

LONDON

Chickenshed Theatre
Chase Side, Southgate, London N14 4PE
tel 020-8292 9222
email info@chickenshed.org.uk
website www.chickenshed.org.uk
Twitter @CHICKENSHED_UK
Managing Director Louise Perry

Produces theatre for all ages as well as running successful education courses, outreach projects and membership programmes.

Colour House Theatre
Merton Abbey Mills, Watermill Way,
London SW19 2RD
tel 020-8542 5511
email info@colourhousetheatre.co.uk
website www.colourhousetheatre.co.uk
Facebook www.facebook.com/The
ColourHouseTheatre
Twitter @ColourHouseThtr
Founder and Chief Executive Peter Wallder, *Resident Artistic Director* Charlie Shakespeare

Grade II-listed building in the riverside setting of Merton Abbey Millls, seating 50–70 people. The resident children's theatre has staged over 100 original musical adaptations of famous fairy tales during the past 25 years. The Children's Theatre achieved charitable status in 2008. The one-hour shows run at the weekends and school holiday days (except July and August). The Theatre also has evening shows, music and comedy nights and is available to hire for events and private parties.

Polka Theatre
240 The Broadway, London SW19 1SB
tel 020-8543 4888
email peter@polkatheatre.com
website www.polkatheatre.com
Twitter @polkatheatre
Artistic Director Peter Glanville

Theatre of new work for children up to the age of 12, with targeted commissions. Now open following extensive redevelopment. Founded 1967.

The Questors Theatre
12 Mattock Lane, London W5 5BQ
email enquiries@questors.org.uk
website www.questors.org.uk
Facebook www.facebook.com/questorstheatre/
Twitter @questorstheatre
Executive Director Andrea Bath

Largest independent community theatre in Europe. Produces 15–20 shows a year, specialising in modern and classical world drama. Visiting productions hosted too. No unsolicited scripts. Also runs a youth theatre for young people aged between 6–18, as well as summer workshops.

Theatre-Rites
Unit 3, Energy Centre, Bowling Green Walk,
London N1 6AL
tel 020-7164 6196
email info@theatre-rites.co.uk
website www.theatre-rites.co.uk
Facebook www.facebook.com/TheatreRites
Twitter @TheatreRites
Artistic Director Sue Buckmaster, *Executive Producer* Claire Templeton

Creates devised theatre for family audiences and young people using a mix of performance, installation, puppetry, dance and sound. Working within the UK and internationally, the company creates site-specific and touring productions. Founded 1995.

Unicorn Theatre
147 Tooley Street, London SE1 2HZ
tel 020-7645 0560
email hello@unicorntheatre.com
website www.unicorntheatre.com
Facebook www.facebook.com/unicorntheatre
Twitter @unicorn_theatre
Artistic Director Justin Audibert, *Executive Director* Bailey Lock (Helen Tovey, maternity cover)

Produces a year-round programme of theatre for children and young people under 21. In-house productions of full-length plays with professional casts are staged across two auditoria, alongside visiting companies and education work. Rarely commissions plays from writers who are new to it, but it is keen to hear from writers who are interested in working with the theatre in the future.

Do not send unsolicited MSS, but rather a short statement describing why you would like to write for Unicorn along with a CV or a summary of your relevant experience.

REGIONAL

Yvonne Arnaud Theatre Management Ltd
Millbrook, Guildford, Surrey GU1 3UX
tel (01483) 440077
email yat@yvonne-arnaud.co.uk
website www.yvonne-arnaud.co.uk
Twitter @YvonneArnaud
Director and Chief Executive Joanna Read

Producing theatre which also receives productions. Runs activities for education providers throughout the year.

Chichester Festival Theatre
Oaklands Park, Chichester, West Sussex PO19 6AP
tel (01243) 784437
email literary@cft.org.uk
website www.cft.org.uk
Twitter @chichesterFT
Artistic Director Daniel Evans

Stages annual Summer Festival Season April–Oct in the Festival and Minerva Theatres together with a year-round education programme, winter touring programme and youth theatre Christmas show. Does not accept unsolicited scripts. The Learning, Education and Participation (LEAP) department runs a programme events for all ages, including workshops, performances, talks and tours.

Contact Theatre Company
Oxford Road, Manchester M15 6JA
tel 0161 274 0600
website https://contactmcr.com/
Twitter @ContactMcr
Artistic Director and Chief Executive Matt Fenton, *Creative Producer* Roxy Moores

Multidisciplinary arts organisation focused on working with and for young people aged 13 and above. Offers a range of free projects, from writing to music and drama, including the Contact Young Company ensemble.

Creation Theatre Company
tel (01865) 766266
email boxoffice@creationtheatre.co.uk
website www.creationtheatre.co.uk
Facebook https://en-gb.facebook.com/CreationTheatre/
Twitter @creationtheatre
Instagram @creationtheatre
Chief Executive Lucy Askew, *General Manager* Charlie Morley

Award-winning producing theatre company, specialising in digital and site-specific inventive theatre in extraordinary locations. Creators of Creation Home Delivery, live & interactive online drama classes for ages 5–16, designed to inspire a life-long love of stories and storytelling. No unsolicited manuscripts.

Derby Theatre
15 Theatre Walk, St Peter's Quarter, Derby DE1 2NF
email creatives@derbyplayhouse.co.uk
website www.derbytheatre.co.uk/about-us/in-good-company
Twitter @DerbyTheatre
Artistic Director and Chief Executive Sarah Brigham, *Creative Learning Director* Caroline Barth

Regional producing and receiving theatre. The In Good Company programme offers opportunities for theatre-makers and companies in the region.

The Dukes
Moor Lane, Lancaster LA1 1QE
tel (01524) 598500
email ask@dukes-lancaster.org
website https://dukes-lancaster.org/
Twitter @TheDukesTheatre
Chief Executive Karen O'Neill

Producing theatre and cultural centre. Its Young Writers scheme was launched in January 2017. See website for up-to-date information about the theatre's productions and programming approach.

The Edge Theatre and Arts Centre
Manchester Road, Chorlton, Manchester M21 9JG
tel 0161 282 9776
email info@edgetheatre.co.uk
website www.edgetheatre.co.uk
Twitter @TheEdgeMcr
Artistic Director and Chief Executive Janine Waters, *Musical Director* Simon Waters

Produces and presents theatre for all ages, including families and children. Musical and children's theatre specialities. 70-seat flexible theatre space and studio spaces. Also runs classes, courses and workshops in theatre, dance, music, writing and other creative genres, including: Theatre Club for ages 6–8; Edge Youth Theatre for ages 9–12; Aspire for young people with learning challenges aged between 13–17; and Edge Youth Dance. Founded 2011.

The Egg
Sawclose, Bath BA1 1ET
tel (01225) 823409 (reception and administration)
email egg.reception@theatreroyal.org.uk
website www.theatreroyal.org.uk/the-egg
Twitter @theeggbath

Part of the Theatre Royal Bath. Purpose-built theatre for young people and their families. Hosts and produces shows for children and young people alongside a year-round participation and outreach programme for people aged 0–21. Opened 2005.

Everyman Theatre Cheltenham
7 Regent Street, Cheltenham, Glos. GL50 1HQ
tel (01242) 512515

email admin@everymantheatre.org.uk
website www.everymantheatre.org.uk
Twitter @Everymanchelt
Creative Director Paul Milton

Regional presenting and producing theatre promoting a wide range of plays. Small-scale experimental, youth and educational work encouraged in The Studio Theatre. Contact the Creative Director before submitting material.

Leeds Children's Theatre

c/o The Carriageworks Theatre, The Electric Press, 3 Millennium Square, Leeds LS2 3AD
email enquiry@leeds-childrens-theatre.co.uk
website www.leeds-childrens-theatre.co.uk
Twitter @LeedsCT

Oldest established Children's Theatre society in the UK. Its members (both adults and children) bring live theatre to young people, often for the very first time. Many of the plays produced are based on well-known children's literature. Stages two productions each year at the purpose-built Carriageworks Theatre, typically in spring (March/April) and late autumn (November). Welcomes school groups as well as families and friends. Founded 1935.

Leeds Playhouse

Playhouse Square, Quarry Hill, Leeds LS2 7UP
tel 0113 213 7700
website https://leedsplayhouse.org.uk
Twitter @LeedsPlayhouse
Artistic Director James Brining

Seeks out the best companies and artists to create theatre in the heart of Yorkshire. Its Artistic Development programme, Furnace, discovers and supports new voices, while developing work with established practitioners. It provides a creative space for writers, directors, companies and individual theatre-makers to refine their practice at all stages of their career. The Creative Engagement team works with more than 12,000 people every year reaching out to refugee communities, young people, students, older people and people with learning challenges.

Live Theatre

Broad Chare, Quayside,
Newcastle upon Tyne NE1 3DQ
tel 0191 232 1232
email info@live.org.uk
website www.live.org.uk
Facebook www.live.org.uk/index.php/creative-opportunities/children-young-people/schools-teachers
Twitter @LiveTheatre
Executive Director & Joint Ceo Jacqui Kell, *Artistic Director & Joint Ceo* Jack McNamara

New writing theatre company and venue. Stages three to six productions per year of new writing, plus touring plays from other new writing companies. The

Live Youth Theatre programme is free and open to young people between the ages of 10 and 25. CPD and Inset support for teachers is also available.

Norwich Puppet Theatre

St James, Whitefriars, Norwich NR3 1TN
tel (01603) 629921 (box office), (01603) 615564 (admin.)
email info@puppettheatre.co.uk
website www.puppettheatre.co.uk
Facebook www.facebook.com/NorwichPuppetTheatre
Twitter @norwich_puppet
Instagram @norwichpuppettheatre

Home to a professional theatre company which creates family puppet shows. The company tours to schools and venues around the country and occasionally internationally. As a venue, the Theatre also presents a programme of puppetry performances and workshops for family and adult audiences. Norwich Puppet Theatre is also a charity and a creative engagement organisation with an extensive outreach programme.

Nottingham Playhouse

Nottingham Playhouse Trust Ltd, Wellington Circus, Nottingham NG1 5AF
tel 0115 941 9419
website https://nottinghamplayhouse.co.uk/get-involved/young-people/
Twitter @NottmPlayhouse
Artistic Director Adam Penford, *Chief Executive* Stephanie Sirr, *Amplify Producer* Craig Gilbert

Seeks to nurture new writers from the East Midlands primarily through its Artist Development programme, Amplify. Also offers a range of groups and youth theatres for young people aged two and above; see website above for full details.

Queen's Theatre, Hornchurch

Billet Lane, Hornchurch, Essex RM11 1QT
tel (01708) 443333
email info@queens-theatre.co.uk
website www.queens-theatre.co.uk
website www.queens-theatre.co.uk/get-involved/youth-theatre/
Twitter @QueensTheatreH
Executive Director Mathew Russell

Regional theatre with a rich heritage, working in Outer East London, Essex and beyond. Each annual programme includes home-grown theatre, visiting live entertainment and inspiring learning and participation projects.

The Queen's Youth Theatre Programme (QYouth) provides the opportunity for young people aged 6–18 to develop creativity, confidence and teamwork, as well as offering valuable opportunities to perform on the Queen's Theatre stage and elsewhere. Younger members begin with the QSteps Programme before moving on to the Young Company Programme, which offers performance, technical and dance opportunities for those who wish to develop further a range of theatre skills. Founded 1953.

Royal Shakespeare Company

The Royal Shakespeare Theatre, Waterside, Stratford-upon-Avon, Warks. CV37 6BB
tel (01789) 296655
email literary@rsc.org.uk
website www.rsc.org.uk
website https://37plays.co.uk/
Facebook www.facebook.com/thersc
Twitter @TheRSC
Artistic Director Emeritus Gregory Doran, *Acting Artistic Director* Erica Whyman, *Head of Literary* Pippa Hill

Produces a core repertoire of Shakespeare alongside new plays and the work of Shakespeare's contemporaries on its two main stages, the RST and the Swan Theatre. In addition, its studio theatre, The Other Place, produces festivals of cutting-edge new work. For all its stages, the Company commissions new plays, new translations and new adaptations that illuminate the themes and concerns of Shakespeare and his contemporaries for a modern audience. The Literary department does not accept unsolicited work but rather seeks out writers it wishes to work with or commission, and monitors the work of writers in production in the UK and internationally. Writers are welcome to invite the Literary department to readings, showcases or productions by emailing the address above.

In 2023, the *37 Plays* national playwriting project will be launched, via which authors of any age are invited to tell their story. The winning entries will be staged across the UK and online in Autumn 2023; submissions will be accepted from 1 January 2023.

Sherman Theatre

Senghennydd Road, Cardiff CF24 4YE
tel 029-2064 6900
website www.shermantheatre.co.uk/theatre-makers/
Twitter @shermantheatre
Executive Director Julia Barry, *Artistic Director* Joe Murphy

Produces two Christmas productions (for ages 3–6 in English and Welsh and an actor/musician-led production for ages 7+) and actively seeks high-quality work for children and young people as part of its programming. Participatory work with youth theatres. Founded 2007.

Theatr Clwyd

Mold, Flintshire CH7 1YA
tel (01352) 344101
email writers@theatrclwyd.com
website www.theatrclwyd.com
Twitter @ClwydTweets

Largest producing theatre in Wales, creating up to fourteen productions each year in English, Welsh and bilingually. Productions are a mix of classic plays, contemporary revivals, musicals and new writing. Will consider plays by writers, particularly Welsh, Wales-based or with Welsh themes, and usually offers six writing residencies each year. No literary department, so authors will need to be patient when waiting for a response to an unsolicited script.

Theatr Clwyd

Mold, Flintshire CH7 1YA
tel (01352) 344101
email together@theatrclwyd.com
website www.theatrclwyd.com
Twitter @clwydtweets
Artistic Director Tamara Harvey, *Executive Director* Liam Evans-Ford, *Director of Creative Engagement* Gwennan Mair Jones

Aims to be a leading force in developing projects, nurturing writers, offering compelling revivals and the best new writing. The Creative Engagement team produces work for children, young people and their communities.

Visible Fictions

Suite 325/327, 4th Floor, 11 Bothwell Street, Glasgow G2 6LY
email laura@visiblefictions.co.uk
website https://visiblefictions.co.uk
Twitter @visiblefictions
Artistic Director Dougie Irvine, *Producer* Laura Penny

Accessible theatre for young people and adults. Also works in creative learning settings – community, educational, institutional and professional – to create bespoke and immersive projects.

TOURING COMPANIES

Arad Goch

Stryd y Baddon, Aberystwyth, Ceredigion SY23 2NN
tel (01970) 617998
email post@aradgoch.org
website www.aradgoch.cymru
Twitter @AradGoch
Artistic Director Jeremy Turner

Performs in Welsh and English and tours nationally throughout Wales, and occasionally abroad. The company is particularly interested in enabling children and young people to recognise and appreciate their own unique cultural identity through theatre. Some of the company's work is based on traditional material and children's literature, but it also commissions new work from experienced dramatists and new writers. Arad Goch performs in theatres and other locations, including schools, and also offers seminars/workshops for students and teachers. The company has its own production house in Aberystwyth which is used by other arts and community organisations and where it programmes a variety of participatory activities for young people. It organises the biennial 'Agor Drysau–Opening Doors' Wales International Festival of Performing Arts for Young Audiences (www.agordrysau.cymru). Founded 1989.

Booster Cushion Theatre

75 How Wood, Park Street, St Albans, Herts. AL2 2RW
tel (01727) 873874
email admin@booster-cushion.co.uk
website www.booster-cushion.co.uk
Facebook www.facebook.com/boostercushiontheatre
Twitter @BoosterCushion
Director Philip Sherman

Comical theatre company formed especially to re-tell traditional tales to primary-school pupils and their families using surprising Big Books. BCT has performed to over 500,000 people in schools, libraries, museums and theatres across the UK using pop-up books up to 3m tall and concertina books over 5m wide.

All productions are solo performing shows using mime, voice and some sign language. They involve a high level of audience participation. Each show is completely portable and can be performed inside or outside; technical requirements are minimal. Founded 1989.

Boundless Theatre

Big Local Works, 4 Market Place, South Bermondsey, London SE16 3UQ
tel 020-7072 0140
email hello@boundlesstheatre.org.uk
website www.boundlesstheatre.org.uk
website https://boundlesstheatre.org.uk/projects/accelerator/
Instagram @boundlessabound
Artistic Director and Ceo Rob Drummer

Creates new plays with and for audiences aged 15 to 25. Tours the UK and internationally. Its Accelerator programme helps new voices develop their work; there is a cash bursary of £2,500, alongside other sources of support. Founded 2001 (as Company of Angels).

Cahoots NI

Cahoots NI, Cityside Retail Park, 100–150 York Street, Belfast BT15 1WA
tel 028-9043 4349
email info@cahootsni.com
website www.cahootsni.com
Facebook www.facebook.com/Cahoots NI
Twitter @CahootsNI
Artistic Director Paul McEneaney, *Creative Engagement Manager* Emma Wilson

Professional children's touring company which concentrates on the visual potential of theatre and capitalises upon the age-old popularity of magic and

illusion as an essential ingredient in the art of entertaining. It aims to provide inspiring theatrical experiences for children and to encourage appreciation of the arts in young audiences from all sections of society via outreach work. The company has performed in Ireland, the UK, the US and Asia in theatres, schools and healthcare settings. Founded 2001.

Catherine Wheels Theatre Company

Brunton Theatre, Ladywell Way, Musselburgh EH21 6AF
tel 0131 653 5255
email admin@catherinewheels.co.uk
website www.catherinewheels.co.uk
Facebook www.facebook.com/CatherineWheelsCompany
Twitter @cwheelstheatre
Artistic Director Gill Robertson

Producing company that tours the UK and internationally, performing for children and young people. One of the founders of the Theatre in Schools Scotland initiative.

Fevered Sleep

15A Old Ford Road, London E2 9PJ
tel 020-3815 6430
email info@feveredsleep.co.uk
website www.feveredsleep.co.uk
Facebook www.facebook.com/feveredsleeponline/
Twitter @feveredsleep
Instagram @feveredsleep
Artistic Directors Sam Butler, David Harradine

Creates performances, installations and digital art for children and adults that the company describes as 'collaborative, participatory, research-led art'. Founded 1996.

Kazzum Arts

Oxford House, Derbyshire Street, London E2 6HG
tel 020-7749 1123
email hello@kazzum.org
website www.kazzum.org
Facebook www.facebook.com/Kazzum/
Twitter @KazzumArts
Instagram @kazzumarts
Artistic Director Alex Evans, *Executive Director* Lauren Irving

Provides opportunities for children and young people to explore their creativity at times in their lives when they are most in need of support. Kazzum facilitates innovative, playful and multi-disciplinary projects which encourage social and reflective skills, enabling young people to foster positive relationships and experience an increased sense of wellbeing. Founded 1989.

Konflux Theatre in Education

4100 Park Approach, Thorpe Park, Leeds LS15 8GB
tel (01937) 832740

Theatre

Theatre

email info@konfluxtheatre.com
website www.konfluxtheatre.com
Twitter @KonfluxTheatre
Artistic Director Anthony Koncsol

Theatre in Education company and Arts Award Supporter. Works with approx. 700 schools each year, building close working relationships with teachers and other education professionals and ensuring its programmes and their delivery are tailored to the needs of the organisation. Konflux offers over 70 curriculum-based Play in a Day® workshops designed to build confidence and promote team work. They give pupils the opportunity to learn through drama, increase their acting skills and present a performance back to peers and parents. Founded 1998.

Little Angel Theatre
14 Dagmar Passage, London N1 2DN
tel 020-7226 1787
email info@littleangeltheatre.com
website www.littleangeltheatre.com
Twitter @LittleATheatre
Artistic Director Samantha Lane

Committed to working with children and families through schools, the local community and the wider community through its extensive touring programme. Little Angel Theatre develops innovative projects, implements improved access to their creative work, increases opportunities for participation and provides stimulating learning and creativity for all using puppetry. Productions last approx. one hour. Termly activities are run for children, families and schools, including INSET training for teachers. Regular introductory and professional development courses are held throughout the year for teenagers and adults.

The London Bubble
(Bubble Theatre Company)
5 Elephant Lane, London SE16 4JD
tel 020-7237 4434
email admin@londonbubble.org.uk
website www.londonbubble.org.uk
Twitter @LBubble
Instagram @bubbletheatre

Aims to provide the artistic direction, skills, environment and resources to create inspirational, inclusive and involving theatre for the local community and beyond. Also runs a number of groups for children and young people as well as an adult drama group.

M6 Theatre Company
Studio Theatre, Hamer C.P. School,
Albert Royds Street, Rochdale, Lancs. OL16 2SU
tel (01706) 355898
email admin@m6theatre.co.uk
website https://m6theatre.co.uk/
Twitter @M6Theatre
Artistic Director Gilly Baskeyfield

Touring theatre company specialising in creating and delivering innovative theatre for young audiences.

Oily Cart
Smallwood School Annexe, Smallwood Road,
London SW17 0TW
tel 020-8672 6329
email oilies@oilycart.org.uk
website www.oilycart.org.uk
Twitter @oilycart
Artistic Director Ellie Griffiths, *Executive Director* Zoë Lally

Touring company staging interactive, sensory shows across the UK and internationally. Reimagines theatre for young audiences to make it more inclusive, and all productions are created for and with children and young people, regardless of age or perceived ability. Considers scripts from new writers, but at present all work is generated from within the company. Founded 1981.

The Pied Piper Theatre Company
1 Lilian Place, Coxcombe Lane, Chiddingfold,
Surrey GU8 4QA
tel (01428) 684022
email info@piedpipertheatre.co.uk
website www.piedpipertheatre.co.uk
Twitter @PiedPiperLive
Artistic Director Tina Williams

Specialises in bringing new writing for children to the stage. Typically tours one show a year in the UK, sometimes two, and occasionally tours in Europe and Asia. Founded 1984.

Prime Theatre
(formerly Sixth Sense Theatre for Young People)
c/o The Wyvern Theatre, Theatre Square,
Swindon SN1 1QN
tel (01793) 614864
email info@primetheatre.co.uk
website www.primetheatre.co.uk
Twitter @PrimeTheatreUK
Artistic Director Mark Powell

Professional theatre company prioritising work with young people. Prime Theatre produces both issue-based and creative theatre productions and performs in schools, theatres and arts centres in the South-West region and beyond. These productions are supported by additional young people-led work, workshops, training sessions and other projects.

Proteus Theatre Company
Proteus Creation Space, Council Road, Basingstoke,
Hants RG21 3DH
tel (01256) 354541
email info@proteustheatre.com
website www.proteustheatre.com
Twitter @proteustheatre
Artistic Director and Chief Executive Mary Swan

Small-scale touring company particularly committed to new writing and new work, education and community collaborations. Produces up to three touring shows per year plus community projects. Founded 1981.

Replay Theatre Company
East Belfast Network Centre,
55 Templemore Avenue, Belfast BT5 4FP
tel 028-9045 4562
email info@replaytheatre.co.uk
website www.replaytheatre.co.uk
Twitter @ReplayTheatreCo
Artistic Director Janice Kernoghan-Reid, *Lead Artist Inclusion* Andrew Stanford, *Research and Evaluation Officer* Cristal Palacios

Innovative, high-quality work for audiences under the age of 19, including school groups, children and young people with disabilities, and families. Each show is shaped through creative consultation with its intended audience, and those who live and work with them. Tours locally, nationally and internationally. Founded 1988.

Rhubarb Theatre
7 Queensway, Leadenham, Lincoln LN5 0PF
tel (01400) 275133
email info@rhubarbtheatre.co.uk
website www.rhubarbtheatre.co.uk
Artistic Directors Kirsty Mead, Philip Mead

Professional indoor theatre and street theatre predominantly aimed at family audiences (age 5+). Productions are newly created stories that include original music and lots of theatrical devices, i.e. masks, puppetry, dance, song, movement and mime. Most of Rhubarb's street shows are wordless and suitable for booking overseas. Tours nationally and performs in a host of different small- to middle-scale venues, including theatres, arts centres, village halls, rural touring schemes and schools, undertaking approx. 200 performances a year. Other activities include walkabout, interactive storytelling, workshops and teaching. Founded 2004.

Spectacle Theatre Ltd
c/o The Factory, Jenkin Street, Porth CF39 9PP
tel (01443) 681024
email steve.spectacletheatre@gmail.com
website www.spectacletheatre.co.uk
Facebook www.facebook.com/Theatr-Spectacle-Theatre
Twitter @SpectacleTheat1
Manager/Creative Director Steve Davis

Community theatre company. Bilingual performances, workshops, training and mentoring.

Tell Tale Hearts
c/o 4 Oxspring Road, Penistone, Sheffield S36 8AB
email info@telltalehearts.co.uk
website www.telltalehearts.co.uk
Facebook www.facebook.com/TellTaleHeartsTheatreCo
Twitter @TellTaleHeart
Artistic Director Natasha Holmes

Produces participatory theatre for primary-school pupils and younger years in a range of settings, from theatres to schools and community venues. Also runs workshops, INSET training and offers other consultancy services. Note that the Tell Tale Hearts rarely produces theatre from written work; it is a devising company and actively seeks out collaborations with contributing artists. Occasionally works with a writer as part of its collaborative team, but this is to produce new work. Contact the Artistic Director before sending any work in order to gauge interest. Founded 2003.

The Theatre Company Blah Blah Blah
Interplay Theatre, Armley Bridge Road,
North Lane House, North Lane, Leeds LS6 3HG
tel 0113 426 1394
email info@blahs.co.uk
website www.blahs.co.uk
Twitter @theatreblahs
Artistic Director Deborah Pakkar-Hull, *Executive Creative Director* Iain Bloomfield

Theatre in Education company which specialises in touring theatre for children and young people and residency work in schools. Founded 1985.

Theatr Iolo
Chapter, Market Road, Canton, Cardiff CF14 3HS
tel 029-2061 3782
email hello@theatriolo.com
website www.theatriolo.com
Twitter @theatriolo
Artistic Director Lee Lyford

Theatre company for children and young people. Aims to create high-quality experiences that are stimulating, surprising and meaningful for children and their accompanying adults.

Theatre Centre
The Albany, Douglas Way, Deptford,
London SE8 4AG
tel 020-7729 3066
email admin@theatre-centre.co.uk
website www.theatre-centre.co.uk
Facebook www.facebook.com/TheatreCentreUK
Twitter @TClive
Artistic Director Rob Watt, *Executive Director and Ceo* Emma Rees

Young people's theatre company producing plays and workshops which tour nationally across the UK. Productions are staged in primary and secondary schools, arts centres and other venues. Keen to nurture new and established talent, encouraging all writers to consider writing for young audiences. Also runs creative projects and manages writing awards: see website for details. Founded 1953.

Theatre Hullabaloo

The Hullabaloo, Borough Road, Darlington DL1 1SG
tel (01325) 405681
email info@theatrehullabaloo.org.uk
website www.theatrehullabaloo.org.uk
Twitter @hullabalootweet
Artistic Producer Miranda Thain

Specialist theatre company that creates, promotes and tours work for young audiences, with a particular emphasis on early years. Encourages greater awareness of the value of theatre to children and young people by working with academic researchers, teachers and others through courses, events and publications. Tours professional theatre productions to schools and venues across the North East and nationally. Dedicated children's theatre and family venue, The Hullabaloo, offers theatre for children, creative play installations and more.

Travelling Light Theatre Company

Barton Hill Settlement, 43 Ducie Road,
Lawrence Hill, Bristol BS5 0AX
tel 0117 377 3166
email info@travellinglighttheatre.org.uk
website www.travellinglighttheatre.org.uk
Facebook www.facebook.com/travellinglighttheatre
Twitter @tl_theatre
Artistic Producer Heidi Vaughan, *Executive Director* Dienka Hines

Professional theatre company producing work for young audiences. Collaborates with many different arts organisations to create original, cross-artform productions that inspire and engage young people. Tours to theatres and festivals throughout the UK and abroad as well as to local schools. Also runs an extensive participation programme engaging with 0–25 year-olds through youth theatre groups, holiday and school projects, work experience, placements and mentoring. Founded 1984.

Tutti Frutti Productions

Shine, Harehills Road, Harehills, Leeds LS8 5DR
tel 0113 388 0027
email emma@tutti-frutti.org.uk
website www.tutti-frutti.org.uk
Twitter @tuttifruttiprod
Artistic Director Wendy Harris, *Executive Director* Emma Killick

Professional theatre for family audiences (age 3+ and families/carers). Productions are adaptations of well-known stories or specially commissioned new shows with a focus on diversity, and have a very physical movement-based style with original music. Tours nationally and internationally and performs in a host of different small- and middle-scale venues in isolated or deprived areas, including theatres, arts centres, village halls, rural touring schemes and schools, undertaking approx. 250 performances a year. Also creates local arts engagement projects for children. Founded 1991.

Societies, prizes and festivals

Society of Authors

The SoA is the UK trade union for all types of writers, illustrators and literary translators at every stage of their careers.

Founded in 1884, the Society of Authors now has over 12,000 members. Members receive unlimited free advice on all aspects of the profession, including confidential clause-by-clause contract vetting, access to professional and geographic author communities, and a wide range of exclusive offers. It campaigns and lobbies on the issues that affect authors and holds hundreds of events online and across the UK each year, offering opportunities for authors to network and learn from each other. It manages more than 50 literary estates, the income from which helps to fund the organisation's work. In addition, since the beginning of the Covid-19 pandemic, they have distributed more than £1.4 million in hardship grants.

Members

SoA members include household names, such as Malorie Blackman, Neil Gaiman, Lenn Sissay and Joanne Harris, but they also include authors right at the start of their careers. Amongst the SoA membership are academic writers, biographers, broadcasters, children's writers, crime writers, dramatists, educational writers, ELT writers, health writers, ghostwriters, graphic novelists, historians, illustrators, journalists, medical writers, non-fiction writers, novelists, poets, playwrights, radio writers, scriptwriters, short story writers, translators, spoken word artists, YA writers and more.

Membership

The Society of Authors
24 Bedford Row, London WC1R 4EH
tel 020-7373 6642
email info@societyofauthors.org
website www.societyofauthors.org
Chief Executive Nicola Solomon
There are two membership bands: Full and Associate membership.

Full membership is available to professional writers, poets, translators and illustrators working in any genre or medium. This includes those who have: had a full-length work traditionally published, broadcast or performed commercially; self-published or been published on a print-on-demand or ebook-only basis and who meet sales criteria; published or had broadcast or performed an equivalent body of professional work; or administrators of a deceased author's estate.

Authors at the start of their careers are invited to join as Associates.

Associate membership is available to anyone actively working to launch a career as an author. This includes: authors who are starting out in self-publishing but who are not yet making a profit; authors who have been offered a contract for publication or agent representation but who are not yet published; students engaged on a course of at least one academic year's duration that will help them develop a career as an author, as well as other activities that mark the early stages of an author's career. Associate members enjoy all the same services and benefits as Full members.

Membership is subject to election and payment of subscription fees.

The subscription fee (tax deductible) starts at £27 per quarter, or £19 for those aged 35 or under. From the second year of subscription there are concessionary rates for over 65s who are no longer earning a significant amount of income from writing.

The benefits available to all SoA members include:

• assistance with contracts, from negotiation and assessment of terms to clause-by-clause, confidential vetting;

• unlimited advice on queries, covering any aspect of the business of authorship;

• taking up complaints on behalf of members on any issue concerned with the business of authorship;

• pursuing legal actions for breach of contract, copyright infringement and the non-payment of royalties and fees, when the risk and cost preclude individual action by a member and issues of general concern to the profession are at stake;

• conferences, seminars, meetings and other opportunities to network and learn from other authors;

• regular communications and a comprehensive range of publications, including the SoA's quarterly journal, *The Author*;

• discounts on books, exclusive rates on specialist insurance, special offers on products and services and free membership of the Authors' Licensing and Collecting Society (ALCS; see page 411);

• Authors with Disabilities and Chronic Illnesses – a peer support network for authors living and working with health challenges;

• Comics Creators Network – a professional support network for all types of comics creators;

> 'It does no harm to repeat, as often as you can, "Without me the literary industry would not exist: the publishers, the agents, the sub-agents, the accountants, the libel lawyers, the departments of literature, the professors, the theses, the books of criticism, the reviewers, the book pages – all this vast and proliferating edifice is because of this small, patronised, put-down and underpaid person."' – *Doris Lessing*

• Children's Writers and Illustrators Group – a professional community of writers and illustrators who create content for the children's publishing market;

• Educational Writers Group – protecting the interests of educational authors in professional matters, especially contracts, rates of pay, digitalisation and copyright;

• Poetry and Spoken Word Group – a new, increasingly active group to which all new member poets are subscribed on joining SoA;

• Scriptwriters Group – representing members working in radio, TV, film and games development;

• Society of Authors in Scotland – organises a varied and busy calendar of activities in Scotland through a committee of volunteers;

• Translators Association – a source of expert advice for individual literary translators and a collective voice representing the profession;

• Carers Network – a new group designed to help keep writers writing when they take on caring responsibilities for someone with an illness or disability.

The SoA also coordinates a growing network of over 40 local author communities across the UK.

Campaigning and lobbying

The SoA is a voice for authors and works at a national and international level to improve terms and treatment of authors, negotiating with all parties including publishers, broadcasters, agents and governments. Current areas of campaigning include contract terms, copyright, freedom of expression, tax and benefits arrangements and Public Lending Right

(PLR; see page 396) – which the SoA played a key role in establishing. With the ongoing impacts of the Covid-19 pandemic and Brexit, the SoA continues to lobby for better terms, benefits and rights for authors and other creative professionals.

In the UK the SoA lobbies parliament, ministers and departments and makes submissions on relevant issues, working closely with the Department for Culture, Media and Sport and the All Party Parliamentary Writers Group. The SoA is a member of the British Copyright Council and was instrumental in setting up ALCS. They chair the Creators for Rights Alliance (CRA), a partnership of unions and member organisations from across the creative industries, working together on common interests such as copyright, payment and credit, and in 2022 launched the cross-industry 'Pay the Creator' campaign. It is recognised by the BBC in the negotiation of rates for authors' contributions to radio drama, as well as for the broadcasting of published material.

The SoA is a member of the European Writers' Council and applies pressure globally, working with sister organisations as part of the international Authors' Foundation.

The SoA also works closely with other professional bodies, including the Association of Authors' Agents, the Booksellers Association, the Publishers Association, the Independent Publishers Guild, the British Council, the National Union of Journalists and the Writers' Guild of Great Britain.

Awards and grants

The SoA supports authors through a wide range of awards and grants. Over £120,000 is given in prizes each year and more than £280,000 is distributed in grants.
The SoA administers:
• the annual SoA Awards – ten prizes for poetry, fiction and non-fiction, awarding authors at the beginning of their careers as well as those well established;
• two audio drama prizes: the Imison Award for a writer new to radio drama and the Tinniswood Award;
• awards for translations from Arabic, Dutch/Flemish, French, German, Greek, Italian, Spanish and Swedish into English;
• the Authors' Foundation and K Blundell Trust, which give grants to assist authors working on their next book;
• the Francis Head Bequest and the Authors' Contingency Fund, which assist authors who, through physical mishap, are temporarily unable to maintain themselves or their families;
• the *Sunday Times* Charlotte Aitken Young Writer of the Year Award;
• the ALCS Educational Writers' Awards.

WGGB (Writers' Guild of Great Britain)

The WGGB is the TUC-affiliated trade union for writers.

WGGB represents writers working in film, television, radio, theatre, books, poetry, animation, comedy and videogames. Formed in 1959 as the Screenwriters' Guild, the union gradually extended into all areas of freelance writing activity and copyright protection. It comprises professional writers in all media, united in common concern for one another and regulating the conditions under which they work.

Apart from necessary dealings with Government and policies on legislative matters affecting writers, the WGGB is, by constitution, non-political, has no involvement with any political party and members pay no political levy.

WGGB employs a permanent general secretary and other permanent staff and is administered by an Executive Council of around 20 members.

WGGB agreements

WGGB's core function is to negotiate minimum terms in those areas in which its members work. Those agreements form the basis of the individual contracts signed by members. It also gives individual advice to its members on contracts and other matters and maintains a welfare fund to help writers in financial trouble.

Membership

The Writers' Guild of Great Britain
First Floor, 134 Tooley Street, London SE1 2TU
tel 020-7833 0777
email admin@writersguild.org.uk
website www.writersguild.org.uk
Facebook www.facebook.com/thewritersguild
Twitter @The WritersGuild
General Secretary Ellie Peers

Full membership: Members pay approximately 1.2% of earnings from professional writing using a banding system (min. £198, max. £2,000 p.a.).

Candidate membership: £108 p.a. restricted to writers who have not had work published or produced at WGGB-approved rates.

Student membership: £30 p.a. for student writers aged 18 or over, studying at BA level or below.

Affiliate membership: £300 p.a. for people who work professionally with writers, e.g. agents, technical advisers.

Members receive a weekly email newsletter. The WGGB website contains full details of collective agreements and WGGB activities, plus a 'Find a Writer' service and a dedicated Members' area; information is also made available on Twitter and Facebook. Other benefits include: legal advice and contract vetting; free training; member events, discounts and special offers (subject to membership tier).

Television

WGGB negotiates minimum terms agreements with the BBC, ITV, Pact (Producers' Alliance for Cinema and Television) and TAC (representing Welsh-language television producers).

WGGB TV agreements regulate minimum fees, residuals and royalties, copyright, credits and general conditions for television plays, series and serials, dramatisations and adaptations, soaps, sitcoms and sketch shows. One of the WGGB's most important achievements has been the establishment of pension rights for members. The BBC, ITV and independent producers pay a pension contribution on top of the standard writer's fee on the understanding that the WGGB member also pays a contribution.

The switch to digital television, video-on-demand and download-to-own services, mobile phone technology and the expansion of the BBC's commercial arm have seen WGGB in constant negotiation over the past decade. WGGB now has agreements for all of the BBC's digital channels and for its joint venture channels. In May 2012 it signed new agreements with the BBC extending minimum terms over online services such as iPlayer. From April 2015 the first payments under the Writers Digital Payments scheme (a not-for-profit company) were paid out to writers whose work had been broadcast on BBC iPlayer and ITV Player. In 2016 WGGB negotiated a 75% fee increase for writers working under its 2003 Pact agreement, and also started work on rewriting the agreement. In 2017 it negotiated a new script agreement for television and online with the BBC.

Film

In 1985 an agreement was signed with the two producer organisations: the British Film and Television Producers' Association and the Independent Programme Producers' Association (now known as Pact). Since then there has been an industrial agreement covering UK film productions and pension fund contributions have been negotiated for WGGB members. The Agreement was renegotiated in February 1992 and consultations on an updated arrangement are in progress.

Radio

WGGB has a standard agreement for Radio Drama with the BBC, establishing a fee structure that is reviewed annually. It was comprehensively renegotiated in 2005 resulting in an agreement covering digital radio. In 1985 the BBC agreed to extend the pension scheme already established for television writers to include radio writers. WGGB has special agreements for Radio 4's *The Archers* and for BBC iPlayer. A separate agreement covers the reuse of old comedy and drama material on digital BBC Radio 4 Extra. It has also negotiated rates for podcasts.

Books

WGGB fought for the loans-based Public Lending Right (PLR, see page 396) to reimburse authors for books lent in libraries. The scheme is now administered by the British Library; WGGB is represented on its advisory committee. WGGB has a Books Committee, which works on behalf of book writers and poets. Issues affecting members include authors' earnings, self-publishing, print-on-demand services and ebooks.

Theatre

In 1979 WGGB, together with the Theatre Writers' Union, negotiated the first industrial agreement for theatre writers. The Theatres National Committee Agreement (TNC) covers the Royal Shakespeare Company, the Royal National Theatre Company and the English Stage Company at the Royal Court. When their agreement was renegotiated in 2007, WGGB achieved a long-standing ambition of a minimum fee of £10,000 for a new play; this has since risen to £12,997.

In June 1986, a new agreement was signed with the Theatrical Management Association (now UK Theatre), which covers 95 provincial theatres. In 1993, this agreement was comprehensively revised and included a provision for a year-on-year increase in fees in line with the Retail Price Index. The agreement was renegotiated in 2015.

Societies, prizes and festivals

After many years of negotiation, an agreement was concluded in 1991 between WGGB and the Independent Theatre Council (ITC), which represents 200 of the smaller and fringe theatres as well as educational and touring companies. This agreement was revised in 2002 and the minimum fees are reviewed annually. WGGB is currently talking to the ITC about updating the agreement. The WGGB Theatre Committee holds an annual forum for Literary Managers and runs the Olwen Wymark Theatre Encouragement Award scheme.

Videogames

WGGB counts games writers amongst its members and holds regular networking events for them, as well as celebrating their achievements at the annual Writers' Guild Awards. The union publishes guidelines for games writers and those who work with them, outlining best practice in this growing area.

Other activities

WGGB is in touch with Government and national institutions wherever and whenever the interests of writers are in question or are being discussed, for example, submitting evidence to a Parliamentary Inquiry on the lack of working-class writers. It holds cross-party Parliamentary lobbies with Equity and the Musicians' Union to ensure that the various artforms they represent are properly cared for, and writers' voices are heard during, for example, the Brexit transition and the Covid-19 pandemic. Working with the Federation of Entertainment Unions, WGGB makes its views known to bodies, such as Arts Council England and Ofcom on a broader basis.

WGGB is an active affiliate of the British Copyright Council, Creators' Rights Alliance and other organisations whose activities are relevant to professional writers. An Anti-Censorship Committee has intervened strongly to protect freedom of speech.

Internationally, WGGB plays a leading role in the International Affiliation of Writers Guilds, which includes the American Guilds East and West, the Canadian Guilds (French and English) and the Irish, Mexican, French, Israeli, South African and New Zealand Guilds. When it is possible to make common cause, the Guilds act accordingly. WGGB takes a leading role in the Fédération des Scénaristes d'Europe.

On a day-to-day basis, WGGB gives advice on contracts, and takes up issues that affect the lives of its members as professional writers. Other benefits include access to free and discounted training, exclusive events and discounts and a dedicated online members' area. Full members are entitled to submit a profile for inclusion in the WGGB online *Find A Writer* directory; pay no joining fee for membership to Writers Guild of America East or West; and are eligible for Cannes accreditation. Regular committee meetings are held by specialist WGGB Craft Committees and its active branches across the UK organise panel discussions, talks and social events.

Recent campaigns include Equality Writes, following an independent report commissioned by WGGB and launched in 2018 which revealed the shocking lack of gender equality in the UK screen industries. In 2022 phase two of the campaign will focus on the under-representation of ethnically diverse screenwriters. The union has also campaigned on bullying and harassment in the creative industries. In 2019 it declared a 'climate emergency' and pledged to put the climate crisis at the heart of everything it does.

Each year WGGB presents the Writers' Guild Awards, covering all the areas in which its members work. These are the only cross-media awards in which writers are honoured by their peers.

Alliance of Independent Authors

The ALLi is a professional association of self-publishing writers and advisors.

The Alliance of Independent Authors (ALLi) is a global organisation with a mission of fostering ethics and excellence in self-publishing and advocating for author-publishers globally.

Founded in 2012 at the London Book Fair by author, poet and creative entrepreneur, Orna Ross, ALLi is headquartered in London but with members all over the world. In addition to its member services, the organisation offers outreach education to the self-publishing community through its popular online Self-Publishing Advice Center, which features a blog, podcast, bi-annual online conference and series of guidebooks.

ALLi has an Advisory Board of successful author-publishers, educators and service providers, and an active Watchdog desk which runs a publicly available ratings board of the best and worst self-publishing services. It also publishes an annual Directory of its Partner Members (https://selfpublishingadvice.org/best-self-publishing-services/): vetted self-publishing services, from large global players like Amazon KDP and Ingram Spark to local freelance editors and designers. Many of these offer discounted services to ALLi author members.

ALLi advocates for the interests of independent, self-publishing authors within and outside the literary, publishing and bookselling industries, and works with ambassadors, other authors associations and grassroots organizations to promote diversity and accessibility. Other campaigns include 'Open Up To Indie Authors', which urges booksellers, festivals, prize-giving committees, libraries, book clubs and corporate media to include author–publishers in their programmes; and 'AskALLi', which pledges to answer any self-publishing question anyone might have. In 2022, ALLi introduced a new organisational membership, offering specialist advice and expertise in self-publishing to national, local and genre authors' organizations that align with ALLi's ethos for independent authors.

Membership

The Alliance of Independent Authors
email info@allianceindependentauthors.org
website www.allianceindependentauthors.org,
https://selfpublishingadvice.org

ALLi offers three grades of membership:

Author membership (£89 p.a.) is open to writers or translators of books for adults who have self-published a full-length title (55,000+ words) or series of shorter books; writers of children's/young adult books who have self-published one or more titles.

Authorpreneur membership (£119 p.a.) is open to full-time self-publishing authors who earn their living from their author business and can show evidence of 50,000 book sales in the last two years; applications are assessed.

Associate membership (£69 p.a.) is open to writing/publishing students with an interest in self-publishing and non-published writers (or translators) preparing a book for self-publication.

Benefits include self-publishing advice, guidance and community; vetted services, service ratings and watchdog desk; legal and contract appraisal; discounts and deals; professional and business development; campaigns and advocacy.

Societies, prizes and festivals

Society of Children's Book Writers & Illustrators

The Society of Children's Book Writers & Illustrators (SCBWI) is the only international professional organisation dedicated to serving people who write, illustrate and translate for children and young adults, and share a vital interest in children's literature, magazines, film, television and/or multimedia. Our mission is to support the creation and availability of quality children's books in every region of the world.

Society of Children's Book Writers and Illustrators

Whether you are a professional children's writer or illustrator, or a newcomer to the field, SCBWI has plenty to offer you, from local to national to international events, from advice on getting your first deal to help in navigating your career as a writer or illustrator. Established in 1971, SCBWI now has over 26,000 members in 70 regional chapters worldwide; SCBWI serves as a consolidated voice for members within the publishing industry. Membership benefits include professional development and networking opportunities, marketing information, events, publications, online profiles, grants and awards. Through awards, events and publications they give established writers, illustrators and translators tools and resources to manage their careers, as well as educating those just starting out.

What does SCBWI British Isles do?

SCBWI British Isles is a dynamic and friendly chapter of over 1000 members, which aims to support aspiring and published writers and illustrators and provide opportunities for them to network, market their work, hone their craft, make industry connections and develop their careers. Events include an annual two-day conference, a fiction and picture book retreat, an annual Agents' Party, the Industry Insiders series (six talks a year in London aimed at professional development on a variety of topics), the Illustrators' masterclass series (Saturday workshops with a hands-on craft element), sketch and scrawl crawls, author masterclasses, webinars, PULSE events (SCBWI PULSE provides professional development opportunities for published members) and an author and illustrator showcase. A network of regional organisers run local critique groups, workshops and social events across the British Isles. SCBWI British Isles is committed to offering free and subsidised places to attend and participate in all of its events and initiatives for authors and illustrators traditionally underrepresented in publishing.

Further information

Society of Children's Book Writers & Illustrators
website www.scbwi.org, www.britishisles.scbwi.org
Co-Regional Advisors (Co-chairs) Natascha Biebow and Kathy Evans
email ra@britishscbwi.org
Membership Coordinator Anita Loughrey
email membership@britishscbwi.org
Membership £95 p.a.; £65 p.a. for students

What SCBWI does for its members

• SCBWI is a professional guild. It speaks as a consolidated global voice for professional children's writers and illustrators. In recent years, SCBWI has successfully lobbied for such issues as new copyright legislation, equitable treatment of authors and artists and fair contract terms.

• It offers a showcase of authors and illustrators' work through the Find a Speaker Directory, Featured Illustrator Showcase and Member Awards, Celebrations & Achievements Showcase (www.scbwishowcase.org).

• It keeps members up to date with industry developments through the SCBWI PULSE series of events, with opportunities to learn more about the 'business' of writing and illustrating, including marketing and publicity, school and festival visits, and exclusive networking events with librarians and booksellers.

• It offers members invaluable exposure to editors, art directors and agents through one-to-one manuscript or portfolio reviews at the annual conference and retreats, the members-only Agents' Party, the Slush Pile Challenge and biennial SCBWI Undiscovered Voices (www.undiscoveredvoices.com) competitions.

• It supports professional development for members to hone their craft through the Master-class series, conference workshops and highly-successful critique groups.

• It gives members increased visibility online with a free profile on its website, which is a point of call for agents, art directors and editors.

• It provides support and a network of like-minded people, helping to answer members' queries through a variety of online resources, including a popular social networking site.

• It facilitates networking opportunities with professionals worldwide.

• Publications include the *Bulletin*, the SCBWI international magazine, *Insight* and *PRO-Insider* e-newletters, weekly *Words & Pictures* newsletter blog with weekly content (www.wordsandpics.org) and resources including annual publications and market guides and *The Book: The Essential Guide to Children's Publishing*.

• Website resources include book launch parties, members' bookshop, discussion boards, illustrator gallery, find-a-speaker search facility, webinars and podcasts.

Awards and grants

The SCBWI administers a number of awards and grants:

• The Golden and Crystal Kite Awards are for the most outstanding books published by SCBWI members each year, voted for by SCBWI peers.

• The Sid Fleischman Humour Award is presented to authors whose work exemplifies the excellence of writing in the genre of humour.

• The annual Spark Award recognises excellence in a children's book published through a non-traditional publishing route.

• The Book Launch Award provides authors or illustrators with $2,000 in funds to help the promotion of their newly published work and take the marketing strategy into their own creative hands.

• The Emerging Voices Award fosters the emergence of diverse voices in children's books.

• Out from the Margins Award for early career underrepresented creators of children's literature.

- Volemos: The Meg Medina Grant for authors of Hispanic/Latinx/Ibero-American heritage who are in the early stages of their career (between 1 and 3 traditionally published books) or not yet traditionally published.
- Ezra Jack Keats Showcase Prize for a promising BIPOC illustrator.
- For Translators: Work-in-Progress Grants to assist children's book writers and illustrators in the completion of a specific project currently not under contract.
- Ann Whitford Paul - Writer's Digest Manuscript Award is an annual award given to the manuscript of the Most Promising Picture Book manuscript.
- SCBWI PJ Library Jewish Stories Award is an award sponsored by the PJ Library to encourage the creation of more high-quality Jewish children's literature.
- Karen Cushman Late Bloomer Award – An award for a work-in-progress from an unpublished author over age 50.
- A. Orr Fantasy Grant – Awarded to young adult and middle-grade writers working in the fantasy or science fiction genre.
- BIPOC Scholarship offers an all-expense paid trip to the Winter or Summer Conference for Black, Indigenous, and People of colour.
- Bologna Illustrators Gallery (BIG) is given bi-annually to an illustrator of promise. The winner is announced at the New York Conference, and the winning art is displayed prominently at the SCBWI Bologna Book Fair booth.
- The Multi-Cultural Work-in-Progress Grant assists writers in the completion of a manuscript featuring a voice traditionally underrepresented in children's books.
- The Magazine Merit Awards are presented for outstanding original magazine work for young people.
- The Sue Alexander Most Promising New Work Award is for the best manuscript submitted for individual critique at the LA conference.
- The Martha Weston Grant encourages authors and illustrators to nurture their creativity in a different genre of children's books.
- The Lee Bennett Hopkins Poetry Award recognises and encourages the publication of an excellent book of poetry or anthology for children or young adults (given every three years).
- The Jane Yolen Mid-List Author Grant honours the contribution of mid-list authors.
- Several Work-in-Progress Grants are available each year to assist children's book writers and illustrators in the completion of a specific project currently not under contract, in the categories of Picture Book Text, Chapter Books/Early Readers, Middle Grade, Young Adult Fiction, Nonfiction, and Multicultural Fiction or Non-Fiction.
- Don Freeman Work-in-Progress Grant is to assist illustrators in the completion of a book dummy or portfolio.
- Narrative Art Award given annually to an illustrator of promise based on a given prompt.
- Tome DePaola Award awards artists with a cash prize of $2,500, in memory of beloved author-illustrator Tome DePaola.
- The Portfolio Award is presented to the best art portfolio on view at the Juried Portfolio Display at the LA conference.
- There are four Student Illustrator Scholarships for full-time graduate and undergraduate students of children's book illustration.
- There are two Student Writer Scholarships to the Summer and Winter conferences for full-time university students in an English or Creative Writing programme.

• There are six Annual Conference Scholarships to attend the annual SCBWI-BI conference.
• A number of scholarship places are awarded at all British Isles region events for under-represented groups in children's publishing, including: SCBWI British Isles members who have financial need; SCBWI British Isles members and non-members who identify as BAME, LGBTQIA+, disabled or working class. SCBWI British Isles also offers scholarship memberships to the All Stories Mentorship programme and Undiscovered Voices competition for participants who have been traditionally underrepresented in children's publishing.

See also...

Seven Stories – The National Centre for Children's Books

At Seven Stories the rich heritage of British children's books is collected, explored and celebrated.

seven stories
National Centre for Children's Books

Once upon a time an idea was born on the banks of the Tyne to create a national home for children's literature – a place where the original work of authors and illustrators could be collected, treasured and celebrated. After ten years of pioneering work by founding directors Elizabeth Hammill and Mary Briggs, that dream became a reality. In August 2005 Seven Stories, the Centre for Children's Books, opened in an award-winning converted seven storey Victorian granary in the Ouseburn Valley, a stone's throw from Newcastle's vibrant quayside. Seven Stories is now officially known as The National Centre for Children's Books, following approval by Arts Council England in 2012. It is the only accredited museum in the UK that specialises in children's books.

The collection

At the heart of Seven Stories is a unique and growing collection of manuscripts, artwork and other pre-publication materials. These treasures record the creative process involved in making a children's book and provide illuminating insights into the working lives of modern authors and illustrators. The collection focuses on work created in modern Britain. It already contains thousands of items by authors such as Peter Dickinson, Michael Morpurgo, Enid Blyton, Berlie Doherty, Jan Mark, Philip Pullman, Michael Rosen, Robert Westall and Ursula Moray Williams; illustrators like Edward Ardizzone, Faith Jaques, Harold Jones, Anthony Maitland, Pat Hutchins, Helen Cooper, Jan Ormerod and Jane Ray; and editors and other practitioners such as Kaye Webb. Many more bodies of work are pledged. A catalogue of the collection is available via the Seven Stories website.

Exhibitions

A celebration of creativity underpins the Seven Stories project: its collection documents the creative act, and its exhibitions and programmes interpret this original material in unconventional but meaningful ways. The aim is to cultivate an appreciation of books and their making, and inspire creativity in its audience.

Seven Stories has been mounting exhibitions since 1998 – first in borrowed venues and now in its own home. Here it provides the only exhibition space in the UK wholly dedicated to showcasing the incomparable legacy of British writing and illustrating for children. With exhibitions changing every year, Seven Stories have showcased the impressive work of children's authors such as Judith Kerr, Michael Morpurgo and David McKee. Their latest exhibition, *Where Stories Come From*, opened in 2020 and explores the idea that every story fits into one of seven basic story plots.

Throughout its seven storeys – from the Studio to the bookshop and café to the Artist's Attic, visitors of all ages are invited to engage in a unique, interactive exploration of creativity, literature and art. In this ever changing literary playground and landscape for the imagination, they can become writers, artists, explorers, designers, storytellers, readers or collectors, in the company of storytellers, authors, illustrators and Seven Stories' own facilitators and learning team.

Seven Stories aims to place children, young people and their books at the heart of the UK's national literary culture. An independent educational charity, it is committed to access for all and has initiated several innovative participation projects. The centre has developed close links with the Newcastle and regional communities, and is working with the Children's Literature Unit in the Department of English Literature, Language and Linguistics at Newcastle University to develop the Seven Stories collection and maximise its potential for research and display.

Seven Stories is dedicated to the celebration of children's literature. It is supported by Arts Council England and Community Foundation Newcastle Culture Investment Fund.

Further information

Seven Stories – The National Centre for Children's Books
30 Lime Street, Ouseburn Valley, Newcastle upon Tyne NE1 2PQ
tel 0300 330 1095
email info@sevenstories.org.uk
website www.sevenstories.org.uk

Public opening hours Thurs–Tues 10am–5pm, Sun 10am–4pm, Open daily during school holidays.

Admission charges General admission free. Event tickets start at £6.50.

Please check the website for the most up-to-date opening and booking information.

See also...

- *Society of Children's Book Writers & Illustrators,* page 330
- *The Children's Book Circle,* page 336
- *Federation of Children's Book Groups,* page 337

Societies, prizes and festivals

The Children's Book Circle

The Children's Book Circle is open to anyone who has a passion for children's books; the activities of the organisation are introduced here.

Are you passionate about children's books? Since 1962, the Children's Book Circle (CBC) has provided an exciting forum for lively debate on important issues in the children's book world, as well as opportunities to socialise and build a network within the industry. Membership is open to publishers, librarians, authors, illustrators, agents, teachers, booksellers and anyone with an active interest in the field. The CBC caters to both creators and consumers of children's books and holds events throughout the year for aspiring authors and illustrators alongside industry-led panels, talks and meet-ups. It's not a route into getting published, but it will give you opportunities to engage with people from the industry in an informal and enjoyable context.

> **Further information**
>
> **The Children's Book Circle**
> *website* www.childrensbookcircle.org.uk
> *Facebook* www.facebook.com/childrensbookcircle
> *Twitter* @ChildBookCircle
> *Membership* £25 p.a.; students £20 p.a.; corporate membership (up to five staff covered) £100 p.a. Includes free or discounted entry to all events. Non-member tickets can also be purchased for individual events from the website.

The CBC meets regularly at venues in central London and frequently invites guest speakers to debate key issues relating to the world of children's books. Previous events have included panel discussions on the importance of diversity and the rise of licensing in children's books, and 'Meet and Critique' evenings for aspiring authors and illustrators to discuss their projects with industry experts. Social drinks and the ever-popular Pub Quiz are fast becoming part of the CBC calendar and are a great chance to catch up with industry contacts and make new ones.

The CBC is also the proud host of the annual **Eleanor Farjeon Award** (sponsored by the estate of Eleanor Farjeon) and the **Patrick Hardy Lecture**. The Eleanor Farjeon Award recognises an outstanding contribution to the world of children's books. Recent winners include The Centre for Literacy in Primary Education (CLPE), Michael Morpurgo, Keats Community Library and Terry Pratchett (posthumously). The Patrick Hardy Lecture is delivered each year at the same event by a distinguished speaker and has previously been presented by Nicola Davies, Lauren St John, Lauren Child, Verna Wilkins (founder of Tamarind Books) and Michael Rosen.

A yearly membership gives you discounted access to all CBC events and keeps you up to date via the newsletter. CBC welcome enthusiasts of children's books from all backgrounds and aims to be as widely representative as possible.

See also...
* *Society of Children's Book Writers & Illustrators*, page 330
* *Seven Stories – The National Centre for Children's Books*, page 334
* *Federation of Children's Book Groups*, page 337

Federation of Children's Book Groups

'The Federation of Children's Book Groups, has, in its own quiet, single-minded way, done more for reading than almost anyone else' – *Anthony Horowitz*

The achievements of the Federation of Children's Book Groups were publicly recognised in 2011 when it was nominated for and subsequently won the Eleanor Farjeon Award (see page 363). Its aim is simple: to bring children and books together, promote children's books and inspire a love of reading through its national and local events. If you are a parent, carer, author, illustrator or professional with a passion for encouraging children to read, the Federation will be of interest to you.

Federation history

The Federation of Children's Book Groups was formed in 1968 by Anne Wood to coordinate the work of the many different children's book groups already in existence across the country and in 2018, it celebrated 50 years of bringing children and books together.

Celebrating its 40th anniversary in 2020, the Children's Book Award is the only national award voted for entirely by children. Throughout the year Federation Testing Groups read and vote on new fiction supplied by publishers. Each year 100,000 votes are cast involving nearly 250 schools and families across the UK. A shortlist (Top Ten) is drawn up with four picture books in the Younger Children category, three shorter novels for Younger Readers and three novels for Older Readers, with children from all over the UK voting in their groups or online. You do not have to be a member to vote in the Top Ten. The Award has a track record of identifying future bestsellers: the first Overall Winner was *Mr Magnolia* by Quentin Blake; other winners include *The Hunger Games*, and the *Harry Potter* and *Percy Jackson* books. For over ten years the Award was supported by Red House, with award ceremonies held at a number of prestigious venues, including the Queen Elizabeth Hall, in London as part of the Imagine Children's Festival (see page 207).

In 1976 National Tell-A-Story-Week was established and it has now grown into National Share-A-Story-Month (NSSM), which takes place each May. It enables groups to focus on the power of story and to hold events which celebrate all forms of storytelling. The theme in 2022 is 'Belonging'. The website hosts the NSSM pack, full of ideas and activities, which is sent to each book group and can also be downloaded by non-members.

In 1977, the first Federation anthology was published, and since then they have compiled booklists covering the whole age range from picture books to the latest teen and young adult novels; these are available on request free of charge via the website.

In 2010 the Federation created National Non-Fiction Day to celebrate the quality and variety of information books available for children; this takes place on the first Thursday of each November, with a host of events focused on non-fiction. It has expanded to be

Societies, prizes and festivals

National Non-Fiction November and further details can be found on the website. The theme for 2021 was 'Heroes' and there are always resources to download for free.

Each year the Federation holds a conference: three days of author and illustrator events, panel discussions and seminars enable group and individual members, publishers, authors, illustrators, teachers, librarians and booksellers to meet and exchange ideas. Delegates are inspired by meeting others who share their passion. The 2020 and 2021 conferences were cancelled due to the coronavirus lockdown, however in 2019, Lewes and Oxted hosted the conference, with the theme 'Opening Doors' and a wide range of speakers including Frank Cottrell Boyce, Nick Sharratt, Jane Ray, Francesca Simon, Guy Puzey, Holly Smale and a whole crowd of poets. See http://fcbg.org.uk/conference/ for more details about future events.

The Children's Book Groups

Federation Book Groups exist throughout the UK: from Plymouth to Dundee, from Ipswich to St David's and from Harrogate to Lewes. Their activities are as varied and diverse as the groups themselves, serving their own community's needs, including author and illustrator visits, bonfire parties, museum and library events, book swaps and parties. But, above all, FCBG are passionate about children's books, bringing together ordinary book-loving families, empowering parents, grandparents, carers and children to become enthusiastic and excited about all kinds of good books. Some book groups are based around schools run by enthusiastic librarians and teachers. You can still be a member of the Federation if there is no book group near you. Individual and professional membership enables everyone to participate in sharing their passion for children's books.

Further information

Federation of Children's Book Groups
Wakananai Firs Road, Mardy, Abergavenny,
Wales NP7 6NA
tel 07591 380434
email info@fcbg.org.uk
website http://fcbg.org.uk

See also...
- *Society of Children's Book Writers & Illustrators*, page 330
- *Seven Stories – The National Centre for Children's Books*, page 334
- *The Children's Book Circle*, page 336

National Literacy Trust

Authors and artists can spark a lifelong love of reading – it just takes one book. Jonathan Douglas explains how the National Literacy Trust encourages and supports young readers.

Writers and artists are essential to the National Literacy Trust's mission to raise literacy levels in the UK. We work to improve reading, writing, speaking and listening abilities in the most disadvantaged communities. Creators are not just our natural allies, they are key partners in our campaign to make a difference. It goes without saying that a literacy charity cannot exist without books.

Further information

National Literacy Trust
68 South Lambeth Road, London SW8 1RL
tel 020-7587 1842
email contact@literacytrust.org.uk
website https://literacytrust.org.uk
Facebook www.facebook.com/nationalliteracytrust
Twitter @Literacy_Trust

The literacy challenge in the UK is significant. 27% of children left primary school in England in 2019 unable to read well, rising to 42% for disadvantaged children. This is deeply concerning, not just because it highlights the attainment gap between children from low-income families and their peers. Children need good literacy to succeed at school, to enter the job market as they grow up, and to be able to support their own children's learning as adults. The intergenerational cycle of low-literacy negatively impacts social mobility, meaning a levelled-up society is difficult to achieve.

Authors have the power to transform the way a child engages with books and in doing so unlock a lifetime of benefits. Our research shows that visits from authors to schools have a tangible impact on literacy skills: twice as many children and young people who had a writer visit to their school read above the expected level for their age compared with their peers who didn't have such a visit. What's more, children who have had an author visit to their school also have higher levels of confidence in their reading and enjoy reading and writing more.

We often talk about the magic of school visits. Following a brilliant World Book Day tour from bestselling author and illustrator Rob Biddulph in Manchester, one teacher told us: 'Many of my class ... have very little opportunity to meet an author, never mind visit a library. I was delighted so many were excited by his books – so much so, they have saved up to buy them.' This is just one example of how, by working together, we can do extraordinary things to address the depth of the literacy challenge.

We are grateful when writers ask how they can collaborate with us, and are always looking for support with our campaigning. As a charitable organisation, we are thankful to the people who help us spread the word about our initiatives. Every new like, comment or share is vitally important in helping us reach the people who need our assistance. We launch new research with sharing in mind, so please do visit our website and social pages.

One growing challenge we need writers' and artists' support addressing is the disconnect between creators and the young people who read their work. The lack of diversity is a problem: one in three children and young people do not see themselves reflected in the pages they read. Children from lower socioeconomic backgrounds, in particular minority ethnic communities, are less likely to read for pleasure and more likely to face literacy

Societies, prizes and festivals

challenges – and our research shows these are the children who are least likely to see themselves represented in books. We know that books that are representative resonate and can spark a child's lifelong love of reading. What's more, representation will strengthen engagement, supporting more young people from diverse communities to see themselves as readers.

Following the launch of our diversity research, we worked with well-known children's authors and artists to find out when they first saw themselves in a story. Dapo Adeola, award-winning illustrator and designer, told us that a very recent reading of *So Much*, by Trish Cooke and Helen Oxenbury, 'was the first time I felt truly seen in a book.' Author Bali Rai added, 'I always thought books were about other people.'

In the coming year, we will focus on supporting one million children and young people whose literacy and learning has been disproportionately affected by the coronavirus pandemic. We know that the progress made in narrowing the literacy attainment gap over the last decade has been negated due to Covid-19.

Approximately 380,000 (1 in 11) disadvantaged children don't own a book of their own, so we have spent the three national lockdowns distributing nearly 300,000 books to address this issue. We rely on the generosity of authors and their publishers to allow us to do this – and there is so much more to be done.

The unequal impact of school closures highlights the urgent need for our work helping children, young people, families, teachers and communities. Our Arts Council England-funded project 'Connecting Stories' is an excellent example of our response to the pandemic. Publishers large and small are donating books and writers' time to encourage children in 14 areas with low literacy levels to read for pleasure, enjoy their local libraries, and boost their wellbeing. On World Book Day 2021, Cressida Cowell virtually visited hundreds of Connecting Stories schools to increase pupils' access to literacy experiences and books, and shared tips on how they can become authors and illustrators.

As the country recovers from the pandemic and schools and libraries reopen, we hope children will have greater access to books and their brilliant benefits. In the meantime, we will continue our work developing programmes, resources, activities and materials to give children across the country the best chance to develop literacy skills that will help them throughout their lives.

Jonathan Douglas CBE is the Chief Executive of the National Literacy Trust.

See also...

Societies, associations and organisations

The societies and associations listed here include appreciation societies devoted to specific authors, professional bodies and national institutions. Some also offer prizes and awards (see page 359).

AccessArt

6 West Street, Comberton, Cambridge CB23 7DS
tel (01223) 262134
website www.accessart.org.uk

A UK Charity which aims to inspire and enable high-quality visual arts teaching, learning and practice. The AccessArt website features over 850 unique resources to inspire practice.

Action for Children's Arts

c/o Mousetrap Theatre Projects,
33 Shaftesbury Avenue, London W1D 7EH
website www.childrensarts.org.uk
Facebook www.facebook.com/ActionChildrensArts
Twitter @childrensart
Membership £30 p.a. individual; from £50 p.a. organisation

A membership charity organisation that values children, childhood and the arts. It embraces the UN Convention on the Rights of the Child:

• by campaigning for the right of all children in the UK to experience high-quality arts as an integral part of their childhood;
• by connecting people within and across the cultural and education sectors, across art forms and across the regions and nations of the UK;
• by celebrating achievement, dedication and best practice in artistic activity for and with children.

(AFEPI) Association of Freelance Editors, Proofreaders and Indexers of Ireland

email info@afepi-ireland.com
website www.afepi-ireland.com
Twitter @AFEPI_Ireland

AFEPI Ireland is a professional organisation for publishing and editorial freelancers in Ireland. It fosters high standards in editing, proofreading and indexing; protects the interests of its members; and helps to match authors, indie writers, publishers, businesses, public bodies and charitable organisations with suitable editorial freelancers. Membership is available to experienced professional editors, proofreaders and indexers. For services for publishers and authors, see the online directory of freelance professional editors, proofreaders and indexers based in Ireland and Northern Ireland. Founded 1985.

Louisa May Alcott's Orchard House

Orchard House, 399 Lexington Road, PO Box 343, Concord, MA 01742, USA
email admin@louisamayalcott.org
website www.louisamayalcott.org
Facebook www.facebook.com/louisamayalcottsorchardhouse
Twitter @LouisaMayAlcott

A not-for-profit historic site dedicated to public education and historic preservation, providing guided tours, educational programmes and special events that honour and interpret the legacy of the Alcotts, a unique 19th-century family who contributed to the fields of literature, education, philosophy, art and social justice. Founded 1911.

Alliance of Independent Authors – see page 329

American Booksellers Association

333 Westchester Avenue, Suite S202, White Plains, NY 10604, USA
tel +1 800-637-0037
email info@bookweb.org
website www.bookweb.org
Twitter @ABAbook

A national non-profit trade organisation that works with booksellers and industry partners to ensure the success and profitability of independently owned book retailers and to assist in expanding the community of the book. Provides education, information dissemination, business products and services, creates relevant awareness programmes and engages in public policy. Founded 1900.

American Society of Composers, Authors and Publishers

website www.ascap.com

An organisation founded and governed by its members, it is the leading performance rights organisation representing more than 850,000 songwriters, composers and music publishers.

Arts Council/An Chomhairle Ealaíon

70 Merrion Square, Dublin D02 NY52,
Republic of Ireland
tel +353 (0)1 618 0200
website www.artscouncil.ie/home

The national development agency for the arts in Ireland. Founded 1951.

Arts Council England

tel 0161 934 4317
website www.artscouncil.org.uk
Facebook www.facebook.com/artscouncilofengland
Twitter @ace_national

The national development agency for arts and culture in England, distributing public money from the government and the National Lottery. In 2022 Arts Council England will invest over £500 million from government funding and the National Lottery to deliver its objectives. Through its schemes organisations, artists, events and initiatives can receive funding to help achieve the Council's mission of providing art and culture for everyone. There are nine regional offices: Newcastle, Leeds, Manchester, Nottingham, Birmingham, Cambridge, Brighton, Bristol and London. Visit the website for information on funding support and advice, an online funding finder and funding FAQs. Founded 1946.

Arts Council of Northern Ireland

Linen Hill House, 23 Linenhall Street,
Lisburn BT28 1FJ
tel 028-9262 3555
email info@artscouncil-ni.org
website www.artscouncil-ni.org
Chief Executive Roisín McDonough

Promotes and encourages the arts throughout Northern Ireland. Artists in drama, dance, music and jazz, literature, the visual arts, traditional arts and community arts can apply for support for specific schemes and projects. The value of the grant will be set according to the aims of the programme. Artists of all disciplines and in all types of working practice, who have made a contribution to artistic activities in Northern Ireland for a minimum period of one year within the last five years, are eligible.

Arts Council of Wales

Bute Place, Cardiff CF10 5AL
tel 03301 242733
website https://arts.wales
Twitter @Arts_Wales_

The official body that funds and develops the arts in Wales. The funding it distributes comes from both the Welsh Government and the National Lottery; most funding goes to artists and art organisations carrying out programmes of work across Wales. Founded 1994.

North Wales Regional Office
Princes Park II, Princes Drive, Colwyn Bay LL29 8PL

Mid and West Wales Regional Office
The Mount, 18 Queen Street, Carmarthen SA31 1JT

Association for Library Service to Children

American Library Association, 225 N Michigan Ave, Suite 1300 Chicago, IL 60601, USA
tel +1 800-545-2433
email alsc@ala.org
website www.ala.org/alsc
Twitter @wearealsc

Develops and supports the profession of children's librarianship by enabling and encouraging its practitioners to provide the best library service to US children.

Association for Scottish Literature

c/o Dept of Scottish Literature,
University of Glasgow, 7 University Gardens,
Glasgow G12 8QH
tel 0141 330 5309
email office@asls.org.uk
website www.asls.org.uk
President David Goldie, *Secretary* Craig Lamont, *Director* Duncan Jones
Membership £65 p.a. individuals; £18 p.a. UK students; £100 p.a. corporate

ASL promotes the study, teaching and writing of Scottish literature and furthers the study of the languages of Scotland. Publishes annually *New Writing Scotland*, an anthology of new Scottish writing; an edited text of Scottish literature; a series of academic journals; and the eZine *The Bottle Imp*. Also publishes *Scotnotes* (comprehensive study guides to major Scottish writers), literary texts and commentaries designed to assist the classroom teacher, and a series of occasional papers. Organises two conferences a year. Founded 1970.

Association of American Literary Agents

302A West 12th Street, Suite 122, New York, NY 10014, USA
email assistant@aalitagents.org
website aalitagents.org

A professional organisation of over 415 agents who work with book authors and playwrights. Founded 1991.

Association of American Publishers

455 Massachusetts Avenue, NW Suite 700,
Washington DC 20001, USA
tel +1 202-347-3375
email info@publishers.org
website https://publishers.org
Twitter @AmericanPublish

AAP is the largest trade association for US books and journal publishers, providing advocacy and communications on behalf of the industry and its priorities nationally and worldwide. Founded 1970.

The Association of Authors' Agents

c/o David Higham Associates, 7-12 Noel Street, London, W1F 8GQ
tel 020-7434 5900
website www.agentsassoc.co.uk
President Catherine Clarke, Secretary Camille Burns

The AAA exists to provide a forum which allows member agencies to discuss issues arising in the profession; a collective voice for UK literary agencies in public affairs and the media; and a code of conduct to which all members commit themselves. Founded 1974.

Association of Canadian Publishers

174 Spadina Avenue, Suite 306, Toronto, ON M5T 2C2
tel +1 416-487-6116
email admin@canbook.org
website https://publishers.ca
Executive Director Kate Edwards

Represents approximately 115 Canadian-owned and controlled book publishers from across the country. Founded 1976.

The Association of Illustrators

Somerset House, Strand, London WC2R 1LA
tel 020-7759 1010
email info@theaoi.com
website www.theaoi.com
Facebook www.facebook.com/theaoi
Twitter @theaoi

Trade association which supports illustrators, promotes illustration and encourages professional standards in the industry. Presents an annual programme of events and holds an annual competition, exhibition and tour of the World Illustration Awards in partnership with the Directory of Illustration (www.theaoi.com/awards). Founded 1973.

Australia Council

PO Box 576, Pyrmont, NSW 2009
tel +61 (0)2 9215 9000
website www.australiacouncil.gov.au
Ceo Adrian Collette

Provides a broad range of support for the arts in Australia, embracing music, theatre, literature, visual arts and crafts, dance, indigenous arts, community and experimental arts.

Australian Copyright Council

PO Box 1986, Strawberry Hills, NSW 2012
tel +61 (0)2 9101 2377
email info@copyright.org.au
website www.copyright.org.au
Facebook www.facebook.com/AustralianCopyrightCouncil
Twitter @AusCopyright
Chief Executive Officer Eileen Camilleri

Provides easily accessible and affordable practical information, legal advice, education and forums on Australian copyright law for content creators and consumers. It represents the peak bodies for professional artists and content creators working in Australia's creative industries and Australia's major copyright collecting societies, including the Australian Society of Authors, the Australian Writers' Guild and the Australian Publishers Association.

The Council advocates for the contribution of creators to Australia's culture and economy and the importance of copyright for the common good. It works to promote understanding of copyright law and its application, lobby for appropriate law reform and foster collaboration between content creators and consumers. Founded 1968.

Australian Publishers Association

60/89 Jones Street, Ultimo, NSW 2007
tel +61 (0)2 9281 9788
website www.publishers.asn.au
Twitter @AusPublish

The APA is the peak industry body for Australian book, journal and electronic publishers. Founded 1948.

Australian Writers' Guild

Level 4, 70 Pitt Street, Sydney, NSW 2000
tel +61 (0)2 9319 0339
email admin@awg.com.au
website www.awg.com.au

The professional association representing writers for stage, screen, radio and online and has protected and promoted their creative and professional interests for 60 years. Founded 1962.

Authors Aloud UK

72 Castle Road, St Albans, Herts. AL1 5DG
tel (01727) 893992
email info@authorsalouduk.co.uk
website www.authorsalouduk.co.uk
Facebook www.facebook.com/Authors-Aloud-UK-497942623573822
Twitter @AuthorsAloudUK
Instagram @AuthorsAloudUK
Directors Naomi Cooper, Annie Everall

An author booking agency which brings together authors, illustrators, poets, storytellers and trainers with schools, libraries and festivals in the UK and internationally, to promote enthusiasm for reading, both for enjoyment and information. Works with children's authors who wish to visit schools and libraries, in person and virtually, and who are published by mainstream children's publishers. Also arranges author tours and book related events for publishers and other organisations.

Authors' Licensing and Collecting Society Ltd – see page 411

Enid Blyton Society

email tony@enidblytonsociety.co.uk
website www.enidblytonsociety.co.uk

Provides a focal point for collectors and enthusiasts of Enid Blyton through its magazine *The Enid Blyton Society Journal* (three p.a.) and the website. Founded 1995.

Book Marketing Society

email admin@bookmarketingsociety.co.uk
website www.bookmarketingsociety.co.uk
Twitter @BMSoc

Launched with the objective of becoming the representative body of marketing within the book industry. It provides a forum for sharing best practice, inspiration and creativity across the sector through regular awards and a lively programme of member meetings, development workshops, masterclasses and social events. Anyone who works for a book publisher, book retailer or book wholesaler is eligible for membership, including those working in associated areas of the publishing and book retailing industry.

Books Council of Wales/Cyngor Llyfrau Cymru

Castell Brychan, Aberystwyth, Ceredigion SY23 2JB
tel (01970) 624151
email castellbrychan@books.wales
website https://llyfrau.cymru/en
website www.gwales.com
Ceo Helgard Krause

A national charity which supports and develops the publishing industry in Wales. It promotes literacy and reading for pleasure through a range of public campaigns, activities and events across Wales, often working in partnership with schools, libraries and other literary organisations. The Council works with publishers to nurture new talent and content in Welsh and English as well as offering specialist editing, design, marketing and distribution services. It administers grants to publishers and independent booksellers. Partly funded by the Welsh Government through Creative Wales and from the commercial operations of its wholesale book distribution centre. Founded 1961.

The Booksellers Association

6 Bell Yard, London WC2A 2JR
tel 020-7421 4640
email mail@booksellers.org.uk
website www.booksellers.org.uk
Twitter @BAbooksellers
President Hazel Broadbrook

A membership organisation for all booksellers in the UK and Ireland, representing over 95% of bookshops. Key services include National Book Tokens and Batch Payment Services. Founded 1895.

BookTrust

G8 Battersea Studios, 80 Silverthorne Road, London SW8 3HE
tel 020-7801 8800
email query@booktrust.org.uk
website www.booktrust.org.uk
Twitter @Booktrust
Ceo Diana Gerald, *Chair of Trustees* John Coughlan

The UK's largest children's reading charity, dedicated to getting children reading because children who read are happier, healthier, more empathetic and more creative; they also do better at school. BookTrust gets children reading in lots of different ways, but its priority is to get children excited about books and stories.

BookTrust reviews at least one children's book each day and runs the Blue Peter Book Awards, Waterstones Children's Laureate, BookTrust Storytime Prize and BookTrust Lifetime Achievement Award. In 2019, it launched BookTrust Represents, a project to promote authors and illustrators of colour.

BookTrust Represents

G8 Battersea Studios, 80 Silverthorne Road, London SW8 3HE
tel 020-7801 8826
email booktrust.represents@booktrust.org.uk
website www.booktrust.org.uk/booktrustrepresents
Twitter @Booktrust

A project to support and promote authors and illustrators of colour and to reach more readers through school visits, special events and festivals. The project also supports aspiring and new authors and illustrators of colour with training, mentoring, events and an online community. Find out more about the project and the associated research into the ethnicity of authors and illustrators in the UK on the website.

The British Council

Bridgewater House, 58 Whitworth Street, Manchester M1 6BB
tel 0161 957 7755
website www.britishcouncil.org
Twitter @BritishCouncil
Chief Executive Scott McDonald, *Director of Arts* Skinder Hundal

The UK's international organisation for cultural relations and educational opportunities. It builds connections, understanding and trust between people in the UK and other countries through arts and culture, education and the English language. It finds new ways of connecting with and understanding each other through the arts, to develop stronger creative sectors around the world that are better connected with the UK. Working in close collaboration with book trade associations, the Literature team participates in major international book fairs.

It works with hundreds of writers and literature partners in the UK and collaborates with offices overseas to broker relationships and create activities which link artists and cultural institutions around the world. It works with writers, publishers, producers, translators and other sector professionals across literature, publishing and education. The Visual Arts team shares UK visual arts around the world, connecting professionals internationally through collaborative exhibition programmes, digital networking, training and development and delegations. It manages and develops the British Council Collection and the British Pavilion at the Venice Biennale.

Canadian Authors Association

192 Spadina Avenue, Suite 107, Toronto,
ON M5T 2C2
tel +1 705-955-0716
email apurcell@canadianauthors.org
website www.canadianauthors.org
Facebook www.facebook.com/
canadianauthorsassociation
Twitter @canauthors
Executive Director Anita Purcell

A membership-based organisation for writers in all areas of the profession. Branches across Canada that provide writers with a wide variety of programmes, services and resources to help them develop their skills in the craft and business of writing. Founded 1921.

The Canadian Children's Book Centre

Suite 200, 425 Adelaide Street West Toronto,
ON M5V 3C1
tel +1 416-975-0010
email info@bookcentre.ca
website https://bookcentre.ca
Facebook www.facebook.com/kidsbookcentre
Twitter @kidsbookcentre
Instagram @kidsbookcentre

A national, not-for-profit organisation, that is dedicated to encouraging, promoting and supporting the reading, writing, illustrating and publishing of Canadian books for young readers. CCBC programmes, publications and resources help teachers, librarians, booksellers and parents select the very best for young readers. Founded 1976.

Canadian Publishers' Council

Suite 6060, 3080 Yonge Street, Toronto,
ON M4N 3N1
tel +1 647-255-8880
email dswail@pubcouncil.ca
website https://pubcouncil.ca
Twitter @pubcouncil_ca
President David Swail

Represents the interests of Canadian publishing companies that publish books and other media for schools, colleges and universities, professional and reference markets, the retail and library sectors. Founded 1910.

Canadian Society of Children's Authors, Illustrators & Performers

720 Bathurst Street, Suite 503, Toronto, ON M5S 2R4
tel +1 416-515-1559
email office@canscaip.org
website www.canscaip.org
Twitter @CANSCAIP
Administrative Director Helena Aalto
Membership $85 p.a. member; $45 p.a. friend

A membership-based non-profit organisation that supports the professional development of Canada's community of authors, illustrators and performers for children and teens. Founded 1977.

The Lewis Carroll Society

email secretary@lewiscarrollsociety.org.uk
website https://lewiscarrollsociety.org.uk
Facebook www.facebook.com/groups/68678994062
Twitter @LewisCarrollSoc
Membership £25 p.a. UK; £30 p.a. Europe; £35 p.a. elsewhere; special rates for students and institutions

Promotes interest in the life and works of Lewis Carroll (Revd Charles Lutwidge Dodgson, 1832–98) and to encourage research. Activities include regular meetings, exhibitions and a publishing programme that includes the first annotated, unexpurgated edition of his diaries in nine volumes, the Society's journal *The Carrollian*, a newsletter, *Bandersnatch* and the *Lewis Carroll Review*. Founded 1969.

Lewis Carroll Society of North America

email secretary@lewiscarroll.org
website www.lewiscarroll.org
Facebook www.facebook.com/LCSNA
Twitter @AliceAmerica
President Linda Cassidy, *Secretary* Sandra Lee Parker
Membership $42 p.a.

An organisation of Carroll admirers of all ages and interests. It is dedicated to furthering Carroll studies, increasing accessibility of research material, and maintaining public awareness of Carroll's contributions to society. The Society has a worldwide membership and meets twice a year. The Society maintains an active publication programme and members receive copies of the Society's magazine *Knight Letter*. An interest in Lewis Carroll or a simple love for Alice (or the Snark for that matter) qualifies for membership. Founded 1974.

The Center for Children's Books

501 East Daniel Street, Champaign, IL 61820, USA
tel +1 217-244-9331
email ccb-asst@illinois.edu
website https://ccb.ischool.illinois.edu
Twitter @iSchoolCCB

CCB houses a non-circulating collection of more than 16,000 recent and historically significant trade books for children, plus review copies of nearly all trade books published in the USA in the current year.

There are over 1,000 professional and reference books on the history and criticism of literature for youth, literature-based library and classroom programming, and storytelling. The collection is available for examination by scholars, teachers, librarians, students and other educators.

Centre for Literacy in Primary Education

Webber Street, London SE1 8QW
tel 020-7401 3382/3
email info@clpe.org.uk
website https://clpe.org.uk
Facebook www.facebook.com/
CentreforLiteracyinPrimaryEducation
Twitter @clpe1

The CLPE is a small independent charity working with all those involved in teaching literacy in primary schools. Aims to raise the achievement of children by helping schools to teach literacy more effectively and by showing teachers how quality children's literature can be placed at the heart of all learning.

Chartered Institute of Editing and Proofreading

Apsley House, 176 Upper Richmond Road, London SW15 2SH
tel 020-8785 6155
email office@ciep.uk
website www.ciep.uk
Facebook www.facebook.com/EditProof
Twitter @The_CIEP

The CIEP is a non-profit body promoting excellence in English language editing. It sets and demonstrates editorial standards, and is a community, training hub and support network for editorial professionals – the people who work to make text accurate, clear and fit for purpose. The CIEP publishes an online directory of experienced editorial professionals and also runs online courses and workshops in copyediting, proofreading and related skills, for people starting an editorial career and those wishing to broaden their competence.

As well as professional practice, training covers business skills for the self-employed. It also offers in-house training to businesses and organisations on various writing-related skills. The Institute will be instrumental in developing recognised standards of training and accreditation for editors and proofreaders. The CIEP was known as the Society for Editors and Proofreaders before being awarded its Royal Charter in 2019. It has close links with and works alongside other bodies in the publishing sector. Founded 1988.

The Children's Book Circle – see page 336

The Children's Book Council and Every Child A Reader

54 West 39th Street, 14th Floor, New York, NY 10018, USA
email cbc.info@cbcbooks.org
website www.cbcbooks.org
website www.everychildreader.net

The CBC is the non-profit trade association of North American publishers and packagers of trade books and related materials for children and young adults. Every Child a Reader is its charitable component that sponsors Children's Book Week, which celebrated 100 years in May 2019; the Children's & Teen Choice Book Awards; Get Caught Reading; and the National Ambassador of Young People's Literature, in conjunction with the Library of Congress.

The CBC offers children's publishers the opportunity to work together on educational programming, diversity advocacy, and national literacy and public awareness campaigns. The CBC connects member publishers to librarians, teachers, booksellers and caregivers across the country, providing reading lists, student resources and community outreach in coordination with prominent national organisations.

The Children's Book Council of Australia

Level 2 State Library of Queensland, Stanley Place, South Brisbane, QLD 4101
email admin@cbca.org.au
website www.cbca.org.au
Facebook www.facebook.com/theCBCA
Twitter @theCBCA

Aims to foster children's enjoyment of books through managing the Children's Book of the Year Awards; providing information on and encouragement to authors and illustrators; organising exhibitions and activities during Children's Book Week; supporting children's library services; and promoting high standards in book reviewing, along with promoting greater equity of access to reading through community projects.

The Children's Book Guild of Washington DC

email membership.cbg@gmail.com
website www.childrensbookguild.org
Facebook www.facebook.com/bookguilddc
Twitter @BOOKGUILDDC

A regional association of writers, artists, librarians and other specialists dedicated to the field of children's literature. Its aims are to uphold and stimulate high standards of writing and illustrating for children; to increase knowledge and use of better books for children in the community; and to cooperate with other groups having similar purposes. Founded 1945.

Children's Books Ireland

17 North Great George's Street, Dublin D01 R2F1, Republic of Ireland
tel +353 (0)1 872 7475

email info@childrensbooksireland.com
website www.childrensbooksireland.ie
Ceo Elaina Ryan, *Deputy Ceo* Jenny Murray,
Programme & Events Manager Aoife Murray

A national charity that champions every child's right to develop a love of reading. They aim to engage young people in reading, foster a greater understanding of books for young people and act as a core resource for those with an interest in books for children in Ireland. They champion and celebrate the importance of authors and illustrators and work in partnership with the people and organisations who enhance children's lives through books. Core projects include: the Children's Books Ireland International Annual Conference; the KPMG Children's Books Ireland Awards and its Junior Juries' programme for school groups and book clubs; the annual Children's Books Ireland Recommended Reads, a guide to the best books of the year; nationwide Book Clinics; various book gifting initiatives including the Every Child A Reader Reading Communities; Bookseed and *Inis* magazine in print and online – a forum for discussion, debate and critique of Irish and international books. Also administers the Laureate na nÓg project on behalf of the Arts Council and runs live literature events throughout the year. Founded 1996.

Children's Literature Association
ChLA, One Glenlake Parkway NE, Suite 1200, Atlanta, GA 30328, USA
tel +1 630-571-4520
email info@childlitassn.org
website https://chla.memberclicks.net
Twitter @chlatweets
Membership From $45 p.a. (dependent on income)

An organisation encouraging high standards of criticism, scholarship, research and teaching in children's literature.

Contact An Author
2 Burns Close, Carshalton SM5 4PY
tel 020-8642 0884
email info@contactanauthor.com
website https://contactanauthor.co.uk
Facebook www.facebook.com/contactanauthor
Twitter @contactanauthor
Instagram @contactanauthor

An author-booking agency that connects children with compassionate and creative people to enhance education. Helps schools, libraries, festivals and organisations all over the world to book authors for their events. Its mission is to celebrate books and help to arrange as many author visits as possible. Always happy for authors to join. Founded 2006.

Coram Beanstalk
Coram Campus, 41 Brunswick Square,
London WC1N 1AZ
tel 020-7729 4087
website www.beanstalkcharity.org.uk
Facebook www.facebook.com/Beanstalkreads
Twitter @beanstalkreads
Instagram @beanstalkreads

Recruits, trains and supports volunteers to provide consistent, one-to-one reading support to children aged 3–13 who need help. Reading helpers give them the support they need to improve their reading skills, reading ability and confidence. Also provides training to people within the school community who want to help children learn to read for pleasure whilst improving their reading skills.

Creative Scotland
British Council, 1 Redman Place, London E20 1JQ
tel 0161 957 7755
email enquiries@creativescotland.com
website www.creativescotland.com
Twitter @BritishCouncil, @BritishArts

The public body that supports the arts, screen and creative industries across all parts of Scotland on behalf of everyone who lives, works or visits there. Through distributing funding from the Scottish Government and the National Lottery, Creative Scotland enables people and organisations to work in and experience the arts, screen and creative industries in Scotland by helping others to develop great ideas and bring them to life. Creative Scotland supports writers and publishers based in Scotland through a range of funds and initiatives.

Creative UK
1st Floor, College House, 32-36 College Green, Bristol, BS1 5SP
tel 033-3023 5240
email info@wearecreative.uk
website www.wearecreative.uk
Facebook www.facebook.com/WeAreCreativeUK
Twitter @WeAreCreativeUK
Instagram @wearecreativeuk

Creative UK champions the creative industries and their ability to catalyse social and economic change. Empowers innovators and entrepreneurs by bringing them together. Provides financial, business development and skills training to enable them to reach their full potential without compromising their ideas. Creative UK merges the insights and expertise of the Creative Industries Federation and Creative England.

Roald Dahl's Marvellous Children's Charity
tel (01494) 890465
email enquiries@roalddahlcharity.org
website www.roalddahlcharity.org
Facebook www.facebook.com/roalddahlcharity
Twitter @RoaldDahlFund

The Charity helps to make life better for seriously ill children in the UK. The Roald Dahl Nurses provide support to children with serious illnesses and their families. The Charity believes that every child should have the best possible healthcare.

The website is illustrated with the artworks of Quentin Blake, Roald Dahl's principal illustrator and President of the charity, and includes full information about the author, his life and his works.

The Roald Dahl Museum and Story Centre
website www.roalddahl.com/museum
Facebook www.facebook.com/roalddahlmuseum
Twitter @roalddahlmuseum

Houses Roald Dahl's unique archive and is situated in the Buckinghamshire village where Roald Dahl lived and worked for 36 years. The Museum features interactive galleries and the Story Centre provides activities and events to inspire young writers.

Walter de la Mare Society
email info@walterdelamare.co.uk
website www.walterdelamare.co.uk
Membership £10 p.a.

Established to promote the study and deepen the appreciation of the works of Walter de la Mare (1873–1956) through a magazine, talks, discussions and other activities. Founded 1997.

Discover Children's Story Centre
383–387 High Street, Stratford, London E15 4QZ
tel 020-8536 5555
email bookings@discover.org.uk
website https://discover.org.uk
Facebook www.facebook.com/
DiscoverChildrensStoryCentre
Twitter @Discover_Story

The UK's first hands-on creative literacy centre for children aged 0–11 years and their families, carers and teachers. Discover's mission is to spark children's and adults' imagination, curiosity and creativity in a magical and stimulating environment through creative play. It offers a variety of programmes including creative family events led by children's writers and illustrators, community and education projects, school workshops and artist residencies. Support is given to new and upcoming artists working with children and families. Artists are also commissioned to create multisensory installations, exhibitions and sets for performative storytelling.

Editors' and Proofreaders' Alliance of Northern Ireland
email info@epani.org.uk
website www.epani.org.uk
Twitter @epa_ni
Coordinator Averill Buchanan

Aims to establish and maintain high professional standards in editorial skills in Northern Ireland. For services for authors, see our directory of freelance professional editors, proofreaders and indexers.

Empathy Lab
email info@empathylab.uk
website https://www.empathylab.uk
Facebook www.facebook.com/EmpathyLabUK
Twitter @EmpathyLabUK

A non-profit with a mission to raise an empathy-educated generation. EmpathyLab builds children's empathy, literacy and social activism through high-quality literature. Their strategy is built on scientific evidence showing that empathy is learnable and that reading is a crucial tool to build this skill. EmpathyLab provides training, free resources, an in-depth schools programme and an annual Read for Empathy Book Collection. One of their four main programmes is Empathy Day, which takes place in June each year. Empathy Day Live! is a free online festival led by children's authors and illustrators. Founded 2014.

English Association
University of Leicester, Leicester LE1 7RH
tel 0116 229 7622
email hello@englishassociation.ac.uk
website www2.le.ac.uk/offices/english-association
President Rob Penman

A membership body for individuals and organisations passionate about the English language and its literatures. Membership includes teachers, students, authors, writers and readers, and is made up of people and institutions from around the world. Its aim is to further the knowledge, understanding and enjoyment of English studies, and to foster good practice in their teaching and learning at all levels by:
• encouraging the study of English language, literature and creative writing;
• working towards fuller recognition of English as core to education;
• fostering discussion about methods of teaching English at all levels;
• offering timely conferences and lectures alongside a uniquely diverse and extensive portfolio of publications; and
• responding to national consultations and policy decisions about the subject.

Federation of Children's Book Groups –
see page 337

Federation of European Publishers
Chaussee d'Ixelles, 29/35 Box 4, 1050 Brussels, Belgium
tel +32 2770 1110
email info@fep-fee.eu
website www.fep-fee.eu
Twitter @FEP_EU

Represents the interests of European publishers on EU affairs; informs members on the development of

EU policies which could affect the publishing industry. Founded 1967.

Forward Arts Foundation

020-7845 4655
email info@forwardartsfoundation.org
website www.forwardartsfoundation.org

Promotes appreciation and engagement with poetry through programmes and initiatives that run throughout the year. As well as advocating for the positive social impact of poetry and growing poetry audiences, the Foundation supports and celebrates poets. Works closely with schools and libraries, organises National Poetry Day each year and runs the Forward Prizes for Poetry.

The Gaelic Books Council/Comhairle nan Leabhraichean

32 Mansfield Street, Glasgow G11 5QP
tel 0141 337 6211
email alison@gaelicbooks.org
website www.gaelicbooks.org
Director Alison Lang

Stimulates Scottish Gaelic publishing by awarding publication grants for new books, commissions new works from established and emerging authors and provides editorial advice and guidance to Gaelic writers and publishers. Has a bookshop in Glasgow that stocks all Gaelic and Gaelic-related books in print. All stock is listed on the website. Founded 1968.

The Greeting Card Association

United House, North Road, London N7 9DP
tel 020-7619 9266
email hello@gca.cards
website www.gca.cards
Facebook www.facebook.com/GreetingCardAssociation
Twitter @GCAUK
Instagram @GCA_UK
Chief Executive Amanda Fergusson

The trade association for greeting card publishers. See website for information, including teachers' resources, lesson plans and card-making projects for children of all ages. Official magazine: *Progressive Greetings Worldwide*. Founded 1919.

Guernsey Arts Commission

Candie Museum, Candie Road, St Peter Port, Guernsey GY1 2UG
tel (01481) 709747
email info@arts.gg

The Commission's aim is to help promote, develop and support the arts in Guernsey through exhibitions, a community arts programme and public events.

House of Illustration

2 Granary Square, Kings Cross, London N1C 4BH
email info@houseofillustration.org.uk
website https://houseofillustration.org.uk
Twitter @illustrationHQ

House of Illustration, soon to evolve in to the Quentin Blake Centre for Illustration, is the UK's centre for illustration. When it reopens at its new central London site in 2023, it will be the world's largest public arts space dedicated to the art of illustration in all its forms. It will also become a permanent home for the archive of its founder, Sir Quentin Blake, after whom it will be renamed. Until it reopens, House of Illustration's work continues offsite and online through a series of education and events programmes and touring exhibitions.

IBBY

Nonnenweg 12, CH–4055, Switzerland
tel +41 61-272 2917
email ibby@ibby.org
website www.ibby.org
Facebook www.facebook.com/ibby.international
Twitter @IBBYINT
Instagram @ibby.international

IBBY (the International Board on Books for Young People) is a non-profit organisation which represents an international network of people from all over the world who are committed to bringing books and children together. Its aims are:

• to promote international understanding through children's books;
• to give children everywhere the opportunity to have access to books with high literary and artistic standards;
• to encourage the publication and distribution of quality children's books, especially in developing countries;
• to provide support and training for those involved with children and children's literature; and
• to stimulate research and scholarly works in the field of children's literature.

IBBY is composed of National Sections all over the world and represents countries with well-developed book publishing and literacy programmes, and other countries with only a few dedicated professionals who are doing pioneer work in children's book publishing and promotion. Founded 1953.

IBBY UK

119 Victoria Road, London N22 7XG
website www.ibby.org.uk
Facebook www.facebook.com/IBBYUK
Twitter @IBBYUK

IBBY (the International Board on Books for Young People) is a unique international alliance of everyone interested in children's literature including academics, librarians, publishers, booksellers, writers, illustrators, teachers, literacy workers, parents and others.

Imaginate

30B Grindlay Street, Edinburgh EH3 9AX
tel 0131 225 8050
email info@imaginate.org.uk
website www.imaginate.org.uk
Chief Executive Belinda McElhinney, *Festival Director* Noel Jordan

The national organisation in Scotland which promotes, develops and advocates for theatre and dance for children and young people. Works to enable more children in Scotland to experience work that is deeply engaging, innovative and inspiring, and believes that all children deserve the opportunity to develop their creativity, emotional intelligence and reach their true potential. Imaginate's work falls into three strands:

• The Edinburgh International Children's Festival, a celebration of the world's best theatre and dance for young audiences, attracting 17,000 children, parents, teachers and industry professionals annually.
• A year-round programme for schools. Delivers Theatre in Schools Scotland, the national touring programme of high-quality, affordable performances for schools, in partnership with National Theatre of Scotland. Also delivers focused projects to develop children's and teachers' creativity, including a partnership with six disadvantaged Edinburgh schools.
• A year-round Creative Development Programme for artists who make theatre and dance for children. This includes projects to develop artistic practice and support productions, networking events, mentoring and a Go and See Fund.

Imaginative Book Illustration Society

email ibissec@martinsteenson.co.uk
website www.bookillustration.org
Membership enquiries Martin Steenson

IBIS was established to encourage research into, and to facilitate, the exchange of information on book and periodical illustrations, the artists and their publishers. The Society has a worldwide membership including artists, collectors, bibliographers, writers and general enthusiasts. Whilst IBIS embraces all aspects of illustrative art, the main emphasis is on the illustration of texts in English since the 1830s. Founded 1995.

Independent Publishers Guild

PO Box 12, Llain, Login SA34 0WU
tel (01437) 563335
email info@independentpublishersguild.com
website www.independentpublishersguild.com
Chief Executive Bridget Shine
Membership open to new and established publishers from all sectors and of all sizes, plus suppliers and service providers.

The IPG is the UK's largest network of publishers and has served, supported and represented independents for 60 years. It delivers two popular annual conferences featuring speakers from across publishing and beyond, a range of other events and numerous resources to help members do better business. Coordinates the Independent Publishing Awards, a mentoring scheme, collective stands at book fairs and training via the IPG Skills Hub, and provides members with weekly ebulletins, a business support helpline and special deals on publishing products and services. Founded 1962.

Independent Theatre Council

The Albany, Douglas Way, London SE8 4AG
tel 020-7403 1727
email admin@itc-arts.org
website www.itc-arts.org
Twitter @itc_arts
Membership £190 p.a.

Enables the creation of high-quality professional performing arts by supporting, representing and developing the people who manage and produce it. It has around 500 members from a wide range of companies, venues and individuals in the fields of drama, dance, opera, musical theatre, puppetry, mixed media, mime, physical theatre and circus. Founded 1974.

International Authors Forum

5th Floor, Shackleton House, 4 Battle Bridge Lane, London SE1 2HX
tel 020-7264 5707
email luke.alcott@internationalauthors.org
website www.internationalauthors.org
Twitter @IntAuthors
Executive Administrator Luke Alcott

Represents authors around the world and has a membership made up of over 70 authors' organisations from every continent. Campaigns for authors' rights at the UN and national levels. Organises events, publications and collaborates with other organisations representing authors to promote the importance of creative work financially, socially and culturally. Keeps members up to date with international developments in copyright law.

International Publishers Association

23 Avenue de France, 1202 Geneva, Switzerland
tel +41 22-704 1820
email info@internationalpublishers.org
website www.internationalpublishers.org
Facebook www.facebook.com/InternationalPublishersAssociation
Twitter @IntPublishers
President Bodour Al Qasimi, *Secretary-General* José Borghino

The IPA is a federation of national, regional and international publishers associations. It promotes and protects publishing worldwide, with a focus on copyright and freedom to publish. Its membership comprises 89 organisations from 73 countries worldwide. Founded 1896.

Irish Writers Centre

19 Parnell Square, Dublin D01 E102, Republic of Ireland
tel +353 (0)1 872 1302
email info@writerscentre.ie
website https://irishwriterscentre.ie
Facebook www.facebook.com/irishwritersctr
Twitter @IrishWritersCtr
Director Valerie Bistany

National resource centre for Irish writers, which supports and promotes authors at all stages of their development. Runs workshops, seminars and events related to the art of writing, which are run by established writers across a range of genres. Also hosts professional development seminars for writers, and provides space for writers, writing groups and other literary organisations. Founded 1991.

The Kipling Society

Bay Tree House, Doomsday Garden, Horsham, West Sussex RH13 6LB
email michaelrkipling@gmail.com
website www.kiplingsociety.co.uk
Chairman Prof. Jan Montefiore
Membership £29 p.a. UK; £31 p.a. Europe; £35 p.a. rest of world; £10 p.a. student (worldwide)

Encourages discussion and study of the work and life of Rudyard Kipling (1865–1936) by assisting in the study of his writings, holding discussion meetings, publishing a quarterly journal and website (with a Readers' Guide to Kipling's work), maintaining a Kipling Library at Haileybury School in Hertfordshire and running an annual writing competition.

The C.S. Lewis Society (New York)

84–23 77th Avenue, Glendale, NY 11385–7706, USA
email subscribe@nycslsociety.com
email csarrocco@aol.com
website www.nycslsociety.com
Secretary Clare Sarrocco

The oldest society for the appreciation and discussion of C.S. Lewis (1898–1963). Founded 1969.

Literature Wales

Glyn Jones Centre, Wales Millennium Centre, Bute Place, Cardiff CF10 5AL
tel 029-2047 2266
email post@literaturewales.org
website www.literaturewales.org
Facebook www.facebook.com/LlenCymruLitWales
Twitter @LitWales

Literature Wales is the national company for the development of literature in Wales. Working to inspire communities, develop writers and celebrate Wales' literary culture, its vision is a Wales where literature empowers, improves and brightens lives. Activities include the Wales Book of the Year Award, the Children's Laureate Wales and Bardd Plant Cymru schemes, creative writing courses at Tŷ Newydd Writing Centre, the professional development scheme Representing Wales, writer's bursaries and mentoring, the National Poet of Wales initiative, and more. The organisation is a member of the Arts Council of Wales' Arts Portfolio Wales.

Little Theatre Guild of Great Britain

tel (01207) 545280
email caroline.chapman1816@gmail.com
website www.littletheatreguild.org
Secretary Caroline Chapman

Promotes closer cooperation amongst the little theatres constituting its membership, acts as a coordinating and representative body on behalf of the little theatres, maintains and advances the highest standards in the art of theatre, and assists in encouraging the establishment of other little theatres.

LoveReading4Kids

PTC International Ltd, Turnbridge Mills, Quay Street, Huddersfield HD1 6QT
tel 020-3004 7204
website www.lovereading4kids.co.uk
Facebook www.facebook.com/lovereading4kids
Twitter @lovereadingkids

A book recommendation site for children's books ranging from toddlers to teens. Ensures that whatever their age or interest, there is a steady stream of book recommendations available. Offers a variety of free services for parents and anyone who is interested in buying the best books for children. Supports parents, teachers and school librarians in helping engender a lifelong love of reading in children. The website features Kids' Zone, an area designed specifically for children, with competitions, quizzes and book-related material. Founded 2005.

LoveReading4Schools

PTC International Ltd, Turnbridge Mills, Quay Street, Huddersfield HD1 6QT
tel 020-3004 7204
website www.lovereading4schools.co.uk
Facebook www.facebook.com/lovereading4schools
Twitter @lr4schools

A book recommendation website which promotes a love of books and reading to all by offering the tools, advice and information needed to help members and browsers to find their next book, including time-strapped teachers and librarians in schools to help engender a lifelong love of reading in their students. Publishes book lists of relevance to schools including lists of inspirational books, cultural books, reluctant readers recommendations and books related to mental health and wellbeing.

The Mythopoeic Society

website www.mythsoc.org

A non-profit international literary and educational organisation for the study, discussion and enjoyment of fantastic and mythic literature, especially the works of Tolkien, C.S. Lewis and Charles Williams. 'Mythopoeic' (myth-oh-PAY-ik or myth-oh-PEE-ik) means 'mythmaking' or 'productive of myth' and aptly describes much of the fictional work of the three authors who were also prominent members of an informal Oxford literary circle (1930s–50s) known as the Inklings. Membership is open to all scholars, writers and readers of these literatures. The Society sponsors three periodicals: *Mythprint* (a bulletin of book reviews, articles and events), *Mythlore* (scholarly articles on mythic and fantastic literature), and *Mythic Circle* (a literary annual of original poetry and short stories). Each summer the Society holds an annual conference, Mythcon. Founded 1967.

National Association for the Teaching of English

Office 6, 197–201 Manchester Road, Altrincham, Manchester WA14 5NU
tel 0330 333 5050
email admin@nate.org.uk
website www.nate.org.uk
Twitter @Natefeed

NATE is a professional association for English teachers that works regionally, nationally and internationally at all key stages. It works to: promote standards of excellence in the teaching of English from early years to university; research curriculum design and assessment; promote innovative and original ideas that have practical classroom outcomes; support teachers' professional development through access to current research, publications and national and regional conferences; provide an informed national voice on matters concerning the teaching of English and its related subjects; and encourage sharing and collaboration between teachers and learners of English and its related subjects. Founded 1963.

National Association of Writers and Groups

Old Vicarage, Scammonden, Huddersfield HD3 3FT
email info@nawg.co.uk
website www.nawg.co.uk
Facebook www.facebook.com/NAWGNews
Twitter @NAWGnews
Secretary Chris Huck
Membership £50 p.a. per group; £25 p.a. individuals

NAWG aims to advance the education of the general public throughout the UK, including the Channel Islands, by promoting the study and art of writing in all its aspects. Publishes *LINK*, a bi-monthly magazine, and a bi-monthly newsletter; holds the Festival of Writing annually in August/September; runs competitions with cash prizes (open to all but free for members); and facilitates online workshops. New members always welcome. Founded 1995.

National Association of Writers in Education

Tower House, Mill Lane, off Askham Fields Lane, Askham Bryan, York YO23 3FS
email admin@nawe.co.uk
website www.nawe.co.uk
Twitter @NaweWriters
Membership £75 p.a. professional; £37.50 professional graduate; £30 p.a. student/associate/overseas

National membership organisation which aims to further knowledge, understanding and enjoyment of creative writing and to support good practice in its teaching and learning at all levels. NAWE promotes creative writing as both a distinct discipline and an essential element in education generally. Its membership includes those working in Higher Education, the many freelance writers working in schools and community contexts, and the teachers and other professionals who work with them. It runs a national database of writers, produces a weekly opportunities bulletin, publishes two journals – *Writing in Education* and *Writing in Practice* – and holds a national conference (this was online in 2022). Professional membership includes public liability insurance cover.

National Centre for Research in Children's Literature

website https://ncrcl.wordpress.com
Twitter @NCRCL

NCRCL members work on a range of projects related to children's literature and the culture of childhood, publishing in such diverse areas as: ethics and metaphysics; adolescent fiction; memories of childhood reading; the Robinsonade; Romantic childhood; print culture; graphic novels; and the literature of food. News of regular conferences and events hosted by the NCRCL can be found on the NCRCL Blog. Founded 1995.

National Centre for Writing

Dragon Hall, 115–123 King Street, Norwich NR1 1QE
email info@nationalcentreforwriting.org.uk
website https://nationalcentreforwriting.org.uk
Facebook www.facebook.com/NationalCentreforWriting
Twitter @WritersCentre

Celebrates and explores the artistic and social power of creative writing and literary translation. An ongoing programme of innovative collaborations engages writers, literary translators and readers in projects that support new voices and new stories and respond to the rapidly changing world of writing.

Based at the historic Dragon Hall in Norwich, where workshops and mentoring are regularly available for writers at all levels, both face-to-face and online. Projects range from the Desmond Elliott Prize to vibrant festivals such as the City of Literature strand of Norfolk & Norwich Festival. Founded 2018.

National Literacy Trust – see page 339

National Society for Education in Art and Design

3 Masons Wharf, Potley Lane, Corsham, Wilts. SN13 9FY
tel (01225) 810134
email info@nsead.org
website www.nsead.org
Twitter @NSEAD1
General Secretary Michele Gregson

The leading national authority concerned with art, craft and design across all phases of education in the UK. Offers the benefits of membership of a professional association, a learned society and a trade union. Has representatives on national and regional committees concerned with art and design education. Publishes International Journal of Art and Design Education online (3 p.a.; Wiley Blackwell) and AD magazine for teachers. Founded 1888.

The Edith Nesbit Society

21 Churchfields, West Malling, Kent ME19 6RJ
email edithnesbit@gmail.com
website www.edithnesbit.co.uk
Membership £10 p.a. individual; £12 p.a. joint; £15 p.a. organisations

Promotes an interest in the life and works of Edith Nesbit (1858–1924) by means of talks, a regular newsletter and other publications, and visits to places associated with her. Founded 1996.

New Writing North

3 Ellison Terrace, Ellison Place, Newcastle upon Tyne NE1 8ST
email office@newwritingnorth.com
website https://newwritingnorth.com
Facebook www.facebook.com/newwritingnorth
Twitter @NewWritingNorth

Supports writing and reading in the North of England. Commissions new work, creates development opportunities and nurtures talent. Founded 1996.

Newcastle University Library

Philip Robinson Library, Jesmond Road West, Newcastle upon Tyne NE2 4HQ
tel 0191 208 7662
email libraryhelp@ncl.ac.uk
website www.ncl.ac.uk/library
Facebook www.facebook.com/NULibraries
Twitter @nclroblib

A modern academic library with multi-disciplinary collections, including historical children's books. The Library's Special Collections hold many unique archives and rare books. These materials provide great scope for original research for many subject areas and the potential to complement teaching and learning at the university. There are a number of collections and archives dedicated to children's literature. See website for details.

The Office for Standards in Education, Children's Services and Skills

Piccadilly Gate, Store Street, Manchester M1 2WD
tel 0300 123 1231
email enquiries@ofsted.gov.uk
website www.gov.uk/ofsted

Ofsted is a non-ministerial government department. It regulates and inspects to achieve excellence in the care of children and young people, and in education and skills for learners of all ages. It regulates and inspects childcare and children's social care, and inspects the Children and Family Court Advisory and Support Service (Cafcass), schools, colleges, initial teacher training, further education and skills, adult and community learning, and education and training in prisons and other secure establishments. It assesses council children's services, and inspects services for looked after children, safeguarding and child protection.

Pathways Into Children's Publishing

Pop Up Projects, 5 City Garden Row, London N1 8DW
email pathways@pop-up.org.uk
website https://pathways-org.com
Facebook www.facebook.com/PathwaysINTO
Twitter @PathwaysINTO
Instagram @PathwaysInto

Two-year illustration programme for talented artists from under-represented backgrounds who want to become the next generation of children's illustrators. The programme is designed and organised by Pop Up Projects, with support from over 20 publishers and leading universities.
    Pathways also runs a series of Masterclasses and Short Courses for all aspiring illustrators looking to improve their practice and learn about creating successful children's books. The courses are run by award-winning illustrators and highly-experienced publishers and provide practical, creative advice as well as a real insight into children's publishing.

Pen to Print

tel 020-8227 2267
email pentoprint@lbbd.gov.uk
website https://pentoprint.org/
Facebook www.facebook.com/OfficialPentoPrint
Twitter @Pen_to_Print
Instagram @officialpentoprint

A free writer development programme based in libraries. As an Arts Council-funded programme, it provides a safe, collaborative environment to develop writers' authentic voices. Aspiring writers, especially those from backgrounds that are under-represented in publishing, are encouraged to reach communities with their stories and inspire potential in others. Free activities include:

• classes and workshops;
• competitions including The Book Challenge;
• author talks;
• ReadFest literary festival
• *Write On!* magazine (print)
• *Write On! Extra* magazine (online)
• *Write On! Audio* podcast

PICSEL (Picture Industry Collecting Society for Effective Licensing)
112 Western Road, Brighton, East Sussex BN1 2AB
tel (01273) 746564
email info@picsel.org.uk
website www.picsel.org.uk

A not-for-profit collecting society that ensures that all visual artists, creators and representative rights holders of images receive fair payment for various secondary uses of their works. It works to ensure that all licence fees collected are distributed equitably, efficiently and in a transparent manner. Founded 2016.

The Poetry Book Society – see page 204

The Poetry Society – see page 204

Poetry Society Education – see page 208

Pop Up Projects: Transforming Lives Through Literature
5 Paper Mill Buildings, City Garden Row, London N1 8DW
email info@pop-up.org.uk
website www.pop-up.org.uk
Facebook www.facebook.com/popupfestival
Twitter @PopUpFestival
Instagram @Pop_Up_Projects

A non-profit national literature and publishing organisation which believes that all children should find themselves, and discover others, through the stories they read. Their work includes creating courses and training for aspiring children's book illustrators and writers from under-represented backgrounds, publishing books for children and young people that celebrate difference, and providing author-led programmes in special educational needs schools. Founded 2011.

The Beatrix Potter Society
email info@beatrixpottersociety.org.uk
website www.beatrixpottersociety.org.uk

Promotes the study and appreciation of the life and works of Beatrix Potter (1866–1943) as author, artist, diarist, farmer and conservationist. Regular lecture meetings, conferences and events in the UK and USA. Quarterly newsletter. Small publishing programme. Founded 1980.

Publishers Association
First Floor, 50 Southwark Street, London SE1 1UN
tel 020-7378 0504
email mail@publishers.org.uk
website www.publishers.org.uk
Twitter @PublishersAssoc
President Nigel Newton, *Ceo* Stephen Lotinga

A member organisation for UK publishing, representing companies of all sizes and specialisms – including children's books. Their members produce digital and print books, research journals and educational resources across genres and subjects. The Publishers Association exists to champion publishing to the wider world and to provide their members with everything they need to thrive. They have helped change laws, improved business conditions and inspired people to become publishers. Founded 1896.

Publishers Association of New Zealand
Level 6, 19 Como Street, Takapuna, Auckland 0622
tel +64 (0)9 280 3213
email admin@publishers.org.nz
website www.publishers.org.nz
Twitter @Publishers_NZ

PANZ represents book, educational and digital publishers in New Zealand. Members include both the largest international publishers and companies in the independent publishing community.

Publishing Ireland/Foilsiú Éireann
63 Patrick Street, Dun Laoghaire, Dublin A96 WF25, Republic of Ireland
website www.publishingireland.com
Facebook www.facebook.com/PublishingIreland
Twitter @PublishingIRL
General Manager Orla McLoughlin

Publishing Ireland enables publishers to share expertise and resources in order to benefit from opportunities and solve problems that are of common concern to all. It comprises most of the major publishing houses in Ireland with a mixture of trade, general and academic publishers as members. Founded 1970.

Publishing Scotland
Scott House, 10 South St Andrew Street, Edinburgh EH2 2AZ
tel 0131 228 6866
email enquiries@publishingscotland.org
website www.publishingscotland.org
Chief Executive Marion Sinclair

A network for trade, training and development in the Scottish publishing industry. The 2022 theme for their annual programme of events is Year of Stories, spotlighting stories inspired by and written in Scotland. Founded 1973.

The Arthur Ransome Society Ltd

9 Merro Avenue, Poole BH12 1PY
email tarsinfo@arthur-ransome.org
website www.arthur-ransome.org

Exists to celebrate the life, promote the works and diffuse the ideas of Arthur Ransome (1884–1967), author of the world-famous *Swallows and Amazons* series of books for children. The Society seeks in particular to encourage children and others to engage, with due regard to safety, in adventurous pursuits; educate the public generally about Ransome and his work; sponsor research in relevant areas; be a communications link for those interested in any aspect of Arthur Ransome's life and works. Founded 1990.

Read for Good

26 Nailsworth Mills, Avening Road, Nailsworth, Glos. GL6 0BS
tel (01453) 839005
email reading@readforgood.org
website www.readforgood.org
Facebook www.facebook.com/readforgood
Twitter @ReadforGoodUK
Instagram @readforgood

The charity aims for all children in the UK to be given the opportunity, space and motivation to develop their own love of reading, benefiting them throughout their lives. Runs a Readathon programme in thousands of schools and a hospital programme, which focuses on the supply of books and storyteller visits to brighten up the days of 150,000 children in the UK's 30 main children's hospitals.

The Reading Agency

24 Bedford Row, London WC1R 4EH
tel 07584 643543
email info@readingagency.org.uk
website www.readingagency.org.uk
Twitter @readingagency

A charity whose mission is to tackle life's big challenges through the proven power of reading. Works closely with public libraries, publishers, health partners and volunteers to bring reading programmes to children across the UK. Funded by Arts Council England, The Reading Agency supports a wide range of reading initiatives for children including the Summer Reading Challenge, run in partnership with libraries, which helps get around three-quarters of a million children into libraries each year; and Chatterbooks reading clubs, which help children build a lifelong reading habit.

RNIB National Library Service

RNIB, Northminster House, Northminster, Peterborough PE1 1YN
tel 0303 123 9999
website www.rniblibrary.com
website https://readingservices.rnib.org.uk
website www.rnibbookshare.org

The largest specialist library for readers with sight loss in the UK. It offers a comprehensive range of books and accessible information for children and adults in braille and Talking Books. Books are also available for download in audio and braille from RNIB Reading Services. RNIB Bookshare opens up the world of reading in Education for learners with a print-disability, including those with dyslexia or who are blind or partially sighted.

The Malcolm Saville Society

11 Minster Court, Windsor Close, Taunton TA1 4LW
email mystery@witchend.com
website www.witchend.com
Facebook www.facebook.com/MalcolmSaville
Twitter @MSavilleSociety
Membership £15 p.a. UK; £17.50 p.a. Europe; £21 p.a. elsewhere

Promotes interest in the work of children's author Malcolm Saville (1901–82). Regular social activities, library, book and merchandise sales and a magazine (up to 4 p.a.). Founded 1994.

Scattered Authors' Society

email scatteredauthorssociety@gmail.com
website www.scatteredauthors.org

Provides a forum for informal discussion, contact and support for professional writers in children's fiction. Founded 1998.

School Library Association

1 Pine Court, Kembrey Park, Swindon SN2 8AD
tel (01793) 530166
email info@sla.org.uk
website www.sla.org.uk
Facebook www.facebook.com/schoollibraryassociation
Twitter @uksla

The SLA is a UK-focused charity which supports everyone involved in school libraries. It believes that every pupil is entitled to effective school library provision and the educational, emotional and developmental benefits that come with it. Provides training, networking and an information service, publishes guidelines for school library and resource centres, book lists and a quarterly journal which includes current book and digital resources for all school-age children.

Scottish Book Trust

Sandeman House, Trunk's Close, 55 High Street, Edinburgh EH1 1SR
tel 0131 524 0160
email info@scottishbooktrust.com
website www.scottishbooktrust.com
Facebook www.facebook.com/scottishbktrust

Twitter @ScottishBkTrust

Scotland's national agency for the promotion of reading, writing and literature. Programmes include: Bookbug, a free universal book-gifting programme which encourages families to read with their children from birth; an ambitious schools programme including national tours, the virtual events programme Authors Live and the Bookbug Picture Book Prize; the Scottish Teenage Book Prize; the Live Literature funding programme, a national initiative enabling Scottish citizens to engage with authors, playwrights, poets, storytellers and illustrators; a writer development programme, offering mentoring and professional development for emerging and established writers; and a readership development programme featuring a national writing campaign, as well as Book Week Scotland, during the last week in November. Founded 1998.

Scottish Storytelling Forum

Scottish Storytelling Centre, 43–45 High Street, Edinburgh EH1 1SR
tel 0131 652 3273
email reception@scottishstorytellingcentre.com
website www.scottishstorytellingcentre.com
website www.storytellingforum.co.uk
Facebook www.facebook.com/ScotStoryForum
Twitter @ScotStoryCentre, @scotstoryforum

Scotland's national charity for oral storytelling, established to encourage and support the telling and sharing of stories across all ages and sectors of society, in particular those who, for reasons of poverty or disability, are sometimes excluded from artistic experiences. The Scottish Storytelling Centre is the Forum's resource and training centre which presents a year-round programme of storytelling and traditional arts events, workshops and the Scottish International Storytelling Festival in the autumn. The Storytelling Network has over 150 professional storytellers across Scotland. Founded 1992.

Seven Stories – The National Centre for Children's Books – see page 334

Society for Storytelling (SfS)

Lytchett House, 13 Freeland Park, Wareham Road, Poole, BH16 6FA
tel 07942 344259
email membership@sfs.org.uk
website www.sfs.org.uk
Facebook www.facebook.com/societyforstorytelling
Twitter @sfs_uk
Instagram @sfsintheuk

SfS is a registered charity and community organisation for both professional and non-professional oral storytellers. It provides information on oral storytelling, events, storytellers and traditional stories. Its volunteers have specialist knowledge of storytelling in education, health, therapy and business settings. To increase public awareness of the art of storytelling it promotes National Storytelling Week. The SfS provides a network for anyone interested in the art of oral storytelling whether they are full-time storytellers, use storytelling in their work, tell stories for the love of it or just want to listen. It holds an annual conference and produces a quarterly newsletter. Founded 1993.

Society of Artists Agents

website https://saahub.com
Twitter @SaaAgents

Formed to promote professionalism in the illustration industry and to forge closer links between clients and artists through an agreed set of guidelines. The Society believes in an ethical approach through proper terms and conditions, thereby protecting the interests of the artists and clients. Founded 1992.

The Society of Authors
– see page 323

Society of Children's Book Writers and Illustrators (SCBWI) – see page 330

Society of Editors

Stationers Hall, Ave Maria Lane, London EC4M 7DD
tel 07599 954636
email office@societyofeditors.org
website www.societyofeditors.org
President Alison Gow
Membership From £60 to £230 p.a. depending on category

Formed from the merger of the Guild of Editors and the Association of British Editors, the Society of Editors has members in national, regional and local newspapers, magazines, broadcasting and digital media, journalism education and media law. It campaigns for media freedom, self regulation, the public's right to know and the maintenance of standards in journalism.

Society of Young Publishers

c/o The Publishers Association, First Floor, 50 Southwark Street, London SE1 1UN
email sypchair@thesyp.org.uk
website www.thesyp.org.uk
Twitter @SYP_UK, @SYPIreland, @SYP_LDN, @SYPNorth, @SYP_Oxford, @SYPScotland, @SYP_SouthWest
Instagram @syp_uk, @syp_london, @oxford_syp, @sypscotland, @syp_southwest
Membership £30 p.a. employed standard; £24 p.a. student/unemployed; £18 p.a. digital membership

The SYP supports those of any age looking to get into publishing, or those within the first ten years of their career who are looking to get ahead. It is made up of six regional committees (Ireland, London, North, Oxford, Scotland and South West), and a UK team responsible for the organisation's oversight. These committees organise mentorship schemes for current and aspiring publishers based in the UK and Ireland. Two annual conferences are held, as well as numerous in-person and digital events each month – including socials, career panels and more. The website is routinely updated with articles and guides on how to progress in the publishing industry. Founded 1949.

Speaking of Books

44 Blackheath Park, London SE3 9SJ
tel 07931 929325
email elle@speakingofbooks.co.uk
website www.speakingofbooks.co.uk
Twitter @speakingofbks

Arranges school visits by writers, illustrators, poets and storytellers, plus other high-quality speakers and workshop facilitators. Also provides speakers for festivals and events relating to literacy and the arts.

Spread the Word

The Albany, Douglas Way, London SE8 4AG
tel 020-8692 0231 ext. 249
email hello@spreadtheword.org.uk
website www.spreadtheword.org.uk
Facebook www.facebook.com/spreadthewordwriters
Twitter @STWevents
Instagram @spreadthewordwriters

London's writer development agency, helping writers make their mark on the page, the screen and in the world. Kick-starts the careers of London's best new writers, and energetically campaigns to ensure mainstream publishing truly reflects the diversity of the city. Supports the creative and professional development of talent, by engaging those already interested in literature and those who will be, and by advocating on behalf of both.

The Robert Louis Stevenson Club

website https://robert-louis-stevenson.org/rls-club

Aims to foster interest in Robert Louis Stevenson's life (1850–94) and writings through various events and a quarterly newsletter. Founded 1920.

The Story Museum

42 Pembroke Street, Oxford OX1 1BP
tel (01865) 807600
email hello@storymuseum.org.uk
website www.storymuseum.org.uk
Facebook www.facebook.com/TheStoryMuseum
Twitter @TheStoryMuseum

The Story Museum celebrates story in all forms and explores their enduring power to teach and delight. It aims to inspire present and future generations by providing great ways of engaging with great stories. Also runs an active education and outreach programme alongside exhibition and events. The Museum houses nine story-themed gallery and activity spaces including a flexible performance space.

Story Therapy CIC

1 Sugworth Lane, Radley, Abingdon-on-Thames, Oxon OX14 2HZ
email admin@storytherapyresources.co.uk
website www.storytherapyresources.co.uk
Facebook www.facebook.com/storytherapy
Twitter @StoryTherapy
Contact Hilary Hawkes

A non-profit social enterprise creating resources, especially story-themed, that support children's emotional health and mental wellbeing. Founded 2016.

The Swedish Institute for Children's Books

email info@barnboksinstitutet.se
website www.barnboksinstitutet.se

Svenska barnboksinstitutet is a research and information centre for children's and YA literature with a special library open to the public. Founded 1965.

The Tolkien Society

website www.tolkiensociety.org
Facebook www.facebook.com/TolkienSociety
Twitter @TolkienSociety
Membership £30 p.a. online or £10 p.a. students; Postal: £35 p.a. UK; £40 p.a. EU; £50 p.a. rest of world; add £15 p.a. for family membership

An educational charity and literary society devoted to the study and promotion of the life and works of J.R.R. Tolkien.

United Kingdom Literacy Association

Room 9 c/o VAL, 9 Newarke Street, Leicester LE1 5SN
tel 0116 254 4116
website www.ukla.org
Twitter @The_UKLA
Membership £65 p.a. individuals; £30 p.a. concessionary

UKLA is a registered charity, which has as its sole object the advancement of literacy in education. It conducts research into literacy education and encourages teachers and librarians to take an active role in finding and sharing a wider range of books that children will love. Members receive access to a community focused on improving literacy, resources and guides, literacy journals, *English 4-11* magazine and conference discounts. Founded 1963.

Voice of the Listener & Viewer

The Old Rectory Business Centre, Springhead Road, Northfleet DA11 8HN
tel (01474) 338716
email info@vlv.org.uk
website www.vlv.org.uk
Facebook www.facebook.com/VLVUK

Twitter @vlvuk
Administrator Lucy Regan
Membership From £30 p.a.; academic, corporate and student rates available

VLV's mission is to campaign for accountability, diversity and excellence in UK broadcasting, seeking to sustain and strengthen public service broadcasting to the benefit of civil society and democracy in the UK. It holds regular conferences and seminars and publishes a bulletin and an e-newsletter. Founded 1983.

Writers Advice Centre for Children's Books

Shakespeare House, 168 Lavender Hill, London SW11 5TG
tel 020-7801 6300
email info@writersadvice.co.uk
website www.writersadvice.co.uk
Facebook www.facebook.com/writersadvice
Twitter @writersadvice
Managing Editor Louise Jordan

Dedicated to helping new and published children's writers by offering both editorial advice and tips on how to get published. The Centre also runs workshops, an online children's writing correspondence course and publishes a small list of its own under the name of Wacky Bee Books (www.wackybeebooks.com). Founded 1994.

WGGB (Writers' Guild of Great Britain) – see page 326

Writing East Midlands

The Garage Studios, Unit 4, 41-43 St Mary's Gate, Notts. NG1 1PU
tel (01157) 934110
email info@writingeastmidlands.co.uk
website https://writingeastmidlands.co.uk
Facebook www.facebook.com/WritingEM
Twitter @WritingEM
Instagram @writingeastmidlands

Removes barriers and encourages equal access to writing and publishing by supporting writers throughout their careers. Services include workshops and writing courses, mentorships and career development, MS appraisals, organising festivals, conferences and events, and facilitating residencies for writers in schools, libraries and museums. Also works with specific groups of under-represented people such as refugees, migrants, domestic abuse survivors, offenders and the elderly.

Young at Art

Cotton Court, 30–42 Waring Street, Belfast BT1 2ED
tel 028-9023 0660
website www.youngatart.co.uk
Twitter @Young_at_Art

Coordinates the annual Belfast Children's Festival as well as a wide variety of projects that encourage children and young people to enjoy the arts, develop awareness of its impact on their lives, and have a say in what their arts provision should be. These include engagement programmes, workshop programmes, commissions, seminars, training, research and online resources. Founded 2000.

Young V&A

Cambridge Heath Road, London E2 9PA
tel 020-7942 2000
email young@vam.ac.uk
website www.vam.ac.uk/info/young
Facebook www.facebook.com/youngvam
Twitter @young_vam

Young V&A (formerly the V&A Museum of Childhood) is currently closed as the site is transformed into a new world-leading museum of design and creativity for children and young people.
Aims to inspire young people to be active citizens and creative change-makers in their communities; to empower educators to drive forward creative education in art, design and performance from early years to secondary school; to connect young people with the creative ingenuity of designers, entrepreneurs, innovators, inventors and each other; and to influence the sector through child-centred museum practice. Opens Summer 2023.

Youth Libraries Group

CILIP, 7 Ridgmount Street, London WC1E 7AE
email secretary.YLG@cilip.org.uk
website www.cilip.org.uk/ylg
Twitter @youthlibraries
Secretary Alison Cassels

YLG is open to all members of the Chartered Institute for Library and Information Professionals (CILIP) who are interested in children's work. At a national level its aims are:

• to influence the provision of library services for children and the provision of quality literature;
• to inspire and support all librarians working with children and young people;
• to liaise with other national professional organisations in pursuit of such aims.
At a local level, the YLG organises regular training courses, supports professional development and provides opportunities to meet colleagues. It holds an annual conference and judges the YOTO Carnegie and Kate Greenaway Awards (see page 369).

Children's book and illustration prizes and awards

This list provides details of prizes, competitions and awards relevant to children's writers and artists. Check individual websites for entry guidelines and deadlines.

Academy of British Cover Design: Annual Cover Design Competition

website https://abcoverd.co.uk
Twitter @ABCoverD

This annual competition awards covers produced for any book published between 1 January and 31 December each year, by any designer in the UK, for a UK or overseas publisher. Ebooks are eligible. Designers may enter their own work or the work of other designers. There are ten categories: Children's, Young Adult, Sci-fi/Fantasy, Mass Market, Literary Fiction, Crime/Thriller, Non-Fiction, Series Design, Classic/Reissue and Women's Fiction. A cover can only be submitted in one category unless it is entered as an individual cover and again as part of a series design. Entry is free.

ALCS Educational Writers' Award

The Society of Authors, 24 Bedford Row, London WC1R 4EH
tel 020-7373 6642
email prizes@societyofauthors.org
website www.societyofauthors.org/ALCS-award

This is an annual award alternating each year between books in the 5–11 and 11–18 age groups. It is given to an outstanding example of traditionally published non-fiction (with or without illustrations) that stimulates and enhances learning. The work must have been first published in the UK, in the English language, within the previous two calendar years. The total value of the prizes is £2,000.

The Alligator's Mouth Award for Illustrated Early Fiction

2A Church Court, Richmond, Surrey TW9 1JL
tel 020-8948 6775
email award@thealligatorsmouth.co.uk
website www.thealligatorsmouth.co.uk/award

This award celebrates highly illustrated early fiction. The children's book prize, launched by The Alligator's Mouth and the Bright Agency in 2018, celebrates the best books for 6-8-year-olds and champions authors and illustrators. The Award's official partner is the books wholesalers Gardners. The award is open to books first published in the UK in English from the last year which have illustrations on the majority of the internal spreads. Entry form, submissions criteria and entry rules can be downloaded from the website. Longlist announced in March. The winner of the prize receives The Alligator's Mouth Award trophy. 2021 winner: Sophy Henn for *Pizazz* (Simon & Schuster Children's UK). 2020 winner: Adam Stower for *King Coo: The Curse of the Mummy's Gold* (David Fickling Books).

The Hans Christian Andersen Awards

International Board on Books for Young People, Nonnenweg 12, CH–4055, Switzerland
tel +41 61 272 2917
email ibby@ibby.org
website www.ibby.org
Facebook www.facebook.com/ibby.international
Twitter @IBBYINT
Instagram @ibby.international

This Award is the highest international recognition given to an author and an illustrator of children's books. Given every other year by IBBY, the awards recognise lifelong achievement and are presented to an author and an illustrator whose complete works have made an important, lasting contribution to children's literature. The selection criteria include the aesthetic and literary qualities of writing and illustrating, as well as the ability to see things from the child's point of view and the ability to stretch the child's curiosity and imagination. The complete works of the author and of the illustrator are taken into consideration. The Author's Award has been given since 1956 and the Illustrator's Award since 1966.

Association for Library Service to Children Awards

American Library Association, 225 N Michigan Ave, Suite 1300, Chicago, IL 60601, USA
tel +1 800-545-2433 ext. 2163
email alsc@ala.org
website www.ala.org/alsc/awardsgrants/bookmedia
Facebook www.facebook.com/Associationforlibraryservicetochildren
Twitter @wearealsc

The following awards are administered by ALSC:

• The Caldecott Medal (named in honour of the 19th-century English illustrator Randolph Caldecott) is awarded annually to the artist of the most distinguished US picture book for children.
• The Newbery Medal (named after the 18th-century British bookseller John Newbery) is awarded annually

to the author of the most distinguished contribution to US literature for children.

• The Geisel Medal (named after the world-renowned children's author a.k.a. Dr Seuss) is given annually to the author(s) and illustrator(s) of the most distinguished contribution to the body of children's literature known as beginning reader books published in the USA during the preceding year.

• The Robert F. Sibert Informational Book Medal is given annually to the author of the most distinguished informational book published in English during the preceding year.

• The Children's Literature Legacy Award honours authors and illustrators published in the US whose books have made a substantial and lasting contribution to literature for children.

• The Excellence in Early Learning Digital Media Award is given to a digital media producer that has created distinguished digital media for an early learning audience.

• The Batchelder Award is awarded annually to an outstanding children's book translated from a language other than English and originally published in a country other than the United States.

• The Belpré Awards are presented annually to a Latino/Latina writer and illustrator whose work best portrays, affirms and celebrates the Latino cultural experience.

• The Odyssey Award is given for the best audio book produced for children and/or young adults. Co-administered with YALSA and Booklist.

Bardd Plant Cymru (Welsh-Language Children's Poet Laureate)

Books Council of Wales, Castell Brychan, Aberystwyth, Ceredigion SY23 2JB
tel (01970) 624151
email castellbrychan@books.wales
website https://llyfrau.cymru/en/

Aims to raise the profile of poetry amongst children and to encourage them to compose and enjoy poetry. During his/her term of office the bard will visit schools as well as help children to create poetry through electronic workshops. The scheme's partner organisations are: S4C, the Welsh Government, the Books Council of Wales, Urdd Gobaith Cymru and Literature Wales.

J.M. Barrie Award

email admin@childrensarts.org.uk
website www.childrensarts.org.uk/celebrate
Twitter @childrensarts

The Action for Children's Arts J.M. Barrie Award is given annually to a children's arts practitioner or organisation for a lifetime's achievement in delighting children whose work, in the view of the trustees, will stand the test of time. 2021 winner: Michael Rosen.

The Bath Children's Novel Award

PO Box 5223, Bath BA1 0UR
email info@bathnovelaward.co.uk
website www.bathnovelaward.co.uk
Twitter @bathnovelaward

This annual international prize is for unpublished or independently published writers of novels for children or young adults. Submissions: first 5,000 words plus one-page synopsis. Entries open June until November. Entry fee: £29 per novel with sponsored places available for low-income writers. Children and teenagers vote for the shortlist, with the winner chosen by a literary agent. Prize: £3,000 plus introductions to literary agents.

Blue Peter Book Awards

BookTrust, G8 Battersea Studios,
80 Silverthorne Road, London SW8 3HE
tel 020-7801 8843
email bluepeter@booktrust.org.uk
website www.booktrust.org.uk/what-we-do/awards-and-prizes/

Awarded annually, winners are shortlisted by a panel of expert adult judges, then a group of young *Blue Peter* viewers judge the two categories, which are: the Best Story and the Best Book with Facts. Winning books are announced on *Blue Peter* in March. Founded 2000.

International Award for Illustration Bologna Children's Book Fair – Fundación SM

email illustratori@bolognafiere.it
website www.bolognachildrensbookfair.com

The aim of the award is to support the illustration work of young artists, the special quality of whose work has yet to be acknowledged. This annual award is granted to one of the young illustrators selected each year from the Bologna Children's Book Fair Illustrators Exhibition. Founded 2009.

BolognaRagazzi Award

Piazza Costituzione 6, 40128 Bologna, Italy
tel +39 051-282111
email bolognaragazziaward@bolognafiere.it
website www.bolognachildrensbookfair.com/premi/bolognaragazzi-award/8382.html
Facebook www.facebook.com/BolognaChildrensBookFair
Twitter @BoChildrensBook

One of the world's most highly regarded international prizes in the sector of children's publishing, it celebrates the finest illustrated children's books and honours the best productions in terms of their graphic and editorial qualities, providing an international launch pad for authors and illustrators thanks to the high profile recognition that the winners receive during the fair. There are four main award categories: Fiction, Non-fiction, Opera Prima (for unpublished authors and illustrators) and Comics. Special categories are introduced each year (Poetry for 2022). A special New Horizons award is made to a particularly innovative book. Founded 1966.

The Bookbug Picture Book Prize

Scottish Book Trust, Sandeman House,
Trunk's Close, 55 High Street, Edinburgh EH1 1SR
tel 0131 524 0160
email info@scottishbooktrust.com
website www.scottishbooktrust.com/bpbp

Scotland's national picture book prize which
recognises the favourite picture book of children in
Scotland by writers and illustrators resident in
Scotland. Visit the Scottish Book Trust website for
more details.

Books Are My Bag Readers Awards

website www.nationalbooktokens.com/vote

Curated by bookshops and chosen by readers,
categories include Fiction, Non-fiction, Poetry,
Young Adult Fiction, Children's Fiction,
Breakthrough Author and Readers' Choice. Reader's
choice is nominated exclusively by readers.

BookTrust Storytime Prize

BookTrust, G8 Battersea Studios,
80 Silverthorne Road, London SW8 3HE
tel 020-7801 8826
email StoryTimePrize@booktrust.org.uk
website www.booktrust.org.uk/what-we-do/awards-
and-prizes/

An annual prize to celebrate the best books for
sharing with young children aged 0–5 with a
particular focus on books that have a wide appeal to
parents and carers across our diverse nation, and for
stories which can be read and enjoyed over and over
again. The prize is run in collaboration with the
CILIP Youth Library Group (YLG) and the
shortlisted titles are shared with families by public
librarians across the UK to find the best book.
Publishers are invited to enter up to five books per
imprint. See website for further details and timings.

The Branford Boase Award

8 Bolderwood Close, Bishopstoke, Eastleigh,
Hants SO50 8PG
tel 023-8060 0439
email anne.marley@tiscali.co.uk
website www.branfordboaseaward.org.uk

An annual award of £1,000 is made to a first-time
writer of a full-length children's novel (age 7+)
published in the preceding year; the editor is also
recognised. Its aim is to encourage new writers for
children and to recognise the role of perceptive
editors in developing new talent. The Award was set
up in memory of the outstanding children's writer
Henrietta Branford and the gifted editor and
publisher Wendy Boase who both died in 1999.
Closing date for nominations: end of December.

Caledonia Novel Award

email caledoniaaward@gmail.com
website https://thecaledonianovelaward.com/

Award for unpublished and self-published novelists.
Novels can be of any genre for adults or young
adults. The award is open to writers of any
nationality who are over 18. Entries cost £25, with the
winner receiving £1,500, and the writer of the best
novel from the UK and Ireland winning a free place
on a writing course at Moniack Mhor Creative
Writing Centre. The Award provides a number of
sponsored places to eligible, low-income writers who
are unable to afford the fee. For more information,
see the competition rules on the website.

The Carmelite Prize

c/o Hachette Children's Group, Carmelite House,
50 Victoria Embankment, London EC4Y 0DZ
email carmeliteprize@hachettechildrens.co.uk
website www.hachettechildrens.co.uk/imprint/
hcgdivision/page/the-carmelite-prize-2020/
Twitter @HachetteKids

An annual award run by Hachette Children's Group
which recognises excellence in children's book
illustration, with the aim of encouraging and
inspiring the next generation of illustrators for
children's stories. The competition is open to all
students aged 18 and over who are studying
illustration and design in the UK in further or higher
education. Entrants are asked to submit illustrations
for a supplied picture book text. The winner and two
runners-up will be chosen from the top five entries:
1st prize: £1,000; 1st runner-up: £500; 2nd runner-
up: £250. See website for full terms and conditions.

Carnegie Medal – see The Yoto Carnegie Greenaway Awards

The Caterpillar Poetry Prize

Ardan Grange, Milltown, Belturbet,
Co. Cavan H14 K768, Republic of Ireland
tel + 353 (0)87 2657251
email enquiries@thecaterpillarmagazine.com
website www.thecaterpillarmagazine.com

The Caterpillar Poetry Prize is for a single
unpublished poem written by an adult for children.
The writer of the winning poem receives €1,000 and
has their poem published in *The Caterpillar*. The
prize is open to anyone over the age of 16. The entry
fee is €14 and writers can submit as many poems as
they like. Closing date 31 March. For full entry details
and guidelines, see the website.

Cheltenham Illustration Awards

email eevans@glos.ac.uk
website www.cheltenham-illustration-awards.com

The awards are divided into two sections: Student
(aged 18 and over) and Emerging and Established
Illustrators. Entries must relate to that year's theme.
The selected work will be showcased in an exhibition
and published in the *Cheltenham Illustration Awards
Annual*, which will be distributed to education
institutions and publishers.

The Children's Book Award

email childrensbookaward@fcbg.org.uk
website https://FCBG.org.uk/childrensbookaward
Twitter @FCBGNews

Awarded annually to authors and illustrators of children's fiction published in the UK. Children participate in the judging of the award and their votes are the deciding factor. Awards are made in the following categories: Books for Younger Children, Books for Younger Readers and Books for Older Readers. Founded 1980.

The KPMG Children's Books Ireland Awards

Children's Books Ireland,
17 North Great George's Street, Dublin 1 D01 R2F1, Republic of Ireland
tel +353 (0)1 872 7475
email info@childrensbooksireland.ie
website www.childrensbooksireland.ie

Leading annual children's book awards in Ireland. The awards are: the Book of the Year, the Eilís Dillon Award (for a first children's book), the Honour Award for Fiction, the Honour Award for Illustration, the Judges' Special Award and the Junior Juries Award. Schools and reading groups nationwide take part in the Junior Juries programme: participating groups make their own selection of suitable titles from the books shortlisted for the awards in March, using a specially devised activity pack to guide them in their reading; each group then votes for their favourite book. Closing date: November for work published between 1 January and 31 December of an awards year. Shortlist announced in March; winners announced in May. Founded 1990.

The Children's Laureate

BookTrust, Studio G8, Battersea Studios,
80 Silverthorne Road, London SW8 3HE
tel 020-7801 8800
email childrenslaureate@booktrust.org.uk
website www.childrenslaureate.org.uk
Twitter @UKLaureate

The idea for the Children's Laureate originated from a conversation between (the then) Poet Laureate Ted Hughes and children's writer Michael Morpurgo. The post was established to celebrate exceptional children's authors and illustrators and to acknowledge their importance in creating the readers of tomorrow. Quentin Blake was the first Children's Laureate (1999–2001), followed by Anne Fine (2001–03), Michael Morpurgo (2003–05), Jacqueline Wilson (2005–07), Michael Rosen (2007–09), Anthony Browne (2009–11), Julia Donaldson (2011–13), Malorie Blackman (2013–15), Chris Riddell (2015–17), Lauren Child (2017–19) and Cressida Cowell (2019–22). Founded 1999.

CLiPPA (Centre for Literacy in Primary Poetry Award)

CLPE, 44 Webber Street, London SE1 8QW
tel 020-7401 3382/3
email info@clpe.org.uk
website https://clpe.org.uk/poetry/CLiPPA
Facebook www.facebook.com/
CentreforLiteracyinPrimaryEducation/
Twitter @clpe1
Instagram @clpe.org.uk

CLiPPA is an award that honours excellence in children's poetry. Organised by the Centre for Literacy in Primary Education (CLPE), it is presented annually for a book of poetry published in the preceding year. The book can be a single-poet collection or an anthology. Submissions deadline: end of January/early February. Founded 2003.

Copy*right* Essay Prize

The Copyright Licensing Agency Ltd, 5th Floor, Shackleton House, 4 Battle Bridge Lane, London SE1 2HX
email CLAcompetitions@cla.co.uk
website https://cla.co.uk/essayprize

The annual competition is open to 16–19 year olds based in UK schools and colleges who are asked to write a 1,500 word essay around subjects concerning copyright and intellectual property. 1st prize: £300; 2nd prize: £200; 3rd prize: £100. Each year the CLA will set a specific essay question that the students must respond to. See website for more details. Founded 2020.

Costa Book Awards

The Booksellers Association, 6 Bell Yard, London WC2A 2JR
tel 020-7421 4640
email costabookawards@booksellers.org.uk
website www.costa.co.uk/costa-book-awards
Contact Rowan Mansell

The awards celebrate and promote the most enjoyable contemporary British writing. There are five categories: Novel, First Novel, Biography, Poetry and Children's, plus one overall winner. Each category is judged by a panel of judges and the winner in each category receives £5,000. Judges then choose the Costa Book of the Year from the five category winners. The overall winner receives £30,000. There is also a seventh award, the Short Story Award, given for a single short story. Total prize money for the Costa Book Awards is £60,000. Submissions must be received from publishers. Shortlist announced: November. Closing date: end of June. For full eligibility and submission guidelines, see the website. Founded 1971.

English Association English 4–11 Children's Book Awards

The English Association, University of Leicester, Leicester LE1 7RH

tel 0116 229 7622
email hello@englishassociation.ac.uk
website https://englishassociation.ac.uk/english-4-11-picture-book-awards/

Awarded to the best children's picture books of the year. Categories are Fiction and Non-fiction in the age ranges 4–7 years and 7–11 years. The winning books are chosen by the editorial board of *English 4–11*, the journal for primary teachers published by the English Association and the United Kingdom Literacy Association from a shortlist selected by a panel of teachers and primary education specialists. Founded 1995.

Etisalat Award for Arabic Children's Literature
email info@uaebby.org.ae
website www.etisalataward.ae
Facebook www.facebook.com/EtisalatAward
Twitter @EtisalatAward

The prize of 1.2 million UAE dirhams is open only to children's literature written in the Arabic language; translated content is not eligible. The Award has widened its scope since its inception, adding new categories in order to highlight the individual achievements of writers, illustrators and publishers. The value of the Award is distributed between four fixed categories and a fifth which changes every two years. Also runs the Warsha-Etisalat Workshops for Children's Books, an initiative aimed at nurturing a new generation of Arab authors, illustrators and publishers of Arabic children's books.

FAB Prize for Undiscovered Talent
email prize@fabfaber.co.uk
website www.fabprize.org
Twitter @FaberChildrens

Set up by Faber Children's and Andlyn Literary Agency, this is an annual competition for unagented and unpublished writers and illustrators from Black, Asian and/or non-white minority ethnic backgrounds. Now with the additional backing of BookTrust and the Association of Illustrators, the competition winners and runners up are not only offered mentoring, but also exposure to literary agents and editors alongside access to training and shadowing schemes. The prize offers a unique opportunity to kick-start a writing or illustrating career and get a foot in the door. Entries must be text or artwork for children aged 1–18 years. 1st prize of £1,500 for text and £1,500 for illustration. Founded 2017.

The Eleanor Farjeon Award
Facebook www.facebook.com/childrensbookcircle
Twitter @ChildBookCircle

An annual award which may be given to an individual or an organisation. Librarians, authors, publishers, teachers, reviewers and others who have given exceptional service to the children's book industry are eligible for nomination. It was instituted in 1965 by the Children's Book Circle (page 336) for distinguished services to children's books and named after the much-loved children's writer Eleanor Farjeon.

The Klaus Flugge Prize
website www.klausfluggeprize.co.uk
Twitter @KlausFluggePr
Instagram @klausfluggeprize

This prize is awarded to the most promising and exciting newcomer to children's picture book illustration. It honours the work of publisher Klaus Flugge in the field of illustration and children's picture books, and the winning debut illustrator receives £5,000.

Foyle Young Poets of the Year Award – see page 209

Kate Greenaway Medal – see The Yoto Carnegie Greenaway Awards

Indie Book Awards
6 Bell Yard, London WC2A 2JR
tel 020-7421 4656
email emma.bradshaw@booksellers.org.uk
website www.booksaremybag.com/IndieBookAwards/About
Facebook www.facebook.com/booksaremybag
Twitter @booksaremybag
Instagram @booksaremybag

The Indie Book Awards are the only awards given to an author or illustrator on behalf of independent bookshops. The awards showcase the best paperback reads for the summer. Awards are given in four categories: Fiction, Non-fiction, Children's Fiction and Picture Book. For entry guidelines and shortlist details see the website.

Invisible Prize for Illustrators
email info@picturehooks.org.uk
website www.picturehooks.org.uk/the-invisible-prize/

A biennial award which acknowledges the quiet reach and huge influence of the illustrator, particularly in encouraging a love of reading from a young age. Founded 2020.

Jhalak Children's & YA Prize
email info@jhalakprize.com
website www.jhalakprize.com/childrens-ya
Twitter @jhalakprize

Awarded annually, this prize seeks out the best books by British or British resident BAME writers and awards one winner £1,000. Entries can be for fiction, non-fiction, short story, graphic novel, poetry, picture books and all other genres intended for children and young adult readers. Started by authors

Sunny Singh and Nikesh Shukla and Media Diversified, with support from The Authors' Club and a prize donated by an anonymous benefactor, the prize exists to celebrate the achievements of writers of colour. For submission guidelines and details of key dates see the website. Founded 2020.

The Kelpies Prizes for Writing and Illustration

Floris Books, Canal Court, 40 Craiglockhart Avenue, Edinburgh EH14 1LT
email kelpiesprize@florisbooks.co.uk
website https://discoverkelpies.co.uk/kelpies-prizes/

Annual awards for emerging writers and illustrators who are committed to developing their skills and creating quality books for children. The Kelpies Prizes are open to anyone who lives or works in Scotland. The winners will receive £500 cash, 9 months of mentoring with an experienced editorial or design team, and consideration for a publishing contract with Floris Books. Submit writing or illustration samples and entry form online; see website for full details. Closing date: end February.

Kindle Storyteller Award

website www.amazon.co.uk/
b?ie=UTF8&node=12061299031

Open to submissions of new English-language books in any genre. Titles must be previously unpublished and be available as an ebook and in print via Kindle Direct Publishing. The award shortlist is decided by reader feedback and a panel of industry judges. The winning author will receive £20,000. Competition entry period runs from 1 May to 31 August.

Lancashire Book of the Year Award

tel 0300 123 6703
website www.lancashire.gov.uk/libraries-and-archives/libraries/lancashires-book-of-the-year/

This annual prize is awarded to the best work of fiction for children in the 12–14 year group, published in the UK. It is the longest-running regional book award in the country and the award is voted for by Year 9 students in high schools around the county of Lancashire. Winner announced in September.

The Astrid Lindgren Memorial Award

Swedish Arts Council, PO Box 27215, SE–102 53 Stockholm, Sweden
tel +46 8-51926400
email literatureaward@alma.se
website https://alma.se/en/

An award to honour the memory of Astrid Lindgren, Sweden's favourite author, and to promote children's and youth literature around the world. The award is five million Swedish kronas, the world's largest for children's and youth literature, and the second-largest literature prize in the world. It is awarded annually to one or more recipients, regardless of language or nationality.

Authors, illustrators, storytellers and promoters of reading are eligible. The award is for life-long work or artistry rather than for individual pieces. The prize can only be awarded to living people. The winner is selected by a jury based on nominations for outstanding achievement from selected nominating bodies around the world. Administered by the Swedish Arts Council. Founded 2002.

Little Rebels Children's Book Award

email info@letterboxlibrary.com
website https://littlerebels.org/
Twitter @littlerebsprize

Recognises children's fiction for readers aged 0–12 years which promotes social justice or social equality, challenges stereotypes or is informed by anti-discriminatory concerns. The award is given by the Alliance of Radical Booksellers. Winning prize: £2,000. See website for submission guidelines. Founded 2010.

The Macmillan Prize for Illustration

Macmillan Children's Books, 6 Briset Street, London EC1M 5NR
email macmillanprize@macmillan.co.uk
website www.panmacmillan.com/macmillanprize

Three prizes are awarded annually for unpublished children's book illustrations by art students in higher education institutions in the UK. Prizes: 1st: £1,000; 2nd: £500; 3rd: £250. Founded 1985.

The Mythopoeic Fantasy Award for Children's Literature

email awards@mythsoc.org
website www.mythsoc.org

This award honours books for younger readers (from young adults to picture books for beginning readers), in the tradition of The Hobbit or The Chronicles of Narnia. The Mythopoeic Awards are chosen from books nominated by individual members of the Mythopoeic Society and selected by a committee of Society members. Authors, publishers and their representatives may not nominate their own books for any of the awards, nor are books published by the Mythopoeic Press eligible for the awards. The Mythopoeic Society does not accept or review unsolicited manuscripts.

New Anglia Manuscript Prize

website https://laxfieldliterary.com/new-anglia-manuscript-prize/

Sponsored by the National Centre for Writing in Norwich, this debut novel prize is open to unpublished writers from Suffolk and Norfolk. There is no fee to enter and submissions open in early October and close in early December. Applicants must submit a completed manuscript of at least

30,000 words. Winning entries are awarded £500 and receive representation from Laxfield Literary Associates. Founded 2020.

New Zealand Book Awards for Children and Young Adults
c/o NZ Book Awards Trust,
72 Te Wharepōuri Street, Wellington 6023
tel +64 (0)27 773 9855
email childrensawards@nzbookawards.org.nz
website www.nzbookawards.nz/new-zealand-book-awards-for-children-and-young-adults

Annual awards to celebrate excellence in, and provide recognition for, the best children's books published in New Zealand. Awards are presented in six categories: Picture Book, Junior Fiction (the Wright Family Foundation Esther Glen Award), Young Adult Fiction, Non-Fiction (the Elsie Locke Award), Illustration (the Russell Clark Award) and te reo Māori (the Wright Family Foundation Te Kura Pounamu Award). Each of these awards carries prize money of $7,500. The overall prize, the Margaret Mahy Book of the Year award, carries a further prize of $7,500. A $2,000 prize (The NZSA Best First Book Award) is also awarded to a previously unpublished author or illustrator. Eligible books must have been published in New Zealand between April and March in the period preceding the awards' August ceremony date.

North East Book Award
Cramlington Learning Village, Cramlington, Northumberland NE23 6BN
tel (01670) 712311
email earmstrong@cramlingtonlv.co.uk
website https://northeastbookaward.wordpress.com
Contact Eileen Armstrong

Awarded to a book written by a UK/Ireland resident author and first published in paperback the previous year. The shortlist is selected by school librarians, teachers and the previous year's student judges. The final winner is decided entirely by the student judges (Year 7/8) and is announced in June. The 2021 winner was *Things the Eye Can't See* by Penny Joelson (Electric Monkey).

North East Teen Book Award
Cramlington Learning Village, Cramlington, Northumberland NE23 6BN
tel (01670) 712311
email earmstrong@cramlingtonlv.co.uk
website https://northeastteenagebookaward.wordpress.com
Contact Eileen Armstrong

Awarded to a book written by a UK/Ireland resident author and first published in paperback during the previous year. The shortlist is selected by school librarians, teachers and the previous year's student judges. The final winner is decided entirely by the student judges (Year 9+) and is announced in March. The 2021 winner was *Hideous Beauty* by William Hussey (Usborne).

Nottingham Children's Book Awards
Nottingham Library Service, Culture and Libraries, Aspley Library, Nottingham NG8 5DD
tel 0115 915 2844
email charlotte.blount@nottinghamcity.gov.uk
website www.nottinghamcity.gov.uk/ncba
Facebook www.facebook.com/NottmLibraries
Twitter @readingnottm
Contact Charlotte Blount

Nottingham children aged 2–4 years choose their favourite picture books from books published the previous year. The shortlist of titles is drawn up by the end of July with the help of local schools and nurseries. In the autumn, library staff visit settings to read the three books to pre-school children asking them to vote for their favourite. Families can also vote in libraries and via the website. The winner is announced at the beginning of December. Founded 1999.

Oscar's Book Prize
Lower Ground Floor, 111 Charterhouse Street, London EC1M 6AW
email info@oscarsbookprize.co.uk
website www.oscarsbookprize.co.uk

This £10,000 prize supported by Amazon and The National Literacy Trust, in partnership with the *Evening Standard*, is awarded to the preschool book published in the UK in the previous year that the judges consider to be the best.
    Publishers may enter up to five books per imprint. Collections and anthologies are not eligible. Previously published, self-published books and ebooks are not eligible. Full terms and conditions and a digital entry form are available on the website. Previous winners include Rachel Bright and Jim Field, Gemma Merino, John Dougherty and Laura Hughes and Steve Antony. Founded 2013.

The People's Book Prize
website www.peoplesbookprize.com
Facebook www.facebook.com/pages/The-Peoples-Book-Prize/200637717319384
Twitter @PeoplesBkPrize
Founder & Prize Administrator Tatiana Wilson, *Patron Emeritus* Frederick Forsyth, *Founding Patron* Dame Beryl Bainbridge

Awards are given in six categories: Fiction, Non-fiction, Children's, First-time Author (the Beryl Bainbridge First Time Author Award), TPBP Best Achievement Award and TPBP Best Publisher Award. Titles must be submitted by publishers, with a limit of three titles per category, per collection.

Phoenix Award

Children's Literature Association,
One Glenlake Parkway NE, Suite 1200, Atlanta,
GA 30328
tel +1 630-571-4520
email info@childlitassn.org
website www.childlitassn.org

This Award is presented by the Children's Literature Association (ChLA) for the most outstanding book for children originally published in the English language 20 years earlier which did not receive a major award at the time of publication. It is intended to recognise books of high literary merit. Founded 1985.

The Queen's Knickers Award

The Society of Authors, 24 Bedford Row,
London WC1R 4EH
tel 020-7373 6642
email prizes@societyofauthors.org
website www.societyofauthors.org/Prizes/Society-of-Authors-Awards/The-Queens-Knickers-Award
Twitter @Soc_of_Authors

An annual prize, generously funded by the author of *The Queen's Knickers*, Nicholas Allan, for outstanding children's illustrated books for ages 0–7. The prize recognises books that strike a quirky, new note, in any combination of words and/or pictures and in any physical format including pop-ups, flap books and board books. Submissions must be made by the print publisher. The winner receives £5,000 as well as a golden Queen's Knickers badge, and the runner-up receives £1,000 and a silvered badge. The prize will be shared between the author and illustrator if applicable. Closing Date: 30 November.

The Royal Society Young People's Book Prize

The Royal Society, 6–9 Carlton House Terrace,
London SW1Y 5AG
tel 020-7451 2500
email sciencebooks@royalsociety.org
website https://royalsociety.org/grants-schemes-awards/book-prizes/young-peoples-book-prize/
Facebook www.facebook.com/theroyalsociety
Twitter @royalsociety

This prize is open to books for under-14s that have science as a substantial part of their content, narrative or theme. An expert adult panel choose the shortlist, but the winner is chosen by groups of young people in judging panels across the UK. The winning entry receives £10,000 and shortlisted entries receive £2,500. Entries open in December each year. Pure reference works including encyclopedias, educational textbooks and descriptive books are not eligible. The Prize is offered thanks to the generosity of an anonymous donor. Founded 1988.

Rubery Book Award

PO Box 15821, Birmingham B31 9EA
email enquiries@ruberybookaward.com
website www.ruberybookaward.com

An annual award for published books on any subject, including children's books, with prizes totalling £2,800 (Book of the Year receives £2,000 and category winners £200 each). Books published by independent presses and self-published books are eligible. See website for entry fees and submission guidelines.

SCBWI Awards and Grants – see Society of Children's Book Writers & Illustrators

Scholastic Laugh Out Loud Book Awards

email laughoutloud@scholastic.co.uk
website https://shop.scholastic.co.uk/lollies
Twitter @lolbookawards

Known as The Lollies, the Laugh Out Loud Book Awards are awarded to books in three categories: Best Picture Book, Best Book for 6–8-year-olds and Best Book for 9–13-year-olds. A judging panel selects four books to make up a shortlist for each category, but winners are decided entirely by children's votes, with voting taking place via the website and promoted through Scholastic Book Clubs and Book Fairs. See website for full entry and submission guidelines.

Searchlight Writing for Children Awards

email hello@searchlightawards.co.uk
website www.searchlightawards.co.uk
Facebook www.facebook.com/WritingAwards
Twitter @WritingAwards

The Searchlight Awards is an annual international competition for aspiring authors writing for children or young adults. There are two competition categories: Best Children's Picture Book (text only) and Best Novel Opening for Children or Young Adults. Entries open: 1st March 2022 until 22nd August 2022. Entry fee: £9 – picture book; £14 – novel opening. Winners are chosen by high-profile industry judges. 1st prize: £500 – picture book; £1000 – novel opening. The top 10 stories in both categories will feature in an agent/publisher pitch book and be published in an anthology. See website for further details and submission guidelines. Founded 2021.

Sheffield Children's Book Award

Schools Library Service, Stadia Technology Park,
60 Shirland Lane, Sheffield S9 3SP
tel 0114 250 6840
email jennifer.wilson@sheffield.gov.uk
website www.sheffield.gov.uk/home/libraries-archives/book-awards

Presented annually in November to the book chosen as the most enjoyable by the children of Sheffield.

Categories include: Baby Books, Toddler Books, Picture Books, Emerging Reads, Shorter Novel, Longer Novel and Young Adult.

Wilbur Smith Adventure Writing Prize

The Wilbur & Niso Smith Foundation, Unit 9, 5-7 Wells Terrace, London N4 3JU
email submissions@wilbur-niso-smithfoundation.org
website www.wilbur-niso-smithfoundation.org/awards/intro
Facebook www.facebook.com/WNSmithFoundation
Twitter @Wilbur_Niso_Fdn

An international writing prize that supports and celebrates today's best adventure writing. The Prize is open to writers of any nationality, writing in English. Awards are presented for fiction in three categories: Best Published Novel (prize: £10,000); Best Unpublished Manuscript (prize: a publishing deal with Bonnier Books UK) and Author of Tomorrow (prizes: £150–£1,000 depending on age category, plus book tokens and digital publication). The Author of Tomorrow award seeks to find the adventure writers of the future and is open to young people across the world (in age categories 16–21 years, 12–15 years and age 11 and under) who have completed a short piece of adventure writing in English. Submission guidelines, eligibility criteria, entry fees, shortlist dates and details of the previous winners for each category can be found on the website.

The Stephen Spender Prize

41 Wellington Square, Oxford, OX4 2JF
email prize@stephen-spender.org
website www.stephen-spender.org/stephen-spender-prize/

Annual competition for poetry in translation, with categories for young people (14 and under, 16 and under, and 18 and under) as well as an open category for adults and an annually rotating spotlight highlighting a language spoken widely in the UK. Translate into English any poem from any language. Overall winner will win a £1,000 cash prize. All entrants must be UK or Irish citizens or residents, or pupils at a British School overseas. Founded 2004.

The Edward Stanford Travel Writing Awards

Stanfords, 7 Mercer Walk, Covent Garden, London WC2H 9FA
tel 020-7836 1321
website https://www.stanfords.co.uk/edward-stanford-travel-writing-awards

Administered by Stanfords, a specialist retailer of maps, travel books and other travel accessories, the Awards recognise exceptional travel writing published in the previous year. The categories include The Stanford Dolman Travel Book of the Year; Fiction, with a Sense of Place; Photography Travel Book of the Year; Illustrated Travel Book of the Year; Food

and Drink Travel Book of the Year; Children's Travel Book of the Year; Bradt Travel Guide's New Travel Writer of the Year; and Outstanding Contribution to Travel Writing. The winner of Travel Book of the Year is awarded £2500, and the winner in each category receives a personalised hand made globe trophy by Lander & May globe makers. Deadline for entries is January each year, shortlists are published in February and winners are announced in March. See the website for submissions details.

The Times/Chicken House Children's Fiction Competition

Chicken House, 2 Palmer Street, Frome, Somerset BA11 1DS
tel (01373) 454488
email competitions@chickenhousebooks.com
website www.chickenhousebooks.com
Twitter @chickenhsebooks
Contact Kesia Lupo

This annual competition is open to unpublished writers of a full-length children's novel (age 7–18). Entrants must be over 18 and novels must not exceed 80,000 words in length. The winner will be announced in *The Times* and will receive a worldwide publishing contract with Chicken House with a royalty advance of £10,000. The winner is selected by a panel of judges which includes children's authors, journalists, publishers, librarians and other key figures from the world of children's literature. For competition opening and closing dates, consult the Chicken House website.

Tir na n-Og Awards

Books Council of Wales, Castell Brychan, Aberystwyth, Ceredigion SY23 2JB
tel (01970) 624151
email wbc.children@books.wales
website https://llyfrau.cymru/en/gwobrau/tir-na-nog
Facebook www.facebook.com/LlyfrDaFabBooks
Twitter @LlyfrDaFabBooks

Established with the intention of promoting and raising the standard of children's and young people's books in Wales. Three awards are presented annually by the Welsh Books Council and are sponsored by the Chartered Institute of Library and Information Professionals Cymru/Wales:

• The best English-language book of the year with an authentic Welsh background. Fiction and factual books originally in English are eligible; translations from Welsh or any other language are not eligible. Prize: £1,000.
• The best original Welsh-language book aimed at the primary school sector. Prize: £1,000.
• The best original Welsh-language book aimed at the secondary school sector. Prize: £1,000. Founded 1976.

Christopher Tower Poetry Prize – see
page 209

Societies, prizes and festivals

UKLA Book Awards

tel 07933 724030
website www.ukla.org/awards/ukla-book-award

The only UK children's book awards voted for by teachers. The Awards encourage teachers and school librarians to increase their knowledge of recently published children's books and to share them with their students. The selection committee are looking for books which can be read aloud, studied, discussed and inspire creative classroom activities. Teachers are looking for books which evocatively express ideas and offer layered meanings through the use of language, imaginative expression and rich illustration/graphics.

The V&A Illustration Awards

Victoria & Albert Museum, London SW7 2RL
email villa@vam.ac.uk
website www.vam.ac.uk/info/va-illustration-awards

These annual awards are open to illustrators living or publishing in the UK and students who have attended a course in the UK over the last two years. Awards are made in the following categories: book illustration, book cover design and illustrated journalism. Winners each receive a trophy and £3,000. Founded 1972.

The Warwick Prize for Women in Translation

email womenintranslation@warwick.ac.uk
website https://warwick.ac.uk/fac/cross_fac/womenintranslation
Coordinators Chantal Wright and Holly Langstaff

Aims to address the gender imbalance in translated literature and increase the number of international women's voices accessible to a British and Irish readership. Awarded annually to the best eligible work of fiction, poetry, literary non-fiction, work of fiction for children or young adults, graphic novel, or play text, written by a woman, translated into English by a translator (or translators) of any gender, and published by a UK or Irish publisher. The £1,000 prize is divided between writer and translator/s. Founded 2017.

Waterstones Children's Book Prize

Waterstones, 203–206 Piccadilly, London W1J 9HD
email childrensbookprize@waterstones.com
website www.waterstones.com

The aim of the prize is to reward and champion new and emerging children's writers, voted for by booksellers. There are three categories: Illustrated Books, Books for Younger Readers and Books for Older Readers. Submission criteria:

Illustrated Books. Illustrated books authored and illustrated by the same person: The author/illustrator may not have previously published more than two titles of any fiction genre worldwide (educational titles are exempt). Author/illustrator partnerships:

Neither the author nor illustrator may have previously solely published more than two titles of any fiction genre (which includes picture books) worldwide (educational titles are exempt). Author/illustrator partnerships may not have previously published more than two titles together.

Books for Younger Readers and *Books for Older Readers.* No more than one previously published title of any fiction genre worldwide (educational titles are exempt). The title must make sense as a standalone novel. If the title is illustrated, and the illustrator matches submission criteria for Illustrated Books, then the illustrator will be considered eligible for this category. Narrative non-fiction is also eligible for submission.

There will be an overall winner from the category winners.

Wildlife Photographer of the Year

The Natural History Museum, Cromwell Road, London SW7 5BD
website www.nhm.ac.uk/visit/wpy/competition.html

This annual competition is for photographers of all experience levels, aged 18 and over. There are 16 categories, ranging from Animal Portraits to Photojournalism and Urban Wildlife to Underwater Photography. The Grand Title award is given to the photographer whose individual image is judged to be the most striking and memorable. Prizes range in value depending on the category. The Young Wildlife Photographer of the Year recognises photographers aged 17 and under. See website for submission guidelines.

World Illustration Awards

Association of Illustrators, Somerset House, Strand, London WC2R 1LA
tel 020-7759 1010
email awards@theaoi.com
website www.theaoi.com/world-illustration-awards
Facebook www.facebook.com/theaoi
Twitter @theaoi
Instagram @WorldIllustrationAwards

Presented in partnership with the *Directory of Illustration*, the awards programme sets out to celebrate contemporary illustration across the globe. A panel of international judges create a 500 strong longlist and shortlists 200 projects, which are celebrated in an online showcase, a printed catalogue and with an online industry events programme. For submission guidelines, categories and prizes, see the website.

YA Book Prize

email caroline.carpenter@thebookseller.com
website www.thebookseller.com/ya-book-prize-2021
Facebook www.facebook.com/YABookPrize
Twitter @yabookprize

First prize to specifically focus on fiction for young adults. Organised by *The Bookseller*, in partnership with the Edinburgh International Book Festival. Open for titles published between 1st January and 31st December of the previous year. Author must be living in the UK or Ireland at publication. Winner receives £2,000. Founded 2014.

The Yoto Carnegie Greenaway Awards

CILIP, 7 Ridgmount Street, London WC1E 7AE
tel 020-7255 0650
email ckg@cilip.org.uk
website www.ckg.org.uk

Nominations for the following two awards are invited from members of CILIP (the library and information association), who are asked to submit one title per Medal, accompanied by an explanation of how the book they have selected meets the Medal criteria. The awards are selected by librarian judges from the Youth Libraries Group of CILIP. One title from each shortlist will receive a prize awarded by children who take part in the Awards shadowing scheme who vote for their favourites.

Carnegie Medal

Awarded annually for an outstanding book for children (fiction or non-fiction) written in English and first published in the UK during the preceding year or co-published elsewhere within a three-month time lapse. The Yoto Carnegie Medal winner is awarded £5,000 prize money from the Colin Mears Award annually.

Kate Greenaway Medal

Awarded annually for an outstanding illustrated book for children first published in the UK during the preceding year or co-published elsewhere within a three-month time lapse. Books intended for older as well as younger children are included, and reproduction will be taken into account. The Colin Mears Award (£5,000) is awarded annually to the winner of the Yoto Kate Greenaway Medal.

YouWriteOn.com Book Awards

tel 07948 392634
email edward@youwriteon.com
website www.youwriteon.com

Arts Council-funded site publishing awards for new fiction writers. Random House and Orion, the publishers of authors such as Dan Brown and Terry Pratchett, provide free professional critiques for the highest rated new writers' opening chapters and short stories on YouWriteOn.com each month. The highest rated writers of the year are then published, three in each of the adult and children's categories, through YouWriteOn's free paperback publishing service for writers. The novel publishing awards total £1,000. Writers can enter at any time throughout the year: closing date is 31 December each year. Previous YouWriteOn.com winners have been published by mainstream publishers such as Random House, Orion, Penguin and Hodder, including Channel 4 TV Book Club winner and bestseller *The Legacy* by Katherine Webb. Founded 2005.

Societies, prizes and festivals

Prize winners

This is a selection of high-profile literary prize winners from the last year presented chronologically. See individual awards websites for details. Entries for many of these prizes are included in the *Yearbook*, starting on page 359.

starting on page 359.

April 2021

BolognaRagazzi Award
Home by Lin Lian-En (Fiction); *One of a Kind* by Neil Packer (Non-fiction); *Mesto pro kazdeho* by Osamu Okamura, illustrated by David Bohm and Jiri Franta (New Horizons); *Neighbours* by Kasva Denisevich (Opera Prima)

May

KPMG Book of the Year Award
Savage Her Reply by Deirdre Sullivan, illustrated by Karen Vaughan

Tir na n-Og Awards
Sw Sara Mai by Casia Wiliam (Primary); *#helynt* by Rebecca Roberts (Secondary)

Scottish Teenage Book Prize (Scottish Book Trust)
Evernight by Ross MacKenzie

YA Book Prize
Loveless by Alice Oseman

June

The Macmillan Prize for Children's Picture Book Illustration
Ants by Cara Rooney

The CILIP Carnegie Medal
Look Both Ways by Jason Reynolds

The CILIP Kate Greenaway Medal
Small in the City by Sydney Smith

July

Lancashire Book of the Year Award
The Loop by Ben Oliver

UKLA Book Awards
Look Up! by Nathan Bryon, illustrated by Dapo Adeola (3–6+ years); *Check Mates* by Stewart Foster (7–10+ years); *Run Rebel* by Manjeet Mann and *The Last Paper Crane* by Kerry Drewery (11–14+ years)

CLiPPA (Centre for Literacy in Primary Poetry Award)
On the Move, Poems About Migration by Michael Rosen

Branford Boase Award
Orphans of the Tide by Struan Murray (and his editor Ben Horslen)

October

Mythopoeic Fantasy Award for Children's Literature (USA)
Wizard's Guide to Defensive Baking by T. Kingfisher

January 2022

Costa Children's Book of the Year
The Crossing by Manjeet Mann

BookBug Picture Book Prize (Scottish Book Trust)
Inch and Grub by Alastair Chisholm, illustrated by David Roberts

February

Scholastic Laugh Out Loud Book Awards
101 Bums by Sam Harper, illustrated by Chris Jevons (Picture book); *Cats React to Science Facts* by Izzi Howell (Book for 6–8 year-olds); *The Super Miraculous Journey of Freddie Yates* by Jenny Pearson, illustrated by Rob Biddulph (Book for 9–13 year-olds)

March

Blue Peter Book Awards
The Last Bear by Hannah Gold (Best Story); *Invented by Animals* by Christiane Dorian, illustrated by Gosia Herba (Best Book with Facts)

Opportunities for under-represented writers

There has been an acknowledgement across the publishing industry that many voices have not found it easy to be heard and promoted amongst the many hundreds and thousands of books published every year. Publishers, agents, authors and prize-awarding organisations have collectively started to actively encourage and nurture a more diverse range of writers who have new stories to tell. There has been an increase in open submissions, prizes, bursaries and other schemes aimed at previously less represented groups. Some of the more established awards have full entries in this *Yearbook* (as indicated below) and some of the newer ones are listed in full here.

PRIZE AND AWARDS

The Cheshire Novel Prize
website https://cheshirenovelprize.com
Facebook www.facebook.com/cheshirenovelprize
Twitter @prize_novel
Instagram @cheshirenovelprize

Only accepts entries from under-represented writers. Every unsuccessful entrant will receive at least one paragraph of feedback explaining why they were not longlisted. Submit a one-page synopsis and the first 5,000 words of a novel for adults or young adults (not children). Entry fee £25; sponsored entries are available for low-income writers. 1st prize: £1,500; 2nd prize: £500.

The Diverse Book Awards
email hello@thediversebookawards.co.uk
website www.thediversebookawards.co.uk

Administered by The Author School to celebrate diversity in book publishing in the UK and Ireland. There are 3 fiction award categories: Adult, YA and Children's. Entries can be traditionally or self-published but must have been published in the preceding year. The winner in each category receives a trophy as well as access to a range of opportunities including marketing workshops, inclusion in Pen&Inc magazine, panel spots, festival appearances and bookshop signings. Founded 2020.

Golden Egg Award – see page 380

Jhalak Children's & YA Prize – see page 363

The London Writers' Awards
The Albany Centre, Douglas Way, London SE8 4AG
email bobby@spreadtheword.org.uk
website www.spreadtheword.org.uk/projects/london-writers-awards

Award programme set up by Spread the Word for London-based prose writers who identify as being from a background currently under-represented in publishing: disabled, LGBTQIA+, working class or writers of colour. The awards are given across four genres: literary fiction, commercial fiction, narrative non-fiction and YA/children's (including middle-grade and YA fiction, excludes picture books). *Founded* 2018.

SCBWI Diversity Awards and Grants – see Society of Children's Book Writers & Illustrators

The Times/Chicken House Children's Fiction Competition – see page 367

EVENTS, BURSARIES AND OTHER SCHEMES

All Stories
email info@allstories.org.uk
website www.allstories.org.uk
Facebook www.facebook.com/AllStoriesWrite
Twitter @AllStoriesWrite
Instagram @allstorieswrite

A mentorship programme for children's writers from under-represented writers supported by the ALCS, Arts Council England and SCBWI. Under-represented is used broadly and includes writers who are people of colour, disabled, neurodiverse, LGBTQ+, working class or socio-economically marginalised; the programme is also intended for those who would not otherwise be able to pay for a membership. Opportunities available include feedback and support from experienced editors, writing workshops from award-winning authors and book career guidance for students.

Societies, prizes and festivals

The Malorie Blackman Scholarships for Unheard Voices

website www.citylit.ac.uk/malorie-blackman-scholarships

Three annual awards worth up to £1000 each, to fund one year's study within the Creative Writing department at City Lit. Writers are welcome from under-represented groups, including (but not exclusive to) people with disabilities, from minority backgrounds and communities, who are members of the LGBTQ+ community, who are from lower socioeconomic backgrounds or who are from BAME backgrounds.

BookTrust Represents – see page 344

Creative Access

3rd Floor, 2 Waterhouse Square, 140 Holborn, London EC1N 2AE
email info@creativeaccess.org.uk
website www.creativeaccess.org.uk
Facebook www.facebook.com/CreativeAccessUK
Twitter @_CreativeAccess
Instagram @_CreativeAccess

A social enterprise and one of the UK's leading diversity organisations which helps those from under-represented communities to secure paid training opportunities and full-time jobs in the creative industries and support them to progress into leadership roles. Working with leading creative organisations across the UK, Creative Access provides a range of services to help support employer partners create inclusive workplaces; including recruitment of trainees and permanent staff, mentoring programmes and employer training. Founded 2012.

Curtis Brown Creative – see page 380

Elevate Mentoring Scheme

2 Green Barton, Swyre, Dorchester, Dorest DT2 9DN
tel (01308) 897374
email helen@cornerstones.co.uk
website https://cornerstones.co.uk/elevate

An Arts Council funded scheme that pairs low-income and/or under-represented writers with specialist editors best suited to help them develop their craft.

Emerging Writers Programme

tel 020-7766 4765
email emergingwriters@londonlibrary.co.uk
website www.londonlibrary.co.uk/about-us/ll-emerging-writers

Open to all writers above the age of 16, the Programme offers writers, in all genres, one year's free membership of The London Library and includes writing development masterclasses, literary

networking opportunities, peer support and guidance in use of the Library's resources. The Virago Participation Bursary (funded by Virago Books) is awarded as part of the Programme for black female and black non-binary writers to assist with any financial issues that might prevent them from accessing the full Programme.

Future Bookshelf

website www.thefuturebookshelf.co.uk
Twitter @FutureBookshelf

Part of Hachette UK's 'Changing the Story' programme, this free creative writing resource is for under-represented writers, providing tips and exercises on writing a book and inspiring content from authors, agents and experienced editors.

HarperCollins Author Academy

Westerhill Road, Bishopsbriggs, Glasgow G64 2QT
email enquiries@harpercollins.co.uk
website www.harpercollinsacademy.co.uk
Facebook www.facebook.com/HarperCollinsPublishersUK
Twitter @harpercollinsuk
Instagram @harpercollinsuk

A training programme for writers from BAME backgrounds who are under-represented in publishing. Courses run twice a year for six weeks and are available in three genres: Fiction, Non-Fiction and Writing for Children. All successful applicants also receive publishing masterclasses and support from a mentor. Applicants must not be represented by a literary agent and should apply online to one of the three courses. Founded 2021.

Inscribe

website www.peepaltreepress.com/inscribe
Twitter @INSCRIBEwriters

Supporting writers of colour in England to professionally advance their creative work and their careers through coaching, mentoring, workshops, residentials, training, newsletters, publications and general advice.

Megaphone Writer Development Scheme

email megaphone.write@gmail.com
website https://megaphonewrite.com
Twitter @MegaphoneWrite

An Arts Council England funded project which offers a year of one-to-one mentoring and masterclasses for writers of colour based in England who are writing a novel for children or teenagers.

The Octopus Scheme

email hello@thenovelry.com
website www.thenovelry.com/scholarships

Established by the Novelry to offer fully funded scholarships for places on their Ninety Day Novel course for under-represented writers. Applicants can include writers from a low-income background, primary carers, ex-offenders, writers with a disability, writers of colour and writers from the LGBTQIA+ community. Successful applicants will also receive one year's Novelry membership and one-to-one membership with a tutor. Applicants should email a 500-word sample of their writing and a personal statement explaining how they are under-represented, why they are applying and how they think they will benefit from the course. Scholarships are sponsored by authors including Sophie Kinsella, Rachel Joyce and Ajay Chowdhury.

TLC/Arts Council England Free Reads Scheme

East Side, Platfrom 1, Kings Cross Station, London N1C 4AX
tel 020-3751 0757 ext. 800
email info@literaryconsultancy.co.uk
website www.literaryconsultancy.co.uk/editorial/ace-free-reads-scheme
Director Aki Schilz

In 2001, TLC received funding from Arts Council England to enable the provision of bursaried manuscript assessments for writers from low-income households. The scheme is known as the Free Reads Scheme and offers access to TLC's core services to writers who might not be able to afford them. Free Reads are selected by a range of literature development bodies from across the UK, and there are currently seventeen organisations benefitting from the scheme. For detailed submission guidelines and eligibility information, see the website.

WriteNow Programme

WriteNow - The Penguin Random House Group, 20 Vauxhall Bridge Road, London SW1V 2SA
email writenow@penguinrandomhouse.co.uk
website www.penguin.co.uk/company/creative-responsibility/writenow/Whats-on-offer.html
Twitter @PenguinUKBooks

A programme by PRH which aims to nurture and publish new, unpublished writers from under-represeneted communities. Its workshops provide the aspiring writer with tools, contacts, information and access to getting published. Opportunities include publishing workshops; mentoring and feedback from Penguin editors; and advice from authors, literary agents and publishing professionals. 18 of the programme's writers have been published by Penguin, and a further 25% of shortlisted writers have since signed a deal with another publisher. The programme is open to writers of adult fiction or fiction for children aged 0–12 (picture books, chapter books and middle grade).

Writers & Artists

Bloomsbury Publishing plc, 50 Bedford Square, London WC1B 3DP
tel 020-7631 5985
email AccessWA@bloomsbury.com
website www.writersandartists.co.uk/accessible-to-all
website www.writersandartists.co.uk/bursary-opportunities

Bursary places with a combined total of £4,000 are available to help ensure that everything W&A offers – events, writing courses and editing services – is accessible to all. See the website for more details and eligibility.

Societies, prizes and festivals

Children's literature festivals and trade fairs

Some of the literature festivals in this section are specifically related to children's books and others are general arts festivals which include literature events for children.

Aspects Irish Literature Festival

email arts@ardsandnorthdown.gov.uk
website www.aspectsfestival.com
Twitter @aspectsfestival

An annual celebration of contemporary Irish writing with novelists, poets and playwrights. Includes readings, children's events and exhibitions.

Aye Write! Glasgow's Book Festival

Glasgow Life, Commonwealth House,
38 Albion Street, Glasgow G1 1LH
email ayewrite@glasgowlife.org.uk
Takes place May

Brings together the best undiscovered local talent with a wealth of established writers from the city and nationwide. A free children's festival runs in tandem with the main festival. Creative writing workshops and masterclasses are on offer at the Festival. Founded 2005.

Baillie Gifford Borders Book Festival

Harmony House, St Mary's Road, Melrose TD6 9LJ
email info@bordersbookfestival.org
website www.bordersbookfestival.org
Facebook www.facebook.com/bordersbookfestival
Twitter @BordersBookFest
Instagram @bordersbookfest
Takes place Summer

An annual festival with a programme of events featuring high-profile and bestselling writers, including a Family Festival programme. Winner of the Walter Scott Prize for Historical Fiction is announced during the festival. Founded 2004.

Barnes Children's Literature Festival

website www.barneskidslitfest.org
Facebook www.facebook.com/BarnesKidsLitFest
Twitter @kidslitfest
Takes place June

The Barnes Children's Literature Festival is London's largest dedicated children's literature festival with more than 100 family friendly events, performances and workshops. Some of the best known names writing for children are featured including Julia Donaldson, Sir Michael Morpurgo, Dame Jacqueline Wilson, Cressida Cowell, Michael Rosen, Lauren Child, Axel Scheffler, Francesca Simon, David Almond and many more.

Bath Children's Literature Festival

tel (01225) 614180
email info@bathfestivals.org.uk
website https://bathfestivals.org.uk/childrens-literature
Twitter @bathkidslitfest

Europe's largest annual dedicated children's literature festival.

Beyond the Border: Wales' International Storytelling Festival

tel (02921) 660501
email info@beyondtheborder.com
website www.beyondtheborder.com

An international festival celebrating oral tradition and bringing together storytellers, poets and musicians from around the world. This is the largest event of its type in the UK and features storytelling, poetry, music, singing, theatre, circus and film.

Bologna Children's Book Fair

Piazza Costituzione 6, 40128 Bologna, Italy
tel +39 051-282111
email bookfair@bolognafiere.it
website www.bolognachildrensbookfair.com
Facebook www.facebook.com/BolognaChildrensBookFair
Twitter @BoChildrensBook
Takes place Spring

Held annually, this is the leading children's publishing event. Publishers, authors and illustrators, literary agents, app developers, e-publishing professionals, licensors and licensees and many other members of the children's content community meet in Bologna. Attendees buy and sell copyrights, establish new contacts and strengthen their professional relationships, discover new illustrators, develop new business opportunities, learn about the latest trends and developments and explore children's educational materials, including new media products. Entry is restricted to professionals in children's content.

Bradford Literature Festival

University of Bradford, Richmond Road,
Bradford BD7 1DP
email info@bradfordlitfest.co.uk
website www.bradfordlitfest.co.uk
Facebook www.facebook.com/bradfordlitfest

Twitter @BradfordLitFest
Founder & Director Syima Aslam
Takes place 24 June–4 July 2022

An annual arts event and year-round cultural outreach programme that hosts a diverse range of authors, poets, speakers, musicians and artists from Bradford, the UK and around the world. Taking place over 10-days, the programme includes over 400 events with a mix of topic-led events, author talks, poetry line-ups, live music, film, theatre and more. The Festival operates an extensive Ethical Ticketing Policy, offering free or discounted tickets to those who might otherwise be unable to attend the festival. Founded 2014.

Budleigh Salterton Literary Festival
10 Fairfield Close, Exmouth EX8 2BN
tel (01395) 262635
email festival@budlitfest.org.uk
website hhttps://budlitfest.org.uk
Facebook www.facebook.com/
BudleighSaltertonLiteraryFestival
Twitter @BudleighLitFest
Director Annie Ashworth, *Chair* Sue Briggs

Held beside the sea on the beautiful Jurassic Coast, the Festival takes place over 5 days in September. It features leading writers and celebrities, events for families and workshops for writers. The Festival has an outreach programme in schools and is one of the biggest literary festivals in the South West. Founded 2009.

Cambridge Literary Festival
Old Divinity School, University of Cambridge, St Johns Street, Cambridge CB2 1TP
tel (01223) 515335
email hello@cambridgeliteraryfestival.com
website https://cambridgeliteraryfestival.com
Facebook www.facebook.com/CamLitFest
Twitter @camlitfest
Takes place April and November

From poetry to politics, fiction to finance, history to hip-hop and comedy to current affairs, Cambridge Literary Festival brings an eclectic mix of today's best writers, thinkers and speakers to Cambridge all year round. Founded 2003.

Cardiff Children's Lit Fest
County Hall, Cardiff CF10 4UW
email events@cardiff.gov.uk
website www.cardiffkidslitfest.com
Twitter @CDFKidsLitFest
Takes place March/April

The Cardiff Children's Literature Festival is an annual event aimed at young people who appreciate the magic of books and grown-ups who want to write them. The festival includes events with local and national authors and comprises a number of educational sessions for schools.

The Times and Sunday Times Cheltenham Literature Festival
The Brewery Quarter, High Street, Cheltenham GL50 3FF
tel (01242) 850270
email boxoffice@cheltenhamfestivals.com
website www.cheltenhamfestivals.com/literature
Facebook www.facebook.com/cheltenhamfestivals
Twitter @cheltlitfest
Takes place October

This annual festival is one of the oldest literary events in the world. The festival features adult, family and schools programmes for everyone with around 500 events over 10 days. Events for families and schools include presentations from the very best children's authors and illustrators alongside workshops, shows, storytellers, story trails, discussions and free drop-in craft activities. Founded 1949.

Chiswick Book Festival
St Michael & All Angels Church, Bath Road, Bedford Park, Chiswick, London W4 1LW
website www.chiswickbookfestival.net
Facebook www.facebook.com/chiswickbookfestival
Twitter @W4BookFest
Instagram @chiswickbookfestival
Takes place September

A non-profit festival which aims to bring writers and readers together to support reading-related charities. Since its inception it has raised over £109,000. A range of literary events are hosted each year, covering history, poetry, biography, fiction, thrillers, gardens, food, wine, politics, creative writing and self-help. Children's book events are also central to the festival, encouraging a love of both reading and writing. Founded 2009.

Creative Folkestone Book Festival
Quarterhouse, Mill Bay, Folkestone, Kent CT20 1BN
tel (01303) 760740
email info@creativefolkestone.org.uk
website www.creativefolkestone.org.uk/folkestone-book-festival
Facebook www.facebook.com/CreativeFolkestone
Twitter @CreativeFstone
Instagram @CreativeFstone

Folkestone Book Festival holds a special place amongst the UK book festivals' scene. Taking place annually, the festival is an opportunity to gather, tell stories and exchange ideas on the beautiful Kent coast.

Derby Book Festival
13 Lavender Row, Darley Abbey, Derby DE22 1DF
email hello@derbybookfestival.co.uk
website www.derbybookfestival.co.uk
Takes place Over 10 days in May/June and a weekend in November for it's Autumn edition

Celebrates the joy of books and reading for all ages and interests, with a programme featuring great writers, poets, historians, politicians, illustrators, storytellers and musicians. Each year the festival welcomes internationally celebrated bestselling authors as well as a broad range of local writing talent. In addition to its core programme of events, the organisers operate community-focused projects across Derby and in schools. Founded 2015.

Edinburgh International Book Festival

Edinburgh College of Arts, 74 Lauriston Place, Edinburgh EH3 9DF
tel 0131 718 5666
email admin@edbookfest.co.uk
website www.edbookfest.co.uk
Twitter @edbookfest
Takes place August

The largest public celebration of the written word in the world. In addition to a unique independent bookselling operation, around 1,000 UK and international writers appear in over 900 events for adults and children. Programme details available in June. Founded 1983.

Edinburgh International Children's Festival

30B Grindlay Street, Edinburgh EH3 9AX
tel 0131 225 8050
email info@imaginate.org.uk
website www.imaginate.org.uk
Takes place May/June

The Edinburgh International Children's Festival presents the world's best theatre and dance for young audiences aged 0–15, with performances that are deeply engaging, innovative and inspiring. With an emphasis on striking visual productions, the international programme continuously goes beyond expectations of children's and young people's work. The shows include a mix of theatre and dance and attract an audience of over 17,000 children, families and schools every year. The Festival is also one of the best places for programmers from all over the world to see work of the very highest standard and regularly attracts over 300 industry delegates.

Hay Festival

The Drill Hall, 25 Lion Street,
Hay-on-Wye HR3 5AD
tel (01497) 822620
email submissions@hayfestival.org
website www.hayfestival.com
Facebook www.facebook.com/hayfestival
Twitter @hayfestival
Instagram @hayfestival
Takes place May; Hay Festival Winter Weekend takes place in Novemeber

This annual festival of literature and the arts in Hay-on-Wye, Wales, brings together writers, musicians,

film-makers, historians, politicians, environmentalists and scientists from around the world to communicate challenging ideas. Hundreds of events over ten days. Within the annual festival is a festival for families and children, HAYDAYS, which introduces children, from toddlers to teenagers, to their favourite authors and holds workshops to entertain and educate. Programme published April.

I AM Writing Festival

email hello@iaminprint.co.uk
website https://iaminprint.co.uk
Twitter @IAMinprint
Instagram @IAMinprint
Directors Sarah Post, Elane Retford
Takes place June

A festival for writers working towards publication. The festival hosts a variety of creative writing workshops, talks and panels featuring debut and bestselling authors, agents and publishers across all children's book genres from picture books to YA and covering all abilities from beginner to those querying. Includes competitions, the opportunity for manuscript feedback from top literary agents and the chance to network with other writers and published authors in a supportive, friendly environment. Founded 2022.

Ilkley Literature Festival

9 The Grove, Ilkley LS29 9LW
tel (01943) 601210
email info@ilkleylitfest.org.uk
website www.ilkleyliteraturefestival.org.uk
Facebook www.facebook.com/ilkleylitfest
Twitter @ilkleylitfest
Director Erica Morris, *Coordinator* Becky Wholley
Takes place October

One of the UK's longest-running and widest-ranging literature festivals with over 150 events, from author discussions to workshops, readings, literary walks, children's events and a festival fringe. Founded 1973.

Imagine: Writers and Writing for Children

Southbank Centre, London SE1 8XX
tel 020-7960 4200
website www.southbankcentre.co.uk/whats-on/festivals-series/imagine-childrens-festival
Twitter @southbankcentre
Takes place February

An annual festival celebrating writing for children featuring a selection of poets, storytellers and illustrators.

Independent Bookshop Week

website www.booksaremybag.com/IndependentBookshopWeek
Facebook www.facebook.com/booksaremybag
Twitter @booksaremybag

Instagram @booksaremybag
Takes place 18–25 June 2022

An annual celebration of independent bookshops, part of the Books Are My Bag campaign to promote all high street bookshops in the UK and Ireland and the idea of shopping locally and sustainably.

Jewish Book Week

36 Gloucester Avenue, London NW1 7BB
tel 020-7284 5910
email info@jewishbookweek.com
website https://jewishbookweek.com
Twitter @JewishBookWeek
Festival Director Claudia Rubenstein
Takes place February/March

A 10-day festival of writing, arts and culture, with contributors from around the world and sessions in London and nationwide. Includes events for children and teenagers. Founded 1952.

Laureate na nÓg/Ireland's Children's Laureate

Children's Books Ireland,
17 North Great George's Street, Dublin 1 D01 R2F1, Republic of Ireland
tel +353 (0)18 727475
email info@childrenslaureate.ie
website www.childrenslaureate.ie
Laureate na nÓg Project Manager Ruth Ní Eidhin

This is a project recognising the role and importance of literature for children in Ireland, established to engage young people with high-quality literature and to underline the importance of children's literature in Ireland's cultural and imaginative life. It was awarded for the first time in 2010. The laureate participates in selected events and activities around Ireland and internationally during their three-year term.

The laureate is chosen in recognition of their widely recognised high-quality children's writing or illustration and the positive impact they have had on readers as well as other writers and illustrators. Laureate na nÓg 2010–12, Siobhán Parkinson; 2012–14, Niamh Sharkey; 2014–16, Eoin Colfer; 2016–18, P.J. Lynch; 2018–20, Sarah Crossan; 2020–23, Áine Ní Ghlinn.

London Literature Festival

email customer@southbankcentre.co.uk
website www.southbankcentre.co.uk
Facebook www.facebook.com/southbankcentre
Twitter @southbankcentre
Takes place 20–30 October 2022

The Southbank Centre is a world-leading space for literature and the spoken word. The annual London Literature Festival combines the best of the year-round literature events with an engaging festival programme, encompassing free public programming, thematically focused talks and debates, newly commissioned performances and a family offer to coincide with the half-term school holiday. Founded 1967.

Manchester Children's Book Festival

Manchester Metropolitan University,
All Saints Building, Manchester M15 6BH
email mcbf@mmu.ac.uk
website www.mmu.ac.uk/mcbf
Facebook www.facebook.com/MCBFestival
Twitter @MCBFestival
Instagram @mcbfestival

A festival of year-round activities celebrating the very best writing for children, inspiring young people to engage with literature and creativity across the curriculum and offering extended projects and training to ensure the event has an impact and legacy in classrooms. Founded 2009.

Marlborough Literature Festival

email general@marlboroughlitfest.org
website www.marlboroughlitfest.org
Facebook www.facebook.com/MarlboroughLitFest
Twitter @MarlbLitFest
Festival Patron Sir Simon Russell Beale
Takes place 29 September–2 October 2022

An annual literary festival in the market town of Marlborough, celebrating the best in writing and reflecting the legacy of writers linked to the town such as Siegfried Sassoon, John Betjeman and William Golding. The festival champions new and upcoming writers as well as established names and offers a varied programme of events for all ages, including fiction, non-fiction, poetry, children's events and creative writing workshops in local venues in and around Marlborough. The festival has a strong outreach programme, delivering free author talks to local primary and secondary schools to encourage a love of reading in children and young people as well as various projects to support the wider local community. LitFest remains a charity run by a small committee of volunteers.

Monty Lit Fest

Montgomery Town Hall, Broad Street, Montgomery, Powys SY15 6PH
email enquiries@montylitfest.com
website https://montylitfest.com
Facebook www.facebook.com/montylitfest
Twitter @montylitfest
Instagram @montylitfest
Takes place June

A diverse programme of events aim to bring together a wide range of audiences to celebrate writers who live in or write about Wales. Founded 2016.

National Poetry Day

email info@forwardartsfoundation.org
website https://nationalpoetryday.co.uk
Facebook www.facebook.com/PoetryDayUK

Societies, prizes and festivals

Twitter @PoetryDayUK
Instagram @nationalpoetryday
Takes place First Thursday in October

Organised by the Forward Arts Foundation to encourage poetry reading and writing. Combines poetry recommendations and teaching resources with nationwide events to highlight the artistic and social value of poetry. Each year explores a different theme. Founded 1999.

Off the Shelf Festival of Words Sheffield

Cathedral Court, 46 Church Street, Sheffield S1 2GN
tel (01142) 223895
email offtheshelf@sheffield.ac.uk
website www.offtheshelf.org.uk
Takes place 14–30 October 2022

A lively, diverse festival featuring children's authors and illustrators with activities and events for children, young people and families. Events in Sheffield and South Yorkshire.

Oundle Festival of Literature

email kidlithillfield@live.com
website www.oundlelitfest.org.uk
Facebook www.facebook.com/
OundleFestivalOfLiterature
Twitter @OundleLitEvents
Festival Director Helen Shair
Takes place early March

Kid Lit Week includes a writing competition and events for infant and junior school aged children. The Festival also runs a programme of all year round events aimed at exciting, informing, entertaining and educating a wide variety of people through talks, discussions and workshops by award-winning and local authors and poets. The Festival uses a variety of venues in the market town of Oundle.

FT Weekend Oxford Literary Festival

c/o Critchleys, Beaver House,
23–28 Hythe Bridge Street, Oxford OX1 2EP
email info@oxfordliteraryfestival.org
website https://oxfordliteraryfestival.org
Takes place March/April

An annual festival for both adults and children held in venues across the city and university. Presents topical debates, fiction and non-fiction discussion panels, and adult and children's authors who have recently published books. Topics range from contemporary fiction to discussions on politics, history, science, gardening, food, poetry, philosophy, art and crime fiction.

Richmond upon Thames Lit Fest

Orleans House Gallery, Orleans Road,
Twickenham TW1 3BL
tel 020-8831 6000

email artsinfo@richmondandwandsworth.gov.uk
website www.richmondliterature.com
Twitter @richmondlitfest
Takes place November

An annual literature festival featuring a diverse programme of authors in venues across the borough. The festival includes an exciting programme of author events for children and families as well as opportunities to explore creativity in literature through workshops and interactive sessions.

Scottish International Storytelling Festival

43–45 High Street, Edinburgh EH1 1SR
tel 0131 556 9579
email reception@scottishstorytellingcentre.com
website www.scottishstorytellingcentre.co.uk
Festival Director Donald Smith
Takes place October

A celebration of Scottish storytelling set in its international context, complemented by music, ballad and song. Takes place at the Scottish Storytelling Centre and partner venues across Edinburgh and Scotland.

The Self-Publishing Conference

tel 0116 279 2299
email books@troubador.co.uk
website www.selfpublishingconference.org.uk
Twitter @Selfpubconf

The UK's only dedicated self-publishing conference. This annual event covers all aspects of self-publishing from production through to marketing and distribution. The conference offers plenty of networking opportunities and access to over 16 presentations. Founded 2013.

Shanghai Children's Book Fair

email ccbf@bfchina.net
website www.ccbookfair.com/en
Facebook www.facebook.com/ccbookfair
Twitter @ccbookfair
Takes place November

The only fair fully dedicated to books and specific contents for children aged from 0–16 in Asia Pacific. Offers unique opportunities for face-to-face interaction with publishers, popular authors, translators and illustrators from the region. Founded 2013.

StAnza: Scotland's International Poetry Festival

tel (01334) 475000 (box office)
email stanza@stanzapoetry.org
website www.stanzapoetry.org
Facebook www.facebook.com/stanzapoetry
Twitter @StAnzaPoetry
Instagram @stanzapoetry

Festival Director Lucy Burnett
Takes place March

The festival is dedicated to programming a wide diversity of poetries and poets, alongside other art forms such as music and visual art. It is international in focus and as of 2022 has adopted a hybrid format, including both live and digital events. Founded 1997.

Stratford-upon-Avon Literary Festival
email info@stratfordliteraryfestival.co.uk
website www.stratlitfest.co.uk
Facebook www.facebook.com/stratfordlitfest
Twitter @StratLitFest
Instagram @stratfordlitfest
Takes place May with events in autumn

The Festival is a feast of workshops, panel discussions, celebrity and best-selling author events. A charity, the festival also runs a programme of educational events and projects for families and regional schools aimed at entertaining and inspiring children and encouraging literacy, as well as events in the community and bedtime story writing workshops in prisons.

The Summer Festival of Writing
4 Acer Walk, Oxford OX2 6EX
tel 0345 459 9560
email info@jerichowriters.com
website https://jerichowriters.com/events/summer-festival-of-writing
Takes place June–August

A three-month online festival for all writers providing the opportunity to connect with others from across the world. Writers will have the opportunity to hear from literary agents, publishers and professional authors. This includes pitching work to literary agents; receiving live feedback from industry professionals; and entering writing competitions.

Wigtown Book Festival
Wigtown Festival Company, 11 North Main Street, Wigtown DG8 9HN
tel (01988) 402036
email mail@wigtownbookfestival.com
website www.wigtownbookfestival.com
Facebook www.facebook.com/WigtownBookFestival
Twitter @WigtownBookFest
Takes place 23 September–2 October 2022

An annual celebration of literature and the arts in Scotland's National Book Town. Includes author events, theatre, music, film and children's and young people's programmes.

Wimbledon Book Fest
35 Wimbledon Hill Road, London SW19 7NB
email info@wimbledonbookfest.org
website www.wimbledonbookfest.org
Takes place June and September 2022

London's leading literary festival aims to foster a space for art and culture within the community. Guest speakers include writers from all genres, with a focus on inspiring stories, diversity and inclusion. Runs educational workshops and projects for young people during the festival and throughout the year. Founded 2006.

World Book Day
email wbd@education.co.uk
website www.worldbookday.com
Facebook www.facebook.com/worldbookdayuk
Twitter @WorldBookDayUK
Ceo Cassie Chadderton
Takes place First Thursday in March

World Book Day changes lives through a love of books and shared reading. Its mission is to promote reading for pleasure, offering every child and young person the opportunity to have a book of their own. Reading for pleasure is the single biggest indicator of a child's future success – more than their family circumstances, their parents' educational background or their income. Aim to encourage more children, particularly those from disadvantaged backgrounds, to form a life-long habit of reading for pleasure and the improved life chances this brings them.

The Writers' Weekend
website https://writersweekend.uk
Facebook www.facebook.com/WritersWkend
Twitter @WritersWkend
Director Sara Gangai
Takes place June/July

A conference for emerging writers, working in all genres and at all levels. Attendees participate in writing workshops, informative talks and one-to-one appointments with top literary agents to pitch their manuscripts. The Weekend is full of opportunities to network with fellow writers, published authors, agents and editors, attend panels, discuss topics of interest in small groups and share writing at open mics to a supportive and friendly crowd. The keynote speakers change every year. In addition to the Weekend, four competitions are also held.

YALC (Young Adult Literature Convention)
email yalc@showmastersevents.com
website https://londonfilmandcomiccon.com/yalc
Facebook www.facebook.com/ukYALC
Twitter @yalc_uk
Takes place Annually in July

YALC is a celebration of the best YA books and authors. It is an interactive event where YA fiction fans can meet their favourite authors, listen to panel discussions and take part in workshops. YALC is run by Showmasters, which runs the London Film and Comic Con. Lots of opportunities available for promotional activities. Founded 2014.

Children's writing courses and conferences

Contact your local library, college or university for further information about the courses that might be most suited to you and the stage you are at with your writing. While many courses are now going ahead in person once more, some may have an online component.

Blue Elephant Storyshaping
email hello@blueelephantstoryshaping.com
website www.blueelephantstoryshaping.com
Editor, Coach and Mentor Natascha Biebow MBE

Offers one-to-one coaching, individual manuscript reviews and marketing advice to writers of picture books up to middle grade fiction. The Cook Up a Picture Book online course offers coaching and mentoring, and is aimed at picture book writers who wish to fine-tune their work, plus illustrators who would like to write and illustrate. The Small-Group Coaching Course is a six-week course featuring weekly, one-to-one detailed editorial feedback and top tips on key aspects of picture book craft and publishing. The aim is to create at least one marketable picture book. There is the opportunity to submit to an editor or agent at the end of this course. See website for full details of services available.

Curtis Brown Creative
28–29 Haymarket, London SW1Y 4SP
tel 020-7393 4201
email cbccourses@curtisbrown.co.uk
website www.curtisbrowncreative.co.uk
Facebook www.facebook.com/CurtisBrownCreative
Twitter @cbcreative
Instagram curtisbrowncreative

Creative writing school offering courses in London and online. Over 160 students to date have subsequently signed publishing deals; alumni include Jessie Burton, Jane Harper, Nicholas Searle and Bonnie Garmus. Subjects covered include fiction, memoirs, short stories, screenwriting and children's picture books. Curtis Brown also runs the Breakthrough Writers' Programme, which offers free courses, mentoring and scholarships for under-represented writers.

The Federation of Children's Book Groups Conference
email info@fcbg.org.uk
website www.fcbg.org.uk/conference
Twitter @FCBGnews
Takes place April

Held annually, guest speakers include well-known children's authors as well as experts and publishers in the field of children's books. Publishers also exhibit their newest books and resources.

The Golden Egg Academy
The Wool House, 6 Cork Street, Frome, Somerset BA11 1BL
email info@goldeneggacademy.co.uk
website www.goldeneggacademy.co.uk
Twitter @TheGEAcademy
Founder and Managing Director Imogen Cooper

Runs writing courses for authors who want to develop their writing to publication standard. All courses are run online and include: Write Your Successful Children's Novel; Writing for Children and Young Adults; Work on Your Novel and two new picture book courses launching in 2022. Selective courses comprise virtual workshops, one-to-one editorial surgeries and regular online group seminars.

Students also have the opportunity to meet industry professionals and benefit from presentations by some of the best writers in their field. Fiction writers enjoy an exclusive non-binding 'First Look' deal with Chicken House; picture book writers enjoy an exclusive non-binding 'First Look' deal with Andersen Press and Peters, Fraser and Dunlop. Also runs the Golden Egg Award for BAME, LGBTQ+, disabled and financially disadvantaged groups. Winners are awarded a free place on the twelve-week Write Your Successful Children's Novel course with runners-up awarded a six-month subscription to the Golden Egg Club. The Club gives writers the opportunity to benefit from talks by industry professionals, editor Q&As and a range of other writer-based events. It is designed to offer writers low-cost access to support from the industry and is particularly useful for those new to the children's book world.

IBBY Congress
Nonnenweg 12, CH-4055-Basel, Switzerland
tel +41 61-272 2917
email ibby@ibby.org
website www.ibbycongress2022.org
Twitter @IBBYINT

IBBY's biennial international congresses bring together IBBY (the International Board on Books for Young People) members and other people involved in children's books and reading development from all over the world. The congresses are excellent occasions to make contacts, exchange ideas and open horizons. Every two years a different National Section hosts the Congress. Several hundred people attend the lectures, panel discussions, seminar sessions and workshops on current congress themes. An IBBY International Congress also serves as a framework not only for the General Assembly and other meetings, but also for the presentation of different exhibitions and celebrations such as the Hans Christian Andersen Awards and the IBBY Honour List. The 38th IBBY will take place in Putrajaya, Malaysia, in September 2022.

Jericho Writers
4 Acer Walk, Oxford OX2 6EX
tel 0345 459 9560 / +1 646-974-9060 (US)
email info@jerichowriters.com
website https://jerichowriters.com
Twitter @JerichoWriters
Instagram @JerichoWriters
Founder Harry Bingham

Inclusive online writing organisation offering editorial services and events for all genres, including writing for children, and tutored courses. Also available: guidance for self-publishers, masterclasses, AgentMatch (a database of over 1,000 literary agents), a free community for writers to connect, and expert guides to writing and publishing.

The London School of Journalism
tel 020-7432 8140
email admin@lsjournalism.com
website www.lsj.org/courses/distance-learning/
writing-for-children

Part of the School's distance learning programme, this year-long course guides the writer as they work in their chosen genre, including picture books, story books, early readers, teenage fiction, activity books, non-fiction and books for the education market. Students will learn how to construct a story that children will enjoy reading, how to create believable characters and realistic dialogue.

Oxford University Day and Weekend Schools
Oxford University Department of Continuing Education, Rewley House, 1 Wellington Square, Oxford OX1 2JA
tel (01865) 270368
email ppdayweek@conted.ox.ac.uk
website www.conted.ox.ac.uk/about/day-and-
weekend
Contact Day School Administrator

Creative writing courses including Writing for Young Adults. Topics vary from year to year. Courses always held on Fridays.

SCBWI-BI Annual Conference and Masterclass Series
email scbwi@scbwi.org
website https://britishisles.scbwi.org/masterclasses/
website www.scbwi.org
Twitter @scbwi
Instagram @scbwi_british_isles
Contact Natascha Biebow

Annual conference offering a mix of inspiration, networking and fun for writers and illustrators, both published and unpublished. The most recent Winter conference took place via Zoom in March 2022 but featured a range of events including keynote speakers, industry panels and breakout sessions. Check website for information on future events.

SCBWI-BI Writers' Events
email araevents@britishscbwi.org
website https://britishisles.scbwi.org/events
Twitter @scbwi
Instagram @scbwi_british_isles

Online listings of retreats and other writing and literary events across the UK organised by the Society of Children's Book Writers and Illustrators.

Swanwick, The Writers' Summer School
Hayes Conference Centre, Swanwick, Derbyshire DE55 1AU
tel (01290) 552248
email secretary@swanwickwritersschool.org.uk
website www.swanwickwritersschool.org.uk
Facebook www.facebook.com/SwanwickWriters
Twitter @swanwickwriters

Extensive choice of courses, talks and workshops. Offers several highly subsidised places for writers aged between 18 and 30, and assistance for writers unable to afford the full course fee. Full details of the programme and information on how to apply for the TopWrite Programme and Assisted Places Scheme are available on the website.

Tŷ Newydd Writing Centre
Tŷ Newydd, Llanystumdwy, Cricieth, Gwynedd LL52 0LW
tel (01766) 522811
email tynewydd@literaturewales.org
website www.tynewydd.wales
Twitter @ty_newydd

Residential creative writing courses for writers of all abilities over the age of 16. Courses cover everything from poetry and popular fiction to writing for the theatre and developing a novel for young adults. No qualifications are necessary; staff can advise on the suitability of courses. Also offers courses for schools, corporate courses and awaydays for companies. Tŷ Newydd is also home to Nant, the writers' retreat cottage located on site. Run by Literature Wales, the national organisation for the development of literature in Wales.

Writers & Artists

Bloomsbury Publishing plc, 50 Bedford Square, London WC1B 3DP
tel 020-7631 5985
email writersandartists@bloomsbury.com
website www.writersandartists.co.uk
Facebook www.facebook.com/WritersArtistsYearbook
Twitter @Writers_Artists
Contacts James Rennoldson, Clare Povey

Runs online and offline masterclasses, conferences and writing courses throughout the year. These are run independently or in collaboration with literary festivals, universities and charities such as Book Aid International, Literature Works and the Open University. An annual How to Write for Children & Young Adults conference is held in February, while writing courses – which cover a variety of genres – take place on weekday evenings. Writers' & Artists' (W&A) also offers a range of editing services, and works regularly with literary agents to provide guidance on the submission process. The W&A platform is free to join, contains hundreds of writing and publishing advice articles, and offers a lively community area and personalisation features.

UNIVERSITY COURSES

Bath Spa University

Newton Park, Newton St Loe, Bath BA2 9BN
tel (01225) 876180
email admissions@bathspa.ac.uk
website www.bathspa.ac.uk/courses/course-index-a-z/

Offers a variety of postgraduate courses on subjects including Creative Writing, Writing for Young People, Travel and Nature Writing, Scriptwriting, and Children's Publishing.

University of Central Lancashire

School of Art, Design and Fashion,
University of Central Lancashire, Preston PR1 2HE
tel (01772) 893364
email mstuart1@uclan.ac.uk
website www.uclan.ac.uk

Offers MA Children's Book Illustration, a taught master's course which explores the practice of illustration for children's picture and story books. The course is designed to encourage the pursuit of a unique and personal line of research into an artist's chosen area of children's book illustration. Many graduates have gone on to careers as published illustrators. The course runs both full and part time.

University of Chichester

Bishop Otter Campus, College Lane, Chichester, West Sussex PO19 6PE

tel (01243) 816000
email h.frey@chi.ac.uk
email h.dunkerley@chi.ac.uk
website www.chi.ac.uk
Contacts Prof. Hugo Frey (Head of Department), Prof Hugh Dunkerley (MA Creative Writing Programme Coordinator)

Offers MA and PhD Creative Writing. Students work with practising writers. Specialisms include: novels, short stories, creative non-fiction, writing for children, screenwriting and poetry. Hosts regular visits by high-profile writers, editors and agents. Visiting Professors: Kate Mosse and Alison MacLeod. Many students go on to publish and win prizes.

University of Cumbria

Fusehill Street, Carlisle CA1 2HH
tel 0808 291 6578
email enquirycentre@cumbria.ac.uk
website www.cumbria.ac.uk
Facebook www.facebook.com/universityofcumbria
Twitter @CumbriaUni

Courses offered include MA Creative Writing, MA Literature, Romanticism and the English Lake District, MA Graphic Novel and Children's Book Illustration.

University of London, Goldsmiths

Goldsmiths, University of London,
London SE14 6NW
tel 020-7919 7171
website www.gold.ac.uk
Facebook www.facebook.com/GoldsmithsUoL
Twitter @GoldsmithsUoL
Instagram @goldsmithsuol

Postgraduate courses include Artists' Film and Moving Image, Art Psychotherapy, Arts and Learning, Black British Literature, Children's Literature, Children's Illustration, Computer Games Art and Design, Creative and Life Writing, Creative Writing and Education, Digital Media, Dramaturgy and Writing for Performance, Film and Screen Studies, Filmmaking, Fine Art, Journalism, Performance Making, Radio, Script Writing and Translation.

The Manchester Writing School at Manchester Metropolitan University

Arts & Humanities Building, Cavendish Street, Manchester M15 6BG
tel 0161 247 1787
email writingschool@mmu.ac.uk
website www.mmu.ac.uk/english/mcr-writing-school
Twitter @McrWritingSchl
Creative Director Professor Carol Ann Duffy, *Contact (admission and general enquiries)* James Draper

Courses offered include Master of Fine Arts (MFA) and Master of Arts (MA) in Creative Writing with specialist routes in Novel, Poetry, Writing for

Children & Young Adults, Scriptwriting and Creative Non-Fiction. Campus-based and international online distance learning, available to study full-time (MA: one year, MFA: two years) or part-time (MA: two years; MFA: three years). September and January enrolment. Scholarships available (including Joyce Nield Fund for non-UK Commonwealth students). Evening taught, with strong industry links. MFA students complete a full-length book/script. MA in Publishing presented in collaboration with the iSchool at Manchester Met and industry partners. PhD in Creative Writing, including PhD by practice.

Nottingham Trent University
School of Arts and Humanities, Clifton Lane, Nottingham NG11 8NS
tel 0115 848 4200
email rory.waterman@ntu.ac.uk
email hum.enquiries@ntu.ac.uk
website www.ntu.ac.uk/course/english-linguistics-creative-writing
Twitter @ntuhum
Programme Leader Dr Rory Waterman

Offers a long-established and practice-based MA Creative Writing. Close links to the writing industry, an annual anthology, a programme of guest talks and workshops and many successful graduate writers. Diverse module options include: Fiction, Poetry, Writing for Stage, Radio and Screen, and Children's and Young Adult Fiction.

Plymouth Marjon University
Derriford Road, Plymouth, PL6 8BH
tel (01752) 636890
email admissions@marjon.ac.uk
website www.marjon.ac.uk/courses/ma-literature-for-children/

Offers MA Literature for Children and Young Adults, which includes creative writing modules.

University of Roehampton
Grove House, Roehampton Lane, London SW15 5PJ
tel 020-8392 3000
website www.roehampton.ac.uk
Facebook www.facebook.com/roehamptonuni
Twitter @RoehamptonUni
Instagram @uni_roehampton

Postgraduate courses include Children's Literature, Journalism, Creative Writing, Screenwriting, Publishing and Film Practices.

University of Southampton
Avenue Campus, Highfield Road, Southampton, Hampshire SO17 1BF
tel 023-8059 5000
email enquiries@southampton.ac.uk
website www.southampton.ac.uk/courses/creative-writing-masters-ma
Course Leader Carole Burns

Offers MA Creative Writing and Publishing, which includes a core module on Writing for Children and Young People.

University of Suffolk
Waterfront Building, 19 Neptune Quay, Ipswich IP4 1QJ
tel (01473) 338833
website www.uos.ac.uk/courses/pg/ma-creative-and-critical-writing

Offers MA Creative and Critical Writing, which includes a module on Children's Literature: Through the Looking Glass.

Publishing practice
Editing your work

If you are publishing, via a traditional publisher or independently, editing your work is an essential part of the process. This article outlines what is involved.

What is editing?

Broadly speaking, editing involves refining your writing ('copy') to make it as readable as possible and thus ready to be published. There are four main editorial stages:
• **Manuscript assessment/critique** is an initial assessment of the strengths and weaknesses of your work, with general suggestions for improvement.
• **Developmental/structural editing** gives more in-depth feedback on aspects of your work such as pace, writing style and appropriate language for your readership, and technical features such as characterisation (fiction) or reference styles (non-fiction).
• **Copy-editing** focuses on the detail, accuracy, completeness and consistency of your text, including grammar, spelling and punctuation.
• **Proofreading** is the final check of the layout and also picks up anything overlooked earlier.

Should I edit my work before submitting it to an agent or publisher?

Most fiction is not submitted direct to a publisher but will find its way to a commissioning or acquisitions editor via a literary agent (see the articles in this *Yearbook* in the *Literary agents* section, which starts on page 211). Some specialist non-fiction can be submitted directly to an appropriate publisher. The listings under *Children's book publishers*, starting on page 22, will indicate if a company accepts unsolicited scripts. In all cases it is important to follow the agent or publisher submission guidelines.

You should always check any submission for basic spelling and grammatical mistakes ('typos') and to ensure that there are no blatant inconsistencies or factual inaccuracies. It is up to you whether you pay a professional editor to do this for you, but you are unlikely to need a full copy-edit of your whole work at this stage. It may help, though, to have an outsider or beta-reader give you feedback.

What if I am self-publishing?

Self-published authors do not have to obtain or pay for editorial advice, but if you want to sell a book that looks as good and reads as well as a professionally produced one, you are unlikely to achieve this on your own. There are a host of individuals and companies available to review and edit your work at all stages in the writing process, and to guide you through design and layout to publication and marketing.

When engaging a professional editor, be cautious and read the small print about what services are being offered and what qualifications the provider has to do the job. Decide what type of help you require and employ people with a track record and recommendations. Importantly, agree a fair price for the work. If you seek out the cheapest offering you are unlikely to get the best result. Writers & Artists offer editorial services for authors.

Look also at the advice, rates, and directory of editorial professionals provided by the Chartered Institute of Editing and Proofreading (www.ciep.uk).

What happens during editing?

While processes differ from publisher to publisher, the sequence of events from draft manuscript to published copy is roughly similar. If you are self-publishing and working direct with an editor the sequence of events will be determined by which services you buy. You should not have your manuscript designed or typeset before it has been edited.

• If your work needs structural or developmental editing the publisher or freelance editor will make suggestions and you will need to revise your work accordingly.

• You will then submit the finished work for copy-editing. You should make sure you follow your publisher's style and formatting guidelines or ask your freelance editor to devise a style guide for you. This will save time in the detailed copy-edit because the text will be made consistent in line with this style guide. The editor or publisher may ask you to answer queries that arise during copy-editing.

• When the text is finalised it will be sent for typesetting or layout. If you are publishing independently, unless you are very experienced, you should find a reputable professional to do your interior page layout for print and ebook and commission a professional cover designer.

• You may be sent one or more sets of proofs of the layout, or your publisher may handle this stage. Again, if you are self-publishing then checking the proofs carefully is up to you. See the handy checklist in the **Common mistakes** box.

• Your work is now ready for publication – and the all-important marketing.

What are the differences between copy-editing and proofreading?

Copy-editing and proofreading are crucial stages in the publishing process and, while the two can often be confused or referred to interchangeably, there are important differences. The copy-editing function normally takes place when your work is complete but before typesetting or design, allowing substantial revisions to be made at minimal cost. Proofreading, on the other hand, typically takes place after your work has been copy-edited and typeset and serves to 'fine-polish' the text to ensure that it is free from editorial and layout inaccuracies.

Copy-editing

This is the essential stage for all writers and should be done after you are happy with the general structure and content of your work. As this is the detailed, line-by-line edit, if you rewrite or add material after this stage your work will need to be edited again. The aim of copy-editing is to ensure that whatever appears in public is accurate, easy to follow, fit for purpose and free of error, omission, inconsistency and repetition. This process picks up embarrassing mistakes, ambiguities and anomalies, alerts you to possible legal problems and marks up your work for the typesetter/designer. Typically, copy-editing involves:

• checking for mistakes in spelling, grammar and punctuation;
• creating a style sheet; applying consistency in spelling, punctuation, capitalisation, etc;
• making sure the text flows well, is logically ordered and is appropriate for your target audience;

• marking up or formatting the structure for the designer – e.g. headings, tables, lists, boxed items, quotes;
• checking any illustrations and figures correspond with what's written in the text;
• checking that any bibliographical references and notes are correctly ordered and styled and that none are missing;
• making sure you have any necessary introductory pages (prelims);
• querying obvious errors of fact, misleading information or parts that are unclear.

How much editing your copy will require (and therefore how long it will take) depends on a number of factors, including:
• the complexity of the subject matter;
• how consistent you have been;
• whether you have correctly followed a publisher's house style (or your own);
• the quality of your writing.

In the past, manuscripts were copy-edited on paper, which was labour-intensive and time-consuming. Nearly all copy-editing is carried out electronically, usually using Microsoft Word (or sometimes a bespoke publishing system). Suggested changes are usually made using the Track Changes function; queries for the author or publisher are often inserted

Common mistakes to look out for when editing and proofreading

• Punctuation mistakes, especially with direct speech and quotations.
• Inadvertently repeated words, e.g. 'and and . . .'.
• Phrases used inappropriately, e.g. 'should of' instead of 'should have' or 'compare to' instead of 'compare with'.
• Apostrophe misuse, e.g. its/it's and plurals (*not* banana's).
• Words with similar spelling or pronunciation but with different meanings used incorrectly, e.g. their/they're/there and effect/affect.
• Mixed use of past and present tenses.
• Use of plural verbs with single subjects (or vice versa), e.g. 'one in five children *are...* ' instead of 'one in five children *is...*' or '[the company] *has* 100 employees and [the company] *provide* free childcare' instead of 'provides' (or 'have' and 'provide').
• Obvious factual errors, e.g. 'the Battle of Hastings in 1766'.
• Inconsistent use of abbreviations and acronyms.
• Abbreviations/acronyms that have not been defined at least once in full.
• Missing bullet points or numbers in a sequenced list.
• Typing errors, e.g. '3' instead of '£'.
• Inconsistent layout of names, addresses, telephone numbers and email/web addresses.
• Incorrect or no use of trademarks, e.g. 'blackberry' instead of 'BlackBerry™'.
• References in the text that do not correspond to footnotes.
• Inaccurate or inadequate cross-referencing.
• Index listings not found on the page given in the index.
• Text inadvertently reordered or cut during the typesetting process.
• Headings wrongly formatted as body text.
• Running heads (at the top of pages) that do not correspond to chapter headings.
• Fonts and font sizes used incorrectly.
• Formatting inconsistencies such as poorly aligned margins or uneven columns.
• Captions/headings omitted from illustrations, photographs or diagrams.
• Illustrations/photographs/diagrams without appropriate copyright references.
• Widows and orphans, i.e. text which runs over page breaks and leaves a word or a line stranded.

using Comments. Copy-editors and publishers work in different ways. You may be asked to work through the changes and comments accepting, rejecting or answering each one; you may be sent a 'clean' edited version to approve; or you may just be sent queries to answer.

Proofreading

As this is the final check for errors and layout problems, you should not make major changes at this stage. You will normally receive proofs as pdf documents, which should be marked up using in-built commenting tools. Learn how to use the strikeout, insertion and commenting tools in your preferred pdf program (the free version of Adobe Reader, for example, will be sufficient). Proofs may be marked-up using proof correction marks (see below), but this is now less common – check with your publisher or editor which method you are expected to use. Some publishers still work with hard copy paper proofs, or you may prefer to work this way yourself, in which case it will be useful to learn to use the main proof correction marks.

What are proofreading symbols and why do I need to know them?

Proofreading symbols (proof correction marks) are the 'shorthand' that some copy-editors and proofreaders use for correcting written material and they are set by the British Standards Institution (BSi). Typesetters, designers and printers also sometimes use these as part of correcting page layout, style and format.

If you are sent a set of page proofs using this method it is important that you have at least a basic understanding of the main marks so that you can interpret corrections that have been made or add your own corrections quickly, uniformly and without any ambiguity. The main proof correction marks you need to know are shown in the tables which follow.

Using the marks

• When proofreading, make a mark in the text to show exactly where the correction needs to be made. The marginal mark is used to specify what needs to be done.
• If there is more than one mark in a line, mark from left to right and use both margins if you need to.
• Every marginal mark should be followed by an oblique stroke, unless it is already followed by the insert mark or the amendment is a delete symbol.
• Circle any comments or notes you write in the margins to distinguish them from the corrections.
• For copy-editing, marks are made in the text only.

Handy proofreading tips

Effective proofreading takes time and practice but by following these tips you'll be able to spot mistakes more quickly and accurately:
• Set aside adequate time for proofreading. It requires concentration and should not be rushed.
• Before starting on a proofreading task, make sure you have easy access to a dictionary and thesaurus, and ensure that you have any relevant style guides for spellings, use of capitals and format/design.

Proof-correction marks

These marks conform to BS 5261C: 2005. In the tables below, 'character' means a letter or individual mark in the text; 'matter' means the content and could be text, a table or a picture.

Marks/symbols for general instructions

INSTRUCTIONS	MARGIN	TEXT
Leave the text in its original state and ignore any marks that have been made: stet (Latin for 'let it stand')	⊘	‗ ‗ ‗ ‗ under the characters to be left as they were
Query for the author/typesetter/ printer/publisher	⍰	A circle should be placed around matter to be queried
Remove non-textual marks	✗	A circle should be placed around marks to be removed
End of change	/	None

Marks/symbols for inserting, deleting and replacing text

INSTRUCTIONS	MARGIN	TEXT
Matter to be inserted	New matter, followed by ⅄	⅄
Additional matter supplied separately	⅄ followed by a letter in a diamond which identifies ◇A additional matter	⅄
Delete a character (and close up)	⌒	/ through the character
Delete text (and close up)	⌒	⊢—⊣ through text
Character to replace marked character	New character, followed by /	/ through the character
Text to replace marked text	New text, followed by /	⊢—⊣ through text

Marks/symbols for grammar and punctuation

INSTRUCTIONS	MARGIN	TEXT
Full stop	⊙	⅄ at insertion point or / through character
Comma	،	As above
Semi-colon	;	As above
Colon	⊙	As above
Hyphen	⊢—⊣	As above
Single quote marks	⸀ or ⸂	As above
Double quote marks	⸌⸍ or ⸜⸝	As above
Apostrophe	⸌	As above
Ellipses or leader dots	⟨⋯⟩	As above
Insert/replace dash	Ⓝ Size of dash to be stated ⊢—⊣ between uprights	As above

Marks/symbols for altering the look/style/layout of text

INSTRUCTIONS	MARGIN	TEXT
Put text in italics	⌣	___ under text to be changed
Remove italics, replace with roman text		Circle text to be changed
Put text in bold	∿∿∿	∿∿∿ under text to be changed
Remove bold		Circle text to be changed
Put text in capitals	≡	≡ under text to be changed
Put text in small capitals	=	= under text to be changed
Put text in lower case	≠ or ≠	Circle text to be changed
Change character to superscript	Y under character	| through character to be changed
Insert a superscript character	Y under character	∧ at point of insertion
Change character to subscript	∧ above character	| through character to be changed
Insert a subscript character	∧ above character	∧ at point of insertion
Remove bold and italics		Circle text to be changed
Paragraph break	⌐	⌐
Remove paragraph break, run on text	∽	∽
Indent text	⊏	⊏
Remove indent	⊐	⊐
Insert or replace space between characters or words	Y	∧ at relevant point of insertion or | through character
Reduce space between characters or words	↑	|
Insert space between lines or paragraphs	Mark extends into margin	—(or)—
Reduce space between lines or paragraphs	Mark extends into margin	→ or ←
Transpose lines	S	S
Transpose characters or words	⊔⌐	⊔⌐
Close space between characters	◠	character ◠ character
Underline words	(underline)	⬭ circle words
Take over character(s) or word(s) to next line/column/page	Mark extends into margin	⊏
Take back character(s) or word(s) to previous line/column/page	Mark extends into margin	⊐

• If possible, proofread the document several times and concentrate on different aspects each time, e.g. sense/tone, format, grammar/punctuation/use of language.
• Always double-check scientific, mathematical or medical symbols as they can often be corrupted during the typesetting process. Accented characters and currency symbols can also cause problems.
• If possible, have a version of the pre-typeset, copy-edited text to refer to while you proofread – it might help solve minor inaccuracies or inconsistencies more quickly.

Further resources

Butcher, Judith; Drake, Caroline and Leach, Maureen, *Butcher's Copy-editing: The Cambridge Handbook for Editors, Copy-editors and Proofreaders* (Cambridge University Press, 4th edn 2006)

Butterfield, J., *Fowler's Dictionary of Modern English Usage* (Oxford University Press, 4th edn 2015)

Hunter, Margaret, *Proofreading or Copyediting? A Quick Guide to Using Editorial Professionals* (CIEP 2020; https://www.ciep.uk/resources/factsheets/#POE)

Ritter, R.M., *New Oxford Dictionary for Writers and Editors: The Essential A-Z Guide to the Written Word* (Oxford University Press, 2nd revised edn 2014)

The Chicago Manual of Style: The Essential Guide for Writers, Editors, and Publishers (University of Chicago Press, 17th edn 2017; www.chicagomanualofstyle.org/home.html)

Waddingham, Anne (ed.), *New Hart's Rules: The Oxford Style Guide* (Oxford University Press, 2nd edn 2014)

The Chartered Institute of Editing and Proofreading (CIEP) offers training, mentoring, support and advice for editors and proofreaders and a freely searchable directory of editorial professionals, www.ciep.uk (see page 346)

This article has been written by three professional editors. **Lauren Simpson** (lauren.simpson73@gmail.com) has over 20 years' experience as an editor, writer, publishing consultant and proofreader. She is currently the Managing Editor at Globe Law and Business. **Margaret Hunter** (daisyeditorial.co.uk) offers copy-editing, proofreading and layout services to businesses, organisations and independent authors. She served on the CIEP Council from 2015 to 2021. **Gerard M-F Hill** (much-better-text.com) served on the CIEP Council from 2007 to 2016 and co-led its successful bid for chartership. He has worked as a copy-editor, indexer, proofreader, consultant and ghostwriter.

ISBNs: what you need to know

The Nielsen BookData ISBN Agency for UK & Ireland receives a large number of enquiries about the ISBN system. The most frequently asked questions are answered here; for more information visit www.nielsenisbnstore.com.

What is an ISBN?

An ISBN is an International Standard Book Number and is 13 digits long.

What is the purpose of an ISBN?

An ISBN is a product number, used by publishers, booksellers and libraries for ordering, listing and stock control purposes. It enables them to identify a particular publisher and allows the publisher to identify a specific edition of a specific title in a specific format within their output.

Contact details

Nielsen BookData ISBN Agency for UK and Ireland
3rd Floor, Midas House, 62 Goldsworth Road, Woking GU21 6LQ
tel (01483) 712215
email isbn.agency@nielseniq.com
website www.nielsenisbnstore.com

Does an ISBN protect copyright?

A widely held belief is that an ISBN protects copyright. It doesn't, it is an identifier, a product code. The copyright belongs to the author. In general, publishers don't tend to buy copyrights for books. They license the copyrights, which the author retains.

What is a publisher?

The publisher is generally the person or organisation taking the financial and other risks in making a product available. For example, if a product goes on sale and sells no copies at all, the publisher loses money. If you get paid anyway, you are likely to be a designer, printer, author or consultant of some kind.

What is the format of an ISBN?

The ISBN is 13 digits long and is divided into five parts separated by spaces or hyphens.
• Prefix element: for the foreseeable future this will be 978 or 979
• Registration group element: identifies a geographic or national grouping. It shows where the publisher is based
• Registrant element: identifies a specific publisher or imprint
• Publication element: identifies a specific edition of a specific title in a specific format
• Check digit: the final digit which mathematically validates the rest of the number
The four parts following the prefix element can be of varying length.
Prior to 1 January 2007 ISBNs were ten digits long; any existing ten-digit ISBNs must be converted by prefixing them with '978' and the check digit must be recalculated using a Modulus 10 system with alternate weights of 1 and 3. The ISBN Agency can help you with this.

Do I *have* to have an ISBN?

There is no legal requirement in the UK and Ireland for an ISBN and it conveys no form of legal or copyright protection. It is simply a product identification number.

Why should I use an ISBN?

If you wish to sell your publication through major bookselling chains, independent book-shops or internet retailers, they will require you to have an ISBN to assist their internal processing and ordering systems.

The ISBN also provides access to bibliographic databases, such as the Nielsen BookData Database, which use ISBNs as references. These databases help booksellers and libraries to provide information for customers. Nielsen BookData has a range of information, electronic trading and retail sales monitoring services which use ISBNs and are vital for the dissemination, trading and monitoring of books in the supply chain. The ISBN there-fore provides access to additional marketing opportunities which could help sales of your product.

Where can I get an ISBN?

ISBNs are assigned to publishers in the country where the publisher's main office is based. This is irrespective of the language of the publication or the intended market for the book.

The ISBN Agency is the national agency for the UK and Republic of Ireland and British Overseas Territories. A publisher based elsewhere will not be able to get numbers from the UK Agency (even if you are a British Citizen) but can contact the Nielsen BookData ISBN Agency for details of the relevant national Agency.

If you are based in the UK and Ireland you can purchase ISBNs online from the Nielsen BookData ISBN Store: www.nielsenisbnstore.com.

How long does it take to get an ISBN?

If you purchase your ISBNs online from the Nielsen BookData ISBN Store you will receive your ISBN allocation within minutes. If you are purchasing ISBNs direct from the ISBN Agency via an off-line application, it can take up to five days. The processing period begins when a correctly completed application is received in the ISBN Agency and payment is received.

How much does it cost to get an ISBN?

Refer to www.nielsenisbnstore.com or email the ISBN Agency: isbn.agency@nielseniq.com.

What if I only want one ISBN?

ISBNs can be bought individually or in blocks of ten or more; visit the ISBN Store to find out more.

Who is eligible for ISBNs?

Any individual or organisation who is publishing a qualifying product for general sale or distribution to the market. By publishing we mean making a work available to the public.

Which products do NOT qualify for ISBNs?

Any publication that is without a defined end should not be assigned an ISBN. For example, publications that are regularly updated and intended to continue indefinitely are not eli-gible for an ISBN.

Some examples of products that do not qualify for an ISBN are:
• Journals, periodicals, serials, newspapers in their entirety (single issues or articles, where these are made available separately, may qualify for ISBN);

Publishing practice

- Abstract entities such as textual works and other abstract creations of intellectual or artistic content;
- Ephemeral printed materials such as advertising matter and the like;
- Customised print-on-demand publications (Publications that are available only on a limited basis, such as customised print-on-demand publications with content specifically tailored to a user's request shall not be assigned an ISBN. If a customised publication is being made available for wider sale, e.g. as a college course pack available through a college book store, then an ISBN may be assigned);
- Printed music;
- Art prints and art folders without title page and text;
- Personal documents (such as a curriculum vitae or personal profile);
- Greetings cards;
- Music sound recordings;
- Software that is intended for any purpose other than educational or instructional;
- Electronic bulletin boards;
- Emails and other digital correspondence;
- Updating websites;
- Games.

Following a review of the UK market, it is now permissible for ISBNs to be assigned to calendars and diaries, provided that they are not intended for purely time-management purposes and that a substantial proportion of their content is textual or graphic.

What is an ISSN?

An International Standard Serial Number. This is the numbering system for journals, magazines, periodicals, newspapers and newsletters. It is administered by the British Library, *tel* (01937) 546959; *email* issn-uk@bl.uk; *website* www.bl.uk/help/Get-an-ISBN-or-ISSN-for-your-publication#

Where do I put the ISBN?

The ISBN should appear on the reverse of the title page, sometimes called the copyright page or the imprint page, and on the outside back cover of the book. If the book has a dust jacket, the ISBN should also appear on the back of this. If the publication is not a book, the ISBN should appear on the product, and on the packaging or inlay card. If the publication is a map, the ISBN should be visible when the map is folded and should also appear near the publisher statement if this is elsewhere.

I am reprinting a book with no changes – do I need a new ISBN?
No.

I am reprinting a book but adding a new chapter – do I need a new ISBN?
Yes. You are adding a significant amount of additional material, altering the content of the book.

I am reprinting a book with a new cover design – should I change the ISBN?
No. A change of cover design with no changes to the content of the book should not have a new ISBN.

I am changing the binding on the book to paperback rather than hardback. Do I need a new ISBN?

Yes. Changes in binding always require new ISBNs even if there are no changes to the content of the book.

I am changing the price – do I need a new ISBN?

No. Price changes with no other changes do not require new ISBNs and in fact must not change the ISBN.

Public Lending Right

Under the PLR system, payment is made from public funds to authors and other contributors (writers, illustrators/photographers, translators, adapters/retellers, ghostwriters, editors/compilers/ abridgers/revisers, narrators and producers) whose books (print, audiobook and ebook) are lent from public libraries. Payment is annual; the amount authors receive is proportionate to the number of times that their books were borrowed during the previous year (July to June).

How the system works

From the applications received, the PLR office compiles a database of authors and books (the PLR Register). A representative sample of book issues is recorded, consisting of all loans from selected public libraries. This is then multiplied in proportion to total library lending to produce, for each book, an estimate of its total annual loans throughout the country. The estimated loans are matched against the database of registered authors and titles to discover how many loans are credited to each registered book for the calculation of PLR payments, using the ISBN printed in the book (see below).

Parliament allocates a sum each year (£6.6 million for 2020/21) for PLR. This fund pays the administrative costs of PLR and reimburses local authorities for recording loans in the sample libraries (see below). The remaining money is divided by the total estimated national loan figure for all registered books in order to work out how much can be paid for each estimated loan of every registered ISBN.

Further information

Public Lending Right – British Library
Boston Spa, Wetherby, West Yorkshire LS23 7BQ
tel (01937) 546030
website www.bl.uk/plr
website www.plrinternational.com
Contact Head of PLR Operations

The UK PLR scheme is administered by the British Library from its offices in Boston Spa. The UK PLR office also provides registration for the Irish PLR scheme on behalf of the Irish Public Lending Remuneration office.
    Application forms, information and publications are all obtainable from the PLR Office. See website for further information on eligibility for PLR, loans statistics and forthcoming developments.

British Library Advisory Committee for Public Lending Right

Advises the British Library Board, the PLR Head of Policy and Engagement and Head of PLR Operations on the operation and future development of the PLR scheme.

Limits on payments

If all the registered interests in an author's books score so few loans that they would earn less than £1 in a year, no payment is due. However, if the books of one registered author score so high that the author's PLR earnings for the year would exceed £6,600, then only £6,600 is paid. (No author can earn more than £6,600 in PLR in any one year.) Money that is not paid out because of these limits belongs to the fund and increases the amounts paid that year to other authors.

The sample

Because it would be expensive and impracticable to attempt to collect loans data from every library authority in the UK, a statistical sampling method is employed instead. The sample represents only public lending libraries – academic, school, private and commercial libraries are not included. Only books which are loaned from public libraries can earn PLR; consultations of books on library premises are excluded.

The sample consists of the entire loans records for a year from libraries in more than 30 public library authorities spread through England, Scotland and Wales, and whole data is collected from Northern Ireland. Sample loans represent around 20% of the national total. All the computerised sampling points in an authority contribute loans data ('multi-site' sampling). The aim is to increase the sample without any significant increase in costs. In order to ensure representative sampling, at least seven libraries are replaced every year and a library cannot stay in the sample for more than four years. Loans are totalled every 12 months for the period 1 July–30 June.

An author's entitlement to PLR depends on the loans accrued by his or her books in the sample. This figure is averaged up to produce first regional and then finally national estimated loans.

ISBNs

The PLR system uses ISBNs (International Standard Book Numbers) to identify books lent and correlate loans with entries on the PLR Register so that payments can be made. ISBNs are required for all registrations. Different editions (e.g. 1st, 2nd, hardback, paperback, large print) of the same book have different ISBNs. See *ISBNs: what you need to know* on page 392.

Authorship

In the PLR system the author of a printed book or ebook is any contributor such as the writer, illustrator, translator, compiler, editor or reviser. Authors must be named on the book's title page, or be able to prove authorship by some other means (e.g. receipt of royalties). The ownership of copyright has no bearing on PLR eligibility. Narrators, producers and abridgers are also eligible to apply for PLR shares in audiobooks and e-audio-books.

Co-authorship/illustrators. In the PLR system the authors of a book are those writers, translators, editors, compilers and illustrators as defined above. Authors must apply for

---

Summary of the 39th year's results

Registration: authors. When registration closed for the 39th year (30 June 2021) there were 57,924 authors and assignees.

Eligible loans. The loans from UK libraries credited to registered books – approximately 33% of all library borrowings – qualify for payment. The remaining loans relate to books that are ineligible for various reasons, to books written by dead or foreign authors, and to books that have simply not been applied for.

Money and payments. PLR's administrative costs are deducted from the fund allocated to the British Library Board annually by Parliament. Total government funding for 2020/21 was £6.6 million. The amount distributed to authors was just over £6 million. The Rate per Loan for 2020/21 was 11.26 pence.

The numbers of authors in various payment categories are as follows:

*301	payments at	£5,000–6,600
371	payments between	£2,500–4,999.99
814	payments between	£1,000–2,499.99
835	payments between	£500–999.99
2,996	payments between	£100–499.99
15,071	payments between	£1–99.99
20,388	TOTAL	

* Includes 217 authors whose book loans reached the maximum threshold

registration before their books can earn PLR and this can be done via the PLR website. There is no restriction on the number of authors who can register shares in any one book as long as they satisfy the eligibility criteria.

Writers and/or illustrators. At least one contributor must be eligible and they must jointly agree what share of PLR each will take based on contribution. This agreement is necessary even if one or two are ineligible or do not wish to register for PLR. The eligible authors will receive the share(s) specified in the application.

Translators. Translators may apply for a 30% fixed share (to be shared equally between joint translators).

Editors and compilers. An editor or compiler may apply to register a 20% share if they have written at least 10% of the book's content or more than ten pages of text in addition to normal editorial work and are named on the title page. Alternatively, editors may register 20% if they have a royalty agreement with the publisher. In the case of joint editors/compilers, the total editor's share should be divided equally.

Audiobooks. PLR shares in audiobooks are fixed by the UK scheme and may not be varied. *Writers* may register a fixed 60% share in an audiobook, providing that it has not been abridged or translated. In cases where the writer has made an additional contribution (e.g. as narrator), she/he may claim both shares. *Narrators* may register a fixed 20% PLR share in an audiobook. *Producers* may register a fixed 20% share in an audiobook. *Abridgers* (in cases where the writer's original text has been abridged prior to recording as an audiobook) qualify for 12% (20% of the writer's share). *Translators* (in cases where the writer's original text has been translated from another language) qualify for 18% (30% of the writer's share). If there is more than one writer, narrator, etc the appropriate shares should be divided equally.

Dead or missing co-authors. Where it is impossible to agree shares with a co-author because that person is dead or untraceable, then the surviving co-author or co-authors may submit an application to register a share which reflects their individual contribution to the book.

Transferring PLR after death. First applications may not be made by the estate of a deceased author. However, if an author registers during their lifetime the PLR in their books can be transferred to a new owner and continues for up to 70 years after the date of their death. The new owner can apply to register new titles if first published one year before, or up to ten years after, the date of the author's death. New editions of existing registered titles can also be registered posthumously.

Residential qualifications. To register for the UK PLR scheme, at the time of application authors must have their only home or principal home in the UK or in any of the other countries within the European Economic Area (i.e. EC member states plus Iceland, Norway and Liechtenstein).

Eligible books

In the PLR system each edition of a book is registered and treated as a separate book. A book is eligible for PLR registration provided that:
- it has an eligible author (or co-author);
- it is printed and bound (paperbacks count as bound);
- it has already been published;
- copies of it have been put on sale, i.e. it is not a free handout;

• the authorship is personal, i.e. not a company or association, and the book is not crown copyright;
• it has an ISBN;
• it is not wholly or mainly a musical score;
• it is not a newspaper, magazine, journal or periodical.

Audiobooks. An audiobook is defined as an 'authored text' or 'a work recorded as a sound recording and consisting mainly of spoken words'. Applications can therefore only be accepted to register audiobooks which meet these requirements and are the equivalent of a printed book. Music, dramatisations and live recordings do not qualify for registration. To qualify for UK PLR in an audiobook contributors should be named on the case in which the audiobook is held; or be able to refer to a contract with the publisher; or be named within the audiobook recording.

Ebooks. Previously only ebooks downloaded to fixed terminals in library premises and then taken away on loan on portable devices to be read elsewhere qualified for PLR payment. Information provided by libraries suggested that the vast majority of ebook and digital audio lending was carried out 'remotely' to home PCs and mobile devices, which meant the loan did not qualify for PLR.

On 27 April 2017 the Digital Economy Bill, which included provision to extend the UK PLR legislation to include remote loans of ebooks from public libraries, received Royal Assent. The new arrangements took effect officially from 1 July 2018, and remote ebook loans data is now collected, and the first payments arising from the newly eligible loans were made in February 2020. The PLR website provides updated information on this legislation.

Statements and payment

Authors with an online account may view their statement online. Only registered authors with an offline account and no registered email address receive a statement posted to their address if a payment is due.

Sampling arrangements

To help minimise the unfairness that arises inevitably from a sampling system, the scheme specifies the eight regions within which authorities and sampling points have to be designated and includes libraries of varying size. Part of the sample drops out by rotation each year to allow fresh libraries to be included. The following library authorities were designated for the year 1 July 2021–30 June 2022 (all are multi-site authorities). This list is based on the nine government regions for England plus Northern Ireland, Scotland and Wales. The composition of the PLR library authority sample changes annually and not all regions have to be represented each year.

• East – Peterborough
• East Midlands – Nottinghamshire, Rutland
• London – Bromley, Croydon, Greenwich, Lewisham
• North East – Northumberland
• North West & Merseyside – Bury, Lancashire, St Helens, Trafford
• South East – Bracknell Forest, Medway, Oxfordshire, South Hamptonshire, West Sussex
• South West – Gloucestershire, Isle of Wight, Plymouth, Shropshire, Wiltshire
• West Midlands – Dudley, Wolverhampton

- Yorkshire & The Humber – Calderdale, Kingston Upon Hull, Leeds, North Lincolnshire
- Northern Ireland – The Northern Ireland Library Authority
- Scotland – Highland, Stirling
- Wales – Bridgend, Carmarthenshire, Newport, Powys.

Participating local authorities are reimbursed on an actual cost basis for additional expenditure incurred in providing loans data to the PLR Office. The extra PLR work mostly consists of modifications to computer programs to accumulate loans data in the local authority computer and to transmit the data to the PLR Office.

Reciprocal arrangements

Reciprocal PLR arrangements now exist with the German, Dutch, Austrian and other European PLR schemes. Authors can apply for overseas PLR for most of these countries through the ALCS (Authors' Licensing and Collecting Society; see page 411). The exception to this rule is Ireland. Authors should now register for Irish PLR through the UK PLR Office. Further information on PLR schemes internationally and recent developments within the EC towards wider recognition of PLR is available from the PLR Office or on the international PLR website.

Glossary of publishing terms

advance

Money paid by a publisher to an author before a book is published which will be covered by future royalties. A publishing contract often allows an author an advance payment against future royalties; the author will not receive any further royalties until the amount paid in advance has been earned by sales of the book.

advance information (AI) sheet

A document that is put together by a publishing company to provide sales and marketing information about a book before publication and can be sent several months before publication to sales representatives. It can incorporate details of the format and contents of the book, key selling points and information about intended readership, as well as information about promotions and reviews.

backlist

The range of books already published by a publisher that are still in print.

blad (book layout and design)

A pre-publication sales and marketing tool. It is often a printed booklet that contains sample pages, images and front and back covers which acts as a preview for promotional use or for sales teams to show to potential retailers, customers or reviewers.

blurb

A short piece of writing or a paragraph that praises and promotes a book, which usually appears on the back or inside cover of the book and may be used in sales and marketing material.

book club edition

An edition of a book specially printed and bound for a book club for sale to its members.

co-edition

The publication of a book by two publishing companies in different countries, where the first company has originated the work and then sells sheets to the second publisher (or licenses the second publisher to reprint the book locally).

commissioning editor

A person who asks authors to write books for the part of the publisher's list for which he or she is responsible or who takes on an author who approaches them direct or via an agent with a proposal. Also called acquisitions editor or acquiring editor (more commonly in the USA). A person who signs-up writers (commissions them to write) an article for a magazine or newspaper.

copy-editor

A person whose job is to check material ready for printing for accuracy, clarity of message and writing style and consistency of typeface, punctuation and layout. Sometimes called a desk editor.

copyright

The legal right, which the creator of an original work has, to only allow copying of the work with permission and sometimes on payment of royalties or a copyright fee. An amendment to the Copyright, Designs and Patents Act (1988) states that in the UK most works are protected for 70 years from the creator's death. The 'copyright page' at the start of a book asserts copyright ownership and author identification.

distributor

Acts as a link between the publisher and retailer. The distributor can receive orders from retailers, ship books, invoice, collect revenue and deal with returns. Distributors often handle books from several publishers. Digital distributors handle ebook distribution.

double-page spread

Two facing pages of an illustrated book.

editor

A person in charge of publishing a newspaper or magazine who makes the final decisions about the content and format. A person in book publishing who has responsibility for the content of a book and can be variously a senior person (editor-in-chief) or day-to-day contact for authors (copy-editor, development editor, commissioning editor, etc).

endmatter

Material at the end of the main body of a book which may be useful to the reader, including references, appendices, indexes and bibliography. Also called back matter.

extent

The number of pages in a book.

folio

A large sheet of paper folded twice across the middle and trimmed to make four pages of a book. Also a page number.

frontlist

New books just published (generally in their first year of publication) or about to be published by a publisher. Promotion of the frontlist is heavy, and the frontlist carries most of a publisher's investment. On the other hand, a backlist which continues to sell is usually the most profitable part of a publisher's list.

imprint

The publisher's or printer's name which appears on the title page of a book or in the bibliographical details; a brand name under which a book is published within a larger publishing company, usually representing a specialised subject area.

inspection copy

A copy of a publication sent or given with time allowed for a decision to purchase or return it. In academic publishing, lecturers can request inspection copies to decide whether to make a book/textbook recommended reading or adopt it as a core textbook for their course.

ISBN

International Standard Book Number.

ISSN

International Standard Serial Number. An international system used on periodicals, magazines, learned journals, etc. The ISSN is formed of eight digits, which refer to the country in which the magazine is published and the title of the publication.

literary agent

Somebody whose job is to negotiate publishing contracts, involving royalties, advances and rights sales on behalf of an author and who earns commission on the proceeds of the sales they negotiate.

moral right

The right of people such as editors, authors or illustrators to have some say in the publication of a work to which they have contributed, even if they do not own the copyright.

out of print or o.p.

Relating to a book of which the publisher has no copies left and which is not going to be reprinted. Print on demand technology, however, means that a book can be kept 'in print' indefinitely.

packager

A company that creates a finished book for a publisher.

PDF/pdf

Portable Document Format. A data file generated from PostScript that is platform-independent,

application-independent and font-independent. Acrobat is Adobe's suite of software used to generate, edit and view pdf files.

picture researcher

A person who looks for pictures relevant to a particular topic, so that they can be used as illustrations in, for example, a book, newspaper or TV programme.

prelims

The initial pages of a book, including the title page and table of contents, which precede the main text. Also called front matter.

pre-press

Before a book goes to press.

print on demand or POD

The facility to print and bind a small number of books at short notice, without the need for a large print run, using digital technology. When an order comes through, a digital file of the book can be printed individually and automatically.

production controller

A person in the production department of a publishing company who deals with printers and other suppliers.

proofreader

A person whose job is to proofread texts to check typeset page presentation and text for errors and to mark up corrections.

publisher

A person or company that publishes books, magazines and/or newspapers.

publisher's agreement

A contract between a publisher and the copyright holder, author, agent or another publisher, which lays down the terms under which the publisher will publish the book for the copyright holder.

publishing contract

An agreement between a publisher and an author by which the author grants the publisher the right to publish the work against payment of a fee, usually in the form of a royalty.

reading fee

Money paid to somebody for reading a manuscript and commenting on it.

recto

Relating to the right-hand page of a book, usually given an odd number.

reprint

Copies of a book made from the original, but with a note in the publication details of the date of reprinting and possibly a new title page and cover design.

rights

The legal right to publish something such as a book, picture or extract from a text.

rights manager

A person who negotiates and coordinates rights sales (e.g. for subsidiary, translation or foreign rights). Often travels to book fairs to negotiate rights sales.

royalty

Money paid to a writer for the right to use his or her property, usually a percentage of sales or an agreed amount per sale.

royalty split

The way in which a royalty is divided between several authors or between author and illustrator.

royalty statement

A printed statement from a publisher showing how much royalty is due to an author.

sans serif

A style of printing letters with all lines of equal thickness and no serifs. Sans faces are less easy to read than seriffed faces and they are rarely used for continuous text, although some magazines use them for text matter.

sensitivity reader

Assesses a manuscript with a particular issue of representation in mind, usually one that they have personal experience of.

serialisation

Publication of a book in parts in a magazine or newspaper.

serif

A small decorative line added to letters in some fonts; a font that uses serifs, such as Times. The addition of serifs keeps the letters apart while at the same time making it possible to link one letter to the next, and makes the letters distinct, in particular the top parts which the reader recognises when reading.

slush pile

Unsolicited manuscripts which are sent to publishers or agents, and which may never be read.

style sheet

A guide listing all the rules of house style for a publishing company which has to be followed by authors and editors.

sub-editor

A person who corrects and checks articles in a newspaper before they are printed.

subsidiary rights

Rights other than the right to publish a book in its first form, e.g. paperback rights; rights to adapt the book; rights to serialise it in a magazine; film and TV rights; audio, ebook, foreign and translation rights.

territory

Areas of the world where the publisher has the rights to publish or can make foreign rights deals.

trade discount

A reduction in price given to a customer in the same trade, as by a publisher to another publisher or to a bookseller.

trade paperback (B format)

A paperback edition of a book that is superior in production quality to a mass-market paperback edition and is similar to a hardback in size 198 x 129mm.

trim size or trimmed size

The measurements of a page of a book after it has been cut, or of a sheet of paper after it has been cut to size.

typesetter

A person or company that 'sets' text and prepares the final layout of the page for printing. It can also now involve XML tagging for ebook creation.

typographic error or typo

A mistake made when keying text or typesetting.

verso

The left-hand page of a book, usually given an even number.

volume rights

The right to publish the work in hardback or paperback (this can now sometimes include ebook).

XML tagging

Inserting tags into the text that can allow it to be converted for ebooks or for use in electronic formats.

Copyright and contracts
Author–Publisher contracts

Publishing contracts can be lengthy, it's helpful to know what types of clauses they are likely to include and why they are there.

If you have an agent, he or she will negotiate your publishing contract on your behalf. Organisations such as the of the Society of Authors (see page 323) and WGGB (see page 326) offer contract review services. A contract is a legal agreement between two parties and exists to protect both author and publisher. It includes clauses on rights and obligations to avoid ambiguity as to the responsibilities of both parties. The clauses in your publishing contract are likely to include those listed below.

Definitions used throughout the contract will often be included at the beginning or in an appendix, and might include terms such as 'Net receipts', 'Hybrid Product', 'First Serial', 'Territory', and 'Electronic Book'.

Legal operation and enforcement of the contract is covered by a few standard clauses, such as those relating to 'Interpretation', 'Arbitration', 'Confidentiality', 'Notices' and 'Entire Agreement'.

Free to publish

The author confirms that she is able to enter into the agreement and that the book she is writing is a unique, new property, her own work and will not contain any legally compromising material. Note that the first example below indicates the style of legalese in which your contract is likely to be couched:

Exclusivity 'The Author hereby grants to the Publishers during the legal term of copyright the sole and exclusive licence to publish the said work in volume form.'

Warranty and indemnity are confirmed, meaning the author states that she is freely able to enter into the agreement, is the sole author, owns the rights in the 'work' and that it is unique, i.e. has not been published elsewhere previously and does not contain any libellous or defamatory material or content that isn't hers to include, i.e. that is someone else's copyright and that the author has cleared permissions with the copyright holder for any part of somebody else's work being reproduced in the book. The author agrees to cover any legal costs, other fees or losses if she is in any way in breach of the warranty.

Territory

This is the geographical areas where the book can be sold, for example UK and Europe, or North American, or World territories.

Rights

Legal Term is the period that the contract covers, from date of signature of the contract by both parties or until rights are reverted to the author.

Granting and Reversion An author agrees that the publisher is allowed to publish their Work during the legal term. Rights might revert (back to the author) automatically when sales dip below a minimum annual level, of say fifty copies. An author may negotiate to have rights in their book reverted and will be able to purchase any remaining stock. At that stage the contract is also formally terminated.

Termination might also occur if either party breaches any of the terms of the contract, for example if the author fails to deliver a manuscript of the quality expected on time and if it is found to be plagiarised. Late delivery alone would not usually be grounds for termination, but an author should always inform the agent or publisher if a contracted delivery date cannot be fulfilled.

Copyright Notice and Infringement This covers how the author's name will appear in the book, i.e. © name of author, 20XX. These clauses confirm that copyright in the Work is the property of the author. They will also make it clear that, if the publisher decides to protect the copyright of a book insofar as it threatens the value of the rights sold to a publisher, the author will assist the publisher (at the publisher's expense).

Subsidiary rights include:
• Anthology and quotation rights
• Broadcast reading and audiobook rights
• Digital and electronic rights
• Dramatisation, film, documentary, television sound broadcasting video or other mechanical reproduction rights
• English language rights (royalty exclusive)
• First serial rights (first place e.g. in a magazine where an extract from an original Work is serialised or published)
• Large print, educational, reprint or paperback rights licensed to a book club or to another publisher
• Micrography reprography, merchandising and manufacturing rights
• Second serial rights (rights sold subsequent to the first serial rights, see above)
• Single-extract or digest or book condensation rights
• Translation rights (royalty exclusive)
• US rights (royalty exclusive)

Each set of rights will be subject to a royalty percentage, payable to the author when these rights have been exercised. Some rights are held back or retained by an agent or author, so they might be exploited at another time and be subject to negotiation with a third party after publication. These tend to be the potentially more lucrative rights if exploited, such as dramatisation and film, translation or audio. Some 'hybrid' authors will license print rights to a publisher but retain digital book rights to allow them to self-publish in that format; a contract would make clear in which territories each edition might be sold.

Practicalities

Delivery – this will include a realistic delivery date and the specifications as to what will be delivered in what format (e.g. complete digital manuscript), to what extent (70,000 words including any endmatter) and accompanied by any material (extracts, quotations) for which copyright might need to be cleared.

Payments

Advances The advance is an example of financial goodwill, a pact that author and editor have cemented through the contract to agree to work together and to make money from the activity. It is usually paid in two or three equal tranches, payable on signature of the contract, on delivery and approval of the final manuscript, and on first publication. The advance against royalties means a payment made before any actual revenue from sales of your book have been received.

Royalties are the fees paid to an author on the sale of copies of their book and are subject to sliding scales, so that as a book becomes more successful an author benefits more. As more and more copies are sold the investment the publisher made in producing the first print run will be recouped; subsequent runs might become very profitable for the publisher and rightly an agent will argue for an author to profit from this success too. Such rising royalty rates for a published price contract might look something like this:

• **on home sales:** 7.5 per cent of the published price on the first ten thousand (10,000) copies sold; 10 per cent of the published price up to twenty thousand (20,000) copies sold and 12.5 per cent of the published price on all copies sold thereafter, such royalty not to be deemed a precedent between the Publishers and Author or agent;

• **on home sales where the discount is 52.5 per cent or more:** four-fifths (4/5ths) of the prevailing royalty; on home sales where the discount is 60 per cent or more: three-fifths (3/5ths) of the prevailing rate.

Free and presentation copies will be provided to the author (anywhere between six and fifteen free copies) on publication and to potential reviewers as part of a promotional campaign; royalty payments are not made against these gratis copies. Authors may purchase copies of their own book at discount.

Payment process, accounting periods and other details about how and when the publisher will remunerate the author (or their agent on the author's behalf) will be included.

Publishing process

Author corrections and their proofreading responsibilities might be clearly laid out, covering what checking tasks an author will be expected to undertake and when and which might be carried out and paid for by the publisher, such as having an index prepared or clearing permissions for images or quotations. It might also include a clause in which the publisher 'reserves the right to charge the Author' for the cost of author corrections to page proofs if these are over and above the usual level of alterations. Such costs might be debited against the author's royalty account.

Promotion clauses advise that a publisher shall advertise, promote and market the Work as they deem appropriate 'in their sole discretion'. If you feel strongly as an author that you wish to be consulted about any aspect of promotion or cover design you could ask for such clauses to be modified. The most you are likely to get is an amendment that agrees an author will be 'consulted' and asked to 'agree' to the publisher's plan and that their agreement 'will not be unreasonably withheld'.

Publication date might not be firmly set when the contract is signed but the publisher's commissioning editor should have a clear idea of what quarter they would like the book to appear in. An agreement would usually stipulate that the book should be published within twelve months of date of delivery and acceptance 'unless prevented by circumstances over which they have no control or unless mutually agreed'.

New and updated editions for non-fiction titles might be referred to, defining what would constitute a 'new' rather than a 'revised' edition and how much new content it might include, say at least 10 per cent new material. The author would be offered first refusal on preparing a new edition, but the publisher would want to include a clause to allow them to ask another writer to complete such a project if they perceived there was a market for it, but the original author was unable or unwilling to take on the commission.

The contract should not daunt an author. It is supposed to be a joint declaration and not biased in favour of one party or the other.

By **Alysoun Owen**, Editor of the *Writers' & Artists' Yearbook* and author of the *Writers' & Artists' Guide to Getting Published* (Bloomsbury 2019).

Copyright Licensing Agency Ltd

The Copyright Licensing Agency (CLA) is a non-profit body established to help organisations to legally copy and share extracts from published works.

It is recognised by the government (www.gov.uk/copyright-licensing-agency-licence) as the collective licensing body for the reuse of text and images from books, journals and magazines. More information on collective licensing bodies can be found at: www.gov.uk/guidance/licensing-bodies-and-collective-management-organisations.

It licenses on behalf of its four members: ALCS (the Authors' Licensing and Collecting Society), PLS (Publishers' Licensing Services), DACS (The Design and Artists Copyright Society) and PICSEL (Picture Industry Collecting Society for Effective Licensing).

CLA's licences permit limited copying, including photocopying, scanning and emailing of articles and extracts from books, journals and magazines, as well as digital copying from electronic publications, online titles and websites. CLA issues its licences to schools, further and higher education, businesses and government bodies. The money collected is distributed to the copyright owners to ensure that they are fairly rewarded for the use of their intellectual property. It gives licensees protection against the risk of copyright infringement and includes an indemnity against legal action, offering a simple solution to copyright compliance.

How CLA helps creators and users of copyright work

CLA provides content users with access to millions of titles worldwide. In return, CLA ensures that creators, artists, photographers and writers, along with publishers, are paid royalties for the copying, sharing and re-use of limited extracts of their published work.

Further information

The Copyright Licensing Agency Ltd
5th Floor, Shackleton House,
4 Battle Bridge Lane, London SE1 2HX
tel 020-7400 3100
email cla@cla.co.uk
website www.cla.co.uk

Through this collective licensing system CLA provides users with the simplest and most cost-effective means of obtaining authorisation for the use of their work.

CLA has licences which enable digitisation of existing print material, enabling users to scan and electronically send extracts from print copyright works as well as copy digital electronic and online publications, including websites.

Who is licensed?

CLA offers licences to three principal sectors:
• education (schools, further and higher education);
• government (central departments, local authorities, public bodies); and
• business (businesses, industry and the professions).

The licences meet the specific needs of each sector and user groups within each sector. Depending upon the requirement, there are both blanket and transactional licences available. Every licence allows copying from most print and digital books, journals, magazines and periodicals published in the UK.

The international dimension

Many countries have established equivalents to CLA and the number of such agencies is set to grow. Nearly all these agencies, including CLA, are members of the International Federation of Reproduction Rights Organisations (IFRRO).

Through reciprocal arrangements covering 38 overseas territories, including the USA, Canada and most EU countries, CLA's licences allow copying from an expanding list of international publications. CLA receives monies from these territories for the copying of UK material abroad, passing it on to UK rights holders.

Distribution of licence fees

The fees collected from licensees are forwarded to ALCS, PLS, DACS and PISCEL for distribution to publishers, writers and visual artists. The allocation of fees is based on subscriptions, library holdings and detailed surveys of copying activity (see www.cla.co.uk/who-we-represent and read the 'Distribution Model Report'). CLA has collected and distributed over £1.5 billion as royalties to copyright owners since 1983. For the year 2020/21, £78.2 million was paid to creators and publishers in the UK and abroad.

Copyright made simple

The CLA exists to simplify copyright for content users and copyright owners. They help their customers to legally access, copy and share published content while making sure copyright owners are paid royalties for the use of their work.

Their rights, licences and innovative digital services (including the Digital Content Store for Higher Education; and the Education Platform for UK schools (www.educationplatform.co.uk)) make it easy for content users to use and manage digitalised content and digital versions of books. By doing so they simplify access to the work of 100,000 authors, 25,000 visual artists and 3,500 publishers and play an important part in supporting the creative industries.

Authors' Licensing and Collecting Society

ALCS is the rights management society for UK writers.

ALCS is the largest writers' organisation in the UK with a membership of over 114,000. In the financial year of 2020/21, it paid 110,000 writers over £38.3 million (net) in royalties. Once you've paid your £36 lifetime membership fee, whatever you've earned in secondary royalties is paid into your bank account during twice yearly distributions. You can be part of this organisation which is committed to ensuring that writers' intellectual and moral rights are fully respected and fairly rewarded. ALCS represents all types of writers and includes educational, research and academic authors drawn from the professions, scriptwriters, adapters, playwrights, poets, editors and freelance journalists, across the print and broadcast media.

Established in 1977, ALCS (a non-profit company) was set up in the wake of the campaign to establish a Public Lending Right (see page 396) to help writers protect and exploit their collective rights. The organisation now represents the interests of all UK writers and aims to ensure that they are fairly compensated for any works that are copied, broadcast or recorded.

Internationally recognised as a leading authority on copyright matters and authors' interests, ALCS is committed to fostering an awareness of intellectual property issues among the writing community. It maintains a close watching brief on all matters affecting copyright, both in the UK and internationally, and makes regular representations to the UK government and the European Union.

ALCS collects fees that are difficult, time-consuming or legally impossible for writers and their representatives to claim on an individual basis, money that is nonetheless due to them. To date, it has distributed over £570 million in secondary royalties to writers. Over the years, ALCS has developed highly specialised knowledge and sophisticated systems that can track writers and their works against any secondary use for which they are due payment. A network of international contacts and reciprocal agreements with foreign collecting societies also ensures that UK writers are compensated for any similar use overseas.

The primary sources of fees due to writers are secondary royalties from the following:

Membership

Authors' Licensing and Collecting Society Ltd
5th Floor, Shackleton House,
4 Battle Bridge Lane, London SE1 2HX
tel 020-7264 5700
email alcs@alcs.co.uk
website www.alcs.co.uk
Chief Executive Owen Atkinson

Membership is open to all writers and successors to their estates at a one-off fee of £36. Members of the Society of Authors, the Writers' Guild of Great Britain, National Union of Journalists, Chartered Institute of Journalists and British Association of Journalists have free membership of ALCS. Operations are primarily funded through a commission levied on distributions and membership fees. The commission on funds generated for Ordinary members is currently 9.5%. Most writers will find that this, together with a number of other membership benefits, provides good value.

Photocopying and scanning

The single largest source of income, this is administered by the Copyright Licensing Agency (CLA; see page 409). Created in 1982 by ALCS and the Publishers' Licensing Services (PLS), CLA grants licences to users for copying books and serials. This includes schools, colleges, universities, central and local government departments, as well as the British Library, businesses and other institutions. Licence fees are based on the number of people who benefit and the number of copies made. The revenue from this is then split between the rights holders: authors, publishers and artists. Money due to authors is transferred to ALCS for distribution. ALCS also receives photocopying payments from foreign sources.

Foreign Public Lending Right

The Public Lending Right (PLR) system pays authors whose books are borrowed from public libraries. Through reciprocal agreements, ALCS members receive payment through a number of overseas Public Lending Right (PLR) schemes, currently from Germany, Belgium, the Netherlands, France, Austria, Estonia and Ireland. Please note that ALCS does not administer the UK Public Lending Right; this is managed directly by the UK PLR Office (see page 396).

Simultaneous cable retransmission

This involves the simultaneous showing of one country's television signals in another country, via a cable network. Cable companies pay a central collecting organisation a percentage of their subscription fees, which must be collectively administered. This sum is then divided by the rights holders. ALCS receives the writers' share for British programmes containing literary and dramatic material and distributes it to them.

Educational recording

ALCS, together with the main broadcasters and rights holders, set up the Educational Recording Agency (ERA) in 1989 to offer licences to educational establishments. ERA collects fees from the licensees and pays ALCS the amount due to writers for their literary works.

Other sources of income include a blank tape levy and small, miscellaneous literary rights.

Tracing authors

ALCS is dedicated to protecting and promoting authors' rights and enabling writers to maximise their income. It is committed to ensuring that royalties due to writers are efficiently collected and speedily distributed to them. One of its greatest challenges is finding some of the writers for whom it holds funds and ensuring that they claim their money.

Any published author or broadcast writer could have some funds held by ALCS for them. It may be a nominal sum or it could run into several thousand pounds. Either call or visit the ALCS website – see **Membership** box for contact details.

DACS (Design and Artists Copyright Society)

Established by artists for artists, DACS is the UK's leading visual artists' rights management organisation.

Established by artists for artists, DACS is a not-for-profit visual arts rights management organisation. It collects and distributes royalties to visual artists and their estates through its different services, including Payback, Artist's Resale Right and Artimage Services, and also campaigns on behalf of their rights.

Contact details

DACS
33 Old Bethnal Green Road, London E2 6AA
tel 020-7336 8811
email info@dacs.org.uk
website www.dacs.org.uk
Membership Free to join

DACS is part of an international network of rights management organisations. Today DACS acts as a trusted broker for over 180,000 artists worldwide and in 2020 it distributed £15.2 million in royalties to artists and estates. See website for more information about DACS and its services.

Payback

Each year DACS pays a share of royalties to visual artists whose work has been reproduced in UK magazines and books or broadcast on UK television channels. DACS operates this service for situations where it would be impractical or near impossible for an artist to license their rights on an individual basis, for example when a business wants to photocopy pages from a book that features their work.

Artist's Resale Right

The Artist's Resale Right entitles artists to a royalty each time their work is resold for €1,000 or more by an auction house, gallery or dealer. DACS ensures artists receive their royalties from qualifying sales not just in the UK but also from other countries in the European Economic Area (EEA). Since 1 January 2012 in the UK, artists' heirs and beneficiaries can now benefit from these royalties. (See website for details of eligibility criteria.)

Artimage Services

This service benefits artists and their estates when their work is reproduced for commercial purposes, for example on t-shirts or greetings cards, in a book or on a website. DACS can take care of everything on behalf of the artist, ensuring terms, fees and contractual arrangements are all in order and in their best interests. Artists who use this service are also represented globally through the DACS international network of rights management organisations.

Copyright facts

• Copyright is a right granted to visual artists under law.
• Copyright in all artistic works is established from the moment of creation – the only qualification is that the work must be original.

• There is no registration system in the UK; copyright comes into operation automatically and lasts the lifetime of the visual artist plus a period of 70 years after their death.

• After death, copyright is usually transferred to the visual artist's heirs or beneficiaries. When the 70-year period has expired, the work then enters the public domain and no longer benefits from copyright protection.

• The copyright owner has the exclusive right to authorise the reproduction (or copy) of a work in any medium by any other party.

• Any reproduction can only take place with the copyright owner's consent.

• Permission is usually granted in return for a fee, which enables the visual artist to derive some income from other people using his or her work.

• If a visual artist is commissioned to produce a work, he or she will usually retain the copyright unless an agreement is signed which specifically assigns the copyright. When visual creators are employees and create work during the course of their employment, the employer retains the copyright in those works.

Money, tax and benefits
Managing your finances: a guide for writers

Chartered accountants Jonathan and Louise Ford of Writers Tax Limited set out a clear view of the various financial issues that a writer needs to understand and consider at each stage of their writing career, with helpful links and valuable advice.

In some ways the financial issues of being a writer are no different to pursuing any other occupation. You earn money for your skill, you deduct the costs you have incurred earning your money, and you pay tax on what's left. However, there are several factors that, in combination, make the situation of a writer unique; many writers have income from multiple sources, as well as overseas tax issues and matters concerning copyright.

We'll look at the different stages of a writer's career and the financial aspects s/he may need to consider as their career develops: 1) getting started – unpaid writing done for love not money; 2) paid writing often running alongside traditional employed income; 3) paid writing as main source of income; 4) life-long considerations.

Stage 1: getting started

When you're at an early stage of your writing career and not earning any money from it, there is little you need to do to stay compliant. However, there are still some important things you can consider.

Setting up a dormant limited company

If you are planning to write a book and you would like the royalty income of that book to be held in a limited company, then consider setting up a company even before you start writing. This will allow you to write the book on behalf of your company. If you wait to set the company up until the book is complete, and publishers are interested, then you would have to transfer the copyright of the book to the company at market value; this

Do I need an accountant?

If your financial situation is straightforward, there may be no need for you to appoint an accountant. If you are employed, then PAYE usually does a reasonable job of collecting the right amount of tax. Your writing income may be quite modest so it should be straightforward to deal with and – if the numbers are not very big – it may not cause too many issues if you get things wrong. To help you as your career develops, a good accountant can do the following:

- Deal with HMRC on your behalf;
- Submit your tax returns on time, so you don't get penalties for being late;
- Make sure you are claiming for the things you can claim for (and not claiming for things you shouldn't);
- Advise you on ways of saving tax legitimately;
- Help you to keep your records accurately;
- Help you to avoid nasty surprises and unexpected tax bills;
- Be on hand for all your tax related questions.

Anybody can call themselves an accountant, even if they have no qualifications or experience. Try to choose someone who is a member of a professional accountancy body, such as ICAEW, ICAS, AAT, ACCA or CIOT. It is also worth getting recommendations from other writers. Social media groups can be a useful source when looking for accountants who act for lots of writers and understand their needs.

could cause issues in terms of valuing the copyright and can create a tax problem that could have been avoided. To decide whether this is right for you, you need to weigh up the cost and hassle of having a dormant limited company against the possible future advantages.

Creative averaging

There are a number of conditions you need to satisfy to be eligible for creative averaging; more details are available on HMRC Helpsheet HS234. One such condition is that you cannot use your first year of trading as part of any creative averaging calculation. Using the example given in the box, Theo would need to be submitting information to HMRC about his writing business from the 2019/20 tax year to be able to claim Creative Averaging in 2021/22.

Loss relief against other income

It is possible for a sole trader to make a loss and to set that loss against other income. This can be beneficial for tax reasons. For example, if an author makes a loss of £5,000 and they also have *employed income* of £30,000, they could offset the £5,000 loss against their employed income so that they only have to pay tax on £25,000. To be able to offset losses against other income, you need to be able to show HMRC that the loss has been incurred on a commercial basis with a view to making a profit. A vague idea that one day you might write a book on Greece would not be sufficient evidence to get a tax deduction on the costs of your holiday.

Creative averaging example

Theo earns nothing in the tax year 2019/20 while he is writing his novel.

In 2021/22 his book is published and he makes a profit of £30,000. Without creative averaging his tax bill in 2020/21 would be nothing, but in 2021/22 he would owe £3,486 income tax and £1,997.48 in National Insurance – a total of £5,483.48.

If he elects to use creative averaging, his £30,000 profit would be split across both tax years, giving him a total tax bill of £1,153.60 in 2020/21 and of £1,133.48 in 2021/22. By choosing to use creative averaging, Theo would have saved £3,194.40 over the two tax years.

Pre-trading expenses

If you haven't been reporting expenditure to HMRC as losses, then it is still possible to get tax relief for 'pre-trading expenditure'. The relief allows you to claim for expenditure incurred within seven years of starting to trade and, in effect, gives tax relief as if it was incurred on the first day of trading. The 'wholly and exclusive' rule will still apply, so it is important to be able to link the expenditure you are claiming to the income you are receiving. The stronger the link, the more likely HMRC are to accept it. In order to maximise any possible pre-trading expenditure claim, it is important to try and keep records and receipts *just in case* you might need them in the future.

Stage 2: paid writing as additional income

Most writers at this stage will still be running their writing business as a sole trader (or freelancer – there is no difference in terms of tax). Legally you don't need to do anything to set up as a sole trader. As soon as you start writing with a view to making a profit, you've become a sole trader. The tax system is very flexible. You can have a part-time employed job, be a partner in a bookshop and be a published author, all at the same time. Important things to consider at this stage are:

Registering with HMRC

If you earn more than £1,000 from self-employment you need to register as a sole trader with HMRC. You can do this at www.gov.uk/register-for-self-assessment/self-employed. You need to register by 5 October in your second tax year (tax years run from 6 April to 5 April).

For example, if you started on 20 November 2021 (tax year 2021/22) then you would need to register with HMRC by 5 October 2022 (tax year 2021/22). You would then get sent a tax return to complete by 31 January 2023 if filing online or 31 October 2022 if filing by paper.

Submitting a tax return

The tax system is called Self Assessment and this means that it is necessary for you to assess what rules and regulations apply to your tax position. There are a range of penalties that HMRC levy and, although it is possible in certain circumstances to appeal the penalties, it is well worth doing all you can to avoid them in the first place.

Keeping records

A self-employed person needs to keep records for at least 5 years from 31 January following the tax year they relate to. For example, if you have transactions in the tax year to 5 April 2022, you need to keep your records until 31 January 2028. You can keep records digitally or on paper. You should keep copies of bank statements, contracts, receipts for expenditure you are claiming for and any invoices you have raised. It is also worth keeping a note of any unusual non-business transactions. If you win £1,000 at the races or get a generous gift from Aunt Ethel, you want to be able to prove this wasn't undeclared income from writing.

It is usually a good idea to have a separate business bank account that you use just for your writing income. This will help to keep things organised and could give you a little more privacy, as your accountant – and possibly HMRC – don't have to look through all your private outgoings.

HMRC Self Assessment penalties

Late filing

Up to 3 months late £100, plus

after 3 months £10 per day for 90 days, plus

after 3 months penalties accrue at regular intervals based on 5% of the tax due or £300 – whichever is the greater.

You can estimate your penalty at www.gov.uk/estimate-self-assessment-penalties.

Late payment of tax

5% of tax due if not paid within 30 days with further 5% penalties every 6 months.

Interest is also charged (currently 3%).

Incorrect returns

Penalties are charged for tax returns that HMRC consider to be incorrect. There is an appeals process. The penalties are all behaviour based and are as follows:

• Careless errors – 0% to 30% of the additional tax due.

• Deliberate errors – 20% to 70% of the additional tax due.

• Deliberate and concealed errors – 30% to 100% of the additional tax due.

Claiming expenses

A writer pays tax on their profit. Profit is income less allowable costs, often referred to as 'expenses'. Sometimes people talk about things being 'tax deductible', which means they can be deducted from your profit before calculating the tax bill, rather than being deducted from your tax bill. For example, if a higher-rate tax payer spends £100 on stationery, this is tax deductible and so it will reduce her profits by £100 and save income tax at 40%, i.e. £40.

Trading allowance

You can claim a £1,000 Trading Allowance against your self-employed income instead of claiming for expenses you have incurred. You cannot claim the Trading Allowance and expenses at the same time. Claiming the Trading Allowance would be suitable when the Trading Allowance is more than the expenses incurred. However, you can't use the Trading Allowance to turn your profit into a loss. There are also restrictions to prevent you from using the Trading Allowance if the income is received from a business controlled by you, or by someone connected to you.

What can you claim for?

The rule is that an expense must be 'wholly and exclusively' for the purpose of your business. Typical costs are:
• Accountancy
• Advertising costs
• Agent commission
• Bank charges
• Computing and IT costs
• Printing, postage and stationery
• Professional subscriptions
• Internet and telephone
• Software subscriptions
• Research costs
• Travel

Some costs may have an element of private use. In this case, HMRC will allow the cost to be apportioned provided you can justify the calculation. For example:
• Motor expenses – may be apportioned according to business use.
• Home as office – apportioned according to rooms and time spent in use.
Alternatively, you may be able to use HMRC Simplified Expenses. You can find more details at www.gov.uk/simpler-income-tax-simplified-expenses.

Cloud bookkeeping

Recent years have seen the development of relatively cheap, simple bookkeeping packages like Xero and Quickbooks. These allow you to link up your business bank account to your accounting records, so you can quickly and accurately keep track of your income and expenditure. They have the advantage of being regularly backed up, less prone to error, and easy to use. You can also store your receipts and paperwork digitally. As the UK moves towards a new system of reporting called Making Tax Digital from April 2024 (delayed from the original date of 2023), it will become more important to be able to easily record and report your income.

Prizes and bursaries

There are many prizes and awards open to authors and other creatives, and entering competitions or seeking awards is a normal part of these professions and a good way for them to obtain extra income from their work. Such prizes are usually taxable. However, there are exceptions. When a prize is unsolicited, and awarded as a mark of honour, distinction or public esteem in recognition of outstanding achievement in a particular field, it won't be taxable. For example, if your publisher or agent enters you for a competition without your knowledge or consent, any prize money received should not be taxable.

Payments on account

For self-employed people the tax system can require payments on account of tax to be made every six months. Each payment on account is half of the previous year's tax bill.

For example: Jo's first year of trading is the tax year 2020/21; she owes tax of £4,000 for the 2021/22 tax year which is due for payment by 31 January 2023. Also, on 31 January 2023 she'll need to pay a payment on account of £2,000 towards her 2022/23 tax bill. She'll have to make a further payment of £2,000 in July 2023. Her actual tax bill for 2022/23 is £5,000. In January 2024 her payments will be:

	£
Tax due for tax year 2022/23	5,000
Less:	
Payment on account - paid 31 January 2023	2,000
Payment on account - paid 31 July 2023	2,000
Balance for 2022/23	1,000
Add:	
Payment on account for 2023/24 (50% of £5,000)	2,500
Total due 31 January 2024	3,500

When income is rising, payments on account can catch out the unwary, as each January there is both a shortfall of tax and a new, higher payment on account to pay. A sensible approach is to save for your tax throughout the year and to complete your tax return early in the tax year, so you have plenty of notice if the bill is higher than expected.

When income is falling (or ceasing) then it is possible to make a claim to HMRC to reduce payments on account so that you don't pay tax in advance that is more than necessary. If the payments on account you make are more than your tax bill, these will be offset against your next payments on account or refunded to you.

Setting up a limited company as a 'money box'

If you already have a paid job, then it's possible that your additional income from writing may take your total income into a higher tax band. If you don't need the money now, setting up a limited company could mean that the company pays corporation tax at a lower rate.

For example, Jamie earns £50,000 through his employment; he also receives £1,820 in Child Benefit in respect of his two children. He earns a further £10,000 in profit as a writer. He doesn't need to access the additional money now and is happy to leave it in his company. His tax liability as a sole trader can be compared with that of the limited company as follows:

Money, tax and benefits

Sole trader	£
Income tax on £10,000 @ 40%	4,000
High Income Child Benefit Tax Charge	1,820
Total due	5,820

Limited company	£
Corporation tax on £10,000 @ 19%	1,900
Total due	1,900

Although this is an extreme example, it shows that through using a limited company Jamie has saved £3,920 of tax on £10,000 of income. Once Jamie wants to take the money out of the company, it will be taxable on him personally, but he can control the amount paid so that it is covered by his personal allowance entirely or subject to a lower rate of tax than he is paying now. If Jamie's plans are to build up a savings buffer, so that one day he can take the plunge and become a full-time writer, then this could be of real benefit.

Stage 3: writing as main source of income
Typically, a writer at this stage will either be self-employed or trade through a limited company. A limited company has to be 'incorporated' at Companies House and, once it is set up, it exists as a legal entity. It can enter into contracts, have a bank account, and exist without you. It is possible to trade both as a sole trader and through a limited company. It may even be the case that an author has some of their books taxed as a sole trader and other titles taxed within a limited company.

Issues on incorporation
If you do trade through a limited company, it is important to ensure that the underlying paperwork is correct. Here are some issues to bear in mind:
• For a company to receive copyright income, it must be legally entitled to the income. This can be achieved by ensuring the company exists before the book has been written and a service contract is in place between the director (i.e. the author) and the company.
• It isn't sufficient to simply 'bank' any proceeds into your company. All contracts need to be properly drawn up in the company's name.
• If you simply give your copyright to your company, it can create a tax issue; HMRC will expect you to pay income tax on the market value of the gift and will also expect the

IR35

IR35 was introduced in April 2000 to stop the practice of employees setting up a limited company (a 'personal service company') and invoicing their employer for their work rather than being paid as an employee. This practice led to a large tax saving for both the employer and the employee.

IR35 only applies to limited companies, so a writer who is trading as a sole trader can ignore it. From April 2021 both public entities and larger private companies will have to look at the status of people working through personal service companies and, if necessary, deduct tax and National Insurance.

For most writers operating through a personal service company, it will be clear that they are not working for anyone as disguised employment. For other writers the situation may be more uncertain. For example, a copywriter with their own company providing weekly content for a client who describes them as their 'Content Manager', pays them a regular salary, expects them to attend meetings on site and doesn't allow a substitute, may be caught by the IR35 rules.

The IR35 rules are complex and, if caught by the rules, your limited company has to pay out most of the money it receives as a salary to the employee – together with Employers National Insurance.

Specialist help should be sought if you think your company may be affected by IR35.

company to pay tax on the income it receives. In effect, the same income could be taxed twice.

• It is possible to sell the copyright to the company. This results in a better tax position, as the company would be able to get some tax relief for the cost of the copyright, but it will require a valuation of the copyright which brings with it costs and some uncertainty.

• Once your company owns the copyright, royalty income is 'locked' into being paid to the company. If you wished to own the copyright personally, it would need to be transferred out of the company at a fair value. You may find you have a company for a much longer time than you first anticipate, because it may not be practical to close it down until the copyright has a negligible value.

VAT

VAT (Value Added Tax) is a tax that businesses are required to charge their customers for goods or services. A writer is no different from any other business and therefore must charge VAT when supplying writing services. The standard UK rate of VAT is currently 20%. VAT is a complicated subject and much of it is beyond the scope of this book. However, there are some key things a writer should be aware of.

A VAT-registered business usually submits a quarterly VAT return within one month and seven days of the end of the VAT quarter. Any VAT due is then paid by the same deadline. Being VAT-registered is not entirely bad news; a VAT-registered business has to charge VAT on their relevant services, but they can also claim back VAT on things they buy for their business. For example, in the VAT quarter ending 31 December 2022 a writer gets a publishing deal for £10,000 plus £2,000 of VAT. Their agent charges them £1,500 plus £300 VAT, and they buy a computer for writing for £500 plus £100 VAT. They would submit a VAT return to HMRC by 7 February 2023 and pay over £1,600, as follows:

	£
VAT charged	2,000
Less:	
VAT on agent's fees	300
VAT on computer	100
Paid to HMRC	1,600

Although this may make you feel worse off, especially when you are paying £1,600 to HMRC, you are in fact better off by £400 – this being the difference between the VAT you have been paid and the VAT you have paid out.

VAT registration threshold

A business needs to register for VAT when the level of sales exceeds the VAT threshold. The VAT threshold is currently £85,000 and it applies to the last 12 months. To know whether you need to register or not, you have to look back at your cumulative sales over the last 12 months and, if these exceed the VAT threshold, you must register. You are also required to register if you believe your sales in the next 30 days alone will be more than the VAT threshold – for example if you bag a big publishing deal.

Some writers will make an early 'protective' VAT registration, so that they know they are registered and don't have to worry about tripping over the VAT threshold. It is important to remember that the turnover figure is not necessarily the amount you receive. For example, a writer gets an advance of £10,000; their agent deducts 15% plus their VAT

Sole trader or limited company – the key differences

Sole trader	Limited company
Starting up	
Nothing legal required	Must be incorporated at Companies House
Closing down	
Nothing legal required	Must be formally struck off at Companies House
Legal protection	
None – you and the business are one and the same	Limited liability (but watch out for contracts that pass on liabilities to directors)
If you are sued, then all your assets are at stake	If the company is sued, then only the assets of the company are at stake
Tax on profits	
Income tax paid depending on total earnings from all sources in the year; rates may be 0%, 20%, 40% or 45% depnding on income	Corporation tax paid. Rate is currently 19%, although this is due to rise in 2023
Tax on profits extracted	
Not applicable – you pay tax on profit whether extracted or not	Dividend tax due at rates of 0%, 7.5%, 32.5% or 38.1% depending on income
National Insurance	
Pay Class 2 National Insurance and Class 4 National Insurance	Only pay National Insurance on salaries paid to employees if they earn over the limit
Reporting	
Must complete an individual Self Assessment tax return each year	Must file accounts each year with Companies House.
	Must submit a Confirmation Statement each year to Companies House
	Must file a corporation tax return each year with HMRC
	May have to run a payroll and report to HMRC
	Likely that director/shareholder will have to complete an individual
	Self Assessment tax return each year
Separate business bank account	
Advisable	Essential
VAT	
Can be VAT registered; it is a person that is VAT registered, not a business, which may have unintended consequences	Can be VAT registered
Creative averaging	
Can be used	Cannot be used
Why choose this one?	
Simple; cheap; you want to take all the money out of business when it's earned, not concerned about legal liability; provides legal liability protection	Save tax if you don't require all the money or are able to take advantage of splitting income

and so the writer only receives £8,200. The figure that counts towards the VAT threshold is £10,000.

Finally, you do not need to include employment income in your turnover calculation or non-UK income (such as royalties from Amazon).

Voluntary registration

You can voluntarily register for VAT even if your sales are under the VAT registration threshold. The reason you may want to do this is to recover the VAT you are being charged – typically by your agent. For example, a writer gets a publishing deal for £25,000; their agent charges 15% commission plus VAT. If they are not VAT-registered, they'll lose the agent VAT of £750 but, if they are VAT-registered, they'd be able to recover this.

Being in the 'VAT club' will allow you to recover VAT on all your other business expenditure, such as computer costs and accountancy fees. Whether it is a good idea to register early depends on your circumstances. If you're not incurring much VAT, then it may not be worth the hassle.

What to include in your sales for VAT

You need to include all your UK sales and any foreign sales collected by your UK publisher. You can exclude any direct foreign sales (such as Amazon self-publishing or sales you or your agent have agreed with a foreign publisher). If you're a sole trader, you can exclude any employed income. But, if you are self-employed as something else too (e.g. you're both a plumber and a writer), you need to aggregate both sets of income. The VAT registration belongs to the *person* not the *business*.

Claiming back VAT

When you first register for VAT, you can reclaim VAT on goods purchased up to four years prior to registration provided those goods are still held when registration takes place. VAT on services supplied in the six months prior to registration may also be reclaimed. To claim VAT you'll need a valid VAT receipt; a credit card receipt isn't enough, and a VAT inspector will disallow any expenditure that you can't produce a valid VAT receipt for – even if it's obvious that you would have paid VAT.

Not all expenditure has VAT charged on it:

Usually has VAT	Usually has no VAT
Agent commission	Trains, planes and taxis
Accountancy fees	Software subscriptions from overseas
Stationery	Postage
Computers and UK software	Entertainment
Internet and mobile phone	Insurance

Withholding tax and double taxation relief

Writers will often receive some or, in the case of an author selling via Amazon Kindle Direct Publishing (KDP), most of their income from an overseas source. Many foreign countries will charge a 'withholding tax' on such royalty payments, for example 30% in the case of the USA. Once withholding tax is paid, it is often not cost effective to try to recover it from the country in question, as doing so may require local professional advice and tax returns to be submitted to the country in question.

It is often possible to avoid any withholding tax being deducted in the first instance by completing the information required by the overseas publisher, so they don't have to apply withholding tax. Amazon KDP has an online tax interview to make it as easy as possible for you to comply. Other publishers in other countries will have to follow their own rules and will often ask for a Certificate of Residence to prove you are a UK tax payer. There are more details on applying for a Certificate of Residence at www.gov.uk/guidance/get-a-certificate-of-residence.

If you do suffer withholding tax, then it may be possible to use the foreign tax you have paid to offset against your tax liability on the same income when you complete your tax return. This may give you a worse result, though, as you will pay tax at the highest rate between the two countries. For example, if you are a UK basic rate tax payer and suffer 30% in the US, that will cover the 20% tax you would have to pay in the UK. You would not get a refund of the additional 10%. But, if you are a higher rate tax payer paying 40% tax, you would have to pay the additional 10% tax in the UK.

Stage 4: Lifelong considerations

As a writer's career becomes more established, there are other financial considerations.

Pensions

State Pension

To qualify for the new State Pension, you need a minimum of 10 qualifying years and at least 35 qualifying years to receive the maximum payments. You can check your pension entitlement online at www.gov.uk/check-state-pension. If you have gaps in your pension contribution history, then you can consider making voluntary contributions.

Writers' Guild Pension Fund

For their members writing for TV, radio and film, WGGB (Writers' Guild of Great Britain) have negotiated agreements with the BBC, ITV and PACT so that pension contributions are made to the Writers' Guild Pension Fund. In return for the writer making a contribution to the fund, the production company will also make a contribution, in addition to the writer's fee. More details are available from WGGB (see page 326 for contact details).

Private pensions

If you have been employed, you may have an occupational pension from your employment in place. Most writers who have been self-employed will depend upon their own pension arrangements using 'defined contribution' schemes. Contributions to a private pension by an individual are made net of basic rate income tax. This means that a contribution of £80 actually means the amount invested is £100, with £20 being claimed by the pension company from the Government. A higher-rate tax payer would save another £20 in income tax, making the cost of putting £100 into a pension just £60. There are rules regarding how much you can invest each year and many people will need professional advice as to what scheme they invest in.

Insurances

Being a self-employed writer does mean that you don't have the same safety net that many employees may have. It is sensible to think about how you and your family would manage if you died or, through injury or illness, were unable to continue to earn a living. There are insurance policies that are available to help.

- **Life insurance** can provide a lump sum or a monthly income for a period of time if you die.

- **Critical illness insurance** can provide a lump sum or a monthly income for a period of time if you are diagnosed with a critical illness.

- **Income protection insurance** can provide a monthly income if you are unable to work due to ill health.

Wills

Making a will is important for a number of reasons. Amongst other things, you can specify who inherits your assets, make tax efficient choices, and provide instructions as to who looks after your minor children. A writer also needs to consider what happens with any copyright they hold as part of their estate. Copyright can last up to 70 years after death, so it may represent a valuable asset. You may also have particular instructions as to what happens to your personal papers and unpublished works. It is also worth thinking about what happens with digital assets such as blogs, social media accounts, online videos, and access to cloud storage services like Dropbox. A bit of forward planning may save a lot of trouble for the people dealing with your estate.

Further advice: useful websites

HMRC
www.gov.uk/government/organisations/hm-revenue-customs

Institute of Chartered Accountants in England and Wales
www.icaew.com

Institute of Chartered Accountants Scotland
www.icas.com
These author associations offer support and advice on financial matters to their members.

National Union of Journalists
www.nuj.org.uk

Society of Authors
www.societyofauthors.org (see page 323)

WGGB (Writers' Guild of Great Britain)
https://writersguild.org.uk (see page 326)
Accountancy and business software tools include:

Sage
www.sage.com/en-gb/cp/accounting

Quickbooks
https://quickbooks.intuit.com/uk

Xero
www.xero.com/uk

Jonathan Ford BSC FCA MSWW and **Louise Ford** BA FCA are the directors of Writers Tax Ltd, a firm of chartered accountants that specialises in helping authors, scriptwriters and other professional writers with their tax and accountancy needs, which they established in 2020. They both qualified as chartered accountants with Price Waterhouse in Liverpool. Jonathan worked at Grant Thornton and later as Financial Controller at Mersey TV before setting up his own company. See their website https://writers.tax for more information.

Money, tax and benefits

National Insurance contributions

Sarah Bradford sets out the facts about National Insurance, explaining the principle that underlies it, the various classes of contribution payable by workers, both employed and self-employed, the related benefit entitlements and information on current rates and earnings thresholds.

Nature of National Insurance contributions

The payment of National Insurance contributions secures access to the state pension and to contributory benefits. This is the contributory principle of National Insurance. National Insurance contributions are payable by employed earners and their employers and also by self-employed earners. People who do not have any earnings or whose earnings are not sufficient to trigger a liability to pay National Insurance contributions can choose to pay National Insurance contributions voluntarily to maintain their contributions record.

If sufficient National Insurance contributions of the right type are paid or credited for a tax year, the year will be a qualifying year for National Insurance purposes. A person needs 35 qualifying years in order to receive the full state pension when they reach state pension age. Where a person has at least ten qualifying years, they will receive a reduced state pension.

Classes of National Insurance

There are various different classes of National Insurance contribution. The class (or classes) that you pay will depend on whether you are an employed earner, a self-employed earner, an employer or a voluntary contributor. Contributions may be earnings-related, payable on profits or payable at a flat rate, depending on the class.

The different classes of contribution are shown in the box below. Class 1, 2 and 4 contributions are only payable once earnings exceed certain thresholds and limits. The rates and thresholds applying for 2021/22 are set out in the box on page 432.

Contributions payable by writers and artists

As for other earners, the class of National Insurance payable by writers and artists depends on whether they are a self-employed earner or an employed earner. This is not something

Classes of National Insurance

Nature of contribution	Payable by
Class 1 Earnings-related	Employed earners (primary Class 1 contributions) Employer (secondary Class 1 contributions)
Class 1A Earnings-related	Employer on taxable benefits in kind and taxable termination payments and sporting testimonials
Class 1B Earnings-related	Employer on items included within a PAYE Settlement Agreement and on the tax due under that agreement
Class 2 Flat rate	Self-employed earners
Class 3 Flat rate	Voluntary contributions
Class 3A Variable amount	Payable between 12 October 2015 and 5 April 2017 voluntarily by those who reached state pension age before 6 April 2016 to boost their state pension
Class 4 Profits-related	Self-employed earners

that they can choose – it will depend on the facts of the engagement. It is important that the employment status of the writer or artist is categorised correctly as this will affect not only what class (and therefore how) they pay, but also what benefits they are entitled to.

Categorisation – employed earner *v* self-employed earner

To ensure that writers and artists pay the correct class of National Insurance contributions, it is important they are correctly categorised. Employed earners will pay Class 1 National Insurance contributions, whereas self-employed earners will pay Class 2 and Class 4 contributions.

A worker's categorisation depends on the characteristics of the engagement. In many cases, it will be clear whether a worker is an employed earner or a self-employed earner. For example, a writer who is employed by a publishing firm and has a contract of employment will be an employed earner and will pay Class 1 National Insurance contributions on their earnings, whereas a freelance writer who undertakes commissions for a variety of people and is paid a fee for each commission will be a self-employed earner and will pay Class 2 and Class 4 contributions.

Characteristics of employment

The following characteristics apply to an engagement where the worker is an employee:
• the person is required to work regularly unless they are unwell or on leave;
• they are expected to work a minimum number of hours a week and expect to be paid for the time that they work;
• a manager or supervisor is responsible for their workload, and will say when a job should be finished or how it should be done;
• they must do the work themselves – they can't send someone else to do it instead;
• the business deducts tax and National Insurance from their pay;
• they are entitled to paid holiday;
• they are entitled to statutory payments;
• they can join the business' pensions scheme;
• they are subject to grievance and disciplinary procedures;
• the contract sets out the procedure applying in the event of redundancy;
• they work at the business premises or at a location specified by the business;
• they only work for that business or, if they have another job, it is completely separate;
• the offer letter and contract refer to the 'employee' and the 'employer'.

For example, a staff writer who is paid a salary and contracted to work 35 hours a week would be an employed earner.

Characteristics of self-employment

The following characteristics indicate that the writer or artist is a self-employed earner:
• they are in business for themselves and are responsible for the success or failure of the business and can make a profit or a loss;
• they decide what work they take on and where and how they do it;
• they can hire someone else to do the work;
• they are responsible for fixing unsatisfactory work in their own time;
• they agree a fixed price for a job – the fee is the same regardless of how long it takes them to do the work;
• they use their own money to buy any equipment needed and to cover the running costs of the business;

• they work for more than one client.

A writer who is commissioned to write specific articles for different publications and who works for a number of publishers, being paid a fee for each article, would be a self-employed earner.

Marginal cases

It will not always be clear whether a writer or artist is an employed earner or a self-employed earner. In this situation, it is necessary to look at the overall picture and see whether, on balance, the writer or artist is employed or self-employed. It should be noted that there is not one single definitive test, rather a question of seeing what characteristics of employment and what characteristics of self-employment are present.

In reaching a decision, the following factors need to be considered:

• The nature of the contract and the written terms – a contract for *services* indicates employment and a contract of *service* indicates self-employment.
• The nature of the engager's business and the nature of the job.
• Right of substitution – a right to send a substitute indicates self-employment.
• Mutuality of obligation – for a contract for services there must be minimum mutual obligations; the employer is obliged to offer work and the employee is obliged to do that work.
• Right of control – a high degree of control (on the part of the employer) over how and where the worker performs the work suggests employment.
• Provision of equipment – the provision by the worker of their own equipment suggests self-employment.
• Financial risk – a person who is self-employed bears a higher degree of financial risk than an employee.
• Opportunity to profit – a person who is self-employed has the opportunity to profit if they do the job quicker or under-budget.
• Length of engagement – while this is not a decisive factor, an open-ended contract is more likely to indicate employment.
• Part and parcel of the organisation – a worker who is seen as 'part and parcel' of the organisation is likely to be an employee.
• Entitlement to benefits – a worker who is entitled to employee-type benefits, such as a pension, is more likely to be an employee.
• Personal factors – a highly skilled worker may not need supervising but may still be an employee.
• Intention – while intention alone cannot determine status, it can be useful in forming an opinion on whether the worker is employed or self-employed.

Check Employment Status for Tax (CEST) tool

HMRC have produced a tool – the Check Employment Status for Tax (CEST) tool – which can be used to reach a decision on whether a writer or artist is employed or self-employed. The tool asks a series of questions on the engagement, which must be answered honestly, in order to reach a decision. As long as the information provided is accurate and represents the reality of the engagement, HMRC will stand by the decision that is reached. The CEST tool is available on the Gov.uk website at www.gov.uk/guidance/check-employment-status-for-tax.

Workers providing their services through a personal service company

Anti-avoidance rules apply where services are provided through a personal limited company or another intermediary to an end client. There are two sets of rules to consider – the off-payroll working rules and the IR35 rules. The rules that apply depend on the nature of the end client.

• Off-payroll working rules

The off-payroll working rules were introduced from 6 April 2017. They apply from the date when services were provided through an intermediary to a private sector body. The rules were extended from 6 April 2021, and from that date they also apply when the end client is a medium or large private sector organisation.

The end client must carry out a status determination to ascertain whether the worker would be an employee of the end client if they provided their services to them directly. Where this is the case, the end client must deduct tax and National Insurance from payments made to the worker's personal company (after adjusting the bill for VAT and the cost of any materials), and report this to HMRC. The worker receives credit for the tax and National Insurance on payment made to them by their personal limited company. They do not need to consider the IR35 rules because the off-payroll working rules apply instead.

• IR35

From 6 April 2021 onwards, the IR35 rules only apply where a worker provides their services to a small private sector organisation through an intermediary, such as a personal service company. The worker's personal service company must determine whether the worker would be an employee of the small private sector organisation if they provided their services directly. If the answer is 'yes' the IR35 rules apply. The intermediary must calculate the deemed employment payment at the end of the tax year, and account for tax and National Insurance on that payment to HMRC.

Employed earners – Class 1 National Insurance

Class 1 National Insurance is payable on the earnings of an employed earner. The employed earner pays primary contributions and the secondary contributor (which is generally the employer) pays secondary contributions. The payment of primary Class 1 National Insurance contributions by the employed earner is the mechanism by which the employed earner earns the right to the state pension and contributory benefits. Secondary Class 1 contributions, payable by the employer, do not earn benefit entitlement – they are akin to a tax on the employee's earnings.

Contributions are calculated by reference to earnings for the earnings period on a non-cumulative basis; no account is taken of earnings previously in the tax year, only those for the earnings period. The earnings period will normally correspond to the pay interval. However, directors have an annual earnings period, regardless of their actual pay frequency. The employer must deduct primary contributions from the employee's pay and pay them over to HMRC together with tax deducted under PAYE and the employer's secondary contributions.

From 6 April 2023, earnings that are liable to Class 1 National Insurance contributions will also attract a liability to the Health and Social Care Levy which is being introduced from that date to raise funds for health and adult social care costs. The levy will be payable by both employees and employers at the rate of 1.25% on earnings that are liable for Class

1 National Insurance. Unlike primary Class 1 National Insurance contributions, liability for the Health and Social Care Levy will not cease when the contributor reaches state pension age.

• Primary Class 1 National Insurance

Primary Class 1 National Insurance contributions are payable by employees aged 16 and over until they reach state pension age (which depends on their date of birth). No contributions are payable until earnings reach the *lower earnings limit* (set at £123 per week, £533 per month, £6,396 per year for 2022/23). They are then payable at a notional zero rate until earnings reach the primary threshold. This is important as it secures the year as a qualifying year for National Insurance purposes (as long as earnings are paid above the lower earnings limit for each earnings period in the tax year). Where earnings are below the lower earnings limit, the year is not a qualifying year (although may become one if the worker receives National Insurance credits or pays voluntary contributions).

Contributions are payable on earnings above the *primary threshold* at the main primary rate of 12% until earnings reach the *upper earnings limit*. The primary threshold is set at £190 per week (£823 per month) from 6 April to 2022 to 5 July 2022 and at £242 per week (£1,048 per month) for 2022/23. The annual primary threshold is £11,908. The upper earnings limit is set at £967 per week, £4,189 per month and £50,270 per year for 2022/23. Contributions are payable at the additional primary rate of 2% on earnings above the upper earnings limit. For 2022/23 only, the main primary rate is set at 13.25% and the additional primary rate is set at 3.25%. The rates were increased by 1.25% for 2022/23 only pending the introduction of the Health and Social Care Levy. They are due to revert to 12% and 2% respectively from 6 April 2023 when the Health and Social Care Levy comes into effect.

• Secondary Class 1 contributions

Secondary contributions are payable by the secondary contributor, which in most cases is the employed earner's employer. They are payable on the earnings of an employee aged 16 and above; unlike primary contributions, the secondary liability does not stop when the employed earner reaches state pension age.

Contributions are payable at the secondary rate of 13.8% on earnings in excess of the *secondary threshold* (set at £175 per week, £758 per month, £9,100 per year for 2022/23). For 2022/23 only, the secondary rate is set at 15.05%, having been increased by 1.25% for 2022/23 only pending the introduction of the Health and Social Care Levy. The rate is due to revert to 13.8% from 6 April 2023 when the Health and Social Care Levy comes into effect.

A higher secondary threshold applies to the earnings of employees under the age of 21 (the upper secondary threshold for under 21s), to those of apprentices under the age of 25 (the apprentice upper secondary threshold) and to armed forces veterans in the first year of their first civilian employment since leaving the armed forces. Each of these thresholds are aligned with the upper earnings limit for primary Class 1 purposes (set at £967 per week, £4,189 per month and £50,270 per year for 2022/23). A separate secondary threshold applies to the earnings of a new Freeport employee (employed by an employer with physical premises in a Freeport tax zone). This threshold is set at £481 per week, £2,083 per month and £25,000 per year. These thresholds only apply for secondary Class 1 purposes; the employee or apprentice pays the usual primary contributions.

Eligible employers can claim the Employment Allowance which is offset against their secondary Class 1 National Insurance liability. To qualify, their secondary Class 1 National Insurance liability must be less than £100,000 for 2021/22. Companies where the sole employee is also a director do not qualify for the allowance. The Employment Allowance is set at £5,000 for 2022/23 (capped at the employer's secondary Class 1 liability where this is lower).

• Earnings for Class 1 purposes

Class 1 contributions are calculated on the earnings for the earnings period. The definition of 'earnings' includes any remuneration or profits derived from the employment. This will include payments of wages and salary, but will also include other items such as statutory sick pay, statutory payments, and certain share-based remuneration. Comprehensive guidance on what to include in earnings for National Insurance purposes can be found in the HMRC guidance CWG2 *Employer further guide to PAYE and National Insurance contributions*. The 2022/23 edition is available on the Gov.uk website at www.gov.uk/ government/publications/cwg2-further-guide-to-paye-and-national-insurance-contributions/ 2022-to-2023-employer-further-guide-to-paye-and-national-insurance-contributions.

• Class 1A National Insurance contributions

Class 1A National Insurance contributions are employer-only contributions payable on taxable benefits in kind and also on taxable termination payments in excess of the £30,000 tax-free threshold and taxable sporting testimonials in excess of the £100,000 tax-free threshold. They are payable at the Class 1A rate, which for 2022/23 is set at 15.05%.

• Class 1B National Insurance

Class 1B National Insurance contributions are employer-only contributions payable in place of the Class 1 or Class 1A liability that would otherwise arise on items included within a PAYE Settlement Agreement (PSA), and also on the tax due under the PSA. The Class 1B rate is aligned with the secondary Class 1 rate and is set at 15.05% for 2022/23.

Self-employed earners – Class 2 and Class 4 National Insurance contributions

Where a writer or artist is a self-employed earner, they will pay Class 2 contributions, and also Class 4 contributions on their profits. Class 2 and Class 4 National Insurance contributions are payable via the Self Assessment system and must be paid by 31 January after the end of the tax year to which they relate (i.e. by 31 January 2024 for 2022/23 contributions).

• Class 2 National Insurance contributions

Class 2 National Insurance contributions are flat-rate contributions payable by self-employed earners whose profits exceed the *small profits threshold*, set at £6,515 for 2022/23. Class 2 National Insurance contributions are payable at the rate of £3.05 per week for 2022/ 23. The payment of Class 2 contributions is the mechanism by which a self-employed earner earns entitlement to the state pension and contributory benefits. Contributions must be paid for the full year for the year to be a qualifying year. A person whose profits from self-employment are below the small profits threshold can pay Class 2 National Insurance contributions voluntarily. This is a cheap way to build up pension entitlement.

• Class 4 National Insurance contributions

Class 4 National Insurance contributions are payable by self-employed earners on their profits. They do not provide any benefit entitlement, and in effect are a tax on profits. No

National Insurance rates and thresholds 2022/23

National Insurance class	Rate or threshold
Class 1	
Lower earnings limit	£123 per week
	£533 per month
	£6,396 per year
Primary threshold: 06/04/22 to 05/07/22	£190 per week
	£823 per month
	£11,908 per year
Primary threshold: 06/07/22 to 05/04/23	£242 per week
	£1,048 per week
	£11,908 per year
Secondary threshold	£175 per week
	£757 per month
	£9,100 per year
Upper earnings limit	£967 per week
	£4,189 per month
	£50,270 per year
Upper secondary threshold for under 21s	£967 per week
	£4,189 per month
	£50,270 per year
Apprentice upper secondary threshold	£967 per week
	£4,189 per month
	£50,270 per year
Veterans upper secondary threshold	£967 per week
	£4,189 per month
	£50,270 per year
Freeport upper secondary threshold	£481 per week
	£2,083 per month
	£25,000 per year
Primary (employee) contributions	
On earnings between the primary threshold and the upper earnings limit	13.25%
On earnings above the upper earnings limit	3.25%
Secondary (employer) contributions	
On earnings above the relevant secondary threshold	15.05%
Class 1A and Class 1B	
Contribution rate (employer only)	15.05%
Class 2	
Flat rate contribution	£3.15 per week
Small profits threshold	£6,725 a year
Class 3	
Flat rate contribution	£15.85 per week
Class 4	
Lower profits limit	£9,880 a year
Upper profits limit	£50,270 a year

contributions are payable on profits below the *lower profits threshold*, set at £11,908 for 2022/23. Class 4 contributions are payable at the rate of 10.25% on profits between the lower profits limit and the *upper profits limit*, set at £50,270 for 2022/23, and on profits in excess of the upper profits limit, at the additional Class 4 rate of 3.25%.

From 6 April 2023, self-employed earners will also be required to pay the Health and Social Care Levy at the rate of 1.25% of earnings liable to Class 4 National Insurance contributions. The Class 4 rates will revert to 9% and 2% from 6 April 2023 when the Health and Social Care Levy comes into effect.

Voluntary contributions – Class 3

A person can pay voluntary Class 3 contributions to plug gaps in their contributions record. For 2022/23, Class 3 contributions are payable at the rate of £15.85 per week. Where a person has profits from self-employment below the *small profits threshold* (set at £6,725 for 2022/23), they can instead pay Class 2 contributions voluntarily; at £3.15 per week for 2022/23 this is a much cheaper option.

Maximum contributions

Where a person has more than one job, or is both employed and self-employed, there is a cap on the contributions that are payable for the year. The calculations are complex.

National Insurance credits

National Insurance credits are available in certain circumstances where people are unable to work or because they are ill. There are two types of credit. Class 1 credits count towards state pension and contributory benefits, while Class 3 credits only count towards the state pension. Further detail on National Insurance credits can be found on the Gov.uk website at www.gov.uk/national-insurance-credits.

Benefit entitlement

The payment of National Insurance contributions (and the award of National Insurance credits) earns entitlement to the state pension and certain contributory benefits. Only the payment of primary Class 1, Class 2 and Class 3 contributions confer benefit entitlement. Benefit entitlement depends on the class of contribution paid.

Benefit entitlement

Class of contributions	Benefit entitlement
Primary Class 1 (employed earner)	State Pension, contribution-based Jobseeker's Allowance, contribution-based Employment and Support Allowance, Maternity Allowance and Bereavement Payment, Bereavement Allowance, Widowed Parent's Allowance, Bereavement Support Payment.
Class 2 (self-employed earners)	State Pension, contribution-based Employment and Support Allowance, Maternity Allowance and Bereavement Allowance.
Class 3 (voluntary contributions)	State Pension and Bereavement Payment, Bereavement Allowance, Widowed Parent's Allowance.

Sarah Bradford BA (Hons), FCA CTA (Fellow) is the director of Writetax Ltd, and the author of *National Insurance Contributions 2022/23* (and earlier editions) published by Bloomsbury Professional. She writes widely on tax and National Insurance contributions.

Money, tax and benefits

Index

Writers &Artists

A FREE WRITING PLATFORM TO CALL YOUR OWN

- Exclusive discounts
- Regular writing competitions
- Free writing advice articles
- Publishing guidance
- Save margin notes
- Share your writings
- Bursary opportunities

REGISTER NOW

WWW.WRITERSANDARTISTS.CO.UK

THE WRITERS' & ARTISTS' GUIDES

The bestselling Writers & Artists brand provides up-to-date, impartial and practical advice on how to write and get published.